The Writings

of

T. Austin-Sparks

Volume III

A limited edition

MINISTRY

Ministry
All *new* material in this edition
© 1999 by SeedSowers Publishing House
Reprinted 2000
Printed in the United States of America
All rights reserved

Published by: The SeedSowers
                     P.O.Box 285, Sargent, GA 30275
                     1-800-228-2665
                     www.seedsowers.com

Library of Congress Cataloging-in-Publication Data

Sparks, T. Austin
        Ministry / T. Austin-Sparks
        ISBN 0-940232-66-9
        1. Spiritual Life.   1. Title

Times New Roman 12pt

MINISTRY

by
T. Austin-Sparks

This volume contains eight of T. Austin-Sparks' books, all on the subject of Ministry.

Book I: The School of Christ (1945)

Book II: The Incense Bearer (1935)

Book III: The More Excellent Ministry (1967)

Book IV: Pioneers of the Heavenly Way (1953)

Book V: Prophetic Ministry (1954)

Book VI: God Hath Spoken (1949)

Book VII: The Stewardship of the Mystery— Vol. 1 (1940)

Book VIII: The Stewardship of the Mystery— Vol. 2 (1964)

The years listed above are those when, in the author's bimonthly magazine *A Witness and a Testimony*, a first notice of each book or booklet appeared. Very many of the titles had already appeared earlier as articles or series in that magazine.

Preface

T. Austin-Sparks is one of the great figures of the twentieth century who ministered outside of the organized church. For over forty years he held forth at Honor Oak in London, England. The conferences he spoke at, both in Europe and America, have had a profound influence on our time.

Brother Sparks published over one hundred books and pamphlets. The majority of them have ceased to be available to the Christian family. This has been a great loss, as the content of his message has placed him in the category of only a few men of the last one hundred years.

T. Austin-Sparks and Watchman Nee, more than any other men, have influenced the lives of believers who are outside traditional churches. We have felt very strongly that all of brother Sparks' books and pamphlets should be brought back into print if at all possible.

This is the third volume of a series that will ultimately contain all of his ministry that found its way into books.

Read T. Austin-Sparks. It is our hope that in republishing his works, his ministry will take wings again, and the influence of his word will spread across the English-speaking world. Hopefully this will give his message a greater influence than ever before.

We send these volumes forth with a prayer that what he ministered will become realities in the 21st century.

The SeedSowers

The School of
Christ

Preface to the Third and Revised Edition

The ministry contained in this little book has been wrought on the anvil of deep and drastic dealings of God with the vessel. It is not *only* doctrinal; it is experiential. Only those who really mean *business* with God will take the pains demanded to read it. For such, two words of advice may be helpful. Firstly, try to remember all through that the spoken form is retained. The messages were given in conference, and the reader must try to get into the spirit and mind of listening, and not only reading. In speaking, the messenger can see by the faces before him where repetition or reemphasis or fuller elucidation is called for. This explains much that would not be the character of a precisely literary production. It has its difficulties for readers, but it also has its values.

Then, my advice is that not too much, indeed not a lot, should be attempted at once. Almost every page requires thinking about, and weariness can only overtake if too much is read without quiet meditation.

Of all the books that have issued from this ministry, I regard this one as that which goes most deeply to the roots and foundations of our life in Christ with God.

May He make the reading of it result in a fuller understanding of the meaning of Christ.

T. AUSTIN-SPARKS
London
July 1964

CONTENTS AND SYNOPSES

I
THE FOUNDATION OF SPIRITUAL EDUCATION

Reading: Ezekiel 40:2-4; 43"10-11; Matthew 3:17; 11:25-30; John 1:51; Luke 9:23; Ephesians 4:20-21

The basic word out of those read, for our present purpose, is Matthew 11:29—

"Take my yoke upon you, and learn of me."

Learn of me. The Apostle Paul, in a slightly different form of words, gives us what the Lord Jesus meant—

"Ye did not so learn Christ" (Eph. 4:20)

Leaving out one very little word makes all the difference and gives the true sense. The Lord Jesus, while He was here, could only put it in an objective way, for the subjective time had not arrived: and so He had to say, *"Learn of me."* When the subjective time came, the Holy Spirit would lead the apostle to leave out the 'of' and say 'learn Christ'.

I am quite sure that many of you will immediately discern that is just the flaw in a very great deal of popular Christianity today—a kind of objective imitation of Jesus which gets nowhere, rather than the subjective learning Jesus which gets everywhere.

So for this little while we are to be occupied with the School of Christ, into which school He brought the twelve, whom He chose *"that they might be with him and the he might send them forth"* (Mark 3:14). They were first of all called disciples, which simply means they come under discipline. Before ever we can be apostles, that is, sent ones, we have to come under discipline to be disciples, to be taught ones, and that in an inward way. It is into this school that every one who is born from above is brought, and it is very important that we should know the nature of it, what it is that we are going to learn, and the principles of our spiritual education.

The Object of Our Schooling is First Comprehensively Presented

Coming into this school, the very first thing that the Holy Spirit, the great Teacher and Interpreter, does for us, if we are truly brought under His hand, is to show us in a comprehensive way what it is that we have to learn, to present to us the great object of our education. We read those passages in Ezekiel which I think have a great bearing upon this matter. In a day when the true expression of God's thought in the midst of his people had been lost and God's people were out of immediate touch with Divine thoughts, away in that far country, the Spirit of God laid His hand upon the prophet. He took him in the Spirit in the visions of God back to Jerusalem, and set him upon a high mountain, and gave him that presentation of a new temple, forth from which would flow a river of life to the ends of the earth. Then He followed this up by going into the whole thing in the most minute detail, and later instructed the prophet to show the house to the house of Israel with a view to bringing about a recovery of spiritual life in conformity to that great comprehensive and detailed revelation of God's thought, that they should first of all be ashamed.

It is a much-disputed matter whether the temple of Ezekiel will yet literally be set up on the earth. We will not argue about that. But of this one thing we need have no question, that all that Ezekiel saw has its spiritual counter part and fulfilment in the Church which is His Body; spiritually it is all in Christ. And God's method with His people, in order to secure a full expression of His thought, is first of all to present the perfect Object; and this He did when at the Jordan He rent the heaven and said, *"This is my beloved Son in whom I am well pleased."* He presented and attested that which was the full, comprehensive and detailed expression of His thought for His people. The Apostle Paul, in words familiar to us, expressly voices the fact—

"Whom he foreknew, he also foreordained to be conformed to the image of his Son" (Rom. 8:20).

"This is my beloved Son in whom I am well pleased"—*"Conformed to the image of his Son"*. There is the presentation and the attestation and the declaration of Divine purpose in relation to Him. Therefore I repeat, the Holy Spirit's first object is to acquaint us with what is in view in our spiritual education; namely, that He is to reveal Christ in us and then afterward to get to work to conform us to Christ. To learn Christ we must first see Christ.

The Pre-eminent Mark of a Life Governed by the Spirit

The mark of a life governed by the Holy Spirit is that such a life is continually and ever more and more occupied with Christ, that Christ is becoming greater and greater as time goes on. The effect of the Holy Spirit's work in us is to bring us to the shore of a mighty ocean which reaches far, far beyond our range, and concerning which we feel—Oh, the depths, the fulness, of Christ! If we live as long as ever man lived, we shall still be only on the fringe of this vast fulness that Christ is.

Now, that at once becomes a challenge to us before we go any further. These are not just words. This is not just rhetoric; this is truth. Let us ask our hearts at once, is this true in our case? Is this the kind of life that we know? Are we coming to despair on this matter? That is to say, that we are glimpsing so much as signified by Christ that we know we are beaten, that we are out of our depth, and will never range all this. It is beyond us, far beyond us, and yet we are drawn on and ever on. Is that true in your experience? That is the mark of a life governed by the Holy Spirit. Christ becomes greater and greater as we go on. If that is true, well, that is the way of life. If ever you and I should come to a place where we think we know, we have it all, we have attained, and from that point things become static, we may take it that the Holy Spirit has ceased operations and that life has become stultified.

Let us take the example of one who is given to us, I believe, as amongst men, for this very purpose of showing forth God's ways, the Apostle Paul. The words which he used to define and express what happened to him right at the commencement are these: *"It pleased God...to reveal his Son in me"* (Gal. 1:16). Now that man did a very great deal of teaching and preaching. He put out a great deal. He had a long and very full life, not only in the amount that he put out, but in the concentrated essence which has defeated all the attempts to fathom. At the end of that long life, that full life, that man who said concerning its commencement, *"It pleased God...to reveal his Son in me"*, is crying from his heart this cry, *"that I may know him"* (Phil. 3:10); indicating surely that with the great initial revelation and all the subsequent and continual unveilings even being caught up into the third heaven and shown unspeakable things, with all that, at the end he knows nothing compared with what there is to be known. That I may know Him! That is the essence of a life governed by the Holy Spirit, and it is that which will deliver us from death, from stagnation, from coming to a standstill. It is the work of the Spirit in the School of Christ to present and to keep in view Christ in Hi greatness. So God, right at the beginning, brings Christ forth, presents Him, attests Him, and in effect says, This is that to which I will to conform you, to this image!

Yes, but then having the presentation, the basic lessons begin. The Holy Spirit is not satisfied with just giving us a great presentation: He is going to begin real work in relation to that presentation, and we are, under His hand, brought to two or three basic things in our spiritual education.

The Challenge and Meaning of an Open Heaven

My aim, in co-operation with the Lord, is to make everything pre-eminently practical. So we apply the challenge immediately and I ask you. Is the Holy Spirit within you presented God's fulness in His Son in an ever-growing way? Is that the nature of your spiritual life? If not, then you must have some definite exercise before the Lord about it; there is something wrong. The anointing means that, and if that is not the nature of your spiritual life, there is something wrong in your case in relation to the anointing. To Nathanael the Lord Jesus said, "Henceforth" (our old English word is 'hereafter', but I think many people have mistakenly thought that means the 'after life') *"ye shall see the heaven opened, and the angels of God ascending and descending upon the Son of man"*. Hereafter, of course, was the immediate hereafter, the days of the Holy Spirit which were coming so soon. With an open heaven you see, and you see God's meaning concerning His Son.

That open heaven for the Lord Jesus was the anointing. The Spirit descended and lighted upon Him. It was the anointing of the Spirit from the day of Pentecost onward upon Christ within us. That open heaven means a continually growing revelation of Christ.

Oh, let me urge this, I am brought back to urge this. We must not just add other things too soon, but make sure that we are right on these matters. The open heaven at once brings God's revelation in Christ to your very door, makes it available to you, so that you are not dependent in the first place upon libraries, books, addresses [teachings] or anything else. It is there for you. However much the Lord may see good to use these other things for your help and enrichment, you have your own open heaven, your own clear way through, and no closed dome over your head. The Lord Jesus is becoming more and ever more wonderful in your own heart, because *"God, that said, Light shall shine out of darkness" hath "shined in our hearts, to give the light of the knowledge of the glory of God in the face of Jesus Christ"* (2 Cor. 4:6).

The 'Other-ness' of Christ

That being true—and if it is not, perhaps you must just suspend things there until you have had dealings with the Lord—that being true, the Holy Spirit gets to work on that, as I said, to make two or three other things very real to us, the first of which is the altogether 'other-ness' of Christ. How altogether other He is from ourselves. Taking the disciples who went into His School—it was not the School of the Holy Spirit in the same sense as ours is. But the result of their association with the Lord Jesus during those three or three and a half years was just the same—the first thing they learned was how other He was from themselves. They had to learn it. I do not think it came to them at the first moment. It was as they went on that they found themselves again and again clashing with His thoughts, His mind, His ways. They would urge Him to take a certain course, to do certain things, to go to certain places. They would seek to bring to bear upon Him their own judgments and their own feelings and their own ideas. But He would have none of it. At the marriage feast in Cana of Galilee, His own mother, with an idea, said, They have no wine. His reply was, *"Woman, what have I to do with thee? Mine hour is not yet come."* What have to do with thee? That is a weak translation. Far better, *"Woman, you and I are thinking in different realms; we have at the moment nothing in common."* Thus throughout their lives they sought to impinge upon Him with their mentality. No, all the time He was putting them back and showing them how different were His thoughts, His ways, His ideas, His judgments; altogether different. In the end I expect they despaired. He might well have despaired of them had He not known that this was exactly what He was doing in them. Catch that and you have got something helpful. "Lord, why is that I am always caught out, always making a blunder? Somehow or other, I always say and do the wrong thing. I am always on the wrong side! Somehow I never seem to come right in line with You; I despair of ever being right!" And the Lord says, "I am teaching you, that is all; deliberately, quite deliberately. That is exactly what I am bringing you to see. Until you learn that lesson, we shall get nowhere at all. When you have thoroughly learned that lesson, hen we can begin constructive work, but at present it is necessary for you to come to the place where you recognize I am altogether other than you are. The difference is such that we move in two altogether opposite worlds."

This ordinary mind of man, at its best, is another mind. This will of man, at its best, is another will. You never do know what lies behind your motives until the Holy Ghost cleaves right down to the depths of your being and shows you. You may put your feelings and desires into the most devout terms. You may, like Peter, react to a Divine suggestion. *"If I wash thee not, thou hast no part with me"*, and say, *"Not my feet only, but also my hands and my head"*; but it is only self coming up again—*my* blessing. I want the blessing, and so miss the whole point the Master is trying to teach. 'I am trying to teach you self-emptying.' He might have said, 'and you are laying hold of every suggestion of mine for self-filling, to get; and I am trying to say, Give, let go!" This self comes up in the most spiritual (?) way. Self comes up for spiritual blessing We do not know what lies behind. We have to come into a very severe school of the Spirit which eventuates in our coming to discover that our best intentions are defiled, our purest motives are unclean before those eyes. Things that we intended to be for God, somewhere at their spring is self. We cannot produce from this nature anything acceptable to God. All that can ever come to God is in Christ alone, not in us. It never will, in this life, be in us as ours. It will always be the difference between Christ and ourselves. Though He be resident within us, He and He only is the object of the Divine good pleasure and satisfaction. And the one basic lesson you and I have to learn in this life, under the Holy Spirit's tuition and revelation and discipline, is that He is other than we are. And that 'other-ness' is indeed an utter thing. That is one of the hard lessons.

It is certainly one that this world will refuse to learn. It will not have that. That runs directly counter to the whole system of the teaching of humanism—the wonderful thing that man is! Oh no, when you have come to *your* best, there is a gulf between you and the beginnings of Christ that cannot be bridged. If you attain *your* best, you have not commenced Christ. That is utter, but we perhaps hardly need that emphasis. Most of us have learned something.

But let us, while we know this in experience, take the comfort which comes perhaps from being told again exactly what is happening. What is the Lord doing, what is the Holy Spirit doing with us? Well, as a basic thing, He is making us to know that we are one thing and Christ another. That is the most important lesson to learn, for there can be nothing constructive until we have learned it. The first thing, therefore, is the altogether 'other-ness' of Christ as over against ourselves.

The Impossibility of Reaching
God's Standard Ourselves

Then, secondly, the Holy Spirit brings us face to face with the utter impossibility of our ever being that of ourselves. You see, God has set up a standard, God has presented His model, God has given us His object for our conformity and the next thing we come up against is the utter impossibility of being that. Yes, of ourselves it cannot be. Have you not learned that lesson of despair yet? Is it necessary for the Holy Spirit to make you despair again? Why not have one good despair and get it all over? Why despair every few days? Only because you are still hunting round for something somewhere, some rag of goodness in yourself that you can present to God that will please Him, satisfy Him and answer to His requirements. You will never find it. Settle it that *"all our righteousness is as filthy rags"*. Our righteousness, all that trying to be so righteous, the Lord says of it all, *"Filthy rags!"* Let us settle this once for all. If you are looking ahead of what I am saying, you will see what it is leading to. It is leading to the most glorious position. It is leading to that glorious issue mentioned by the Lord Jesus in this way, in those days before things became inward: *"Learn of me...and ye shall find rest unto your souls."* That is the end. But we shall never find rest unto our souls until we have first of all learned the utter difference between Christ and ourselves, and then the utter impossibility of our ever being like Him by anything that we can find in ourselves, produce or do. It is not in us, in ourselves, in that way. So we had better despair our last despair with regard to ourselves. Those two things are basic.

A Final Word and Exhortation

But then the next thing the Holy Spirit will do will be to begin to show us how it is accomplished. We are not going to start on that just now, but stay with the fact that the Holy Spirit can do nothing until these other things are settled. Oh, God is very jealous for His Son. His Son has gone right through the fires over this matter, having accepted manform and a life of dependence. Having voluntarily emptied Himself of that which meant that at any moment He could of Himself work by Deity for His own deliverance, salvation, provision, preservation. Having emptied Himself of that right and said, I let go all My rights and prerogatives and powers of Deity for the time being and I accept man's position of utter dependence upon God as My Father; I meet all that man ever has to meet on man's level!* He met it in every realm in its concentrated form and force and went through without a flaw as man for man, and went back to the throne on the merit of a complete triumph over every force that ever man has to encounter in satisfying God. Do you think that after that God is ever going to forgo His Son, and all that He wrought in man's behalf, and say, Only be at your best and that will satisfy Me? Oh, what blindness to Christ, to God, is this Christianity that is popular today! No, there is only One in this universe concerning whom God can say from His heart *"in whom I am well pleased"*, and that is the Lord Jesus Christ. If ever you and I are going to come into that favour, it will be as "in Christ Jesus", never in ourselves.

When that is learned, or when that part of the education has been taken up, then it is that the Holy Spirit can begin the work of conformity tot he image of God's Son. Well, we have seen lessons one and two in the case of

---

* This does not mean that He emptied Himself of Deity, but of its rights *for the time being*.

the disciples. Through the months and years, they came to see how altogether different He was from themselves, and then came to the place of despair on that very matter as the Lord intended it should be. He foresaw it all. He could not hinder it, He could not save them. He had to allow them to go that way. And right at the end when they were making their loudest protestations about their loyalty, their faithfulness, their endurance, and what they were going to do when put to the test, he said to them all, *"Do ye now believe? Behold, the hour cometh, yea, is come, that ye shall be scattered, every man to his own, and shall leave me alone"* (John 16:31-32). And to one in particular He said, *"The cock shall not crow till thou hast denied me thrice"* (John 13:38) What do you think those men felt when He was crucified and they had all run away, and left Him alone, and the one had denied Him? Do you not think dark despair entered into their souls, not only over their lost prospects and expectations, but despair over themselves. Yes, and He had to allow it. he could take no step to prevent it, it was necessary. And you and I will go the same way if we are in the same school. It is essential. No constructed work can be done until that has got advanced within us.

Well, that sounds terrible, but that ought to be encouraging! After all, it is all constructive in a way. What is the Lord doing with me? He is preparing a way for His Son, He is clearing the ground for bringing in the fulness of Christ. That is what He is doing. He did it with them, and Pentecost and afterward was His answer to what happened on the day when he was delivered up, to all that happened on the day when He was delivered up, to all that happened with them. You say, Then He commenced His constructive work. Yes, He did; after the Cross and Pentecost, things began to change in an inward way, and from that time you begin to see that Christ is now within them transcending what they are by nature. It is not that they become so much better, but it is that Christ within becomes so much more real as a power.

That is all for the moment. Let us bow our hearts today, yield today. It is the School of Christ. I know how challenging it is, challenging to this old man who dies very hard, yields with great difficulty. All our training, teaching, perhaps has been other than this. We have come into this horrible heritage of humanism—to be the best that I can be, to be my best! Well, you must take what I am saying in the sense in which I am saying it. No one is going to think that you can go and just be careless, slovenly, at your worst or less than your best, simply because of what I have said; but you know what I am talking about. At our best we can never pass across that gap between man and Jesus Christ. No, that gap remains, and the only way to get over is to die and to be raised from the dead; but that, for the moment, is another matter.

II
LEARNING THE TRUTH

"Jesus therefore said to those Jews that had believed him, If ye abide in my word, then are ye truly my disciples; and ye shall know the truth, and the truth shall make you free. They answered unto him, We are Abraham's seed, and have never yet been in bondage to any man: how sayest thou, Ye shall be made free? Jesus answered them, Verily, verily, I say unto you, Every one that committeth sin is the bondservant of sin. And the bondservant abideth not in the house for ever: the son abideth for ever. If therefore the Son shall make you free, ye shall be free indeed" John 8:31-36).

"Ye are of your father the devil, and the lusts of your father it is your will to do. He was a murdered from the beginning, and standeth not in the truth, because there is no truth in him. When he speaketh a lie, he speaketh for his own: for he is a liar, and the father thereof" (John 8:44).

"Ye have not known him: but I know him; and if I should say, I know him not, I shall be like unto you, a liar; but I know him, and keep his word" (John 8:55).

"Jesus saith unto him, I am the way, and the truth, and the life" (John 14:6).

"The Spirit of truth: whom the world cannot receive; for it beholdeth him not, neither knoweth him: ye know him; for he abideth with you, and shall be in you" (John 14:17).

"But when the Comforter is come, whom I will send unto you from the Father, even the Spirit of truth, which proceedeth from the Father, he shall bear witness of me" (John 15:26).

"For the wrath of God is revealed from heaven ,t all ungodliness and unrighteousness of men, who hold down the truth in unrighteousness" (Romans 1:18).

"For that they exchanged the truth of God for a lie…" (Romans 1:25).

"If so be that ye heard him, and were taught in him, even as truth is in Jesus" (Ephesians 4:21)

"Put on the new man, which after God hath been created in righteousness and holiness of truth" (Ephesians 4:24).

"These things saith he that is holy, he that is true: (Revelation 3:7).

"These things saith the Amen (= Verily), the faithful and true witness" (Revelation 3:14).

In our previous meditation, we were speaking together about the School of Christ, and we were saying that every true child of God is brought into the School of Christ under the hand of the Holy Spirit, and Spirit of the anointing, and that there the first great work of the Holy Spirit is to present Christ to the heart as God's object for all the Holy Spirit's dealings with us. Thus Christ is first of all presented and attested by God as the object of His pleasure. Then the Holy Spirit makes known the Divine purpose in connection with that inward revelation of the Lord Jesus, namely, that we should be conformed to the image of God's Son. Then we were speaking about two or three basic lessons in the school, things which underlie our education. Firstly, the Holy Spirit takes pains to make all who are under this discipline (for that is the meaning of a disciple) to know in experience, in an inward way in their own hearts, the altogether 'other-ness' of Christ from themselves. Then He also works to bring us to the place where we realize how impossible the situation is part from miracles of God, that of ourselves we can never be like Christ. The one upshot of it all is that this must be something outside ourselves which is God's own doing.

Well, this is all preliminary in the School of Christ, although it seems to me that this preliminary education goes on to the end of our days. At any rate, it seems to be spread over a great deal of our life, though there should be a point reached which represents a definite crisis in the matter, at which a foundation is laid wherein these three things are recognized and accepted, and we shall not get very far until it is so. The person who really does begin to move is the person who has had his final despair over himself, and has come to see quite clearly by the Holy Spirit's illumination that it is *"no longer I, but Christ"*— 'Not what I am, O lord, but what Thou art, that, that alone, can be my soul's true rest': Thy love, not mind; Thy peace, not mine: Thy rest, not mine; Thy everything, nothing of mine; Thy-self! That is the essential foundation of spiritual growth, spiritual knowledge, spiritual education.

'I Am the Truth'

Now, in this meditation, we come to look at the Lord Jesus more closely as God's object and standard for the Holy Spirit's work in us, this 'other-ness' which He represents and we have read a number of passages, all of which, as you noted, bear upon truth. Surely those passages in the Gospels must have played a part in the disciple's education. In the first place there was the statement o declaration made to the Jews—a tremendous thing to be said in the hearing of those disciples. There were Jews who made a profession of believing. The Lord Jesus raises the question of discipleship with them. He said to those Jews who had believed Him (it does not say they had believed *on* Him), *"If ye abide in my word, then are ye truly my disciples; and ye shall know the truth, and the truth shall make you free."* They answered back at once with the counter claim, *"We are Abraham's seed, and have never yet been in bondage to any man."* He presses this matter of the truth, truth in relation to Himself. *"If therefore the Son shall make you free, ye shall be free indeed." "Ye shall know the truth, and the truth shall make you free."* The question of whose seed they were arose, and associated with that the statement *"if therefore the Son shall make you free, ye shall be free indeed".* Do you follow that? Knowing the truth is knowing the Son. Freedom by the truth is by the knowledge of Him.

Then to the Jews—I presume of the more violent type—He said these words of unparalleled strength: *"Ye are of your father the devil, and the lusts of your father it is your will to do. He was a murdered from the beginning, and standeth not in the truth...he is a liar, and the father thereof...when he speaketh a lie, he speaketh of His own."* Tremendously strong language, and all on this question of the truth, the truth as bound up with Himself.

Then, when you come to chapter 14, He is with His disciples alone; and Philip says to Him, *"Lord, show us the Father, and it sufficeth us."* His reply is, *"Have I been so long time with you, and dost thou not know me, Philip? He that hath seen me hath seen the Father."* Another question in the school: *"Lord, we know not whither thou goest; how know we the way?" "I am the way, and the truth..."* I am the truth. The truth is not some *thing*; the truth is a Person. Well, all this is in the School of Christ, bearing upon Christ as the Truth.

I do not know how strongly you feel about the matter, but our object surely is that we should come to feel very strongly about these things. How do you feel about the importance of having a true foundation? And after all, the supreme feature in a foundation is truth, that the thing should be well and truly laid. This foundation has to take a fairly heavy responsibility, no less a responsibility than our eternal well being and destiny, nay, the very vindication of God Himself. Therefore it must be absolutely true and the truth, and it surely behooves us to make very sure of where we are. In other words, to have done with all our unreality, to finish forever with anything that is not genuine and utterly true in our position. It is just this that we are going to press and analyse for a little while now. So great are the consequences that we cannot afford to have anything doubtful in our position.

It is like this. You and I are going to face God sometime. We are going to come face to face with God literally in eternity and then the question is going to arise, Has God at any point failed us? Shall we be able, on any detail, to say, Lord, You failed me, You were not true to Your word? Such a position is unthinkable, that even any being should be able to lay a charge like that at god's door, to have any question as to God's truth, reality, and faithfulness. The Holy Spirit has come for that. If that is true, then the Holy Spirit will deal with all disciples in the School of Christ to undercut everything that is not true, that is not genuine. To make every such disciple to stand upon a foundation which can abide before God in the day of His absolute and utter vindication.

The Need for a True Foundation

But in order that this may be so, you and I, under the Holy Spirit's teaching, have to be dealt with very faithfully. We have to come to the place where we are perfectly adjustable before God, where there is all responsiveness to the Holy Spirit, and nothing in us that resists or refused the Holy Spirit, but where we are perfectly open and ready for the biggest consequence of the Holy Spirit putting His finger upon anything in our lives needing to be dealt with and adjusted. He is here for that.

The alternative to such a work of the Holy Spirit being allowed to be done in us is that we shall find ourselves in a false position. And it is far, far too costly to find ourselves in a false position, even though it only be on certain points. This is a false world we are living in, a world that is carried on upon lies. The whole constitution of this world is a lie, and it is in the very nature of man, though multitudes do not know it, but think they are true. They are trying to build the world on a false foundation. The Kingdom of God is altogether other. It is built upon Jesus Christ, the Truth.

Well now, my emphasis at the moment is upon the need for a true position where we are concerned. Oh for men and women in whom the truth of Christ has been wrought and who will go on with God, no matter what it costs. *"Who shall ascend into the hill of the Lord?"* *"He that speaketh truth in his heart...he that sweareth to his own hurt'*—that is, who takes the position of verity though it cost him dear. We are influenced by all sorts of false considerations, influenced by what others will think and say, especially those in our religious circles, of our tradition; and they are false considerations and false influences. They bind and keep many men and women from going right on with God in the way of light. The issue is a false position at last.

Will you accept it when I say that there is no truth in us? This is one of the things we are going to have to find out under the Holy Spirit's dealings with us, that there is no truth in our minds naturally. We may be the most strongly convinced, and we may be prepared to lay down our lives for our convictions and to put everything into the crucible for what we believe with all our beings is right, is true, and in that very thing we may be utterly wrong. Such was the case with Saul of Tarsus—*"I verily thought with myself, that I ought to do many things contrary to the name of Jesus of Nazareth"* (Acts 26:9). Again, *"The hour cometh, that whosoever killeth you shall think he offereth God service"* (John 16:2)l so zealous for their conviction—That is God's will! God's will!—convinced it is God's will; some to give their own lives on the strength of their conviction, and some to take other people's lives on the strength of their conviction. How far we will go on the strength of conviction and be wrong, utterly wrong, as utterly wrong as we are in earnest. A false conviction; and there is not one human mind incapable of getting into that state. The seeds of that are in human nature, in every one of us; in the mind as to conviction, the heart as to desire. We may think our desire is a perfectly pure and right one, and it may be utterly false. So with our will, just the same. In us by nature there is no truth.

Living by the Truth

I am going to get right down inside this thing. What is a Christian? A Christian is one who was not a very good-tempered person, but is now good-tempered; not a very genial person, but is now very much more genial; a person who was not very zealous, but is now very zealous; a person who is different in disposition from what he was formerly. Is that a true definition of a Christian? Give me a homeopathic cabinet. Bring along to me a very irritable person. Give him a dose of, what shall I say? —nux vomica; in two or three hours he will be a very good-tempered man. Is he a Christian? Give him something else; turn him back to what he was before. Was he saved, and has he back-slidden? Drugs can change a man's temper in a few hours. From being a lethargic, careless, indifferent person, you become alive, energetic, active; from being miserable, discontented, morose, melancholic, disagreeable, irritable, you become amiable, pleasant, relieved from all that nervous strain which was making you like that, and all that disordered digestion which was making you such a boor to live with. For a little while, you have made a Christian with drugs! You see the point.

Where is the truth? If the truth about my salvation lies in the realm of my feelings, my digestive system, my nervous organism, I am going to be a poor Christian; because that will be changing from day to day according to the weather or to something else. Oh no! Truth; where is the truth? *"Not what I am, but what Thou art."* That is where the truth is, *"Ye shall know the truth, and the truth shall make you free."* Free from what? Bondage! What bondage? Satan clapping his chains of condemnation upon you because today you are not feeling up to scratch. You are feeling bad in your constitution, and you are feeling depressed, you are feeling death all around, you are feeling irritable, and Satan comes along and says, You are not a Christian! A fine Christian you are! And you go down under it. Is that the truth? It is a lie! The only answer for deliverance and emancipation is, 'It is not what I am, it is what He is; Christ abides the same'. He is not as I am, varying here in this human life from hour to hour and day to day: He is other.

Forgive me being so strong in my emphasis, but I do feel this is the only way in which we are going to be saved really, Jesus, you see, says, *"I am the truth."* What is the truth? It is that which stands up to all arguments of Satan who is *"a liar and the father of it"*. It is that which delivers us from this false self which we are; and we are a false self. We are a bundle of contradictions. We can never be sure that we are going to be of the same mind for long together, that our convictions are not going to do a right about turn. Oh no, it is not ourselves at all; it is Christ. You see what a false position we could be in if we were on that other level of nature. What a game the Devil could play with us.

I am using these illustrations to try to get to the heart of this. What is the truth? What is true? It is not found in us. We are not true in any part of our being. Christ alone is truth, and you and I have to learn how to live on Christ, and until we have done that the Holy Spirit cannot do the other thing. Perhaps you are saying, Is not a true Christian less ill tempered? Is there no difference at all? Is a Christian right to be irritable and all that? I am not saying that, I am not letting you off on that; I am saying that in the school, until you and I have learned to hold on to Christ by faith, the Holy Spirit has not the ground upon which to work to bring us into conformity to Christ. If we are going to live upon the false basis of ourselves, the Holy Spirit leaves us lone. When we come to live by faith on Christ, then the Holy Spirit can come in and make Christ good in us, and teach us victory and teach us mastery, and teach us by deliverance how not to become a prey to good or bad feelings in ourselves, but to live on another level altogether. I mean this, that you cut the ground from under a great deal when you really get on to the ground of Christ.

Take irritability, for example. Some of you, of course, may never suffer in that way at all, but others do know what that battle is. Well, let us take such a case. Today we feel like that, all nervy, strained and short. What are we going to do about it? Are we going to make that our Christian life or the negation of our Christian life! If we come on to that ground, then Satan is always swift to make the most of it and bring us into terrible bondage and really to kill all spiritual life. But if you will take the position, 'Yes, that is how I feel today, that is my infirmity today, but Lord Jesus, You are other than I am, and I just rest on You, hold on to You, make You my life', you see what you have done. You have cut the ground from under the feet of the Devil altogether, and you will find that there is peace along that line, and rest, and although you may still be feeling bad in the outer part of you, in the inner part you are at rest. The enemy is shut out from the inner part of you, he has no place there. The peace of God stands sentinel over heart and mind through Christ Jesus; the citadel is safe. What Satan is always trying to do is to get into the spirit through the body or soul and to capture the stronghold, the spirit, and bring it into bondage. But we can remain free inwardly when we are feeling very bad outwardly. That is freedom by the truth. That is the truth! Not a thing, not an affirmation, but a Person. It is what Christ is, and He is altogether different from what we are. Well, the Holy Spirit would teach us, as the Spirit of Truth, that it is abiding in Christ that means everything. The alternatives are to get into ourselves, or into other people, or into the world, in a mental way. Abide in Christ and there is rest, there is peace, there is deliverance.

But do not forget that if we mean business with the Holy Spirit, He is not going to allow us to be deceived. I mean that the Holy Spirit is going to expose our true selves. He is going to uncover us and show us thoroughly there is nothing sound in us, nothing to be relied upon in us, in order that He may make it equally clear that it is only in Christ, God's Son, that there is security, and safety and life.

I have a sense of failure in trying to convey to you what I have in my heart. So many people think that the spiritual life, the life of a child of God, is a matter of things. It is a thing called 'the message of the Cross'. It is a thing called 'sanctification'. It is a thing called 'deliverance'. It is a thing called 'death with Christ'—some *thing*. They are trying to get hold of *it*, and there is no deliverance that way at all. It does not work. 'Its' do not work! It is all a matter of the Person, the Lord Jesus, and the Holy Spirit will never save us by an 'it'. He will always bring us to the Person, and make Christ the basis of our life, of our deliverance, of our everything. So the word is *"Christ Jesus...was made unto us wisdom from God, both righteousness and sanctification, and redemption"* (1 Cor. 1:30).

The Abiding Need of Faith

Well, I must close. The work of the Holy Spirit is to conform us to Christ, to cause us to take the form of Christ, to form Christ in us; but Christ will always remain other than we are, so that there will never cease to be a call for faith. Do you expect to reach a point in this earthly pilgrimage when faith can be dispensed with! It is a false hope. Faith will be required as much as ever in your last moments in this life, if not more than at any other time. Faith is an abiding thing for the duration of this life. If that is true, that in itself dismisses any hope whatever of our having the thing in ourselves. That was the first sin of Adam, that choice of his, not to have everything in God, but to have it in himself in independence, to get rid of the idea of faith. So he sinned by unbelief, and the sin that has come in since is traceable to that one thing—unbelief. Faith is the great factor of redemption, or salvation, of sanctification, of glorification; everything is through faith. It undoes the work of the Devil. And faith simply means that we are put into the position where we have not got it in ourselves, we only have it in Another, and can only know it and enjoy it by faith in that Other. Thus Galatians 2:20 always comes with renewed force—*"I have been crucified with Christ; and it is no longer I that live, but Christ liveth in me: and that life which I now live in the flesh I live in faith, the faith which is in the Son of God, who loved me, and gave himself up for me"* (A.R.V.). I live the life in the flesh by faith in the Son of God.

The Lord interpret His word to us.

III
LEARNING BY REVELATION

"In the visions of God brought he me into the land of Israel, and set me down upon a very high mountain, whereon was as it were the frame of a city on the south. And he brought me thither; and, behold, there was a man, whose appearance was like the appearance of brass, with a line of flax in his hand, and a measuring reed; and he stood in the gate. And the man said unto me, son of man, behold with thine eyes, and hear with thine ears, and set thy heart upon all that I shall show thee; for, to the intent that I may show them unto thee, art thou brought hither: declare all that thou seest to the house of Israel" (Ezekiel 40:2-4).

"Thou, son of man, show the house to he house of Israel, that they may be ashamed of their iniquities; and let them measure the pattern. And if they be ashamed of all that they have done, make known unto them the form of the house, and the fashion thereof, and the egresses thereof, and the entrances thereof, and all the forms thereof, and all the laws thereof; and write it in their sight; that they may keep the whole form thereof, and all the ordinances thereof, and do them" (Ezekiel 43:10-11).

"In the beginning was the Word, and the Word was with God, and the Word was God. The same was in the beginning with God. All things were made through him; and without him was not anything made that hath been made. In him was life; and the life was the light of men" (John 1:1-4).

"And the Word became flesh, and dwelt among us (and we beheld his glory, glory as of the only begotten from the Father), full of grace and truth" (John 1:14).

**"And he saith unto him, Verily, verily, I say unto
you, Ye shall see the heaven opened, and the angels of
God ascending and descending upon the Son of man"**
(John 1:51).

God's Answer to a State of Declension

We have observed that, when the Divine thought as
represented by the temple and Jerusalem was forsaken and
lost and the glory had departed, Ezekiel was given and
caused to write the vision of anew heavenly house, a house
in every detail measured and defined from above. In the
same way when the Church of New Testament times had
lost its purity and truth and power, and its heavenly
character and order, and the primal glory of those early
New Testament days was departing, then John was caused
by the Spirit o bring into view the new, wonderful,
heavenly, spiritual presentation, the person of the Lord
Jesus; that new heavenly presentation of Christ which we
have in John's Gospel, his letters, and the Revelation. And
we must remember that the Gospel written by John is, in
point of time, practically the last writing of the New
Testament. Perhaps the real significance of this has not
fallen upon us with due power and impressiveness. We
take up the Gospels as we have them in the New Testament
arrangement of books, and immediately we are put by them
back into the days of our Lord's life on the earth, and from
the standpoint of time that is where we are when reading
the Gospels. For us, all the rest of the New Testament has
yet to be when we are in the gospels, both as to the writings
and the history which followed, all is in prospect. That of
course is almost inevitable, perhaps almost unavoidable;
but we must try to extricate ourselves from that position.

Why was the Gospel of John written? Was it
written just as a record of the life of the Lord Jesus here on
earth to go alongside of two or three other records, that

there might be a history of the earthly life of the Lord Jesus preserved? Is that it? That is practically the sole result for a great many. The Gospels are read with a view to studying the life of Jesus while He was on earth. That may be very good, but I do want to emphasize very strongly that this is not he Holy Spirit's primary intention in inspiring the writing of those Gospels. And this is particularly seen in the case of John's Gospel, written so long after everything else, right at the end of everything; for when John wrote his final writings, the other apostles were in glory. John's Gospel was written when the New Testament Church, as we have said, had lost its original form and power and spiritual life, its heavenly character and Divine order; written in the midst of such conditions as are outlined in the messages to the churches in Asia at the beginning of the Apocalypse, and that can be so clearly inferred from his letters.

What was the object in view? Well, just this: as John writes, things are not as they were, not as God meant them to be. They no longer represent God's thought in and for His people. The order, the heavenly order, has broken down and is breaking down yet more. The heavenly nature has been forfeited and an earthly thing is taking shape in Christianity. The true life is being lost and the glory is departing. To that situation God reacts with a new presentation of His Son in a heavenly and spiritual way; for the features or characteristics of John are heavenliness and spirituality. Is that not true? Oh yes, here is a new bringing into view of His Son. But what a bringing into view! Not just and only as Jesus of Nazareth, but as the Son of Man, Son of God. God revealed and manifested in man, out from eternity with all the fulness of Divine essence, that His people might see.

So we must get to the Holy Spirit's standpoint in the Gospel by John, and in his other writings, and just see this, that God's way of recovery, when His full and original thought has been lost and that heavenly revelation has departed, and the heavenly glory has been withdrawn, is to bring His Son anew into view. Not to bring you back to the technique of the Church or the Gospel or the doctrine, but to bring His Son into view. To bring Christ again in the tremendousness of His heavenly and spiritual meaning before the heart-eyes of His people. That is the answer that is found in John to these conditions that we meet with in the New Testament, which so plainly shows that the Church was losing its heavenly position, and all sorts of things were coming in, and the whole thing was becoming earthly. What will God do? In what way will He save His purpose which seems to be so dangerously near being lost? He will bring His Son into view again. Remember God's answer is always in His Son to every movement. Whether that movement be in the world as it heads up to Antichrist (God's answer to Antichrist will be Christ in the full blaze of His Divine glory), or whether it be in the Church in declension and apostasy, God's answer will be in His Son.

That is the meaning of the opening words of the book of the Revelation. The Church has lost her place, the glory has departed, but God breaks in with a presentation of His Son.

"I am...the Living one; and I became dead, and behold, I am alive unto the ages of the ages, and I have the keys of death and of Hades."

Christ is presented, and then everything is measured and judged in the light of that heavenly Man with the measuring reed in His hand. That is enough really, if we only saw that, and grasped it. Everything for God and for us is bound up with a heart-revelation of the Lord Jesus. Oh, it will not be, as I have said, in trying to recover the New Testament technique. It will not be in a restoration of New Testament truth and doctrine. These are things, and they can be used to form a framework, but they can never guarantee the life, the power, the glory. There are plenty here in this earth who have the New Testament doctrine and technique and order, but it is a cold, dead framework. The life, the glory, is not there; the rapture is not there. No, God's way of the glory is in His Son: God's way of the life is in His Son: God's way of the power is in His Son: God's way of the heavenly nature is in His Son. And that is John's Gospel in a few words, what God is there saying. It is all in the Son, and the need, the only need, is to see the Son. And if you see the Son by God's act of opening the eyes, then the rest will follow. That is John's Gospel again.

"How opened he thine eyes?" Who did this? How did He do it? The man's response or reaction to the interrogation was this, in effect, You are asking me for the technique of things; I am not able to give you the technique, I am not able to explain this thing, but I have the reality, and that is the thing that matters. *"One thing I know that, whereas I was blind, now I see."* It is the light by the life. *"In him was life and the life was the light..."*

We do not want to be able just to give the technique of truth, and expound and define it all. That is not the first thing. The first thing is, the life produces the light and that is in the revelation of the Son: and if I must bring everything to a condensation it is this—firstly, God has shut up everything of Himself within His Son, and it is not possible now to know or have anything of God outside of the Lord Jesus, His Son. God has made this a settled thing. It is final, it is conclusive.

Christ Known Only by Revelation

Secondly, it is not possible to have or know anything of all the fulness which God has shut up in His Son without the Holy Spirit's revelation of that in an inward way. It has to be a miracle wrought by the Holy Spirit within every man and woman if they are to know anything of what God has shut up in Christ. That again summarizes John's Gospel, for there at the centre is a man born blind. He never has seen. It is not a case of restoration with him, it is a giving of sight. It is the first thing. It is going to be an absolutely new world for that man. Whatever he may have surmised or guessed or imagined, or had described to him, actual seeing is going to be something with a new beginning. It is going to be an absolute miracle, producing an absolutely new world, and all his guesses of what that world contained and was like will prove to have been very inadequate when he actually sees. Nothing is going to be seen save by the miracle wrought within.

(1) God has shut up everything of Himself in His Son.

(2) No one can know anything of that save as it is revealed. *"No one knoweth the Son, save the Father; neither doth any know the Father, save the Son, and he to whomsoever the Son willeth to reveal him"* (Matt. 11:27).

Revelation can only come by choice of the Son.

Revelation Bound Up With Practical Situations

The third thing is this. God always keeps the revelation of Himself in Christ bound up with practical situations. I want you to get that. God always keeps the revelation of Himself in Christ bound up with practical situations. You and I can never get revelation other than in connection with some necessity. We cannot get it simply as a matter of information. That is information, that is not revelation. We cannot get it by studying. When the Lord gave the manna in the wilderness (type of Christ as the bread from heaven) He stipulated very strongly that not one fragment more than the day's need was to be gathered, and that if they went beyond the measure of immediate need, disease and death would break out and overtake them. The principle, the law of the manna, is that God keeps revelation of Himself in Christ bound up with practical situations of necessity, and we are not going to have revelation as mere teaching, doctrine, interpretation, theory, or anything as a thing; which means that God is going to put you and me into situations where only the revelation of Christ can help us and save us.

You notice that the Apostles got their revelation for the church in practical situations. They never met around a table to have a Round-Table Conference, to draw up a scheme of doctrine and practice for the churches. They went out into the business and came right up against the desperate situation, and in the situation which pressed them, oft-times to desperation, they had to get before God and get revelation. The New Testament is the most practical book, because it was born out of pressing situations. The Lord gave light for a situation. The revelation of Christ, we might say, in emergencies is the way to keep Christ alive, and the only way in which Christ really does live to His own. You understand what I mean.

Now then, that is why the Lord would keep us in situations which are acute, real. The Lord is against our getting out on theoretical lines with truth, out on technical lines. Oh, let us shun technique as a thing in itself and recognize this, that, although the New Testament has in it a technique, we cannot merely extract the technique and apply it. We have to come into New Testament situations to get a revelation of Christ to meet the situation. So that the Holy Spirit's way with us is to bring us into living, actual conditions and situations, and needs, in which only some fresh knowledge of the Lord Jesus can be our deliverance, our salvation, our life, and then to give us, not a revelation of truth, but a revelation of the Person, new knowledge of the Person, that we come to see Christ in some way that just meets our need. We are not drawing upon an 'it', but upon a 'Him'.

He is the Word. *"In the beginning was the Word"*, and the meaning of that designation is just this, that God has made Himself intelligible to us in a Person, not in a book. God has not first of all written a book, although we have the Bible. God has written a Person. In one of his little booklets, Dr. A. B. Simpson has this illustration, or illustrates this thing in this way. He says that on one occasion he saw the Constitution of the United States written, and it was written on a parchment. He was near to it, and could read all the details of the Constitution of the United States. But as he stood back from that parchment, some yards off, all he could see was the head of George Washington there on the parchment. Then he drew near again and saw the Constitution was so written in light and shadow as to take the shape of the head of George Washington. That is it. God has written the revelation of Himself, but it is in the Person of His Son, the Headship of the Lord Jesus. And you cannot have the constitution of heaven, except in the Person, and the constitution of heaven is the Person in the shape of God's Son.

This is only an affirmation of things. I do trust you will take hold of the fact stated and go to the Lord with this. Do not ask for light as some thing; ask for a fuller knowledge of the Lord Jesus. That is the way, for that is the only living way to know Him: and remember God always keeps the knowledge of Himself in Christ bound up with practical situations. That cuts both ways. We have to be in the situation. The Holy Spirit will bring us, if we are in His hand, into the situation which will make necessary a new knowledge of the Lord. That is one side. The other side is that, if we are in a situation which is a very hard and a very difficult one, we are in the very position to ask for a revelation of the Lord.

IV
THE HOUSE OF GOD

Reading: Ezekiel 40:2-4; 43:10-11

You remember it was at the time when everything which had formerly been God's means of setting forth in type His thoughts in the midst of His people, had been broken down and lost, and the people were far out of touch both spiritually and literally with those things (the temple and Jerusalem, etc.) that the Lord took up His servant Ezekiel, and in the visions of God brought him back to the land, setting him upon a high mountain, and showed him in vision the city, and that great, new, spiritual heavenly house. Very full and very comprehensive and very detailed was the vision and the unveiling that was given, and the prophet was taken to every point, every angle, and through the whole of that spiritual temple step by step; in and out, up and through, and around, the angel with the measuring rod all the time giving the dimensions, the measurements of everything; a most exhaustive definition of this whole spiritual house. And then, further, after being shown all the form and the ordinances, the priesthood, the sacrifices and everything else, the prophet was commanded to show the house to the house of Israel and to give them all the detail of the Divine thought. In our previous meditation we pointed out, in that connection, that whenever there is a departure from Divine thoughts, whenever there is a loss of the original revelation of God, whenever the heavenliness, the spirituality, the Divine power of that which is of God ceases to operate in the midst of His people and whenever the glory departs, the Lord's reaction to such a state of things is to bring His Son anew into view; and we followed through to see how that, in just such a time in the history of the Church in the first days, when things changed from the primal glory, John was used by the Holy Spirit through his

Gospel, his Letters, and the Apocalypse, to bring the Lord Jesus in a full, heavenly, spiritual way anew into view; reminding ourselves, in so doing, that John's Gospel is practically the last New Testament book that was written, so that in spiritual value and significance, it stands really after everything else written in the New Testament. That is to say, it represents God's breaking in again with a fresh presentation of His Son in terms of heavenliness and spirituality, at a time when things have gone astray.

I just want for a few minutes, as I feel constrained, to stay with that: and we have the Gospel of John opened before us, at the first chapter. And note that this is God coming back in relation to the fulness of His thought for His people, and the meaning is just this: Christ is the fulness of God's thought for us, and the Holy Spirit (represented by the angel in Ezekiel), has come with the express object and purpose of giving and leading us into the detail of Christ, so that we get a comprehensive and detailed expression of the Divine thought in Christ and are brought thereunto.

Now you notice with John 1 you get the fresh, great, eternal presentation:

"In the beginning was the Word, and the Word was with god, and the Word was God."

that is the eternal background of Divine thought. Move on a little:

"And the Word became flesh, and tabernacled among us."

That is the Divine thought coming out of eternity and being planted right in the midst in a full and comprehensive way; all God's thoughts summed up in His son, the great Eternal Thought, and centred in the midst of men in the Person of Christ. And then you move (and I am not touching all that lies between these points) to the end of that first chapter and you have by implication something that is very beautiful, if you recognize its significance. It is the word to Nathanael. It is always interesting to notice that it was to Nathanael. Had it been to Peter, James or John, we might well have concluded that it was for a sort of inner circle. But, being Nathanael, he is in the widest circle of association with Christ, and therefore what was said to him is said to every one.

"Ye shall see the heaven opened, and the angels of God ascending and descending upon the Son of man."

Bethel—The House of God

Now for the implication: we are instinctively carried by those words right back to the old Testament, to the book of Genesis, and Jacob immediately comes into view. We remember Jacob on his way between two points, as it were in an in-between place, between heaven and earth; neither wholly of the earth nor wholly of the heaven, but an in-between place. That night, in that in-between place, somewhere in the open he lay down and slept; and, behold, a ladder set up on the earth, the top of which reached unto heaven, and upon it the angels ascending and descending, and above the ladder the Lord; and the Lord spoke to him. And Jacob awaked out of his sleep, and said, Surely the Lord is in this place; and I knew it not: this is none other but the house of God! And he called the name of that place "Bethel", or the House of God.

The Lord Jesus appropriated that and made it to apply to Himself in His words to Nathanael, and, in effect or by implication, said, I am Bethel, the House of God; I am that which is not wholly of the earth, although resting on it; not wholly of heaven in My present capacity, though related to it; I am here between heaven and earth, the meeting place of God and man, the House of God, in Whom God speaks, in Whom God is revealed—He speaks in His House, He is revealed in His House—I am the House of God: the communications of God with this world are in Me, and in Me alone: *"no one cometh to the Father but by me"*. He might well have said, although it is not recorded that He ever did so: the Father comes to no one but by Me.

Now, it is just that House of God, as represented by Christ, that is our thought as leading up to the practical testimony in baptism: Jesus—God's House. We know, of course, that every other house in the Bible is only an illustration of Him. Whether it be the tabernacle in the wilderness or the temple of Solomon, or any subsequent temple which was intended to fulfil the same function, or anything that in more spiritual terms in the New Testament is called the Church, it is not something other than Christ, but it is Christ. In the thought of God it is just Christ and there is nothing other than Christ and nothing extra to Christ which is the Church or the House of God.

The point that we feel the Lord is seeking to emphasize in these meditations is how He has bound up everything in a final way, conclusively and exclusively, with His Son, and that there is nothing to be had of God except in Christ, and by revelation of the Holy Spirit at that, as Christ is revealed by Him in our hearts. So that the Lord Jesus, being God's House, fulfils every function which is in type set forth in these other houses on this earth.

You begin with the Most Holy Place, the Holy of Holies. In Him is the Holy of Holies, where God verily and personally and actually dwells, has His habitation. God is in Christ, and in no other does He dwell in the same sense. It is going to become true that the Father will take up His abode in us. But, beloved, there is a difference. By the Father coming to dwell in us, we are not constituted so many more Christs. We are not in the same sense indwelt by very God as was the Son. The difference we will see in a minute. The indwelling of God in Christ is unique, and the Most Holy Place is in Him alone.

In Him is the oracle; that is, the voice, the voice that speaks with authority, and final authority. The final authority of God's voice is in Christ, and in Christ alone. The three disciples were in a very exalted position, both in their souls and in their bodies, on the Mount of Transfiguration. It was a wonderful, wonderful experience, a tremendous spiritual happening. But even so, when you are in a very exalted and elevated spiritual state, full of spiritual aspirations and spiritual expressions, you may make most grievous mistakes. So Peter, with the purest of motives, the highest intentions, said, *"Lord, it is good for us to be here: if thou wilt, I will make here three tabernacles; one for thee, and one for Moses, and one for Elijah."* And while he yet spake—as though God stepped in and did not give him a chance to finish, but said, Enough of that—while he yet spake, the cloud overshadowed, and there came a voice out of heaven saying, *"This is my beloved Son, in whom I am well pleased; hear ye him."* 'Don't you begin to give expression to your thoughts and ideas here in this position: the final word of authority is in Him; you be silent to Him. Your spiritual ecstasies must have no place here; you must not be influenced by even your most exalted feelings.' God's authoritative voice in Christ is the final word of authority. It is the oracle that is in Him, as in the sanctuary of old. So we may go through all of that tabernacle or temple and take it all point by point, and we see Him as the fulfilment of it all, as the House of God where God is found, and where God communicates.

The Corporate House of God

Now, what is the House of God in its fullest sense, in its corporate or collective sense? It is, to take up that wonderful phrase with its almost two hundred occurrences in the New Testament, all that is meant by "in Christ". If we are in the House of God, we are only in the House of God because we are in Christ. To be in Christ is to be in the House of God, and not to be in Christ Jesus is to be outside of the House of God. He is the House of God. We are brought into Him.

But to be in Christ means a total exclusion of all that is not Christ, and in a previous meditation we strove to make one thing so clear, and that is, the altogether and absolute 'other-ness' of Christ from ourselves, even at our best. How utterly different He is from man, even at man's religious best; different in mind, in heart, in will; different altogether in constitution, so that it take us a whole lifetime, under the tuition of the Holy Spirit, to discover how different we are from Christ and how different absolutely from the beginning. It does not take God a lifetime to discover the difference. He knows it, and therefore He has put the absolute position from His own standpoint right at the beginning. He has, in effect, said, The difference between you and Christ is so utter and final that it is the width and the depth of a grave! It is nothing less than the fulness of death. There is no passing over. Death and the grave are the end. On the one side, therefore, is the utter end of what you are, and if there is to be anything afterward at all, that death must stand between, and anything subsequent can only be by resurrection: So that, in that death, you are regarded as having passed out of the realm of what you are, even at your best, and as having passed into the realm of what He is. The depth of a grave lies between you and Him, and there is no passing over. It is an end. To get into the House of God means that.

The Altar

Thus you notice, coming back to John 1, the truth is here set forth in a representative way. It is more fully and clearly developed later in the New Testament when the

Holy Spirit has come for that purpose—He has come to take up what Christ has said and lead it out into its full meaning—but in John 1, long before you reach the House of God, you have this word reiterated, *"Behold, the Lamb of God, which taketh away the sin of the world."* Before you can get to the House, you have always to come to the altar. That is how it is in the tabernacle and temple. You can never get into the sanctuary, into the House actually until you have come to the altar. The lamb, God's lamb, and the altar, stand and bar your way to the sanctuary, and that lamb speaks of this dying in our stead, this passing out as us. We are identified firstly with Christ in His death, His death as our death. Then in virtue of His precious Blood which is sprinkled all the way from the altar right through to the Most Holy Place, in virtue of that precious Blood there is a way of life. It is His Blood, not ours; not our remedied life, not our improved life, not our life at all, but His. It is Christ and only Christ in the virtue of whose life we come into the presence of God. No High Priest dare come into the presence of God, save in the virtue of precious blood, the blood of the lamb, blood from the altar. Behold the Lamb of God! That stands right across the path to the House, the death in judgment, what we are. Well, these are hints from which you are seeing a great deal more, I expect, than I am able to say.

But what is particularly in view at this moment is this matter of being in Christ, and therefore being in God's House. The House of God is Christ, and if we speak of the House of God as being a corporate or collective thing in which we are, it is only because we are in Christ. Those who are in Christ are in the House of God, and *are* the House of God by their union with Him. They have come into the place where God is, and where God speaks; where God is known, and where the authority of God is in Christ absolutely, and we are carried in thought at once into Colossians, to Paul's word— *"He is the head of the church".* We see the Body and its head. Christ's Headship means the authority of God vested in Him for government.

Baptism

Now you see two things. There is the first step toward the House, namely, the altar, the death, and that is what baptism is intended to set forth. It is that we take our place in Christ representing us, as the end of all that we are in ourselves. It is not only our sins that are taken away; it is ourselves, as so utterly different from Christ. *From God's standpoint*, it is an end of us. Let us understand that. That is God's standpoint. In the death of Christ, God has brought an end to us in our natural life. In Christ's resurrection and our union with Him, *from God's standpoint* it is no longer we who exist. It is only Christ who exists and the Holy Spirit's work in the child of God is to make that which has been established in its finality real in us. We have not to die; we are dead. What we have to do is to accept our death. Failing to see that, we shall all the time be struggling to bring ourselves to death. It is a position taken which is God's settled, fixed and final position so far as we are concerned. That is the meaning of reckoning yourself dead. It is taking the place that God has appointed for us, stepping into it, and saying, I accept the position which God has fixed with regard to myself: the Holy Spirit's business is to deal with the rest, but I accept the end. If ever you and I should come to place where we turn away from the Holy Spirit's dealings with us, what we are doing is something more than just refusing to go on. It is refusing to accept the original position, and that is very much more serious. It really is a reversing of a position which we once took with Him.

Well, now, baptism is that altar where God regards us as having died in Christ, and we simply step in there and say, That position which God has settled with reference to me is the one which I now accept, and I testify here in this way to the fact that I have accepted God's position for me, namely, that in the Cross I have been brought to an end. The Lord Jesus took this way and set baptism right at the beginning of His public life, and, under the anointing of the Spirit, from that moment He absolutely refused to listen to His own mind apart from God, to be in any way influenced by anything arising from the dictates of His own humanity, sinless as it was, apart from God. All the way along He was being governed by the Anointing; in what He said, what He did, what He refused to do: where He went, and when He went; and was putting back every other influence, whether coming from the disciples, or from the Devil, or from any other direction. His attitude was, Father, what do You think about this: what do You want: is this Your time? He was saying, in effect, all the time, Not My will, but Yours; not My judgments, but Yours; not My feelings, but what You feel about it! He had died, in effect, you see; He had been buried, in effect. His baptism had meant that for Him, and that is where we stand.

The Laying on of Hands

But then there is the other thing. When the position has been accepted in death, there is the rising. But as I have said, it is the rising in Christ, and from God's standpoint it is the rising, not only in Christ, but as under the Headship of Christ. Or in other words, under that full and final authority of God vested in Christ, so that Christ is our mind, Christ is our government, His Headship! And when believers in New Testament times had taken the first step in baptism, declaring their death in Christ and had come up out of the waters representative members of the Body, not always the apostles, laid their hands upon their heads and prayed over them, and the Holy Spirit signified that they were in the House. The Anointing which was upon Christ as Head now came upon them in Christ; not a separate anointing, but anointed in Christ (2 Cor. 1:21; 12:13).

But what is the Anointing? What was the Anointing in the case of Christ, when He accepted a representative life and for the time being declined to live and act on the basis of Deity and Godhead, in order to work out man's redemption as Man? What did the Anointing mean? Well, in His case it is so clear. The Anointing meant that He was under the direct government of God in everything and had to refuse to refer or defer to His own judgments and feelings about anything. The Father, by the Anointing, was governing Him in everything, and He, apart from that, was altogether set aside. And when He said, *"If any man would come after me, let him deny himself, and take up his cross daily, and follow me";* or again, *"Whosoever doth not bear his own cross, and come after me, cannot be my disciple"* (Luke 9:23; 14:27), He was only saying in other words, 'You can never learn Me unless the Cross is operating continually to put you out and make way for Me, so that you can accept My mind, and the Cross means that you have to be crucified to your own mind about things; your mind has to come under the Cross; your will has to come under the Cross; your feelings and your ways have to come under the Cross daily. That is how you make a way for learning Me, My mind, My government, My judgment, My everything. That is the school of discipleship, the school of Christ.'

I was saying that, on the resurrection side, the Headship of Christ under the Anointing becomes, or should become the dominating factor in a believer's life, and the laying on of hands on the head is simply again a declaration that this one is under the Headship, this head comes under another Head, this head is subject to a greater Head. Thus far, this head has governed its life, but no longer shall this head govern its life; it is to be subject to another Headship.

This one is brought under Christ as Head in the Anointing. And the Spirit attested that in the first days; the Spirit came upon them, declaring that this one is in the House where the Anointing is, to be under the government of the Head of the House.

The spirit of it all finds expression in that word in the Letter to the Hebrews, *"But Christ as a son, over God's house; whose house are we"* (Heb. 3:6) I think it is unnecessary to say any more. We are just going on the way of the heavenly revelation of Christ; and, in baptism, we take the position of accepting God's position so far as we are concerned, namely, that this is an end of us! If in the future, what we are in ourselves seeks to assert itself, we should revert to this and say, 'We said once for all—an end of us!' Preserve your attitude toward God's position.

Then afterward the gathering around and the laying on of the hands of representative members of the Body is a simple testimony to the fact that in Christ such as bear the testimony are the House of God, under the government of Christ through the Anointing, and that His Headship constitutes us one in Him.

May the Lord make all this true in the case of all of us, a living reality, so that we really have come to Bethel and can say in our rejoicing in Christ, 'Surely the Lord is in this place!' It is a great thing when we come to a spiritual position where we can say, 'The Lord is in this place. I am where the Lord is: this is the House of God!' And that simply means a living knowledge of what it means to be in Christ, under His Headship and Anointing.

V
THE LIGHT OF LIFE

"And, behold, the glory of the God of Israel came from the way of the east: and his voice was like the sound of many waters; and the earth shines with his glory. And the glory of Jehovah came into the house by the way of the gate whose prospect is toward the east. And the Spirit took me up, and brought me into the inner court; and, behold, the glory of Jehovah filled the house" (Ezekiel 43:2,4,5).

"Then he brought me by the way of the north gate before the house; and I looked and, behold, the glory of Jehovah filled the house of Jehovah: and I fell upon my face" (Ezekiel 44:4).

"And he brought me back unto the door of the house; and, behold, waters issued out from under the threshold of the house eastward (for the forefront of the house was toward the east); and the waters came down from under, from the right side of the house, on the south of the altar" (Ezekiel 47:1).

"In him was life; and the life was the light of men" (John 1:4).

"Again therefore Jesus spake unto the, saying, I am the light of the world: he that followeth me shall not walk in the darkness, but shall have the light of life" (John 8:12).

"Jesus answered and said unto him, Verily, verily, I say unto thee, Except one be born from above, he cannot see the kingdom of God" (John 3:3, margin)

"When I am in the world, I am the light of the world" (John 9:5)

"Now there were certain Greeks among those who went up to worship at the feast; these therefore came to Philip, who was of Bethsaida of Galilee, and asked him, saying, Sir, we would see Jesus. Philip cometh and telleth Andrew: Andrew cometh, and Philip, and they tell Jesus. And Jesus answereth them saying, The hour is come, that the Son of man should be glorified. Verily, verily, I say unto you, Except a grain of wheat fall into the earth and die, it abideth by itself alone; but if it die, it beareth much fruit" (John 12:20-24).

"I am come a light into the world, that whosoever believeth on me may not abide in the darkness" (John 12:46).

"...in whom the god of this world hath blinded the minds of the unbelieving, tat the light of the gospel of the glory of Christ, who is the image of God, should not dawn upon them" (2 Corinthians 4:4).

"That the God of our Lord Jesus Christ, the Father of glory, may give unto you a spirit of wisdom and revelation in the knowledge of him; having the eyes of your heart enlightened, that ye may know what is the hope of his calling, what the riches of the glory of his inheritance in the saints, and what the exceeding greatness of his power to us-ward who believe, according to that working of the strength of his might..." (Ephesians 1:17-19).

The light of life! Before coming to a closer consideration of this matter of the light of life, may I just ask a simple but very direct question? Can we all say with truth of heart that we are really concerned to be in God's purpose; to know what that purpose is, and to be found in it? Everything depends upon whether we have such a concern. It is a practical matter. It should immediately swing us clear of just being interested in truth and increasingly our knowledge or information about spiritual things. As we look into our own hearts at this moment—and let us do so, each one of us—can we really say that there is a genuine and strong desire to be in the purpose, the great eternal purpose of God? Are we prepared to commit ourselves to the Lord in relation to that in an utter transaction, by which we now have an understanding with Him that He will stand at nothing so far as we are concerned to secure us in His eternal purpose, whatever it may cost? As the Lord's people, are we ready to just pause and face that, and get right into line with God's end? I know that some of you are there, and that for you there is not much need of exercise about it, but it is quite likely that there are some who have taken things pretty much for granted. That is to say, they are Christians, they are believers, they belong to the Lord, they are saved, they put their faith in Christ, they have had association with Christian institutions and matters for so long, perhaps even from infancy. It is to such that I make this appeal at the outset. Here in God's Word that very phrase is used repeatedly—*"according to his eternal purpose which he purposed in Christ Jesus before the world was"*. Is that the thing which stands foremost on our horizon or is it something remote, dim, in the background? I press this, because we must have something upon which to work. God must have something upon which to work, and if that is the position, then we can go on, and there will be a drawing out of revelation as to that purpose and the way of it. But unless we are in some quite positive position and attitude about it, you will hear a lot of things said and they will simply be things said, more or less of account to you.

The Purpose of God

Well now, given that there is that concern, at least in some measure, which justifies our going on, we ask, What is the purpose of God? What is God's end? And I think it can be put in one way amongst others. We can say that God's purpose is that there shall come a time when He has a vessel in which and through which His glory shines forth to this universe. We see that intimated in the case of new Jerusalem, coming down from God out of heaven, having the glory of God, her light like unto a stone most precious, as it were a jasper stone, clear as crystal, "Having the glory of God"! That is the end which God has in view for a people, to be, in a spiritual sense, to His universe of spiritual intelligences what the sun is to this universe; that the very nations shall walk in the light thereof; no need of sun, no need of moon, for there is no night. And that is only saying that God wills to have a people full of light, "the light of the knowledge of the glory of God". That is the end, and God begins to move toward that end immediately a child of His is born from above. For that very birth, a new birth from above, is the scattering of the darkness and the breaking of the light.

All along our way in the School of Christ, the Holy Spirit is engaged upon this one thing, to lead us more and more into the light, *"of the knowledge of the glory of God in the face of Jesus Christ"*, that it shall be true in our case that *"The path of the just is as the shining light which shineth more and more unto the perfect day"* (mid-day) (Proverbs 4:18). Many people have thought—and, thinking so, have been disappointed—that that means it is going to get easier and easier, brighter and brighter, the more cheerful as we go on. But it does not work out that way. I do not see it to be true in the circumstances and outward condition of saints anywhere at any time. For them the path does not become brighter and brighter outwardly. But if we are really moving under the Spirit's government, we can say with the strongest affirmation, that in an inward way the light is growing. The path is growing brighter and brighter; we are seeing and seeing and seeing. That is God's purpose; until the time comes when there is no darkness at all, and no shadow at all, and no mist at all, but all is light, perfect light: we see not through a glass darkly, but face to face, we know even as we are known. That is God's purpose put in a certain way. Does that interest you? Are you concerned with that?

And that has a crisis and is also a process in spiritual life with a glorious climax in rapture. What I am especially concerned with now is the process.

We read in Ezekiel about the glory of the Lord coming and filling the House, and we have been seeing in previous meditations that the Lord Jesus is that House. He is the great Bethel of God on whom the angels ascend and descend, in whom God is found, in whom God speaks (the place of the oracle), in whom is the Divine authority, the final word. He is the House, and the glory of the Lord is in Him, the light of God is in Him.

The Place of the Shekinah Glory

Looking backward at that tabernacle or that temple of old where the Shekinah glory was found, we mark that that light, that glory which linked heaven and earth like a ladder, had its expression in the Most Holy Place. You know that in the Holy of Holies, everything was curtained around and over, excluding every bit of natural light, so that the place, entered into apart from the Shekinah, would have been black darkness, without light at all; but entered nto while the glory rest upon it, it was all light, it was all

Divine light, heavenly light, the light of God. And that Most Holy Place sets forth the inner life of the Lord Jesus, His spirit where God is found, the light from heaven, the light of what God is in Him. His spirit is the Most Holy Place, in the holy House of God. And it was there, in that Most Holy Place where the light of the glory was, that God said He would commune with His people through their representative. *"I will commune with you above the mercy seat between the cherubim"* (Ex. 25:22). The place of communion—"I will commune". What a lovely word—"commune". There is nothing hard, nothing terrible, nothing fearful about that. "I will commune with you." It is the place where God speaks; in the communion God speaks, makes Himself known. It is the place of speaking. It is called the place of the oracle, the place of the speaking, and that is the Propitiatory, the Mercy Seat, and that is all the Lord Jesus. He, we are told, has been set forth by God to be a propitiatory (Romans 3:25), and in Him God communes with His people. In Him God speaks to and with His people.

But the underlining must be of those words *"in Him"*, for there is no communion with God, no communion of God, no speaking to be heard, no meeting at all, save in Christ. That would be a place of death and destruction for the natural man; hence the terrible warnings given about coming into that place without the right equipment, that symbolic equipment which spoke of the natural man having been altogether covered and another heavenly Man having enfolded him as with heavenly robes, the robes of righteousness. Only so dare he enter into that place: otherwise it was "lest he die..."

If you want to know exactly how that works out, come over to the New Testament and take up the story of the journey of Saul of Tarsus to Damascus. He says, *"At midday, O king, I saw on the way a light from heaven, above the brightness of the sun...And when we were all fallen to the earth, I heard a voice saying unto me...Saul, Saul, why persecutest thou me?"* Then you will remember how they lifted him up and led him into the city, because he was without sight. By the mercy of God, he was without sight only for three days and three nights. God commissioned Ananias to go and visit that blinded man, and say to him, *"Jesus, who appeared unto thee in the way which thou camest, hath sent me, that thou mayest receive thy sight."* Saul of Tarsus would otherwise have been a blind man to the end of his life. That is the effect of a natural man encountering the glory of God in the face of Jesus Christ. It is destruction. There is no place for the natural man in the presence of that light; it would be death. But in John 8 we have those words, "the light of *life*", over against the darkness of death. Well, in Jesus Christ the natural man is regarded as having been entirely put away. There is no place for him there.

No Place for the Natural Man

That means that the natural man cannot come into the light, nor can e come into God's great purpose and be found in that House full of His glory, that vessel through which He is going to manifest that glory to His universe. The natural man cannot come in there: and when we speak about the natural man, we are not just referring to the unsaved man, that is, the man who has never come to the Lord Jesus. We are speaking about the man whom God has reckoned as being put aside altogether.

The Apostle Paul had to speak to Corinthian believers along these lines. They were converted people, saved people, but they were enamoured of this world's wisdom and this world's power; that is, of natural wisdom, knowledge, and the strength that comes by it. Their disposition or inclination was to try to seek to take hold of Divine things and analyse them and investigate them, and probe into them along the lines of natural wisdom and understanding, philosophy, the philosophy and wisdom of this world. So they were bringing the natural man to bear upon Divine things, and the Apostle wrote to them, and in their own language he said, *"Now the man of soul* (not the unregenerate man, not the man who has never had a transaction with the Lord Jesus on the basis of His atoning work for salvation; no, not that man) *'the man of soul receiveth not the things of the Spirit of God, neither can he know them'* (I Corinthians 2:14). The man of the *psuche*, that is the natural man. The newest of our sciences is psychology, the science of the soul: and what is psychology? It has to do with the mind of man; it is the science of man's mind; and here is the word now—I am paraphrasing this because this is exactly what it means—Now the science of the mind can never receive the things of the Spirit of God, neither can it know them. This man is very clever, very intellectual, very highly trained, with all his natural senses brought to a high state of development and acuteness, yet this man is outside when it comes to knowing the things of God: he cannot, he is outside. For the first glimmer of the knowledge of God a miracle has to be wrought, by which blind eyes which never have seen are given sight, and by which light comes as by a flash of revelation, so that it can be said, *"Blessed are thou. . .for flesh and blood hath not revealed it unto thee, but my Father which is in heaven."*

That is stating a tremendous fact. Every bit of real light which is in the direction of that ultimate effulgence, the revealing of the glory of God in us and through us, every bit of it is in Christ Jesus, and can only be had in Him on the basis of the natural man having been altogether put outside, put away, and a new man having been brought into being with a new set of spiritual faculties: so that Nicodemus, the best product of the religious school of his day and of his world, is told, *"Except one be born anew (or from above), he cannot see..."* He cannot see. Well, it resolves itself into this, that to know even the first letters of the Divine alphabet we must be in Christ, and every bit that follows is a matter of learning Christ, knowing what it means to be in Christ.

How We Get the Light of Life
(a) The Crisis

That brings us to this question. What is the way into Christ, or how do we get the light of life? Well, the answer is, of course, briefly, to have the light we have to have the life. The light is the light of life. It is the product of life. All Divine light, true light from God, is living light. It is never theoretical light, mere doctrinal light; it is living light. And how do we get this light of life?

We have these two things brought very much before us in this Gospel of John, namely, Christ in us, and we in Christ. The Lord has given us a beautiful illustration of what that means, and that illustration we have read in chapter 12. What is it to be in Christ? What is it to have Christ in us? What is it to be in the life and in the light? What is it to have the life and the light in us? Well, here it is. There is life in that grain of wheat, but it is just one single grain. I want to get the life that is in that single grain into a whole host of grains, enough grains to cover the earth. How shall I do it? Well, the Lord says, put it into the ground: let it fall into the earth and die; let it fall into the dark earth, and let the earth cover it over. What happens? It immediately begins to disintegrate, to fall apart, to yield itself up, as to its own individual and personal life alone. Presently a shoot begins to break through the earth and up the stalk comes, and eventually there I an ear, a heavy ear, of grains of wheat; and if I could actually see life and look into those grains of wheat, I should see that life which was in the one of every one of them. Then I sow that ear, be it one hundred grains I sow, and I get ten thousand; and I sow them again, and they are multiplied a hundred-fold, and so on until the earth is full; and if I could look with a magnifying glass into every one of those millions and millions of grains, and life was something visible to the eye, I should see that that same original life was the life of every one of them. That is the answer.

How does this life get into us, this light of life? The Lord Jesus says that death must take place, a death to what we are in ourselves, a death of our own life, a death to a life apart from Him. We must go down with Him into death, and there, under the act of the Spirit of God in union with Christ buried, there is a transmission of His life to us. And He, coming up no longer merely as a single grain of wheat, comes up manifold in every one of us. It is the miracle that is going on every year in the natural realm. And it is just exactly the principle by which the Lord gets into us. You see the necessity of our ceasing to have a life apart from the Lord, the necessity of our letting that life of ours go absolutely. That is a crisis at the beginning, a real crisis. Sooner or later, it has to be a crisis.

Some may say, I have not had that crisis. For me becoming a Christian was a very, very simple thing. As a child, I was simply taught, or, at sometime I simply expressed my personal faith in the Lord Jesus in some way, and from that time I belonged to the Lord; I am a Christian! Are you moving on in the growing fulness of the revelation of the Lord Jesus? Are you? Have you an open heaven? Is God in Christ revealing Himself to you in every greater wonder and fulness? Is He? I am not saying that you do not belong to the Lord Jesus, but I am saying to you that the unalterable basis of an open heaven is a grave, and a crisis at which you come to an end of your own self-life. It is the crisis of real experimental identification with Christ in His death, not now for your sins, but as you. Your open heaven

depends upon that. It is a crisis. And so with not one or
two but with many this has been the way. The truth is this,
that they were the Lord's children; they knew Christ, they
were saved, they had no doubt about that. But then the
time came when the Lord, the Light of Life, showed to
them that He not only died to bear their sins in His body on
the tree, but He Himself represented them in the totality of
their natural life, to put it aside. It was the man, and not
only his sins that went to the Cross. That man is you, that
man is me: and many, after years of being Christians, have
come to that tremendous crisis of identification with Christ
as men, as women, as a part of the human race; not only as
sinners, but as a part of a race, natural men, not
unregenerate, but natural men, all that we are in our natural
life. Many have come to that crisis, and from that time
everything has been on a vast, a vaster scale than ever
before in the Christian life. There has been the open
heaven, the enlarged vision, the light of life in a far greater
way.

How does it come about? Just like that, and that
crisis is a crisis for us all. If you have not had that crisis,
you ask the Lord about it. Mark you, if you are going to
have that transaction with the Lord, you are asking for
something. You are asking for trouble; for, as I said before,
this natural man dies hard; he clings tenaciously, he does
not like being put aside. Look at that grain of wheat.
When it has fallen into the ground, look at what happens to
it. Do you think it is pleasant? What is happening? It is
losing its own identity. You cannot recognize it. Take it
out and have a look at it. Is this that lovely little grain of
wheat I put into the ground? What an ugly thing it has
become! It has lost all its own identity, lost its own
cohesiveness; it is all falling to pieces. How ugly! Yes,
that is what death does. This death of Christ as it is
wrought in us breaks up our own natural life. It scatters it,
pulls it to pieces, takes all its beauty away. We begin to

discover that, after all, there is nothing in us but corruption. That is the truth. Falling apart, we are losing all that beauty that was there from the natural point of view, perhaps, as men saw it. It is no pleasant thing to fall into the ground and die. That is what happens.

"But if it die..." If we *died with Christ, we believe that we shall also live with him"* (Romans 6:8). We shall share His life, take another life, and then a new form is given, a new life; not ours, but His. It is a crisis. I do urge upon you to have real dealings with the Lord about this matter. But if you do, expect what I have said. Expect that you are going to fall to pieces. Expect that the beauty you thought was there will be altogether marred. Expect to discover that you are far more corrupt than ever you thought you were. Expect that the Lord will bring you to a place where you cry. Woe is me for I am undone! But then the blessing that will come will jus be this—O Lord, the best thing that can happen for me is that I shall die! And the Lord will say, That is exactly what I have been working at. I cannot glorify that corruption. *"This corruptible must put on incorruption"* (I Corinthians 15:53), and that incorruption is the germ of that Divine life in the seed which yields its own life up, that is transmitted from Him. God is not going to glorify this humanity. He is going to make us like Christ's glorious body. That is far too deep, and too much ahead, but our point is that there has to be this crisis if we are coming to the glory, God's end.

(b) The Process

Then there is going to be a process. The Lord Jesus said, *'If any man would come after me, let him deny himself, and take up his cross daily, and follow me"*, and in so saying He was not wrong in principle. That the Cross is something taken up or entered into once for all is true, as to the crisis in which we say, Lord I accept once for all what the Cross means! But we are going to find that after the crisis, the all-inclusive crisis, day by day the Cross has to be adhered to, and the Cross is working out in those afflictions and sufferings which the Lord is allowing to come upon His people. He has put you in a difficult situation in His sovereignty; a difficult home, business, physical situation, a difficult situation with some relation. Beloved, that is the outworking of the Cross in your experience, in order to make a way for the Lord Jesus to have a larger place. It is going to make a way for His patience, the endurance of Christ, for the love of Christ. It is going to make a way for Him: and you have not to go to your knees every morning and say, Oh, Lord, get me out of this home, get me out of this business, get me out of this difficulty! You are to say, Lord, if this is the Cross in its expression for me today, I take it up today. Facing the situation like that, you will find there is strength, there is victory, the co-operation of the Lord, and there is fruit and not barrenness. It is in that sense that the Lord was right in principle in making the Cross a daily experience. *"Whosoever doth not bear his own cross, and come after me, cannot be my disciple"*—one of My taught ones, one learning Me! So that the taking up of this difficulty, whatever it be, day by day, is the very way in which I am learning Christ, and it is the process of light, the light of life, coming to know, coming to see, coming into fulness. You and I can never see and know apart from the Cross. The Cross has to clear the ground of this natural life. The Lord knows what we would do if He lifted away the Cross from us every day. I wonder what we would do.

It may not be just the later New Testament phraseology, or way of putting it, to speak of our daily cross, bearing my cross daily. The principle may be more truly be that it is the Cross which is given to Him and becomes mine daily. That may be true, but it just works out this way. If the Lord lifted that which is the expression of the Cross for us day by day and took it off our shoulders, it would not be for our good. It would at once clear the way for the uprising of the natural life. You can see when people begin to get a bit of relief from trial. How they throw their weight about! They get on stilts, they are looking down on you; you are wrong, they are right. Pride, self-sufficiency, all comes up. Well then, what about Paul! I look up to Paul as a giant, spiritually. Beside that man we are puppets spiritually. Yet, Paul, spiritual giant that he was, humbly confessed that the Lord sent him a messenger of Satan to buffet him, a stake through his flesh, lest he should be exalted above measure. Yes, spiritual giants can exalt themselves if the Lord does not see to it and take precautions. And in order to keep the way of that great revelation opened and clear, that it might grow and grow, the Lord said, *'Paul, I must keep you down very low, very much under limitation; it is the only way: immediately you begin to get up, Paul, you are going to limit the light, spoil the revelation.'*

Well, there is the principle. The light of life. It is His life: and so again the Apostle says,

"Always bearing about in the body the dying of Jesus that the life also of Jesus may be manifested in our body" (2 Corinthians 4:10).

His life is what we need, and with the life comes the light. It is light by life. There is no other real Divine light, only that which comes out of His life within us, and it is His death wrought in us that clears the way for His life.

I must close there. See again God's end; light, glory, the fulness coming in. It is in Christ. The measure of light, the measure of the glory, is going to be the measure of Christ, and the measure of Christ is going to depend entirely upon what space the Lord can find for Himself in us. And for space to be made for Him, we must come to the place where the utterness of the setting aside of the self-life has been accomplished: and that takes a whole lifetime. But, blessed be God, there is the glorious climax, when He shall come to be glorified in His saints and to be marvelled at in all them that believe. Marvelled at! Having the glory of God! Oh, may something of the light of that glory fall upon our hearts now to encourage and comfort us in the way, to strengthen our hearts to go on in the knowledge of His Son, for His Name's sake.

VI
AN OPEN HEAVEN

We have been led to think in these meditations
about being in the School of Christ, where all the learning,
all the instruction, all the discipline, is toward knowing
Christ, learning Christ; not learning about Christ but
learning Christ. That is the point of greatest difficulty in
trying to make things plain and clear. We could take up
everything there is about Christ as doctrine, as teaching, but
that is not what we are after. That is not what the Lord is
after at all. It is Christ Himself. He Himself is the living,
personal embodiment, the personification of all truth, of all
life and the Lord's purpose and will for us is not to come to
know truth in its manifold aspects, but to know the Person,
the living Person in a living way, and that the Person being
imparted to us, and we being incorporated into the Person,
all the truth becomes living truth rather than merely
theoretical or technical truth.

Just a word of repetition here: and I cannot tell you
with what force this has come to my own heart and how
heavily it rests upon me in its meaning. Whenever things
are in danger of departing from His full, His complete,
thought, God will always seek to bring back a fresh
revelation of His Son. He will not lead to the recapture of
truths as such. He will bring back all that is necessary by a
fresh revelation of His Son, an unveiling or presentation of
His Son in fulness. In that connection we have more than
once said in these meditations that the Gospel written by
John and his Letters and the Apocalypse, are the final
things of the New Testament dispensation. They were
written and brought in when the New Testament Church
was departing from its primal and pristine glory, and purity,
and truth, and holiness and spirituality, and becoming an
earthly Christian system. The Lord's way of meeting that
situation was through these writings which are a new

presentation of His Son in heavenly, Divine, spiritual fulness. It is a coming back to Christ, and the Holy Spirit would do that all the time. He would bring us back to the Person, to show us what that Person represents in a spiritual fulness. It is a coming back to Christ, and the Holy Spirit would do that all the time. He would bring us back to the Person, to show us what that Person represents in a spiritual and heavenly way. We must be very careful that in our passing on from the Gospels to the Epistles, we do not get even unconsciously into the position that we have left elementary things and gone on to something that is not so elementary; that is, that the Epistles are something very much in advance of the Gospels. Emphatically they are not. They are only the opening up of the Gospels. All that is in the Epistles is there in the Gospels, but the Epistles are simply the interpretation of Christ, and the Lord would never have us occupied with the interpretation to the loss of the Person.

All Things in Christ

Now, if I were talking to people who were responsible in the matter of Church building, that would be a very profitable matter with which to stay for a little while; but it just amounts to this for us. We take the Acts and the Epistles as setting forth the technique of the Church and churches and adopt it as a crystallized system of practice, order, form, teaching. And the weakness in the whole position is just this, that that is something as in itself, and the Lord Jesus has been missed and lost. I wonder if you detect what I mean by that? You see, the Holy Spirit's way is to take Christ and open up Christ to the heart, and show that Christ is a heavenly order; not that the Epistles set forth as a manual a heavenly order, but that Christ is that order, and everything in the matter of order has to be kept immediately in relation to the living Person. If it becomes some *thing*, then it becomes an earthly system; and you can make out of the Epistles a hundred different earthly systems all built upon the Epistles. They will be made to support any number of different systems, different interpretations, represented by Christian orders here, and the reason is that they have been divorced from the Person.

You see there are numerous things, numerous subjects, themes, teachings. There is the "kingdom of God", there is "sanctification", there is "eternal life", there is "the victorious life", "the overcomer" or "the overcoming life", there is "the second coming of Christ". These are but a few subjects, themes, truths, as they are called, which have been taken up and developed out of the Scriptures and become things with which people have become very much occupied, and in which they are very interested as things. So certain people hive off around a sanctification teaching, and they are the 'sanctificationists' and it becomes an 'ism'. Others hive off, and they are bounded by the hedge of Second Adventism, the Lord's coming, prophecy, and all that. So you get groups like that. I want to say that would be utterly impossible if the Person of the Lord Jesus was dominant. What is the kingdom of God? It is Christ. If you get right inside of the Gospels you will find that the kingdom of God is Jesus Christ. If you are living in Christ, you are in the kingdom and you know, as the Holy Spirit teaches you Christ, what the kingdom is in every detail. The kingdom is not some thing, in the first place. The kingdom, when it becomes something universal, will simply be the expression and manifestation of Christ. That is all. You come to the kingdom in and through Christ; and the same is true of everything else.

What is sanctification? It is not a doctrine. It is not an 'it' at all. It is Christ. He is made unto us sanctification (1 Corinthians 1:30). If you are in Christ and if the Holy Spirit is teaching you Christ, then you are knowing all about sanctification; and if He is not, you may have a theory and doctrine of sanctification, but it will separate you from other Christians, and it will be bringing any number of Christians into difficulties. Probably the teaching of sanctification as a thing has brought more Christians into difficulty than any other particular doctrine, through making it a thing, instead of keeping Christ as our sanctification.

I am only saying this to try to explain what I mean that it is in the School of Christ that we are to be found, where the Holy Spirit is not teaching us *things*; not Church doctrine, not sanctification, not adventism, not any *thing*, or any number of things, but teaching us Christ. What is adventism? What is the coming of the Lord? Well, it is the coming of the *Lord*. And what is the coming of the Lord? Well, such a word as this will give us the key: *"He shall come to be glorified in His saints, and to be marvelled at in all them that believed"* (2 Thessalonians 1:10). You see, it is the consummation of something that has been going on in an inward way. How then do I best know that the coming of the Lord draws nigh? Not best of all by prophetic signs, but by what is going on within the hearts of the Lord's people. That is the best sign of the times, namely, what the Spirit of God is doing in the people of God. But maybe you are not interested in that. You would far sooner know what is going to happen between Germany and Russia, whether these two eventually are going to become a great confederacy! How far does it get us? Where has all the talking about the revived Roman Empire got us? That is adventism as a thing. If only we keep close to Him who is the sum of all truth, and move with Him and learn Him, we shall know the course of things. We shall know what is imminent. We shall have in our heart whisperings of preparation. The best Advent preparation is to know the Lord. I am not saying that there is nothing in prophecy: don't misunderstand me. But I do know that there are multitudes of people who are simply engrossed in prophecy as a thing whose spiritual life counts for nothing, who really have no deep inward walk with the Lord. We have seen it so often.

I shall never forget on a visit to a certain country going into one of the big cities where I was to speak for a week. Everything was so arranged that my first message was timed to follow the last message of a man who had had a week before me, and he had been on prophecy for the whole week. I went into the last meeting where he gave his final message on the signs of the time. Notebooks were out, and they were taking it all down, fascinated. It was all external, all-objective; such things as the Roman Empire revived and Palestine recovered. You know the sort of thing. Then he finished and they were waiting for some more, and the notebooks were ready. The Lord put it right into my heart that the first word was to be, *"And every one that hath this hope set on him purifieth himself, even as he is pure"* (1 John 3:3); to speak on the spiritual effect of that spiritual hope. They were not interested in that. The notebooks were closed, pencils put away, there was no interest as I sought in the Lord to be very faithful as to what all this should mean in an inward way, in adjustment to the Lord, and so on. They were only longing for the meeting to close. When I finished——they hardly waited for me to finish——they were up and out.

Oh no, it is the Lord, and the Holy Spirit would bring us back to the Lord, and it is not, after all, coming back to nonessentials, to elementary things, to come back to Christ. It is coming on to the only basis upon which the Holy Spirit can really accomplish all God" will and purpose, to be in the School of Christ where the Holy Spirit is teaching us Christ; and the Holy Spirit's way of teaching Christ is experimental.

The Need of a New Set of Faculties

Now, here is where we become so seemingly elementary. You see, the very nature of this school requires the most drastic change in ourselves. It is impossible to get into the School of Christ, where the Holy Spirit is the great tutor, until the greatest change has taken place in us. We have to be made all over again or that school will mean nothing. We cannot come in here with any hope of learning Christ in the smallest way until a whole new set of faculties has been given to us. We have to have faculties given to us which we do not possess naturally. *"Except one be born from above, he cannot see the kingdom of God"* (John 3:3); and that is the Lord's way of stating a tremendous fact.

That kingdom is one in which certain things obtain with which I have no correspondence at all, with which naturally I have no power of communication. Take a walk round the garden. Walk down by the potatoes and vegetables and talk about, well, anything you like. What would the potatoes thing about you? What would the cabbages say about you? They neither hear nor understand what you are talking about, whatever it is. Their kind of life is not your kind of life. They are not constituted in your kingdom. There is no correspondence between them and you at all. They have not the capacity, the gift, the qualification, for the most elementary things that you may be talking about. You may be talking about such foolish things as dress, ordinary everyday things: they do not know. It is like that. There is just as great a divide between us and the kingdom of God. *"The natural man receiveth not the things of the Spirit of God: for they are foolishness unto him; and he cannot know them..."* (1 Corinthians 2:14). The divide is so utter that if you and I were brought in our natural state right into the place where the Spirit of God was speaking, unless that Spirit of God wrought a miracle in us, the whole thing would be of another world. And is it not so? You believers, go out into this world and talk about the things of the Lord and see men gape at you! It is all foreign to them. It is like that. *"Except one be born from above, he cannot see the kingdom of God."* To get into this school, something has to happen to us, and that means that we have to be constituted anew, with altogether other qualifications and abilities for the things of God. That is the nature of this school. It is the School of the Spirit of God.

I know that is very elementary, but, after all, is not that the thing that is being pressed on us all the time? It is being brought home to us how that we may hear words, and yet that they may not mean anything to us. We need our capacity for spiritual understanding enlarged more and more. We are naturally handicapped in this whole matter.

The Breaking of the Self-Life

There is one passage that I cannot get away from. It has been with me for a long time. It has been here as the basis of our meditation. It is John 1:51, and it seems to me that those are words which introduce us to the School of Christ, namely, those words of the Lord Jesus to Nathanael. I think it would be helpful to read the whole section from verse 47:

"Jesus saw Nathanael coming to him, and saith of him, Behold, an Israelite indeed, in whom is no guile! Nathanael saith unto him, Whence knowest thou me? Jesus answered and said unto him, Before Philip called thee, when thou wast under the fig tree, I saw thee. Nathanael answered him, TEACHER, thou art the Son of God; thou art King of Israel. Jesus answered and said unto him, Because I said unto thee, I saw thee underneath the fig tree, believest thou? Thou shalt see greater things than these. And he saith unto him,

Verily, verily, I say unto you. Ye shall see the heaven opened, and the angels of God ascending and descending upon the Son of man."

Here we are approaching the School of Christ, and there is one thing which is essential before we can even come to the threshold of that school, and that is what is marked by those words. *"Behold, an Israelite indeed, in whom is no guile!"* That put alongside the final words—*"the angels of God ascending and descending upon the Son of man"*—gives us a complete picture of what spiritually lies behind.

At the time when Jacob in guile—you remember the story of his guile—stole the birthright and had to escape for his life, he saw a very great truth, though but dimly as in type or figure, and a truth moreover into which he was not then able to enter. Jacob at that time could never have entered into the meaning of what he saw, namely, the House of God, Bethel; that place where heaven and earth meet, God and man meet, where the glory—united heaven and earth, God and man—is the great link, where God speaks and makes Himself known, where God's purposes are revealed. Why was this the case with Jacob! He was in guile. Let him leave it there then, as he must, and go on, and for twenty years come under discipline, and at the end of twenty years' discipline meet the impact of heaven upon his earthly life, his earthly nature, the impact of the Spirit upon his flesh, the impact of God upon himself at Jabbok, and let that fleshly, natural life be smitten and broken and withered, to bear the mark for the rest of his days of its having come under the ban of God; and then with the Jacob judged, the Jacob smitten, wounded, withered, he can go back and pour out his drink-offering at Bethel, and abide. The guile is dealt with. He is now not Jacob but Israel, in whom, speaking in type and figure, there is no guile. The work was not finished, but a crisis was met.

The Lord is saying here, to put it in a word, just this; to come into the place of the open heaven, where for you God is coming down in communication, and the glory of God abides, and where you enjoy what Bethel means, is nothing else than to come into Me. And to come into Me and abide in Me as the Bethel, the House of God, and have all the good of heaven and of God communicated, means you have come to the place where the natural life has been laid low, broken, withered. You cannot come into His school until that has happened, and it is necessary for the Lord to say to us in Christ as we come to the very threshold of that door, Behold, an Israelite indeed, in whom there is no Jacob; you shall see the heaven opened! To speak of the Jacob-life, is, after all, only another way of saying the self-life; for self is the very essence of the natural life; not just the self-life in its most positive evil forms, but the self-life in its totality. Jacob was in the elect line. He had a knowledge of God historically, but the transition from the natural to the spiritual was through discipline and crisis.

Let me stay with that. Here is the Lord Jesus. No one will dare to say that the self-life in Christ was like our self-life, polluted, corrupted, sinful. Not at all! And yet He had a self-life, a sinless self-life. For Him the self-life simply meant that He could act and speak and think and judge and move out from Himself. That is all. Not with evil intent, not as motivated or influenced by anything sinful or corrupt, but simply independently. He could have done and said a lot of good things independently. But He took the attitude, the position, that, although there was no sin in Him, He could not and would not at any time act or speak apart from His Father. That would be independence, and give the enemy just the opening that he was working for. But we can leave that.

My point is this, that you and I must not think of the self-life *only* as something manifestly corrupt. There is a great deal done for God with the purest motive that is done out from ourselves. There are many thoughts, ideas, judgments, which are sublime, beautiful, but they are ours, and if we did but know the truth, they are altogether different from God's.

And so, right at the very door of His school the Lord puts something utter. It is Jabbok. Jabbok was a tributary of the Jordan, and the implications of Jordan are right there at the very threshold of the School of Christ. He accepted Jordan in order to enter into that school of the Spirit for three and a half years. You and I will not get into that school of the Anointing in any other way. It has to be like that. If you and I are going to learn Christ, it will only be as the Jacob-nature is smitten. I am not talking to you mere doctrine and technique. Believe me, I know exactly what I am talking about.

I know this thing as the greatest reality in my history. I know what it is to have been labouring with all my might for God and preaching the Gospel out from myself for years. Oh, I know; I know what hard labour it is with the dome over your head. How many times have I stood in the pulpit and in my heart have said, If only somehow or other I could get a cleavage through this dome over my head, and instead of preaching what I have gathered from books and put into my notebooks, and having to study it up, I could scrap the whole thing and, with an opened heaven, speak out what God is saying in my heart! That was a longing for years. I sensed there was something like this, but I had not got it until the great crisis of Romans 6 came, and with it the open heaven. It has been different ever since then, altogether different. *"Ye shall see the heaven opened"*; and all that strain has gone, all that bondage has gone, that limitation; there is no dome there. That is my glory today. Forgive that personal reference. I must say it, because we are not here to give addresses. We are right down on the reality of this matter of the Holy Ghost directly and immediately revealing

Christ to us, and that ever-growingly. And this cannot be until we have come to our Jabbok, until the Jacob-life has been dealt with through crisis, and the Lord is able to say, An Israelite indeed, in whom is no Jacob; thou shalt see heaven opened! There is that dome, that closed heaven over us by nature, but, blessed be God! The cross rends the heavens, the veil is rent from top to bottom, and Chris is revealed through the rent veil of His flesh. He is no longer seen as the Man Jesus; He is seen in our hearts in all the fulness of God's consummate thought for man. It is a tremendous thing to see the Lord Jesus, and it is a tremendous thing to go on seeing Him more and more. That is where it begins—Behold, an Israelite indeed, in whom is no guile, no Jacob! Thou shalt see heaven opened!

A New Prospect for a New Man

That word, *"thou shalt see heaven opened"* is the new prospect for a new man. A new man, a new prospect! In the Authorized Version, a word is added which has been left out in the Revised Version. I take it for the simple reason that it is implicit in the original, without the word necessarily being introduced. In the Authorized it says, "Hereafter ye shall see heaven open". In the Revised Version, that first word is left out, and it simply reads, "Ye shall see..." But "ye shall" is something prospective, it is a tense pointing on to a future day. Not 'ye are seeing', but 'ye shall see'. It is a new prospect for a new man; and therein lines a new era. It is the era of the Holy Spirit, for by the coming of the Holy Spirit, the open heaven is made a reality. The Cross effects the opening of the heavens for us, but it is the Holy Spirit who makes it good in us, just as was the case in that typical or symbolic death and burial and resurrection of the Lord Jesus in Jordan, when the heavens were opened to Him. Coming up on new, resurrection ground, He had the open heaven. The Spirit then alighted and abode upon Him, and the Spirit became, shall we say, the channel of communication, making the open heaven all that it should be a matter of communication, intercourse, communion. It is the era of the Spirit, making all the values of Christ real in us. "Ye shall"; and blessed be God, what was prospective for Nathanael is present for us.

That era has come. We are in the era of the Holy Spirit, of the open heaven.

The Mark of a Life Anointed by the Holy Spirit

Now what is then the mark of a life anointed by the Holy Spirit? You remember when Paul went to Ephesus, he found certain disciples and without giving us any explanation of the reason for his question, he immediately said, *"Did ye receive the Holy Spirit when ye believed?"* Their reply was, *"We did not so much as hear whether the Holy Spirit was"* Then Paul's next question is full of significance, taking us back to Jordan, *"Into what then were ye baptized?"* Baptism is bound up with this vital reality. If you do not know the Holy Spirit, what can your baptism have meant? Oh, we were baptized with John's baptism; Oh, I see: well, *"John baptized with the baptism of repentance, saying unto the people, that they should believe on him that should come after him, that is, on Jesus."* Then when they heard that, they were baptized into Christ, and the Holy Spirit came upon them. Thus they came into the School of Christ; and the mark of a life anointed by the Spirit is that you know Christ in this living and ever-growing way.

Oh, listen to this, this is not so elementary and unnecessary as it may seem. Some of us, of course, are very poor scholars, and we take such a long time to learn. It took decades in my case to come to a true realization of this. We know so much, and we discover that our real personal knowledge of Christ is a poor thing. We are constantly brought up against that. At last, sooner or later, you and I are going to come to the place where we exclaim, 'Oh, it is not doctrines and truths and themes and subjects and Scripture as mere matter that I need to know!' It is all very wonderful when you are taken up with it; but let a man come into the fires, into deep trial, into trouble and perplexity and then what about all your doctrines and all your themes, and all your Bible study? What is the value of it? It does not really solve your problem, it does not get you through. This is a tragedy. It is true of many of us who have got certain doctrines, who have gone through the doctrines of the bible and worked them out, and who know what is in the Bible on these things; regeneration, redemption, atonement, righteousness by faith, sanctification, and so on. It is true that after we have gone through them all, and have got them all well worked out, and we come into a terrible spiritual experience, the whole thing counts for nothing, and we come to the place where but for the Lord we could easily throw the whole thing over and say, 'This Christianity does not work!' Yes, for those who have known the Lord for years, so far as the accumulation of truth is concerned, that is about the value of it in an hour of the deepest spiritual distress. The only thing then that can help you is not your beautiful notebooks full of doctrines but, 'What do I know of the Lord personally and livingly in my own heart? What has the Holy Spirit revealed in me and to me, and made a part of me, of Christ? Sooner or later, that is where we are coming to. We are going to be brought back to the living, spiritual knowledge of the Lord; for He alone personally, as revealed in our very being by the Holy Ghost, can save us in the deepest hour. The day will come when we will be stripped of everything but what is spiritually, inwardly known of Christ; stripped of all our mental and intellectual knowledge. Many of those who have been giants in teaching and in doctrine have had a very, very dark hour at the end of their lives, a very dark hour indeed. How they have got through has depended upon the inward knowledge of the Lord as over against mere intellectual knowledge. How can I explain what I mean by that?

Well, for example, you discover something in the realm of food that really does help you. You have gone all round trying everything, all that the food people can provide to help you in a specific malady or weakness, and nothing has helped you. Then suddenly you discover something that really does help you, and the next time you are put to the test you take some of that and find you can go through on that. It is in you, something that gets you through your ordeal. That is what I mean with reference to this question of how and what Christ is to be to us. He is to be in us, that upon which we can rest back in confidence and assurance, and, doing so, He gets us through. We are to know Him in that way. That is the only way in which to learn Christ, and that is experimental. *"Ye shall see the heaven open."* The Holy Spirit has come to make for us an altogether new order of things, so that Christ is being revealed in us as our very life. Ye shall see when the Spirit comes: that is the mark of an anointed life. Ye shall see! And those are great moments when we do see. Some of us have had those great moments in specific connections, and some of us have seen others have their great moments in specific connections. Yet we have known that they knew all about the thing, and have been taught it, and have had it drummed into them for years; and then after years suddenly it has broken upon them, and they have said, 'Look here, I am now beginning to see what has been said all this time!'

I remember a man brought up in a most saintly family, whose father I always used to liken to Charles G. Finney. He was like Charles G. Finney in spirit, soul and body; and one of his sons brought up in that most godly home was a great friend of mine for years. We had real fellowship together, always talking about the things of the Lord. One day—I can see it now right at the corner of Newington Green—I was going to meet him, and as I came toward Newington Green I saw him in the distance. I saw him smile, and we met and shook hands. He was one big smile. "Do you know, I have made a discovery", he said. I said, "What is your discovery?" "I have discovered that Christ is in me!" *"Christ in you, the hope of glory"* has become a reality to me. "Well," I said, "I could have told you that years ago." "Ah, that is the difference," he said: "I see it now, I know it now."

You see what I mean. It is just that. Oh, that the world were full of Christians like that! Is this not the need? But inasmuch as this was said to Nathanael, it must be for us all. It was not said to Peter, James and John up on the Mount of Transfiguration: it was said to Nathanael, one of the general circle. It is for all; and if that wants strengthening, proving, notice what the Lord Jesus said—*"Ye shall see the heaven opened, and the angels of God ascending and descending upon the Son of man."* What has happened? A tremendous transition has taken place in the course of a few sentences. Behold, an Israelite indeed! That is for Israel; for Jacob, yes, the father of Israel; for sons of Jacob, the earthly Israel. Ah, yes, but that is purely within the limitation of earth, purely within the limitation of a people here amongst the nations, and within the limitation of types. Yes, but now for the tremendous transition. The Lord has cancelled out something Nathanael said, "Thou art King of Israel", said he. King of Israel? That is nothing, Thou shalt see greater things than these. *Thou shall see the heaven opened, and the angels of God ascending and descending upon the Son of man!* That is something vastly greater than Israel. Son of Man! That is racial, that is universal; that is for all men who will come in, not just for Israel. Thou shalt see greater things! Heaven opened—and for whom? Not just for Israel, but for all men in Christ. The Son of Man!

That title, Son of Man, simply represents God's thought concerning man. Oh, the great, great thought and intention of God concerning man. The open heaven is for man when he comes into God's thought in Christ. The open heaven is for man: God revealing Himself to man in the Man. It is for all of us. Let no one think that this open heaven, this anointing, is for a certain few. Oh no, it is for everyone. God's desire, God's thought, is that you and I, the most simple, foolish, weak amongst men, the most limited naturally, with the least capacity naturally, should find that our very birthright is an open heaven. In other words, you and I may in Christ know this wonderful work of the Holy Spirit in an inward revelation of Christ in every-growing fulness. That is for us, every one of us. May the most advanced Christian have a new movement toward the Lord in this matter, and all of us really come to this first crisis where the dome over us is cleft and we know an open heaven, the Spirit revealing Christ in our hearts for His glory.

VII
LEARNING UNDER THE ANOINTING

Reading: Matthew 11:20; John 1:51; Matthew 3:16; John 1:4; Romans 8:2; 2 Corinthians 3:16-18

The School of Christ that is, the School where Christ is the great Lesson and the Spirit the great Teacher; in the School where the teaching is not objective but subjective, where the teaching is not of things but an inward making of Christ a part of us by experience—that is the nature of this School.

The Meaning of the Anointing

"Ye shall see the heaven opened." "He saw the heavens opened and the Spirit of God descending upon him." What is the meaning of the anointing of the Holy Spirit? It is nothing less and nothing other than the Holy Spirit taking His place as absolute Lord. The anointing carries with it the absolute lordship of the Holy Spirit, the Spirit as Lord. That means that all other lordships have been deposed and set aside; the lordship of our own lives; the lordship of our own minds, our own wills, our own desires; the lordship of others. The lordship of every interest and every influence is regarded as having given place to the undivided and unreserved lordship of the Holy Spirit, and the anointing can never be known, enjoyed, unless that has taken place. That is why the Lord Jesus went down into Jordan's waters, into death and burial, in type, taking the place of man in representation, from that moment not to be under the government of His own life in any respect as He worked out the will of God, but to be wholly and utterly subject to the Spirit of God in every detail. Jordan's grave set forth the setting aside of every

independent lordship, every other lordship, every other influence, and if you will read the spiritual life of Christ in the Gospels you will see that is was to that position that He was every moment adhering. Many and powerful were the influences which were brought to bear upon Him to affect Him and govern His movements. Sometimes it was the full force of Satan's open assault, to the effect that it was necessary that He should do certain things for His cause, or for His very continuance in life physically. Sometimes it was Satan clothing himself with the arguments and suasions of beloved associates, in their seeking to hold Him back from certain courses, or to influence Him to prolong His life by sparing Himself certain sufferings. In various ways influences were brought to bear upon Him from all directions, and many of the counsel were seemingly so wise and good. For example, with regard to His going up to the feast, it was urged, in effect: It is the thing that everybody is doing: if you do not go up you will prejudice your cause. If you really want to further this cause, you must fall into line with the accepted thing religiously, and you only stand to lose if you do not do that; you will curtail your influence, you will narrow your sphere of usefulness! And what an appeal that is if you have something very much at heart, some cause for god at heart, the success of which is of the greatest importance. Such then were the influences that were beating upon Him. But whether it be Satan coming in all the directness of his cunning, his wit, his insinuation, or whether it be through beloved and most intimate disciples and associates, whatever the kind of argument, that Man cannot be caused to deflect a hair's-breadth from His principle. 'I am under the anointing; I am committed to the absolute sovereignty of the Holy Spirit, and I cannot move, whatever it costs. Cost it my life, cost it my influence, cost it my reputation, cost it everything that I hold dear, I cannot move unless I know from the Holy Spirit that that is the Father's mind and not another mind, the Father's will and

not another will, that this thing comes from the Father.'
Thus He put back everything until He knew in His spirit
what the Spirit of God witnessed. He lived up to this law,
this principle, of the absolute authority, government,
lordship of the anointing, and it was for that that the
anointing had come.

That is the meaning of the anointing. Do you ask
for the anointing of the Holy Spirit? Why do you ask for
the anointing of the Holy Spirit? Is the anointing
something that you crave? To what end? That you may be
used, may have power, may have influence, may be able to
do a lot of wonderful things? The first and pre-eminent
thing the anointing means is that we can do nothing but
what the anointing teaches and leads to do. The anointing
takes everything out of our hands. The anointing takes
charge of the reputation. The anointing takes charge of the
very purpose of God. The anointing takes complete control
of everything and all is from that moment in the hands of
the Holy Spirit. We must remember that if we are going to
learn Christ, that learning Christ is by the Holy Spirit's
dealing with us, and that means that we have to go exactly
the same way as Christ went in principle and in law.

So we find we are not far into the Gospel of John,
which is particularly the Gospel of the spiritual School of
Christ, before we hear even such as He saying, *'The Son
can do nothing of himself'*. *'The words that I say unto you
I speak not from myself.' The works that I do are not Mine;
'the Father abiding in me doeth his works'*.

"The Son can do nothing out from himself." You
see, there is the negative side of the anointing; while the
positive side can be summed up in one word—the Father
only. Perhaps that is a little different idea of the anointing
from what we have had. Oh, to be anointed of the Holy
Spirit! What wonders will follow; how wonderful that life
will be! The first and the abiding thing about the anointing
is that we are imprisoned into the lordship of the Spirit of

God, so that there can be nothing if He does not do it. Nothing! That is not a pleasant experience, if the natural life is strong and in any way ascendant. Therefore Jordan must be there before there can be an anointing. The putting aside of that natural strength and self-life is a necessity, for the anointing does carry with is essentially the absolute lordship of the Spirit.

You notice the issue of that in 2 Corinthians 3:16. *"When it shall turn to the Lord"*, when the Lord is the object in view, *"the veil is taken away, and we all with unveiled face beholding as in a mirror the glory of the Lord are transformed into the same image. . .even as from the Lord the Spirit"*, or *"the Spirit which is the Lord"*. You are in the School and you can see Christ and learn Christ; which is being transformed into the image of Christ under the lordship of the Spirit. "When it shall turn to the Lord", when the Lord is our object in view! But with us, with us Christians, with us very devoted, very earnest Christians, what a long time it takes to get the Lord as the sole object. Is that saying a terrible thing? We say we love the Lord; yes, but we do love to have our own way as well, and we do *not* love to have our way thwarted. Have any of us yet reached that point of spiritual attainment where we never have a bad time at all with the Lord? Oh no, we are still found at the place where we so often think it is in the interests of the Lord that our hearts go out in a certain direction, and the Lord does not let us do it, and we have a bad time; and that has betrayed us absolutely. Our hearts were in it. It was not easy, absolutely easy and simple for us to say, "Very well, Lord, I am just as pleased as though you let me do it, I delight always to do thy will! We are disappointed the Lord does not let us do it; or if the Lord delays it, what a time we go through. Oh, if we could only get at it and do it! The time is finding us out. Is that not true of most of us? Yes, it is true. We do come into this picture, and that just does mean that, after all, the Lord is not as verily our object as we thought He was. We have another object alongside and associated with the Lord; that is, something that we want to be or to do, somewhere we want to go, something we want to have. It is all there, and the Holy Spirit knows all about it. In this School of Christ, where God's objective is Christ, only Christ, utterly Christ, the very anointing means that it has to be Christ as Lord by the Spirit. The anointing takes that position. Well, so much for the moment for the meaning of the anointing. It was true in Him, and it has to be true in us.

"Lordship" and "Subjection"

If we are going to graduate in this School, graduate to the glory, the ultimate full glory of Christ, to be the competent instrument in His Kingdom for government, the one way of learning that spiritual, Divine, heavenly government which is His destiny for the saints, is subjection to the Holy Spirit. That is a very interesting word, that word 'subjection', in the New Testament. I think it has been rather mishandled and given a wrong and unpleasant meaning. The idea of subjection is usually that of being crushed down underneath, being put under all the time, suppression. *"Wives, be in subjection to your own husbands."* That is now interpreted as, 'You have to get down underneath'; and the word does not mean that at all. How shall we seek to convey what the Greek word for subjection or submission really implies? Well, write down the number 1; and then you are going to write subjection or submission. How are you going to write it. Not by putting another 1 underneath. The word means 'putting alongside it or after it'. No. 1 is the primary number, it stands in front of all that comes after, and governs and gives value to all the rest. Subjection means that He in all things has the pre-eminence. We come after and take our value from Him. It is not being crushed down, but deriving everything from

Him as the first one: and you never derive the benefits until you know subjection to Christ. That is to say, you come after, you take second place, take that place by which you derive all the benefit; you get the value by taking a certain place. The Church is not subject to Christ in that repressive sense, not down under His heel or His thumb, but just coming after, alongside, He having the pre-eminence, and the Church, His Bride, deriving all the good from His pre-eminence from His having the first place. The Church second, yes,; but who minds a second place if you are going to get all the values of the first by having second place? That is subjection. The Lord's idea for the Church is that she should have everything. But how will she get it? Not by taking the first place, but by coming alongside the Lord and in all things letting Him have the pre-eminence. That is submission, subjection. The lordship of the Spirit is not something hard that strips us, takes everything from us, and keeps us down there all the time so that we dare not move. The lordship of the Spirit is to bring us into all the fulness of that headship. But we do have to learn what that lordship is before we can come into that fulness. It is of His fulness we receive.

The trouble ever was, from Adam's day till ours, that it is not someone else's fulness that man wants, it is his own; to have it in himself and not in another. The Holy Spirit cuts that ground from under our feet and says, It is His fulness, it is in Him. He must have His place of absolute lordship before we can know of His fulness. That is enough I think, for the moment, on the meaning of the anointing. Do you grasp it? The Lord give us grace to accept the meaning of Jordan in order that we may have the open heaven and, by the open heaven, the anointing which brings in all heaven's fulness for us. But it does mean the absolute lordship of the Spirit. Lesson No. 1 in the School—oh, that is not Lesson No. 1, that is the very ground of coming into the School, that is a preliminary examination. We never get into the School until we accept the lordship of the Holy Spirit. That is why so many do not get on very far in the knowledge of the Lord. They have never accepted the implications of the anointing, never really come down into Jordan. Their progress, their learning, is very slow, very poor. Find a person who really knows the meaning of the Cross, of Jordan, in the clearing of the way for the lordship of the Spirit, and you will find quick growth, you will find spiritual development far ahead of all others. It is very true. That is the preliminary, the entrance examination.

The First Lesson in the School of Christ

But when you are in, Lesson No. 1 begins here. It is but a reiteration of what has been strongly said in earlier meditation. The firs lesson in the School of Christ which the Holy Spirit takes up to teach us is what we have called the altogether 'other-ness' of Christ from ourselves. This may be not only the first lesson but a continuous lesson throughout life. But this is the one thing with which the Holy Spirit begins, the altogether 'other-ness' of Christ from what we are. Will you take up the Gospel of John with that one thought in mind and read it again, quietly and steadily. How different Christ is from other people, even from His disciples. You can expand from John's Gospel to all the Gospels with that one thought. It will be an education to you if the Holy Spirit is with you as you read. How utterly different He is! That difference is again and again affirmed. *"Ye are from beneath; I am from above"* (John 8:23). That is a difference, and that difference becomes a clash all the way along; a clash of judgments, a clash of mentalities, a clash of minds, a clash of ideas, a clash of values; a clash in everything between Him and others, even with His disciples who are with Him in the School. His nature is different. He has a heavenly nature, a Divine nature. No one else has that. He has a heavenly mind, a heavenly mentality. They have an earthly mentality, and the two cannot meet, at any point. When the last word has been said, there is a big, big gap between the two. He is so utterly other.

Now, you say, that being so, we are at a very great disadvantage. He is one thing and we are another. But that is just the nature and meaning of this School. How is that problem going to be resolved? Well, it is just resolved like this, that He is all the time speaking about a time when He will be in them and they will be in Him, and when that time comes, in the innermost and deepest reality of their being, they will be altogether other than what they are in every other part of their being. That is to say, there will be in them that which is Christ, that which is Christ in all that He is as the absolutely Other. Sometimes they will think that the best thing to do is this, but that altogether Other inside keeps saying in effect, Get on with it! The outer man says, It is madness! I am only courting disaster! The inner Man says, You are to do it! These two cannot be reconciled. He is within and He is altogether other, and our education is to learn to follow Him, to go His way, *"If any man will come after me, let him deny himself. . .and follow me."* Deny himself: your arguments, your judgments, your common sense sometimes. Follow Me!—and Christ is vindicated every time. Men have done the maddest things from this world's standpoint and have been vindicated. This is no suggestion that you should go and begin to do mad things. I am talking about the authority of Christ within, the difference of Christ from ourselves, and this is the first lesson the Holy Spirit would teach anyone coming into the School of Christ, that there is this great difference, this great cleavage, that He is one thing and we are quite another; and we can never be sure that we are on the right line save as we submit everything to Him.

This is why prayer has to have such a large place in the life of a child of God, and this is why prayer had such a large place in His life when He was here. The prayer life of the Lord Jesus is, in a certain realm and sense, the biggest problem that you can face. He is Christ, He is the Son of God, He is under the anointing of the Holy Spirit, and He is without sin in His person, and yet, He must spend all the night in prayer after a heavy and long day's work. Again and again you come upon Him in prayer. Why must He pray? Because there are other influences at work, there are other things which are seeking to call for consideration and response and obedience, and He must keep all the time in line with the anointing, in harmony with the Spirit under whose government He has placed Himself, because He can decide nothing out from Himself. If He must do that, what of us? We are not even on His sinless level. We have all that in our very natures which works violently against God, God's mind, God's will. How much the more necessary then is I for us to have a prayer life, by which the Spirit is given an opportunity of keeping us straight, keeping us on the line of Divine purpose, keeping us in the ways of the Lord, and in the times of the Lord.

Beloved, if there is one thing that a child of God will learn under the Holy Spirit's lordship, it is this thing, namely, how different He is from us, how different we are from Him, how altogether other. But, blessed be God, now in this dispensation, if we are truly children of God, the altogether Other is not merely objective but within. That is the second phase of this matter of the 'other-ness', The first phase is the fact of the difference. Will you accept this? Will you now, at this very point, this moment, just settle this? The Lord Jesus is altogether other than I am: even when I think I am most perfectly right. He may still be altogether other, and I can never, never rely upon my own sense of rightness until I have submitted my rightness to Him! That is very utter, but it is very necessary. Many of

us have learned these lessons. We are not talking out of a
book, we are talking out of our own experience. We have
been quite sure at times that we were right and we have
gone forward to follow out our rightness in that judgment,
and we have come to grief, and we have got into an awful
fog of perplexity and bewilderment. We were quite sure
we were right, but look where we have been landed! And
when we come to think about it, and put it before the Lord,
we have to ask ourselves, how much did I wait on the Lord
and wait for the Lord about that thing. Were we not a bit
precipitate with our own sense of rightness? And this is
David and the ark all over again. David's motive was all
right and David's sense of God's purpose was all right.
That God wanted the ark in Jerusalem was right enough,
but David got the thing into his soul as an idea, and it
worked itself up as a great enthusiasm within him, and so
he made the cart. The motive, the good motive, the good
idea, the devout spirit, got him into most awful trouble.
The Lord smote Uzzah, and he died before the Lord, and
the ark went into the house of Obededom, and tarried there,
all because man had a good and right idea, but had not
waited on the Lord. You know the sequel. Later on, David
said to the heads of the Levites, *"Sanctify yourselves, both
ye and your brethren, that ye may bring up the ark of the
Lord, the God of Israel, unto the place that I have prepared
for it. For because ye bare it not at the first, the Lord our
God made a breach upon us, for that we sought him not
according to the ordinance."* The instruction was there all
the time, but he had not waited on the Lord. If David had
brought his devout enthusiasm quietly before the Lord, He
would have directed him to the instruction He had given to
Moses, and said, in effect, "Yes all right, but remember,
this is how it is to be carried." There would have been no
death, no delay, things would have gone right through.

Yes, we may get a very good idea for the Lord, but
we have to submit it to the Lord, to be quiet sure it is not

our idea for the Lord, but the Lord's mind being born in us. It is very important to learn Christ; He is so other.

You see, this divides Christians very largely into two classes. Christians can be, in the main, divided into these two classes. There is that very large class of Christians whose Christianity is objective, is outward. It is a matter of having adopted a Christian life, that now they do a lot of things which they once would not do. They go to meetings, they go to church, they read the Bible, lots of things that they used not to do; and they now do not do quite a lot of things they once did. That is what holds good more or less in that class. It is now a matter of no doing and doing, not going and going, being a good Christian outwardly. That is a big class with its various degrees of light and shade, a very big class of Christians indeed.

There are others who are in this School of Christ, for whom the Christian life is an inward thing of walking with the Lord and knowing the Lord in the heart, in greater or lesser degree. That is the nature of it, a real inward walk with a living Lord in their own heart. There is a great deal of difference between those two classes.

The Spirit's Law or Instrument of Instruction

Well now, I must come to a close. The altogether 'other-ness'; by what means does the Spirit make that 'other-ness' known to us?—for the Spirit does not speak to us in audible language and words. We do not hear an outside voice saying, 'This is the way, walk ye in it!" then how are we to know? Well, it is in what the Apostle Paul calls "the law of the Spirit of life in Christ Jesus". *"In him was life; and the life was the light."* How are we to know, by what means are we to be enlightened on this matter, on the difference between our ways, our thoughts, our feelings, and the Lord's? How are we to have light? The life was the light. *"He that followeth me shall not walk in*

the darkness, but shall have the light of life" (John 8:12).
*"The law of the Spirit of life in Christ Jesus made me free
from the law of sin and of death."* Then the Spirit's
instrument, if I may call it that, of our education is life in
Christ. That is to say, we know the mind of the Spirit on
matters by quickening, by sensing, discerning life. Divine
life, the Spirit of life. Or, on the other hand, if we are alive
to the Lord, we know when the Spirit is not in agreement
with anything by a sense of death, death in that direction.

That is the thing that no one can teach us by words,
by giving us a lesson. But it is a thing we can know. You
know it by reactions, violent reactions often. You have
taken a course, and you get a bad reaction. You strive in a
certain direction to realize a certain thing, and if only you
would stop for a moment and look at it, you know that you
are trying to bring that about. You know quite well that
this thing is not spontaneous, that this lacks the spontaneity
which is a mark of the Lord. You know the Lord is not
coming through there. You know quite well that you have
no sense of spontaneity and peace. It has to be forced, to
be driven, to be made to happen. More or less, I think,
every one of you who is a true child of God knows what I
am talking about. But remember, this is the Spirit's
instrument in the School for teaching Christ—life. The
mark of a Spirit-governed, Spirit-anointed, man or woman
is that they move in life, and that they minister life, and that
what comes from them means life. And they know by that
very law of life where the Lord is, what the Lord is in, what
he Lord is after, what the Lord wants. That is how they
know. No voice is heard, no objective vision is seen, but
deep in the spirit life arbitrates, the Spirit of life.

How necessary it is for us to be alive unto God in
Christ Jesus. How necessary it is for us to be all the time
laying hold on life. If Satan can only bring his spirits of
death to bear upon us and bring our spirit under the
wrappings of death, he will cut off the light at once and

leave us floundering; we do not know where we are, what to do. He is always seeking to do that, and ours is a continuous battle for life. Everything for the realization of God's purpose is bound up with this "life". This "life" is potentially the sum of all Divine purpose. Just as in the seed there is the life, not only of the seed, but of a great tree, and that life, if but released, will eventuate in that great tree, so in the life given to us in our spiritual infancy, our new birth, there is all the power of God's full and final and consummate thought. And Satan is out, not just to cut off our life, but to prevent God's final interests and concerns in the full display which is in that life which is given to us, that eternal life given to us now. The Spirit is always concerned with that life, and He would say to us, 'Guard that life: do not allow anything to come to interfere with that life: see that whenever there is something that grieves the Spirit and arrests the operation of that life, you immediately resort to the precious Blood which stands as a witness against all the death, that precious Blood of Jesus, the incorruptible life, the witness in heaven to victory over sin and death, by which you can be delivered from that arresting hand of Satan. That precious Blood is the ground upon which we must stand to deal with everything that grieves the Spirit and checks the operation of life, by which we come to know, and know in this living way, Christ in ever-growing fulness. The Lord help us.

VIII
THE GOVERNING LAW OF DIVINE LOVE

Reading: John 1:4; 2:3; 3:3; 4:13-14; 5:5-9; 6:33-35; 9:1-7; 11:1-6, 17, 21, 23, 25-26.

A Zero Point

All these passages which we have read are really a sequence. They are the outflow of the first. *"In him was life; and the life was the light of men."* And you will notice that they all represent a zero point. The mother of Jesus said unto Him, 'They have no wine: there is nothing to draw upon! The next chapter is only another way of saying the same thing. Nicodemus came to Jesus and sought to commence at a point which he considered to be a good point from which to begin negotiations with the Lord Jesus, but it was a point far in advance of that which the Lord Jesus could accept: so He took him right back to zero, and said: Ye must be born again. We cannot start at any point beyond that. If you and I are going to come into any kind of living relationship, we must get right back there: we must come to zero and start from zero. *"Ye must be born again."* For except a man be born anew, he cannot see. It is no use our starting at some point where, after all, we are incapacitated from seeing. Chapter 4 is but another way of setting forth the same truth. The woman after all is found to be bankrupt, at zero. Jesus gradually draws her out and the final expression from her side is, in effect, "Well, I don't know anything about that, I have not anything of that; I have been coming here every day, day after day, but I know nothing about what you are talking of! She is down to zero: and then He says, "That is where we begin. The water that I shall give is not the drawing upon your own resources at all, not bringing something out of your well, it is not something that you can produce and I improve upon and make better. No, it is something which comes solely and only from Myself; it is a new act altogether apart from you; it is the water that I shall give. We begin all over again in this matter.

Then in chapter 5 the Holy Spirit is careful to make perfectly clear that this poor fellow was in a hopeless state, that every effort was abortive, every hope was disappointed. For thirty and eight years, a lifetime, the man had been in that state, and there is the note of despair in the man. The Lord Jesus does not say to him, "Look here, you are a poor cripple; I am going to take you in hand, and after a court of treatment I will have you on your feet, I will make those old limbs over anew, I will improve on your condition." Not at all. In an instant, in a moment, it is a start again. The effect of what He does is as though the man were born again. This I not curing the old man, this is making a new man, in principle. This is something that comes in that was not there before, and could not be produced before, the ground of which was not there, something which was uniquely and solely Christ's doing. It was zero, and He began at zero.

Chapter 6—a great multitude. Whence shall we buy bread enough for this multitude? Well, the situation is quite a hopeless one, but by His own act He meets the situation, and then follows on with His great teaching to interpret what He has done in feeding the multitude. He says, "I am the Bread which came down out of heaven. There is nothing here on this earth than can meet this need. It has to come out of heaven. Bread out of heaven for the life of the world: otherwise the world is dead. We begin at zero. (The loaves and fishes may represent our small measure of Christ which can be increased.)

Chapter 9—the man born blind. Not a man who has lost his sight and is having his sight recovered. That is not the point at all. The glory of God is not found in improving, the glory of God is found in resurrection. That is what is coming out here. The glory of God is not found in our being able to produce something or put something into God's hands, something of ours, that He can take up and make use of. The glory of God is something solely out from God Himself, and we can contribute nothing. The glory of God comes out of zero. The man was born blind. The Lord Jesus gives him sight; he never had sight before.

Then chapter 11 gathers it all up. If you like to sit down and look at Lazarus, you will find that Lazarus is the embodiment of *"They have no wine"*. He is the embodiment of *"Ye must be born again"*. He is the embodiment of *"the water that I shall give shall be in him..."* He is the embodiment of a bankrupt state; in the grave four days; but the Lord is coming to that. Lazarus is the embodiment of chapter 6: *"I am the living bread which came down out of heaven...for the life of the world"*. Lazarus is the embodiment of chapter 9, a man who is without sight, who is given sight by the Lord Jesus. Lazarus gathers it all up. But if you notice, in gathering up everything, the Holy Spirit is very careful to stress and emphasize one thing, namely, that the Lord Jesus will not touch the thing until it is far, far removed from any human remedy. He will not come on to the scene, or into association with it, until from all human standpoints it is bankrupt, it is at zero. And this is not a questions of lack of interest, lack of sympathy, or lack of love, for here the Spirit again points out that love was there. But love is bound by a law.

The Governing Law—The Glory of God

Divine love is bound by a law. Love has a law where God is concerned. God' love is under a law. God's love is under the law of the glory of God, and He can show His love only in so far as showing His love is going to be to His glory. He is governed by that. In all the showings of

His love, His object is that He may be glorified, and the glory of God is bound up with resurrection. *"Said I not unto thee, that if thou wouldest believe, thou shouldest see the glory of God?"* *"Thy brother shall rise again."* The glory of God is in resurrection, and therefore love demands that everything shall come to the place where only resurrection will meet the situation; no curing of things, no remedying of the old man.

Oh, let me start right back at the beginning if it is necessary. There are still a lot of people in this world who think that there is something in man that can contribute to the glory of God and that Christianity is only the bringing up out of man of something that is for the glory of God. That is a long, long-standing fallacy and lie. It is not true. Call it what you like; it goes by various names, such as 'the inner light' or 'the vital spark'. The Word of God all the way through is coming down tremendously on this thing. I start at zero, and zero for me means that I can contribute nothing. Everything has to come from God. The very face that the gift of God is eternal life means that you have not got it until it is given to you. You are blind until God gives you the faculty of sight. You are dead until God gives you life. You are a hopeless cripple until God does something for you and in you which you can never do. Unless God does this thing, unless this act takes place, well, there you lie. Spiritually, that is how you are. You can contribute nothing. Nicodemus, you have nothing to give, you must be born again; I cannot take you at the point at which you come to Me! Woman of Samaria, you have nothing, and you know it and confess it: that is where I begin! Man of Bethesda, you can do nothing, and you know it: then it all rest with Me! If ever there is to be anything, it rests with Me! Lazarus, what can you do now, and what can anybody make of you? If I do not come right in as out from heaven and do this thing, then there is nothing but corruption!

This is one of the great lessons that you and I have to learn in the School of Christ, that God begins for His glory at zero, and God will take pains through the Holy Spirit to make us to know that it is zero; that is, to bring us consciously to zero, and make us realize it is all with Him. You see, the end is always governing God, and the end is His glory. Take that word through this Gospel again—the glory of God in relation to Christ. We were saying in a previous meditation that God's great end for us in Christ is glory, fulness of glory. Yes, but then there is this—that no flesh should glory before Him. And where does that come?—*"He that glorieth, let him glory in the Lord"* (1 Corinthians 1:29-31). And what is that connected with?—He *"was made unto us wisdom from God, and righteousness and sanctification, and redemption: that, according as it is written, He that glorieth, let him glory in the Lord"*. It is a question of what He is made to be. No flesh is to glory before Him. *"My glory will I not give to another"* (Isaiah 42:89, 48:11). Therefore it is all the Lord's matter and He will retain it in His own hands. *"And when he had heard...he abode two days...where he was"* (John 11:6). In love, governed by love, that the glory of God might be revealed, He kept away.

Have we got settled on this? We take so long to learn these basic elementary lessons. We do still cling to some sort of idea that we can produce something, and all our miserable days are simply the result of still hoping that we can in some way provide the Lord with something. Not being able to find it, but breaking down all the time, we get miserable, perfectly miserable. It takes us so long to come to the place where we do not fully and finally settle this matter, that if we lived as long as ever man lived on this earth, we shall not be able to contribute one iota which can be acceptable to God, and which He can take and use for our salvation, for our sanctification, for our glorification, not a bit. All that He can use is His Son, and the measure of our ultimate glory will be the measure of Christ in us, just that. There will be differences in glory, as one thing differs from another. One glory of the sun, another of the moon, another of the stars. There will be differences in degree of glory, and the difference in degree of glory ultimately will be according to the measure of Christ that each one of us severally has. That in turn depends upon how much you and I by faith are really making Christ the basis of our life, the very basis of our living, of our being, how much the principle of these familiar words has its application in our case, *'Not what I am, but what Thou art'*. Christ is all the glory, *'the Lamb is all the glory in Immanuel's land'*.

Beloved friends, whatever you go away with, go away with this, that from God's standpoint, the glory of life depends entirely upon our faith apprehension, appropriation and appreciation of Christ, and there is no glory at all for us now or in the time to come but on that ground and on that line. I know how simple that is, how elementary, but oh, it is such a governing thing. Glory—that the Lord shall be glorified in us. What greater thing could happen than that the Lord should be glorified in us? The glory of God is bound up with the resurrection, and resurrection is God's unique and sole prerogative. So that if God is to be glorified in us, you and I have to live on Him as the resurrection and the life from day to day, and know Him as that as we go through life.

imself

The Incense Bearer

THE INCENSE BEARER

2 Corinthians 2:14-16

"...and by me sends forth the knowledge of Him, a stream of fragrant incense, throughout the world. For Christ's is the fragrance which I offer up to God, whether among those in the way of salvation, or among those in the way of perdition; but to these it is an odour of death, to those of life." (Conybeare.)

THE MINISTER AND HIS MINISTRY

The Apostle Paul is setting forth one of his conceptions of hat the minister of Christ is, and then what the effect of the ministry. He is thinking here of the minister of Christ as an incense-bearer. The picture at the background of these verses is one with which we are well-acquainted. Verse 14 of II Corinthians 2 brings into view the triumphal procession of the victorious war-lord as he moves from place to place with his captives behind him, celebrating at many points his victory, and using them for the purpose of evidence as to his victory. But also in the procession there are those who carry vessels of incense, and the incense being diffused everywhere speaks in two ways, to two different classes of people.

There are some who are going to celebrate this day of victory by being slain. It was a custom to hold certain notorious or distinguished captives in bondage until the day of the great celebration of the victory, and then that day was marked by their being slain. On the other hand, there were those who were appointed to be released as a distinguishing mark of the day. To the one the incense brought death near, and made them know that their hour had come. To the other the same incense made known that the hour of emancipation, of liberation, was drawing near. The same incense proclaimed death and life, life and death.

In the second part of the picture the Apostle himself passes from the first, where he has been viewing himself as one of those prisoners, led in the triumphal procession, as an object of public exhibition as to the triumph of the great Warrior. He has seen himself as in the train of the triumph of the Lord, being on full view as a demonstration of the greatness of that victory. Now he passes himself into the second part, and takes the place of an incense bearer in the procession, and says that he passes on through the world bearing incense, and that incense is saying two things, having two effects, speaking to two different classes of people. It relates to life and death.

But the Apostle carries that thing inward, and he does not regard himself as simply carrying a censor of incense. He regards himself as that vessel, and as—in a strange, deep, inward way, so as to become a very part of his own being—the incense itself. He thinks of himself as being, not only the giver forth of the sweet savour, but that sweet savour itself; that he is the means by which this effect is registered upon these two different classes of people.

In that presentation of the servant of the Lord there is a deep, strong and solemn word for all of us who stand in that position as the Lord's servants. The thing which is going forth from us, the thing which is the effect of our lives, according to these words, is the knowledge of Christ. Everywhere, not just by us, but because of us, men are coming to a knowledge of Christ. The very object of our being is that Christ should be known because of us. The Divinely appointed way of men coming to know Christ is by our being here, moving amongst men.

THE VITAL ELEMENT IN MINISTRY

That is simple, and perhaps we recognize and accept it, but the extra point which has to be noticed is this, that it is something more than our giving out knowledge concerning Christ; it is that we are to men the knowledge of Christ. There is a very big difference between giving out the truth concerning the Lord Jesus—even in large measure, in a great fulness, truth which cannot be denied because it is the truth—and that strange, deep, indispensable element that we are that truth, that that truth itself takes its power, its strength from the fact that here are those who are the living expression if it; who have gone through the depths, been tested, been tried, been taken from place to place, been subjected to experiences of intense severity, and in the fires have learned Christ, and are therefore themselves the embodiment of the knowledge of Christ. Wherever they go it is not that they have truth to give, but it is that men and women learn Christ because of them, and of them it can be said: It is not what they say only; there is something coming from them. There is an indescribable "something" which is an extra element to what they say. That thing has its reality in their being, and you feel that it is not only the words but the very virtue that comes out when they speak, or by reason of their presence. It is that of which the Apostle is speaking.

That is the real value of any knowledge of Christ which we can give, which others may come to possess by us. It is not that they come through us to know more about Christ, but that there is a ministration of Christ. That is the thing for which we should seek the Lord very earnestly.

THE COSTLINESS OF TRUE MINISTRY

We should recognize that this represents the costliness of ministry. Ministry of this kind is an intensely costly thing. It is so different from being a preacher as a preacher. There may be a glamour about preaching, a fascination about gripping a congregation, and all that sort of thing, which is not costly but gratifying to the flesh; the snare of the limelight, the snare of publicity, the snare of that satisfaction, feeling power over other people, which has robbed preaching of that essential blood, and passion, and anguish. Paul was not a preacher of that kind. It is all very well to talk about Paul as the great preacher and orator, and to try to be another Paul along that line. But to be a Paul is a desperately costly thing, and to minister Christ is a thing into which our very blood will be poured.

This kind of ministry can bring no satisfaction to the flesh. This kind of ministry is not something for which to reach out for ourselves. This kind of ministry is something that we should plead to be delivered from unless our life and heart passion is that Christ Himself—not ourselves, but Christ Himself—should be known. Suffer that word thus to you who minister in the Name of the Lord.

That is the true value of ministry. It is indeed a costly thing, it is a thing of suffering, but it is the thing which goes beyond words, far beyond clever thinking and clever expressing, far beyond that acute needle-like brain that grasps truth and then begins to give it out. It is something which is an extra factor, without which the very best equipment in nature will fail to reach the Divine end. It is, in a word, Christ ministered, not Christ ministered about, but Christ ministered. Paul saw that there was no doubt about it, that this ministry was effective, although effective in two directions. Not always did it result in people leaping into life, but it always resulted in something.

If it plunged some people more deeply into death it was a proof that it was effective. If it brought death home to some consciences that proved its power. To have real spiritual effect demands that this shall be the kind of ministers that we are.

The living knowledge of Christ brought near to us in vessels which have been shaped and wrought through the fires will, in the first place, discover our state and then intensify our state. It is bound to do those two things. The two states are here presented as: In the way of life, and, In the way of death.

THE EFFECTS OF THIS MINISTRY
I. FROM DEATH UNTO DEATH

(a)   As to the Unsaved

Let us get quite clear on this matter. This does not for one moment suggest—let alone support—the idea that some are elected to death and perdition and some are elected to life and salvation. That is not the thought. What is here is this, that there are those who are refusing life, and therefore put themselves in the way of death. There are those who are open to life, and therefore may be in the way of life. It is really a matter of the attitude of the heart. It has nothing to do, in the first place, with the Divine predestination. It has to do with our attitude toward Christ, our attitude toward the knowledge of Christ brought near to us in a living way. It is very simply explained. It can be possible that there are those who are not open to Christ. They have no intention whatever of giving their lives to the Lord. It is far from their meaning that they shall be saved or shall become Christians, however they would put it. It is not their thought or intention. They are not open, they are quite closed. It is quite a settled matter with them that they are not going to be Christians, or religious, or converted, or however they express it. For them the situation is as bad as any situation could be. Christ in a living way is being brought near, and they are not open to Him, and they cannot remain as they are. They are going to be intensified in their position, and more definitely and positively shut up to death by being where Christ is brought near, unless thy change their attitude.

They may not be any more conscious that they are more set, but they are. The coming near of Christ is going to be according to the Word, and according to truth, death unto death, from one measure of death to an intensified measure of death, from one point of distance from Christ and salvation to a removed point, further away from Christ and salvation. If ever the day comes when they do turn and desire the Lord, they will have a tenfold more difficult time than they would have had, and their salvation will be fraught with the most terrific suffering. The infinite peril of that sort of thing is that: "He that being often reproved hardeneth. . .shall suddenly be destroyed, and that without remedy." *"Today* if ye will hear his voice, harden not your hearts." Pharaoh hardened his heart once, twice, thrice at the call of God, and then God came in and shut his heart, and Pharaoh was incapable of opening it, though he may have wanted to. That is the danger of being where Christ is livingly brought nigh and our hearts being closed, unresponsive.

(b) As to the Saved

That does not only operate in the matter of our salvation in the first instance. That operates in the case of believers. It was not only Pharaoh who fell into that awful and tragic and disastrous state; but Israel in the wilderness, who had been saved from Pharaoh, fell into it. The words of Hebrews iii were addressed to Israel in the wilderness, and that whole generation failed to come into God's full purpose and thought. Why? Because there was brought near unto them the purpose of God, the will of God, and they stopped short in their response. They had gone so far, they had come out, and had moved to a certain point, and then they went no further. For some reason or another they ceased to go on with the Lord from a certain point. Do you think they remained the same? The Word of God makes it perfectly clear that they did not just stop there but, having stopped, there set in an intensifying process which eventually made it impossible for them to come into what God had appointed.

The door had been opened to them and set before them. Their hearts had been imperfect in response and abandonment. That led to the issue that when they wanted to enter and made an effort to do so they had not the spiritual life necessary, and the consequences were disastrous. "Too late" is a terrible reality to face. This may apply to the unsaved sinner; but it may also relate to the full object of salvation—the inheritance, the *fulness* of Christ. Truth received and not responded to means spiritual declension and loss of capacity.

It is just possible that we should belong to the Lord, and have gone so far, and then stopped; and yet from the day that we stopped, when we ceased to be obedient, to follow the Lord, to respond to His revealed will, Christ has been brought near to us again and again in a living way, all with a view on the Lord's part to getting us to move from that position, to move on; but, No! Every time there has been the recoil instead. There has been a failure to rise up and say: I am going on with God! Those people do not remain in that condition. All the time, perhaps unconsciously, there is hardening within, which presently will be manifested as a situation which is impossible of overcoming.

There is a passage in the Word which speaks of those who even touch the fire and are not conscious of it; of those upon hose heads there are gray hairs and they know it not: the marks of lost vitality, lost life; time going and not conscious of it. It is a terrible thing to suddenly wake up and find that your life has gone, all that could have been for God no longer possible. As we become older, and are naturally more occupied with the past than with the future (spiritually we do not do that), life holds a great deal more in the past than in the future; we see how much more there might have been, and we regret that we have not made more of the opportunity and of the years. We wake up to the fact that no longer have we the powers for mastering, no longer is it possible for us to make good. Think of that in relation to eternal things! Christ constantly coming near in a living way, and yet all that that means never being entered into.   But, more; that only strengthening our position in death. Oh! Terrible thought! That which is meant for life working out in death. Is this not a very strong appeal to our hearts, that we should rise up and go on, that we should consider our state and say: Am I locked up? Am I becoming incapable of moving? Whereas at one time it might have been difficult, but if I had resolved in the grace of God to move I should have moved, I should have been in a different place from what I am in today, today I am finding it less possible than ever to move, *and*, as things are brought to me, as Christ is brought to me, the truth is brought to me, and appeals are made in my presence, I find myself less inclined to respond! That is a terrible situation, the knowledge of Him meaning death unto death. Oh! Do shake yourself from the dust, if you should be in that position! If you have had Christ brought near in a living way for years, and you have not come into the living value of that, now is the time for you to get before God and say: This must stop; this death regime must end; this bondage must be brought to a conclusion; I must break and go on with God! Seek the grace to fight that thing through, *lest* all that was meant for you by the Lord coming near again and again should be eternally missed.

There is no getting away from the fact that Christ is effective. If He is not effective unto life, He is effective nonetheless. It is impossible for the Holy Spirit to bring Christ near without a result. There is no such thing as God's Word returning to Him void. It *will* accomplish a purpose, and the purpose of Christ is not to leave people where they were, but, if possible, to lead them into life; and, if they will not, to intensify their state, so that in The Day they will have no ground whatever on which to stand. If God condemns He condemns thoroughly, and leaves no room for argument.

II. FROM LIFE UNTO LIFE

The life may be in very simple forms. It may not be in a large measure. It may only require openness of heart, willingness of spirit, but that is toward life, life in its simplest form reaching out, incapable of doing very much, yet open and stretched forth. Ah, yes! The very heart open to the Lord, ready for the Lord. The coming near of the Lord means a ministration of more life. Increase of life requires that the life that is should be active. Even though it be in its simplest and smallest forms, yet to be active.

It is only a state of heart. Are you dead, or are you alive? Are you indifferent, or are you reaching out? The Lord draws near to minister more of Himself in life to every heart open to Him. It is wonderful and blessed to see what happens when the heart is open and the spirit is pure. There may not be a great deal of energy, a great deal of understanding, a great deal of instruction, a great deal of truth and teaching, but the most blessed results are not always in the realm where there is a great comprehending of truth, but more often in the realm where there is a simplicity, honesty, and openness of spirit. Some people are far too well informed to *live*. Some people's heads are the great obstruction to their spiritual enlargement. It is noticeable today that the Lord is not particularly active amongst the people who know such a lot, and He is not seeming to working to lay hold of the clever people, the well informed people, the people who are recognized as the authorities. The Lord is moving in a wonderfully blessed way amongst people whose hearts are open, whose spirits are simple, and who have little to throw off in order to go after Him. Are we active to the Lord in heart? Are we really going on, or have we come to a standstill? Have we never started?

Here is Christ brought near, and there can be an increase of Christ, an increase of Divine life. It ill depend upon whether you are open, whether you are not very concerned, not particularly interested, passive, perhaps antagonistic; or whether—not that you have a great deal of ability, or knowledge, or understanding of the meaning of it all—but whether your heart is open and reaching out to the Lord. Marvellous things can happen if you are in that state. It is not that you should have a perfect understanding of everything, not that you should have confidence in yourself, that having moved you can keep going, but it is that your heart is livingly toward the Lord; then everything is possible. That is the way of life (and to be in the way of life may only mean at its beginnings, that you are reaching out for the Lord), that is the direction of life. That you are in that state is the way of life; that you are obeying whatever light the Lord has given you; that you are obedient to everything that He has made known to you as His will, that is the way of life, and the way of an increase of life.

The way of death may be, at its beginning, no intention whatever of being the Lord's; or, at some point further on, where the Lord has said in your heart: That is My way for you; that is My will for you! You have perhaps

not said, "No, Lord" in as many words, but that is what
your life is saying. That, No! has now been hanging over
your life for perhaps five, ten years, perhaps longer. It is
not that you have never said positively: I will never be
obedient; I am not going that way! It may be that you are
simply doing nothing. That is a negative! That is, No! It
is not Yea! to the Lord. The issues are tremendous. When
we think that there may never be a presentation of Christ
without one of two results: we may either increase or
decrease; we may be more positive or less so; we are either
in a fuller way of death or a fuller way of life; it is a
tremendous thing. It is impossible to get away from the
alternatives.

The Apostle felt the solemnity of this, and surely we
feel the solemnity of it! The Apostle was so deeply
conscious of, and moved by, the solemnity of this position
that he said: "Who is sufficient for these things?" Think of
it, that wherever I go the effect of my life is more life or
more death! It is serious to be bound up with anybody's
life.

So we would entreat, and would plead, lest it should
be death unto death. Open the heart! Reach out to the
Lord! Move in obedience to every bit of light which He
has given, and it shall be a savour of life unto life.

The More
Excellent
Ministry

Publisher's note:

This 1998 reprint has retained the original English form as presented by the Author.

Table of Contents

Chapter 1
The True Source of All Ministry . . .
Union With Christ

Reading: Leviticus 8:22-24; Romans 12:1-2; John 17:19.

Referring to this passage in chapter 8 of the book of Leviticus, it is important to note what happened at that particular point in the consecration of Aaron and his sons to the priesthood. The ram of consecration was brought; Aaron and his sons laid their hands upon it; and then it was slain, its blood was shed. That blood was then taken and put upon them at different points of their beings.

There we have two sides of consecration. The shedding of the blood is the death side, and the sprinkling of the blood is the life side. The blood poured out is the life poured out, delivered up, let go or taken away. Sprinkling is the making active and energetic of the ministry in a living power. When you recognize that, you understand what consecration is, and also the meaning of the laying on of hands, the act of identification with a life poured out, a life yielded up, a life let go, a life taken away unto death. In the act of sprinkling a new position is represented, implying that now there is no longer anything of the self life, but all is livingly of God, active by God, and unto God alone. That is consecration.

Chapter 17 of the Gospel by John is known to us familiarly as the High-Priestly prayer of the Lord Jesus. He is there, in effect advancing to the altar in an act of consecration of Himself, in the behalf of His sons, whom He is seeking to bring to glory, that they may behold His Glory, and that the glory which He had might be theirs. Here is undoubtedly that which is represented by Aaron and hi sons. The High Priest is consecrating Himself, as He says, that they also may be consecrated. The rest of the prayer is a wonderful exposition of the inner meaning of this part of Leviticus 8. In the little while at our disposal we shall seek to understand it more clearly.

The whole man has come into the realm of consecration on both its sides; the death side, and the life side; the life poured out, and the life taken again; the life let go, and the life resumed. But on another basis; the whole man is involved, as represented by his ear, his hand, his foot. That has a simple and direct message to our hearts.

The Government of the Ear

We begin with ear. "...upon the tip of Aaron's right ear." That means that the Lord is to have supreme control of the ear, that we must come on to the ground where the ear is dead to every other controlling voice, every other governing suggestion, and is alive unto God, and unto God alone. It is quite clear that, in some way, the governing faculty of every life is the ear; not necessarily the outward organ, but that by which we listen to suggestions, that, as we say, to which we 'give ear'. The suggestions may arise from our own temperament and make-up; the constraining things in our life may be our natural inclination; the pull and the draw of our constitution; deep-seated ambitions, inclinations, interests, which are not cultivated nor acquired, but which are simply in us because we are made that way. To listen to these is to have our lives governed by our own interests. Or it may be other things, such as the suggestions, the desires, the ambitions of others for us; the call of the world; the call of human affections; consideration for the likes of others. Oh, how many things may come to us like the activity of a voice, to which, if we listen, we shall become slaves and servants, and the ear, and the life with it, become so governed.

This illustrative truth in Leviticus 8 says, definitely and emphatically, to you and to me, that that shedding, that slaying, was the slaying of our ear and our hearing in respect of all such voices, and that sprinkling meant that we now have a ear only for the Lord, and He is to have the controlling voice in our life. The right ear, as the right hand, is the place of honour and power so far as the hearing and the speaking are concerned. Then you and I, if we say that we are consecrated men and women, mean that we have brought the death of Christ to bear upon all the government and domination of voices which arise from any quarter save from the Lord Himself. We are not to consult the voice of our own interests, our own ambitions, our own inclinations, or the voice of anyone else's desires for us. We must have an ear only for the Lord. That is consecration.

It is a solemn and direct word for everyone, and perhaps especially for the younger men and women, whose lives are more open now to be governed by other considerations, because life lies before them. It may happily be that the sense of responsibility about life is uppermost; the feeling is that it might be disastrous to make a mistake, and along with it there is a strong ambition to succeed and not to have a wasted life. Herein is your law for life, and although the course of things may be strange, and the Lord's ways oft times perplexing, and you may be called upon in a very deep way to give ear to the exhortation addressed to us in the book of Proverbs, 'trust in the Lord with all thine heart, and lean not unto thine own understanding," nevertheless, in the outworking, you will find that God's success has been achieved, and, after all, what matters more than that, or as much as that? The course may be very different from what you expected, or thought, or judged would be the reasonable way for your life, but that does not matter so long as God has been successful in your life, so long as your life has been a success from God's standpoint. This is the secret, an ear alive only unto Him, and dead to everything that comes from any quarter other than the Lord Himself.

Chapter 17 of John's Gospel is an exposition of that. "They are not of the world, even as I am not of the world." If we were of the world, we should take the judgments of the world for our lives; what the world would suggest to be the course of greatest success, prosperity, advantage. The spirit of the world does sometimes get into our own hearts, and suggests to us that it would be fatal for us to take this course or that to give heed to that voice is to become conformed to this age. "I beseech you therefore, brethren, by the mercies of God, to present your bodies a living sacrifice, holy, acceptable to God, which is your reasonable service": and from the outset the point of supreme government is the ear. The ear must be put under the blood, to be God's vehicle of government. It means that we must have a spiritual ear. As children of God we have, by reason of our new birth, a spiritual faculty of hearing, and we must take heed to develop it as the Lord would have us do.

It means that the ear must be a listening ear. Many people hear, and yet do not hear; they have ears and they hear, but yet they hear not, because they do not listen. The Lord says many things to us, and we do not hear what He is saying, although we know He is saying something. There must be a quiet place for the Lord in our lives. The enemy will fill our lives with the voices of other claims, and duties, and pressures, to make it impossible for us to have the harvest of the quiet ear for the Lord. That ear must be an ear that is growing in capacity. The child has an ear, and it hears, but it does not always understand what it hears. A babe hears sounds, and you notice the signs of the babe having heard a sound, but that babe does not understand the sound that it hears. As it grows, it begins to know the meaning of those sounds. In the same way there must be a spiritual ear, a consecrated ear, marked by the

same features of growth and progress. Then, further, this
ear must be an obedient ear, so that hearing we obey. Thus
God governs the life from the outset.

The Work of Our Hands

Then we come to the thumb: "...and upon the
thumb of his right hand..." The order is quite right, the ear
first and the hand next. The Lord must have the place of
honour and strength in the activities of our life, in the work
of our life. Now this all sounds very elementary, but we
must listen for the Lord's voice in it. The point is that in
whatever we are doing, or about to do, in all our service,
there must be death to self; no self-serving, no world-
serving, no serving for our own gratification, pleasure,
advantage, honour, glory, position, exaltation, reputation.
In the death of our Offering we died to all that, and now our
hand, in whatever it does—and it may have to work in this
world's business, to do a multitude of uninteresting things
of a very ordinary character—whatever activity of life it
has to engage in, on the one side, our hand is to be dead to
self, and on the other side, to work with the Lord's interests
in view, "Whatsoever thy hand findeth to do; do it with thy
might. . ." (Ecclesiastes 9:10) You will remember how
much the Apostle warned about service being done to men,
as by men pleasers, and not as unto the Lord. He was
speaking largely to the slave of those days. When the slave
system obtained—and the slaves had to do many, many
things that must have gone much against the grain—he said
to them: Fulfill your service, not as unto those men who are
your masters, but as unto the Lord. We must question
ourselves as to why we are in any given place, or what it is
that moves us to desire any particular place or work. What
is the governing motive of our ambition for service?
Before God we must be able to say that any personal or
worldly consideration is dead, and that our service now is

not only not a reluctant, nor resigned giving of ourselves to what we have to do, but a ready applying of ourselves to even difficult, hard, unpleasant and uninteresting things for the Lord's pleasure.

Do write this word in your heart, that the Lord will not, indeed cannot, exalt you and give you something else, something more fruitful, more profitable, more glorious for Himself, until in that least, that mean, that despised, that irksome, maybe even revolting place and work, you have rendered your service utterly as unto Him, even if it has meant a continual self-crucifixion. That is the way of promotion. This is the way in which we come into a position where the Lord gets more out of our lives than we imagine He is getting. There is a priestly ministry in doing that difficult and unpleasant thing as unto the Lord, but we do not se that we are priests at the time. The idea of being girded with a linen ephod, at the same time when you are scrubbing floors and washing dishes, and other like things, is altogether remote from your imagination. Yet there is a testimony being borne which is effective, of which, maybe, you have no consciousness. It may come to light one day. Someone may say: I proved that Jesus Christ is a reality, simply by seeing the way in which you did what I know you naturally hated doing; it was wholly distasteful to you, you had no heart for it, but you did it in such a way that it convinced me that Christ is a living reality. That is no imagination and sentiment, it is true to life. The Lord has His eye upon us.

The Directed Walk

Next we consider the toe, "…and upon the great toe of his right foot." That means that the Lord is to have the direction of our lives, that all our outgoings and our stayings are to be controlled alone by the Lord's interests. We are not always being bidden to go. Sometimes the going is a relief, it is staying which is so difficult. We are so eager to go, and yet often the Lord has a difficulty to get us to go in His way. However the case may be, it is a simple point, it is a direct word. Our going has been rendered dead to all but the Lord, and our staying also. Our life has been poured out, has been let go, has been taken away, that is, the life which is for ourselves, of ourselves. Life has been taken up on another level.

The Supreme Example

Apply that to the great High Priest. Had He ever an ear for Himself or for the world? Had He not a ear for the Father alone? Trace His life through again. Satan came to Him in the wilderness, and began to speak. We do not know how this took place. We know that the Lord must have spoken of the matter secretly and confidentially to some, for no one had been with Him, He had been alone. We do not know whether Satan appeared in physical form, and spoke with an audible voice, but the probability is that it was not so, and that he wrought rather by inward suggestion, the strong bearing down upon the Lord Jesus of certain other considerations, every one of which was in His Own interest. There is no doubt whatever that Satan spoke to Him in some way, and He heard what Satan said, but His ear was crucified, and the power of that voice was paralyzed by his consecration to the Father. In effect He triumphed on this ground: I have no ear for you, My ear is for the Father alone!

Satan came in other forms, not always openly, but under cover. Thus a beloved disciple would sometimes serve him for a tool: "Be it far from thee, Lord: this shall never be unto thee" (Matt. 16:22). The Lord turned and said, "Get thee behind me, Satan"; He recognized that as the voice of self-consideration, self-preservation; He was dead to that; this way of the Cross was the Father's way for

Him; He had an ear for Him only. And so it was, all the way through.

Was it true of His service? Did He for a moment seek His Own ends by His works, Hi Own glory by what He did? No! Even in tiredness and weariness and exhaustion, if there were interests of the Father to be served, He was alive to those interests, never consulting His Own glory, or His Own feelings; and I have no doubt that His feelings were sometimes those of acute suffering. We read of Him as 'bearing wearied.' We know what that is, and how in weariness we would not only sit on the well, but remain sitting on the well, even though some demand were being made upon us. If we are the Lord's, we must be governed by the Lord's interests, and brush aside all the rising suggestions of looking after ourselves. So it was with Him in all His goings. He submitted His going or His staying to the Father. His brethren would argue that He should go up to the feast, but He does not yield to their persuasions and arguments. His one criterion is, what does the Father say about this? His mother entreats Him at the marriage in Cana, and says they have no wine. His unlooked reply is, "What have I to do with thee?" In other words, what does the Father say about this? So His whole life was, on the one hand, dead to self, to the world, and, on the other hand, alive only to God. And what a fruitful life, what a God-satisfying life!

There is a oneness with Christ in consecration. "For their sakes I consecrate myself, that they themselves also may be consecrated in truth." "I beseech you therefore. . .present your bodies a living sacrifice, holy, acceptable to God, which is your spiritual worship..." That is our priesthood.

Will you listen to that word? Will you take that work to the Lord in prayer? Will you get down before Him with it? Perhaps it is a word to bring about an end to a struggle, a light, a conflict; an end to restlessness, chafing, a lack of peace, lack of joy. You may have been fretted, you may have been thinking of your life as being wasted, and you are all in a ferment. Are you reaching out for something? Are you being governed by your own conception of things, by what other people think of you, by what the world would do, or what others would do, if they were in your place? These are not the voices for you to heed. What does the Lord say? Wait upon that; rest in that. You may not understand, but be sure a life on this basis is going to be God's success. Do you want God's success? God may do something through you for which you are temperamentally, constitutionally, altogether unfit, and for your part you have thought that, because you are made in a certain way, that must govern your direction in life. Not at all! Come, then, let us get down before Him on this matter, to deal with consecration, if needs be, all anew.

Chapter 2
The Experience of Ministry. . .
Pictured by Elijah

Reading: I Kings 17

What we have in view, of course, in the first place, is the servant of the Lord. Once more God is found reacting to a state of things amongst His Own people, rising up in Divine discontent, and, as always, laying His hand upon an instrument for recovery.

So Elijah stands before us to represent such an instrument, and, in God's dealings with him, we see the ways and the principles by which a servant of the Lord is made an effectual servant, in relation to the purpose of God.

The Sovereign Choice of God

The first thing related to any such instrument is the sovereignty of God. There is never any adequate, natural explanation for the choice and appointment by God of His servants. There may be things in the chosen instrument which will be turned to account, when they are wholly sanctified and brought under the government of God's Spirit, but when all has been said, we have to recognize that God's choice of His instruments is always a sovereign choice, and not because there is anything naturally in the instrument to warrant His choosing that instrument and selecting it from others. He acts sovereignly in choosing and appointing for His purpose. But, although that may be true, and although God may go beyond choosing and may endue that instrument with spiritual power, yet the instrument must be controlled and disciplined continually by the hand of God. Otherwise that servant of the Lord, or that instrument, will be found following in the direction of his own soul, following his own judgments, being influenced by his own feelings. The intent and motive may be very good, it may be very godly, but that does not dispense with the necessity of that instrument being continuously under the hand of God, for government and for discipline.

That is what comes very clearly before us at the outset in the case of Elijah. There is no doubt about God's sovereign choice, and there is no question as to God having endued Elijah with Divine power. Nevertheless, we see him at every step under the hand of God, and those steps are all steps which are a disciplining of the man himself. God is dealing with His servant all the time, and bringing him, all the way along, under His hand, so that he never becomes something in himself, but has everything in the Lord, and only in the Lord. We make a great mistake if we think that it is enough to have the Divine thought as to Divine purpose, that is, to have the knowledge of what God desires to do. That is not enough, that knowledge of what desires to do. That is not enough, that knowledge of the thought of God is not sufficient. There has to be a dealing with us in relation to that Divine thought, and that dealing with us is usually in a way which is altogether beyond our understanding.

If God were dealing with us as sinners, that is, if He were dealing with us because of certain personal sins and personal faults, we could quite clearly understand that; but when He is dealing with us in relation to Divine purpose, as His servants, His dealings with us go far beyond our understanding. We are taken out into a realm where we do not understand what the Lord is doing with us, and why the Lord takes certain courses with us. We are out of our depth, we are altogether baffled, and we are compelled—that is, if we are going on with God—to believe that God knows what He is doing: we have just to move with Him according to whatever light we may have, and believe that these dealings with us, o far beyond our understanding, are somehow related to that purpose with which we are called, and that the explanation waits some distance ahead, and we will find it when we get there. God does not explain Himself when He takes a step with us. God never comes to a servant of His and says, "Now I am going to take you through a certain experience which will be of this particular character, and the reason for this is so-and-so." Without any intimation from the Lord we find ourselves in a difficult situation, which altogether confounds us, puts us beyond the power of explaining that experience, and God takes us through without any explanation whatever until we are free, until the purpose for which that experience was given is reached, and then we have the explanation.

The point is, that even an instrument, sovereignly taken up by God in relation to His purpose, while knowing His main thought as to His purpose, still needs to be kept every moment, at every step, under God's hand, to be disciplined in relation to that thought, to be governed entirely by God.

Elijah, great man as he was, outstanding in the history of God's movements, was brought to that very point where, although He knew that God had laid hold of him, and although he knew what God's intention was, he could not, by his own initiative and by his own energy, freely go on to fulfill his mission. He could not move more than one step at a time, and even so that step had to be definitely governed by God. He could only take that step under the Divine direction. You see it here in this chapter to begin with. He had to take just one step, and then the next, and that by Divine direction, nothing beyond that. The Lord does not turn even His greatest servants loose with an idea. He does not liberate His most mightily used instruments to take a free course, even though they may know what God is after.

Divine Authority

Some of the reasons for that are clear. Elijah's ministry was one of Divine authority. There were powers at work which were more than human powers. The case with Israel was not simply one of spiritual declension. It was not merely that the people had lost a measure of spiritual life and were on a lower level than they should be, so that they had to have a deepening of the spiritual life. That was not the position at all. Baal had a mighty footing in Israel, and the evil powers, the forces of darkness, were back of this state of things. The situation demanded more than merely spiritual help to Israel. Something more than a ministry of exhortation and of spiritual food, something more than a convention for the deepening of spiritual life was called for. A ministry of Divine authority was needed, to deal with a spiritual situation back of the condition in which the people were found. There were mightier forces at work than merely human faults and failings. The might power of Satan was there represented by Israel's state. Elijah, therefore, must needs fulfill a ministry of Divine authority, and the very first public utterance indicates that that is what his ministry was:

"As the Lord, the God of Israel liveth, before whom I stand, there shall new be dew nor rain these years, but according to my word"—I Kings 17:1

There is a position, and there is an authority by reason of that position. James say that by Elijah's prayer the heavens were closed. That is going beyond the merely earthly, human situation. And again, by his prayer the heavens were opened. That is authority in heaven.

Secret Preparation

Now that ministry of authority was born in secret preparation before it came out in public expression. The Apostle James tells us quite definitely that "...Elijah was a man of like passions with us, and he prayed fervently (you have no mention of that in the historic record in the book of Kings) that it might not rain; and it rained not on the earth for three years and six months. And he prayed again; and the heaven gave rain..."

There is a secret history with God. He came into his public ministry with abrupt announcement. He simply stood there upon the platform of the universe, as it were, and made his declaration. But that is not all. There is a secret history with God behind that. All such ministry of Divine authority has its beginning hidden from the public eye, has its roots in a secret history with God. That kind of ministry, born out from that secret history with God, needs very special government by God to preserve its safety, to safeguard it from all those forces which can destroy it, and that is why Elijah, having such a ministry, needed to be governed in every step by God. There must be no generalization of movement in his case, there must be specific movements, God dictating every step. So God preserves that authority as He produces it, that is, by a hidden life. Such a life and such a ministry must not be exposed, otherwise it will be destroyed.

Separation from the Self-life

So the Lord said to Elijah, "Get thee hence..." Hence? Where from? From this exposure, this publicity, this open place with all its dangers. "Get thee hence, and turn thee eastward, and hide thyself by the brook Cherith, that is before Jordan." Hide thyself. Geography may have little to do with it. What is here spiritually is "hide thyself." Cherith means separation or cutting off, and that is linked with Jordan. Cherith is a tributary of the Jordan. We know what Jordan stands for, the death of the self-life. In the major sense, the Lord" servants have been to Jordan; that is, the self-life has been set aside; but they have to keep near Jordan, and Jordan has to govern them at every step. The most paralyzing thing to a ministry of Divine authority is "thyself." It is, in other words, the strength of our own souls.

Elijah was a strong-minded man, a strong-willed man, a man capable of very strong and drastic actions, of pouring out a great deal of his own soul-life with great heat, and the self-life of a servant of God is a great peril to the spirit. Paul makes it perfectly clear that, at an advanced point in his ministry and in his spiritual life, when God had entrusted him with visions and revelations unspeakable, which it was not lawful for a man to utter, the main and most immediate peril and menace to the ministry of that revelation was himself. "Lest I should be exalted above measure..." Then the self-life had not been eradicated from Paul! Paul was not clear of the peril of doing great damage to purely spiritual ministry, and God had to take a special precaution against the self-life of His own servant, not the sinful life in its old sense, but the self-life. "Lest I should be exalted..." I...exalted! What is that? That is the exaltation of the ego, the self. What dangers are in that "I", and how truly it stands in peril of getting into an exalted place, a place of power, a place of influence, a place of authority. It is in this sense that the Lord has to say, "Hide thyself," "get to the place of cutting off, of separation."

This was so different from what you might expect. You see, here is a man having had this deep, secret preparation with God in much prayer, who finds himself brought out in Divine authority to make a great announcement which represents a crisis in the purpose of God. You would expect that, from that point, he would go straight on from strength to strength, from place to place, would at once become a recognized authority, a recognized servant of God, and be very much before the public eye. But God would guard against any servant of His taking up a Divine purpose and a Divine commission in himself, taking it up in his own energy. That will destroy it, and there must be a hiding, a very real hiding. If a geographical hiding is God's way of getting a spiritual hiding, well, be it so. If God chooses to send us out of the realm of public life and ministry into some remote and hidden place, in order to take us away from the imminent peril of our becoming something, of our being taken up to be made something of, our going on in the strength of our own self-life, that is all well and good; but whether it be geographical or not, the word of the Lord to all His servants would always be, Hide thyself!

Adjustableness

Then you see, connected with that, as a part of it, the servant of the Lord must be found always in the place where he is pliable, where the Lord can get a ready and immediate response. The servant has no programme, therefore there is nothing to upset. He has no set course, therefore the Lord has nothing to break. He is moving with God, or standing with God, just as the Lord directs. He must be mobile in the hands of the Lord, that is, capable of being moved at any time, in any way, without feeling that everything is being broken up and torn to pieces.

"Get thee hence...and hide thyself by the brook Cherith...and it came to pass..." that the brook would not dry up, and the fact that the Lord told Elijah to go to the brook Cherith did not mean that the Lord was going to preserve the brook forever. It was a step. I do not promise you that you will stay there always. I am not saying that that is your last abiding place, and that you will settle down there forever. That is your next step: go there and be ready for anything else that I want."

This is a spiritual condition, of course. No one is going to take this literally. If we were to begin to apply this literally, s to our businesses here on earth, we might get into confusion; but we have to ready in spirit for the Lord to do anything that He likes, and never to feel that there is any contradiction when the Lord, having directed us in one way, now directs us in another. It is a matter of being in the hands of the Lord, without a mind of our own made up, though the way be hidden from our own reasoning, from our own will, from our own feelings, hidden from all our soul-life, so that the Lord has a clear way with us.

The brook dried up! Well, are you dependent on the brook? If so, you are in a state of utter confusion when the brook dries up. Are you dependent upon the Lord? Very well, let all the brooks dry up and it is quite all right. Dependence on the Lord is a governing and an abiding law of true spiritual power. Elijah has been spoken of and written of as the prophet of power. If that is true in any special way, he was very certainly the prophet of dependence.

That relationship to the Lord made it possible for the Lord to do other things, and to lead him on into new realms of revelation and experience. OH, what a thing adjustableness is! If we are not adjustable, how we prevent the Lord from bringing us into his full revelation and purpose.

Those disciples of John the Baptist were adjustable, and because of that they came to know the Lord Jesus. You will remember those disciples of John who followed Jesus, and said, "Master, where dwellest thou?" He said, "Come and see." Now had they been fixed and settled, saying, "We are John's disciples and we must stand by him; we must stay with John, and move with him; let Jesus have His Own disciples, but we stand by John." They would have lost a great deal. But they were open and adjustable, and moved beyond John.

Those other disciples of John whom Paul found at Ephesus many years afterward, to whom he said, "Did ye receive the Holy Ghost when ye believed?" were adjustable. When they heard what Paul said, they were baptized into the Name of the Lord Jesus. They were ready to go on from John to Christ, and so they came into the greater fulness (Acts 19).

Unless we are adjustable we shall miss a great deal. Elijah was adjustable, and so God could lead him on. The Lord allowed the brook to dry up because He had something more for His servant to learn, and something more to do through him, and so He said, "Arise, get thee to Zarephath...I have commanded a widow woman there to sustain thee." He went to Zarephath, and was made a blessing by his obedience.

Experience of Resurrection

Then he was brought by his new movement of obedience and faith into a new exercise, a new perplexity, a new trial; for the woman's son died. The woman was a widow with one son. The death of the son meant for her loss of everything. It happened while Elijah was there, being looked after by this woman, and he was there in his obedience to the Lord. He had done this in obedience to the Lord, and now, in the line of obedience to, and of faith in, the Lord, the Lord allowed this catastrophe to come into the very home to which he had been sent. It clearly raised a big question in Elijah's heart. "God sat me here, I know that! God raised me up and commissioned me, and in the course of the fulfilling of my commission He brought me into this situation! There is no doubt about the Lord having led this way, and no where I am, having done what the Lord told me, having taken the course that He indicated, and everything has come into death and confusion; there is a terrible contradiction here!" All sorts of questions can arise when you get in a position like that, and you can begin to go back on your guidance, begin to raise questions as to whether, after all, you were led, or whether you made mistake in your guidance. Do that, and you only get more and more into the mire. What is all this about? God had a revelation for Elijah beyond anything that he had yet received. He was going to bring him into something more than he had yet known. He was going to show his servant that He is the God or resurrection; and that has to be wrought, in a deep way, into the very being of His servant, through trial, through perplexity, through bewilderment. Thus the Lord allows the widow's son to die, and the house to be filled with consternation, and all concerned to ask big questions.

The prophet goes up to his chamber and brings the thing before the Lord, and lays hold of God, and so relates himself to this situation that he and the situation are one, and the boy's resurrection is the prophet's resurrection. There is identification of the prophet with the situation in death, and then in resurrection. The mighty meaning of the power of His resurrection, with new experience of that for the servant of God, was an essential lesson, if this authority was to be maintained, and this ministry to work out to its ultimate meaning in the overthrow of the powers of death, which were working destruction. The servant of God must go through it all in his own heart.

This discipline of Zarephath was relative to the whole ministry of the prophet. Zarephath means testing and refining, and it was indeed a refining fire. But Elijah came out, and everybody else concerned came out, into a new place in resurrection.

The Lord write these things on our hearts, and show us how they still remain as spiritual values connected with the reaching of God's end, the fulfilling of His purpose.

Chapter 3
The Stewardship of Ministry...
The Steward's Vital Position

Reading 1 Cor. 4:1-2; 1 Cor. 9:17; Titus 1:7-8; Col. 1:25; 1 Tim. 1:4.

The subject of our meditation is to be that of stewardship. A steward is a man who, on the one hand, stands in a living relationship to all that his Lord has, and, on the other hand, in an equally close relationship to all who look to his Lord for the supply of their needs, or to receive somewhat of His bounty. So that the steward is a very responsible person. He is responsible for the reputation of his master. What the world knows of his master will very largely accord with what the steward is, and what the world or the household receives of enrichment and good, will depend very much upon him. That is a very simple illustration, but that, and very much more, is what is bound up with this word "steward," or "stewardship."

The Apostle Paul spoke of himself as a steward, as having been entrusted with a stewardship, and it is impressive to note that he applies the term to the believers in the Corinthian church or assembly. We can quite readily understand and appreciate that Paul should be a steward, but when he addresses the people in the Corinthian assembly and says to them: "Let a man so account o us, as of ministers of Christ, and stewards of the mysteries of God" (1 Cor 4:1), thus bringing them all in, surely that is transferring the designation to very ordinary believers. We cannot, therefore, evade the issue by saying, Well, that applies to special people like Paul! It clearly applies to ordinary people, like the Corinthians and ourselves, and the exhortation is that men should be able to regard us, to take account of us as stewards.

The Fact of Responsibility

That speaks of something more than merely having a standing as believers. We might perhaps think the world must take account of us as Christians; they will do so in any case if we make a profession! But this Divine thought takes us much further. It brings us out into a place of specific and definite responsibility in two connections; firstly, to the Lord, binding up the Lord's interests with us in an active way; secondly, in alike practical way, to man. We are stewards, we stand in a place between, with a responsibility in two directions.

The Lord's people need to be reminded, from time to time, of the fact of their responsibility. There is a tremendous responsibility resting upon everyone who is related to the Lord, because that relationship is never a passive one, or ought never to be so. It is not the case that we are just members of a family, and there the matter begins and ends. Membership of the family, in the household of faith, is but one phase of truth, of the teaching of the Word of God. It has its own special meaning and value. The fact that believers are called by a variety of designations, and that the various designations seem to counter one another, presents no actual conflict when it is seen that they are but so many aspects of a whole, and not mutually exclusive. For instance, in the case of earthly relationships, for one to be a member of a family would preclude one from being the steward of the household but with the spiritual relationship it is not so. We have to keep the family relationship in its own place, to recognize that it brings its own responsibility and obligations, and has its own meaning and value; but with that in its place, you yet find yourself, in another direction, in the position of a steward, where you come into a great and specific responsibility. This holds good of all. We are all called to be stewards: that is God's thought for every one of us.

Such an observation leads us to one or two important considerations.

The Qualification for Stewardship

A fact which should be very helpful to us is that all the Lord's dealings with us are with the design of making us such stewards as it is required we should be. A steward has to be qualified for his stewardship. A steward must be a man of certain definite characteristics. The fulfillment of his stewardship will demand experience. He cannot step into a true spiritual stewardship at will. There has to be a real preparation, a real development, a real endowment for such a stewardship. If you read carefully the connection in Paul's mind between the stewardship and its fulfillment, you will see that the connection is a very practical one, a very active one, a very deep one. He was conscious of the need of special enablement, special gifts, special qualifications, and for such equipment he had to go through special experiences. Stewardship is a matter of training, and deep training at that.

In order to make us able stewards, the Lord takes us into many different kinds of experiences; into extraordinary, unusual experiences, into such a variety of experiences as come to none but His Own people. No one else goes through quiet the same variety of experiences. There are features about the experiences of God's people which are uncommon. Other people in the world may go through certain sufferings which are seemingly like the sufferings of believers: they may know the difficulty of poverty, the difficulty of maintaining their position in the world; outwardly there may be a similarity; but in reality, on the inward side, there are elements associated with the experiences of believers which are not associated with the experiences of the world; theirs are peculiar. They have factors of a spiritual character associated with them, which are entirely foreign to the ungodly, to the unbelieving. With the experience of a believer there comes a challenge which does not come to the unbeliever, there is a demand to be faced which in the case of the world is not there. I believe that we go through a great many things as the Lord's people which we should never go through if we were not His people. It is simply because we are the Lord's that we go that way. The explanation is not merely that we have to face an enemy when we take sides with the Lord. We have further to take into account the fact that the Lord allows the enemy to do what he does.

(1)   An Experimental Knowledge of the Need

To what end is this? We have already shown that what governs the Lord in His dealings with us, His mysterious dealings, His strange leadings, His unique permissions, is His design of making us stewards. How do those things accomplish such an end? A steward must know the needs of the people to whom he is to minister. He must know of their needs, and he must know the nature of their needs. The man of God is not just an official. He is not someone taken out of a crowd and put into office, and set a daily task which can be learned by studying a manual. He has to have a vital relationship with the whole position, and he must know, in a living, experimental way, the nature of the needs to which he has to minister. Between him and those to whom he is to minister his Master's riches, there must be a sympathy of heart by way of inward understanding. He must know the variety of their needs, for what he would give to one would never do for another; what he might give to quite a number would be altogether out of place to give to others. He will find, as the physician finds, that no two cases are exactly alike, because no two temperaments are exactly alike. A dozen people may have the same complaint, but it may be needful to treat each one differently, because of different temperamental factors in each case. The true physician is one who not only takes the complaint into account, but the person who has the complaint. It is like that with the steward. There has to be an understanding of the need, of the situation; there must be a heart-understanding, a sympathy.

The Lord deals with us in order that we might be able to minister in an apt way. His stewards are to be men of understanding, who can touch the various needs, who can reach the heart, so that the Lord's children are saying: That just fits me! That ouches my case! That person must know! That one must have been through it! Who has been telling him about me? Yes, the Lord knows, and He would take you and me through experiences such as will make us stewards in a living way: and that is what He is doing. The steward must understand the universal needs, the variety of needs, and must understand in a way that no one can who merely studies from the outside. The Lord's way of training His stewards is to take them **through** things: and who is better able to meet the need than the One who has known that need Himself?

(2)   An Experimental Knowledge of the Resource

Then the steward has not only to understand the nature of the need to be met, but he must have an equal knowledge of the resources with which he is to meet it. He must know the quality of that which is at his command, the nature of it, the values that are in it. Here again, we can never know the values of the things of God unless we have gone through experiences in which we have put them to the test, and proved them. No one really knows the value of Divine things who has not proved their value in his own life.

The stewardship of the Gospel is something more than our seeing the Gospel of the grace of God in the New Testament, as a system of truth, as something which embraces in a formula certain matters such as forgiveness of sins, justification by faith, and all the other elements of the Gospel: it is something more than that. The stewardship of the Gospel implies that the Gospel has become wrought into the very being of the steward, and that the steward himself is rejoicing in it. Such a steward can come out of the treasure house and meet the household, and meet those beyond, and say: I have something here of tremendous value; I am rejoicing in it myself; I know it, and I can assure you I am not giving you something that has simply been taken hold of and passed on apart from experience; it is not something that is the result of my studies, gleanings from other minds, what the commentators and "authorities" say. I am up-to-date in my personal knowledge and benefit of this matter.

What is true of the Gospel is true of the many-sided mysteries of God. That is another stewardship of which Paul speaks. You and I are led into the mysteries of God, into the depths, to discover those secrets, in order that we may come out with the treasures of darkness. Ah, but what darkness it is while we are there! No treasures seem to abound in the darkness. All seems death, and desolation. Poverty and starvation seem to reign. But to come out with the treasures of darkness, **treasures** of darkness, constitutes stewardship. Stewards are men and women who have been through the dark, and have discovered treasures and have the treasures of darkness to pass on.

(3)   Faithfulness

How much have you to dispense? Are you sure that you are dispensing what you have? The Lord did not lead you through that trial, through that darkness, through that strange experience, just for your own sake. The Lord has not dealt with you as He has, in order that you should be shut up to yourself, to enjoy the result alone. He had done that to constitute you a steward. If you and I will only allow that fact to govern us in the days of difficulty and trial, it will help us through. We should hold fast to the fact that the trial is to mean enrichment for the Lord's people, and an increase of equipment and qualification for stewardship. There are so many who have a measure of spiritual wealth and are not making it available for others; others are not getting the benefit of it. They have a knowledge of the Lord that has come through experience, and if only they would get alongside of others, those others would get some of the good of the Lord's dealings with them, would be blessed, and enriched. Ask the Lord to release you into your stewardship within your measure. We are not speaking of an official, organized service for God, where you have to be continually ministering to others, whether you have the resources with which to do or not. That is all false, and puts strain upon you; you may well revolt against that kind of thing. We simply have in mind the way in which the Lord creates living contacts. Children of God may cross your path in dire need, and may all the time be looking for the person who can help them. They have been crying to the Lord to meet the need, and have been watching to see how the Lord would answer. They may cross your path, and you talk upon all sorts of ordinary things; they pass on their way, and you have failed in your stewardship. They have not received that for which they have been asking, and the steward has disappointed the Lord, and those who were looking to the Lord. Let us ask the Lord to give us release from our tied-up state, to fulfill this stewardship.

The Lord's Word is: "...it is required in stewards, that a man be found faithful," not eloquent, intellectual, with a strong personality, none of those things. What is your mental conception of a steward? One who has a great facility of speech, who finds no difficulty in talking? No! "...it is required in stewards, that a man be found **faithful**." I believe that the greatest virtue in the eyes of God is faithfulness; it embraces everything. Faithfulness is after God's own heart.

Take a passing glance at this steward—Paul the Apostle. "Demas forsook me..."; (II Tim. 4:10); "...all that are in Asia turned way from me..." (II Tim. 1:15). Look at him when everything which would inspire to faithfulness is breaking down. He is left practically alone. He has more enemies than ever. And now the tragedy, the pathos is that so many of his enemies are those to whom he has been most used. While there were enemies without it was not so difficult, but now the very people for whom he has spent himself have become his enemies. But there is no though, no hint, no suggestion of giving up. His word is, "...faithful unto death..." This steward was faithful. You cannot say that, when he died, the situation outwardly testified to tremendous success. It did not look like that at all. Paul's life was not vindicated up to the hilt. No! He died largely a lonely man, but faithful. "...it is required in stewards, that a man be found faithful." But what enrichment of others may follow from the meeting of that requirement, costly as it is. Paul is not dead! I only hope that Paul knows of all that has sprung from his ministry, all that his ministry means to us. The Lord has met us through His servant, and we never, never get to the depths or anywhere near the bottom of the fulness of Christ that has come through Paul. We shall go on, and, if we live twice or three times the length of our present life, we shall still be making discoveries of what we owe to Paul's faithfulness as a steward. That has been going on century after century.

That is faithful stewardship, and although the steward may be called away from his earthly stewardship, the stewardship goes on. Faithfulness is always rewarded beyond our wildest dreams. May the Lord maintain us in faithfulness, even though that faithfulness may sometimes involve us in an appearance of utter failure. The Lord make us good stewards.

Pioneers of the Heavenly Way

Publisher's note:

Pioneers of the Heavenly Way originally published from 39 Honor Oak Road, London in 1953

The year of publication as given is from when, in the author's bimonthly magazine *A Witness and a Testimony*, a first notice of this book or booklet appeared. Very many of the titles published had already appeared earlier as articles or series in that magazine.

Where a new title's date of publication is not known, + signifies the year of the magazine article or series from which, some unspecified time later, that new publication was reproduced.

1998 Christian Books Publishing House / SeedSowers
P O Box 285
Sargent
GA 30275

CONTENTS

CHAPTER ONE

THE FACT AND NATURE OF THE HEAVENLY WAY

" These all died in faith, not having received the promises, but having seen them and greeted them from afar, and having confessed that they were strangers and pilgrims on the earth. For they that say such things make it manifest that they are seeking after a country of their own. And if indeed they had been mindful of that country from which they went out, they would have had opportunity to return. But now they desire a better country, that is, a heavenly : wherefore God is not ashamed of them, to be called their God : for he hath prepared for them a city "
(*Hebrews xi. 13 — 16*).

SOME TIME BEFORE these messages were given, desiring to be quiet and away from many things, I went down into the country with my heart very much to the Lord for His word. In the early hours of the morning it seemed as though the heavens opened and everything became alive : it all opened up wonderfully, and centred in one phrase —' Pioneers of the Heavenly Way '. That really does sum up the verses that we have just read, and, while we are going to think and perhaps say much about the heavenly way, it is this matter of pioneering the heavenly way that will be our main concern. It is necessary, to begin with, for us to consider to some extent the heavenly way itself, but I repeat that it is this whole tremendous business of *pioneering* that way that I believe to be the main concern of the Lord, and hence of ourselves, at this time.

THE EARTH RELATED TO HEAVEN

The Bible begins with the heavens: "In the beginning God created the heavens and the earth"—not 'the earth and the heavens'; the heavens come first. The Bible closes with the holy city, new Jerusalem, coming down from God out of heaven (Rev. xxi. 2); and, just as heaven stands at the beginning and at the end, so everything in between, in the Word of God, from the beginning to the end, is from heaven and to heaven. As it is in the natural realm, so it is in the spiritual. The heavens govern the earth and the earthly, and the earthly has to answer to the heavenly. It is the heavens, it is heaven, that is ultimate: everything has to be in the light of heaven, to answer to heaven, to come out from heaven. That is the sum of the Word of God, the whole content of the Scriptures.

This world, this earth, is not unrelated and alone. However important it may be in the Divine scheme of things —and certainly it is an object of great heavenly concern; perhaps the greatest things in the universe have taken place on this earth: God has come here in flesh, has lived here, has given Himself for this world; the great drama of eternal counsels has to do with this earth—nevertheless it is not apart, alone, it is related to heaven, and all its significance is by reason of that relationship. It takes its significance and importance from being related to something greater than itself—to heaven.

The Bible teaches that God is located in heaven. " God is in heaven " (Eccles. v. 2): that is the declaration. It teaches that there is a system, an order, in heaven, which is the true one and which is the ultimate one. In the end, it will be the reproduction of a heavenly order upon this earth which will be the consummation of all the counsels of God. Christ came down from heaven and returned to heaven. The Christian, as a child of God, is born from heaven and has his life centred in heaven, and the life of the child of God will be consummated in heaven. The Church, that masterpiece of God, is of heavenly origin, of heavenly calling, and of heavenly destiny. In all these things, and in many others, " the heavens do rule " (Dan. iv. 26). This great factor of heaven governs everything.

CHILDREN OF GOD RELATED TO HEAVEN

As for ourselves, if we are children of God our whole education and history is related to heaven. That is one of the matters we must follow out presently in greater detail ; but let it be said, and let it at once be recognised, that our whole history and education as children of God is related to heaven—and by that I do not mean simply that we are going to heaven. We are *related* to the kingdom of the heavens, by birth, by sustenance and by eternal vocation. All our education, I have said, is related to heaven. All that you and I have to learn is as to how it is done in heaven ; as to what the Lord meant when He said, " Thy will be done, as in heaven, so on earth " (Matt. vi. 10)— a great comprehensive fragment covering all the education of the child of God, for that prayer begins with " Our Father who art in heaven ". For as things are in heaven, so they must be here ; but a whole lifetime of education, deep and drastic training, is involved in conformity to heaven.

The Bible of the Christians in New Testament times was the Old Testament. When we read in the New Testament, as we so often do, about the Scriptures—" that the Scriptures might be fulfilled ", " as it is written in the Scriptures ", and so on—it was the Old Testament that was referred to. The Old Testament was the only Scripture, the only Bible, of the first Christians, the Christians of the first decades. They had not got our New Testament. For them the Old Testament was the Bible, and it was continuously drawn upon, referred to, taken up and used in order to exemplify the spiritual experience of Christians. This letter to the Hebrews, from which we quoted at the outset, is just that. From beginning to end it is packed with the Old Testament ; the Old Testament is being unceasingly used to illustrate and set forth the meaning of the spiritual life of the New Testament Christian.

A PILGRIMAGE RELATED TO HEAVEN

And what we find in the Old Testament is a pilgrimage, all the way through : a pilgrimage in relation to heaven. Let us step right back to the beginning. You see, the Divine intention in creation was that such a harmony should obtain between heaven and earth that God could be here in this world in pleasure, in happiness, in rest, just as much as He could be in His heaven. He made it for His pleasure, He made it for Himself, He made it that He might come and go in perfect satisfaction and rest and

joy. The first picture is of God being pleased to come to
the world which He had created. He made it, it was His
work, and we are told that when He had made it He entered into His rest. His rest was found in being here in
His creation.

Ah, but since the tragedy of the fall, heaven and earth
have lost their harmony ; they are now at variance. This
world is in conflict with heaven. Everything here on this
earth has been changed. So far as the world is concerned,
God has no pleasure in being in it or coming to it. *His presence here is in testimony, not in fulness*—in testimony
that this is His rightful place, in testimony to the fact that
" the earth is the Lord's, and the fulness thereof " (Ps.
xxiv. 1), in testimony that He made it for His own pleasure. But God is here *only* in testimony, in token. He must
have that testimony, but He is not now here in fulness. In
a very real sense and in a very large degree, God is outside of this world, and there is conflict between heaven
and the world ; and even while there is testimony here,
that very testimony is here and not here. It is outside. The
very vessel of the testimony of God's presence is something that does not belong here. Here it has no dwelling ;
here it has no city. It is ' in ', but not ' of '. It is a stranger
in this world. So it has been since the fall.

Now the whole history of Divinely apprehended instruments for that testimony, whether they be individual
or whether they be corporate, is the history of spiritual
pioneering in relation to heaven. Have you grasped that?
Let me repeat it. The whole history of vessels Divinely
chosen and apprehended for the testimony of God, whether they be individual or corporate, is the history of pioneers breaking a way, cleaving a way through, doing

something which was new so far as this world was concerned, breaking fresh ground, making fresh discoveries
in relation to heaven ; pioneers of a heavenly realm. How
much history is gathered into a statement like that!

FOR PILGRIMS THE CENTRE OF GRAVITY
IS IN HEAVEN

Let us look at one or two of the features of this pioneering vocation. First of all, those who are called from heaven,
apprehended by heaven, to serve the heavenly purpose,
find that their centre of gravity has been inwardly and
spiritually changed and transferred from this world to
heaven. Inside there is a deep-seated sense that we do not
belong here, that this world is not our resting-place, that
this is not our home and this is not our centre of gravity ;
we are not drawn to it inwardly. Within the spirit of the
pioneer there is this sense of conflict with what is here, of
being at variance with it and unable to accept it. I repeat :
inwardly and spiritually, the centre of gravity has been
transferred from this world to heaven. It is an inborn consciousness, and it is the first thing in this heavenly calling, the first effect, the first result of our calling from on
high. We are going to come back to that again later on.

And we can test by this. Of course, it is true of the simplest child of God. The first consciousness of one born,
truly born, from above, is that the centre of gravity has
changed. Somehow or other, inwardly, we have moved
from one world to another. Somehow or other, that to
which we have hitherto been related by nature no longer
holds us : it is no longer our world. Put it how we will,
that is the consciousness, and unless it is so there is some-

thing very doubtful about any profession of faith in the Lord Jesus. And this inborn sense of a new centre of gravity has to grow and grow and grow and make it more and more impossible for us to accept this world in any way. Again I say, it is a test of our spiritual progress, of our pilgrimage and our advance in it. But that is elementary after all.

THE HEAVENLY REALM UNKNOWN TO US BY NATURE

Again, that other realm, the consciousness of which has come into our hearts, the gravitation toward which has commenced in our spirits, is an entirely unknown world to us by nature. To nature it is another realm altogether —different, unfamiliar, unexplored. It does not matter how many have gone on before us, it does not matter how many there are who have started on this way and gone a long way in it: for every individual it is an altogether new world and it can only be known by experience. We may derive values from the experience of others, and thank God for all those values, but with all their experiences they cannot get *us* one step further on that way. For us it is new, utterly new, and strange. We have to learn everything about it from the beginning.

That makes pioneering—what pioneering always is— a lonely way. No one can hand down to us a heritage. We have to obtain our own in that world, strange and unknown as it is; demanding basically a new constitution according to that world, with capacities that are not possessed by nature. No man by searching can find out God (Job xi. 7); we have not the capacity. It must be born in us from heaven. We have got to make the discovery for ourselves of everything. We have to discover God for ourselves, in every detail of His willing relationship to the human heart.

Light may come through testimony, light may come through the Scriptures, help may come through counsel, inspiration may come to us from those who have ploughed through and gone ahead, but in the last analysis we have got to possess our own spiritual plot in the heavenly country, subdue it, cultivate it and exploit it. You know that is true; that you are going that way in the spiritual life. You are having to find out for yourself. Oh, how we long for somebody to be able to pick us up and put us through on the good of their experience! The Lord never allows that. If really and truly we are on the heavenly road—if we have not just started and sat down or given up: if we are moving on the heavenly road, we are all pioneers. There will be values in it which others will come into because we have pioneered, but there is a sense in which every one, no matter how far behind, has got to make discoveries for himself, and it is best so. Ultimately, there is nothing second-hand in the spiritual life.

PIONEERING FRAUGHT WITH COST AND CONFLICT

So we come to the third feature of this pioneering. All pioneering is fraught with great cost and suffering, and, this being a spiritual course or way, the cost of this pioneering is mainly inward.

Perplexity ; yes, perplexity. I have been reading a translation of a message by our brother Watchman Nee. In it he says, in effect, ' There was a time when I had such a high idea of the Christian life that I thought for a

Christian to be perplexed was all wrong ; a Christian to be cast down—that is all wrong ; a Christian to despair— that must be all wrong ; what kind of Christian is that? And when I read Paul saying he was perplexed and in distress and in despair it constituted a real problem for me, in the light of what I had taught myself a Christian ought to be ; but I had to see there was nothing wrong with it, after all.' Yes : a Christian, and such a Christian as the Apostle Paul, perplexed, and cast down, and in despair. That is the way of pioneers.

Perplexed. What does perplexity imply? It implies a need for capacity or comprehension in some realm in which at present there is none. There is a realm that is beyond you. It does not mean that you will always be perplexed in the same measure over the same thing. You will grow out of your perplexity on this matter, and you will understand ; but there will be to the end perplexity, in some measure, simply because heaven is bigger than this world, vaster than this natural life, and we have to grow and grow. Perplexity is the lot of pioneers.

Weakness. Brother Nee asks, ' A Christian in weakness and confessing to being weak? What kind of a Christian is that? ' Paul speaks much about weakness, and about his own weakness—meaning, of course, that there is another kind of *strength* which is not our own, which has to be discovered ; something that we do not know naturally. It is the way of pioneers : to come to a wisdom which is beyond us and which for the time being means perplexity ; to a strength which is beyond us and which for the time being means weakness in ourselves. We are learning, that is all. It is the way of the pioneer, but it is costly. The cost is inward, like that, in so many ways.

But while it is inward, it is also outward. This letter to the Hebrews is just full of these two aspects of the pilgrimage. "*These all . . . confessed that they were strangers and pilgrims on the earth*" *(Heb. xi. 13)*. It was a spiritual journey, a transition from the earthly to the heavenly, that the Apostle was writing about. There was an inward aspect. But there was the outward aspect for them, and it is the same for us. The whole trend of nature, if left to itself, is downward. Leave things to themselves, and down they go, in all nature. Is that not true? A beautiful garden will become a wild desolation, a riot and a chaos, in no time, if you take the upward-ordering hand from it. And that is true of us in a spiritual way—gravitation earthward, always wanting to settle down, always wanting to end the conflict and the fight, always wanting to get out of the atmosphere of stress in the spiritual life. The whole history of the Church is one long story of this tendency to settle down on this earth and to become conformed to this world, to find acceptance and popularity here and to eliminate the element of conflict and of pilgrimage. That is the trend and the tendency of everything. Therefore outwardly, as well as inwardly, the pioneering is a costly thing.

You are up against the trend of things religiously. See again this letter to the Hebrews. The trend was backward and downward to the earth, to make of Christianity an earthly religious system, with all its externalities, its forms, its rites, its ritual, its vestments ; something here to be seen and to answer to the senses. It was a great pull on these Christians ; it made a great appeal to their souls, to their natures, and the letter is written to say, ' Let us leave these things and go on '. We are pilgrims, we are strangers, it is the heavenly that matters—you recall that great paragraph about our coming to the heavenly Jerusalem (chapter xii. 18 — 24).

But it is a costly and a suffering thing to come up against the religious system that has 'settled down' here. It is, I sometimes feel, far more costly than coming up against the naked world itself. The religious system can be more ruthless and cruel and bitter; it can be actuated by all those mean things, contemptible things, prejudices and suspicions, that you will not even find in decent people in the world. It is costly to go on to the heavenlies, it is painful; but it is the way of the pioneer, and it has to be settled that that is how it is. The phrase in this letter is, " Let us therefore go forth unto him without the camp" (Heb. xiii. 13)—and I leave you to decide what is the camp referred to there; it is not the world. " Unto him without the camp " means ostracism, suspicion.

"These all died in faith, not having received the promises, but having seen them and greeted them from afar " —is that not the vision of the pioneer—always seeing and greeting from afar; hailing the day, though it might be beyond this life's little day; greeting the day of realisation?—" and having confessed that they were strangers and pilgrims on the earth. For they that say such things make it manifest that they are seeking after a country of their own. And if indeed they had been mindful of that country from which they went out, they would have had opportunity to return. But now they desire a better country, that is, a heavenly : wherefore God is not ashamed of them "—God is not ashamed of the people who are on the pilgrimage with Himself to His end; He calls them His own and He is " called their God "—and " he *hath prepared for them a city" (Hebrews xi. 13 — 16).*

That is a marvellous summary, when you come to think about it. "These all"—what a comprehensive "all"! And covering them all, it says of them that they had seen something—and having seen they could never rest, to their last day and their last breath on this earth. They were still pilgrims, they could never rest, this was in them the call of the unseen. It is something that must come into us from heaven in order to get us to heaven. Have you got it?

Well, as we shall see, that is the key to everything, it explains everything. It is the guarantee—oh, blessed be God for this, would that more of the Lord's people knew it in greater power!—it is the guarantee that all that is in us of longing and of craving and of quest, born of the Spirit of God, is going to be realised.

Are you hungry? Are you longing? Are you dissatisfied? That is itself a prophecy of more to come. Are you contented? Have you settled down? Is your vision short and narrow? Can you just go on here? Can you accept things as they are? Very well, you will be left to it, you will not get very far. God calls Himself the God of those who are pilgrims. He is the God of pilgrims, and, divesting ourselves of all the mentality of a literal pilgrimage—if you like, of a literal heaven, for I do not know where heaven is, but I know that there is a heavenly order of things and that I am being dealt with in relation thereto every day of my life—let us leave out the literal side, and see the spiritual, which is so real ; and let us ask the Lord to put this spirit of pilgrimage in us mightily.

You will find as you go on that, whereas at one point in your spiritual life everything was so wonderful and so full that you felt you had reached the end of everything, there will come a time when that will be as nothing, and you look back upon it as mere infancy. Things that you were able to read then and feed upon: you say, ' How was I able to find anything in this at all? ' Do not mistake me : there is nothing wrong with that, that is all right for people at that point—but you have gone on, you must have something more. We ought to be growing out of things all the time, going beyond. We ought to be people of the beyond. That is probably the meaning of the word ' Hebrew '. This letter is called the letter to the Hebrews, and it speaks about pilgrims and strangers, and if the word ' Hebrew ' means a person from beyond, well, we are people from beyond, our home and our gravitation is beyond. We are pilgrims here, pilgrims of the beyond.

May the Lord make this helpful, and on the one hand move us out of any lethargy or false contentedness, or undue longing to reach an end here, and, on the other, keep our eyes and our hearts with those who have pioneered before, seeing and greeting, and, if needs be, dying, in faith.

CHAPTER TWO

THE CRISIS AS TO THE EARTHLY AND THE HEAVENLY

Reading : Numbers xiii. 1—3, 17—23, 27—33 ;
xiv. 1—3.

WE HAVE BEEN CONSIDERING the fact and nature of the heavenly way. The Bible begins with the creation of the heavens and the government of the heavens. It ends with the emergence from heaven of that which has been formed by heaven, according to heavenly principles : the holy city, new Jerusalem, coming down from God out of heaven, fulfilling this word which we have read in Hebrews xi. 16—" God hath prepared for them a city ".

THE CLASH BETWEEN THE EARTHLY AND THE HEAVENLY

We remind ourselves here that a characteristic of the Old Testament at every stage is the clash and contrast of two worlds, of two orders : the heavenly and the earthly. All the way through the Old Testament we have this element —of heaven challenging this world, and apprehending, in this world, that which it will take out and constitute according to its own, heavenly, order and nature. It does not require a very profound knowledge of the Old Testament to confirm that. Your minds run quickly over its story and you recognise that you are in the presence of a clash all the time, a conflict. It is this conflict between heaven and earth. Heaven is not satisfied with this world—very much to the contrary. Heaven is against what is here in this world; but heaven is seeking to take what it can out of this world to reconstitute according to its own standards : and so, while you find the opposition of heaven, the challenge of heaven, you at the same time find heaven, right from the beginning, as it were laying hold of people—a line of individuals and a nation—in order to detach them from the world, even while here in it, and by a deep process to make them a completely different type and kind of people from everyone else ; apprehending them, in other words, for heavenly purposes.

The Old Testament men were *pioneers* of the heavenly way. We have already seen a little of what that involves, but it is upon that particular point that we want to focus all our emphasis just now. It is not only that there *is* a heavenly way which is different—we know that, we know it in our hearts if we have been born from above, we are learning as we go on how different the heavenly way is from every other way—but the focal point at this time is this : that there is such a thing as *pioneering* that heavenly way, *being called into a relationship with heaven* in ordei to cleave a way, to take possession, to make it possible foi God's full meaning to be understood, interpreted ; a ministry to others who shall follow on. We said earlier that there is a sense in which everyone born from above is a pioneer, because for every such one the way is a new way, which they and they alone can follow : no one can do it for them ; it is a new way for everyone. Our present occupation is with the vocational aspect of this.

There is no doubt about it that the majority of the Lord's children know little, very little, about the heavenly way. Organized Christianity has become very largely an earthly thing, with earthly standards and conceptions and resources: therefore it has become spiritually very limited. In comparison with the heavens, this world is a very, very small thing. I mean that spiritually as well as illustratively. The kingdom of the heavens is a vast thing, far greater than any conception of man. God's thoughts are as the heavens are high above the earth in range, outbounding all earthly conceptions, and not until we get well away from this earth do we realise on the one hand how miserably small we are and on the other hand in what a very much greater realm it is possible to move than that in which we do move—I mean spiritually. The great, great need of this time is that the people of God, the Church of God, should come into its true heavenly position, with its heavenly vision and vocation.

Now there is a great deal in that statement, but it all means that someone, some people, have got to pioneer the way for the Church back again to the realm where it once was at the beginning, the realm which it has lost in succumbing to that persistent tendency earthward. I say, a pioneering instrument is needed, and the way is a costly way.

Now let me repeat, the Old Testament men were pioneers of the heavenly way. That is what is explicitly stated by the writer in this letter to the Hebrews, particularly in the passage which we have read. Heaven has its own standard and basis, and earth cannot provide that. One of the great key-words of the Old Testament is ' sanctify ', and sanctify means to separate, make holy, consecrate, set apart, and in the main that is a spiritual and inward thing, dividing between heaven and earth. God has divided those two things, put them apart, and there is to be this putting apart in a spiritual way, inwardly, also. So you find that these men of the Old Testament were men who were set apart in this sense: something was done right at the very centre of their being which separated them from this world and committed them to a course which was altogether different from and contrary to the course of this world; and if, under pressure, under strain, by deception inadvertently, consciously or unconsciously, they touched this earth, they were at once in confusion—they knew at once in their inner being that they were out of the way, and the only thing was somehow to get back. You see that again and again. Heaven witnessed against their position; they were in trouble. Not until they got back could they go on. They were being ruled by another standard, but oh, how different was that standard, and how difficult to understand!

Consider Cain and Abel. From this world's standpoint, Cain's was a very worthy procedure. Looked at from the standpoint of the religious man of this world, it is difficult to see what was wrong with Cain, or how much more right was Abel, or how absolutely right and absolutely wrong these two were. Yet how utterly right Abel was is shown by the issue. One got through to heaven. That is the fact. He got through to God and he got through to heaven, and the other one had a closed heaven and a rejecting God.

You say, What is the standard? Just the difference between heaven and earth, that is all. Heaven's basis and standard of access is altogether different from earth's—

even religious earth's. The religious man may have the same God, worship the same God, bring his offering to the same God, and yet get no way to heaven, no way at all on the heavenly road. Heaven has its own basis and standards and provision, and earth can neither find nor provide that. It is different. That is the fact that we are up against when it is a case of getting to heaven. I am not talking about geographical location, but about getting through to God, finding an open way with heaven. You can only come on heaven's own provision, and that will entirely and utterly upset all your own natural calculations. You have to find something that nature cannot provide. If you, like Cain, reason this thing out according to religious reason, and come on that ground, you do not get anywhere. *"By faith Abel offered unto God a more excellent sacrifice than Cain, through which he had witness borne to him that he was righteous, God bearing witness in respect of his gifts"* (Heb. xi. 4). Heaven attested.

I am not dealing with all the nature and detail of these things. I am pointing out a fact—that heaven's standards and judgments are altogether different, and they are going to throw us completely into confusion when we try to come, even in a religious way, into heaven. Nicodemus may be the most perfect representation of the religious system, but he cannot get anywhere where heaven is concerned. Heaven makes its own provision for access, and you have to have heaven's provision. You may ask a thousand Why's. There is the fact.

PIONEERS ARE LEADERS

Let us now turn to our reading from the book of Numbers. It is at the point of the sending over of the spies, and the focus of the whole incident is upon two men : Joshua and Caleb. Now, mark you, all the twelve heads of fathers' houses—princes in Israel (a significant term), typically representative men—were called to be pioneers of the heavenly way. The principle of their headship and princeliness was that they were to be pioneers. That is the pioneer principle. If you are a true pioneer, you are a leader, you are a prince in character. But only two of them justified their calling ; only two of them became what all the rest were supposed to be—pioneers. Very often it just works out like that. It is the minority, the very, very clear minority, that does the work. The others have the name, but they are not doing it ; the others have the official position, but they are not doing it. The point is—where is it being done? Here it was Joshua and Caleb.

A LINK WITH THE PAST

Now let us spend some time in taking account of the significance of these two men, Joshua and Caleb. To begin with, we will look at them as a link with the past. The intention of God which was taken up by them harked back to His covenant with Abraham, so that with Joshua and Caleb Abraham comes very much into evidence. You are at once compelled to look back and take fresh stock of the significance of Abraham, as taken up by these two : because, you see, the point at which Joshua and Caleb came into view was a critical point, an hour of very great crisis. The whole question now is—Is God's purpose going to be realised in this people, or is it not? That is no small issue ; a real crisis has arisen. And *they* are the deciding factor.

There are three features of the place of Abraham as it comes in here.

A SPIRITUAL AND HEAVENLY SEED

First of all, there is the feature of a spiritual and heavenly seed. Do get that—a spiritual and a heavenly seed. We, to-day, are in a position of very great advantage. We have now, through the Holy Spirit, the full significance of Abraham. We have our New Testament and all that the New Testament says about Abraham. We have the full revelation through the Apostle Paul, and we are now able to see from our New Testament—we have not to go back to the Old Testament for all our knowledge—we can see now, with our New Testament in our hand, the full significance of Abraham ; on this point we have much extra light.

A spiritual and heavenly seed. You see how that bears upon Joshua and Caleb, and how they take it up. But this other seed of Abraham is not spiritual and it is not heavenly. It has come down to earth. In these thirteenth and fourteenth chapters of Numbers that we have read, the reactions of this people—how gross they are, how earthly, how lacking in spiritual vision and life and aspiration! They are swayed entirely by the earthly—by the sight of the eyes, by things here, the difficulties, the people, the mountains. For them there is no way. For Joshua and Caleb the mountains were a way, not a hindrance. There was a heavenly way. But these others see nothing of that, they are earthly.

A heavenly and spiritual seed—that is the thought of God in Abraham made clear to us in the New Testament.

AN EXCLUSIVE SEED

But what more light have we got on this? That it was something exclusive. Paul argues that out in his letter to the Galatians. *"Now to Abraham were the promises spoken, and to his seed. He saith not, And to seeds, as of many; but as of one"* (*Gal. iii. 16*). It was exclusive. We will see in a minute where that led to; but note that this, so far as Abraham was concerned, was tied up inseparably and exclusively with Sarah. It was permissible in those times for a man to have more than one wife, but God was shutting this thing up to Sarah. Abraham, under stress and pressure, tried it along another line, by another means —with Hagar; but here was one of these points of which I was speaking a little earlier: a failure, a slip, a mistake, a blunder, under trial, under pressure, under duress; getting off the heavenly line and rueing it—and history has rued it to this day. He had to get back to Sarah. God has shut this thing up, it is an exclusive matter. Not Hagar, and not others, but *this* one.

SUPERNATURAL IN BIRTH AND MAINTENANCE

And this seed carries all the marks of the heavenly. It is supernatural in birth; impossible along the line of nature. That is Isaac: and Abraham was shut up to that, shut up to an intervention of heaven. This cannot have an existence, let alone a history, unless heaven sees to it. God was very particular about that. Sometimes God shows how particular He is about the right thing by letting us see the awfulness of the wrong thing. God does not just let a wrong thing go; a mistake, a slip, go as such. We are plagued sometimes to the end of our lives by a wrong step. God will keep that, so that we may see—No, the right way is an important way ; it is not just an option. The heavenly is *the* way, and any alternative to that is not just allowed to pass as though it did not matter. We discover that it does matter ; and so it was here. Heaven must do this, or it will never be done, because it is in the heavenly way. What a lot we have to learn, and are learning, about that principle! It explains a great deal that is happening in our lives. God has us in hand.

THE PRINCIPLE OF DEATH AND RESURRECTION

Yes, but not only was Isaac a heavenly product by the intervention of heaven, by a miracle, but you see God is going to press that right through to the ultimate in demanding the offering of Isaac as a sacrifice. Isaac was born by a miracle, by the intervention of heaven, but something still further had to be done: he had to die and be raised from the dead. This mighty thing of God must come in and ratify that. What Paul says in Romans i. 4, " declared to be the Son of God with power, according to the spirit of holiness, by the resurrection of the dead ", could well be rendered ' ratified the Son of God . . . by resurrection ' ; and that is Isaac, ratified heavenly.

That has very much of our own spiritual history in it. We have not only been born again by a miracle and heaven's intervention ; this has been ratified all the way along. God is demanding the maintenance of that by resurrection life, and resurrection life has no meaning unless we know something of death. God is keeping us on heavenly ground. That is the meaning of Isaac: not only

putting us on heavenly ground, but keeping us on heavenly ground by constant expressions of resurrection, when
only resurrection will save the situation.

After all, no matter what it was at the beginning of our
Christian life—that we had a wonderful experience of
conversion and can put down in a notebook when it happened and where—that may be good, but it has to be
ratified continually by the expression of resurrection. We
have got to be kept on that ground. And that is the pioneer way. The way of pioneering the heavenly way is
knowing again and again the meaning of death and its
direness, in order to know the meaning of resurrection and
its greatness. It is the pioneer way. The Church has gone
that way ; many a revelation of God has gone that way ;
many a child of God has gone that way—in order to keep
the heavenly way alive and stop this ' dry-rot ' of earthliness which is always seeking to sap the Christian life. We
know how true that is.

Abraham came to know that his real inheritance was in
heaven. I always think it is a very wonderful thing, this
aspect of Abraham's life and experience, under the hand
of God : that no doubt when he first set out, at the command of God, he interpreted those promises in a very
earthly and limited way. No doubt to begin with his expectation was that they would be fulfilled and realised in
this way and in that ; but the longer he lived the more he
became aware that it was not this way or that, it was
something more than he had thought when he started,
something very much more and very much other. He went
on, and he is one of those here included in this word—
" *These all died in faith, not having received the promises,
but having seen them and greeted them from afar . . . But*

now they desire a better country, that is, a heavenly ". When God said, ' I will bring you to a country ' (Gen. xii. 1), Abraham in the first place thought that that was earthly ; in the end he saw it was not. He came to *see*, to have perception : for the Lord Jesus said, *" Your father Abraham rejoiced to see my day ; and he saw it, and was glad "* (*John viii. 56*). *" Having seen them and greeted them from afar "*. And so Paul brings us back here, in his letter to the Galatians—*" to thy seed, which is Christ "*. *" He saith not, And to seeds, as of many ; but as of one, And to thy seed, which is Christ "* (*Gal. iii. 16*). Christ was the answer to everything of inheritance for Abraham.

But Christ, the heavenly Christ, is the very embodiment of all that is heavenly. We know not Christ after the flesh. Christ is essentially heavenly. You see the heavenly nature of this seed. You can crowd all that into Joshua and Caleb. Who will be the people that will inherit, go over and possess? Not this earthbound, earth-minded crowd. They will perish in their earth, their earth will be their prison and their tomb. They will be replaced by another generation with a different constitution—represented by Joshua and Caleb, the first of a new generation—who will possess. They are the pioneers of the heavenly way and the heavenly fulness. But how deeply they had to suffer for it. *"All the congregation bade stone them with stones "* (*Num. xiv. 10*). Pioneering is always a way of suffering and cost, even amongst—not the worldlings—but those who go by the name of the people of God.

Well, the pioneer of the heavenly way will always be like this: heavenly as a seed, and constantly ratified as heavenly by the necessity for repeated interventions of heaven to extricate, to deliver, to keep going. It is true to the spiritual life. We would not have gone on more than a little way, we would have stopped, it would have been again and again the end of us, if heaven had not intervened, if it had not been that God had ratified the fact that we belong to heaven. And He is doing it.

Well, all this is so clearly seen to be fulfilled in Christ, this Heavenly Seed. His birth was by heaven's intervention, a miracle. At His baptism heaven broke in again and ratified, " This is my beloved Son ". His Cross?—that does not look very much like an intervention of heaven. But wait a minute: do not forget that the New Testament never talks about the Cross of Christ on the death side alone. In the New Testament the Cross has twin sides— death, resurrection. *" Ye by the hand of lawless men did crucify and slay : whom God raised up " (Acts ii. 23 — 24).* The world has done all that it can do, has exhausted itself upon Him. The powers of evil have exhausted themselves. What more can be done? Ah, now heaven comes in and spoils it all and raises Him: ratifies that He belongs to heaven and not to this world. He is not the property, the plaything, either of this world or of the evil powers that govern this world. He belongs to heaven: and heaven intervenes, and not only raises Him, but takes Him up and out and sets Him over.

His spiritual history is the spiritual history of the pioneer of the heavenly way. He is *the* Pioneer. " Within the veil ; whither as a forerunner Jesus entered for us " (Heb. vi. 19 — 20), says this letter to the Hebrews.

A LINK BETWEEN FAILURE AND REALISATION

One other thing with which to close this present phase as to the backward aspect of Joshua and Caleb to Abraham. They, like Abraham and all the pioneers, were a link between failure and realisation. You look at the world at the time when " the God of glory appeared unto our father Abraham " (Acts vii. 2) in Ur of the Chaldees. You look at the world and you look for that which is of heaven, and where will you find it? Where is all God's thought for something heavenly? It seems that once more it has disappeared. There seems to be no testimony at all to this heavenly thought of God—a heavenly people, a heavenly testimony, something that represents and expresses heaven's thought. Where is it? " The God of glory appeared unto our father Abraham ", and he became the link between the failure and the realisation.

Joshua and Caleb took that up. Here is the story of the failure in the wilderness. But for them, where is the heavenliness? But for them, where is God's thought? Yet God has not given it up. It may seem to have well-nigh disappeared ; it has been like that again and again. But heaven intervenes, and secures a link between the failure and heaven's triumph. That link is the pioneer. The Lord must have an instrument like that to set over against the failure and to open the heavenly way again to realisation.

You are probably wondering, ' What has this to do with me?' You are saying,' Yes, these are all wonderful ideas : it is quite true, it is quite clear that it is true in the Bible : but how does it affect us? ' Well, it just does. One does not like dwelling in a critical way upon a situation, and whatever is said in this direction always leaves room for something very precious of the Lord still in the earth. It is to speak quite broadly. We will put it this way. The great need of Christians to-day is to be recovered for the full heavenly thought of God. They have settled down to something less. They have become involved in something less and largely other. It has always been like that. The New Testament was written almost entirely because of it. The Lord's people are always at least in peril of doing that—at least in peril. They do gravitate spiritually toward this world and lose their heavenly testimony in one way or another. The pressure is always there to bring down, and the Lord needs lives that have *seen*—that have become like those of whom we were thinking in our last meditation, for whom the centre of gravity of life has been transferred from this world to heaven, within whom there is this sense—whether they can interpret it or not, whether they can put it into a system of truth, doctrine, Bible teaching, or not—there is this sense that they are in the line of some great destiny which is beyond what this world can provide, that they have been gripped by something that they can only say is the heavenly calling, which has held them. I am going to say more about that later on ; but the Lord needs a people like that, who just cannot be satisfied with things as they are : it is not just a matter of the mind, of the reason, at all. It is inside of them ; they know that God has done something. Because God has done something, they are committed to something far greater than the poor limits of this life and this world. They have been inwardly linked on with something tremendous. I say again, they may not be able to preach it, but they know it. We shall never be useful to God beyond our vision, our true God-inwrought vision, beyond our own reach of heart. Our measure of vision will determine the measure of our usefulness. Oh, for the immeasurable measure of heaven in the heart of a people ! That is the need to-day.

Let me close by saying again that, while that is the

heavenly calling of which the Apostle speaks so much, it is the most difficult way—it is fraught with every kind of difficulty ; but it is the real, it is the true, and it is the ultimate, for heaven is a nature, a power, a life, an order, which is destined to fill this world and this universe.

CHAPTER THREE

ABRAHAM—A GREAT PIONEER

Reading : Hebrews xi. 13 — 16

WE RETURN NOW to Abraham as one of the representative pioneers of the heavenly way. We begin by reiterating one thing which was so true of Abraham, but which must be true, and is always true, of every spiritual pioneer, of every one who is moving on to explore and exploit the heavenly kingdom : that is, his sense, his deep, inborn sense, of *destiny*. Stephen has told us, concerning Abraham, that " The God of glory appeared unto our father Abraham " (Acts vii. 2) when he was in Ur of the Chaldees. We do not know how the God of glory appeared unto him. It may have been in one of those theophanies common to the Old Testament and common to Abraham's later life when God came to him in man-form. We do not know. But we do know from his whole life that the effect of it was to bring to birth in him this tremendous sense of destiny—the sense of destiny which uprooted him from the whole of his past life, and which created in him a deep unrest, unrest of a right kind, a deep and a holy discontent.

Discontent may be all wrong, but there is a right kind of discontent. Would to God many more Christians had

35

it! There was started in Abraham an urge which grew and grew through the years and made it impossible for him to settle down and accept anything less than the full meaning of God. He could not accept a second-best in relation to God. Of course, the consciousness of that had to grow. He had to come progressively to realise what it meant. It came in this way : that he arrived at a certain place, and perhaps thought that here was it, and then he found it was not, and he had to move ; and then perhaps he thought, ' Now, this is it—but no, it is not. There is still—I do not know what it is, I cannot define, explain, but I know within me there is still something more that God has '. *" Not that I have already obtained, or am already made perfect : but I press on "* (*Phil. iii. 12*) ; it was this urge through the ages—so very real in the case of the man whose words I have just quoted. He was never able to accept God's second-best. God has a second-best. Again and again in history God has found it impossible to realise His ' first best ', His very best. People would not go on. He said, ' All right, you shall have My second-best ', and they had it ; but pioneers never do that. Abraham could not do it.

Now, do not misunderstand or misinterpret this. This was not natural or temperamental instability. Do not think that, if you are a person who is never contented, that is a Divine discontent. It may be temperamental. You may be one of those people who can never stick at a thing for very long, who are always jumping from one thing to another. You will be an entire misfit, both in the world and in the kingdom of God. It was not that sort of thing with Abraham. There was something of heaven working in him, the proof of it being that he was always on the upward move ; he was not on the horizontal, he was on the upward move. He was making progress, not only on the earth level, but spiritually, all the time.

Now you see, alongside of Abraham there was Lot, and Lot was a man who was always seeking security *here*. He sought the city; he sought a house. He disliked this tent life. He wanted to be settled in this world, and he sought to be settled. But Lot was the weak man with all that. Abraham who was always moving in a tent was the strong man. This was not natural at all, it was spiritual. This urge from heaven, this mighty working of a spiritual force in Abraham brought him into the very hard school of the heavenly. To the natural, to the earthly, to the flesh, the heavenly is a very hard school, and Abraham was brought into it by this urge from heaven.

THE CONFLICT BETWEEN THE SPIRITUAL AND TEMPORAL

In the first place, there was the conflict between the spiritual and the temporal, the conflict between the seen and the unseen—and that is a very fierce conflict. In Abraham's life it was sometimes pressed to a very fine issue. You see, on the one hand Abraham was blessed of the Lord, he was prospered of the Lord, there were the signs that the Lord was with him. There was increase, enlargement, great enlargement, yes, embarrassing enlargement. His flocks and his herds multiplied; he was a very prince in the land—and yet, and yet, that very blessing of the Lord was at times brought to the point where the whole thing could in a moment be wiped out—by famine, acute, devastating famine. Why had God blessed and increased and enlarged, and then allowed something that could wipe it all out in no time? That is rather a difficult problem, is it not? Would it not have been better to have been kept small and limited than to see all this threatened? Abraham found the problem very acute. It was that that brought about one of his failures. He went down to Egypt.

It was a hard school.

What does it mean? It seems that God gives with one hand and takes away with the other: prospers and blesses —and then throws in something that threatens to destroy the blessing. Is God a contradiction? Is He denying Himself? You know the temptations at such times to try to interpret. Are we, after all, but the pawns in a game? Are we, after all, but the children of chance, of fortune or misfortune? After all, is the Lord in this? Can this really explain the Lord, a consistent God?

It is a hard school. But, you see, it is wholly in keeping with what God is doing.

What is He doing?

Well, if He blesses, there are two things bound up with it. In the first place, Abraham's blessing and prosperity and increase and enlargement had to find its support from heaven and not from earth. God is introducing the great heavenly principle. Oh, the Lord may bless and enlarge, but God forbid that ever we should assume that now we can support ourselves, now we can carry on, now we have got going and can maintain our going by our own momentum. He will see to it that, however He may bless, if a thing is of Himself—however great, however enlarged, however increased it may be—it can perish at any moment if heaven does not look after it. That is a lesson. Do not presume; do not take anything for granted. Live every moment out from heaven. As truly in the day of blessing as in the day of adversity, cling to heaven.

And then there is this other factor. God was so training Abraham that he could be safe for blessing, and that is something—to be safe for blessing. Such discipline, such trial of faith, such testing! And yet it does not matter to Abraham how much God blesses him, he does not allow his blessings to obscure the heavenly vision and halt him on the way. That is a tremendous triumph. Oh, the devastating perils of blessing! Perhaps you may feel that you do not know much about those perils as yet. But God wants to make us safe for His heavenly kingdom, safe for spiritual enlargement, safe for being used mightily; and we are never safe if things less than God's ultimate can hold us up, never safe if the good is the enemy of the best. With Abraham it is perfectly clear, that, whether in prosperity or adversity, he was never allowed to settle and never allowed to seem to have arrived. If at any time he did feel he had now arrived, that was very quickly exploded. *"These all died in faith, not having received ... but having seen ... and greeted ... from afar"*.

Another thing about Abraham is this: that he never allowed the apparent difficulties, however great they were, ultimately to stay his spiritual onward and upward march. We will come back to that again in a moment. Do you not see how all that was taken up by Joshua and Caleb? Think again about Joshua and Caleb. These were most certainly men who had been in that school. If they had not been, they would never have taken the next generation into the land. God only knows what those men went through. You see, the story is told in so few verses, about the spies going

out, and the minority report, and the taking up, or proposal to take up, stones, to stone these men and kill them.
But you have got to add to that the long, long years while
that whole generation was dying out, with only two men
holding on to the heavenly vision. That is a hard school.
They might easily have lost heart and given up and said,
' It is a hopeless outlook '; but they did not: the heavenly
had got a grip upon them in their innermost being and
held them. It held them, even in the greatest adversity, and
they came through ; they ' overcame the world '.

THE CONFLICT BETWEEN THE SPIRITUAL AND CARNAL

Then, again, with Abraham there was the conflict
between the spiritual and the carnal: not only between
the spiritual and the temporal, but between the spiritual
and the carnal. This conflict came right inside what we
may call the domestic circle. It was in the family, in the
blood. It was in Lot. I am speaking spiritually. I interpret
Lot as representing something that is not only objectively
in the Christian family (which is of course quite true) but
is in our own natures, subjectively, the carnal setting up
conflict with the spiritual, the earthly with the heavenly.

Here, you see, is Lot, and he is of the same blood as
Abraham ; but right in the blood, right in the family—if
you like, right in the Christian family—there is this streak
of carnality: Lot and his worldliness, his worldly-minded-
ness, his worldly vision, his worldly ambition, his worldly
longings. There is no heavenly vision with Lot ; and he is
right alongside, so closely alongside, Abraham. Abraham
finds this menace of an argument against his spiritual
course right in his blood. It is there ; it is in us, and it is in

the Christian family. It is right alongside, very near all the time—this craving to settle down, to have things here and now—quick returns—things seen—the gratification of the soul ; that rest which is not rest, but which we think of as rest.

Many of you know what I am talking about. You know how sometimes naturally we crave for rest, and we try to get it—and we do not get it until we get to the Lord. We find our real rest in the things of heaven, not in having holidays. But there it is, and it is always trying to draw us away, get us away, make us run away. ' Oh, to get out of it ! If only we could live on some island alone—how restful, how peaceful ! To get away from it all !' And it never happens. Our rest is in heavenly things. We only find our real satisfaction in the things of the Lord. You Christians go and have a surfeit of the world : you know you will come back and say, 'No more of that !' You know you cannot do it. But that craving is with us all the time. The carnal influence is in our blood. And it is in the whole Christian family—the Lot side, that wants to have a Christianity of this world, always dragging and pulling downward and away from the heavenly. Abraham knew all about that.

That constitutes the very ground of this pioneer work, pioneering for the things of the Spirit. It is this warring against the things of the flesh, as though we were always carrying about a corpse, some lifeless thing to be dragged about and subdued every day. We have to say to ourselves, ' Come on, none of that ! ' It is the way of the pioneer. You can settle down, but you will lose your heavenly inheritance. The carnal has very, very subtle ways—very ' spiritual ' ways.

Is that a contradiction? It is a spurious spirituality, but what is interpreted as spirituality. I think of the great battle that Paul, the heavenly man, had with the Corinthians, the earthly church. And yet the Corinthians were supposed to be spiritual. They had all the spiritual gifts ; they had the miracles, the healing, the tongues. But Paul said, " I . . . could not speak unto you as unto spiritual, but as unto carnal " (I Cor. iii. 1). The carnal can have very ' spiritual ' ways, apparently. The fact is that their carnality was taking hold of spiritualities, and making the spiritualities serve their carnality ; giving them soulish gratification, in display, in show, in demonstrations ; pulling the heavenlies down to the earth. Do not let us blame the Corinthians. How we long to see, how we long for evidences and proofs ! Why do these things gather such a following? Because there is something in human nature that is gratified, and it is so infinitely more difficult to walk the heavenly way where you do not see and you do not know ; but that is the way of the spiritual pioneer who is going to inherit for others.

THE PROOF OF THE REALITY OF HEAVENLY VISION

Finally, the proof of Abraham's vision : the proof of this sense of destiny being real, true, genuine, being really of God, and not just his imagination : how is that proof given in his case?

(a)   FAITH IN THE GOD OF THE IMPOSSIBLE

First of all, Abraham's attitude toward the impossible. As we said in the last chapter, the New Testament gives us the full story. In the Old Testament it looks as though he gave way, broke down in the presence of the impossible.

We shall come to that in a minute. The New Testament tells us quite emphatically that Abraham looked the impossible squarely and straightly in the face and believed that it was possible. His attitude to the impossible over Isaac proved that there was something more than just imagination ; there was something mighty in his sense and consciousness of destiny. If we give up when a situation begins to appear to be impossible—that is the ultimate test of whether we really have had registered in us a sense of heavenly vocation. The fact is that, although you feel you want to give up, you are not allowed to give up. Something in you just does not let you give up. You have been on the point of writing your resignation a hundred times. Again and again you have said, ' I am going to get out of this ; I cannot go on any longer or any further ; I am finished ' ; but you have gone on, and you are going on, and you know quite well that there is something in you stronger than all your resolutions to resign. How necessary is that sense in us—and it is proved to be something, not of ourselves, but of God. " According to the power that worketh in us " (Ephesians iii. 20)—it is that.

(b) CAPACITY FOR ADJUSTMENT WHEN MISTAKES ARE MADE

Then consider Abraham's capacity for adjustment when he made mistakes. This man, this pioneer, made mistakes, and they were big mistakes. What is the temptation of a servant of God who makes a glaring blunder ; of one carrying responsibility who makes a terrible mistake? What is the immediate reaction? ' Oh, I am evidently not fit for this, I am not called to this ; God has got hold of the wrong person, I was never meant for this ; I had better find another job, I had better get out.' But although Abraham made the mistakes—and they were very bad ones, grievous lapses and failures not excused in the Bible, shown to be what they were, never rubbed out by God; there they are on record—and not only on record in the written Word, but on record in history: look at Ishmael to-day!—although they were seen for what they were, there was that in Abraham which reacted to adjust. 'I have made a mistake in going down to Egypt; but I will not give up in self-despair and refuse to go back again; I will get back. I have made this mistake over Ishmael—I must get back and recover my ground.' He was a great man for recovery and adjustment in the presence of heartbreaking disappointment with himself.

(c)   THE WORKING OF A HEAVENLY POWER WITHIN

What does all this say? There is a working of a heavenly power in this man. This is not natural, this is not the way of nature. If only we knew the tension and the stress, if only we knew all the hardness of that school that Abraham was in—! I never fail to marvel when I read Paul on Abraham. "*Without being weakened in faith he considered his own body now as good as dead (he being about a hundred years old) . . . yea, looking unto the promise of God, he wavered not through unbelief, but waxed strong through faith, giving glory to God, and being fully assured that, what he had promised, he was able also to perform*" (*Romans iv. 19—21*). "*. . . the faith of Abraham, who is the father of us all . . . before him whom he believed, even God, who giveth life to the dead*" (*Romans iv. 17*). He proved his faith by binding his only son and taking the knife to slay him. In an instant more the son, in whom all the promises were centred, would have been dead. I say, I marvel. It is one thing even for God to do a thing like that—to take away ; it is another thing for us to have to do it, to give it up to God : but Abraham did it. There is something not natural here. This is not the way of the world, the earth. It is the heavenly way. Abraham is pioneering the heavenly way. And so he occupies that tremendous place, not only in the old dispensation, but in this, and for ever. A great pioneer of things heavenly— that is what it means.

That may explain a great deal in our own experience. God needs people like that in this day of terrible downward, down-grade spiritual movement to the world on the part of His Church. With all its good intentions, perhaps even its pure motive, it is nevertheless adopting the framework and form of this world in order to do the work of heaven. There must be a reaction to that, and there must be vessels who can prove that it is not necessary to go to this world. Heaven is sufficient for all things.

CHAPTER FOUR

MOSES

Reading : Hebrews xi. 24 – 27, 13, 16.

GOD HAS ONE GREAT DESIRE—to have what may be termed a ' people of His best '. Until He has such a people, He will never be wholly satisfied. There may be those who will accept His ' second-best '—for He surely often allows a second-best—but only a people set on His *very* best will truly satisfy His own heart. But since the attainment unto His best is a matter fraught with conflict and cost and discipline, and much that is utterly contrary to the whole course of nature, it is not everybody—indeed, it is but a comparative few—who will go on with Him to His best. This is seen in all the Scriptures, and there are some outstanding illustrations of it. They are found in every dispensation.

For example, whilst we are not to say that the generation which perished in the wilderness, which had been brought out in virtue of precious blood and by initial faith—for " by faith they passed through the Red Sea " (Hebrews xi. 29)—whilst we are not to say that that generation represents ultimate and final loss of salvatian, it is nevertheless clear that they lost God's full thought for them, and it was a great and grievous loss, always held up in the Scriptures as an example of tragedy, failure and disappointment. We are not to say that the greater number of those who went into exile in Babylon, in Chaldea, and never returned, were lost eternally to God's salvation. But we do know that the minority came back, and in coming back fulfilled the true intention of God, and are represented as those of whom particularly He is not ashamed. For the others, in the wilderness and in Babylon, there is a certain sense in which God is ashamed ; for these, not so. And thus it is in every dispensation. The call continues, and it is being sounded here to the people of God to be satisfied with no second-best.

But, as we have said, this is not only a call to us to attain. This is a call to a people to pioneer this way for others—for so many of the Lord's people do not know the heavenly way. Strangely enough, though born from above, they do not know the heavenly way. We will not bring in all the proofs of this, but it is true, and perhaps many of us have been like that for a period of our Christian life. It was very largely an earthly thing. Our activities were very earthbound, in a Christian way. Then there came a time of crisis, when we entered into the meaning of an open heaven and were lifted on to an entirely new level of spiritual life and began to learn heavenly things in a new way. These are facts, and all those who are called of God into this heavenly way are not only moving in it with regard to their own spiritual measure, but are called to pioneer the way for those who do not know, even of the Lord's people. That does not mean to preach to them about a heavenly way, to have a special interpretation of Scripture, some doctrine or phraseology. It means that they are called to be in the good of it, to be *there,* and by what they themselves know and experience to be able to help others up from the lower levels of spiritual life.

So we are going to look again at this matter of pioneering the heavenly way, centring our thoughts upon another great pioneer—Moses. There are, of course, many other features of his life besides pioneering, but I think that this really goes to the very centre of the significance of Moses —this fact that he was the pioneer of a heavenly way.

If we look at the life of Moses from an earthly standpoint, we see very much that speaks of disappointment and of failure and of tragedy : for, although, for eighty years —eighty long, trying, testing years of discipline and suffering—he walked the heavenly way or learned the heavenly way, neither he nor the people that he brought out of Egypt entered into the land. That sounds like disappointment, and indeed tragedy. I can never read that record of Moses pleading with God to let him go in, and God's full, final, conclusive refusal, without being deeply stirred. It is a touching thing.

You see, of these people who were constituted a nation by the hand of Moses, who instrumentally owed their existence as a nation to him, not only did that first generation not go into the land and inherit, but their whole history ever since has been one of tragedy. There have been bright spots and periods in that history ; there have been times of glory ; but, taking their history as a whole up to this day, remembering how much they talk about Moses, what they attribute to Moses, how they are always appealing to Moses, it has been a most disappointing history. I repeat: from certain standpoints, the life of Moses bears much that speaks of failure and disappointment and tragedy. But the very fact of his own life and the nature of its termination, the very fact of the generation that perished in the wilderness, the very fact of the nation all through the ages failing and disappointing, is the one most powerful and conclusive argument for another aspect, namely, the Divine truth of the heavenly. They are asserting in a most emphatic way that, if this is all, down here, then it is a poor thing: that there must be some other way than this, there must be some other sequel to this, this is not all. No, there is another standpoint from which to view it—there is the heavenly standpoint, where heaven interprets and governs everything.

Well, let us look at Moses. Firstly, Moses himself and his training. Secondly, Israel under his leadership.

(I) MOSES' TRAINING

(a) SOVEREIGN APPREHENDING

We begin with himself and his training. We are not beginning with his birth. We begin where we read of him in the letter to the Hebrews—Moses in Egypt; and here we are once more met by something that has come up repeatedly in these meditations—that inborn sense of destiny. You cannot get away from it. When you are dealing with God's full purpose and when you are dealing with the work, the service, the ministry, the pioneering in relation thereto, that is always the point at which you have to begin; and it is always there—this deep-down sense of a Divine, sovereign apprehending for something.

Here is this man in Egypt. He is surrounded by all that Egypt has, and students of history know that the glory and the glamour of Egypt were no small thing in Moses' day. He was surrounded by it all. The writer here speaks of " the pleasures of Egypt ". Its pleasures, its amenities, its scholarship, its education : all its privileges, right up to the very house of the king—everything was at the command and disposal of Moses. He was " learned in all the wisdom of the Egyptians " (Acts vii. 22), and he had all the " pleasures " of Egypt to his hand. That was no small thing. Do you say that was nothing to throw away? It was a mighty ' all ' of this world—but this sense of destiny made it as nothing. Although enjoying it all, as far as he could enjoy it, there was a shadow over his enjoyment all the time ; there was a something inside that withheld him from becoming finally content with it. There was within him a sense of restless discontent and dissatisfaction, which really was a working in him of God's unwillingness to be satisfied with anything short of His full purpose. Moses may not have been able to explain or define this strange urge, but it made him know that the ' all ' of Egypt was by no means God's all, and that Egypt could never answer to this call and pull from above and beyond.

Now, that is not exaggeration, and those are not just words. That is Scripture, and that is very testing. For such as are called into the way of God's full thought, His highest and His best, it will be like that. It does not matter what there may be of popularity, worldly position, success, means and resources—everything to hand : if we are truly called according to His purpose, we shall be restless in it all, dissatisfied, and feel, ' After all, is it worth it? There is something more than this.' Test your hearts by that. That is no fiction ; that is fact.

It may be that that fact lies behind your very reading of these words to-day. You could have much in this world if you liked to lay yourself out for it. You could have a way in the world and its pleasures, and other things, if you really went for it. Yes, and perhaps you could get acceptance and position even in the religious world, but to you it has become second-rate. There is something in you—you may not be defining it, perhaps you could not write down what it is—but you know there is something, and unless you discover that something, arrive at that something, life will be a disappointment, for there is a mockery in everything else. If that is true in your case, it is a very hopeful thing, it is a marvellous thing : heaven has come down to lay hold of you in relation to all its meaning. Of course, if you have not got this sense, you will be pleased with all sorts of things less than that, and you will be out for them. But, mark you, if you can be like that, it is a very terrible indictment, for it means that somehow, where you are concerned, that mighty heavenly apprehending has failed.

(b) A CRISIS

So the thing began with Moses inwardly, and that inward thing led to a definite crisis, the crisis of the earthly and the heavenly. The Lord has wonderful ways of producing this crisis. You know it is not always produced and precipitated by some ecstasy—if that is what you are after —the glory of a great light and vision, the enrapturing of your soul, some tremendously wonderful heavenly experience. It does not always happen like that. It did not happen like that with Moses, nor with others. How did it happen?

He went out one day and saw an Egyptian persecuting a Hebrew, and this sense of destiny took possession of him and overmastered him, and so, being evidently of powerful physique, he laid on to the Egyptian and slew him there and then. That was the crisis that precipitated this whole thing. Sometimes we only wake up to the heavenly or are brought face to face with the heavenly by some ghastly misdemeanour or failure; for, almost immediately after this, things were made untenable for Moses in that realm in Egypt, and he had to quit.

But what was inside the crisis, what was the meaning of it, why did God allow it? Moses might have said, ' Why did the Lord allow me to do that? Why did the Lord, who had foreknown me and had in His own foreknowledge called me to His great service, let me make a mess of things like that? Why did He let me become involved by my own act in a thing like murder, to have the stain of murder on my hands?—I who am called to be the emancipator of God's people! Why has the Lord allowed it? ' And the answer would have been: ' That is not the way in which heaven does things, Moses. That is the way the world does things; it is the way the flesh does things. It is not heaven's way of doing things. You, Moses, can never bring out a heavenly people into a heavenly place by earthly methods and means. Learn that once and for all. It may seem a terrible way of dealing with the situation, but there it is, clear and plain. This people, that you are chosen in the foreknowledge of God and by the sovereign act of God and by this sense of destiny in yourself to lead out: this people, chosen to be a heavenly people—how can you get them on to a heavenly level of life if that is your level of life? ' We will come back to that again in a

minute. Heaven breaks in and says wi h terrible emphasis,
' No, Moses. Carnal weapons for carnal ends, but not carnal weapons for spiritual ends ; earthly ways for earthly
ends, but not earthly ways for heavenly ends. Heaven is
governing here and must register itself like this.' What a
lesson for a life ! what a foundation !

Now, you may never have been a murderer, but I have
no doubt but that some at least who read these lines have
learned very deep lessons of this kind : that you just cannot go on with God on that level, you cannot get through
with God along that line, you cannot serve God in His
heavenly purpose in such ways, in the strength of the flesh.
It is so true to principle. Heaven will have none of them ;
it demands its own life, its own nature. That was the
crisis of the heavenly and the earthly in the training of
Moses.

(c) FORTY YEARS IN THE WILDERNESS

And the next phase—to the wilderness, to the " back-
side of the desert " for the next forty years. Oh, surely this
has no place in the economy of God ! Yes, wildernesses
always represent and signify one thing wherever you find
them. They signify self-emptying. Think about that. You
cannot be a very important person in a wilderness. You
cannot be a very self-sufficient person in a wilderness. You
cannot be a self-confident person in a wilderness. A wilderness empties all that out. You are not only in the wilderness : the wilderness gets into you, barren, desolate, unprofitable, useless. And do you not think that that got into
Moses in forty years? What is happening?

It is the negative side of training. It is the cancellation
of Egypt and of the world. Egypt stood for self-sufficiency,

Egypt was always the synonym for independence—and
Egypt had to be emptied out of Moses; he had to be
emptied of the spirit and principle of the world. It had got
inside, and now it was being put out, and just the contrary
to Egypt was coming in. This negative side, as we have
called it, is an integral part of the school of the heavenly
way. It brings us inwardly and spiritually to the place
where we see clearly that there is no profit whatever in us;
where of ourselves we can produce and accomplish nothing. That is the wilderness. Do not misunderstand or
fail to recognise that. It is true to life, true to experience,
and true to heavenly principle. Room has to be made in
us for heaven—for there is no room for heaven in us by
nature.

(d)   THE ORDEAL OF EMANCIPATION

Then the next thing after that—Moses is brought back
to Egypt for the ordeal of emancipation. Now it is the
Lord, not Moses. It is going to be all the Lord now, or
nothing at all. But it is going to be the Lord. *" Now shalt
thou see what I will do " (Exodus vi. 1).* There was a day
when Moses said, ' Now you shall see what I will do ', and
the Egyptian felt the weight of that, and the next day the
Hebrew. But that has gone, and the Lord says, " Now
shalt thou see what I will do ". ' I will do, now you have
stopped.' The position is altered; everything now becomes
possible. There has been a transition from the negative to
the positive. The great ordeal of the emancipation of this
people begins.

The first stage relates to the rod and the hand. Exodus iv
—" What is that in thy hand? " " A rod." ' Very well;
by that rod things are going to be done.' " Put now thine

hand into thy bosom." ' Take it out '—white and leprous. " Put thine hand into thy bosom again." ' Take it out '— clean and whole.

THE ROD

What is the rod? You know that the rod that Moses used was later Aaron's rod, the rod that budded when the test of priesthood was made (Numbers xvii). Twelve rods were put up overnight, representing the tribes. In the morning there were eleven dead rods and one living—the insignia of a living priesthood. And do not forget: priesthood has to do with the spiritual. They are going to have to deal with all the gods of the Egyptians. They are unclean, they are corrupt, they are evil, they are of the devil's company. It needs the mighty power of a holy priesthood to deal with that unclean situation. It is the rod of the word of the Cross. The word of the Cross is a mighty rod.

What is the issue here—the issue that is bound up with this whole ordeal? This is it. The Lord had said, *" the Egyptians shall know that I am Jehovah "* (Ex. vii. 5). That is the issue. Very well then ; begin to apply that in practical ways by the word of the Cross, the word of living priesthood.

Apply it first to the whole realm of nature, of creation. *" I, the Lord, have created "* (Isaiah xliv. 8). The Lord of Calvary is the Lord of creation, and the first application of the word of the Cross is in that realm in Egypt. At the touch of the Lord of creation the world of living things is brought under judgment ; the issue—"I am the Lord ".

The second application is to the heavens—for the Lord made the heavens as well as the earth—and the elements, under the word, are touched. If you look on to Calvary, you will see all these features. When He, the great Pioneer of the heavenly way, went to the Cross, the whole creation was affected. Heaven and earth were involved. There was a great earthquake, and there was " darkness over all the land until the ninth hour ". Creation and the very elements were coming under the impact of Him who is the Word in the Cross. That happened in Egypt, in type.

Then, thirdly, there came the application to hell. What is hell's greatest weapon? Death, " the last enemy " (I Cor. xv. 26). Death is no friend, death is the last enemy, and that was the last judgment of Egypt. Hell's stronghold was broken into ; the power of death was taken hold of for the emancipation of a people. That is what Christ did in the Cross. The word of the Cross is this : that hell has been broken into and death has been apprehended and made to serve the ends of God rather than frustrate them. In Egypt the word by the rod touched the firstborn with death, and hell was stung with its own sting to the very core of its being. But that is not all. That self-same rod led the people out, worked redemption from Egypt and through the Red Sea. " *Lift thou up thy rod, and stretch out thine hand over the sea* " *(Ex. xiv. 16).* The word of the Cross is the word of life triumphant over death. Death is vanquished and life and incorruption are brought to light. By means of the rod of the word of the Cross, through this wonderful ordeal of emancipation, Moses is learning one thing—that *heaven rules* : heaven rules in this creation, heaven rules in heaven, heaven rules in hell ; and in the kingdoms of men heaven rules for the emancipation of the elect. All this is the story of the intervention of heaven.

You wonder why this was graduated as it was. It did

not happen all at once. The effect of the rod was only partial to begin with, but gained in strength and power as it went along.

There are two sides to this. On the one hand, there is the progressive nature of this education : it is gradual. We do not come all at once to see and to know the full power of heaven. We learn it a bit at a time. It is graduated. It goes so far at one time ; it will go farther later on. Are we not learning that? We learn it in simple ways—how heaven is greater than earth, than man, than nature, than the enemy. We are learning, step by step, more and more of the meaning of that tremendous, infinite ascendency of heaven.

But there is the other side. God, by this gradual means, is drawing out the opposing forces, gradually extending them. " I will harden Pharaoh's heart." " I will harden Pharaoh's heart." " I will harden Pharaoh's heart." " Pharaoh shall harden his heart." God could have wiped him out in one stroke, but He is going to extend him to his utmost limit. The power of this world is going to be drawn out to its full extent to meet the infinite power of heaven, and then heaven's superiority will be a very simple thing, after all.

We have so often said this, and it is true. Though we cannot grasp it or see it or calculate it, the truth is that " the power that worketh in us " is " the exceeding greatness of his power " (Eph. iii. 20 ; i. 19). We do not know, we are not able to measure, the immensity of the forces that are against a soul being saved, the immensity of the forces that are set against God's full purpose for His people. We know a little, and we shall know more and more as we go on ; but when it says " the *exceeding* greatness of his pow-

er ", that is not just language : that is an attempt—only
an attempt—by means of language, by superlatives, by
all that human language can do—to arrive at the reality.
"*The exceeding greatness of his power to us-ward who believe, according to that working of the strength of his
might which he wrought in Christ, when he raised him
from the dead*" (*Eph. i. 19, 20*). And that is *to us-ward*.

There is something tremendous here. It is heaven's
superiority over this whole situation to bring a people out
and to bring a people through. We are in that school.
Moses was in that school. He was put through that ordeal
in order that he might progressively, but quite steadily and
definitely, recognise that all that is here in Egypt, all that
Pharaoh represents, is going to be drained to the last drop
of its vitality and be laid in death at last—all of it. Moses
was sometimes apprehensive. Sometimes he came back
from the challenge disappointed. He felt, ' We have not
got there yet, something more is needed yet '. ' All right ',
says the Lord, ' we will have something more '. The Lord
was leading him on in his education ; he was coming progressively to see more and more. Do you not think that,
if God did everything all at once, in one act, we should
miss something, we should take it all for granted, it
would not mean so much to us, it would be just a miracle
of the past? And yet throughout our lifetime God is extending the forces against us in order to prove that His
forces are superior. It is a long schooling, but that is the
way of the heavenly purpose.

THE HAND

From the rod to the hand. " Put now thy hand into thy
bosom." What hand? That hand that had murdered the

Egyptian, that hand stained with blood, that hand of natural strength, that hand of self-sufficiency, that hand which represented the old Moses and his failure, failure under the energy and drive of his own will. ' Put that hand in. What is in your bosom, Moses? *That* is what is yours. Do you think *that* can wield the rod of God? Do you think *that* can bring in the heavenly authority? Oh no, that hand has to be cleansed before you can wield that rod. That bosom must be cleansed, that stain must be removed, all that self-energy and self-sufficiency has to be undercut. Moses, *that leprous hand is what you are like in yourself.'*

Are we not discovering that? What is my heart like? What are we like? Just like that. The more we know and see of ourselves, the more it is like leprosy. But, blessed be God, there is a cleansing. For Moses there was a Divine act of cleansing. In that instant, all the meaning of the Cross, the word of the Cross, took effect in Moses' life— of course in type, in figure. And now that there is a hand cleansed, that is, a heart circumcised, the inner life separated from the fleshly strength and sufficiency, all that can take the word of the Cross, the word of authority. It must be like that. We have no power in the realm of the gods of the Egyptians, those spiritual forces that are actuating this world, no authority at all in that court, no hope of overpowering that strength, unless something has happened for the deliverance of ourselves from our own strength, our own sufficiency, our own hearts.

(II) ISRAEL UNDER THE LEADERSHIP OF MOSES

Then there is that phase, so large that I hardly dare

touch on it at the moment—Israel under the leadership of Moses. It was one long-drawn-out issue of the heavenly and the earthly. All those forty years of the nation in the wilderness were just that—the issue of the heavenly and the earthly being fought out. They had been brought out to be a heavenly people; to have all their resources, all their support and succour, from heaven; to be in this world and not of it. If ever that is true—to be in the world and not of it—it is true in a wilderness.

The Divine thought was the making of a large place for heaven. There was a large place for heaven in that wilderness. Everything from the Divine side was to be heavenly. The people were constituted on heavenly principles. Moses up in the mount was securing those heavenly principles for the constituting of the nation. It was all coming from heaven. Their whole relationship to God in the wilderness, as centred in the tabernacle, came out of heaven: it was the pattern shown in the mount. It was heavenly; nothing was left to man and his judgment at all. Their going from day to day was out from heaven—by means of the pillar of cloud and fire. It was all heavenly. What warfare there was, was heavenly: Moses on the top of the hill, with hands uplifted, the battle going on in the valley. Heaven is directing this warfare: it is heavenly warfare. It was all learning the meaning of the heavenly way, in every aspect.

But they failed to learn those lessons. They would come down to earth, they would reject the heavenly. It was too hard, it was too difficult for the flesh, it was too uncertain. It was such dependence, it was such helplessness so far as self was concerned. They could not help themselves—and we do want to help ourselves in this business. It was all so heavenly. But it was most real. Those who know any-thing about it know that heavenly things are the most real, that spiritual things are far more real than other things. But they would not have the heavenly way, they would have the earthly; and they repudiated it all and perished, on the earth, in the wilderness.

Joshua and Caleb took up all those lessons of the schooling of Moses and Israel, in themselves. They learned the lessons, they apprehended the heavenly truth, and they took the next generation over—a heavenly generation.

Well, all that may be regarded as history, as what is in the Bible: but I am sure that many of you are reading your own history. Is it not so true in principle to what we are going through, to what God is doing with us—defeat-ing us, bewildering us, bringing us to an end, to an empti-ness and helplessness?—and yet, by some mighty power that we do not feel, of which we are not conscious, we are going on; we are being drawn out and drawn up. It is the story of so many survivals, when it would seem that all has gone: that we are lost, we have failed, broken down, disappointed the Lord; there can be no future.

But there is a future. We have continued. There is something from beyond that is all the time holding us on, and it may be that to-day our hearts are more set upon what is of God than ever they were. And why is that? Not because we have been more successful, not because we have been less full of failure and weakness. No; rather because we have learnt the lesson of our own weakness. We know to-day, better than ever we knew it, that " in me, that is, in my flesh, dwelleth no good thing " (Rom. vii .18)—and yet to-day the Lord has a stronger purchase upon us than ever. What is this? This is a mystery. Oh, thank God it is true! Thank God for His sovereign grace! These are the evidences that He has called us with a great calling and that He will not be satisfied until He has brought us right through to His own full end. May we follow on, whatever the cost.

CHAPTER FIVE

JORDAN — A CHANGE OF SITUATION

Reading : Joshua iii ; iv. 1 — 9.

THE PASSAGE OF JORDAN, about which we read in
these verses, is a consummate presentation of what the
Lord is saying to us in this series of studies. It must be
quite clear to us, as we read it, that it represents a pro-
foundly critical point in the history of the people involved,
the culmination of a long process of preparation, the initiation of a new and wonderful phase of their life. Moreover, from abundant New Testament support, we see that
this is a representation of the life of the children of God
and of the would-be children of God in our own time :
that is, the New Testament takes up this incident in the
life of Israel and declares that it was a type, or figure ;
that its real meaning, its abiding meaning, its spiritual
significance relates to the Christian or the would-be Christian.

So that we to-day, at this present time and in our present situation, really stand right into this part of the book
of Joshua. It applies to us. We are not reading ourselves
back so many centuries ago, merely with the idea that
something happened then in Israel's life—that they

passed out of the wilderness into the land of Canaan. We are reading from there on into this present day. We are bringing that right forward and saying, ' That is not then, it is now ; and this is that, or that is how it should be '. The wonderful thing is that that could be now, at this very moment, in experience. When Joshua said, " Sanctify yourselves : for to-morrow the Lord will do wonders among you "—that is possible now, that can be brought right up to date. So let us look at it, for we are keeping closely to all that we have been considering in these past chapters—the pioneering of the heavenly way.

THE OBJECTIVE IN VIEW IN THE TRANSITION

First of all, let us recall the objective, the object in view in this transition, this passage of the Jordan. We are given the spiritual interpretation. It is shown to be an illustration of life in resurrection and heavenly union with Christ. That is the objective to which God has called His people. That is precisely the thing for which the Lord calls us at all, by His grace—resurrection union with Christ : union with Christ on the ground of resurrection life. And not only that, but union with Christ in His heavenly life, by the Holy Spirit ; oneness with Him as in heaven, and all that that means.

That is the objective ; that is the irreducible minimum of God's will for His people. If we do not come to resurrection union with the Lord Jesus, we have not come to any union at all. That is to say, that, for all practical purposes and values, we know nothing really of the meaning of being " joined to the Lord ". There are many who know something of what it is to be in union with a living Christ, but who know perhaps very little, at most not enough, of heavenly union with Him and all that that means. Until we come to that, we have not come to the very object of our salvation, neither have we come to God's satisfaction in saving us. We must see what that means.

TRANSITION

(a) INTO THE AUTHORITY OF CHRIST

Getting the objective clear before us, let us look more closely at the transition. This transition had two aspects. In the first place, it represented a transition from the authority of darkness into the authority of Christ. Up to this point these people had still been under the authority of darkness, notwithstanding that they had been out of Egypt for a good many years. The fact is that, while they had long ago come out of Egypt, Egypt had only just come out of them. It is possible for us to be saved from the world in an outward way and not to be saved from it in an inward way. Egypt had retained a strength inside of them through the years of the wilderness. That generation had constantly been found harking back to Egypt. " Would that we had died by the hand of the Lord in Egypt" (Exodus xvi. 3). 'Oh, that we had stayed in Egypt!' It was still inside, it still had a grip upon them, they still had dreams and imaginations of satisfaction there. They had not come completely and utterly to that emancipation which settles once and for all that there is absolutely nothing back there in that world, nothing at all ; the very thought of it is repugnant, is hateful ; the very thought of it means desolation : they had not come there. There is that, even in Christians, which sometimes, under strain and pressure, makes them begin to think that they

would be better if they were back in the world—they
would have a better time. But this Jordan was the settle-
ment of that. Whatever had lingered and lurked through
all the wilderness years was finished with at the Jordan.
That authority, that inward control, was finally broken
at the Jordan. It was transition, utter transition, from the
authority of darkness into, typically speaking, the authority
of Christ.

Again I am going to say something that I have often
said before. There is such a thing as having and knowing
Christ as your Saviour without knowing Him as your Lord
—that is to say, only for salvation : as Saviour from condemnation, from pending judgment, from hell ; perhaps
Saviour into some of the positive blessings of that position :
and yet—oh, how much more is possible and real for our
knowledge ! It is all too long a gap from the exodus to
the ' eisodus ', the entry ; far too big a space between these
two things. How many, many Christians, after having been
saved for a long time, go to a convention and make Jesus
Christ Lord, discovering that that space between the two
things has been far too long, that this might have been
long ago. Jordan speaks not only of our finding Christ as
our Saviour from judgment and death, but of our finding
Him as Lord—with all that it means that He should be
Lord. It is not until He is Lord that we begin to discover
the riches, the unsearchable riches, that are in Him, like
the wealth of the land.

(b) INTO THE FRUITFULNESS OF LIFE IN THE SPIRIT

The Jordan again represented the transition from the
desolation and barrenness of nature into the fruitfulness

of life in the Spirit. They had lived so much in themselves ;
the self-life, the natural life, had been so much asserting
itself ; their own personal interests, advantages or disadvantages had occupied such a large place on their horizon.
If things in the line of God's purpose were not easy, but
going contrary to nature, they were full of murmurings.
If things went well, of course it was quite natural to be
full of rejoicing. It was nature either way. It was nature
rejoicing because things were easy. It was nature grum-
bling because things were difficult. It was the life of nature
—and what a barren wilderness that was for them, a wilderness outside and inside. And now the Jordan puts a finish to that and represents a transition from that barren,
desolate life in the flesh, in nature, to a life in the Spirit.

For that Man, who presently confronted Joshua as representative of God, was, I believe, no other than the Holy
Spirit, the Spirit of God, the Captain of the Lord's host. He
is that—" Prince of the host of the Lord " (Joshua v. 14),
He called Himself. When those words which we so often
quote, " Not by might, nor by power, but by my Spirit,
saith the Lord of hosts " (Zech. iv. 6), were used by the
prophet, you know that the literal wording there is, " Not
by an army . . . but by my Spirit ". And here is the Captain
of the host of the Lord, the Spirit, and from this time He
is going to take charge—and what a different situation
will obtain ! It will be life in the Spirit. Yes, there will
be fruitfulness now ; not a life without slips and mistakes
—they happen—but a life adjusted to the Spirit. It was
to be a life of progress, a life of enlargement, a life of
constant enrichment, a life of entry upon their inheritance.
" Every spiritual blessing in the heavenlies in Christ "
(Ephesians i. 3). From the barrenness of nature to the

fruitfulness of life in the Spirit: that was the meaning of the transition of Jordan.

THE GREAT PIONEER GOING BEFORE

But then we come to the central focal point of it all: the great Pioneer—this time written with a very big capital—the great Pioneer as represented by the ark of the Lord of the whole earth. Once again, this is not imaginary interpretation. The New Testament warrants, by definite statement, the interpretation that that ark was a type of the Lord Jesus. We will not stay to prove it from the Scripture, but it is so. The ark then typifies Christ. The great transition was going to be made. How would it be made? *"The ark of the covenant of the Lord of all the earth passeth over before you"* (Joshua iii. 11). *"There shall be a space between you and it, about two thousand cubits"* (Joshua iii. 4). It is not possible to estimate exactly what that measurement was, because there are three cubits in the Bible, and we do not know which of them this was (and even if we did, we do not know precisely what the measurement was); but the very smallest measurement here of the cubit would make this over—well over—one thousand feet between the ark and the people.

Why that? 'Keep that space, come not near, keep that mighty space between you and it'—shall we say, 'between you and Him'? Why that great space?

(a)   THE GREATNESS OF CHRIST IN DEATH

Does it not speak, in the first place, of the greatness of Christ in death?—for it says here in parenthesis "Jordan overfloweth all its banks all the time of harvest" (Joshua iii. 15), and this was the time. " Jordan overfloweth all its banks ": a wide inundation beyond its channel, spreading itself out in all directions; and we know so well that that speaks of the waters of death and judgment. It speaks of the Cross of the Lord Jesus. And He stands right in the flood, in the overwhelming inundation of death's power : stands right in it, right in the centre of it, right in its full depth and length and breadth; stems it all.

How great is Christ in death! Death is no small thing. Death is a mighty overwhelming flood. He has plumbed its depths, He has taken its measure, and by dying He has destroyed death. There He is. He stands right into death : death has lost its power: death is thrown back: death is forbidden to move on. The description of that is wonderful. While on the one side there was the mighty wall of water standing up, on the other side, right down to the Dead Sea, all that spoke of death was dried up. How great is Christ in death! Incomparable! He is alone in that. No one else could do it.

(b) THE EXCLUSIVENESS OF CHRIST IN DEATH

Then it speaks of the exclusiveness of Christ: not only the greatness but the exclusiveness of Christ in death. ' There was no other good enough '. Oh, the blasphemy of talking about the death, even the most heroic death, of a soldier, giving his life for his country, being comparable to the death of Jesus! No. Whatever heroism there may be—and there may be a great deal which can be honoured, valued and appreciated—but however great may be the heroism and sacrifice of men, it ' comes not nigh unto' this by two thousand cubits. There is a space between. God has placed that space, and He says, 'This is inviolate: He is apart, nothing can come near to this mighty work of Jesus Christ; no one else has done it, and no one can do it; it must be done by Him alone'.

(c) THE LONELINESS OF CHRIST IN DEATH

Alone. Look at the loneliness of that figure—forgetting for the moment that there were Levites bearing the ark on their shoulders: the description is intended not to bring them into view at all, but to have this ark only in view— to behold it, as it were, afar off. It is a great space. If it were only one thousand feet, that is quite a distance from which to look on a little object like that, a lonely little object right out there. How alone He was in death. " All the disciples left him, and fled " (Matt. xxvi. 56). He said, " Ye . . . shall leave me alone " (John xvi. 32), and they did. And then the deepest pang of all—" My God, my God, why hast thou forsaken me?" (Matt. xxvii. 46). His aloneness in death is portrayed by the ark out there. Behold Him: " Behold, the Lamb of God, which taketh away the sin of the world!" (John i. 29).

Why this aloneness? Well, you see, ' there was no other good enough to pay the price of sin ': there was no other great enough, big enough, to bear the sin of the world. He being the only one who could do it, it involved Him in this utterness of loneliness. Who could bear to know in full consciousness their utter abandonment by God? Thank God, we need never know that. We need never for a moment have the consciousness that God has forsaken us. That is not necessary, and indeed we could not

survive it. But He knew it. It took Him, the Son of God, to
come through that. It is the price He paid as the Pioneer—
the Pioneer of our salvation, the Pioneer of our inheritance, the Pioneer of our possession of all that unto which
God has called us by union with Christ. The Pioneer had
to pay the price of this utter and final aloneness. Is that
not something of the sigh, the cry, in Isaiah liii? Yes, He
is the alone One there, wounded for our transgressions,
smitten of God and stricken, His soul made by God an
offering for sin ; but " He shall see his seed, he shall prolong his days ", and out of that loneliness shall come, in
a mighty multitude, the children of His bereavement
(Isa. xlix. 20).

IDENTIFICATION WITH CHRIST BY FAITH
AND TESTIMONY

The next thing, and the final word for the moment,
is identification with Him by faith and testimony. No,
we cannot literally and actually come into this. Thank
God, it is not necessary. I mean that we are not called to
go through all that He went through, but we are called
to take a faith position, to give attestation to it in a very
practical way. Not just walk in and through and take it
as ours, but to recognise that it is only ours because of
Him, only ours in Him. There is an identification of life
with Him.

And so this identification by faith and testimony is seen
in the commandment of God as to what was to be done.
Out of the bed of the Jordan, out of the place where all
this was transacted by the great Pioneer of redemption,
stones were to be taken, and—notice—by twelve men :

" out of every tribe a man " (Joshua iv. 2). In effect, every man of every tribe is here represented. It is a personal matter for every one. " Every man . . . a stone ". It has to be a personal transaction, a personal testimony, a personal appropriation of it all, a taking of it upon our shoulders as bringing us under all that it means ; our committal to it, our committal to the death of the Lord Jesus, to the fact that in Him we died ; our committal to His burial. " We were buried . . . with him " (Romans vi. 4). Then our committal to His resurrection. The stones in the Jordan signify our union with Him in death and burial ; the stones taken out of the Jordan and built up for a memorial on the other side, our union with Him in resurrection.

But there has to be a practical, personal, individual transaction. " Every man . . . a stone." Have you taken the stone on your shoulder personally? Have you definitely done this? You know how the Apostle Paul tells you that the testimony is borne, it is so familiar. "*We were buried . . . with him through baptism into death : that like as Christ was raised from the dead through the glory of the Father, so we also might walk in newness of life*" *(Romans vi. 4).* That is this story quite clearly, so simply.

Yes, by baptism we declare that we have taken the stone on our shoulders, we have made this our responsibility, we have definitely committed ourselves to all this.

Let me say again—it is not just to be saved from judgment, death and hell, but to be saved unto—not only from, but *unto*—all that which is in the heart of God ; that it is no longer what *we* are going to get, how it is going to affect *us :* that is the old tyranny ; no longer personal circumstances at all. It is what the Lord wants ; it is what will satisfy and glorify Him. That is the passion of the heart that is so committed; and when He gets us through on that matter, gets us over the fence of self-interest, worldly interest, fleshly government, on to the ground where it is all the Lord and what He wants, we shall have found the land flowing with milk and honey, we shall have found the riches of Christ, we shall have come into an opened heaven. So much of our Christian life and work is self-ward. Until it is changed from self to the Lord, fully and utterly, we shall know nothing of the heavenly life of spiritual fulness. But that is what is here represented.

May the Lord find us all making this great transition, this declaration—" Every man . . . a stone ": that Jordan, with all that it means, has got to rest upon our shoulders.

CHAPTER SIX

THE WAY TO GOD'S END

WE ARE NOT GOING TO READ at the moment, but we shall have the book of Joshua open before us, for reference as we go along.

THE END OF THE WAY

It is necessary for us at the outset, before considering the way to the end, to bring the end of the way right into view. We commenced by noting that God began with the heavens and then proceeded to the earth, and at the end of the Bible it is that which comes down out of heaven which consummates the whole process of His activities through the ages, so that the end is a full expression of what is heavenly, or an expression of what is heavenly in fulness. That is the end. We said to begin with that the heavens govern everything. As it is in nature, so it is in the things of the Spirit. Everything is governed by the heavens, and the earth and all that is earthly has to reckon with and answer to what is heavenly.

Get that as a spiritual truth. What is true in the realm of the natural creation is but an expression of the spiritual mind of God: and that means that, just as this world, this earth, is so governed and controlled by heavenly forces and heavenly bodies that if it should get out of right adjustment or relationship with those bodies it would disintegrate, it would cease, it would freeze up or burn up, it would cease to function as an organic whole : the same thing is spiritually true. The whole Bible is taken up with this fact, that what is here is related to what is in heaven, and everything comes out from heaven and has to answer to heaven and keep adjustment to heaven —everything in our lives: because the Holy Spirit, having come down from heaven, is the link between what is here and what is there.

These things are not just abstract ideas. They are the factors which lie right behind everything we have of Divine revelation in the Scriptures. The whole of the Bible from the first verse to the last can be summed up in that one thing—that heaven is challenging this earth, and this earth has got to make an answer to heaven. There are countless details covered by that, but it is a fact ; so that the end of all things will just be that heaven is fully realised in the creation and, especially in a spiritual way, in the people of God. That is the end which we bring into view at once.

Now, in relation to that end, we must note another governing truth. But let me first say something in parenthesis. Some of these phrases are very familiar, and I am always a little afraid that familiarity with phraseology may take something of their edge away. When we use that phrase 'a governing thing', let us stop to get the force of it. It means that, if we are under the *government* of a law, we cannot escape that law. There are laws of nature, in our bodies, in this world. They are there, and if you disregard those laws it does not put them out of operation. You find that in the long run they will break you ; in the long run they find you out. But come into line with them, and they will mean your salvation, your life. They are ' governing ', whether you like it or not. Thus, " Whatsoever a man soweth, that shall he also reap " (Gal. vi. 7). That is a law ; you cannot escape it. There are numerous laws like that. So when we speak of a ' governing ' law or truth, it is something established by God in His universe, and it is best discovered and obeyed.

GOD'S SOVEREIGN CHOICE OF VESSELS

Let us come, then, to this further governing truth, in relation to God's end : that God chooses vessels, individual and collective or corporate, and brings them in a peculiar way sovereignly into relationship with His full end, and then does that in them which He means for a much larger company than themselves. He sovereignly chooses vessels —whether individuals or companies—the Bible is just full of that—and then sets to work with those vessels to do something in an extraordinary way, in a very much fuller way, in order that, by means of what He is doing in such elect vessels, He may reach out to many others beyond them. That is a governing truth. He does something in an elect vessel which is meant for many more than itself or its members.

REPRESENTATIVE VALUES

Now let us stop with that for a moment, because our mentality always needs helping. It might very well be that many of you, reading these lines, would say, ' Well, I cannot see that I am an elect vessel, in that specific way '. You are thinking of the men to whom we have been referring as the pioneers of this heavenly way—Abraham and Moses and so on. You say, ' I am not a Moses or an Abraham ; I do not see how I come into that category at all '.

Well, while it may be that there are individuals among you who are chosen of God for something of this nature beyond the ordinary rank and file, as we say : while that may be true, there is this other side—that you may be a part of a collective or corporate vessel, just a part of it ; and if you are—and most probably you are ; I think I would go as far as to say, ' and you are '—if the Lord has laid His hand upon you and put in you this sense of destiny, of having been called to something more than just ' being a Christian ', a strong sense of calling—if that is in you, you may take it that you are related to a larger purpose. If that is true, you must not just regard yourself, as an individual, and therefore your experiences and God's dealings with you, as though you were the only person, as though you were something very special.

Let me put it the other way round. You may be going through what God is doing with a collective vessel and you may not see, so far as your own individual and personal life is concerned, any meaning for what you are going through. ' Why am I going through this?' Well, because you are a part of a larger whole—that is the answer. So often we find that great pressure upon us individually. When we begin to compare notes, we find that other people spiritually related to us are having the same experience. It is the great law of the Body. '' Whether one member suffereth, all the members suffer with it " (I Cor. xii. 26). What is it all about?

Well, you see, it is collective, it is corporate ; and although we cannot follow it all, to see how it is working out, God is doing something in a related way, and we are a part of that. We are bearing the brunt of something very much bigger than ourselves. That spiritual relatedness is involving us in this larger purpose of God, which has to do with the heavenlies, much bigger than this earth. It is that that makes us one. It is not that we join something, that we have our name on a membership roll, or that something is done to recognise us publicly as a member of a certain company. It is not that. You may be many miles, hundreds or thousands of miles, apart, and yet, because you are bound up with this heavenly thing that God is doing, you may be feeling the repercussions thousands of miles away. Because when you get into heaven all these earthly things disappear ; geography and distances and time all go ; they do not obtain up there.

If only we could get the heavenly conception of the Church ! Oh, how foolish our earthly conceptions of the Church are ! We must get off this earth, and all that is here, as to what is called the Church. You find it is just one unit in heaven. All this does not obtain there. That is where we were when we were speaking about the passage of Jordan in our last chapter. In that Jordan something was left behind. The people moved off earthly ground on to heavenly. We shall come back to that again presently. But that is to be a spiritual reality, a consciousness into which we enter. While we ourselves cannot explain and understand why we may be having such a bad time, the heavenly explanation is that we are involved in something

related to God's fuller purpose, and we are suffering, or
we are going through this experience, in a *related* way ;
and it is very wonderful, as from time to time we meet
others with whom we know spiritual fellowship, how we
find they have been going through exactly the same thing
as we have. The Lord has been saying something to them,
and doing something with them, which is not the ordinary
or the usual thing, but something quite extra.

INTRINSIC VALUES

Now that is all connected with the fact, mentioned
earlier, that God chooses individual or collective vessels,
and does in them that which is meant for a very much
larger company. Those vessels, be they individual or be
they collective, are representative of something that God
is after on a larger scale, in a larger sphere. It begins in
them. I think that is what Paul meant when he said, "in
me as chief [first one] . . . for an ensample " (I Timothy
i. 16). I think he meant by that that he was representative
of what God was going to do through him. All the Lord
was going to do through him in the larger realm, in the
churches, the provinces and the nations, was representative, was in token. God was going to operate in the wider
scale through this man—not by giving him something to
say, but by doing something in him.

That is where we have gone astray. God *does* something
first. He brings into being a living representation of His
fuller thought, by means of peculiar, unusual and extraordinary dealings with a vessel. There is very little that is
ordinary in the life and experience of such a vessel. It is
all extraordinary, unusual. Such representative vessels,

individual or collective, are chosen that in them there shall be established the *essential, intrinsic values* intended for the larger sphere and realm ; something which can be expanded, which is capable of going far beyond itself, capable of great enlargement and expansion.

In chemistry we speak of the ' mother-tincture '. We mean, by that, something you can enlarge upon and distribute. It is of the very essence, the concentrated essence. But the effecting of this kind of thing in any vessel, in order to produce intrinsic values, concentrated essence, is terrific work. There is nothing ordinary about it. Some of you may be able to understand this from experience. God's dealings with you are by no means ordinary dealings. Sometimes you feel that the concentration in your experience is far too concentrated! You wonder how you are going to get through at all under this kind of handling from the Lord.

I am keeping very near to the Bible. Do not think that I am talking outside the Bible. I am talking with the background : this is what the Word of God reveals. This is the experience of Abraham—no ordinary experience ; a concentration of God upon that man. Think of the vast host who have derived the values from that. Abraham more than once got to breaking point, where he could not support it. God had to intervene to get him through. The intrinsic value of heavenliness is the most testing thing that anybody can ever have to do with.

In our nature we are so utterly earthly and earthy in every way. We must *see* things—that is earth ; we must *feel* things—that is earth. We must have all the evidences —we must have so much that is earthly. But God takes us off the earth, right off the earth—I mean in a spiritual way—and dangles us, so to speak, in mid-air. It is a most precarious kind of existence, exceedingly trying. You do not know where you are ; you cannot explain things ; you cannot put your foot down solidly and feel that you are sure about anything. God is upsetting all your powers of reckoning and calculation and interpretation, and making it utterly necessary to have another kind of wisdom and understanding, which does not belong to this earth or world or man at all. It is heavenly. That is the experience of these pioneers of the heavenly way. Hear them crying out of their earthliness, sometimes even complaining to the Lord. Listen to Jeremiah—he is out of his depth. It was the intensive, intrinsic values that God was after.

SPONTANEOUS MINISTRY

Then further, spontaneous ministry. I underline that word ' *spontaneous* '—not organized ministry but *spontaneous* ministry. When it is like that, you have only got to *be* and it happens. Do you understand that? You only have to be like that and it happens. You can no more shut that up than you can shut up the sun.

You notice that that is what the Lord was after at the beginning of His ministry. He first of all got hold of a set of men, individuals, and He put them through it. It was not all so simple as the reading of the story. You may read the Gospels covering the story of three years' companionship between those disciples and the Lord, and you may read the record of those last days on the earth, and then the Cross. Well, it is a tremendous story in itself ; but we have not recorded, because it was not possible to record, all that went on inside those men. Even during those three years, I venture to say that they were again and again at the end of their tether: they did not know where they were, what this meant, what it was leading to. They were all the time trying to bring things within the compass of their own ideas, their own mentality; to interpret in the light of prophecy, and so on; to bring it down and have it according to the text-book. He was beating them all the time, He was a continuous enigma. They could not fathom this Man. He never did things according to the text-book, not even according to Moses. He is upsetting the whole thing. What is He doing? What does He mean?

And then the Cross. You cannot read the depths of their soul-anguish and perplexity in those days. You can only understand it out of your own experience of when the Lord begins to do things like that—getting you out of your depth and contradicting all your expectations, seeming to go entirely the opposite way from what you felt you had a right to expect of Him. He does not do what you expect. Sometimes you are altogether with your back to the wall because of the Lord's dealings with you. He got hold of men who went through that with a very deep experience.

Then through those men He got churches, He got companies of believers, and the business started. There is a peculiar kind of discipline and training which belongs to corporate life, when you cease to be just a separate unit, even as a Christian, and you have to live a related life, come into relationship with other believers and live this corporate life, a heavenly life on earth. The New Testament shows that that is anything but an easy thing. You may think, viewing it objectively, that it is a very lovely thing to be in an assembly; but it is not always lovely. That assembly may be going through it. There is something happening, there is a handling of God there, which is sometimes so deep and terrible that you do not know what the Lord means by it ; you are all registering this. It is a deep way, a suffering way. We suffer together as an assembly ; this is corporate suffering, corporate travail. So these churches were brought into being, and they went through it. They were instructed, too ; but, whatever happened to them in the way of instruction and teaching, there was always the parallel and the corresponding discipline of the Holy Spirit. The Holy Spirit had His hand upon them and was dealing with them in a drastic way. Things were happening.

You say, ' Well, instance that '. Look at all the happenings in Corinth. What was it Paul said to them? " For this cause many among you are weak and sickly, and not a few sleep [have died] " (I Cor. xi. 30). There is a secret spiritual history there. The Holy Ghost has got hold of the situation. They might have looked at it in a natural way. ' Somebody is ill—send for the doctor.' But wait a minute. May there not be some spiritual factor bound up with it? May not the Holy Spirit have something to do with this? Paul says, Yes! It does not mean that everybody who is sick is a spiritual delinquent, but the principle is there. The Church is being dealt with by the Holy Ghost in relation to God's fuller purpose.

The point is quite clear, then, that God gets hold first of individuals and then of companies, and He deals with them in this way: so that, not because they have been given a message or a truth, but because of what God has done in them, they have a spontaneous ministry. It just happens, that is all ; somehow or other, it happens, without our being able to explain it—except thus: that the Holy Spirit has taken account of something and He is using it; He is seeing that what He has done there is expanded, is reaching out. It just happens. Paul said about the church in Thessalonica, " From you hath sounded forth the word of the Lord, not only in Macedonia and Achaia, but in every place . . ." (I Thess. i. 8). Do you think that that necessarily meant that they sent out evangelists? They may have done, but it does not say so. Look at the context. You will see that Paul is saying, ' All over the place in other churches they are talking about you ; I need not speak of you—it is known '. It is spontaneous ministry out of what God does. God takes in hand to get these intrinsic values, and He is not going to waste them.

So the end that God has in view is governing all His dealings with His instruments. Heavenly fulness is His end, and it motivates all His dealings with the instruments that He has chosen in relation to that end. He is bringing to heavenly fulness.

We must realise that nothing with God is an end in itself. Conversion is not an end in itself. It is an awful tragedy to regard conversion as an end in itself and leave it there, feeling quite satisfied. You stop with conversion, and see what happens, with your own or anybody else's. What happens? All the sense of purpose is quenched, all that vitality in the conversion subsides, and you get simply a lot of converted people. They are converted—they have believed on the Lord Jesus ; but they are just a lot of converted people, and probably the greatest problem to-day is a lot of converted people over this earth. They have stopped ; their conversion has become an end in itself.

Assembly life is no end in itself. Gather a company of

the Lord's people in a corporate expression, and let them put their own hedge around and be something to themselves, having a nice time on their own—and the same thing happens. The work of the Lord: if the work of the Lord is an end in itself—that is, so that it becomes some *thing*—oh, here again is a tragedy. We take up the work of the Lord in some way, perhaps missionary work as it is called, or some other kind of specified work, and then that particular thing closes down in itself, that sphere is shut up or that line of things is brought to an end—and you have to start all over again and you have lost everything. The work was something in itself.

Now come back to this—if the Lord has done something in you, in me, or in a company, after this character, with this concentrated essence of heavenliness, nothing is an end in itself. The sphere may change, the form may change, but the thing is there. God has got what He wants and He will find a way for it, if it is there, if it is truly heavenly. We only cut off our own usefulness and ministry when we bring it down to earth. That is a true saying. Make it *your* ministry, *my* ministry, and you have narrowed it right down to earth. It will not move out, it will not realise God's end.

Oh, this possessing of things in the realm of God and making them ours! I want to say here that, if you have a mandate from God, if you have an anointing from heaven, if you have a ministry God-given, and you are not holding it as yours or stickling for its realisation as yours, it will be fulfilled, and neither earth nor hell can stop it. Heaven will see to it. But it must be held in relation to heaven. The anointing is from heaven and everything that the anointing means has to be held in relation to heaven, and then heaven will see to it. Put Paul in prison and his ministry will be fulfilled. It is related to heaven. " The heavens do rule " (Daniel iv. 26). But if we have brought it down to earth somewhere, then heaven is not going to sponsor it. There is a lot of history behind that.

Now, seeing that God's end is heavenly and spiritual fulness, and that it is by the way of progressive enlargement, we should be very concerned as to what that way is. It should really concern us as to what heaven's way is, what is the heavenly way to God's end. " Whatsoever things were written aforetime were written for our learning " (Romans xv. 4), and this book of Joshua is among the things written aforetime for our learning, and gives us a very great deal of light on this matter of the heavenly way. But the heavenly way is so contrary to the earthly way. I do not know what you are expecting to happen, or to experience, when we talk of Gods' end being spiritual fulness, and this being something God is working at. What do you expect to happen? I think the first phase of this book contains quite a lot of light upon that.

THE SERVANT SPIRIT

Just look at Joshua himself. Remember that Joshua here is representative in the thought of God of all God's saints and all God's servants, and what God did in Joshua is what God is going to do in all those to whom he is to minister. God did it in him in relation to the larger company. Well, how does it begin? The book begins like this : *" Now it came to pass after the death of Moses the servant of the Lord, that the Lord spake unto Joshua the son of Nun, Moses' minister . . ."*—that word is really ' attendant'. With all that is in view in this book, you would think that he would get a better start than that. Moses the servant of the Lord, and Joshua just his attendant. He is not brought in with some official title, such as ' the servant of the Lord '. He is not brought in on that official ground at all. All that he is is an attendant. Follow that word through and see where it will lead you. The same word is used of John Mark—" they had also John as their attendant " (Acts xiii. 5). What is an attendant? Well, if there is one thing about an attendant, surely it is that he knows that kind of subjection that makes it possible for him to do as he is told. That is the mighty Joshua that is to be, and that is where he begins.

We are well aware of the great significance of Elisha. What a tremendous place Elisha came to have, with a double portion of Elijah's spirit and greater works than Elijah did! You remember what was said about Elisha. " Elisha .. poured water on the hands of Elijah " (II Kings iii. 11). He was his attendant. That is where he began.

In Joshua chapter x, when Joshua commanded the sun, " Stand thou still ", it says, " there was no day like that before it or after it, that the Lord hearkened unto the voice of a man ". This man is touching heavenly things. That is tremendous. Where does it begin? With Moses' attendant! He has learned subjection: to do as he is told, to do trivial things, to be obedient, to take a humble position. And do not think it was easy for Joshua. Joshua had as much soul as anybody else. There was a time when there were others in the camp prophesying, and it was Joshua who went to Moses and said, " My lord Moses, forbid them ". And Moses said, " Art thou jealous for my sake? would that all the Lord's people were prophets ...!"

(Numbers xi. 26 — 30). Joshua had a soul ; Joshua could assert his own ideas. He was a young man then. But here at last he comes out at the commencement of his great life work ; now he is emerging into the real purpose of the sovereign calling of God: and the narrative begins— " Moses the servant of the Lord . . . Joshua the son of Nun, Moses' minister ". Is that not a principle? There is something in that. We must always remember that the Holy Spirit wrote the Bible—and the Holy Spirit, if He is anything at all, is consistent with spiritual principles. It does not matter in what guise they are found ; it does not matter when, where or how: the principle remains exactly the same.

The Levites commenced this ministry at the age of 25, but they were not allowed to assume full responsibility until they were 30. They were understudies of fully-fledged Levites for five years. This principle of the Attendant is maintained all through the Scriptures. A probationary period or phase always precedes full approval. Fulness is suspended until the particular purpose of that period as an Attendant is learned. It is the inculcating of ability to obey, to take orders, to be in subjection, to serve. We must not assume that we are anything. What we may be has to come naturally out of what we have been made. Do not expect that, if God calls you to serve Him, there will immediately and inevitably be some great demonstration of His power and fulness. Joshua was the Attendant of of Moses long before he was his successor and before the *manifestation* of the spirit of Moses was seen in Joshua. God digs deep, He has no pleasure in superficiality, and the measure of our usefulness in relation to His *full* purpose will be the measure of our discipline by testing. We shall never be *spiritual* leaders until we have learned meekness as faithful Attendants.

Remember, then—succession is never official in the things of heaven. It is never by human selection. It is never assumed by the persons concerned. You cannot assume that you are the successor of what God has been doing. You cannot assume that you come in and have place there, and certainly no one can put you into it. If it is heavenly, succession is sovereign and spiritual. You never know how the Divine sovereignty is going to work, but you can be fairly sure that the Divine purpose is going to work contrary to your expectation, your ideas.

SOVEREIGN GRACE

The next movement was to send spies. Joshua sent out the spies. What was the upshot? ' All the land lies before you : I have given it to you.' " This day will I begin to magnify thee in the sight of all Israel." There is immense fulness in view. Well, then, surely there must be something very dignified about this? No. Rahab, a harlot, is the key to the whole situation. A woman without reputation, or with a bad reputation, who has no status or standing at all in the world of repute : everything is bound up with that. That is sovereign, and that is grace : and you are not going to get into the land of heavenly fulness except through those two things. Even the great Joshua-to-be finds that everything becomes dependent upon a woman of ill-fame.

God has strange ways of humbling us. How often we look for something wonderful and big and glorious and noble, something of repute, in relation to the great things of God: and then God brings us down to having to accept something that has no recognition at all, no acceptance at all; puts us in a position where, if we want commendation, that will not commend us; if we want something that will introduce us as an influence in the realm of usefulness, well, this will not do it. There is no chance of getting anywhere along that line in this world. See what influence that woman had in Jericho. Do you think her word would have carried any weight? Not at all. There was no introduction from high quarters. If this is not of heaven, then everything is against it. We are getting no help. No; rather are we out of court here, we have no way, no ground here, if it is not of heaven. He has not got people with influence at court in this matter. It is all of heaven; it is sovereign or not at all.

And it is of grace, for Rahab is in the genealogy of Jesus Christ. Wonderful! When you come to that New Testament genealogy—Rahab! Oh, grace! What can recommend Rahab? What can put her on the inspired record, into Holy Scripture, in the line of Jesus Christ? Nothing but grace, and that is of heaven. It is all like that. If there is going to be anything of real value, it will be because of sovereign grace, and nothing else; no commendation. We are out of court; we have nothing to support our claim, nothing to go upon naturally. It is right down on the level of Rahab. Think of a great Joshua having to come there. But it is the principle all the time through the Word of God. If only I could show you how again and again it *is* that. You would say, 'Why, God seems to go out of His way to prejudice His own interests, to prejudice the success of His purposes, really to make it difficult. He might at least have chosen a respectable person, even if they were not important or prominent.' But He takes a disreputable person ; He goes out of His way to keep this thing true to principle. It is of heaven or it is nothing, and less and worse than nothing. That woman is the key to Jericho and Jericho is the key to the land. That is the kind of key He uses.

THE NATURAL MAN RULED OUT

When you come to the passage of Jordan and when they are over, Joshua commands that there shall be taken a man representing every tribe of Israel and that they shall take twelve stones and put them in the bed of the Jordan and leave them there. All Israel has been left in the bed of Jordan, every man. That is what he is in God's sight—right down there, and left there. Something is left behind in Jordan. That which goes through and comes out on the other side is a testimony to the fact that something has been left behind, because Gilgal follows immediately. Something has been left behind. We cannot bring that over here ; that has to be left in Jordan. This has no standing over here in heaven. This natural man, this Corinthian idea of man—he is down there, and God has left him there. The waters cover him and flow on, and he is underneath, buried for ever. " They are there, unto this day " (Joshua iv. 9). It is the way of enlargement.

But God has to bring that home to us, and it seems to me that Gilgal was the practical application of the principle implicit in the stones in the river-bed. Those stones represented the union of God's people with Christ in death and burial—the natural man who was so in evidence in the wilderness being put out of sight. Gilgal takes up that truth and applies it perpetually. Colossians ii. 11 – 12 confirms this. We have to experience in our souls—our flesh—the severing work of the Cross—the death of Christ. We can believe all the doctrine of Romans vi, and yet there may be great contradiction of it in ourselves. Heaven will not commit itself to the flesh or natural life. If we are occupied with ourselves ; talking about ourselves, our work, our having been used, and so on, we are not in the full values of an open heaven. It is so easy to slip all unconsciously from giving glory to God to glorifying a piece of work or glorying in the work itself ; and when this happens the atmosphere changes and spiritually sensitive people know that something has happened, a cloud has descended. Heaven is so transparent that no earth-vapour can come there, and heavenly fulness demands transparency in our spirit.

CHAPTER SEVEN

TAKING POSSESSION OF THE HEAVENLY LAND

" And it came to pass, when Joshua was by Jericho, that he lifted up his eyes and looked, and, behold, there stood a man over against him with his sword drawn in his hand : and Joshua went unto him, and said unto him, Art thou for us, or for our adversaries ? And he said, Nay ; but as prince of the host of the Lord am I now come. And Joshua fell on his face to the earth, and did worship, and said unto him, What saith my lord unto his servant ? And the prince of the Lord's host said unto Joshua, Put off thy shoe from off thy foot ; for the place whereon thou standest is holy. And Joshua did so." (Joshua v. 13 — 15).
". . . having the eyes of your heart enlightened, that ye may know what is the hope of his calling, what the riches of the glory of his inheritance in the saints " (Ephesians i. 18).

I WOULD MAKE IT CLEAR at the outset that it is not my purpose to deal with the correspondence between the book of Joshua and the letter to the Ephesians. We are occupied in these studies with one particular thought, around which all this gathers, in which it centres : that is, that God's end is to have heavenly fulness expressed in this earth through and by a people. The whole course of His dealings through the ages, from the time when He established the heavens over the earth, has been, and still is, from man's point of view, like a spiritual pilgrimage, a moving spiritually heavenward: and that means, not to some place, necessarily, but to some order of things according to God's mind—that order to which the Lord Jesus referred when, speaking of the will of God, He said, " as in heaven " (Matt. vi. 10); to have everything as it is in heaven. Toward this there is a heavenly way, a heavenly course, a heavenly journey, and we are seeking to see, amongst other things, the nature of that heavenly way. And then we have seen that, since so many do not know more than the very beginning of that way in conversion, the Lord raises up instrumentalities in whom He does His very deep work in relation to heaven to pioneer the way for others.

Now we pursue this a little further. With the two passages which we have just read, we arrive at a particular point in this matter of coming to heavenly fulness. The second half of the book of Joshua, of course, is occupied with the people coming into the inheritance, the inheritance being divided and apportioned and possessed. Strangely, in the letter to the Ephesians—which corresponds to this—it is put round the other way. It is spoken of as God's inheritance in His people, " the riches of the glory of his inheritance in the saints " (i. 18); and I would like to drop a word on that before we pass on, because it is not different, it is not something else. It is the same thing viewed from the other side.

The Lord comes into His inheritance when, and only when, His people really become a heavenly people. For the Lord to have His inheritance, they must be where they are seen to be in the letter to the Ephesians. When they really take position and possession and truly become a heavenly people, then the Lord has got His inheritance. To see " the riches of the glory of his inheritance in the saints " means, from the other side, that we come to the place where He can see it in us. He cannot see His inheritance in the saints until He sees them in the place where He would have them, until He sees them really the people that answer to His mind as a heavenly people. I am saying this in order to clear up any possible mental difficulty over talking about the people possessing the inheritance, and this word about the Lord possessing His inheritance.

Now, our point is not just the truth of there being an inheritance in Christ, either for us or for the Lord ; not just the truth, set forth in the Word, that, when we are in union with Christ through death, burial and resurrection, and on the other side, we come into the realm of Divine fulness. The point that we are underlining is the point of actually becoming a heavenly people, actually taking possession—not doctrinally, not theoretically, not Biblically, but *actually*. I am quite sure that you behold the truth, you contemplate it, you recognise that it is a wonderful presentation ; I am quite sure that you, in your hearts, embrace the idea ; but the trouble is that all this is known so well—it has been taught to so many, but they are not there. They have not actually come to that position where they *are* this—and what is the use or good of

all our doctrine, teaching, interpretation, contemplation
and all the rest, if we are not there? So we have to look
at the way to, shall I say, *get there,* so that it shall become
an actuality.

THE LORDSHIP OF THE HOLY SPIRIT

And the very first thing after that preparatory work of
which we were speaking a few pages earlier: the Jordan,
the leaving something in the bed of Jordan, our old man
crucified and left there; after leaving him there and letting him be covered over and going away from him:
after that and after Gilgal—that is, the negative side, the
putting off—now comes the positive side, the putting on,
the real, the actual taking possession or entering; the becoming the thing that has always been in view. For this
has always been in view, or it has been ever since coming
out of Egypt. It was mentioned in the song of Moses. Yes,
it was pre-visioned in that great prophetic song on the deliverance side of the Red Sea. It has always been there as
a notion, but it has been remote, somewhere out there,
more or less vivid, as the days have gone on: sometimes
strong and clear and positive and gripping; at other
times fading, weak and far off, an abstract.

But now the whole thing has come right up as a positive present issue, preparation having been made. We
come to this passage which we have just read in Joshua
v. 13 − 15. Joshua, standing over against Jericho, " lifted
up his eyes and looked, and behold, there stood a man
over against him with his sword drawn in his hand ". The
warrior spirit in Joshua evidently rose, and he went to

challenge him: "Art thou for us, or for our adversaries?"
—probably meaning that if he got Yes to the latter part
of his interrogation it was going to be the worse for the
man—for at this point he only saw a man. The answer
revealed that He was more than a man. Joshua capitulated, dropped his attitude of challenge, bowed, worshipped, confessed himself the servant of this One, and asked
for instructions.

Who is this One? As I said in a previous chapter, it
is my own conviction that this One, in this particular part
of the Bible, represents the Holy Spirit in the New Testament. That, I think, could be borne out by quite a lot of
evidence, but, without arguing it from the Scriptures, let
us see how it works out—if it is that—in effect.

There are a number of changes which have taken place
at this point. Up to this point, the course, the way, the
government of the people, had been by the pillar of cloud
and fire. Everybody will accept that that is the Holy Spirit.
That is objective, that is in evidence to the senses, that is
characteristic of the wilderness. When you get over into
the heavenlies, it is all the Spirit; but, although at this
point He was seen, He was never seen again. He disap-
pears from sensual perception, but He is there all through
what happens, very much there, the unseen Prince of the
host of the Lord. That is one change. There are many
other changes. No longer the manna—now the old corn
of the land; the bread of life, the heavenly food, in another sense; that which belongs to another realm: Christ
in resurrection, not Christ in humiliation, the broken
bread. This is Christ in resurrection, the food of a heavenly
people. The one belonged to the wilderness; this belongs

to the land. And so we might go on with the differences. You see, here, in this realm, everything is essentially heavenly, in a new sense ; in other words, it is essentially spiritual ; not sentient, not temporal, but essentially spiritual.

Now Paul says that the Holy Spirit is " an earnest of our inheritance " (Ephesians i. 14): so that the Holy Spirit coming here at this point is the guarantee that this purpose of God is going to be realised. He, although from this point unseen, is the absolute security of all the rest. We said in our last study that the presence of the Holy Spirit in anointing for Divine purpose positively guarantees the realisation of that purpose, not only making it possible, but being the ground of the actuality. How does it become an actuality, as more than a doctrine, a truth, a precept—a present actuality?

God has given us the Spirit as an earnest: the guarantee, the security. The positive side begins with this first —the Holy Spirit presented as Lord. You notice that the American Revised Version (as English A.V.M. and R.V.M.) here says " as prince ", and perhaps it is more true to the original than ' captain '. " As Prince of the host of the Lord " : He is presented in Lordship. The positive side of things begins there—with the absolute Lordship of the Holy Spirit amongst the people of God. He is presented and recognised, and something is done in relation to it. It is not an objective truth, but something that is done positively in relation to it. Joshua went down in absolute surrender and capitulation.

The Cross has led to that. The Cross always does lead to the Lordship of the Holy Spirit. So it is from the Jordan to His Lordship. The Cross demands that. If He is not in His place as Lord, and if there is no capitulation, you had better get back to the Cross—go back and have another look through the waters at those stones which are supposed to represent you. Something has gone wrong, you are not true to the fact of the Cross, if He is not Lord.

But here, in spiritual interpretation, it is taken for granted that the Cross really is an established fact. While there are the faults and the weaknesses of the human life —they come out in Joshua—while there are faults and weaknesses and flaws still there in our humanity, nevertheless, so far as our hearts and our wills and our minds are concerned, the Cross has broken us and made a way for the Holy Spirit. That is what the Cross means : the way of the Lordship of the Spirit is open, and through the Lordship of the Spirit the way to heavenly fulness is open.

What a profound difference there is between man-made ‘ conquests ’ (?)—shall I say, man-made revivals—and the work of the Holy Spirit! What a difference! This book of Joshua is the book of mighty differences. The difference here is such that it just leads man right out of it. He cannot reckon with this thing, he has no place in it, it is simply beyond his powers of calculation. The Lord has precipitated His people into a realm where it is altogether different from man's way of doing things. When the Holy Spirit is Lord you have not got to organize something to get it going. You have not got to plan and devise and scheme, in order to get something going, to make a work of God, to make a revival. It just goes. It is the going of heaven. And it requires you in that position— it requires this absolute government of the Holy Spirit.

In every man-made activity there is always the ' earth touch '—means or methods or people, or all that paraphernalia, to guarantee its success—and the thing goes with a lot of noise and a lot of creaking, and it has to have a tremendous amount of human support, and at any moment it may fade out, if you do not prop it up with something more ; it will collapse if you do not.

Never is it like that in a work of the Spirit. But that earth touch—that is the point. The earth touch always means death, always means arrest. The absolute Lordship of the Holy Spirit demands that the earth touch be finished with—and that is what is meant by Joshua being commanded to take the shoes from off his feet. " What saith my lord unto his servant?" ' Go and conquer the land, go and take possession, go and lead the people in '? Not at all. ' Take your shoes off.' You get your shoes off, Joshua, and all the rest will follow. You destroy the earth touch, and see what will happen. You will only have to walk round Jericho. That is not how men would do it. Think of the tremendous campaign that would have been organized to capture Jericho if left to men ! No, get your shoes off and see what happens.

If you question that interpretation, you have only to see what happened where he put his shoes on, or where Israel put their shoes on, a little later. What happened at Ai? What happened with the Gibeonites? They had got their shoes on, they touched earth : the result—arrest, compromise, limitation. Get your shoes off and keep them off. The principle of the heavenly is the principle of the Holy Ghost's moving on, is the principle of spiritual fulness. ' Put off thy shoe from off thy foot ; for the place whereon thou standest is heavenly ground.' You have no standing here ; the earth has no place here, the world has no place here, men have no place here. This is sacred and sanctified to heaven. From this point heaven takes over. Yes, even from the great instrument raised up to serve the Lord, heaven has taken over. Sovereignty in choice of an instrument never means that sovereignty gives place to human strength. It never condones wrong in the instrument. That works out even with Joshua and Israel, for Joshua, as we said earlier, is representative of all the saints and all the servants of the Lord.

THE HOLY SPIRIT COMMITTED TO GOD'S PURPOSE

But notice this answer that came to his enquiry—" *Art thou for us, or for our adversaries ?* " Which? For us? for them? For this? for that? ' Nay ; I am not for this or for that, I am not for you or for them : I am for the Lord's purpose'. That is the real content of the answer. ' I am not for people, whoever they are : I am for the Lord's purpose. I am not for this work or that work that you are trying to do for the Lord. I am for the Lord's purpose, I am committed to the purpose of God—the eternal purpose.' " *Nay ; but . . .*" Oh, if only we could get the force of that in everything ! We are wanting the Holy Spirit to sponsor our movements, our work, our ministry. We are asking the Holy Spirit if He is 'for us'. He will never say He is. There is a sense in which the Lord is for His people. " If God be for us . . ." But there is another sense in which the Lord says, 'I am not for you but for My purpose in you and through you ; not for you, as you, in behalf of Israel, or Joshua the sovereignly chosen and anointed; I am not for you, I am committed to the purpose of God'.

My point is that we must identify the ground and object of the Holy Spirit's committal. We must know what the Holy Spirit is committed to. There is so much planning and arranging for the Lord, and so much failure on the part of the Lord to come and take it up and fulfil it. How much there is to-day in the world that is being arranged, planned and programmized for the Lord. It does not seem to go. The Lord does not seem to be committing Himself to it. That is just the point. We must identify the object of the Holy Spirit. The object of the Holy Spirit is not to do something and make something on the earth, not to set up something upon, and linked with, this earth, which has 'shoes' on it. To establish something here is not His object at all. The Holy Spirit is committed to something that is absolutely heavenly, and His whole object is to detach everything, in a spiritual and inward way, from this world. That must be shown more fully, perhaps, presently; but note that it is most important to know what it is that God will commit Himself to. He will not commit Himself to anything that is attached to this earth. He will only commit Himself to that which is attached to heaven.

THE HOLY SPIRIT WITH A DRAWN SWORD

Well, now, that being established, the next thing follows—again an extraordinary thing. This One, as Prince of the host of the Lord, is standing with His sword drawn in His hand. 'Oh, this is battle, is it? This is warfare, is it?' And so immediately the Holy Spirit takes charge and there is complete capitulation to Him. The battle is on. Make no mistake about it. Whatever you think about being baptized with the Holy Spirit, and all that that may imply—whatever else it is going to mean, it means immediate and unceasing conflict. It may mean other things, but it means that—a warfare from which there is no discharge, an army from which there is no retiring. Here you will never be pensioned off. You are in it to the end.

Was it not like that with the Lord Jesus? It begins there—Jordan, the open heaven, the Holy Spirit, the wilderness, the devil. Immediately—" Then was Jesus led up " (Mark says ' driven ', or ' impelled ') " of the Spirit into the wilderness to be tempted of the devil " (Matthew iv. 1). No sooner had the heavens been cleft for the advent of the Spirit, on that day called Pentecost, than the war was on. The Church was precipitated into it, and has never been out of it since. If it has, it has been to its own spiritual loss. Somehow this Lordship of the Holy Spirit immediately issues in that. The sword is in hand, and it will never be sheathed until the day's task is done.

Yes, but that is language. The Holy Spirit is not very interested in carnal and physical warfare. The warfare, the conflict, will be after His own kind. It will be spiritual, it will be after the spirit—because spiritual forces are in possession ; and therefore it is spiritual warfare that is going to dispossess. That is one reason why it is so actually and truly a battle. The point hardly needs labouring. We know it. We know that there is not one step, one foot, of spiritual attainment that is not contested ; not one movement or even gesture in the direction of spiritual increase but what there is conflict. It is true. It is spiritual warfare, and the nature of it is altogether beyond our power to comprehend. We think it will come one way—it comes another. It never comes where we expect and in the forms which we think we would recognise. The fact is that we rarely recognise the devil in his assaults. They seem to be so covered in either accident or mishap, or something going wrong—but you have only got to judge of the effect in relation to spiritual life, and you know there is something more of design and intelligence in it than mere circumstances of life. It is spiritual warfare. The Holy Spirit has precipitated this.

Do understand that; it explains so much. How constantly the enemy works by the ' blind spot '! I think that probably by far the greater proportion of his success to-day is by blind spots amongst the Lord's people. Prejudice is called ' caution ', suspicion is ' being watchful '—good names for bad things. The enemy is a past master at that. Your prejudice may be your blind spot which the devil has created. He has found the possibility of creating that, and it is standing right in the way of your own spiritual and heavenly fulness. The Lord's people are caught in that snare to-day, the world over. Enlargement and increase spiritually, in a heavenly way, is being withstood and frustrated by the prejudices and suspicions of God's people. " An enemy hath done this."

Why is it that in the letter to the Ephesians, with all the heavenly fulness presented and in view, and the spiritual conflict in relation to it shown, the Apostle prays that the ' eyes of their hearts may be enlightened ' to see? Why is that necessary? Because of this blinding work and these blind spots; because all can be lost by a prejudice, a bit of closed mind, a bit of suspicion, a bit of false fear, instead of trusting the Holy Spirit and knowing the anointing within which will 'teach you concerning all things' (I John ii. 27) and show you what is right and what is wrong. You feel you must fortify yourself 'in case', and you may be fortifying yourself against the Holy Ghost. That is what so many are doing. That is the realm of the conflict. Spiritually it is like that. It is very sinister and subtle.

But there is another aspect to this spiritual conflict. Why does the *Holy Spirit* bring this about? Why does the *Holy Spirit* precipitate it? You would think that it would come from the enemy quite naturally, but why does the Holy Spirit start it up, or make Himself the occasion of it, every time? We have seen it in the case of the Lord Jesus. Deliberately—for it is a definite and positive and precise statement: " Then was Jesus led up of the Spirit into the wilderness to be tempted of the devil "—the Holy Spirit takes the matter in hand to precipitate it, to bring it about. He did it with the Church—deliberately, knowing what He was doing. The effect of it is as though the Holy Spirit said, ' Now I am going to lead them into battle forthwith, straightway'. Why?

Well, for one thing, because this is a spiritual matter, a spiritual inheritance, because there are spiritual forces in possession and they have to be ousted; but also because we only grow spiritually by conflict. The Lord is interested in us. It is perhaps rather difficult for us, if a speaker stands on a platform and says, ' You are having a bad time because the Lord is interested in you; the devil is being allowed a lot of leash to assail you because the Lord has His highest interests in your well-being '—it is perhaps difficult for us to accept such a statement. The next time the enemy comes and begins to do his terrible work, you will be the last to say, ' Oh, the Lord loves me to-day ' ! We do not do that. But is it not a fact, is it not true to experience, true to history, and therefore true to principle, that we never make any progress spiritually, never increase at all, never grow at all, never go on at all, except by conflict? It is true. The only way we grow is by having something to over-come, where our spiritual life has somehow to get on top of something. It is a law in nature and in grace. There is no progress without contest. Would to God that we should be able to look at it like that every time ! We believe it may be true as a fact—but, oh, save us from being involved in that truth !

That will not do. The Lord is concerned with these people coming *actually* into possession ; not theoretically, not doctrinally, not on the ground of a Bible reading, but *actually* into possession ; and when you really come under the mastery of the Holy Spirit, then you are in the way of the actuality, and the Lord believes in it being actual and very practical.

Jericho is representative : the great example of how it will always be in principle. You have first of all to have a heavenly position, as we have said ; not an earthly position, not man's way of doing things. This is the out-working of that principle which we saw first of all with Abraham, where man tried to act and made an awful mess, because he touched earth ; and again with Moses, where he took things into his own hands, and assailed the

Egyptian and the Hebrew, and made an awful mess. Here is the outworking of the discipline, and Joshua takes up all that spiritual history, and at Jericho we find there are no carnal weapons—no human reason here, nothing left to man here. If this is not heavenly, it is nothing. Things do not happen like this on the earth. We can walk round, not only seven days, but all our lives, and nothing will happen unless we are in a heavenly position, unless heaven is coming in. Jericho is man set aside, altogether excluded. It is heavenly.

Well, that is the basis. And then immediately afterward you find this—that, if the enemy cannot succeed by open resistance, he will try more subtle tactics. He cannot succeed by open resistance if you and I are in our heavenly position and *keep it*—and *keep it*, for that is what Jericho means. They not only took it on the first day but they held it and kept it and ratified it, and seven times on the last day they confirmed it, holding their heavenly position; they did not give up. We do not always get through with the first or second day. There has to be a holding to that position in faith, and the enemy is completely worsted when that position is really held like that. When he is worsted along that line, he must somehow turn it to defeat, if he possibly can, and so he will work subtly.

Is that not the word about the Gibeonites? They worked subtly to make an ' earth touch ' somewhere. It was the same with Achan and Ai, the Babylonish garment and the wedge of gold—an earth touch. The Gibeonites and the covenant made with them constituted another earth touch. We must not think that it is always going to be just open, clear, straightforward spiritual warfare. There is that aspect where we must see where the earth touch is being manœuvred by the enemy—where there is the introduction of something that will make a contact with that which is cursed, and with which God cannot go on.

How is that done? You know, of course, that Gilgal was the place from which they moved out—Gilgal, the place of the rolling away, the place of the flesh set aside. But they did not go back to Gilgal after Jericho. They went straight on to Ai: whereas it was the custom always to go back to Gilgal after any advance or conquest—back to Gilgal and out again from Gilgal. This time they did not go back to Gilgal. They went on.

Let us keep near the Cross, and never assume that because the Lord has blessed and prospered and given success we can go on. Never for a moment must we get away from the Cross. The Cross is not something that lies back there, to be left. It is something to be with us all the time. It is our safety.

This is the heavenly way, the whole nature of the heavenly way, the way to God's end. The Lord keep us in it.

CHAPTER EIGHT

THE SIGNIFICANCE OF LEVITES IN RELATION TO HEAVENLY FULNESS

" And they commanded the people, saying, When ye see the ark of the covenant of the Lord your God, and the priests the Levites bearing it, then ye shall remove from your place, and go after it." (Joshua iii. 3).

FIRST OF ALL, IT IS THIS FRAGMENT—" the priests, the Levites, bearing it ", bearing the ark—that is the key to our present consideration.

In this book of Joshua, the Levites have a large place. They are referred to quite a number of times. Indeed, at one point the whole chapter circles round them, and it is the significance of the Levites in relation to heavenly fulness that I want by the Holy Spirit's help to try to bring to you. Many of us are quite familiar with the history of the Levites, but it is necessary for us just to go over that ground hurriedly to begin with.

In this book of Joshua the Levites are presented in three ways. Firstly, as we have just seen, as bearing the ark of the covenant into the bed of the Jordan and standing there with it, with a two-thousand-cubit space between them and it and the people—a very great distance, as we saw in

chapter V. Then, secondly, in Joshua xiv it is stated that
the Levites were given no inheritance. That is, in the dividing up of the land, unlike the other tribes they were not
apportioned a particular area, they were given no inheritance in the land. But, thirdly, in chapter xxi, the chapter
which circles round the Levites, you find that all the tribes
had to give something of a plot, a place, to the Levites. The
Levites were distributed among all the tribes, and their
place and their portion was not all together in one place,
but in relation to the whole country, so that you might say
the Levites were just scattered all over the land, everywhere, in relation to the rest of the people. Those are the
three things about the Levites, in this book, full of wonderful significance.

LEVITES REPRESENT THE HEAVENLY THOUGHT

What do they signify? Let us go back. You remember
how the Levites came into being as a tribe. It was on the
occasion when Israel departed, when the calf was made,
and they cried, " These be thy gods, O Israel " (Ex. xxxii.
4), and they left the Lord. And Moses came down, heard
and saw, destroyed the calf, stood in the gate and cried,
" *Whoso is on the Lord's side, let him come unto me. And
all the sons of Levi gathered themselves together unto him.
And he said unto them, Thus saith the Lord, the God of
Israel, Put ye every man his sword upon his thigh, and go
to and fro from gate to gate throughout the camp, and slay
every man his brother, and every man his companion, and
every man his neighbour. And the sons of Levi did according to the word of Moses* " (*Exodus xxxii. 26 – 28*). All

earthly considerations were sacrificed to the heavenly interest, all earthly relationships severed for the heavenly
thought; everything of natural sentiment and emotion, all
that was of the mere soul, was slain in the interests of that
which governed the very coming out of the people of God.
For it was in the thought of God that they should be a
heavenly people, and not thus involved in the spiritual
system governing this world. In that alone the Levites are
seen to represent the heavenly thought of God. A very
drastic and utter thing, was it not, that they should do that.

And you remember the Lord never forgot it. Right at
the end of the Old Testament, in the last book, Malachi,
referring to the matter of Baal-Peor, where Phineas maintained the stand for heavenly interests originally taken on
the occasion of the making of the golden calf (Num.
xxv), the Lord said, "My covenant was with him [Levi]
of life and peace" (Malachi ii. 5). 'He did not acknowledge his brethren' (Deuteronomy xxxiii. 9): that is, he
did not look with sympathy even upon his own flesh
when that moved away from God's high thoughts. God
made His covenant with Levi. So at the very outset the
Levites were selected, and separated from all the rest of
Israel, as taking the place of the firstborn in Israel, and
they became the tribe of the firstborn ones; and from that
many of you will at once in your minds leap over to the
letter to the Hebrews—"Ye are come unto . . . the . . .
church of the firstborn who are enrolled in heaven" (Heb.
xii. 22, 23). Here is the heavenly thing coming in again :
the firstborn who are enrolled in heaven—the Levites, the
heavenly thought.

Now we said in chapter V that there was this space of

two thousand cubits at the very least—for we cannot determine at this time which cubit it was of the three : the
distance was over one thousand feet at the very least, and
could easily have been more than three thousand feet ; a
great space between the ark and the people, indicating the
immense distance between Christ and all others in this
work of salvation, of redemption, of deliverance ;—but
the Levites were bearing the ark. You say, ' Is not that a
contradiction? Christ stands in solitary isolation from all.'
But you see the principle of the Levite. He represents the
heavenly thing. This is the heavenly Christ. That is the
principle of the Levites bearing the ark there. This is not
just the earthly Christ, the Jesus of history, a man amongst
men, though greatly better. This is the Heavenly One.

If you want that principle proved, you remember the incident in the days of David, when he consulted with the
elders of Israel to bring up the ark, and made a cart to do
it. He got his idea from the land of the Philistines, where
he had been during the reign of Saul, and where he had
seen them make a cart. They put the ark on a cart, and
tragedy followed. Uzzah died before the Lord. David was
very grieved with the Lord because He had made a breach
that day ; but, being the man he was, always adjustable to
the Lord—one of the glorious things about David was his
adjustability—he did not have a long controversy with the
Lord, or the Lord with David. David got back to the Lord,
and probably tried to argue it out—but the Lord won the
argument. The Lord took him back to the Scriptures and
showed him that the Levites were to bear the ark—it is
not machines, not organizations, but a heavenly people,
that is to carry the testimony of Jesus.

So the Levites are carrying the ark. This heavenliness of things is the principle of the Levite function, and that of course goes to the root of their not having an inheritance in the earth. They do not belong to the earth : they belong to heaven. They are not going to be rooted down here ; but even so, as men representing the heavenly things, they are going to be distributed amongst all the people of God to keep the people of God in touch with heaven. The people of God are always so prone to become earthly. That has been the peril and the tragedy of the Church through the centuries, always gravitating toward this earth, becoming something here after the fashion of man, after the ideas of this world.

THE LORD'S NEED OF LEVITES AMONG HIS PEOPLE

Now we come to our point. The Lord must have those who have been through the suffering, through the Cross, through the sacrifice, through the deep work of separation ; who have not compromised on any considerations of senti- ment or earthly interest: those who have stood and are standing wholly, utterly, at all costs, for His full heavenly thought concerning His Son and concerning the Church. He must have them, and He must distribute them every- where and bring them into vital relationship with His people, in order to keep those people from succumbing to that tendency earthward—from becoming world-bound.

HEADQUARTERS IN HEAVEN

And do you not see that this is exactly what happened in the New Testament? It is quite fascinating to see it.

When you come into the New Testament, you have left types and figures—I expect some of you are rather tired of types and figures ; you get a surfeit of that. It is a grand thing to see the actuality. When you come into Acts, you find this whole thing repeated. What has happened? You begin with the Lord Jesus placed in heaven : headquarters in heaven, every bit of government now in heaven ; and then the Holy Spirit coming to make everything heavenly, to govern everything in relation to heaven. That is what we were speaking about in our last chapter : the Captain of the host of the Lord coming to take everything up in relation to heaven, and then everything moving from heaven.

It moved from heaven first of all in Jerusalem, a mighty movement from heaven, and things were happening. But note the tendency after a time (of course the story is told in a few phrases, but it covers a very considerable period). After a time Jerusalem gravitated earthward, and tended —and not only tended, but actually began—to become an earthly headquarters of the Church. It was only to be, in the Lord's command, the beginning, the commencement spot: "beginning at Jerusalem". Jerusalem was never intended to be the inclusive and final thing, but it constituted itself a kind of headquarters to govern the Church, and you will find that sort of thing developing as you go on in the book of the Acts. Look on a bit to Paul the heavenly man, and see how he repudiates Jerusalem.

However, you come to the seventh chapter of the book of the Acts, the stoning of Stephen, and that is the end of Jerusalem. From that point heaven re-asserts itself to say, ' No ; no earthly centre or headquarters ; headquarters is in heaven '; and at that point they are all scattered from Jerusalem. They are stirred up and thrown out of the nest and go in all directions. Wherever they go, whether it is Philip or whoever it is, they are testifying everywhere to the heavenly Lord, bringing in the heavenly side of things. Yes: everywhere these Levites are placed in relation to the whole world, to keep things in a heavenly way. So it develops like that.

You move on to chapter ix, and it is one of heaven's tremendous movements. Saul has come from Jerusalem, on his way to Damascus—and Jerusalem is *his* headquarters, right enough. He has authority from the High Priest, from the rulers. Jerusalem governs where he is concerned. But he discovers before he gets to the end of the journey that the government is in heaven, not in Jerusalem. The heavens are cleft; there comes a light from heaven and a voice from heaven; and that is the end of earthliness for Saul of Tarsus. From that moment he is a heavenly man —and see how, for ever afterwards, that man is moving in relation to heaven. That could bear following out in detail; but here is a mighty Levite. And so it was no more at Jerusalem, but Antioch. The Lord has moved from Jerusalem. Antioch is a very pure spiritual thing. Jerusalem has become the centre of Christian officialdom—but there is nothing official at Antioch. What you have at Antioch, which now supplants Jerusalem, is a company of men who are fasting and praying: and heaven breaks in, and the Holy Ghost says, " Separate me Barnabas and Saul " (Acts xiii. 2). This is something in relation to heaven, you see. It is wonderful.

So we could go on giving the evidence. But what is the

point? Is it not very clear that from God's standpoint, in God's mind, everything is intended to be related to heaven and governed from heaven? Heavenly fulness is His objective with His people : to make them a heavenly people and to fill with His heavenly fulness. And right at the end we see the new Jerusalem—not the old one, but the new Jerusalem—coming down from God out of heaven, in great heavenly fulness. It is something immense, is that Jerusalem—twelve thousand furlongs in every direction (Revelation xxi. 16). There is great fulness here. All the nations are going to derive their resource from it. The fruit of its tree of life, the waters of its river of life, are for all the nations. Its light is for all the nations. " The nations shall walk amidst the light thereof " (Rev. xxi. 24). This is heavenly fulness, the thing to which the Lord has been working all the time.

He is working now in you and me. I sometimes think that we are two persons, one here and one in heaven. Naturally we are here, but there is something of ourselves ' going up ' all the time, when the Lord is getting in us something more of heaven. It is being stored up there. Is not that perhaps what the Lord meant, when He referred to Himself as " the Son of man, who is in heaven " (John iii. 13), even while He is on earth? There is an aspect of us that is growing in heaven. Do not think of heaven as some remote planet. We are growing in that heavenly thought of things. Something of us is ' going up '.

I believe the Church is like that. The real Church is an invisible thing. You do not know, except by the Spirit, what the Church is really. You cannot say that people attending a certain place are the Church. You cannot say that people who profess certain doctrines and Christian truths are the Church. They may be or they may not be. But if you meet in the Spirit—and that is something intangible—there you have the Church. The Church is like that, and that is its heavenly character—and that is ' going up ', so to speak, all the time, and it is going to come down presently in fulness out of heaven. It is being built in that way now. It is God's will that it should be like that.

But my point now is that the Lord must have that kind of representation, be it in individuals or in companies, to place alongside of all His people here to keep them in touch with heaven, to keep the heavenly things always in view. One of the functions of the Levites was to teach the Word of God—that is, to keep the Lord's people in touch with God's thought. That is functional, not official. You need not call yourself a Levite, any more than ' Reverend '. Do not take on titles, but grasp the principles. If we here on this earth are keeping people in touch with heaven, if we are linked with heavenly things, if people are built up by our presence—not by our preaching necessarily, not by our getting down and saying, ' Now you see this and this . . .' ; no, just by our presence, by our embodiment of the heavenly life and nature and fulness—if they are coming to see God's fuller thought because we are here, we are Levites without the title and that is what the Lord must have.

It may be as individuals. The Lord has the disposing of His people. In this very book, heaven disposed of the people, of the tribes, and said, ' You shall be here, this is your place '. Sovereignly the Lord will dispose of you, and put some of you in Germany, some in Holland, some in England, some in America; and when He has disposed of your life you are there by heaven's appointment, to be a link with heaven, to keep things from settling down spiritually on to this earth level.

That, of course, is also the meaning of churches in the New Testament. That is the Divine idea—to have companies of the Lord's people, planted here and there and everywhere, as a corporate Levitical ministry, to keep heaven near, and to keep things near heaven. Oh, that every church were like that, keeping things near heaven!

Well, that is the beginning. Much more could be said. We could begin now to consider all the letters of the New Testament and to see the outworking. We would begin with Romans xii—for here you have a Levitical principle: " I beseech you therefore, brethren, by the mercies of God, to present your bodies a living sacrifice, holy, acceptable to God, which is your spiritual service. And be not fashioned according to this world ". That is Levitical, the living sacrifice not conformed to this world. So we could go on through it all. But the great issue of our meditations together is this—that we have to be here in relation to heaven, under heaven's government, bringing in heavenly things. We are ministering in relation to heaven. It must be as true of us, in our measure and in our calling, as it was of Paul, that we have a heavenly vision and we are not disobedient unto it. What do we not owe to that dear man for all the sacrifice and the suffering that he knew for heavenly things! But how faithful he was to heaven, right to the end—cast into his prison, on his chain, and talking about nothing else but the heavenly places.

Do you say your situation is too difficult to bring heaven in? Well, there are difficult situations. Daniel's was a difficult situation—his three companions were in a difficult situation ; but they brought heaven in. A grand phrase in the book of Daniel is—" the heavens do rule " (iv. 26). And they proved it. Headquarters is in heaven : not in Babylon, not in Rome, not in Jerusalem or anywhere else, but in heaven. The Lord help us to live up to and out from heaven.

And now, at the end, we bring the specific object of these messages into view once more.

God has but one end which will bring Him complete satisfaction—the ' Fulness of Christ '. That fulness is meant to be found in a people taken out of the nations. By that people in that fulness He purposes to rule the creation in the ages to come. This will not be attained to willy-nilly, but only by infinite cost and conflict now.

All who " come out " do not " enter in " to this ulti-mate. Many will not go all the way, fulfil all the condi-tions, ' make their calling and election sure ', but will enter the Kingdom to inherit in different measures ; smaller or larger.

Unto the fulness of purpose, pioneers are necessary, and the way of the pioneers is a peculiar way, fraught with experiences, sufferings, perplexities, and testings, of which others know little.

But God *must* have His pioneers—individuals or companies ; and these are they who

'WHOLLY FOLLOW THE LORD.'

Prophetic
Ministry

Publisher's note:

Prophetic Ministry originally published from
39 Honor Oak Road, London in 1954

The year of publication as given is from when, in the
author's bimonthly magazine *A Witness and a
Testimony*, a first notice of this book or booklet
appeared. Very many of the titles published had
already appeared earlier as articles or series in that
magazine.

Where a new title's date of publication is not known, +
signifies the year of the magazine article or series from
which, some unspecified time later, that new
publication was reproduced.

1998 Christian Books Publishing House / SeedSowers
P O Box 285
Sargent
GA 30275

CONTENTS

FOREWORD

The function of the Prophet has almost invariably been that of recovery. That implies that his business related to something lost. That something being absolutely essential to God's full satisfaction, the dominant note of the Prophet was one of dissatisfaction. And, there being the additional factor that, for obvious reasons, the people were not disposed to go the costly way of God's full purpose, the Prophet was usually an unpopular person.

But his unpopularity was no proof of his being wrong or unnecessary, for every Prophet was eventually vindicated, though with very great suffering and shame to the people.

If it be true that prophetic ministry is related to the need for the recovery of God's full thought as to His people, surely this is a time of such need! Few honest and thoughtful people will contend that things are all well with the Church of Christ to-day. A brief comparison with the first years of the Church's life will bring out a vivid contrast between then and the *centuries* since.

Take alone the lifetime of one man—Paul.

In the year 33 A.D. a few unknown men, looked upon as poor and ignorant, were associated with one ' Jesus of Nazareth '—which very designation was despicable in the minds of all reputable and influential people. These men, after that Jesus had been crucified, were later found seeking to proclaim His Lordship and Saviourhood, but were handled hardly by all official bodies.

5

In the year that Paul died—67-68 A.D. (34 years later)—how did the matter stand? There were churches in Jerusalem, Nazareth, Caesarea ; Antioch and all Syria ; Galatia ; Sardis, Laodicea, Ephesus and all the towns on the West coast throughout lesser Asia ; in Philippi, Thessalonica, Athens, Corinth, and the chief cities of the islands and the mainland of Greece ; Rome, and the Western Roman Colonies ; and in Alexandria.

The history of *generations* of missionary enterprise, tens of thousands of missionaries, vast sums of money, immense administrative organizations, and much more on the publicity, propaganda, and advocacy side, does not compare at all favourably with the above. We now find ourselves confronted by the end of the whole system of world missions and professional missionaries *as they have existed for a very long time,* and still the world is not evangelized.

Is there a reason for this? We feel—nay, know—that there is. The explanation is not in a difference in Divine purpose or Divine willingness to support that purpose. It is in the difference in apprehension of the basis, way, and object of the work of God.

Some proof of this is recognisable in our own time. In much less than the lifetime of one man in China, churches of a deeply spiritual character sprang into being all over that land ; four hundred of them in a few years. At the time when Communism overran that country a movement was in progress which was not only covering China, but reaching beyond, and as a result living churches are now found in many other parts of the Far East. This was for years a despised, persecuted, and much ostracised work. But since missionary movements and societies have had to leave the country this work has gone on, and, although with many martyrs, is still going on. The man raised up of God lies in prison, but the work is unarrested.

The same kind of thing is taking place in India, and in only a very few years of the life of one God-apprehended man churches of a real New Testament character have come into being all over the country and beyond. The opposition is very great, but the work is of God, and cannot be stopped.

What, again, is the explanation?

The answer is not to be found in the realm of zeal or devotion to the salvation of souls. Rather is it this: that there was at the beginning the supreme factor of an absolutely original and new apprehension of Christ and God's eternal purpose concerning Him. This *revelation* by the Holy Spirit came with devastating and revolutionising power to the Apostles and the Church, and, rather than being a ' tradition handed down from the fathers ', a ready-made system, all set and entered into as such, it was, for every one of them, as though it had only newly dropped from heaven—which, in fact, was true.

This movement of God, brought about by a mighty up-heaving of all traditions and ' old ' things by a practical experience of the Cross, was marked by three features: —

(1) Utter heavenliness and spirituality ;
(2) Universality, involving the negation of all preju-dices, exclusiveness and partiality ; and
(3) The utter Lordship and Headship of Christ *directly* operating by the sovereignty of the Holy Spirit.

This was all gathered into a tremendous and overpow-ering initial and progressive realisation of the immense significance of Christ in the eternal counsels of God, and therefore of the Church as His Body. Anything that corresponds to the results which characterized the beginning will—and does—correspond to the reason, namely, a getting back behind tradition, the set and established system, institutionalism, ecclesiasticism, commercialism, organizationalism, etc., to a virgin, original, new breaking upon the consciousness of God's full thought concerning His Son.

To bring into view this *full* purpose of God was the essence of the Prophet's ministry, and will always be so. We may not now speak of a special class as ' Prophets ', but the function may still be operative, and it is function that matters more than office.

FOREST HILL, LONDON.
JUNE, 1954.   T. A-S.

CHAPTER ONE

WHAT PROPHETIC MINISTRY IS

Reading : Deuteronomy xviii. 15, 18 ; Acts iii. 22 ; vii. 37 ; Luke xxiv. 19 ; Revelation xix. 10 ; Ephesians iv. 8, 11 — 13.

"*He gave some . . . prophets . . . for the perfecting of the saints, unto the work of ministering, unto the building up of the body of Christ* " (*Ephesians iv. 11, 12*).

WE ARE GOING TO CONSIDER the matter of prophetic ministry. " He gave some . . . prophets." But we must at once make some discrimination, for when we speak of prophetic ministry, we find that people are very largely governed by a certain mentality associated with what is called ' prophecy '. They immediately relate the very term ' prophetic ' to incidents, happenings, dates, and so on, lying mainly in the future. That is, they think instantly of the predictive element in prophetic ministry and limit the whole function to that conception.

Now, for the real value of what is before us we must remove from our minds that restricted idea of the preeminence of the predictive aspect in prophetic ministry. It is an aspect, but it is only an aspect. Prophetic ministry is a much larger thing than the predictive.

Perhaps it would be better if we said that the prophetic

function, going far beyond mere events, happenings and dates, is the ministry of spiritual interpretation. That phrase will cover the whole ground of that with which we are now concerned. Prophecy is spiritual interpretation. If you think about it for a moment, in the light of prophetic ministry in the Word of God, I am quite sure you will see how true this is. It is the interpretation of everything from a spiritual standpoint; the bringing of the spiritual implications of things, past, present and future, before the people of God, and giving them to understand the significance of things in their spiritual value and meaning. That was and is the essence of prophetic ministry.

Of course, what we know about prophets in the Scriptures is that they were a special function or faculty amongst the Lord's people, but we must also remember that they often combined their prophetic function with other functions. Samuel was a prophet; he was also a judge, and a priest. Moses was a prophet, but he was other things besides. I believe Paul was a prophet; he was an apostle, an evangelist; he was everything, it seems to me! So that our purpose is to speak not so much of *prophets,* as distinct people, as of prophetic *ministry.* It is the ministry with which we are concerned, and we shall arrive at the instrument better by recognising the ministry fulfilled; we shall understand the vessel better and see what it is, if we see the purpose for which it is constituted. So let me say that it is function, not persons, that we have in view when we are speaking about prophets or prophetic ministry.

I am quite sure that those who have any knowledge whatever of the times, spiritually, will agree with me when I say that the crying need of our time is for a prophetic ministry. There never was a time when there existed so

extensively the need for a voice of interpretation, when
conditions needed more the ministry of explanation. One
does not want to make extravagant statements or to be
extreme in one's utterances, but I do not think it would
be either extravagant or extreme to say that the world to-
day is well-nigh bankrupt of real prophetic ministry in this
sense—a voice that interprets the mind of God to people.
It may exist in some small degree here and there, but in
no very large way is that ministry being fulfilled. So often
our hearts groan and cry out, Oh, that the mind of God
about the present situation could be brought through, in
the first place to the recognition of His people, and then
through His people to others beyond! There is a great
and terrible need for a prophetic ministry in our time.

PROPHETIC MINISTRY RELATED TO THE FULL PURPOSE OF GOD

Recognising that, we must come to see exactly what
this function is. What is the function of prophetic ministry? It is to hold things to the full thought of God, and
therefore it is usually a reactionary thing. We usually find
that the prophets arose as a reaction from God to the
course and drift of things amongst His people ; a call back,
a re-declaration, a re-pronouncement of God's mind, a
bringing into clear view again of the thoughts of God.
The prophets stood in the midst of the stream—usually
a fast-rushing stream—like a rock ; the course of things
broke over them. They challenged and resisted that course,
and their presence in the midst of the stream represented
God's mind as against the prevailing course of things. In
the Old Testament, the prophet usually came into his
ministry at a time when things were spiritually bad and

anything but according to the Divine mind ; the state was
evil, things were confused, mixed, chaotic ; there was much
deception and falsehood, and often things very much worse
than that. Here is the thing to which the prophetic ministry all-inclusively relates—the original and ultimate purpose of God in and through His people ; and when you
have said that, you have got right to the heart of things.
We ask again, What is the prophetic ministry, what is the
prophetic function, to what does it relate?—and the answer all-inclusively is that it relates to the full, original and
ultimate purpose of God in and through His people.

If that statement is true, it helps us at once to see the
need in our time ; for, speaking generally, the people of
God on the earth in our time have confused parts of the
purpose of God with the whole ; have emphasized phases
to the detriment of the whole. They are confusing means
and methods and enthusiasm and zeal with the exact object of the Lord, failing to recognise that God's purpose
must be reached in God's way and by God's means, and
the way and the means are just as important as the purpose : that is, you cannot reach God's end just anyhow,
by any kind of method that you may employ, by projecting your own ideas or programmes or schemes to get to
God's end. God has His own way and means of getting to
His end. God's thoughts extend to and spread over the
smallest detail of His purpose, and you cannot wholly
realise the purpose of God except as the very details are
according to the mind of God.

God might have said to Moses, Build me a tabernacle,
will you? I leave it to you how you do it, what you use ;
you see what I am after ; go and make me a tabernacle.
Moses might have got the idea of what God wanted and
have worked out the kind of thing he would make for God

according to his own mind. But we know that God did not leave a single detail, a peg or a pin's point, a stitch or a thread, to the mind of man. I only use that illustration in order to enforce what I mean, that prophetic ministry is to present God's full, original and ultimate purpose, as it is according to His mind, and hold it like that for God ; to interpret the mind of God in all matters concerning the purpose of God, to bring all details into line with the purpose, and to make the purpose govern everything.

PROPHETIC MINISTRY BY THE ANOINTING

(a) DETAILED KNOWLEDGE OF GOD'S PURPOSES

This involves several things which are clearly seen to be features of prophetic ministry in the Word of God. First of all, it involves the matter of anointing. The meaning and value of anointing is that, firstly, only the Spirit of God has the full and detailed plan in view and can make everything to be true in principle to God's intention. I say only the Spirit of God has that. It is one of the most wonderful things in Scripture, to find that, when you get back to the simplest, earliest—shall we say, the most elementary—expression or projecting of Divine things in the Word of God, everything there is so true in principle to all that comes out later in that connection in greater fulness. It is simply marvellous how God has kept everything true to principle : you never find later, however fully a thing is developed, that there is a change in principle ; the principle is there and you cannot get away from it. When you later take up a more developed matter in the Word of God you find that it is true to the original principle of that matter as it was first introduced.

And God has brought everything into line with those

fixed principles. God does not deviate one little bit. His
law is there and it is unchanging. The Holy Spirit alone
knows all that. He knows the laws and the principles, all
the things which spiritually govern the purpose of God ;
and He alone knows the plan and the details, and can
make everything true to those principles and laws. And
everything has got to be true to them. We may take it as
settled that if in the superstructure there is anything that
is out of harmony with God's original basic spiritual principle, that is going to be a defect which will spell tragedy
sooner or later. The superstructure, in every detail of principle, has to be true to the foundation, to the original. Most
of us are not enlightened as to all that. We are feeling our
way along, we are groping onward, we are getting light,
slowly, very little at a time ; but we are getting light. But
the prophetic ministry is an enlightened ministry, and is
that which, under the anointing, is to bring things back to
that position of absolute safety and security because it is
true to Divine principle.

The anointing is necessary, firstly, because only the
Spirit of God is acquainted with all the thought of God
and He alone can speak and work and bring things about
in true and utter consistency with the Divine principles
which govern everything ; and everything that is from
God must embody those principles. The principle of the
Church—that which governs the Church—is that it is a
heavenly thing. It is not an earthly thing ; it is related to
Christ as in heaven. The Church does not come into being until Christ is in heaven, which means that the Church
has to come, as to Christ in heaven, on to heavenly ground,
in a spiritual way. It has got to leave earthly ground and
really be a heavenly, spiritual thing, while still here, in
relation to Christ in heaven. That is a Divine law and

principle which is so clear in the New Testament. It is
there from " Acts " onward most manifestly.

But this is not something new which has come in with
the New Testament. God has put that law into everything
that points in any prophetic way to the Church and to
Christ. Isaac was not allowed to leave the land and go
abroad to fetch his wife. He had to stay there and the servant had to be sent to bring her to where he was. There
is your law. Christ is in heaven ; the Spirit is sent to bring
the Church to where He is—firstly in a spiritual way, and
then later literally ; but the principle is there. Joseph
passes through rejection and typical death and eventually
reaches the throne, and with his exaltation he receives his
wife, Asenath. Joseph is a clear figure of Christ. It is *on
His exaltation* that Christ receives His Church, His Bride.
Pentecost is really the result of the exaltation of Christ,
when the Church is spiritually brought into living relationship with Himself, the exalted Christ. There is your principle in the simple story of Joseph. You can go on like
that, seeing how God in simple details has kept everything true to principle ; you find His eternal principles are
embodied in the simplest things of the Old Testament,
fulfilling this final declaration that the testimony of Jesus
is the very spirit of prophecy (Rev. xix. 10). There is
something there indicative of a great heavenly truth, which
is the spirit of prophecy pointing to Christ.

I wonder whether you have really been impressed with
the tremendous importance of Divine principle in things.
There is a principle, and the recognition and the honour-
ing of that principle determines the success of the whole.
Now, only the Holy Spirit knows all those Divine principles, only He knows the mind of God, the thoughts of
God, in fulness. Hence, if things are to be held to the full

thought and purpose of God, it can only be under an anointing—which means that the Spirit of God has come to take charge. An anointed ministry means that God the Holy Spirit has become responsible for the whole thing ; He has committed Himself to it. I do not suppose anyone would dispute or challenge the statement of the need for the Holy Spirit, the need for Him to be in charge, for everything to be done by Him. But oh, that means a great deal more than a general truth and a general position.

(b) KNOWLEDGE IMPARTED BY REVELATION

It leads to this second thing in prophetic ministry : By the anointing there comes revelation. We can accept in a general way the necessity of the Holy Spirit's doing everything—initiating, conducting, governing and being the power and inspiration of everything ; but oh ! that is a life-long education, and it brings in the necessity for everything to be given by revelation. That is why the prophets originally were called " seers "—men who saw. They saw what no other men saw. They saw what it was impossible for other people to see, even religious, God-fearing people. They saw by revelation.

A prophetic ministry demands revelation ; it is a ministry by revelation. Later we shall examine that more closely, but I want just to emphasize the fact at this moment. I am not thinking now of revelation extra to the Scriptures. I cannot take the ground of certain ' prophets ' (?) in the Church to-day who prophesy extra to the Scriptures. No, but within the revelation already given—and God knows it is big enough !—the Holy Spirit yet moves to reveal what ' eye hath not seen, ear hath not heard '. That is the wonder of a life in the Spirit. It is a life of constant new discovery ; everything is full of surprise and wonder. A life under the Holy Spirit can never be static ; it can never reach finality here, nor come to the place where the sum of truth is boxed. A life-really in the Holy Spirit is a life which realises that there is infinitely, transcendently, more beyond than all we have yet seen or grasped or sensed. People who *know,* who have come to a fixed place and cannot see—let alone move—beyond their present position, represent a position that is foreign to the mind of the Holy Ghost. Prophetic ministry under the Holy Spirit is a ministry through growing revelation.

A prophet was a man who went back to God again and again, and did not come out to speak until God had shown him the next thing. He did not just go on in his professional office because he was a prophet and it was expected of him. There was nothing professional about his position. When it became professional, then tragedy overtook the prophetic office. It did become professional through the ' schools of the prophets ' set up by Samuel. We must not even confuse these schools of the prophets with true prophetical office. There was a difference between those who graduated in the schools of the prophets and the true prophets represented by such men as Samuel, Elijah, Elisha. Whenever things become professional, something is lost, because the very essence and nature of prophetic ministry is that it is coming by revelation afresh every time. A thing revealed is new ; it may be an old thing, but it has about it something that is fresh as a revelation to the heart of the one concerned, and it is so new and wonderful that the effect with him is as though no one had ever yet seen that, although thousands may have seen it before. It is the nature of revelation to keep things alive and fresh, and filled with Divine energy. You cannot recover an old position by just the old doctrine. You will never recover something of God which has been lost by bringing back the exact statement of the truth. You may be stating the truth of the early days of the New Testament exactly, but you may be far from having the conditions which obtained at such times.

Prophetic succession is not the succession of teaching ; it is the succession of anointing. Something can come in from God, by the operation of God ; there may be something very real, very living, which God effects through an instrumentality, it may be individual or collective, which is alive because God brought it in under His anointing. And then someone tries to imitate it, duplicate it, or later someone takes it up to carry it on ; someone has been appointed, elected, chosen by ballot to be the successor. The thing goes on and grows ; but some vital factor is no longer there. The succession is by anointing, not by framework, even of doctrine. We cannot recover New Testament conditions by re-stating New Testament doctrine. We have to get New Testament anointing. I am not dismissing doctrine ; it is necessary ; but it is the anointing which makes things alive, fresh, vibrant. Everything must come by revelation.

Some of us know what it is to be able to analyse our Bibles and present, perhaps in a very interesting way, the contents of its books and all its doctrines. We can do that with " Ephesians " as well as we can do it with any other book. We can come to " Ephesians " and analyse it and outline the Church and the Body and all that, and be as blind as bats until the day comes when, God having done something in us, something deep and tremendous and terrific, we *see* the Church, we *see* the Body—we *see* " Ephesians "! They were two worlds: one was truth,

exact in technical detail, full of interest and fascination—
but there was something lacking. We could have stated
the truth from beginning to end, but we did not know
what was in it ; and until we have gone through that experience and something has happened in us, we may think
we know, we may be sure we know, we may lay down our
life for it; but we do not know. There is all the difference
between a very keen, clear, mental apprehension of things
in the Word of God, and a spiritual revelation. There is
the difference of two worlds—but it is quite impossible to
make people understand that difference until something
has happened. We shall speak about that ' something that
happens ' later, but here we are stating the facts. By anointing there is revelation, and revelation by anointing is
essential to the seeing of what God is after, both in general
and in detail.

So, building up, we arrive at this. A prophetic ministry
is that which—although much detail has yet to be revealed, even to the most enlightened servants of God—
has, by the Holy Ghost, *seen the purpose of God,* original
and ultimate.

(c) EXACT CONFORMITY TO GOD'S THOUGHTS

And then there is the third thing we find connected with
this anointing. It is that to which we have already referred
in general—*exactness.*

The anointing brings about that *first-hand touch with
God,* which means seeing God face to face. Was it not that
that was the summing up of Moses' life? " There hath not
arisen a prophet since in Israel like unto Moses, whom the
Lord knew face to face " (Deut. xxxiv. 10). And when
that happens you come into the place of direct spiritual

knowledge of God, direct touch with God, the place of the open heaven—you cannot, under any consideration, for any advantage at all, be a person who compromises, who deviates from what has been shown to your heart.

What is it that the Apostle says about Moses? " Moses was faithful in all his house as a servant " (Heb. iii. 5) ; and the faithfulness of Moses is seen particularly and largely in the way in which he was governed exactly by what God said. You know those later chapters of the book of Exodus, bringing everything back again to the word, again and again and again, " as the Lord commanded Moses ". Everything was done as God said ; through the whole system which Moses was raised up to constitute and establish, he was exact to a detail. We know why, of course ; and here is that great, that grand, comprehensive explanation of what I said just now about principles. God has Christ in view all the time, in every detail, and that system that Moses instituted was a representation of Christ to a fraction ; and so it was necessary that in every detail he should be exact. It is a difficult, costly way, but you cannot have revelation, and go on in revelation, and at the same time compromise over details and have things at any point other than exactly as the Lord wants them. You are not governed by diplomacy or policy or public opinion. You are governed by what the Lord has said in your heart by revelation as to His purpose. That is prophetic ministry.

Prophets were not men who accommodated themselves to anything that was comparative in its goodness. They never let themselves go wholly if the thing was only comparatively good. Look at Jeremiah. There was a day in Jeremiah's life when a good king did seek to recover things, and he did institute a great feast of the Passover, and the people did come up in their crowds for the celebration of that Passover, and it was a great occasion apparently. They were doing great things there in Jerusalem, but with all that was going on which was good, confessedly good, Jeremiah did not let himself go. He had a reservation, and he was right. It was seen afterward that this thing was very largely outward, that the real heart of the people had not changed, the high places were not taken away, and Jeremiah's original prophecy had to stand. If the apparent reformation had been the true thing, then Jeremiah's prophecies about the captivity, the destruction of the city, the complete handing over to judgment, would have gone for nothing. Jeremiah held back. He may not have understood, he may have been in perplexity about it, but his heart would not allow him to go wholly with this comparatively good thing. He found out the reason why afterward—that, although it was good up to a point, it did not represent a deep heart change, and so the judgment had to be.

The prophet cannot accept as full and final what is only comparative, though he rejoices in the measure of good that there may be anywhere. We should, of course, be generous to any little bit of good that is in the world— let us be grateful for anything that is right and true and of God ; but oh ! we cannot say that is altogether satisfying to the Lord, that is all that the Lord wants. No, this prophetic ministry is one of utter faithfulness to the thoughts of God. It is a ministry of exactness. That is what the anointing means, and we have said why—it is a *full* Christ who is in view.

That last statement in Revelation xix. 10 sums it all up. It gathers up into one sentence prophetic ministry from the beginning. I suppose prophetic ministry commenced in the day when it was stated of the seed of the woman that it should bruise the head of the serpent, and then passed on to Enoch, who prophesied saying, " Behold, the Lord came . . ." (Jude 14), and so right on from then. It is all gathered up at the end of the Revelation in this thought, that " the testimony of Jesus is the spirit of pro- phecy." That is, the spirit of prophecy from beginning to end is all toward that—the testimony of Jesus. The spirit of prophecy has always had Him in view from its first utterance—" the seed of the woman "—to " Behold, the Lord came " (and how beginning and end are brought to- gether so early on!). All the way through it was always with the Lord Jesus in view, and a full Christ. " He gave . . . prophets . . . till we all attain unto . . . the fulness of Christ." That is the end, and God can never be satisfied with anything less than the fulness of His Son as repre- sented by the Church. The Church is to be the fulness of Him ; a full-grown Man—that is the Church. The pro- phetic ministry is unto that—the fulness of Christ, the finality of Christ, the all-inclusiveness of Christ. It is to be Christ, centre and circumference ; Christ, first and last ; Christ in general and Christ in every detail. And to see Christ by revelation means that you can never accept any- thing less or other. You have seen, and that has settled it. The way to reach God's end, then, is *seeing* by the Holy Spirit, and that seeing is the basis of this prophetic ministry.

I think that that perhaps is enough to show what I said earlier, that if we see the nature of the ministry, we at once see what the vessel is. The vessel may be individuals fulfilling such a ministry, or it may be collective. Later we may say something more about the vessel, but let us not now think technically, in terms of apostles and prophets and so on, as offices. Let us think of them as vital *functions.* God is concerned that the man and the function are identi-

cal, not the man and a professional or official position
with a title, whatever the title may be. The vessel must
be *that,* and *that* must justify the vessel. We will not go
about advertising ourselves as prophets ; but God grant
that there may be raised up a prophetic ministry for a time
like this, when His whole purpose concerning His Son
is brought back into view amongst His people. That is
their need, and it is His.

CHAPTER TWO

THE MAKING OF A PROPHET

PROPHETIC MINISTRY is something which has not come in with time, but is eternal. It has come out of the eternal counsels.

Perhaps you wonder what that means. Well, we remember that, without any explanation or definition, something comes in right at the beginning and takes the place of government in the economy of God, and involves this very function. When Adam sinned and was expelled from the garden, the Word simply says, God " placed at the east of the garden of Eden the Cherubim . . . to keep the way of the tree of life " (Genesis iii. 24).

Who or what are the Cherubim? Where do they come from? We have heard nothing about them before ; no explanation of them is given. It simply is a statement. God put them there to guard the way of the tree of life. They have become the custodians of life, to hold things according to God's thought. For the thoughts of man's heart have departed from God's thoughts and have become evil ; everything has been marred ; and now the custodians of the Divine thought about the greatest of all things for man —Divine life, uncreated life—the custodians of that, the Cherubim, are placed there.

But later we are given to understand what the Cherubim are like : this symbolic, composite representation has a four-fold aspect—the lion, the ox, the man and the eagle ;

and we are given to understand very clearly that the predominant feature is the man. It is *a man*, really, with three other aspects, those of the lion, the ox, and the eagle. The lion is a symbol of kingship or dominion ; the ox, of service and sacrifice ; the eagle, of heavenly glory and mystery. The man, the predominant aspect of the Cherubim—what is that?

We know that throughout the Scriptures the man takes the place, in the Divine order of things, of the prophet, the representative of God. The representation of God's thoughts is *a man*. That was the intention in the creation of Adam in the image and likeness of God—to be the personal embodiment and expression of all God's thoughts. That is what man was created for. That is what we find in *the* Man, the Man who was God manifested in the flesh. He was the perfect expression of all God's thoughts.

Where has this symbolism of the Cherubim come from? It is simply brought in. It comes out from eternity. It is a Divine, an eternal thought, and it takes charge of things, to hold things for God. So that man—and we know that phrase "the Son of man"—is peculiarly related to the prophetic office, and the prophetic function is an eternal thing, which just comes in. It is, in its very nature, the representation of Divine thoughts, and it is to hold God's thoughts in purity and in fulness. That is the idea related to the man, to the prophet, and that is the prophetic function and nature.

THE IDENTITY OF THE PROPHET WITH HIS MESSAGE

But what does that carry with it? Here we come to the most important point of the whole. It is the absolute identity of the vessel with the vessel's ministry. Prophetic ministry is not something that you can take up. It is something that you *are*. No academy can make you a prophet. Samuel instituted the schools of the prophets. They were for two purposes—one, the dissemination of religious knowledge, and the other, the writing up of the chronicles of religious history. In Samuel's day there was no open vision; the people had lost the Word of God. They had to be taught the Word of God again, and the chronicles of the ways of God had to be written up and put on record for future generations, and the schools of the prophets were instituted in the main for that purpose. But there is a great deal of difference between those academic prophets and the living, anointed prophets. The academic prophets became members of a profession and swiftly degenerated into something unworthy. All the false prophets came from schools of prophets, and were accepted publicly on that ground. They had been to college and were accepted. But they were false prophets. Going to a religious college does not of itself make you a prophet of God.

My point is this—the identity of the vessel with its ministry is the very heart of Divine thought. A man is called to represent the thoughts of God, to represent them in what he *is*, not in something that he takes up as a form or line of ministry, not in something that he does. The vessel itself is the ministry and you cannot divide between the two.

THE NECESSITY FOR SELF-EMPTYING

That explains everything in the life of the great prophets. It explains the life of Moses, the prophet whom the Lord God raised up from among his brethren (Deut. xviii. 15, 18). Moses essayed to take up his life-work. He was a man of tremendous abilities, " learned in all the wisdom of the Egyptians " (Acts vii. 22), with great natural qualifications and gifts, and then somehow he got some conception of a life-work for God. It was quite true ; it was a true conception, a right idea ; he was very honest, there was no question at all about his motives ; but he essayed to take up that work on the basis of what he was naturally, with his own ability, qualifications and zeal, and on that basis disaster was allowed to come upon the whole thing.

Not so are prophets made ; not so can the prophetic office be exercised. Moses must go into the wilderness and for forty years be emptied out, until there is nothing left of all that as a basis upon which he can have confidence to do the work of God or fulfil any Divine commission. He was by nature a man " mighty in his words and works " ; and yet now he says, " I am not eloquent . . . I am slow of speech . . ." (Exodus iv. 10). There has been a tremendous undercutting of all natural facility and resource, and I do not think that Moses was merely disagreeable in his reply to God. He did not say in effect, ' You would not allow me to do it then, so I will not do it now.' I think he was a man who was under the Divine discipline and yet on top of it. A man who is really under things and who has become petulant does not respond to little opportunities of helping people. We get a glimpse of Moses at the beginning of his time in the wilderness (Exodus ii. 16, 17) which suggests that he was not of that kind. When there was difficulty at the well, over the watering of the flocks, if Moses had been in a bad mood, cantankerous, disagreeable because the Lord had not seemed to stand by him in Egypt, he probably would have sat somewhere apart and looked on and done nothing to help. But he went readily to help, in a good spirit, doing all he

could. He was on top of his trial. Little things indicate
where a man is.

We go through times of trial and test under the hand
of God, and it is so easy to get into that frame of mind
which says in effect, 'The Lord does not want us, He
need not have us!' We let everything go, we do not care
about anything ; we have gone down under our trials and
we are rendered useless. I do not believe the Lord ever
comes to a person like that to take them up. Elijah,
dispirited, fled to the wilderness, and to a cave in the
mountains ; but he had to get somewhere else before the
Lord could do anything with him. " What doest thou *here,*
Elijah?" (I Kings xix. 9). The Lord never comes to a man
and recommissions him when he is in despair. ' God shall
forgive thee all but thy despair ' (F. W. H. Myers, ' *St.
Paul* ')—because despair is lost faith in God, and God can
never do anything with one who has lost faith.

Moses was emptied to the last drop, and yet he was not
angry or disagreeable with God. What was the Lord doing? He was making a prophet. Beforehand, the man
would have taken up an office, he would have made the
prophetic function serve him, he would have used it. There
was no inward, vital relationship between the man and
the work that he was to do ; they were two separate things ;
the work was objective to the man. At the end of forty
years in the wilderness he is in a state for this to become
subjective ; something has been done. There has been
brought about a state which makes the man fit to be a
living expression of the Divine thought. He has been
emptied of his own thoughts to make room for God's
thoughts ; he has been emptied of his own strength, that
all the energy should be of God.

Is not that perhaps the meaning of the fire and the bush

that was not consumed? It is a parable, maybe a larger parable, but I think in the immediate application it was saying something to Moses. ' Moses, you are a very frail creature, a common bush of the desert, a bit of ordinary humanity, nothing at all of resource in yourself ; but there is a resource, which can carry you on and on, and you can be maintained, without being consumed, by an energy that is not your own—the Spirit of God, the energy of God.' That was the great lesson this prophet had to learn. ' I cannot !' ' All right ', said the Lord, ' but I AM.'

A great deal is made of the natural side of many of the Lord's servants, and usually with tragic results. A lot is made of Paul. ' What a great man Paul was naturally, what intellect he had, what training, what tremendous abilities !' That may all be true, but ask Paul what value it was to him when he was right up against a spiritual situation. He will cry, " Who is sufficient for these things? . . . Our sufficiency is from God " (II Cor. ii. 16 ; iii. 5). Paul was taken through experiences where he, like Moses, despaired of life. He said, " We . . . had the sentence of death within ourselves, that we should not trust in ourselves, but in God which raiseth the dead " (II Cor. i. 9).

A MESSAGE INWROUGHT BY ACTUAL EXPERIENCE

You see, the principle is at work all the time, that God is going to make the ministry and the minister identical. You see it in all the prophets. The Lord stood at nothing. He took infinite pains. He worked even through domestic life, the closest relationships of life. Think of the tragedy of Hosea's domestic life. Think of Ezekiel, whose wife the Lord took away in death at a stroke. The Lord said, ' Get up in the morning, anoint your face, allow not the slightest suggestion of mourning or tragedy to be detected ; go out as always before, as though nothing had happened ; show yourself to the people, go about with a bright countenance, provoke them to enquire what you mean by such outrageous behaviour.' The Lord brought this heartbreak upon him and then required him to act thus. Why? Ezekiel was a prophet ; he had got to embody his message, and the message was this : ' Israel, God's wife, has become lost to God, dead to God, and Israel takes no notice of it ; she goes on the same as ever, as though nothing had happened.' The prophet must bring it home by his own experience. God is working the thing right in. He works it in in deep and terrible ways in the life of His servant to produce ministry.

God is not allowing us to take up things and subjects. If we are under the Holy Ghost, He is going to make us prophets ; that is, He is going to make the prophecy a thing that has taken place in us, so that what we say is only making vocal something that has been going on, that has been done in us. God has been doing it through years in strange, deep, terrible ways in some lives, standing at nothing, touching everything ; and the vessel, thus wrought upon, is the message. People do not come to *hear* what you have to *teach*. They have come to *see* what you *are,* to see that thing which has been wrought by God. What a price the prophetic instrument has to pay !

So Moses went into the wilderness, to the awful undoing of his natural life, his natural mentality ; to be brought to zero ; to have the thing wrought in him. And was God justified?—for after all it was a question of resource for the future. Oh, the strain that was going to bear down upon that life ! Sometimes Moses well-nigh broke ; at times he did crack under the strain. " I am not able to bear all this people alone, because it is too heavy for me " (Num. xi. 14). What was his resource? Oh, if it had been the old resource of Egypt he would not have stood it for a year. He could not stand provocation in Egypt, he must rise up and fight. He broke down morally and spiritually under that little strain away back there forty years before. What would he do with these rebels? How long would he put up with them? A terrific strain was going to bear down upon him, and only a deep inwrought thing, something that had been done inside, would be enough to carry through when it was a case of standing against the stream for God's full thought.

With us, too, the strain may be terrific ; oft-times there will come the very strong temptation—' Let go a little, compromise a little, do not be so utter ; you will get more open doors if you will only broaden out a bit ; you can have a lot more if you ease up!' What is going to save you in that hour of temptation? The only thing is that God has done this thing in you. It is part of your very being, not something you can give up ; it is you, your very life. That is the only thing. God knew what He was doing with Moses. The thing had got to be so much one with the man that there was no dividing between them. The man *was* the prophetic ministry.

He was rejected by his brethren ; they would not have him. " Who made thee a prince and a judge over us?" (Ex. ii. 14). That is the human side of it. But there was the Divine side. It was of God that he went into the wilderness for forty years. It had to be, from God's side. It looked as though it was man's doing. But it was not so. These two things went together. Rejection by his brethren was all in line with the sovereign purpose of God. It was the only way in which God got the opportunity He needed to reconstitute this man. The real preparation of this prophet took place during the time that his brethren repudiated him. Oh, the sovereignty of God, the wonderful sovereignty of God! A dark time, a deep time ; a breaking, crushing, grinding time ; emptied out. It seems as if everything is going, that nothing will be left. Yet all that is God's way of making prophetic ministry.

A MESSENGER DIVINELY ATTESTED

I expect that Moses at the beginning would have been very legalistic, laying down the law—' You must do this and that '—and so on ; an autocrat or despot. When, after those years, we find him coming off the wheel, out of the hands of the Potter, he is said to be " very meek, above all the men that were upon the face of the earth " (Num. xii. 3), and God could stand by him then. He could not stand by him on that day when he rose up in a spirit of pride, arrogance, self-assertiveness. God had to let that work itself out to its inevitable consequence. But when Moses, as the meekest of men, the broken, humble, selfless man, was challenged by others as to his office—at such a time Moses did not stand up for his position, his rights ; he just handed the matter over to the Lord. His attitude was, ' We will allow the Lord to decide. I have no personal position to preserve : if the Lord has made me His prophet, let Him show it. I am prepared to go out of office if it is not of the Lord.' What a different spirit! And the Lord did stand by him marvellously and mightily on those occasions, and terribly so for those who opposed themselves (Numbers xii. 2ff.; xvi. 3ff.).

PROPHETIC MINISTRY A LIFE, NOT TEACHING

Well, what is a prophet? what is the prophetic function? It is this. God takes hold of a vessel (it may be individual or it may be collective: the function of prophetic ministry may move through a people, as it did through Israel), and He takes that vessel through a deep history, breaking and undoing, disillusioning, revolutionising the whole mentality, so that things which were held fiercely, assertively, are no longer so held. There is developed a wonderful pliableness, adjustableness, teachableness. Everything that was merely objective as to the work of God, as to Divine truth, as to orthodoxy or fundamentalism; all that was held so strongly, in an objective, legalistic way, as to what is right and wrong in methods—it is all dealt with, all broken. There is a new conception entirely, a new outlook upon things; no longer a formal system, something outside you which you take up, but something wrought in an inward way in the vessel. It is what the vessel is that is its ministry. It is not what it has accepted of doctrine and is now teaching.

Oh, to get free of all that horrible realm of things! It is a wretched realm, that of adopting teachings, taking on interpretations, being known because such and such is your line of things. Oh, God deliver us! Oh, to be brought to the place where it is a matter of *life*—of what God has really done in us, made of us! First He has pulverised us, and then He has reconstructed us on a new spiritual principle, and that expresses itself in ministry: what is said is coming from what has been going on behind, perhaps for years and even right up to date.

Do you see the law of prophetic function? It is that God keeps anointed vessels abreast of truth by experience. Every bit of truth that they give out in word is something that has had a history. They went down into the depths and they were saved by that truth. It was their life and

therefore it is a part of them. That is the nature of prophetic ministry.

A PROPHET, TOLERANT BUT UNCOMPROMISING

Reverting to what I was saying about the change in
Moses : you can see a reflection of it in the case of Samuel.
I think Samuel is one of the most beautiful and loveable
characters in the Old Testament, and he is called a prophet. Do you notice that although his own heart is utterly
devoted to God's highest and fullest thought, and inwardly
he has no compromise whatever, yet he shows a marvellous charity toward Saul during those early months? (It
seems not to have gone much beyond a year, the first year
of Saul's reign, during which it seems that Saul really did
seek to show some semblance of good.) And yet you must
remember that Saul represents the denial of the highest
of all things—the direct and immediate government of
God. Such government was repudiated by Israel in favour
of a king—" Make us a king to judge us like all the
nations ", they said. God said to Samuel : " They have not
rejected thee, but they have rejected me " (I Samuel viii.
5 — 7).

Kingship was a Divine principle as much as prophecy
was. The lion is there with the man. The monarch, representing God's thought of dominion, is there. But with
Saul it is on a lower level. His coming in represented the
bringing down of that Divine thought to the level of the
world : " like all the nations "—a Divine thought taken
hold of by carnal men, dragged down to the world level ;
and Samuel knew it. In his heart he could not accept that,
and he complained to God about it ; he was against this
thing, for he saw what it meant. But how charitable he
was to Saul as long as he could be !

Why do I say that? Because there is a condition like that existing to-day. Divine things have been taken hold of by men carnally, and brought down to an earth level; the direct government of the Holy Spirit has been exchanged for committees and boards and so on. Men have set up the government in Divine things and are running things for God. The way of the New Testament, that in prayer and fasting the mind of the Lord is secured, is hardly known. Well, those who are spiritual, who know, who see, who understand, cannot accept that. But they must be very charitable. A true prophet, like Samuel, will be charitable as long as possible, until that wrong thing takes the pronounced and positive form of disobedience to light given. The Lord came to Saul through Samuel and gave him clearly to understand what he had to do. It was made known to him with unmistakable clearness what God required of him, and he was disobedient. Then Samuel said, ' No more charity with that!' He was implacable. " Because thou hast rejected the word of the Lord, he hath also rejected thee from being king" (I Samuel xv. 23). Samuel went as far as he could while the man did the best he could. That is charity.

Of course, types are always weak and imperfect, but you can see the truth there. The prophet Samuel showed a great deal of forbearance with things that were wrong, even while in his heart he could not accept them. He hoped that light would break and obedience follow and the situation be saved. We have to be very charitable to all that with which we do not agree.

The point is this—Moses had to learn that; he had to be made like that. We are better fitted to serve the Lord's purpose, we are truer prophets, when we can bear with things with which we do not agree, than when in our zeal we are iconoclasts, and seek only to destroy the offending thing. The Lord says, ' That will not do.'

In all that we have said we have emphasized only one thing—that prophetic ministry is a function. Its function is to hold everything in relation to God's full thought—but not as holding a ' line ' of things, in an objective and legalistic way. You do not take something up. You can only do it truly as God has wrought into you that thing for which you are going to stand, and in so far as it has been revealed in you through experience, through the handling of God—God has taken you through it, and you know it like that. It is not that you have achieved something, but rather that you have been broken in the process. Now you are fit for something in the Lord.

CHAPTER THREE

A VOICE WHICH MAY BE MISSED

" For they that dwell in Jerusalem, and their rulers, be-
cause they knew him not, nor the voices of the prophets
which are read every sabbath, fulfilled them by condemn-
ing him " (Acts xiii. 27).

THE ABOVE STATEMENT as a whole carries a significance
which embraces a very great deal of history, but its direct
and immediate implication is that if the people referred
to—the dwellers in Jerusalem and their rulers—had been
in the good of the most familiar things, they would have
behaved very differently from the way in which they did
behave. Every week, Sabbath by Sabbath, extending over
a very great number of years, they heard things read ; but
eventually, because of their failure to recognise what they
were hearing, they acted in a way entirely opposed to those
very things, though under the sovereignty of God fulfilling
them in so doing.

Surely that is a word of warning. It represents a very
terrible possibility—to hear repeatedly the same things,
and not to recognise their significance ; to behave in a way
quite contrary to our own interests, making for our own
undoing, when it might have been otherwise.

The point is this—that there is a voice in the prophets
which may be missed, a meaning which may not be appre-

hended, and the results may be disastrous for the people concerned. " The voices of the prophets ": that suggests that there is something beyond the mere things that the prophet says. There is a ' voice '. We may hear a sound, we may hear the words, and yet not hear the voice ; that is something extra to the thing said. That is the statement here, that week by week, month after month, and year after year, men read the prophets audibly, and the people who heard the reading did not hear the voices. It is the *voice* of the prophets that we need to hear.

As you go through this thirteenth chapter of the Acts you are able to recognise that this little fragment is in a very crucial context. This chapter, to begin with, marks a development. There in Antioch were certain men, including Saul, and the Holy Ghost said: " Separate me Barnabas and Saul for the work whereunto I have called them." That was a new development, a moving out, something far-reaching, very momentous ; but you are not through the chapter before you come upon another crisis, which became inevitable when in a certain place a great crowd came together, and the Jews, refusing to be obedient to the Word, stirred up a revolt. The Apostles made this pronouncement: " It was necessary that the word of God should first be spoken to you. Seeing ye thrust it from you, and judge yourselves unworthy of eternal life, lo, we turn to the Gentiles " (vs. 46) ; and they quoted a prophet (Isaiah xlix. 6) for their authority: " I have set thee for a light of the Gentiles." These were epochs in the history of the Church ; and the Jews, as a whole, were turned from, and the Gentiles in a very deliberate way were recognised and brought in, because of this very thing—that the Jews had heard these prophets Sabbath by Sabbath but had not heard their voices.

Big things hang upon hearing the voice. Failure to hear may lead to irreparable loss. Very big things concerning Israel have come into the centuries since the time of Acts xiii. It is not my intention to launch out on matters of prophecy concerning the Jews, but my point is this. On the one hand, it was no small thing to fail to hear the voices of the prophets. On the other hand, you notice that the Gentiles rejoiced. It says here, " As the Gentiles heard this, they were glad, and glorified the word of God." Well, on both sides, it is a great thing to fail to hear what could be heard if there were an ear for hearing, and it is a great thing to hear and give heed. I think that is a sufficiently serious foundation and background to engage our attention.

OLD TESTAMENT PROPHETS IN THE NEW TESTAMENT

Let us now look more closely at this matter of " the voices of the prophets ". A fact of very great significance is this, that the prophets have such a large place in the New Testament. I wonder if you have taken account of how large that place is. You will not need to be reminded of how largely the Gospels call upon the major prophets, as they are called. " That it might be fulfilled which was spoken by the prophet . . ."—how often that statement alone occurs in the Gospels. It came in from the birth of the Lord Jesus, and in that connection alone on several occasions the major prophets are quoted. But when you move from the Gospels into the Acts and the Epistles, you move largely into what are called the minor prophets— not minor because they were of less account than the others, but because the record of their writings is smaller. It is tremendously impressive and significant that these

minor prophets should be drawn upon so extensively in
the New Testament; they are quoted over fifty times.

PROPHETS MEN OF VISION

From that general significance, two factors emerge. One
as to the prophets themselves: why do they have so large
a place in the New Testament? Well, the answer to that
will be largely another question. What do prophets signify? They are the 'seers' (I Samuel ix. 9); they are the men
who see and, in seeing, act as eyes for the people of God.
They are the men of vision; and their large place in the
New Testament surely therefore indicates how tremendously important spiritual vision is for the people of God
throughout this dispensation. Of course, the other thing
is the vision itself, but I am not concerned just now to
speak about what the vision was and is—that, with other
aspects, may come later. At the moment, I feel the Lord
is concerned with this factor—the tremendous importance
of spiritual vision if the people of God are to fulfil their
vocation. It resolves itself into a matter solely of vision unto vocation, and the vocation will not be fulfilled without
vision.

VISION IMPARTS PURPOSE TO LIFE

So for a moment let us dwell upon the place of vision—
and you will not think that I am talking about 'vision-
ariness'. No, it is something specific, it is *the* vision, it
is something clearly defined. The prophets knew what they
were talking about—not merely abstract ideas, but something very definite. Vision is something quite specific,
something with which the Lord is concerned and which

has become a mighty, dominating thing in the life of those who have it; clear, distinct, precise, specific; taking hold of and mastering and dominating them, so that the whole purpose of existence itself is gathered into it. Such people are at the place where they know why they have an existence, they know the purpose for which they are alive and are able to say what it is, and their horizon is bounded by that thing; they, with their whole life in all its aspects, are gathered into that, poised to that. It is an object which governs everything for them. It is not just living on this earth and doing many things and getting through somehow; but everything that has a place in life is linked with this definite, distinct, all-governing objective. It is such a vision which gives meaning to life.

It is not necessary for me to take you through Israel's history as governed by that very truth. You know quite well that, when Israel was in a right position, that is how things were—focused, definite, with everybody centred in one object. And, before we go further, let us say again that all these prophets—men who were the eyes of God for a people, and signifying to that people God's thought and purpose concerning them, their Divine vocation, God's interpretation of their very existence—these prophets who embodied that are all brought into the New Testament dispensation and into the Church, with this clear implication, that that is how the Church is to be if it is to get through. The Church is to be a *seeing* thing, dominated by a specific object and vision, knowing why it exists, having no doubt about it, and poised in utter abandonment thereto, bringing all other things in life into line with that. Our attitude has to be that, while in this world we necessarily have to do this and that, to earn our living and do our daily work, yet there is something governing all else:

there is a Divine vision. These things have to bend to that one Divine end.

That is the first implication of the fact that the prophets have such a large place in this dispensation. We cannot now stay to follow that out in detail from the Word, but it would be very helpful to go through the New Testament, and see how the bringing in of the prophets is made to apply to the varied aspects of the Church's life. It is very impressive.

VISION A UNIFYING FACTOR

The prophets are governing this dispensation in this way. This vision, *the* vision, was the very cohesiveness and strength of Israel. When the vision was clearly before them, when their eyes were opened and they were seeing, when they were in line with God's purpose, when they were governed by that end to which God had called them, they were one people, made one by the vision. They had a single eye. That little phrase, " If . . . thine eye be single . . ." (Matthew vi. 22), has a great deal more in it than we have recognised. A single eye—it unifies the whole life and conduct ; it will unify all your behaviour. If you are a man or a woman of one idea, everything will be brought into that. Of course, that is not always a very happy thing, though in this case it is. People who are obsessed and, as we say, ' have a bee in their bonnet ', with nothing else to talk about but one thing, are often very trying people. But there is a right way, a Divine way, in which the people of God should be people of a single eye, a single idea ; and that singleness of eye brings all the faculties into co-ordination.

During the rare periods when Israel was like that, they

were a marvellously unified people. On the other hand, you can see how, when the vision faded and failed, they disintegrated, became people of all kinds of divided and schismatic interests and activities, quarrelling amongst themselves. How true is the word: "Where there is no vision, the people perish (go to pieces)" (Proverbs xxix. 18). And so it was with Israel. See them in the days of Eli, when there was no open vision. What a disintegrated, dis-united people they were! That happened many times. The vision was a solidifying, cohesive power, making a people solidly one, and in that oneness was their strength, and they were irresistible. See them over Jordan in their assault upon Jericho! See them moving triumphantly on! While they were governed by one object, none could stand before them. Their strength was in their unity, and their unity was in their vision. The enemy knows what he is doing in destroying or confusing vision: he is dividing the people of God.

VISION A DEFENSIVE POWER

What a defensive power is vision like that! What little chance the enemy has when we are a people set upon one thing! If we have all sorts of divided and personal interests, the enemy can make awful havoc. He does not get a chance when everybody is centred upon one Divine object. He has to divide us somehow, distract us, dis-integrate us, before he can accomplish his work of hindering God's end. All those features of self-pity, self-interest, which are ever seeking to get in and spoil, will never get in while vision is clear and we are focused upon it as one people. It is tremendously defensive. The Apostle spoke about being "in diligence not slothful; fervent in

spirit ; serving the Lord " (Romans xii. 11). Moffatt trans-
lates " fervent in spirit " as " maintaining the spiritual
glow ". Being centred upon an object wholeheartedly is
a wonderfully protective thing. Such a condition in a
people closes the breaches and resists the encroachments
and impingements of all kinds of things which would distract and paralyse.

VISION MAKES FOR DEFINITENESS AND GROWTH

Vision was like a flame with the prophets. You have to
recognise that about them, at any rate—that these men
were flames of fire. There was nothing neutral about
them ; they were aggressive, never passive. Vision has that
effect. If you have really seen what the Lord is after, you
cannot be half-hearted. You cannot be passive if you see.
Find the person who has seen, and you find a positive life.
Find the person who does not see, is not sure, is not clear,
and you have a neutral, a negative, one that does not
count. These prophets were men like flames of fire because
they saw. And when Israel was in the good of the Divine
calling, Israel was like that—positive, aggressive. When
the vision faded, they came to a standstill, turned in upon
themselves, went round and round in circles, ceased to
get anywhere.

This aggressiveness, this positiveness, which is the fruit
of having seen, provides the Lord with the ground that
He needs for a right kind of training and discipline. It
does not mean that we shall never make mistakes. You
will see in the New Testament—and I hope you will not
charge me with heresy—that even a man as crucified as
Paul could make mistakes. Peter, a man so used and so
chastened, could make mistakes. Yes, apostles could make

mistakes. And prophets could make mistakes. "What doest thou here, Elijah?" (I Kings xix. 9). 'You have no business to be here '—that is what it means. Yes, prophets and apostles could make mistakes, and they did ; but there is this about it—because they had seen, and were utterly abandoned to that which they had seen of the Lord's mind, the Lord was abundantly able to come in on their mistakes and sovereignly overrule them and teach His servants something more of Himself and His ways.

Now, you never find that with people who are indefinite. The indefinite people, those who are not meaning business, who are not abandoned, never do learn anything of the Lord. It is the people who commit themselves, who let go and go right out in the direction of whatever measure of light the Lord has given them, who, on the one hand, find their mistakes—the mistakes of their very zeal— taken hold of by Divine sovereignty and overruled ; and, on the other hand, are taught by the Lord through their very mistakes what His thoughts are, how He does things, and how He does not do them. If we are going to wait in indefiniteness and uncertainty and do nothing until we know it all, we shall learn nothing.

Have you not noticed that it is the men and women whose hearts are aflame for God, who have seen something truly from the Lord and have been mightily gripped by what they have seen, who are the people that are learning? The Lord is teaching them ; He does not allow their blunders and their mistakes to engulf them in destruction. He sovereignly overrules, and in the long run they are able to say, ' Well, I made some awful blunders, but the Lord marvellously took hold of them and turned them to good account.' To be like this, with vision which gathers up our whole being and masters us, provides the Lord with the ground for looking after us even when we make mistakes —because His interests are at stake, His interests and not our own are the concern of our heart. The prophets and the apostles learned to know the Lord in wonderful ways by their very mistakes, for they were the mistakes, not of their own stubborn self-will, but of a real passion for God and for what He had shown them as to His purpose.

VISION GIVES ASCENDENCY TO GOD'S PEOPLE

And then note that the very ascendency of Israel was based upon vision. They were called of God to be an ascendent people, above all the peoples of the earth, set in the midst of the nations as a spiritually governmental vessel. The Lord did promise that no nation should be able to take headship over them. His thought for them was that they should be " the head, and not the tail " (Deut. xxviii. 13). But that was not going to happen willy-nilly, irrespective of their condition and position. It was when they had the vision before them clearly, corporately, as an entire people—dominated, mastered, unified by the vision— it was then that they were head and not tail, it was then that they were in the ascendent.

And that brings in these prophets again. (We think now of the later prophets of Israel.) Why the prophets? Because Israel had lost their position. Assyria, Babylon and the rest were taking ascendency over them because they had lost their vision. It is in the minor prophets, as they are called, that you have so much about this very matter. " My people are destroyed for lack of knowledge " (Hosea iv. 6). That is a note to which all the prophets are tuned. Why this state of things? Why is Israel now the underdog of the nations? The answer is—lost vision. The prophet comes to try to get them back to the place of the vision. The prophet has the vision, he is the eyes of the people: he is calling them back to that for which God chose them, to show them anew why He took them from among the nations.

VISION NEEDED BY EVERY CHILD OF GOD

All this is but an emphasis upon the place of vision. It may not get you very far; you may wonder what it all leads to. You are saying now, ' Well, what is the vision?' That is not the point at the moment; that can come later. The point is that that is the necessity, the absolute necessity, for the Church to-day—for you, for me; and let me say at once that, while it is pre-eminently a corporate thing—that is, it is something which is to be in a people, even though that people be but a remnant, a small number amongst all the people of God—while pre-eminently a corporate thing, it must also be personal. You and I individually must be in the place where we can say, ' I have seen, I know what God is after!'

If we were asked why the Church is as it is to-day, in so large a measure of impotence and disintegration, and what is needed to bring about an impact from heaven by means of the Church, could we say? Is it presumption to claim to be able to do that? The prophets knew; and remember that the prophets, whether they were of the Old Testament or of the New Testament, were not an isolated class of people, they were not some body apart, holding this in themselves officially. They were the very eyes of the body. They were, in the thought of God, *the people* of God. You know that principle; it is seen, for instance, in the matter of the High Priest. God looks upon the one

High Priest as Israel, and deals with all Israel on the ground of the condition of the High Priest, whether it be good or bad. If the High Priest is bad—" And he showed me Joshua the high priest . . . clothed with filthy garments " (Zechariah iii. 1 — 5)—that is Israel. God deals with Israel as one man.

The prophet is the same ; and that is why the prophet was so interwoven with the very condition and life of the people. Listen to the prophet Daniel praying. Personally he was not guilty ; personally he had not sinned as the nation had sinned ; but he took it all on himself and spoke as though it were his responsibility, as if he were the chief of sinners. These men were brought right into it. There is such a oneness between the prophets and the people in condition, in experience, in suffering, that they can never view themselves as officials apart from all that, as it were talking to it from the outside ; they are in it, they *are* it.

My meaning is this, that we are not to have vision brought to us by a class called ministers, prophets and apostles. They are here only to keep us alive to what we ought to be before God, how we ought to be ; constantly stirring us up and saying, ' Look here, this is what you ought to be.' It ought therefore to be, with every one of us personally, that we are in the meaning of this prophetic ministry. The Church is called to be a prophet to the nations. May I repeat my enquiry—it is a permissible question without admitting of any presumption—could you say what is needed by the Church to-day? Could you interpret the state of things, and explain truly by what the Lord has shown you in your own heart? I know the peril and dangers that may surround such an idea, but that is the very meaning of our existence. It will be in greater or lesser degree in every one of us, but, either more or less, we have the key to the situation. God needs people of that sort. It must be individual.

VISION CALLS FOR COURAGE

But remember it will call for immense courage. Oh, the courage of these prophets! —courage as over against compromise and policy. Oh, the ruinous effects of policy, of secondary considerations! ' How will it affect our opportunities if we are so definite? Will it not lessen our opportunities of serving the Lord if we take such a position?' That is policy, and it is a ruinous thing. Many a man who has seen something, and has begun to speak about what he has seen, has found such a reaction from his own brethren and amongst those where his responsibility lay, that he has drawn back. ' It is dangerous to pursue that any further.' Policy! No, there was nothing of that about the prophets. Are we committed because we have seen?

There will be cost; we may as well face it. There is a little fragment in Hebrews ix—" They were sawn asunder." A tradition says that that applied to the prophet Isaiah—that he was the one who was sawn asunder. Read Isaiah liii. There is nothing more sublime in all the literature of the Bible, and for that he was sawn asunder. Was he right? Well, we to-day stand on the ground, and in the good, of his rightness. But the devil does not like that, and so Isaiah was sawn asunder. There are tremendous values bound up with seeing, and with uncompromising abandonment to the vision, but there is very great cost also.

We will leave it there for the time being; but we must have dealings with the Lord and say, ' How much have I seen? After all I have heard of the prophets week by week, after all the conventions, the conferences, the meetings I have been attending, have I heard the *voice* of the prophets after all? I have heard the speakers give their messages and addresses: have I heard the voice? ' The effect will be far-reaching if we have. If we have not, it is time we got to the Lord about it. This must not go on! What happened in Acts xiii? Hearing they did not hear ; but where there was a hearing, oh, what tremendous things happened, what tremendous values came!

CHAPTER FOUR

A VISION THAT CONSTITUTES A VOCATION

*"For they that dwell in Jerusalem, and their rulers, be-
cause they knew him not, nor the voices of the 'prophets
which are read every sabbath, fulfilled them by condemning him" (Acts xiii. 27).*

WE POINTED OUT at the beginning of the previous
chapter that the above statement indicates that there
is something more to be heard than the audible reading
of the Word of God. " The voices of the prophets." What
were the prophets saying?—not, what were the actual
words used by the prophets, the sentences and statements,
the form of their pronouncements, but what did it all
amount to *in effect ?* These dwellers and rulers in Jerusalem could have quoted the prophets without difficulty :
they probably could have recited the contents of all the
books of the prophets. They were well-drilled in the content of the Old Testament Scriptures, but they never
stopped and asked the simple questions : ' What does it
amount to? What really is the implication? What were
these men after?' And because they never did that, they
never got further than the letter.

VOCATION MISSED BECAUSE VISION LOST

We are asking those questions now. What is that which
is within and behind and deeper than the written and

51

spoken utterances of the prophets? We know that the prophets were dealing with a situation which by no means represented the Lord's mind regarding His people. I could
make it stronger than that, and say the situation was very
far from the Lord's thought; but I have present conditions in mind, rather than any extreme state of things,
and so I simply say that the condition did not then, nor
does it now, really represent the Lord's mind and intention where His people were and are concerned. The prophets were dealing with such a situation, and, because it
was like that, the real vocation of the people of God was
not being fulfilled. They were failing in that for which the
Lord had really brought them into being. Whereas they
ought to have been a people of tremendous spiritual
strength in the midst of the nations, with a real impact
of God upon the nations, with a note of great authority
which had to be taken account of—" Thus saith the
Lord ", declared in such a way that people really had to
heed—whereas it ought to have been like that, they were
failing. There was weakness and failure. The prophets
sought to get down to the root of that situation, to get
behind that deplorable condition and that tragic failure.
To get there, of course, they had to work their way
through a lot of positive factors in the condition. There
were all the things to which the prophets referred—sins
and so on; but the prophets were solid as one man on one
particular thing, that back of these conditions, resulting
in this main failure, the cause was lost vision. The people
had lost their original vision, the vision which had at one
time been clearly before them.

When God laid His hand upon them and brought them
out of Egypt, they had a vision. They saw the purpose and
intention of God. It became the exultant note of their

song on the farther side of the Red Sea. I am not going to stay for the moment with what that purpose was. But they were a people to whom God had given a vision of His purpose concerning them, both as to themselves and as to their vocation. They had lost it, and this was the result; and the prophets, in dealing with that, lighted solidly upon this one thing: 'Your vocation in its fulness of realisation and accomplishment rests upon your vision, and fulness of vocation requires fulness of vision.' That means that if your vision becomes less than God's fulness, you will only go so far, and then you will stop. If you are going right on and through to all that God meant in constituting you His vessel, you must have fulness of vision; God is never satisfied with anything less than fulness. The very fact that you cannot go any further than your vision leads you is God's way of saying, 'You must have fulness of vision if you are coming to fulness of purpose and realisation.'

Now, that is the very foundation of the thing with which we are occupied just now. The prophets were always speaking about this matter. We previously quoted Hosea iv. 6: "My people are destroyed for lack of knowledge: because thou hast rejected knowledge, I will also reject thee, that thou shalt be no priest to me." That is only saying in other words, 'My people go to pieces for lack of vision; you have closed your eyes to My purpose which I presented to you; I have no further use for you'; and that is a very strong statement. It links with another passage: "Israel is swallowed up: now are they among the nations as a vessel wherein none delighteth" (Hosea viii. 8, A.R.V.).

If you want to get the full force of that, look at a word in Jeremiah's prophecies. "Is this man Coniah a despised broken vessel? is he a vessel wherein none delighteth? wherefore are they cast out, he and his seed, and are cast into the land which they know not? O earth, earth, earth, hear the word of the Lord. Thus saith the Lord, Write ye this man childless, a man that shall not prosper in his days ; for no more shall a man of his seed prosper, sitting upon the throne of David, and ruling in Judah " (Jer. xxii. 28 — 30, A.R.V.). " Israel . . . among the nations as a vessel wherein none delighteth." " Coniah . . . a vessel wherein none delighteth . . . Write ye this man childless." There is no future for a vessel like that. We might well say of Israel as of Coniah, " Write this man childless." That is an end. A continuation, going right through without that arrest, demands fulness of vision.

VISION, NOT KNOWLEDGE OF FACTS, QUALIFIES FOR VOCATION

Do give heed to this, especially my younger brothers and sisters in Christ. The fulfilment of that into which you are called through the grace of God—what you may call the service of God, the work of the Lord ; what we will sum up as Divine vocation—*must* rest upon a vision which the Lord has given you : a vision, of course, that is not just something in itself but is *the* vision which He has given concerning His Church. You must have that. Then the measure in which you will go right on and through to fulness will be the measure of your vision—the measure in which you have come personally to possess that Divine vision. There can be all sorts of things less than that which lead you into Christian work. You may hear an appeal for workers, an appeal for missionaries, an appeal to service, based upon some Scripture—" Go ye into all the world, and preach the gospel "—and so on. And with the accompaniments of that appeal you may be moved, stirred up, feel very solemn ; something may happen in the realm of your emotions, your feelings, your reason, and you may take that as a Divine call. Now, I am not saying that no one has ever served the Lord properly and truly on that basis : do not misunderstand me : but I do want to say there can be all that, and in a very intense form, and yet it can be not your own but someone else's vision which has been passed over to you, and that will not do.

' But ', you say, ' there is the Scripture—" Go ye into all the world, and preach the gospel ".' Remember, those to whom those words were addressed had all the facts about Christ—the incarnation, the virgin birth, His life, His teaching, His miracles, His Cross, and all the accompanying heavenly attestations. Some of those very men —John's disciples—were there when the voice from heaven said, " This is my beloved Son ". Others were on the mountain when again the voice said, " This is my beloved Son ". They saw the transfiguration, and they saw Him in resurrection. Is that not enough with which to go out to the world—all that mass of mighty facts? Surely they can go and proclaim what they know? But no— " Tarry ye in Jerusalem ".

What was it eventually that constituted them men who could fulfil and obey that command to go? ' Well ', you say, ' of course it was the presence of the Holy Spirit.' Perfectly true. But was there not something else? Why the forty days after His resurrection? Do you not think that they were getting through the externals, the events, and *seeing* something—seeing what no human eye could see, what could never be seen by any amount of objective demonstration? If the Apostle Paul is anything to go

by in this matter, he will tell us perfectly plainly that his
whole life and ministry and commission were based upon
one thing: " It was the good pleasure of God . . . to reveal his Son in me, that I might preach him among the
Gentiles ". " I make known to you, brethren, as touching the gospel which was preached by me, that it is not
after man. For neither did I receive it from man, nor was
I taught it, but it came to me through revelation of Jesus
Christ ". (Galatians i. 15, 16 ; 11, 12.)

All the other things may be facts which we possess by
reading our New Testament. We have it all and we may
believe it as the substance of Christianity. That does not
constitute us missionaries to go out and proclaim the facts
of Christ—facts though they be. That is not it. How many
have done so! How far have they gone? They go so far
and then stop. We cannot stay to dwell upon the limitation. Dear friends, there is terrible limitation in the
Church just now, limitation of the knowledge of the
Lord, even on the part of many who have been the Lord's
servants for a long period of years. There are many
Christians, even of years' standing, to whom it is actually
difficult to talk about the things of the Lord.

THE VISION—GOD'S FULL PURPOSE IN REDEMPTION

But reverting to Israel: you do not find anything concerning Israel that suggests or indicates that they came
out of Egypt, and were in the wilderness and later in the
land, to declare as their gospel that God brought them
out of the land of Egypt. That was not their message. Of
course, it is recounted many times, but that was not their
message, not what they were proclaiming. What was it
that was always in their view? It was what they were

brought out for. It was God's vision in bringing them out. So many of us have settled down to preach just the ' coming out ' side—salvation from sin, from the world. It goes just so far, but the Church does not get very far with that. It is good, it is right, of course ; it is a part of the whole ; but it is only a part. It is the full vision that is needed to go right through. Oh, the pathos associated with the lives of many of the Lord's servants! They come to a standstill, in a realm of limited life and power and influence, because their vision is so small. Is that not true?

What am I saying to you? First of all, if you are going right through, to serve the Lord in any full way, you must have revealed to your own heart God's purpose concerning His Son. You will have to be able to say that God has ' revealed His Son in you ', in this sense, that you see, not merely your own deliverance from sin, but God's purpose concerning His Son unto which you are saved—the big thing, the full thing. You are only a fragment in it. That is the basis of service, of vocation ; and these very Apostles were held back until there broke upon them the full blaze of the meaning of Christ risen and ascended —the vision of the glorified Christ and all that that signified in the eternal purpose of God. Then they went out, and we find their message was always, not the gospel of God concerning personal salvation, but " the gospel of God . . . concerning his Son ", Jesus Christ. They had seen, not the historic Jesus, but the glorified Christ of God ; and they had not just seen Him as an objective vision, but His true significance had broken in upon them.

What a change it represented from the old days, when they were always thinking in terms of the coming Messiah who would set up a temporal kingdom on this earth, with themselves seated on His right hand and on His left! They

would be notable people down here on this earth, and
would oust the Romans from their country! That thing on
the earth was their full and only vision—fighting with
literal arms, revolting against literal usurpers of their
country.

But oh, what a vast change when they saw His kingdom! Now, the thing which had held them in its grip
simply went, not to be thought of any longer. Seeing His
kingdom! He had said, "There are some of them that
stand here, who shall in no wise taste of death, till they
see the Son of man coming in his kingdom" (Matthew
xvi. 28). What is the kingdom? It is Christ, far above all
rule and authority, the centre and the goal of all Divine
counsels from eternity. That is language, of course—mere
words; but the import needs to be apprehended. You
must have vision in your own heart before you can be
a servant of God who will get very far, and you have to
have growing vision in order to get right through. Come
back to Hosea. "My people are destroyed for lack of
knowledge" (Hosea iv. 6). What does he say a little
later? "Let us know, let us follow on to know the Lord"
(Hosea vi. 3). It is growing, progressive vision that brings
us through to God's full end. It must be like that—not
being contented with two or three facts about Christ and
salvation, but having the eyes of our hearts enlightened
to see Him.

What I am saying, of course, is a statement of facts.
I cannot give you anything, I cannot bring you into it;
but I can, I trust, influence you a little in the direction
of going to the Lord and saying, 'Now, Lord, if Thou
needest me, I am available, I am at Thy disposal; but
Thou must lay the foundation, and open my eyes, and
give me the requisite vision that will mean that I do not

only go out and preach things about Christ.' Something very much more than that is needed.

That is the first thing, and it applies to us all, not only to those who are going out into what we call 'full-time service '.

ISRAEL'S VOCATION—TO EXPRESS GOD'S PRESENCE AMONG THE NATIONS

Saying that, I am able to come to the next thing for the moment. What was the vision that Israel had lost and to which the prophets were seeking to bring the people back? The vision was this—the very vocation for which God had laid His hand upon Israel, the meaning of their existence as Israel. What was that?

The movement of God was like this. Here are nations and peoples spreading all over the earth. Out from those nations God takes one solitary individual, Abram, and places him, so to speak, right at the centre of the nations. That is the spiritual geography of it. And then God raises up from that man a seed, and constitutes his seed a nation right in the midst of the nations ; distinct from the nations, perfectly distinct, but in the midst. Then God constitutes that nation on heavenly principles—a corporate body constituted on heavenly, Divine, spiritual principles, with God Himself in the midst—with the result that all the other nations gather round to look on.

And what do those nations take account of? Not of the preaching of this nation in their midst ; you have nothing about their preaching at all—that is, the proclaiming of doctrines and truths. But the onlookers become aware that God, the only true and living God, is there. There is no mistaking it, they cannot get away from it, they have to

recognise it: God is there. Because this people is so constituted, God is there, and there is a registration of God
all around, wherever these people come. Ah, even before
they come, something is beginning to happen. Listen to
Rahab! What did she say to the spies? Israel has not arrived yet, but she says, ' We know all about you. We know
what you signify. We have heard all about it.' Already
the fear of this people is ahead of them. There is something of spiritual power there which does not have to be
preached in words. The people are there, with God in their
midst—because God has His heavenly thoughts and principles as the very constitution of their life. He is there ;
the rest follows.

Now I have gathered into that statement the whole of
the Bible, Old and New Testaments. As to the Old Testament, what was Israel's Divine vocation? Not primarily
to say things about God, but to be as God in the midst of
the nations. " God is in the midst of her ; she shall not be
moved " (Psalm xlvi. 5). ' The Lord is here!' How much
that counted for! That was their vocation. You may say
that in the Old Testament it was type ; but oh, it was much
more than type, it was very real ; it was a fact.

THE CHURCH'S VOCATION—TO EXPRESS THE LORDSHIP
OF CHRIST

When we come into the New Testament we find ourselves in the presence of a double development. God is
here present in the Person of His Son, Jesus Christ. His
name is Emmanuel—' God with us '—and all who have
to do with Him have to do with God in a very personal
and immediate way. He claims that His very physical body
is the temple of God. Then, through His death, resurrec-

tion, and ascension, He returns in the Person of the Holy Spirit and takes up His residence in the Church, which is His Body. Things then begin to happen quite spontaneously, out from the world of spiritual intelligences—not just because of certain doctrines being preached, but because of that Divine presence.

There are conscious intelligences all around, behind men and nations, and the conflict has started ; not because of what God's people say, but because they are here. Let that be corporate, and you have God's idea of vocation. This is not the dispensation of the conversion of the nations. I wonder even if this is the dispensation of the full evangelization of the nations. We are hoping the Lord may come any day. Half of this world has never heard the name of Jesus yet, after two thousand years. If the Lord is coming to-night, something has to happen if the world is to be evangelized before He comes ! That is not said to stay or weaken evangelization. Let us get on with it and do all that is possible ; but, remember, the Lord has given us His meaning for this dispensation. " This gospel of the kingdom shall be preached in the whole world *for a testimony* unto all the nations ; and then shall the end come " (Matthew xxiv. 14).

Look at your New Testament. It was said, " Their sound went out into all the earth " (Romans x. 18). It was said then that the whole world was touched. But the world has grown a good deal since then. What happened at that time ? The Lord planted nuclei, corporate representations of His Church, first in one nation and then in another, and by their presence the fight broke out. The one thing that Satan was bent upon was to eject that which inoculated his kingdom with the sovereignty of the Lord ; to get it out, break it up, disintegrate it, somehow to nullify

it ; turning those concerned one against another, creating
divisions—anything to spoil, to mar, to destroy their representation of Christ's absolute lordship ; to neutralise
that, to get it out, to drive it out, to do anything to get rid
of this thing inside his kingdom. Satan's kingdom has
acted in this way, as if to say : ' While that thing is here,
we can never be sure of ourselves ; while that is here our
kingdom is divided, it is not whole : let us get it out, in
order to have our kingdom solid.'

God's object is to get into the nations a corporate expression of the lordship of His Son—to have His place
there. I am not saying we are not to preach ; yes, we must
preach, witness, testify ; but the essential thing is that the
Lord must *be* there. There are times—and this will be
borne out by many servants of God—when you cannot
preach, you cannot do anything but hold on where you
are, being there, standing there, keeping in close touch
with heaven there. You can do nothing else, and the waves
break upon you. It has happened many times. Before ever
there has been any advance or development there has been
a long-drawn-out period in which the one question has
been, ' Shall we be able to hold on, to stand our ground?'
Satan has said, ' Not if I can help it ! You will go out if
I can do anything about it !'

The whole question at issue is the foothold of the
heavenly Lord in the nations. Israel was constituted for
that ; the Church is constituted for that. It cannot be done
single-handed by units ; it requires the corporate—the two,
the three ; the more the better, provided there is the unifying factor, the oneness, of a single eye. If double motives
and personal interests come in, they will undo it all. Are
you fighting a lonely battle? You need co-operation, you
need corporate help to fight that battle through and to

hold your ground. Mark you, the enemy will drive you out if he can. Preach if you can ; but if you cannot, that does not mean that you are to quit. Until the Lord says, ' I can do no more here, ' you have to hold on. Do we not know the terrific efforts of the enemy to drive us out? Many of you have gone far enough to know what that means. If he could put you out, he would.

But that is the vision—what the Church is constituted for in relation to the Lord Jesus : so that, in the light of the coming day, you are standing as a testimony of the coming day ; in the nations for a testimony, "until he come whose right it is " to reign, and " the kingdom of the world is become the kingdom of our Lord, and of his Christ " (Rev. xi. 15) ; a foothold unto that time ; an altar built, which testifies : ' This belongs to the Lord : the Lord's rights are here : He has purchased this.' But you will find every kind of contradiction to that in conditions, and every kind of assault from the enemy to try to prove that the Lord has not anything there, that He has no footing, and that you had better get out.

Do you see how necessary it is to have the vision? You cannot do that on enthusiasm—it will not last ; nor on someone else's vision—it will not support you to the end. You must be like this man Paul and those who " endured, as seeing him who is invisible " ; not as having seen Him long ago, but living continually in the light of what you have seen and are seeing—a light which is ever growing.

VISION IS THE MEASURE OF VOCATION

Now, if all this is simple and elementary, it is nevertheless basic. Do you see that vision of God's full purpose concerning His Son, revealed in your own heart in its beginnings, but then growing clearer and fuller, is the

basis of vocation? I do trust that nothing I have said will
have the effect of making you less earnest and devoted in
all simple ways of witnessing, or testifying concerning
salvation ; but do remember that, for fulness, you need
to see very much more than that. You will go just as far
as your vision takes you ; therefore, we all have need of
Paul's prayer that God " may give unto you a spirit of
wisdom and revelation in the knowledge of him ; having
the eyes of your heart enlightened, that ye may know what
is the hope of his calling, what the riches of the glory of
his inheritance in the saints, and what the exceeding greatness of his power to us-ward who believe " (Ephesians i.
17 – 19).

That is the vision. And then, as is written in Isaiah
xxv. 7 (A.R.V.) : ". . . he will destroy (*lit.* swallow up)
in this mountain the face of the covering that covereth
all peoples, and the veil that is spread over all nations."
What does that mean—" this mountain "? What mountain? Well, it is Zion. But has that literal mountain,
Mount Zion, that rocky eminence in Jerusalem, ever
been the instrument of taking the covering veil from off
all faces? Of course it has not! What is Zion? Zion, in
spiritual interpretation, is that people who are living in
the good of the Lord's complete sovereignty. It says in the
immediate context, " He hath swallowed up death for
ever " (vs. 8). It is through His triumph, the triumph of
His Cross and resurrection, that He comes to us. " Ye are
come unto mount Zion " (Hebrews xii. 22). Zion is the
realm of His absolute lordship, and a people living in the
good of His lordship. Then the veil is taken away. What
the Lord wants here and there and there are these nuclei,
these little companies of people living in the good of His
victory, living in the good of His having swallowed up

death victoriously ; and where they are, people will see ; they will be the instrument for taking the veil from other people's faces. Where such a company is found, there you see the Lord. When you come into touch with those people, you come into touch with reality.

So the final appeal is that everything must be adjusted and brought into line with the vision, and the one question for us is this : Are people seeing the Lord? It is not a matter of whether they are hearing what we have to talk about—our preaching, doctrine, interpretation—but : Are they seeing the Lord, are they feeling the Lord, are they meeting the Lord? Oh, I do not ask you in your different locations to gather two or three together to study certain kinds of Bible teaching ; but I do ask you to ask the Lord to constitute you corporately that which will have a spiritual impact, that in which the Lord can be seen, the Lord can be found ; of which it can be said, ' The Lord is there ! ' May that be true of us, wherever we are.

CHAPTER FIVE

WHY THE PROPHET'S MESSAGE IS NOT APPREHENDED

Reading: Acts xiii. 27, 15; II Corinthians iii. 14 – 18; Isaiah liii. 1.

THE PROPHETS WERE READ, as Paul points out here, every Sabbath. It was the fixed custom to read the law and the prophets every Sabbath, and it may be pointed out that it was not just at one particular time in the day that this was done, but all through the Sabbath day the law and the prophets were being read in the synagogues. And yet it says that although the very rulers themselves, as well as the dwellers in Jerusalem who attended the temple, heard that reading of the prophets so continuously, they never heard the *voices* of the prophets. And because they failed to hear that inner something, which was more than just the audible reading of what the prophets had said, they lost everything that was intended for them, as this thirteenth chapter of Acts shows. The Apostles left them and turned to the Gentiles, who had an ear ready to hear.

That is a matter of no small consequence and seriousness. It is evident that it behoves *us* to seek to hear the voices of the prophets, really to know what the prophets were saying. Let us again look at the statement: " . . .

because they knew him not, nor the voices of the prophets." Why did they not know? Why did they not hear? There is one basic answer to that enquiry which is going to occupy us just now, and which brings us down to foundations, really to the root of things.

THE OFFENCE OF THE CROSS

(a) A SUFFERING MESSIAH

The answer to that enquiry is this—because they were not willing to accept the Cross. That is what went to the root of the whole matter. Firstly, they were not willing to admit of a suffering Messiah. They had their own minds well made up, both as to what kind of Messiah their Messiah would be, and as to what He would do, and as to the results of His advent; and anything that ran counter to that fixed mentality was not only not accepted—it was an offence. They could not admit into the realm of their contemplation that their coming Messiah would be a suffering Messiah. Yet the prophets were always speaking about the suffering Messiah. Isaiah, at that point in his prophecies which we know as chapter liii, presents the classic on the suffering Messiah, and yet he opens by saying: "Who hath believed our message?"

I think we need not stay to gather further evidence that that was their attitude. Right the way through it was just that. Paul, in his letter to the Galatians, was dealing with that very thing. Towards the end of the letter he spoke about the offence of the Cross, and he set that over against the Judaizers, who were dogging his steps everywhere and seeking to prejudice his ministry, and at whose hands he was suffering. He ' bore branded on his body the marks of the Lord Jesus' (Galatians vi. 17). Why? Because of his message of the Cross. He said, 'If I were willing to drop that, I could escape all this suffering; it is the offence of the Cross which is the cause of all the trouble' (Galatians v. 11). And all the way through we see the Jews' unwillingness to admit of a suffering Messiah.

(b) THE WAY OF SELF-EMPTYING

But then it went further than that. It became not only a national issue but a personal one. They would not accept the principle of the Cross in themselves. You find that representative individuals of the nation, who came to the Lord Jesus from time to time, were presented with the ffence of the Cross—and off they went again, not prepared to accept it. Nicodemus was very interested in the kingdom which the Messiah was going to set up, which he was expecting and anticipating, but it became a personal matter of the Cross. Before the Lord was through with Nicodemus, He had brought into his full view the serpent lifted up in the wilderness. That was an offence. —Another man, who has become known to us as the rich young ruler, went away very sorrowful because of the offence of the Cross. It was no use for the Lord, at that time, before the Cross had actually taken place, to speak in precise terms about it to other than His disciples, but He applied the principle, which is the same thing. He applied the principle to this young man. 'If, as you say, you are interested in the Kingdom and in eternal life, this is the way: the way of emptying—utter self emptying.' "He went away sorrowful: for he was one that had great possessions" (Matthew xix. 22). The Lord said, "How hardly (with what difficulty) shall they that have riches enter into the kingdom of God!" (Luke

xviii. 24). The offence of the Cross finds them out.

Now here, with the Jews as a whole, they were making the kingdom of God an earthly thing on the principles of this world—and do not let us blame them without blaming ourselves. This is our battle right up to date. It is a matter that finds us all out at heart. Oh, you may not be expecting that through your preaching of Christ a temporal kingdom will be set up and you will get a literal crown to wear and a throne to sit upon—that may not be your outlook or mentality; but are we not, almost every day of our lives, in trouble because the Lord hides from us everything that He is doing and starves our souls of their ambition to see things, to have things? Is that not the basis of a great deal of our trouble? We want to see, we want to have, we want the proofs and the evidences. We do really, after all, want a kingdom that can be appraised by our senses of sight and hearing and feeling—a palpable kingdom, the answer in tangible form to all our efforts and labours; and the opposite of that is a tremendous strain upon faith, and sometimes even brings us to a serious crisis.

Why does not the Lord do this and that, which we think He ought to do? It is simply this soul-craving to have proof and demonstration; and this is why, if there is anything built up in Christian work which is obvious, big, impressive, where there is a great thing being organized and a great movement on foot and all is in the realm of something that can be seen, crowds of Christians flock after it; or if there are manifestations, things that seem to be clear proofs, the crowds will be found there. The enemy can carry away multitudes by imitation works of the Holy Ghost in the realm of demonstrations and proofs. We are so impressionable, we must *possess*; and that is exactly the same principle as that which governed the rulers. They were not prepared for the principle of the Cross to be applied in this way—an utter self-emptying, being brought to an end of everything but the Lord Himself.

THE PROPHETS' THEME—KNOWING THE LORD

Now you see that does bring us to the matter of the voices of the prophets. What was the one thing the prophets were always talking about? It was about *knowing the Lord.* The thing that was lacking amongst the Lord's people in the days of the prophets was the knowledge of the Lord. There were plenty of people who were prepared to have the Lord for what He could do for them, but as for the Lord Himself . . . ah, that was another matter.

What is the Lord after with you and with me? Is He first of all wanting us to do things? The idea of what is of God to-day is chiefly associated with the things which are being done for Him, the work we are engaged in, and so on—that is, with what is objective and outward. But the Lord is not first of all concerned about how much we do. He is far more concerned that, whether we do little or much, every bit of it should come out of a knowledge of Himself. Any amount can be done for the Lord in Christian work and activities, just as you do other work, but it may not proceed from your own deep knowledge of God. The Lord is concerned above all else that we should know Him. " Let not the wise man glory in his wisdom, neither let the mighty man glory in his might, let not the rich man glory in his riches ; but let him that glorieth glory in this, that he hath understanding, and knoweth me " (Jeremiah ix. 23, 24, A.R.V.).

May that not explain the very principle of the Cross

that is being applied to us? The Lord does not satisfy and gratify; along many lines He seems again and again to be saying ' No ' to quite a lot that we crave for ; and, being denied, we often come to the point where we would almost give up everything and allow the biggest questions as to our relationship with the Lord. And yet what He is after all the time, by His denials and witholdings or delays, is to deepen our knowledge of Himself. What matters with the Lord before anything and everything else is not that we should be in any given place doing a lot of Christian work (do not let that stop you serving the Lord !), but that we should be there as one who *knows* the Lord. Our opportunities for serving Him will spring out of our knowledge of Him ; He will see to that. The Lord the Spirit is arranging His own work. He knows where need exists, and when He sees someone who can meet that need He can make the contact.

KNOWLEDGE OF THE LORD BASIC TO ALL USEFULNESS

That is the principle in the New Testament. We see it in the life of the Lord Jesus Himself. That meeting between Christ and the woman of Samaria was not just a casual happening, a pretty story. No, you have principles. The Holy Ghost wrote those narratives, and involved principles in every incident. Here is One who has water to give that the world knows not of, and here is a thirsty woman. God sees to it that the one in need is brought into touch with the One who has the supply. That is a law. If you have not got the supply, it is very largely empty work that is done for the Lord.

The principle of the Cross works out along many lines, in many ways—testing, trying, emptying us, in order to bring us to the place where we know the Lord, and where our joy in the Lord and our enthusiasm and our Christian life are the result of something deeper than the mere momentum produced by doing many things, running about from meeting to meeting, giving addresses, being occupied on the crest of a wave of engagements in Christian work. The Lord does not want it to be like that. I am not saying that you will never be on the crest of a wave, that you will never have your hands full ; but the Lord's way of making us useful servants is so to deal with us as to make us know Him, so that, whether occupied in Christian work in an outward way or not, we are there with a knowledge of the Lord. What is so necessary for us is an increasing measure of the preciousness of the Lord to our own hearts ; that, whether we are able to do anything or not, He should still remain very precious to us. That is what He wants.

That is very simple, but it is basic to everything. You are there in some place where you cannot be always talking about the Lord, where you can do very little ; but if the Lord is precious to you, that is service to Him, and in you He has available a vessel for anything more that He wants. I am sure the Lord will never bring us out and entrust us with responsibilities until He has become very precious to us in the place where we are, even though many other things that we would like are being denied to and withheld from us. It is the principle of the Cross.

Nicodemus comes with all his ' fulness '. He is a man with a great fulness—a ruler of the Jews, in high standing, in a place of influence, and much more. He represents a fulness of a religious kind. Then the Lord virtually says to him : ' You have to let it all go, and start all over again like a newborn babe. You are concerned about the Kingdom of Heaven, but you cannot bring any of that into the Kingdom.' To the rich young ruler He says, in effect, 'You cannot bring your riches in here.' You may have a lot of natural wealth—intellectual, financial, influential, positional, but that does not give you any standing in the Kingdom of Heaven at all. The wealthiest, the fullest, the biggest here in this world receives no more of the glance of the Lord in their direction than the poorest and the weakest. All are brought down here—you must be born again, you must start from zero in this matter of the Kingdom of Heaven. The Kingdom is not a matter of eating and drinking, it is a matter of spiritual measure ; and you start spiritual measure by being born of the Spirit. The new life is utterly spiritual from the very first breath— something that was not before, something new.

Spiritual measure is just *knowing the Lord* ; that is all. Our standing in the Kingdom of Heaven is simply a matter of knowing the Lord, and if we are going to gain higher place it is not going to be at all by preferences, but by the increase of our spiritual measure. People who count in heaven are spiritual people, and what counts is the degree of their spirituality ; and spirituality is knowing the Lord. We may take it that the Lord applies Himself utterly to this matter of bringing us to know *Him.* That is the thing that really does count.

THE CROSS BASIC TO ALL KNOWLEDGE OF THE LORD

They could not hear the voices of the prophets because the prophets were talking about a suffering Messiah, and there was something inside the people which had closed the door ; they were predisposed against anything like that, and so they could not hear. Even the disciples of the

Lord Jesus were in that position. When He began to refer to His Cross they said, " Be it far from thee, Lord :
this shall never be unto thee " (Matthew xvi. 22). A suffering Messiah? Oh, no ! But they did come to the place
where the Cross had its very deep application, where it
meant an end of everything for them. The Lord precipitated that whole question, and you see them after His crucifixion—they have lost their Messianic Kingdom, they
have lost everything, they are stripped and emptied. And
then what happened? They began then to *know*, just began to know, and their knowledge grew and grew ; but
it was of another order entirely. So you find, in the rest
of the New Testament, that, in their own history and in
their instruction of others, two things go together. They
are like the negative and the positive in an electrical circuit—there can be no current without both. The negative
is the application of the principle of the Cross, which says
No, No, No: an end: death to yourself, death to the
world, death to all your own natural life. But the positive
is the Holy Ghost, the Spirit of God, mightily present, but
always hand in hand with the Cross. With those two acting always together, the negative and the positive—the
Cross, and heavenly purpose and heavenly power and
effectiveness—you find that there is movement and an
ever-growing knowledge of the Lord.

We cannot have the knowledge of the Lord—the most
important thing in the mind of God for us—except on
the ground of the continuous application of the Cross,
and that will go right on to the end. Do not imagine that
there will come a day when you have done with the Cross,
when the principle of the Cross will no longer be necessary and when you have graduated from the school where
the Cross is the instrument of the Lord. Such a day never

will be! More and more you will come to recognise the necessity for that Cross. If you are going on into greater fulness of knowledge—I mean spiritual knowledge of the Lord—and therefore greater fulness of usefulness to Him, you must take it as settled that that principle of the Cross is going to be applied more and more deeply as you go on.

Oh, God write that in our hearts! for surely we all know the need of the Cross; and those who have known most about it are conscious most of its need still. We have seen the terrible tragedy of people who knew the message of the Cross in fulness, and who after many years have been a positive contradiction to that very message— marked by self-assertiveness, self-importance, impatience, irritability, so that other people have been unable to live with them. Are you one of those habitually irritable people? I do not mean one of those persons who some-times is overtaken in a fault. The Lord is patient with the upsets that come here and there along the way, but are we habitually irritable, short-tempered, difficult to live with? That is a denial of the Cross, and that has wrecked the life and work of many a missionary.

The Cross will be applied right on to the end, and, al-together apart from our faults and the things in our con-stitution and nature which have to be dealt with, in this coming to know the Lord for still greater usefulness we go from death to death on that side of things. We think of some known to us. We marvel at the way the Lord has been able to use them, the large place into which He has put them, what riches He has given them; but of late they have been plunged into depths of death never known before. It is evidently unto something more, something greater still. It is like that; the knowledge of the Lord re-quires it in an ever-growing way.

KNOWLEDGE AND USEFULNESS SAFEGUARDED BY THE CROSS

But furthermore, there is no *safe* place, apart from the constant application of the principle of the Cross. Safety absolutely demands it. Nothing is safe in our hands. The more the Lord blesses, the more peril there is. The greatest peril comes when the Lord begins to use us. You may say, ' That does not say very much for our sanctification.' It certainly does not say very much for ' eradication '! Well, here is Paul. Did that man know anything about the Cross? Would you say he was a crucified man? If he was not, who was? Did he know the Lord? And with all that he knew of the Cross and the Lord, did he know that he needed the Cross to be applied right on to the end? He will definitely place it on record—". . . that I should not be exalted overmuch, there was given to me a thorn in the flesh, a messenger of Satan to buffet me." " That I should not be exalted overmuch "! (II Cor. xii. 7). And mark you, he is saying that because of the great revelation that had been given him. He was caught up into heaven. It is a most perilous thing to be entrusted with Divine riches, so far as our flesh is concerned. The only safe place is where the Cross is still at work, touching all that is ourselves, touching all our independence of action.

Take all these Apostles—take Peter, a man who would act so independently, who liked to do things on his own and do what he wanted to do. We find it cropping up constantly. He is the man who acts without stopping to ask anybody. We have no hint that he ever got into fellowship with his brother disciples and said, ' I am thinking of doing so and so ; I would very much like you to pray with me about it, and to tell me what you think ; I have no in-

tention of going on unless there is one mind among us.'
Peter never did that sort of thing. He got an idea, and off
he went. The Lord summed him up very well when He
said: " When thou wast young, thou girdedst thyself, and
walkedst whither thou wouldest: but when thou shalt be
old, thou shalt stretch forth thy hands, and another shall
gird thee, and carry thee whither thou wouldest not"
(John xxi. 18). That was Peter before the Cross was inwrought in him. But see him afterwards. Why, in those
early chapters of Acts, do we read " Peter and John ",
" Peter and John ", " Peter and John "? Well, they are
moving together now, there is relatedness. Is it an acknow-
ledgment that Peter felt his need of co-operation and fellowship, that he had seen the perils and disasters into
which independent action led him, even when his intentions and motives were of the best? These are just glimpses
of how the Cross touches us in our impulsive, independent
nature, our self-will, our self-strength. The Cross has to
deal with all that to make things safe for God, and to keep
us moving in the way of increasing knowledge of the Lord,
which, as we have said, lies behind all our value to the
Lord, all our usefulness, all our service.

THE CROSS OPENS THE WAY TO FULL KNOWLEDGE OF THE LORD

The Cross is the only way to spiritual knowledge. Important as study of the Word of God may be in its own
realm, as laying a foundation for the Holy Spirit to work
upon, you never come to a knowledge of the Lord simply
by studying the Bible. The Holy Spirit may use what you
know of the Bible to teach you much, to explain your experiences, to enable you to understand what the Lord is

doing, but you never get this kind of spiritual knowledge merely by study and by teaching.

You must be prepared to let the Cross be so applied to your life that you are broken and emptied and fairly ground to powder—so that you are brought to the place where, if the Lord does not do something, you are finished. If you are prepared for that way, you will get to know the Lord. That is the only way. It cannot be by addresses or lectures. They have their value, but you do not know the Lord spiritually along those lines.

The full knowledge of the Lord is reserved to us who live in this dispensation, because the latter is governed by the Cross. Peter himself had something to say about this : —

" Concerning which salvation the prophets sought and searched diligently, who prophesied of the grace that should come unto you: searching what time or what manner of time the Spirit of Christ which was in them did point unto, when it testified beforehand the sufferings of Christ, and the glories that should follow them. To whom it was revealed, that not unto themselves, but unto you, did they minister these things, which now have been announced unto you . . . ; which things angels desire to look into " (I Peter i. 10 — 12).

There you have two orders—prophets and angels—who did not know certain things which are revealed to us. The prophets knew much, but they were searching diligently to know something they could not discover. ' What does this mean? ' they must have asked themselves. ' The Spirit of God is making us say these things, but what do they mean? ' They sought diligently to know that which was reserved for us. Why could they not know? Because full knowledge is based upon the Cross, and the Cross had not taken place then. And angels, too, desire to look into these things. Can it be true? We thought angels knew everything! Surely angels have far more knowledge and intelligence than we have about these things? They do not know. "Which things angels desire to look into." Why do they not know? Angels have had no need of the Cross ; the Cross has no meaning for them personally. It is on the basis of the Cross that full knowledge is entered into. Does that need any further argument?

THE CROSS SECURES POSITIVE, NOT ONLY NEGATIVE, RESULTS

So then, the Holy Spirit, in order to bring us to the full knowledge of the Lord and by means of that growing knowledge to make us useful to the Lord, must constantly work by means of the Cross in principle ; and my closing word is this. The work is not all negative ; the Lord works on a positive basis. You may think that the Lord is always saying No, that He is always against you, that the Cross is suppressive ; but no, it is a positive instrument in the hands of the Spirit of God. God is working on a positive line. The fact is that, if ever the Holy Spirit brings us into a new knowing of the meaning of the Cross, He is after something more. That is the law of the Spirit of life.

You must remember that the Lord Jesus, in His resurrection, was not left just where He was before. Before He died He was on this earth, and then He died ; and Paul refers to His raising from that death in these words : " the exceeding greatness of his power to us-ward who believe, according to that working of the strength of his might which he wrought in Christ, when he raised him from the dead, and made him to sit at his right hand in the heavenly

places, far above all " (Ephesians i. 19 — 21). The resurrection carries Him through to the " far above all, " and
the principle of resurrection is always that of rebound—we
may go down very deep, more deeply than ever we have
known before, but the Spirit of God is intending that that
shall issue in our being higher than ever before. So do not
be afraid when you are feeling very empty, very finished,
very much at the end. Ask the Lord that if this is truly the
working of His Cross it shall be succesful in what He
intends for you ; and if it is successful, you will be on
higher ground afterward than ever you were before.

THE NEED FOR A DEFINITE TRANSACTION WITH THE LORD

We have said from time to time that the Cross does
involve a crisis. For some this may be an overwhelming
experience, the biggest thing that has happened in your
life, even bigger than your conversion. It was so for some
of us as we moved from the apprehension of the substi-
tutionary aspect of the Cross, where we saw only what
Christ had done *for* us, to the apprehension of our union
with Christ in death, burial and resurrection. Whether or
not you have a big crisis which divides your life in two,
you must have a point of transaction with the Lord where
you recognise that the Cross is in principle an utter, all-
inclusive reality that, sooner or later, is going to run to
earth the last vestige of that self-life which is the ground of
Satan's power. It is best at some point to have this understanding : ' I rejoice in the fact of Thy death for me, and
I am saved on the ground of that death and my faith in it.
But I died in Thee—that was Thy thought about me as a
son of Adam. I could not bear to have all that that means

brought to me at once, but I recognise that it has to be worked out as grace enables, and that sooner or later I shall have to come to an utter end ; and I therefore commit myself to all Thou dost mean by the Cross.'

A transaction of that kind is necessary. Do not begin to kick when the Lord begins to work it out. He takes you at your word, but He is doing it with the definite object in view of getting you to a higher and fuller knowledge of Himself. Out of that growing knowledge of Him, the growing preciousness of the Lord, all real service will issue. It is not what we *do*, but what we *have*, that is the secret of service.

CHAPTER SIX

THE KINGDOM, AND ENTRANCE INTO IT

"For they that dwell in Jerusalem, and their rulers, because they knew him not, nor the voices of the prophets which are read every sabbath, fulfilled them by condemning him" (Acts xiii. 27).

"Verily I say unto you, Among them that are born of women there hath not arisen a greater than John the Baptist : yet he that is but little in the kingdom of heaven is greater than he. And from the days of John the Baptist until now the kingdom of heaven suffereth violence, and men of violence take it by force. For all the prophets and the law prophesied until John. And if ye are willing to receive it, this is Elijah, that is to come. He that hath ears to hear, let him hear" (Matthew xi. 11 — 15).

"The law and the prophets were until John : from that time the gospel of the kingdom of God is preached, and every man entereth violently into it" (Luke xvi. 16).

I THINK WE CAN RECOGNISE that the common link between Acts xiii. 27 and Matthew xi. 13 is "all the prophets." In the one case they heard not the voices of the prophets ; in the other it is said (vs. 15), "He that hath ears to hear, let him hear."

THE PROPHETS PROPHESIED OF THE KINGDOM

First of all, we must understand the meaning of this whole statement in Matthew xi—" all the prophets . . . prophesied until John." What did they prophesy? Of course, they prophesied many things. One paramount concern in their prophecies was that relating to the coming King and the Kingdom. So much was that so that in the New Testament the matter of the Kingdom is taken for granted. When you open the New Testament and begin to read in the Gospels, you find that no explanation is given. The Kingdom is not introduced as something of which people were unaware. You find from amongst the people those who came to the Lord Jesus and used the very phrase, and you find the Lord Himself, although the matter was not mentioned by others who came to Him, using the phrase ' the Kingdom' without any introduction or explanation.

Nicodemus was a case in point. We have nothing in the narrative to indicate that Nicodemus said anything at all about the Kingdom. He started by saying: " Rabbi, we know that thou art a teacher come from God." There was nothing about the Kingdom in that. The Lord Jesus interrupted there and said: " Except one be born anew, he cannot see the kingdom of God." (John iii. 2, 3.) Evidently that was the thing that was in the mind of Nicodemus, and the Lord knew it. You see, it is a thing taken for granted in the New Testament; and although later (as we find in the book of the Acts and subsequently) the true heavenly explanation is given, or there is some teaching concerning its true meaning, the Kingdom is something that is already very much in the minds of the Jewish people, and of course it has come from the prophets. The prophets had much to say concerning the Kingdom, and some of them had something very definite to say about the King. We will not try to prove that. It is a statement which you can easily verify.

What did the prophets prophesy? Inclusively, they prophesied concerning the King and the Kingdom. What was the culmination of the prophets in that comprehensive connection? It was John the Baptist. He gathered them all up; he was, so to speak, the inclusive prophet. What was John the Baptist? He was the terminal or turning point between all that had been and that which was now going to be, between the Old Testament and the New. That is the statement here—" all . . . prophesied until John." Until John; now—from John. What was the message of John? " Repent ye ; for the kingdom of heaven it at hand " (Matthew iii. 2). But alongside that, the great outstanding note of John is, " Behold, the Lamb of God, that taketh away the sin of the world!" (John i. 29). Those are not two different things ; they are one. " The kingdom . . . is at hand ": " Behold, the Lamb of God!"

THE KINGDOM PRESENT IN CHRIST

What was the issue, then, from John's time—the issue which sprang into new meaning, new force, because it had become an immediate one ; no longer that of prophecy but now the issue of actuality? It was the Kingdom of Heaven. " The law and the prophets were until John : from that time the gospel of the kingdom of God is preached." The prophets had prophesied it ; now it is preached as having come, and having come with " the Lamb of God, that taketh away the sin of the world."

What, then, is the Kingdom of Heaven? We have led

up to this step by step, and when we answer this final question we shall see clearly what it was that these Jewish rulers and dwellers in Jerusalem never saw, though they heard the prophets week by week.

I am going to press the challenge of this again. I feel that it is a very solemn thing that ever the Kingdom of Heaven should have come near to anyone. You see, the Lord is eventually going to judge everyone on their opportunity. The opportunity has been given—and contact is opportunity. The very availability of the Kingdom is opportunity. What is done with opportunity? The Lord Jesus walked in the midst of the Jewish nation three and a half years. His very presence among them was their opportunity—and what a terrible, terrible consequence followed their failure to make good their opportunity!

Now there may be someone in this category who reads these words. Through reading them, there has become available to you, even if never before (but surely we could hardly say that), the gospel of Jesus Christ—the knowledge of the fact of the Lord Jesus and His Cross. To have ever had that within your reach is enough to settle your eternal destiny. If the Kingdom of Heaven is come near—within the compass and range of your life, to your knowledge—that is the ground upon which your eternal destiny may be settled. Of course, there was very much more in the case of these people, and their condemnation was so much the more. The prophets prophesied in their hearing, and yet because of something in their own make-up, because of some reaction from themselves, the rulers and the people never heard what they were hearing; they never recognised that here was something which had very great implications, and that they must find out what those implications really were. They did not take the attitude—

'If there is something here which concerns me, I must know what it is.'

You could hardly ask for less than that, could you?—but the very absence of that kind of reaction to the presence of the gospel, as I have said, may be the ground upon which judgment will take place. It did in their case, and a terrible judgment it was! What a judgment, these two thousand years of Jewish history! "Your house is left unto you desolate" (Matthew xxiii. 38). Was there ever a story of more awful desolation than the story of the Jews since then? But, even so, that is only a *parable* of desolation ; something here on this earth. What must desolation in the spiritual and eternal sense mean—forsaken of God, and knowing it? It is a solemn message, and of course it paves the way to this other part, the "violent" entering into the Kingdom. This is something to take seriously, something about which you cannot afford to be careless or indifferent.

What is the Kingdom? The answer to that can be given in three or four quite brief statements. What did the Kingdom of Heaven prove to be? I repudiate that system of interpretation which claims that a literal, earthly, temporal kingdom was offered to the Jews at this time. I do not believe it. It would have been a poor sort of thing for the people of whom we read in the Gospels to have had the kingdom in their hands—not much glory or satisfaction to God in them! Look at Palestine to-day, and see what kind of kingdom it would be in the hands of those people! What is possible for the world when that kind of thing gets the kingdom? No, I repudiate the interpretation of a temporal kingdom being offered to Israel by Jesus at that time. But what did the Kingdom of Heaven, which was preached in the days of John the Baptist, prove to be and to mean, as the Lord Jesus interpreted it, and later the Apostles?

WHAT THE KINGDOM IS

(a) A NEW LIFE

First of all, the Kingdom of Heaven was a new life, altogether other than that which men knew anything about in all their history from Adam onward. That is what the Lord meant in His own first reference to the Kingdom, when speaking to Nicodemus about his soul's need. " Except one be born anew, he cannot see the kingdom of God "—because it is another life that has come in, as by a birth. It is not just the energizing of an old life. It is not just the swinging over of an old life into new interests, turning from one line of interest to another, from one system of occupation to another : once you were all out for the world, and now with the same life and interest you are all out for Christianity. No, it is another, different life, a life that never was, given from God Himself. The very essence of the Kingdom of Heaven is that it is a heavenly nature in a heavenly life, given as a distinct gift at a crisis. Another life—that is the Kingdom, to begin with.

(b) A NEW RELATIONSHIP

It is a new relationship, a relationship with God : which is not simply that now we become interested in God—that God becomes an object of our consideration and we swing over from one relationship to another because now we have taken up Christianity. No, it is a relationship which is of the essence of this very life itself. We have an altogether new and different consciousness, so far as our relationship to God is concerned. The great truth of the Gospels, especially as emphasized in the Gospel by John, is that a new revelation of relationship with God has come by Jesus Christ. " I manifested thy name unto the men whom thou gavest me out of the world " (John xvii. 6). That name, of which He is always speaking, represented a new relationship—" Father "; not in the sense of a general and universal fatherhood of God and brotherhood of man, but a specific, new relationship which comes about only by the entering of the Holy Spirit into the life in a definite, critical act. " God sent forth the Spirit of his Son into our hearts, crying, Abba, Father " (Galatians iv. 6). When did that happen with you? What was the very first lisp of your new life? " Father ! "—uttered out of a new consciousness. Not now a God who is afar off, unthinkable, all-terrible, of whom you are afraid ; no, " Father ! " When we are " born of the Spirit," there is brought about an entirely new relationship.

(c)   A NEW CONSTITUTION

Then the Kingdom of Heaven is a new constitution. I am not thinking now of a new set of laws and regulations, but of a new constitution so far as you and I are concerned. We are constituted anew, with an entirely new set of capacities which make possible things which were never possible before. It ought to be recognised—and I would have you lay this to heart anew—that the child of God, the member of the Kingdom of Heaven, is the embodiment of a miracle, which means that there are super-natural possibilities and capacities in every such one. What tremendous things go on in the history of a child of God ! When we see fully and clearly at last, we shall recognise them to have been nothing less than Divine miracles again and again. We do not know all the forces which are bent upon the destruction of a child of God, and how much his preserving through to the end represents an exercise of the almighty power of God. Some of us know a little about that: that our very survival is because God has exercised His power over other immense hostile powers, that we are kept by the power of God—and that it takes the power of God to keep us!

The inception of the life of the child of God is a miracle. ' How can a man be born again?' There is no answer to that question except that God does it. " How can this man give us his flesh to eat?" (John vi. 52). That is, how can the child of God be supported throughout, without anything here to help, to succour, to nourish? There is no answer to that either, except that God does it; and if He does not, the child of God, because of the extra forces centred upon him or her for destruction, will simply go under. The consummation of the life of the child of God will be equally a miracle. " How are the dead raised? and with what manner of body do they come ? " (I Corinthians xv. 35). The answer to that is the same—God alone is going to do it.

The whole matter is a miracle from start to finish. It is a new constitution, having in it possibilities and capacities which are altogether above and beyond the highest level of human abilities ; that is, above and over the whole kingdom of earth and nature.

(d)   A NEW VOCATION

Further, it is a new vocation. It is something for which to live, something in which to serve, something to bring

into operation. It becomes the sphere and the means of a
new life-ministry and -purpose. The very consciousness of
a truly born-again child of God is like this—' Now I know
why I am alive! I have been wondering all along why I
was born ; I have grumbled about it, and felt I was hardly
done by in being brought into this world without being
consulted as to whether I wanted to come ; but now I see
there is purpose in it—I have something to live for!' A
truly born-again child of God goes off and tells people that,
after all, it is worth being alive! He has discovered, behind
everything else, that which has Divine intent and meaning
—it never existed as an active thing until he was born
anew and entered into the Kingdom. The Kingdom of
Heaven is a new vocation, a new sense of life-purpose. It
gives to life a meaning. That is the Kingdom.

Is that not altogether a different idea from that which
would make the Kingdom a place with certain laws and
regulations—' You must' and 'You must not '—something objective? " The kingdom of God is within you "
(Luke xvii. 21), and it is after this kind.

(e)   A NEW GRAVITATION—TO HEAVEN, NOT EARTH

It is moreover something from above, and that surely
implies that it is transcendent in every way. It is something
that lives, and it brings life up on to a higher level. That is,
if the new life comes from above, from heaven, it will
always gravitate back to its source, and if this new life
works in us, it will be lifting us, pulling us upward to
God. It will so work that we shall feel first of all that this
world is not our home. It was our home ; everything for us
was here until that happened ; we saw nothing beyond.
Now we do not belong to it, we belong somewhere else ;

and in some strange way we are steadily moving further and further away from this earth. We find that we become less comfortable here every day. You are in the Kingdom if you have something like that experience. If you can be comfortable and happy and content to go on here you ought to have grave doubts as to where you are as regards the Kingdom. But if you are increasingly conscious that inwardly the distance is growing between you and all that is here, then the Kingdom is truly at work, the Kingdom of Heaven has come.

THE KINGDOM COME BUT ALSO COMING

Now, another thing: the Kingdom has come, but it is always coming. We have entered, but we ought to be always entering. There is a little word at the end of the letter to the Hebrews—" Wherefore, receiving a kingdom that cannot be shaken . . . " (Hebrews xii. 28). The literal sense there is—" being in the course or process of receiving a kingdom that cannot be shaken . . . " It has come, but it is coming; and it is at that point that I think we all need to recognise a difference, to discriminate between two things—between conversion and salvation.

Have you ever made that distinction? There is all the difference between conversion and salvation. Conversion is a crisis, something that happens perhaps suddenly, in a moment, and it is done. Salvation? That is something that has commenced; but you find also that the New Testament speaks about " receiving the end of your faith, even the salvation of your souls " (I Peter i. 9), thus indicating that salvation is still future. Some people have built a false doctrine upon this, teaching that you cannot know you are saved until you are at the end, because it is spoken of in the future tense. But we are saved, and we are being saved. We have entered the Kingdom by conversion, but salvation is a far greater thing than conversion. Oh, salvation is a vast thing, and is only another word for the Kingdom—the Kingdom coming all the time. A spiritual babe who has just received Divine life has not got everything, except potentially. It has conversion, it has new birth. Would you say that a little babe has everything it is intended to have? Potentially, in the life, all is there. But how much more there is to be known of what that life implies, of all that it carries with it and may lead to, of all the capacities that are there!

That is the difference between conversion and salvation. The Kingdom is a vast kingdom—" His kingdom is an everlasting kingdom " (Daniel iv. 3). " Of the increase of his government . . . there shall be no end " (Isaiah ix. 7). ' No end ' simply means eternally expansive. Can you make just a geographical matter of that? Surely not. It must be spiritual—the vast inexhaustible resources of God for His own people. It will take eternity to know and to explore all those resources, the dimensions of His Kingdom.

THE KINGDOM SUFFERS VIOLENCE

Now, having in a very imperfect way considered what the prophets were talking about and what you and I have come into touch with, let us see what can be missed. Let us look at these other words: " The law and the prophets were until John: from that time the gospel of the kingdom of God is preached, and every man entereth violently into it " (Luke xvi. 16). " From the days of John the Baptist until now the kingdom of heaven suffereth violence, and men of violence take it by force " (Matthew

xi. 12). It "suffereth violence." That does not simply mean that it permits of violence. It really means that it calls for violence, and it is men of violence that take it by force. Luke puts it "entereth violently".

Here is the spirit of citizenship in that Kingdom—"by force." Why? This is not merely an appeal to be in earnest —though it certainly includes that, seeing what a tremendous thing this Kingdom is, and what an immense loss will be suffered if we do not take it seriously. But you see, the Lord Jesus is speaking as in the midst of things which are constantly opposing. There is a whole organized system, expressing tremendous prejudice. He said to them on one occasion: "Woe unto you, scribes and Pharisees, hypocrites! because ye shut the kingdom of heaven against men: for ye enter not in yourselves, neither suffer ye them that are entering in to enter " (Matthew xxiii. 13). There is everything, from devil and men, to obstruct; to enter in requires violence. If you can be hindered, you will be hindered. If you are going to be easy-going, you will give to antagonistic forces all the ground that they want to put you out.

That is why I pointed out that it is not only a once-for-all entering into the Kingdom, but it is a continuous entering. The Kingdom is so much bigger than conversion. Of course, if you are going to be saved at all—I mean saved initially—you will have to mean business for that. You will have to make it a desperate matter, because there will be everything to stop you. But the Kingdom means a very great deal more than merely getting into it, far more than being converted. There is a great deal more in the purpose of God for our lives than we have ever imagined, and if we are to enter into that, violence has to characterize us. We must desperately mean business, and come to the place where we say: 'Lord, I am set upon all that Thou dost mean in Christ. I am set upon that, and I am not going to allow other people's prejudices or suspicions or criticisms to get in the way ; I am not going to allow any man-made system to hinder me ; I am going right on with Thee for all Thy purpose. I am going to do violence to everything that would get in the way.' It calls for violence, and we have to do a lot of violence to get all that God wills for us.

Oh, how easily many lives are side-tracked, simply because they are not desperate enough! They are caught in things which limit—things which may be good, that may have something of God in them, but which none the less are limiting things, and do not represent a wide open way to all God's purpose. The only way for us to come into all that the Lord means—not only into what we have seen but into all that He has purposed—is to be desperate, to be men of violence ; to be men who say, ' By God's grace, nothing and no one, however good, is going to stand in my way ; I am going on with God.' Have that position with the Lord, and you will find that God meets you on that ground.

No men—not even Paul himself—knew all that they were going to know. Paul was constantly getting fuller unveilings of that unto which he was called. He received something fairly strong and rich at the beginning ; then, later, he was shown unspeakable things (II Corinthians xii. 4). He was growing in apprehension. But why? Because he was a man of violence. God meets us like that. "With the perverse thou wilt shew thyself froward" (Psalm xviii. 26). That, in principle, means that God will be to you what you are to Him. He will mean business if you mean business. There is a vast amount in the Kingdom that we have never suspected. Do believe that. There is more for all of us to know than anybody on this earth knows—far more than the very greatest saints, the most advanced Christians, know of the purpose of God.

Paul intimates that. In his Philippian letter he makes it clear that, even at the end of his life, he has yet to apprehend, he needs still to know. " That I may know . . ." (Philippians iii. 10). There is far more to know. Do you believe that? Are you going to allow your life simply to be boxed up within the measure that you know, or within the measure of other people? No—it is the measure of Christ that is God's end. " Till we all attain unto the unity of the faith, and of the knowledge of the Son of God, unto a fullgrown man, unto the measure of the stature of the fulness of Christ " (Ephesians iv. 13). No movement, no society, no evangelical organization, no church on this earth has come to that yet, but that is the objective in view. But God requires, in order to bring us to fulness, that we be men of violence, that we really mean business, that we say to everything that gets in the way—and oh, the plausible voices, which nevertheless are subtly influenced by prejudices!—' Stand thou aside : I am going on with God, I am going to allow nothing to stand in the way.'

" The gospel of the kingdom is preached." Can you imagine those Judaizers speaking to the people about Jesus? ' Be careful ; mind you don't get caught! Our advice to you is to steer clear of that—don't get into too close touch with Him!' All that was going on. Paul was up against it all the time. He was tracked down throughout his journeys by these very people who, following on his heels, said, ' Be careful—it is dangerous !' The Lord Himself experienced the same kind of thing ; and He said : " the kingdom . . . suffereth violence." It calls for violence ; you will not get in to begin with, and you will certainly not get in in growing fulness, unless you are one of those people who do violence to everything that stands in the way of God's full purpose as revealed in Christ. You will not even know what that purpose is, God will not be able to reveal to you the next part of it, unless He finds that you are one after this kind—entering in violently.

Are you like that? Well, if we are passive, there is everything to be lost ; if we mean business, there is everything to be gained. The Lord make us men and women like that, lest we be numbered among those of whom it is said that they " have ears to hear, and hear not " (Ezekiel xii. 2).

CHAPTER SEVEN

THE CONTRAST BETWEEN
THE OLD DISPENSATION AND THE NEW

*"For they that dwell in Jerusalem, and their rulers, because
they knew him not, nor the voices of the prophets which
are read every sabbath, fulfilled them by condemning him"
(Acts xiii. 27).*

IN A WAY, THAT VERSE IS THE KEY to the whole of the
book of the Acts, for this book is really an interpretation
and exhibition of the principle that is at the heart of that
statement—that is, that there is the Bible with its verbal
statements, its record of utterances and activities of God
through men, and it can be read and re-read for a lifetime,
as it was in the case of the people referred to here, and yet
the real significance may be missed. In other words, there
is in it something more than the actual verbal statements.
You may have the statements, the letter, the volume, the
whole record, and you may know it as such, as these Jewish rulers did, and yet you may be missing the way, you
may be moving on a plane altogether other than that
which God intended. This book of the Acts, from beginning to end, shows that there was something more in the
mind of God when He inspired men of old to speak and to
write than is discernible in the actual words which they
used, and which requires the activity of the Spirit of God
if it is to be heard and grasped and understood, and if it is

97

going to work out as things worked out in this book—in power, in effectiveness.

There is much of the Old Testament in the book of the Acts, and in the New Testament as a whole. The prophets are very much quoted, but see the difference between the effect of the words as used in the book of the Acts and the effect upon those who merely heard or read the actual utterances of the prophets. The Holy Ghost has come ; and He is not making another Bible, He is using the old one ; but it is a new book with a new meaning and a new effect, and you are amazed at times at the way in which He uses Scripture. You never saw that it meant that ; it is something altogether beyond a former apprehension, although you knew that Scripture quite well in a way. There is a difference, and it is a crucial one.

So these people in Jerusalem and their rulers heard every Sabbath the prophets, but failed to hear their voice. They missed something—the voice of God coming through, the meaning of God in what was being said, as distinct from the mere statements. It is possible for a company to be gathered together and for one to be speaking the word of the Lord, and for some merely to hear the words and go away and say, ' He said so and so,' repeating what was actually said in verbal statements. It is at the same time possible for others to say, ' I never saw it like that before ; I knew that passage of Scripture, but I never saw that!' Something, not only of a fresh recognition but of living value, has been detected. That is the difference between the words of the prophets and the voice of God through the words of the prophets.

So, as I have said, this verse in chapter xiii is, in a way, a key to this whole book. It makes this discrimination, which is so very important, between the letter and the spirit, between the statements and the Divine meaning in the statements. One is death and gets nowhere. The other is life and goes right through.

ALL PROPHECY POINTS TO THE LORD JESUS

Let us now glance at the book of the Acts. We go right back to the first chapter with this principle in mind. It might be well for us to be reminded, in parenthesis, that, speaking broadly, the whole Bible (but for a few verses) closes upon a comprehensive statement about this very matter. In Revelation xix. 10, we are told that " the testimony of Jesus is the spirit of prophecy." What does that mean? It simply means this—that all the way through the Bible, from the beginning onward, there has been a predictive element in this sense, an element of implication, something implied beyond the actual words said at the time. In it all there has been a pointer onward. It may be an historic incident, something quite local and immediate in itself as to time, place and persons concerned, but in no part of the Bible is only the local and present in view. There is something more—there is an implication, there is a pointer onward ; and if you could see where all these pointers point to, you would find it was Jesus. He is implied in everything, everywhere.

When we speak of prophecy, do not let us limit our thoughts to certain times and certain men of the Old Testament. True, we have been, and are very often, occupied with the prophets whose books are included in the ' prophetic' section of the Old Testament, but we have to expand beyond that. Moses was called a prophet (Deuteronomy xviii. 15), and Samuel was a prophet (I Samuel iii. 20), and even David in the New Testament is called a prophet (Acts ii. 30). The spirit of prophecy embraces more than a certain class of men whom we designate prophets. The spirit of prophecy goes right back, as far back as Enoch ; no, further back than that—to Genesis iii. 15, concerning the seed of the woman : that is the spirit of prophecy. So, if we remember that prophecy is something so far-reaching and all-inclusive, and bearing upon the Lord Jesus, I hope we are able to see something of Divine meaning as being more than verbal statement.

With that parenthesis, let us come to the first chapter of the Acts.

THE HOLY SPIRIT'S HIDDEN MEANING IN THE SCRIPTURES

" They therefore, when they were come together, asked him saying, Lord, dost thou at this time restore the kingdom to Israel?" (Acts i. 6).

We pointed out in a previous chapter how much the prophets were occupied with this matter of the Kingdom. These disciples of the Lord Jesus had their whole idea of the Kingdom from the prophets, and so their question is based upon a certain kind of mental apprehension of the teaching of the prophets. They had deduced certain things from what the prophets said, and they bring this question even at this late hour—" Dost thou at this time restore the kingdom to Israel? And he said unto them, It is not for you to know times and seasons, which the Father hath set within his own authority. But ye shall receive power, when the Holy Spirit is come upon you : and ye shall be my witnesses both in Jerusalem, and in all Judaea and Samaria, and unto the uttermost part of the earth. And when he had said these things, as they were looking,"—

He restored the Kingdom, ascended His throne? No—
" he was taken up ; and a cloud received him out of their
sight " (Acts i. 6 — 9).

Everything begins there in the way of spiritual understanding, because this statement of the Lord Jesus indicated that a new dispensation was being inaugurated
which was different from that which the disciples had expected from the teaching of the prophets. This was the dispensation of the Holy Spirit, and they were going to
discover that the Holy Spirit had meanings about the
Old Testament prophecies which they had never imagined
were there. Not until the Holy Spirit took hold of the
Word of God did they know the prophets at all. And then
we shall see that when He really took hold of the Scriptures and began to apply them and open them up and give
the Divine meaning, things happened which not only
were unexpected but were utterly contrary and opposed
to the fixed mentality of the disciples, and which required
a complete shattering of their mentality, the abandonment of established positions on their part. It is tremendously challenging if the Holy Spirit gets hold of the
Word of God and then gets hold of us. There are going
to be revolutionary changes in our whole outlook and procedure, and this book of the Acts is just full of that.

THE COMING OF THE SPIRIT—A NEW ORDER
INTRODUCED

It is the dispensation, or stewardship, of the Holy
Ghost. The words ' dispensation ' and ' stewardship ' mean
an economy, an order ; how things are done in this régime.
We find that, in this dispensation, when the Holy Spirit
came, He began to change things, because He was in

charge. You may become a member of the staff of a business, and when you arrive you find things are done in such and such a way. Times are set and fixed like this; this is how things are done in this régime. And then a new Managing Director arrives, and he sees this prevailing order, and he registers at once that it is an imperfect system, that it is not producing the fullest results for which the business exists. He begins quietly but very strongly to take charge, and things begin to change, and the old set people who have been in that régime for years do not like these changes, and they begin to kick. They will not have it; they revolt and begin to fight against this new order. Some, who are more open-spirited, who are not so fixed and settled, begin to see his mind, his vision, and although they stumble on difficulties from time to time, and come up against the implications of this tremendous change—like Peter, over the visit to Cornelius (Acts x)—and it wants just a little battle to get over the old prejudice, nevertheless, they have their battle, get over their difficulties, and fall into line, and so the great change takes place with wonderful results. Things begin to happen; the original purpose of the business is now beginning, in a wonderful way, to be realised and fulfilled.

That is exactly what happened when the Holy Spirit came in on the day of Pentecost. There was an existing, fixed, established order, but it was not reaching God's end. It was not, as we say, 'delivering the goods'. The Holy Ghost came, with all the full knowledge of the Divine mind; He entered in and began His work of realising the real Divine concept; He took hold. So He divided the people. Some—these that dwelt in Jerusalem, and their rulers—would not have the new order. Well, all right—they lose it all. But others came into the fellowship

of the Holy Ghost, " joined unto the Lord . . . one spirit "
(I Corinthians vi. 17), with wonderful results.

A VITAL CONTRAST—THE LETTER AND THE SPIRIT OF SCRIPTURE

The point is: first of all, it is a new dispensation; and
next, the Holy Ghost is in charge. His being in charge has
to be recognised, with all that it means. And, being in
charge, by His activities He reveals and evolves the very
object of God from all eternity, and seeks to bring it out
in this dispensation. As for the cleavage—well, it was
an historic cleavage then, but it is a cleavage which spiritually has been going on all through the dispensation. It is
a dividing between men of the letter and men of the spirit.
That movement, that tendency, toward a fixed position is
constantly recurring, bringing that which is of God into
imprisonment, within organized limitations which frustrate the whole counsel of God. I have an article before
me—I wish I could quote it all; I cannot—but there are
some things in it which express what is in my heart better
than anything that I could say myself. It was written by a
Member of the British Parliament.

' There are many classifications into which men and
women may be divided—as upper, middle or lower class;
rich, well-to-do and poor; religious, sceptical and atheist;
. . . and so forth and so on. But, as I think, the only cate-
gorization which really matters is that which divides men
as between the Servants of the Spirit and the Prisoners of
the Organization. That classification, which cuts right
across all other classifications, is indeed the fundamental
one. The idea, the inspiration, originates in the internal
world, the world of the Spirit . . . the idea having embodied

itself in the organization, the organization then proceeds gradually to slay the idea which gave it birth. In the field of religion a prophet, an inspired man, will see a vision of truth. He expresses that vision as best he may in words. Upon what his disciples understand of the prophet's message, an organization, a church, will be built. The half-understood message will crystallize into a creed. Before long the principle concern of the church will be to sustain itself as an organization. To this end any departure from the creed must be controverted and, if necessary, suppressed as heresy. In a few score or a few hundred years what was conceived as a vehicle of a new and higher truth has become a prison for the souls of men. And men are murdering each other for the love of God.

' One moral to be drawn, it would not be wholly facetious to suggest, might be that the first rule for any organization should be a rule providing for its dissolution within a limited period of time . . . When we are members of an organization, as such, our attitude to it should be one of partial detachment. We must be above it even while we are in it. We should reckon on being in almost perpetual rebellion within it. Above all we should regard all loyalties to organization as tentative and provisional. We must be Servants of the Spirit, not Prisoners of the Organization. We must keep in touch with the sources of life, not lose ourselves in the temporary vehicles.'

' This world is a bridge. Ye shall pass over it, but ye shall build no houses upon it.'

Is that not just what you have in the Acts and all the way through—the crystallizing of our apprehension of truth, our interpretation, the partial perception, the statement in the letter, something fixed, embodying that which was of the Spirit of God in the beginning, but not allowing it to go beyond those bounds now? Anything more, anything other than that, is called heresy; this is the last word. It may be embodied in an organization, in what is called a church, a sect, a denomination, and if you go beyond that, well, you are said to be all wrong. The great difference between men of the organization and men of the Spirit is what you have here in the Book of the Acts.

THE LORDSHIP OF THE SPIRIT ESSENTIAL TO PROGRESS

The point is this: the fulness of Divine purpose demands that the Holy Spirit be continually in charge, that He be allowed to be completely in the place of government, and that we do not put anything in His place—nothing whatsoever; not a ' church ', not a fixed order— so that at any point or in any way we could say, ' That is not what we teach, that is not what we have been brought up to believe, that is not what our church believes and teaches.' To do that is to put something in the way of the Holy Ghost. The Holy Ghost must be in charge and must be free. It was on those very points that the Apostles themselves had firstly their battles and then their enlargements. We shall see that as we go on. The full Divine purpose is going to take shape when the Holy Spirit is in charge with us.

And then there is something infinitely greater than times and seasons. Be careful about times and seasons; they have a wonderful and pernicious way of bringing you into limitations. Many people are dwelling in times and seasons. But they have done that all the way through the centuries. Let us watch, observe, take note; but be careful. Things have been happening, for example, in Palestine. We were told that the times of the Gentiles ended when General Allenby entered Jerusalem ; that a new Cæsar had arrived to reconstitute the Roman Empire when Mussolini set up his great empire in Rome ! That sort of thing has been going on for centuries, and it is all based upon times and seasons.

The point is this—not that there are no times and seasons, not that there are not movements in the plan of God which have their particular characteristics and can be noted, but that there is something infinitely greater than that. It is the heavenly and not the earthly aspect that is in view in the Book of the Acts. That is why I stayed at that point—" When he had said these things . . . he was taken up". From that point it became a heavenly matter. Later the apostle Paul will use a phrase like this : " The Spirit searcheth all things, yea, the deep things of God " (I Corinthians ii. 10). " The Spirit searcheth . . . the deep things of God": that is something transcendently greater than times and seasons ; and if the Holy Spirit really is in charge, there is no fathoming what God has to reveal. " Things which eye saw not, and ear heard not, and which entered not into the heart of man." It is out there, into that vast realm, that the Holy Spirit would bring us, and we must be very careful that we do not clamp down on the Holy Spirit with man-made, man-constituted institutions. We must keep out in the open with the Spirit, and it is there that our surprises will begin—yes, and our very real discipline.

THE PROPHETS' ULTIMATE MEANING SPIRITUAL AND HEAVENLY

Those referred to in Acts xiii. 27, or those of whom they were typical, had a kind of apprehension of the Scrip-

tures. There was no doubt at all about their devotion to
the Word of God. They were fundamentalists of a rabid
kind, as far as the inspiration of the Scriptures was concerned. They stickled for the Scriptures ; they dotted all
the 'i's and crossed all the 't's. Many among them were
particular about the smallest detail in the realm of outward observances, even to the point of fussy fastidious-
ness. Because the law ordained that a tithe of all the fruit
of the land was the Lord's, they tithed meticulously even
their mint and other herbs—but at the same time overlooked the things that were inward and which mattered
much more to the Lord, such as judgment, mercy and
faith (Matthew xxiii. 23). That was their apprehension,
their mentality, their position. They saw everything on the
horizontal. It was a matter of the exact technique of
Scripture.

What was the result? Well, they were perpetuating an
earthly system with the Word of God. Their ' church ' was
the ' church of Israel ', the ' Israelitish church '—and you
can put in the place of Israel any other denominational
title that you like. That church had its own particular
forms, its vestments, its ritual, its liturgy, and all according to the Scriptures. It had its reading of the prophets
every Sabbath. It had the whole system ; but it was right
down here on this earth and as dead as anything could be.
It was purely formal ; it was not getting through to God's
end at all. Scriptural, in a sense, though it was, it was failing to realise the eternal counsels of God. When the Holy
Ghost came, He did not sweep away the prophets, the Old
Testament. He took them up and showed that there was
something more—something more than all that earthly,
perfect technique of the Word of God, with all its accompaniments—without which all that other would have to

be set aside. And it is going to be set aside. It fails to reach
God's end, therefore it passes out ; and that is the issue of
the Book of the Acts—the great transition. There is a
Divine meaning back of all that, and when you have the
Divine meaning, you can dispense with the other—it can
go. If you have the thing in the really spiritual sense and
realm, in the living and heavenly way, it does not matter
about the other ; that just drops out and falls away.

That is what happened in the Book of the Acts. You
can hardly see the point at which it happened, but there is
such a point. The Apostles did go on attending the temple
and the synagogues for a little while, and then they ceased
to do so. They were continuing for a time, but then it was
as though they were steadily, quietly, moving out, and
eventually they were out. Something had happened. They
had come into the real thing and the initial thing had gone.
The one led to the other, but it had served its purpose.
They came into the heavenly good and meaning of it all ;
it was not a matter of technique now.

There are many who will say about the fixed orders and
rituals : 'Of course, we do not regard this as everything ;
it is only symbolic. We do remember that it implies and
points to something else, and it is that something else we
are thinking of.' Yes, but is it not true that, when the Holy
Ghost comes, as He came then, and gets possession, and
you go on with Him, more and more the emphasis of the
merely outward and earthly and temporal aspects of Christianity fade away, and you become increasingly occupied
with the glory of the reality? The Jesus of history gives
full place to the Jesus of the Spirit, of heaven. That is exactly what is meant by " the voices of the prophets ".

So, on the day of Pentecost, you start with Joel. Everybody in Jerusalem was saying, "What meaneth this?"

(Acts ii. 12). They were all bewildered, without any understanding or perception ; and Peter, with the eleven, stood up and said: "This is that which hath been spoken through the prophet Joel" (vs. 16). "This is that . . ." What a crushing blow it was to tradition, what an upheaval it created in Israel, this—with its implications of Jesus of Nazareth! And the Apostle went on, quoting freely from the Old Testament. He quoted David. That sermon of his on the day of Pentecost was just full of Old Testament quotations. But who ever saw that—who ever knew that that was the meaning of it!

You see the point. It is something that really needs to come to us with tremendous force, because even New Testament Christianity can be reduced again to an earthly system of exact technique. You can write your manuals on New Testament procedure. You can have it exactly according to the letter—but it is all on the horizontal, it becomes legalistic, it ties up the Holy Ghost. Although the intention may have been to be more exactly according to Scripture, that the Lord might have a fuller way, it does not always result in that. The whole thing must be baptized in the Holy Ghost and lifted clean off the earthly level, becoming something entirely heavenly.

OUR RESPONSIBILITY TO YIELD TO THE SPIRIT

Now I think we can rightly say that, when the disciples asked, "Lord, dost thou at this time restore the kingdom to Israel?", they were seriously and genuinely exercised. The Scriptures must be fulfilled ; what was written must happen. I think the disciples were very much occupied with this, burdened and perplexed ; they wanted to know how things were going to work out. The Lord said, in effect: ' Do not worry about that. The Holy Ghost is coming and He will take all responsibility for everything—times and seasons and everything else. He is coming with the whole purpose of God in His hands, and He will work it out. You can be at rest—it is all right.' Those who get this earthly idea and conception of a system become terribly worried and burdened to work it out—burdened with the awful responsibility of this ' New Testament Church ', of having things exactly as the Scriptures say! If the Holy Ghost were in charge, the burden would go. *He* is doing it. All that we are called upon to do is to get into the hands of the Holy Spirit, get completely free from all this harness, free to the Spirit of God. Matters will work out all. right.

And even if the Holy Spirit comes up against some stones in us and for a time there is some conflict, He is more than equal to that situation. He is more than equal to Peter and his never having eaten anything unclean. When the Lord gave Peter that vision of the sheet let down with all manner of fourfooted beasts and creeping things and said, "Rise, Peter; kill and eat", Peter in effect quoted Scripture to the Lord ; he quoted Leviticus xi, with its commandments concerning the unclean beasts which must not be eaten. ' Lord, here is Scripture for my position; my position is soundly founded upon the Word of God!' What are you going to do with that? Now, listen—*I am not saying nor even implying that the Holy Ghost will ever call upon us to do something contrary to the Scriptures.* He never will. But He will very often show us that the Scriptures mean something that we never saw them to mean. Leviticus xi had a meaning that Peter had not seen. He had taken the letter and the literal meaning of those things. He never saw the Divine, spiritual meaning at the back of that. Cornelius had never received the Holy Spirit, and therefore an angel spoke to him. Peter had received the Holy Spirit on the day of Pentecost, and it was the Spirit who was speaking to Peter. The Holy Ghost had this matter in hand, and was dealing with the difficulties in Peter, even in his fundamentalism, to lift him off a merely temporal, earthly ground to a heavenly. Peter was living under an open heaven ; and there are tremendous changes when you get there. It does not all happen at once.

THE HOLY SPIRIT ' UPON ' AND ' IN '

Just one further word for the present. You notice here that there was a double operation of the Holy Spirit. In chapter ii, the Spirit lighted 'upon' them. These cloven tongues as of fire sat upon them ; and then it says, " They were all filled with the Holy Spirit, and began to speak with other tongues, as the Spirit gave them utterance." ' Upon ' and ' in '. I do not want to be technical, contradicting what we have been saying about too much technique, but there is a meaning in the ' upon ' and the ' in '. The coming ' upon ' is the sovereignty of the Holy Spirit in relation to God's eternal purpose. That is, the Holy Spirit hàs come as the custodian and administrator of the eternal counsels of God, of the purpose of God from eternity, and, coming like that, He imposes (I trust that it is not the wrong word to use) the purpose of God upon the vessel. He gathers the vessel into the purpose in a sovereign way. It is as though He circled around and took charge of the vessel in an outward way and said, ' This is the vessel of the eternal purpose of God.' He takes charge of it, comes ' upon ' for that.

But then He entered ' in ' also, and they were filled, and

this had a further meaning. It meant this, that the inward life of the vessel must correspond to the outward purpose. That is tremendous. You see, the old dispensation was not like that, and this is the problem that the prophets were dealing with all the time. The outward form was there. Israel had their temple, they were offering their sacrifices, they were going through all the ritual, but their inward life was far from corresponding to that. God had to say, through the prophets, ' Away with your sacrifices—I do not want them!' (cf. Isaiah i. 10 — 14). The Lord Jesus took that up. "Sacrifice and offering thou wouldest not, but a body didst thou prepare for me; in whole burnt offerings and sacrifices for sin thou hadst no pleasure: then said I, Lo, I am come (in the roll of the book it is written of me) to do thy will, O God " (Hebrews x. 5 — 7).

Formalism never does the will of God ; merely external system, however much it corresponds to the technique of the letter, never does the will of God ; and the Holy Ghost was having none of that. He did not come in sovereignty to take up a lot of new people in a new dispensation, and give them forms and order, and make them do things in such and such a manner, merely in an outward way. He was going to have the inner life of the Church corresponding to the purpose. You find before long that He very severely comes upon anything that does not correspond. Ananias and Sapphira will know you cannot carry on in an outward way, pretending all is right. The Holy Ghost has seen inside the contradiction, and is not allowing it to pass.

Many want the coming 'upon' because they want to feel the power, feel themselves taken up, manipulated and moved. There has been a great deal of that sort of thing, which has not carried with it an inward correspondence.

But the Lord's end can never be reached fully while there is any lack of true consistency between the purpose of God and the life of the people called to that purpose. " I . . . beseech you to walk worthily of the calling wherewith ye were called " (Ephesians iv. 1). Oh, I do beg of you to have continuous dealings with God on this matter of the indwelling Spirit—not just for purposes of service, or power, but for purposes of life.

One of the tragedies of many Christians and many servants of God is this, that they can believe and give expression to things which are positively false, and propagate those things and do harm to other Christians by propagating them, and yet the Holy Ghost never seems to be able to make them aware that they are not telling the truth. I do not mean in Bible teaching, but in relation to other servants of God, and other work that God is doing. The solemn fact that there are such prejudices, suspicions, criticisms, misrepresentations, and so on, ought to drive us to the Lord with earnest appeal—' Oh, Lord, it is no good my being engaged in Thy work, doing a lot of things for Thee, being prominent among men, perhaps, and well known for my Christian service, if yet, after all, the Holy Ghost cannot correct me within, put me right, give me a bad time when I say something not true. Save me from saying anything that does not correspond with the truth, or of which my inward life is a contradiction.' The Spirit within is to adjust us to the purpose of God. If we habitually, constantly, fall into ways which are not according to the Spirit, so that we become known for that kind of unpleasantness, we had better ask the Holy Spirit to do a deeper work in us. It is no use our having the deep things of God, while people know us as most difficult to get on with, always making life unpleasant for others. It will not do ; it is a contradiction of the indwelling Spirit. He does not want us to have the system of things merely outwardly. We must have the inner life to correspond.

So we see that He came ' upon ' to possess for the purpose of God, and He came ' within ' to see that everything in the inner life corresponded to that purpose.

CHAPTER EIGHT

THE CRY OF THE PROPHETS FOR HOLINESS

"For they that dwell in Jerusalem, and their rulers, because they knew him not, nor the voices of the prophets which are read every sabbath, fulfilled them by condemning him" (Acts xiii. 27).

WE WERE TAKING NOTE, in our last chapter, of a contrast which is marked between the old dispensation and the new: of how much there is to be missed if there is a continuing in the fixed order of the old, and how much there is to be gained by moving into the essential nature of the new. This is found focused for us in the passage we have read.

Without repeating too much of our previous meditation, may I just say that it is perfectly clear in the New Testament, from the Book of the Acts onwards, that the people in the new dispensation, the dispensation of the Holy Ghost, were required to keep completely free from everything set, from everything of a conclusive position, *excepting fundamental facts of the faith.* So far as their mentality was concerned—yes, their religious, traditional mentality, the mentality which had been formed by their very birth into Israel, by all that they had received through training and teaching from their infancy upward—they were to be always open to the Lord even for the revolutionary. They

115

were called upon to come into a place where that no longer held them, but where the Lord was perfectly free to do the revolutionary thing in them and make them revise all their thinking—in the light, not of anything contradictory, but of God's fuller meaning in all that they knew of the Word of God ; where they acknowledged that the Lord really had ' more light and truth to break forth from His Word '—indeed, so much more as to make all that they already knew seem as nothing.

You find, therefore, that this necessity precipitated crises in their spiritual course, and sometimes brought them to a standstill, where a tremendous conflict was set up ; but the Holy Spirit was sufficiently in possession to win, and to be able to carry them further. That happened with Peter, on the housetop at Joppa. It happened with Saul of Tarsus. There is no doubt about it that, in acting as he did, Saul was acting upon the basis of the Old Testament Scriptures. He thought he had the full support of the Word of God for what he was doing. When he met Jesus of Nazareth out from heaven as he went to Damascus, although he capitulated there and then and acknowledged Jesus as his Lord, his great problem was, ' How am I going to reconcile my Old Testament with this?' He went away into Arabia, and probably for two years he was occupied there with the reconciliation of the Old Testament with the fact of Jesus as Christ and Lord. And he got well through, came back from his desert, and, caught in the resistless stream of the Spirit, became a mighty servant of God.

We want to go on a little further now. We are saying that here, in this new dispensation as represented in the Book of the Acts, the prophets are being re-interpreted, or their inner meaning is being brought to light, with all that that inner meaning implies. We know that the inauguration of the dispensation on the day of Pentecost was accompanied by a quoting of the prophets. It began with Joel—" This is that which hath been spoken through the prophet Joel" (Acts ii. 16)—and went on with other Old Testament quotations pointing to that time. Now, either by direct citation or fulfilment (as clearly seen in the case of the Joel prophecy) or by an unmistakable implication, the prophets are here brought in in many connections.

CHRIST ALONE THE MEASURE OF WHAT IS OF GOD

You pass from chapter ii of the Book of the Acts, and go on to chapter v—the very terrible, dark story of Ananias and Sapphira. Where did the prophets come in in that?

In the first chapter of the Book of Ezekiel, you have what was introduced spiritually on the day of Pentecost. There you have that wonderful, though difficult, vision of the living creatures, the wheels full of eyes, the Spirit in the wheels, the Spirit of life going, always going: the Spirit, life, eyes, and the irresistible movement from heaven in relation to the Man upon the throne. " Acts " begins there. The Lord Jesus was received up, out of this world ; and in relation to that Man in the throne there is this going on here, touching the earth and yet detached from it ; touching, but not fixed here ; a heavenly thing. And that is moving with tremendous directness and deliberation. That is like the second chapter of " Acts ". The Man in the throne ; the wheels, the eternal counsels of God, the goings of God from eternity ; the living creatures, the Church ; the life within, the Spirit of life there, with His perfect vision—" full of eyes ". Is that not what is here?

Yes ; but that is the beginning of " Ezekiel ". At the
other end of his prophecy you have this—away, up from
the earth—a vision, a picture, of a temple, a spiritual
house, very fully depicted and defined, with every detail
marked. The man who leads the prophet round goes
measuring, measuring, giving the measure of every detail. This house is all of the Holy Ghost. It is all a measure of Christ, in every part. This thing is not on the earth ;
it is heavenly measurement. Before you can have the river
issuing from the sanctuary, flowing on in increasing volume, deepening and widening, making everything on its
banks to live, and swallowing up death in victory as it
proceeds, you have to have the house utterly according to
God ; and then the one overall statement about it is : " the
whole limit thereof round about shall be most holy "
(Ezekiel xliiii. 12). It is all of God ; it is all of Christ, His
risen, exalted Son. It is out from Him, through a Church
constituted on a heavenly pattern, that the life flows ; and
it is flowing here in " Acts ".

HOLINESS THE LAW OF WHAT IS OF GOD

Now Ananias and his wife violate the very governing
law of that house—holiness ; and what happens? That is
where Israel failed to hear the voices of the prophets. We
said, in our previous meditation, that they carried on the
external formalities of the temple, the daily services, the
ritual and the liturgy, adopted the forms and the vestments, but the inner life did not correspond. It was the
cry of the prophets that a system was being maintained
and preserved out of relation to the inner life of the
people. The prophets throughout are crying for holiness.
The trouble lay there. And what does this matter of holi-

ness really mean? When you really get to the heart of it, what is it? " Why hath Satan filled thy heart to lie to the Holy Spirit?" (Acts v. 3). That is the unholiness. The act of Ananias and Sapphira implies something deeper—that sinister mind behind ; Satan finding an opportunity of getting into these holy precincts, this heavenly realm, corrupting and polluting, and establishing his lie. " He is a liar, and the father thereof ", said the Lord (John viii. 44). A lie right in the presence of the Holy Ghost! The life of the Spirit and the Spirit of life do not just go on ignoring conditions. They require that first of all everything shall be constituted on God's heavenly pattern ; that is only saying, constituted on the pattern of Christ His Son ; that it shall be really an expression and representation of the Lord Jesus by the Holy Spirit.

THE SPIRIT SPONTANEOUSLY REPRODUCES THE NATURE OF CHRIST

Now, I am not going back behind what I said earlier. I am not saying that we must take the Bible in its letter and phrases and make a mould, a scriptural mould, which we think is the New Testament order. That is not the point at all. Development did not come about in the beginning in that way. Every fresh reproduction of the Church, in any part of the Roman Empire or beyond, in the days of the Apostles, came about, not by taking thither a fixed mould and trying to pour people into that mould and to reproduce the shape of things that existed somewhere else. It began with life—life from heaven—" the Holy Ghost sent forth from heaven " (I Peter i. 12). And wherever the believers went, two things were imperative: firstly, baptism, as a testimony to the fact that

an old order was finished, and that everything now had
to have as new a beginning as anybody must have who has
died and been buried ; and secondly, the gift of the Holy
Ghost, the Spirit of life, coming to take up residence within those concerned.

When the Holy Spirit comes in and has His way, He
relieves you of all the responsibility of New Testament
order ; you have no more burden and responsibility about
that than a tree has in producing leaves and fruit. No tree
ever spends hours and hours worrying and fretting, ' How
can I bring forth some leaves? how can I develop my
fruit?' It just lives—it yields to the life process ; and the
rest happens. That was the glorious spontaneity of New
Testament churches—they just came about. And the Lord
must have them like that—constituted from heaven by the
Holy Ghost ; not man bringing his form of church and
church government, his mould, his conception of things,
and saying, ' This is our conception of a Bible church.'
No, it is the product of life. As that Spirit of life was allowed to work, things took a certain course and a certain
form, and that was the form of Christ. The Holy Spirit
took responsibility. " I will build my church ", the Lord
Jesus had said (Matthew xvi. 18), and He meant it ; and
He is found doing it here.

THE NATURE OF CHRIST IS UTTER HOLINESS

But remember : Christ, in the innermost expression of
what He is, is very holy. " The holy thing which is begotten ", said the angel to Mary, " shall be called the Son
of God " (Luke i. 35, A.R.V.). He "offered himself without
blemish unto God " (Hebrews ix. 14). He was ". . . in all
points tempted like as we are, yet without sin " (Heb. iv.

15). Christ was and is without sin. He is infinitely holy.
The great antagonist of Christ, that unholy one, is always
seeking to destroy what is of Christ, by introducing a
contradiction, a lie, giving the lie to the holiness of Christ ;
and that is what happened here.

I do feel that this is a very solemn matter for us all.
I have not said this without a very great deal of exercise
in my own heart. It is not an easy thing to say. Some of
us are not ignorant of Satan's devices. Who has a right to
talk about holiness? Who is sufficient in holiness to talk
to other people about it? Holiness is what Christ is. Who
of us could say we are like that?

THE SPIRIT ARRESTED BY CONSCIOUS UNHOLINESS

Unholiness is that which is not consistent with Christ.
It is the opposite of what Christ is ; it is a contradiction of
Christ. The mighty purpose of God, the mighty course of
the Spirit of God—all that has come in with this dispensation—can be suddenly brought under arrest, and a tragedy
occur, if you or I knowingly dabble with unholiness. " His
wife also being privy to it " (Acts v. 2) means that this was
conscious. I am not speaking of the unholiness which is
ours in general—though we are not going to condone or
make light of it. What I am speaking about now is deliberate sin in the very presence of the Holy Spirit. Ananias and
Sapphira deliberately planned to give to the Lord only a
part of the proceeds of their sale, but to represent it as being the whole. If they had been really in the good of the
régime of the Holy Spirit, they would have known the
Spirit saying to them : ' That is not right—it is a contradiction of Christ.' And may we not confidently conclude
that the Holy Spirit did warn them? Were there not two

voices which, though perhaps not audible, yet spoke in them, the one warning from evil, the other suggesting this deceit—the voice of the Spirit and the voice of Satan? They were disposed to listen to the tempter's voice, and Satan ' filled their hearts '. That is the kind of unholiness we are speaking about.

We are in the dispensation of the Spirit. If we are really in the good of this dispensation, that is, if the Holy Spirit is in us, He will tell us—He does tell us. If we will, we can know the mind of the Spirit on all issues of right and wrong. But until we yield to the Spirit, everything is in suspense. The whole life of the Spirit is brought under arrest. The Lord was very positive in laying down the principles for the dispensation. He left us in no doubt as to what His attitude is toward this sort of thing. If He does not act in the same way every time, and if we do not fall down dead, it does not mean that something just as tragic does not take place in us. The Spirit is arrested, and spiritual death comes in, and there is no going on from that time. There is a sense in which, spiritually, we also are ' carried out '.

Yes, this is a solemn matter. Forgive me if I seem to be oppressive, but this matter of holiness is so very pertinent, and so very much bound up with all that we are seeking to see—all the wonderful meaning of the Spirit's being here and of His being able to go right on ; life and fulness, growing depth, increasing vitality, ever fuller knowledge, the swallowing up of death in victory. That is to be the spiritual existence of the Church, but that can all be arrested by some unholiness, known to be such and not dealt with before God, repudiated and refused. Whatever that may mean to you in its particular application, remember that it is a very dangerous thing to have an unsettled controversy with the Holy Ghost—dangerous not only for you, but perhaps for many others who will be affected.

THE PERIL OF PERSISTING IN UNHOLINESS

Oh, the tragedy of a controversy with the Lord not cleared up! Surely, seeing the setting of a matter like this, we must face the specific things from the standpoint of the great background. You have not an adequate motive for dealing with particular points of outstanding unholiness unless you see this whole matter in its great setting. If it is merely something personal, relating only to us, we may or we may not feel it is worth clearing up. But look! The whole course of God's eternal counsels, coming down our way and gathering us in: the mighty purpose of God to be realised in and through us: the far-reaching range of those purposes of God which would find us as their vehicle and channel: all that God would do of making Himself known to us for the sake of others: all brought under arrest because of that! Yes, a personal ministry, a great ministry which might be very far-reaching, may all be set aside—the Lord, in keeping with His own nature, would have to set it aside—if there were a persistence in something about which He had spoken but which was not dealt with. It is a tremendous background.

The psalmist said: "I know, O Lord, that thy judgments are righteous, and that in faithfulness thou hast afflicted me" (Psalm cxix. 75). What did he mean? Evidently he had gone through some severe handling by the Lord, and as he looked at what his wrong involved for the Lord's people—how many were affected and how it touched the Lord's honour—he said: 'Only the faithfulness of God lies behind His dealing with me: He has to be faithful to Himself and faithful to me, and not let me off ; and He has to be faithful to His own nature, His own righteousness, because so much is bound up with it.' May the Lord show us just what that means, and give us grace. Oh, we need protecting, we need safeguarding in this matter of a holy walk with God ; we need to clear up every controversy with Him because there is so much bound up with it.

We see that those that dwelt in Jerusalem, and their rulers and those whom they represented, would not clear up the controversy which God had with them, and they were set aside, and another nation bringing forth the fruits of the Kingdom was brought in. What a loss ! And do you think that the Lord will deal with us differently? It may not be our salvation that will go, but surely our vocation is of some consequence ! The Lord give us grace !

CHAPTER NINE

A RECAPITULATION

WE HAVE BEEN SEEING that in the dispensation of the Old Testament the Holy Spirit was operating as the Spirit of prophecy, making everything a prophecy. He was causing everything within the Divine economy to point onward, to imply something further, which was not clear to those who lived in those times and who were most closely connected with what was being done and said ; and that comprehensive work of the Holy Spirit through those ages was all heading up to what would be the nature, character and purpose of the dispensation in which we live. This dispensation is marked by two outstanding features—two aspects of one thing. It is the dispensation, firstly, of Christ enthroned at the right hand of the Majesty in the heavens, and secondly, of the Holy Spirit here within the Church to make good all that that means. That prophetic activity was many-sided ; that is, it pointed to various characteristics of the age which lay ahead ; and we have been looking at some of those characteristics in the foregoing chapters.

So that now we start here. We have come to and are living in the dispensation of the spiritual fulfilment of what the prophets foretold ; but that fulfilment is not merely and only objective, as in the history of the world or of the Church, in an outward way. That fulfilment is an inward thing, and moreover an inward thing so far as every member of Christ is concerned. It is something which must come down to the youngest. Please do not think that this is for older or more advanced Christians! It involves every one of us equally.

SPIRITUAL VISION

The first thing that the prophets were occupied with, and which has its fulfilment in an inward way in the members of Christ in this dispensation, is spiritual vision. Everything in the purpose of God, for its fulfilment and for our attainment unto it, rests firstly upon this—that the Holy Spirit has become to us the Spirit of revelation, and has made us to see, in its grand outline, what God is after. The details are filled in as we go on.

(a)   THE FACULTY OF SEEING

That has two sides. First of all, there is the faculty of seeing. The prophets had much to say about this. You know that, because of a certain prejudice on the part of the people of Israel, by which they were not disposed to see what God wanted them to see (because they had their own visions and ideas and were not ready for what God wanted), a double judgment was passed upon them, and the Lord closed their eyes. The word was given to Isaiah for this people: "Go, and tell this people, Hear ye indeed, but understand not; and see ye indeed, but perceive not. Make the heart of this people fat, and make their ears heavy, and shut their eyes" (Isaiah vi. 9, 10). That was a judgment, and a terrible one: the very faculty of spiritual sight, of vision, was neutralised. It was a terrible judgment, with terrible consequences; for, as we have seen, the ultimate consequence was that they lost all that God intended, and that was no small thing. It passed away from them. It was given to another nation—a heavenly nation. It is a terrible judgment to have a faculty of spiritual sight nullified; and if that is so, it must be a very great thing in the desire and grace and lovingkindness of the Lord that people should have such vision, such sight.

The faculty for seeing is a birthright of every child of God. Do not think that you have to live the Christian life for a long time, receive much teaching, and reach a certain advanced position, before you begin to see. It is a part of your very new birth. The Lord said to Nicodemus : " Except one be born anew, he cannot *see* the kingdom of God " (John iii. 3). By implication He said, ' When you are born from above, you will see.' The commission to the Apostle Paul was : ". . . unto whom I send thee, to open their eyes " (Acts xxvi. 17, 18). The very symbolical work of the Lord Jesus in the days of His flesh, in opening the eyes of the blind, was pointing on to what was going to happen when He went above and the Holy Spirit came, and men saw. It is a part of your new birth to see. I am not saying that you will see all at once, that you will see all that those who have gone far on with the Lord are seeing ; but the faculty of sight has been given to you. Are you using it? Do you know that it is just as true of your spiritual life as it is of your physical—that you have spiritual eyes, and that they have been opened? If not, get right down to the Lord about this, because something is wrong.

(b) THE OBJECT SEEN

And not only the faculty, but the object, of sight ; it is a part of the vision. There must be a faculty for seeing before there can be an object seen, but, having the faculty, you must have an object to see ; and the object is—what? What was the thing that came to the perception, the recognition, of people, when the Holy Ghost came? What did they begin to see? They began to see the significance of Jesus Christ, and there is one very familiar phrase which indicates what that is—" the eternal purpose ". They are one and the same thing—the significance of Christ, and God's eternal purpose. The purpose of God from eternity is concerning His Son—the place that His Son holds in the very universe according to God's mind ; the tremendous comprehensiveness of Christ ; the tremendous implications of the very being and existence of Christ ; the tremendous consequences that are bound up with Jesus Christ. They did not see it all at once, but they began to see the Lord Jesus. They began to see that this was not just a man among men, not just the man of Galilee. No, He is infin- itely greater than that, overwhelming. This mighty im- pact of a meaning about Jesus Christ is too big to hold, so great that you cannot grasp it. It is overwhelming and devastating. They began to see *that* ; that was their vision. Out of that vision everything else came. Look at them and hear them, recognise what a new and great Christ they have found, what a significant Christ He is, how every- thing is bound up with Him. All destiny is centred in Him ; He is the only consequence.

The prophets had dimly seen something. You will hear a prophet saying: " His name shall be called Wonderful, Counsellor, Mighty God, Everlasting Father, Prince of Peace " (Isaiah ix. 6). Well, that prophet had begun to see something ; and there are other things like that. It is but a beginning, but what they are saying is that this One is going to come into full view. ' We are pointing on to Him ', they say, ' looking on to the day when this One shall come right out into recognition.' And this is that day ; we are in the day of the prophets' fulfilled vision.

These are not merely words, great ideas. It has to be true of you, even though it may be only at its beginnings, that the apprehension of Jesus Christ in your heart is tremendous, is overwhelming. He is your vision, and He has mastered you in the sense of His greatness. We shall never get through without vision. We shall break if we have no vision, or if our vision is arrested. If something interferes with the clearness, the fulness, of our vision, we shall begin to go round in circles, not knowing where we are. The vision will carry us on if it is kept clear and full. Have you got it? When the Holy Spirit came on the day of Pentecost, this tremendous thing happened—they saw the Lord, and in seeing Him they began to be emancipated from everything that was other or less than He. Those who did not see, well, they began to pass out and either became nonentities in the spiritual realm or, because of their prejudices, enemies to those who saw. The instance in John ix was fulfilled in a spiritual sense. The Lord opened the eyes of the man born blind. What happened? The others cast him out. Those who saw in the day of the Spirit's coming were excommunicated by many who were prejudiced. They were cut off. There is always a price attached to seeing.

But that is not our subject now. Simply, what the Lord has been saying to us, in the first place, is that He desires to have, and must have—and therefore He can have—in this dispensation a people with their eyes open, a seeing people who have the faculty in themselves.

(c) VISION TO BE PERSONAL AND INCREASING IN EVERY BELIEVER

Now, the difference between the dispensations is just that. In the old dispensation everything had to be told

to the people. They had to get it secondhand from someone else; it was never their own, it was not original. In
the new dispensation of the Holy Spirit, the thing was in
themselves; the root of the matter was in them. But
Christianity has become very largely a system which has
reverted to the level of the old dispensation. That is, so
many Christians have their lives based upon addresses and
sermons and going to meetings and being told by other
people. How many Christians do you find to-day who are
really living in the good of a throbbing, personal revelation of Jesus Christ? I do not think that is an improper
question. The great need of our day is for the people of
God to be re-established on the basis upon which the
Church was founded in the beginning, a Holy Ghost
basis; and the very beginning of that basis is this—not to
have a lot of information given to Christians, but that the
Christians should have the faculty of spiritual sight within them, should have the capacity for seeing, and should
themselves be seeing. Can you say: ' My eyes are open ;
I am seeing God's eternal purpose, I am seeing the significance of Christ ; I am seeing more and more as to the
Lord Jesus'? Unless it is like that, we shall leave the
Holy Ghost behind, and we shall have to turn round and
go back to find Him where we left Him, because a life in
the Holy Ghost right up to date is a life of continually increasing vision. Vision is absolutely essential, both as to
faculty and as to object.

THE INSTRUMENTALITY OF THE CROSS

(a)   DEATH—THE REMOVAL OF WHAT IS OF MAN

Still recapitulating, we went on next to see that, in
order to keep the faculty alive and the vision growing, the

Holy Spirit has an instrument. He always works by an instrument, and that instrument is the Cross ; that is, the principle of the Cross of the Lord Jesus.

This means, on the one side, the removal of everything that cannot come into the new Kingdom ; getting rid of that which in God's sight is dead and has to be put away —that is to say, the sum total of the self-life. Call it by other names if you like—the flesh, the natural life, the old Adam, and so on. I prefer this designation—the self-principle—because it is very comprehensive : whether it be the self-principle acting in the outward direction, in assertiveness, in imposition, where the self is the impact ; or whether it act in the inward direction, drawing to self. Oh, how many aspects there are of the self-life in both these directions ! We may know some of the more obvious ones, but are we not learning how deeply rooted, with countless fibres, is this self? We never get to the end of it. It spreads its tentacles throughout our whole constitution —' I ', somehow, strong or weak. It is just as bad for it to be weak as to be strong. Self-pity is only a way of drawing attention to ourselves and being occupied with ourselves, and it is just as pernicious as self-assertiveness. It is *self,* all the same ; it belongs to the same root, it comes from the same source. It all comes from that false life of the one who said : " I will ascend into heaven, I will exalt my throne above the stars of God ; and I will sit upon the mount of congregation . . . I will ascend above the heights of the clouds ; I will make myself like the Most High " (Isaiah xiv. 13, 14). ' I ' — ' I ' — ' I ' —. Truly, we cannot exhaust the forms of this self-life.

Now, because it is so many-sided and so far-reaching and so deeply rooted, the Lord cannot deal with it all at once in the active way. He has dealt with it all at once potentially in the Cross of His Son. But now the application of that must go on. You and I must know continually the application of the principle of the Cross to the various forms of the self-life. We must learn both the need for and the manner of its being smitten, stricken, laid low and brought under the hand of God ; and that is the meaning of ' disciple ', that is the meaning of training. It is on that side of things that the Holy Ghost is constantly taking precautions against the self-life. Even in the case of a far-advanced and well-crucified Apostle, it becomes necessary, in the presence of great Divine deposits, for God to take precautions and put a stake in his flesh and give him a messenger of Satan to buffet him, lest he should become exalted (II Corinthians xii. 7). That is very practical. The Holy Ghost uses the principle and the law of the Cross repeatedly and ever more deeply in order to get rid of the rubbish—that which occupies the ground which must be occupied by the Lord Himself. There has to be a lot of clearing of the ground in order to build the new spiritual kingdom within.

(b) RESURRECTION—THE EXPRESSION OF THE LORD HIMSELF

So, on the other side, the corresponding thing is the power of His resurrection, which can never be known except as we know the power of His Cross ; and it is in knowing Him and the power of His resurrection that our education on the positive side is found. Oh, to know Him and the power of His resurrection ! It is a wonderful thing when you and I are brought to the place where on the side of nature—and not feignedly, but very utterly—we are compelled to recognise the awful and terrible reality : ' This is an end of everything. I who have said so much, I who have preached so much, I who have taught so much, I who have done so much—I am at an end.' It is the sentence of death ; no more is possible ; and it is terribly and grimly real. And then God raises the dead! You go on, and there is something more of the Lord than there was before. It is a great thing to see how God does raise the dead again and again. The same person is alive again, and there is more than there ever was, because there has been a greater emptiness than there ever was. It is a very safe position from the Lord's standpoint.

What are we learning, what is the meaning of that way, what is it we are inheriting along the line of such experiences? Just this—we are knowing the Lord, that is all. We are knowing this, that everything is of the Lord,. and whatever is not of Him is nothing at all. It must be of the Lord or there is no more possibility, no hope. We are the most ready to say, ' If it depends upon me, there is nothing more possible ' ; and then the Lord does it. You see what He is doing by the death side of the Cross. He is clearing ground for Himself, and then He is occupying the ground ; He is building Himself up as the risen Lord on the ground which has been purged of our old self. The Holy Spirit uses the Cross to keep the way open, to keep the vision clear and growing.

A NEW LIBERTY

Further, we pointed out that when the dispensation changed on the day of Pentecost, from that moment there was a marvellous emancipation into a new liberty. In the old dispensation the whole order was one of bondage, of thraldom ; people were in a strait-jacket of a religious system. In the new dispensation, the strait-jacket has gone. There is nothing that suggests a strait-jacket in the Book of the Acts. People are out, they are free. There will still be some things to be taken away, like Peter's remnant of tradition in the presence of the call to the house of Cornelius, and so on. But in the main they are out, released, and it is the Holy Spirit who brings that about and demands that it shall be maintained.

The Lord wants and needs such a people to-day, just as then. Firstly, a people of vision ; and then, secondly, a thoroughly crucified people, giving the Lord full scope for all His purpose—a people who, in themselves, have been removed out of the Lord's way. (That is the meaning of the Book of the Acts—that people are out of the Lord's way, and He can move freely.) Then, the Holy Ghost, having effected this liberation, demands that it shall be preserved. We were pointing out earlier that the constant and persistent tendency of man and effort of the enemy is to bring back again into a yoke of bondage, imprisoning the Holy Ghost in some set, crystallized system of things—a Church system, an ecclesiastical system, a man-made religious order, a formality, an organization, and all such things as so often commence with a Divine idea, and then take charge of the Divine idea and make it to serve them instead of everything serving it.

That is the peril, and the Holy Ghost will have none of it. He can only go as far as He has liberty to go. He demands that we be out in a free place with Him ; He demands His own rights as the Spirit of liberty. He will be hampered by nothing. If we try to hamper Him, to put chains on Him, we shall lose His values. He demands that we shall never allow ourselves to be brought into any fixed form or economy or limit of any kind ; that we shall be God's free people. That is not licence. That does not give the individual the right to be a free-lance, nor mean that we can go and do everything that our impulse would suggest, and independently snap our fingers at all spiritual authority. It never meant that. But it does mean that the Lord will not allow us to crystallize His things and put them into a box and say, ' That is the limit.' He demands that we should be ready always to receive and respond to new light. If His new light demands that we make new adjustments—revolutionary adjustments sometimes—we are to be so free in the Lord that we can do it. It is most necessary that we should be like that, as God's free people. It is a very blessed thing to have the expanse of the universe in which to move.

HOLINESS THE CHARACTER OF THE NEW DISPENSATION

Now our next point was that the whole nature of things, characteristic of the dispensation of the Holy Spirit and of all the Spirit's movements, is holiness—that everything shall inwardly correspond to what is outward. Progress can be brought to an abrupt standstill; all this movement of the Spirit of God can be suddenly arrested; there may be an end beyond which there is no advance, if there is some debatable thing between the Holy Ghost and us. We have to keep very short accounts with the Holy Spirit on all matters of question, and He is resident in us for this purpose. Why are there so many things in Christians that are not as the Lord would have them? It is simply because those concerned have not recognised and taken to heart this—that the Holy Spirit is their personal, indwelling Teacher, and they have to listen to Him. How much is lost because of that failure! ' Oh, there is a meeting: I do not think I will go to it—I will go for a walk.' So off you go. In that meeting was the very word God meant you to have! If only you had said, ' I would like to go for a walk, but there is a meeting; I will ask the Lord whether He wants me there.' Something has been lost that you may not recover for yourself, because you failed to ask the Lord.

And so in a thousand different ways. If only we listened to the Holy Spirit, we should make more progress. He talks to us about all sorts of practical matters. For example, we need to be taught by the Spirit in the matter of our merriment—how to be merry without being frivolous, and how to be serious without being long-faced and miserable. We are not going to giggle our way through life, but at the same time the Lord does not want us to be poor, solemn creatures. He does want us to be serious people, but do not think that solemnity is necessarily spiritual life. I read in my morning paper of a poor girl in Australia, who was overtaken of a certain disease which deprived her of the ability to smile. She was brought by air to have an operation in London—and after the operation she could smile! I think a lot of Christians need that operation!

But in this whole matter we have to know the discipline of the Holy Spirit, because spiritual value, spiritual increase, is bound up with it. In matters of holiness, and controversies with the Lord—which may come down to very small points, such as details of dress, the wearing of adornments, and so on—it is remarkable how adjustments are made by many young Christians on these practical matters without anything being said to them by anyone. Who told them to do it? No one; but they came to feel that the Lord would have them do it, that is all. Such people are going on; they are beginning to count for God. I take those points, not to impose law upon you, but to show the principle of the Holy Spirit's being able to speak to us inside on matters where the Lord may not be fully in agreement, and, as He speaks and we respond, we go on. The Holy Spirit adds and adds.

SPIRIT-DIRECTED SERVICE: NO EXCLUSIVISM

As you come into the Book of the Acts further, you find that the Holy Spirit was the Spirit of service. You get to chapter viii, and the movement out from Jerusalem is absolutely spontaneous. Philip goes down to Samaria. Who told him he should go to Samaria? Surely we may say that the Holy Spirit led him there. They moved out under the sovereign control of the Holy Spirit. He was the Spirit of service ; He brought it about. And when you come to chapter x, oh, what a blessed aspect of that development! We find it in keeping with what the prophets, though imperfectly, were made to see. In chapter x the Holy Spirit precipitates the whole matter of going beyond the bounds of Israel out to the Gentiles. How do the prophets come into that? Well, what about Jonah? It is a terrible story, that story in the little book of Jonah. It is not the whole life and work of Jonah, but it is practically all that most people know about him—that he had a fierce quarrel with the Lord. "Doest thou well to be angry? . . . I do well to be angry " (Jonah iv. 9). Think of a man answering God like that! Why? Because the large-hearted grace of God had said, in effect, ' There must be no exclusivism ; I am not bound up wholly and solely with Israel ; my heart embraces the heathen as well ; the whole world is the scope of My grace.' Jonah was so exclusive—there could be nothing beyond his own circle, and he came into controversy with the Lord.

The Lord has scattered here and there through His Word lessons and illustrations which emphasize that.

What about Ruth? She is a Moabitess, a heathen, outside
the pale of Israel. It is the most beautiful romance in the
Bible, that little story of Ruth. What is the Lord saying?
Look at the genealogy of the Lord Jesus, and you will
find Ruth, the Moabitess, there. But if that is impressive,
what about Rahab the harlot, the resident in doomed Jericho, who had faith and expressed it by the scarlet cord in
the window? And in the genealogy of Jesus Christ, Rahab
the harlot has a place. What is God saying? He takes up
in the new dispensation the principle of that prophetic
work of the Holy Spirit through the Old Testament. In
Acts x He precipitates it, as if to say, ' Go out to all ; let
there be no exclusivism.' It is impossible to be people governed by the Holy Spirit and not to have the world in your
heart—not to be concerned for all the Lord's people, and
for all who are not the Lord's people. He will precipitate
that issue. Let us allow that truth to search us deeply.

The point of all that we have been saying is this : that
when the Holy Spirit comes and really has His way, all
these things are spontaneous : they happen : these are the
features of His government. Oh, that the Lord might recover a people like that, free from all set, ecclesiastical,
religious, traditional limits and bounds—a people in the
Spirit! The Lord make us every one to be of that kind.

God
Hath
Spoken

Publisher's note:

God Hath Spoken originally published from
39 Honor Oak Road, London in 1949

The year of publication as given is from when, in the
author's bimonthly magazine *A Witness and a
Testimony*, a first notice of this book or booklet
appeared. Very many of the titles published had
already appeared earlier as articles or series in that
magazine.

Where a new title's date of publication is not known, +
signifies the year of the magazine article or series from
which, some unspecified time later, that new
publication was reproduced.

1998 Christian Books Publishing House / SeedSowers
P O Box 285
Sargent
GA 30275

CONTENTS

"GOD HATH SPOKEN"

Chapter One

The Final Message of God

Preamble

THE "Preface" to any book is intended to serve the purpose of letting its readers know what the writer has to say as to his purpose in writing, and anything that does not really form a part of the subject matter. While it ought to be regarded as important, many people do not read the Preface, and by not doing so, may unintentionally do the writer an injustice. To guard against this risk, I ask at the outset for a careful perusal of what follows.

I am well aware that what will be said will represent for multitudes of Christians to-day no less an upheaval and revolution than that which was presented at the beginning by the transition from Judaism to a fully-fledged Christianity as presented by the Apostles when they were through that transition and interpreted the significance of Christ. If it should cause or result in as violent a reaction and hostility, it will be no surprise.

There are two causes for comfort in such a case: one is the deep sense of Divine urge and commission to write, "whether they will hear or whether they will forbear"; and the other, the knowledge that for a long time and in an ever deepening way there has been a growing realisation on the part of many that all is not well with Christendom, even with evangelical

Christianity. With the exception of two classes of Christians, there is an increasing concern over the actual or comparative weakness and ineffectiveness of the spiritual life and witness of Christians and the churches. This concern shows itself in various ways. Sometimes by enquiries and discussions as to what is wrong, and sometimes in the holding of an increased number of conventions and meetings " for the deepening of the spiritual life."

The two classes excepted are, those who have so organised Christian activity as to have made it all a matter of a tremendous business to be maintained by drive and its own momentum : which unceasing activity is itself thought to be life and power : with the result that there is little time or interest to be given in the matter of spiritual depth, and Divine measure. The other class is comprised of those who are so settled in tradition and a fixed position in doctrine and practice as to make it wellnigh impossible for the Holy Spirit to lead into the way of a greater fulness of Christ. Both of these conditions marked Judaism in the first days, and they both provided a ground for the strong resentment and antagonism from which the Apostles and first believers had to suffer.

It is not too much to say that a time and state of crisis is upon traditional Christianity. This, and its nature, will be shown more fully in what follows; but in concluding the Preamble may I ask that, should you at any point be so vexed as to be inclined to put the whole thing aside, you will just pause and give place to a supposition. Supposing it *should* be right? In the year 1939 many responsible people, governments, and officials, came under severe condemnation because—it was said— they refused to believe facts. For years Germany had been most thoroughly establishing Fifth Column agents and forces in almost every country. But whenever anyone said so and warned the Governments of those countries that it was so, not only was the suggestion repudiated, but evil intent was disbelieved. Well, the persistently disbelieved reports proved true, but it meant suffering, sorrow, and horror unparalleled in history. Supposing that in 1939 someone had prophesied that in less than a year Germany would have defeated and overrun Holland, Belgium, and France, in addition to a number of other European countries, what would have happened to such a prophet? He would have been ridiculed, if not put into prison or an asylum as a defeatist or a lunatic. He, himself, most likely would have been regarded as an enemy agent, as in effect were Jeremiah and other prophets of old. But those " unbelievable " things became actualities. Thus, untold suffering and loss are the price of refusing to entertain a supposition.

But there was another factor of a very subtle nature. It was a studied part of the success of that German technique that the agents should spread abroad the impression

7

that no such evil intent existed. To disarm suspicion and impress with good will was a vital part of the success of the scheme. This has its counterpart in the " heavenlies," and it will only be those who keep much in the secret place with the All-knowing Spirit of God who will be saved from the infinite perils which lie in the way of a superficial optimism which is such a secret weapon of Satan's campaign against the fulness of Christ.

Pause then, and ask, Supposing what is here written should be right? Would it result in *spiritual and eternal* loss or gain? Supposing it should eventually prove to be God's message?

THE LETTER TO THE HEBREWS

(i) The Approach

In the Preamble we have used the word Crisis. The letter which is before us had its occasion in a crisis in two dimensions or phases. Immediately, it was related to those who had taken a real step with Christ and were in peril of resolving Christianity into a Judaism which acknowledged rather than rejected Him. But it also related to the great event which was imminent, in which the whole Jewish system would be swept away, and all the prophecies as to Israel's rejection and scattering would be fulfilled. It is always important to remember that, when God deals with any of His people on a spiritual issue, there is always a literal issue bound up with it sooner or later. He would save us from the historic disaster which He knows to be coming by putting us into a spiritual position where the event will be no disaster *to us*. Thus the crisis is a turning point—as in a critical illness —with life or death as the issue. The letter repeatedly warns and entreats in the light of the tremendous consequences which are in the balances. We may say without fear of being contradicted that some of the most terrible things in the whole Bible are found in this letter. Thus does it become us to note the significance of the opening statements.

God in past times spoke in fragments and various ways, but now He has spoken in fulness and in one all-inclusive way, and that with finality. He will not speak again; He will neither add to nor vary what He has said in the final way. The fragmentary speech of God in past ages had very great consequences involved in man's attitude and reaction; but that was small compared with what is bound up with this final Speech. This kind of approach is preserved like a theme through the whole letter; it comes to the ear in various connections, sometimes beautiful, sometimes terrible. The upshot of it all is this: You have had in your midst and available to you the *full* Revelation of God's mind. For that you are now responsible. That Revelation was, and is, intended to bring you into a certain spiritual position and to govern the entire order of your life. The measure of your spiritual life in terms of Divine satisfaction will be determined by your living apprehension of and obedience to that Revelation. *The degree of your ineffectiveness and unfruitfulness, individually and collectively, will declare the degree of your failure in your apprehension of that Revelation.*

The letter is intended to be tremendously serious. While it contains most glorious things, it is the possibility of missing these (a possibility so nearly becoming an actuality in the case of its first readers) which makes the tone so solemn at times. Thus our approach must be with the shoes off our feet: the shoes of prejudice, self-sufficiency, pride, formalism, and such-like. Having adjusted our approach, we are able to contemplate something of the import or implications of the letter.

(ii) The Implications

It is here that we have to begin to say some of the things not easy to say, and still less easy to accept.

This letter to the Hebrews sets forth the all-inclusive revolution or reconstitution which God made when He brought His Son, Jesus Christ, into the world—that is, the *religious* revolution. This revolution, which was rejected by Judaism, has been almost entirely overlooked or lost sight of by Christendom since Apostolic times. The entire present system of Chris tianity as generally accepted would be impossible if the meaning of this letter were received as a heavenly revelation in the power of the Holy Spirit. That is—if it came into the heart

10

by the Spirit's power with the effect of a revelation in the same way as the Apostle Paul
came to see who " Jesus of Nazareth " is, then
a Christian-Judaism, or Judaistic-Christianity
(which Christendom so largely is) would be
impossible; as it became in his own case. The
letter to the Hebrews is only one other aspect
of the battle fought out in the letters to the
Romans and Galatians. In the light of such
a spiritual eye-opening a whole lot of things
would go: but being a " heavenly vision,"
there would be no tears, no sense of loss, and
no fond farewells. The gain and joy would
rather put all such things into the category of
a worn-out and no-longer-to-be-desired suit of
clothes. In saying this we are only contemplating the full-tide of spiritual life known before
any of these things came into being. These
things only came in when the fulness of the
Spirit had gone out, and being an artificial
substitute they can never but be limiting things
in the realm of Divine purpose. And yet,
behold how these things have become the very
nature of traditional and organised Christianity! So much so that to touch them in
any way which threatens their existence is to
meet something more bitter and formidable
than any persecution from the world. This
is not said carelessly. Religion can be, and
is very largely, a terrible force; and Christianity has become a religion. There are very
few communities of Christians—even the most
evangelical, and spiritual—who wholly escape
the tendency or propensity to persecute or

ostracise other bodies of Christians who might be regarded as rivals in *their* field of activity. All the talk about " sheep-stealing " has little or nothing to do with stealing from *the* fold or *the* Shepherd, but only relates to some private religious fold of organised Christianity.

We have—without mentioning them specifically—spoken of things which would have to go if a true spiritual revelation were received, and doubtless the reader is wondering what those things are. Well, this letter which we are considering will make them plain, so let us come closer to it. On the very face of it there appears for all who have eyes the contrast between Judaism and Christ. Judaism was an earthly religious system: Tabernacle, Temple, Priests, Vestments, Rites, Sacrifices, Feasts, Ministries, Orders, etc. The New Testament, and this letter in particular, has some very clear things to say about this Jewish system.

(i) As to its intent and purpose

It was instituted by God as a copy of things in the heavens. Not that heaven contained such things literally, but just as all visible and created things were intended to embody heavenly laws and principles, so this system was intended to represent the centremost spiritual things of God's universe. But the instrument or type was never intended to do more than serve a purpose *for a time*. It represented a dispensation, or method of God for a period only. Never was it intended to be an end in itself, nor was it meant to be carried on in any detail or respect beyond a

12

certain point in time. God meant it ever and always to be a prophecy of " better things to come," and to be held so loosely as to constitute no difficulty when the " better things " arrived. The letter which is before us affirms that the era of the " better things " had arrived some time since. " God . . . hath at the end of these days spoken . . . in his Son."

But the new era and new order had brought out a new and mightier-than-ever conflict. A very serious and grim part of that conflict was with the religion of tradition, the religion which worshipped the same Lord, and embodied *in a symbolic way* all the truth of the new era. One great warrior apostle was the champion of the new spiritual order—himself one who had been deeply and powerfully embedded in the old system, but by a mighty revelation emancipated from it. He called that revelation " the heavenly vision," and that word " heavenly " defined for ever the nature of the change in the dispensations. Into this battle he was forced by the ubiquitous Judaisers. It was fought in his letters to the Romans and to the Galatians. Whether or not we believe that Paul wrote the letter to the Hebrews, there is no doubt that he had a big part of influence in it, and in it again is the same battle carried on.

If the main feature of Judaism is sought, it will be found to be the resolving of heavenly and spiritual things into a purely earthly system. It is the making of the things of God

13

purely sentient, a matter of the physical and soul senses: sight, sound, feeling, reason, emotion, etc., with the numerous and various complex elements of human constitution. One of the inclusive arguments of this letter is that a religious system based upon the natural senses has no power to bring those who adhere to it to spiritual fulness. Such the Jewish system was, and it failed utterly and tragically. God did not mean it to do more than lead to something other; and in this dispensation even that is set aside and the other has become the first and only thing in God's acceptance. The earthly, natural, and temporal has been supplanted by the heavenly, spiritual and eternal, which lay behind the illustration. The failure was inevitable because it was never intended to be an end in itself, and because of man's condition. It only operated at all in the realm of man's soul, a very unstable and variable thing; whereas everything with God is a matter of man's spirit, *in the first instance*. This is the point of verse twelve of Chapter four, which should be considered with the context preceding.

The whole thought of God, running right through this letter, is spiritual fulness; and any religion—even Christianity—mixing and confusing soul and spirit, the sentient and the spiritual (as did the Christian-Judaism and as does organised Christianity) is doomed to the destiny of Judaism. If we draw upon the soul resources of people to build up Christianity, instead of recognising that " all things

14

are out from God "—that all must first come from Him and have its first point of contact with man in his spirit, which, being renewed (made anew) becomes the vessel and vehicle of all divine things for ever after—no matter how immense may be our structure, it is going to crash when the great " shaking " comes. Christianity now is very largely a built up thing with many Jewish features in it; i.e., outward orders, forms, vestments, titles, buildings and rigidly fixed boundaries of apprehension of truth. Viewed from a heavenly standpoint, it is all so much nonsense, child's-play; albeit so seriously regarded by its children.

It is important to recognise that this letter was addressed to a people who—for a long period—had held the position nationally of a people whom God had taken out of the world unto Himself. It seeks to explain their nature and history in the light of Christ and true spiritual Christianity. It shows that even such a people may make their separation earthly and earthbound, and that for so doing they have been " overthrown," and will—even as Christians—be overthrown again if they repeat in Christianity what their fathers did in Judaism. There is something here much more than typology interpreted and the interpretation accepted as to salvation from sin and judgment; it is the essential and indispensable heavenly relatedness and life of the Lord's people as *inwardly* detached from the natural life even in a religious sense.

Chapter Two

The All-inclusive Object

S O far we have been mainly negative in our approach to the " Letter to the Hebrews," albeit seriously so, and we shall find it necessary as we go on to constantly strike the note of what God's mind concerning His people is *not*.

In commissioning His servant Jeremiah the Lord said that his ministry would be twice as much corrective and destructive as it would be constructive (Jer. i. 10). This indicated how much there was to be got out of the way before God's end could be reached. It was like Nehemiah's " much rubbish " in the way of the constructive work later on. But the best way to the corrective is always the positive, that is, presenting the purpose of God as fully as possible.

So, then, that which governs everything here in this letter, as everywhere else in the New Testament, is the believer's attainment unto

The Fulness of Christ

and the strongest warnings—with terrible examples—are given as to failure in this matter. The fatal weakness of so very much of the Church's work, both in its evangelism and in inside activity, is its failure to realise that God has never been satisfied with just having converts or adherents, but has considered it so important to bring such to spiritual full-growth as to make the abiding monument of Divine Revelation—the New Testament—ninety-nine per cent. a volume for Christians as to their spiritual life after conversion; this, first and foremost, is God's way of saying two things.

Firstly, that the end, apart from the attaining of which His eternal counsels would have broken down, is Christ *in fulness*, not in aspects alone. Secondly, that only a Church which has a large measure of Christ can adequately and effectively fulfil the purpose of the evangel. There is far more of spiritual force to be overcome in and around this world than can be met by the novitiate Church or Christian. Only Christ in fulness can do this, and the measure of effectiveness will ever be according to the measure of Christ. That the " Letter to the Hebrews " has so fully to do with this matter is to be seen from the fact that—in principles—it embraces and comprehends the whole New Testament revelation and meaning, doctrinal and practical. Sit down with it and see if you cannot find in it the essence of " Romans," " Corinthians," " Galatians," " Ephesians," " Philippians," " Colossians " and " Peter." And does it not set the basis for the interrogation of the churches in the " Revelation "?

But to come more immediately to the inclusive object, just take the thought of fulness and read the letter through with this as your guide. When you have done so, and have recognised that it is this which governs all, then start again with this second thought; in what way is Christ revealed here as fulness for our apprehending and attainment? A third question will eventually arise; what adjustments are necessary if that attainment is to be realised? We will seek to answer these questions in order.

Fulness—the Governing Object

God does not believe in either emptiness or partial occupation. This is clearly shown throughout the entire Scriptures. If at any given time He speaks in a particular way, on a particular line, and with a particular emphasis, it is only by way of building up to a whole and bringing all to completeness. This is the point in the first statement in this letter. God has in times past spoken in portions and ways, but all the portions and manners pointed to the whole, and eventually that whole is found to be Christ—His Son. He is not merely another way or form of speech, He is the sum and consummation of all. He has been implicit in all parts, but never complete in any one. All the parts were—in principle—aspects or features of Him. But fulness is not just the combination and co-ordination of the parts as types and figures, manners of speech. Rather is it the Divine *meaning* of all that has gone before. The fulness is spiritual, heavenly, eternal, not temporal, earthly and passing. This is a point which must make us pause and

18

think again. Fulness will be found in the essential nature of God's thoughts, not in their symbolic representation. Thus sonship, when understood, is the greatest revelation ever given by God to man, and the greatest of all Divine thoughts for man. So chapters one and two sum up all in sonship.

First there is the presentation of the Son.

He has been made heir of *all things*.

He was the instrument in the making of the ages.

He is the fulness of the revelation of God

He sustains all things in cohesiveness and being.

He accomplished purification of sins.

He sits at the right hand of God.

He is superior to the angelic orders.

He has inherited an ineffable name.

It is a presentation of Christ on two sides of His being, sonship in two connections—Son of God and Son of man. Only in Paul's letter to the Colossians (chap. i) and John's Gospel (chap. i) is there anything to compare with this as a presentation of the fulness and transcendence of Christ.

The point which we must now make sure of grasping is that, while fulness has ever been God's thought and intention for His creation, there has been no *possibility* of real spiritual fulness since the fall of man until Christ, the Son, was seated at God's right hand after His circuit of humiliation, suffering, death and resurrection. God *begins* from fulness, He does not work towards it. Only in experience does fulness progress, but it is really, in God's mind, working *back* to the initially fixed realisation in Christ. When the Son—the Divine standard of fulness—has been set before us, then sonship in relation to Him (not in Deity but as Son of man, chap. ii) is brought out as to the believing family. All family titles are used: " children," " brethren," " sons," and " God's House."

This not being a detailed exposition of the letter, very much must be left without comment, although it is so valuable. We are governed by one thought.

When the Son and the sons have been presented, and with them God's thought and intention of fulness as governing the creative work, especially in relation to " man " and " the son of man " (ii. 6), then the great and significant phrase is used " Partners in a heavenly calling." By this phrase we are precipitated into the whole object of this letter, its subject matter, and the crisis which it represents.

   i. " The heavenly calling." What is it? The dominion over " the inhabited earth to come (whereof we are speaking)" (ii. 5).

     a. Man, in the first place was intended for this, but he missed it or forfeited it.

     b. Israel was a type of an elect people with this as their destiny. *They* forfeited it (see chap. iii, etc.).

     c. The dominion has been fully secured

20

in " the Son of man," Who is Son of God—" Thy throne, *O God* " (i. 8)—and Who is now " crowned with glory and honour." And this " inheritance " is for the Church.

ii. But there are two factors of major importance.

a. This " heavenly calling " is essentially heavenly and spiritual. It has no connection with this present earth excepting as to spiritual testimony.

b. Its full realisation and fulfilment is " tʰo come," it is future, after this age.

Let us look at these two things more closely. What is the aspect of this letter? It is entirely *upward*! See the heavenly references.

" Heavenly calling," iii. 1; " heavenly gift," vi. 4; " heavenly country," xi. 16; " heavenly Jerusalem," xii. 22; " heavenly things," viii. 5, ix. 23; " passed through the heavens," iv. 14; " higher than the heavens," (" high priest "), vii. 26; " throne of the Majesty in the heavens," viii. 1; " entered into heaven itself," ix. 24; " in heaven a better . . ." x. 34; " enrolled in heaven," xii. 23; " him that speaketh from heaven," xii. 25; " make to tremble the heaven . . ." xii. 26.

So, the Lord and everything of Him is looked at as from below. The counterpart of the whole Old Testament system is seen to be in heaven, and it was only a temporal representation of the heavenly and spiritual reality.

21

Christ is in heaven, and all of our religious bonds with God are through Christ as there. Every bond with the earth is broken, even while we are walking on the earth. Christ in heaven takes the place of all earthly figures and representations in ritual. It is important to recognise that this letter was addressed—in the first place —to a people who for centuries had held the position of a people whom God had taken out of the world unto Himself, explaining their own nature and history in the light of Christianity, showing that even such a people may make their separation earthly and earthbound. Everything here and now is essentially spirit, but it is shown that there can be a false spirituality, a pseudo-spirituality. It was thought by the Jews, as it is thought by multitudes of well-meaning Christians, that the performing of certain rites, the preserving of certain forms, the following of a certain ritual, the wearing of certain garments, the employment of certain instruments, language, tones: and, indeed, the recognition of a set of more or less sentient accompaniments: if bathed in an atmosphere of reverence and solemnity, is spirituality. This letter in which we are meditating most definitely cuts clean in between soul (of which the above is the expression) and spirit (iv. 12). In effect its corrective is that when you have true spirituality you need none of the above; and, indeed, this is the age in which that has all given place to what is purely and solely spiritual. But you can have all that, and not be really spiritual people. The more truly spiritual you are the less you will be impressed by, or taken up with, these things. They will be to you like so much child's play. This can be proved by the fact that in the realms where ritual is the greatest the gap between personal knowledge of the Lord and ritual is also the greatest. Whereas a deep rich life in God is usually found where there is little or nothing of outward forms in the sense of a system of religion.

Let it be noted, as we close this chapter, that it is in this very realm and connection that the appeal, the warnings, the exhortations, and the argument of this letter lie. Not concerning Corinthian sensuality or worldliness or divisions; not the sins of Christians; but the immaturity, childhood (chap. v. 12 to chap. vi. 12) of those who, although "once enlightened," were in danger of having their spiritual life limited and frustrated by becoming conformed to a traditional and fixed earthly religious system which, although instituted by God at one time to serve in the lower classes of the school of the ages, has, with this age, been left behind, and *all* who are of this dispensation begin their spiritual life and education at an entirely different level, and with an entirely superior equipment.

This equipment is twofold, making for such transcendent possibilities and responsibilities; Christ in full revelation; not in types and symbols, but in living reality; actually Himself the Priest, the Sacrifice, the Altar, the Mercy Seat, the Tabernacle, the Holy of Holies, etc.,

23

etc.; and then the Holy Spirit given to make Christ, in all that He is, a living *inward* reality, so that we live in the good of all by the power of the indwelling Holy Spirit. But Christ is infinitely vaster and fuller than has ever been conceived by man, and the growing revelation and apprehension of Him by the energy of the Holy Spirit keeps the believer's life ever moving forward and growing, so that Christianity should never be a static system but an ever-expanding life. Hence the constantly recurring appeal, " Let us go on," " Let us . . . let us . . ."

Chapter Three

The Transcendent Thought of Sonship

H AVING, in our consideration of the message of the " Letter to the Hebrews," identified the all-inclusive object as the fulness of Christ, we proceed to crystallise that object, or see that it is here crystallised, into the Divine meaning of sonship. This thought runs right through the letter, but at points the keynote is struck with particular emphasis.

> *i. THE SON. " Hath at the end . . . spoken*
> *. . . in his Son " (marg.: a son; lit.*
> *sonwise). i. 2.*
> *" Thou art my Son." i. 5.*
> *" But of the Son he saith." i. 8.*
> *" Christ as a son, over his (God's)*
> *house." iii. 6.*

> *ii. THE SONS. ". . . bringing many sons*
> *unto glory." ii. 10.*
> *" My son, regard not lightly the chasten-*
> *ing of the Lord . . . and scourgeth*
> *every son whom he receiveth . . . God*
> *dealeth with you as with sons . . . the*
> *Father of our spirits." xii. 5, 6, 7, 9*
> *(see also " brethren," " children ").*
> *" Ye are come . . . to the church of the*
> *firstborn . . . enrolled in heaven." xii.*
> *22, 23.*

The central truth then, around which all else circles, and in the light of which all else must be read, is the mystery or hidden nature of sonship. There is no greater thing in all Divine revelation than the thought and purpose of sonship. But this letter shows (as do other parts of the New Testament) that sonship is not an initial relationship but an ultimate one. It is not what is meant by being born of God or being a child of God, although sonship is implicit in that, but it is the maturity and therefore responsibility of those born of God; it is just that motive of all the exhortations, entreaties, encouragements, and warnings in the letter, at one point set over against unduly delayed growth in the words " Let us go on to full growth," vi. 1. Let us hasten to mention that we are not thinking or speaking of deity. We are not called to that unique Sonship which belongs to Christ as Son of God in terms of Godhead, but we keep strictly to what is meant by the use made of the words of the eighth Psalm in chapter two of this letter with its backward relation to Adam and its forward relation to Christ and the " many sons," " brethren," " children," " partners." So then, sonship means spiritual full growth which carries with it the placing in responsibility to govern the world to come (ii. 5).

The great implication, if not obvious state- ment, of this letter as a whole is that all " children " of God will not " go on " to realise the full meaning of their birth, but, while they may not lose their life, they may lose their " calling " or the full intention of their birth.

Thus, we are able, by recognising the governing object of this letter, to link up with those things which show what sonship means. There are many such links; we can take but two of them.

The first obvious link is between " Hebrews " and the fourth chapter of John's Gospel.

The New " Hour " of the Son

". . . *the hour cometh, when neither in this mountain, nor in Jerusalem, shall ye worship the FATHER . . . the hour cometh, and NOW IS, when the true worshippers shall worship the FATHER in spirit and truth: . . . God is Spirit: and they that worship him must worship in spirit . . ." (John iv. 21-24). (The emphasis is ours.)*

Now, everyone knows that the all-governing object of John's writings was to bring out Christ's Sonship. A study of relevant words— " Father," " Son," etc., will serve as an initial indication of this.

But a second unmistakable characteristic of those writings is the essentially spiritual nature of everything in relation to Christ. Here is a simple example. With Christ a new " hour," or day, or dispensation has come, and in this new day geography, place, material building, traditional association, religious centre, or ecclesiastical hierarchy have nothing whatever to do with it. It is now an inner relationship of a spiritual nature between Father and son. So chapter four follows chapter three in John. " Hebrews " just develops John iv and gives the so-much-greater range and content of its implication. Thus, in the first place, sonship is a heavenly thing. It takes its rise in heaven: " born from above " (John iii. 3, marg.). Then it is an inward thing like a heavenly well, springing up unto life eternal (John iv. 14), and it is not in any way earthbound. " Neither in this mountain, nor in Jerusalem." It is not historical but eternal; not temporal, but spiritual. As the letter to the Hebrews so quickly passes from the personal to the corporate, from the individual to the family, so in " John " there is a distinct point at which there is a transition from the many personal and individual incidents to the gathering of all those separate features into a corporate company in which the full glory of the Son and of sonship is to be expressed. This consummation is reached in chapter xvii.

Another clearly defined link between " Hebrews " and the Gospels is seen in the Transfiguration, and this sees sonship in its consummation, as what we have just said sets forth its initiation and nature.

The Consummation of Sonship

On the mount of transfiguration three things are noted.

a. Moses and Elijah; corresponding to " divers portions and in divers manners " (Heb. i. 1).

b. Jesus glorified; corresponding to " we see Jesus, . . . crowned with glory and honour " (Heb. ii. 9). (See also II Pet. i. 16—18.)

c. " Hear ye him "; corresponding to " God

. . . hath at the end . . . spoken . . . in his Son " (Heb. i. 2).

Thus we have,

   a. A new dispensation :

   b. Taking its character from Jesus in heaven, glorified.

   c. The absolute fulness and finality of God's work and speech in His Son.

Let us here remind ourselves of the supreme conflict that has ever circled round this matter of sonship. In the case of the Lord Jesus Himself it was the focal point of all the fierce controversy and bitter hatred. It was the point of Satan's personal and direct attack : " If thou be the Son." Later, demons referred to it through their victims of possession. It was the occasion of the Jewish assault, and it headed up in the combined assault of devil, demons, and men, issuing in His crucifixion. Paul not only regarded the Jews as responsible for His death, but said the " principalities and powers " invested Him in the cross, and He stripped them off (Colossians ii. 15).

The battle was carried on against the Church, and almost every New Testament letter has as its object the urge and constraint of believers not to stop short at spiritual infancy or immaturity, but to go on to fulness. This fulness is what is meant by and involved in sonship. There is nothing so feared and hated by Satan and his powers as sonship in its full attainment and expression. As " Prince of this world," having wrested the kingdom and dominion from Adam, he loses it to the Son of God —the Son of man; and the full and universal manifestation of that loss is to come with " the manifestation of the sons of God," that Body of Christ which is " the fulness of him," the " partakers of a heavenly calling " to have dominion over the world to come (Rom. viii. 19; Eph. i. 23; Heb. iii. 1, ii. 5).

Any ministry or instrumentality which has real spiritual full growth and sonship as its anointed function will meet what such has ever met; firstly from the enemy himself directly and nakedly, then from whatever direction and means he can find available. If he cannot *directly* destroy, he will seek Balaam's method of subterfuge. His one persistent method through the ages has been to divert the people of God from the Son to a system.

The Letters to the Hebrews, the Galatians, and the Romans are outstanding instruments of God in relation to this very thing. Thus, early in " Hebrews," in bringing in the sons with the Son, mention is made of a matter which is much more fully developed later. It is that of

Death in Relation to Sonship and Spiritual Fulness

The inclusive statement in this connection is in Chap. ii, vers.: 9, 14 and 15:

" *That . . . he should taste death for (in behalf of) every man." " That through death he might bring to nought him that had the power (hold) of death, that is, the devil; and might deliver all them who through fear of death were all their lifetime subject to bond-age.*"

The question of life and death is later taken up and opened out in relation to priestly function. Aaron and his successors were unable to bring anything to fulness and finality because death broke in in every case and cut their work short. Melchizedek is then introduced as type of another priesthood. " Without father, without mother, without genealogy, having neither beginning of days nor end of life, but made like unto the Son of God . . . after the power of an endless life " (vii. 3, 16 and context).

You will thus see that sonship, eternal life, and spiritual fulness are linked together.

Death is the great enemy of spiritual fulness, but death is—in this letter and everywhere else —not just a physical matter. Israel is here spoken of as having died in the wilderness and is used as a warning to Christians. But the warnings have to do with the *purpose* of salvation in its fulness. Death is a spiritual thing, and it is an enemy ever seeking to ambush the child of God. So this whole letter is one solid and comprehensive document and treatise on the fact that spiritual life can be curtailed, arrested, and thwarted of its possibilities by the child of God being brought down, even in a religious way, to an earthly position with all the trappings of a bygone dispensation, and losing the essentially heavenly and spiritual position. " Dead works " the writer calls them (vi. 1).

In chapter i, verse 5 we have a quotation

31

from the second Psalm related immediately to sonship in Christ.

" Thou art my Son, this day have I begotten thee." That quotation is made again in chapter v, verse 5, in relation to His endless-life Priesthood. In Acts xiii. 33, the same quotation is made as prophetic evidence of the resurrection of Christ, and thus, sonship and resurrection are linked. This does not mean that Christ was not Son before the resurrection, but the New Testament shows that in resurrection there is a feature of sonship which was not there before, namely that Christ is " the firstborn among many brethren " in resurrection. As Peter puts it " hath begotten us . . . by the resurrection of Jesus Christ from the dead." We are not thereby incorporated into Christ as Son of God in the sense of deity, but as Son of man in a new creation family.

For the moment, then, the point is that the new life of resurrection union with Christ as the principle of sonship must not be put into the old wine-skins of earthly traditions and systems, but into the new wine-skins of an entirely heavenly and spiritual order. This was probably the occasion of this letter. It was possibly written as an appeal to the strong section of Hebrew Christians in Jerusalem who found the ever-widening trend of Christianity too much for their conservative habits of Judaistic thought. As the cleavage between the Temple and the Synagogue on the one hand, and the Church and the Apostles on the other, became more marked, the Judaisers were inclined to snap the new ties for the old. The new wine was bursting the old wine-skins, and, like many to-day, they were not prepared for that. But the issues were, and are, infinite.

Thus we have arrived at one of those infinite issues which are exercising most Christians and Christian bodies to-day, the issue of

Fulness of Life in Christ

Yes, life in fulness is the question. Many bodies of Christians who have a great past and a great tradition are deeply concerned with the inadequacy or lack of life amongst them to-day. This poverty of life is leading to great organised efforts, largely outside of the churches, to try to bring fulness about. Its lack has been the occasion for the abnormal development of many spurious and pseudo-spiritual movements and teachings. For want of it multitudes are passing by the churches as things which do not count. In many ways the great enemy has triumphed against the Church by countering its very life impact and testimony. A major and largely inclusive way of this achievement is the specific point of our letter. Make Christianity into another Juda-ism, i.e., an earthly religious system of precepts and practices, and you have made it dead! Is not this the point at chapter vi. 1-6? I am not one of those who believe that the Apostle was there referring to Jewish ordinances. Some of my reasons for this are these. Chapter vi. 1-6 must be read strictly in conjunction with chap-ter v. 12-13. " The rudiments of the first

33

principles (or beginning) of the oracles of God " are the same as " the first principles of Christ," linked together by the " Wherefore." Jewish ordinances were not the first principles of Christ. They were the " dead works " referred to in the phrase " Repentance from dead works." " The teaching of baptisms " does not refer to Jewish " washings." It is the *teaching* as to the difference between John's Baptism (or any other) and baptism into Christ. Acts xix. 1-6 ought to settle this conclusively; and note the context of xviii. 25. (What a pity that the chapters are divided where they are, instead of after xviii. 23!) In this same place (Acts xix. 6) the " laying on of hands " (Heb. vi. 2) is seen as a doctrine of Christ, not a Jewish ordinance. No, the point of the Apostle is that, having laid this sixfold foundation we should " go on to full growth." Life only begins in the foundation; its fulness requires the whole building. The peril is that even the first principles can become another legal system imposed upon people, and thus the things intended to lead to fulness of life may be made an arrest of life. Satan is very clever.

The recovery of life and its constant increase unto final fulness will only be as we get away from mere tradition and earthliness to a new living apprehension of Christ in His fulness as a Divine Representation of God's thoughts for His people; away from types, figures, symbols, to spiritual realities. Even if there are to be expressions of " first principles " they must come out of the living reality, and not be mere

34

forms and things in themselves. We must do nothing with a view to perpetuating forms of doctrine and practice, but the expression must be that of life, and the spiritual meaning and value of everything must be ever growing. Only so shall we " go on to full growth."

Chapter Four

How life is maintained. The principle of the New Covenant

I N our last chapter we laid special emphasis upon the necessity for everything to be preserved in life, as against even Christianity becoming resolved into another system of " dead works." For, what the writer (of the Epistle to the Hebrews) said was necessary as to Judaism in his time, has now become a necessity in relation to much of Christendom, namely " repentance from dead works " (vi. 1).

In this chapter we shall gather our thoughts around a principle which is implicit in the whole purpose and argument of the letter. It is that of how life is preserved and maintained. This is one of the most difficult matters to convey unless there is a real measure of spiritual understanding, and it might well suffer in the same way as did the " many things " regarding Melchizedek in Chapter v. 11. However, the spiritual situation is such to-day as to justify every attempt at solving it.

The first phase of the problem is this; seeing that there is a sum of Christian doctrine and practice embodied in the New Testament, and that certain clearly defined beliefs and practices represent the substance or foundation of Christianity: that these are not to be added to or taken from: is it possible that Christianity should not become a set system, tradition, or form? There are some phrases in the New Testament which would seem to imply that it is such. It would seem impossible to avoid this when once the first newness, novelty, and wonder have passed, and age succeeds age in Christian teaching, work and practice. But to accept such a conclusion and position is really to violate the most vital and crucial facts in New Testament Christianity, and to agree to a state of things which is a caricature and denial or contradiction of Christ. If Christianity *were* a system of truths and practices then the above-mentioned result would be inevitable. But it is *not*! It is a living Person, known only in the power of the Holy Spirit. Yes, and not known all at once, but to be known by continuous and ever-growing revelation of the Holy Spirit. That brings us to our point.

The Old and the New Revelation

In the letter under contemplation, among many comparisons and contrasts between what *was* and what *is*, reference is made to the two Covenants. Before considering the crucial point of difference between them, let us remind ourselves of the nature and meaning of a Biblical Covenant.

Firstly, a Covenant was an expression, revelation, or making known of God's

37

thoughts, mind, desires, and will. In those presentations of God's mind the character and nature of God was made known. When we read the terms we have to say, That is what God is like.

Then, upon that revelation of Himself God offered and moved to bring His people into an active relationship with Himself as to purpose and destiny. He made a Covenant with them on that basis. It was a mutual understanding that—if they accepted the basis—He fulfilled promises.

The Covenant was sealed or ratified by blood. The blood was provided by God and symbolised life. In a way prescribed by God, man—the other party to the Covenant—had to participate by an act of identification with the blood-donor. So it became a case of sharing in one life. It was this that made blood so sacred in Old Testament times. Of course this opens up the whole realm of Blood Covenant, but here we do no more than hint at it. To violate the terms of this Covenant was to rupture the very bond of life. The focal point of all warning and judgment was idolatry, which was spiritual fornication, or—in principle—unlawful mixture of bloods—i.e. life.

Thus we are able to come to the heart of the letter to the Hebrews. These Hebrews would understand it well. Look again at the Blood, the Life, and the Covenant in this letter. Here we are able to appreciate the whole question of sonship, with which we dealt in the last chapter. But here we are brought right up to the all-dominating feature of the Person of Christ.

The Living Person Governs All

No, it is not a new system of truth. It is not a new and superior religion. *It is a Living Person of Whom the truths and practices are but spiritual features.*

Let us look at this briefly in three aspects.

Firstly; the letter to the Hebrews (and indeed the whole New Testament) does not say that we have to come to believe and accept certain doctrines such as those mentioned in chapter vi—Repentance, Faith, Baptism, Laying on of hands, Resurrection of the dead, Eternal Judgment—in order to be New Testament Christians. Although the passage *seems* to contradict that statement, we are very insistent upon it, for it is upon this that we are sure the whole question of life and death rests. It is here also that a very great peril lies in the preaching and propagation of New Testament truth. If these matters have a place, as they certainly do, that place is subsequent to something else. Does it sound strange—in the light of certain Scriptures—to say that, *in the first instance*, we are *not* commissioned to preach repentance? While it may be less surprising to be told that the same is true regarding baptism, etc., yet it is as true of the one as of the other! The Holy Spirit always demands and secures a background of and occasion for precipitating a reaction from man's side, and that ground is not just that men are told that they must do certain things. No, this letter, like all New Testament preaching and teaching, opens with a revelation and presentation of the Person of Christ in living fulness. It was ever and only as people were convicted by the Holy Spirit as to the sovereign supremacy of the Lord Jesus and were actively ready to capitulate utterly to Him that these other things became a living and eager expression of that capitulation. Until people have really seen Christ by Holy Spirit revelation or illumination and conviction, there is no adequate motive for repentance, and the rest. It is not repentance for *sins*! That would make salvation a matter of degree according to the number or nature of the sins. It is all a matter of the Person. " Of sin, because they believe not on me " (John xvi. 9). Hence, New Testament preaching was little more than a proclaiming of Christ—crucified, raised, exalted, glorified—with its implications and challenge. The Holy Spirit's way of overthrowing and uprooting false systems and positions has never been that of exposing the falseness, but that of bringing Christ in His greater fulness into view and convicting concerning Him! It is always positive, never negative. So it is the shadow of a Glorified Man—God's Son—that lies right over all the detail of the letter, and the New Testament as a whole.

Secondly; all the truths and practices are but

Features of the Living Person

and must be seen in the light of the inclusive

40

revelation of Himself. Take the matters referred to in particular in chapter vi. " Baptism " is not an ordinance, it is Christ expressed in death and resurrection as representing the old creation judged and doomed, and the new creation which is wholly out from God without a trace of judgment ground in it. Baptism then is the way in which a believer declares that he or she has been crucified with Christ, and, although living, yet it is not himself or herself but Christ.

The New Covenant, in the first place, is in the blood of Christ, i.e. His life, and in participation in His nature as " firstborn among many brethren." Glance again at chapter ii of this letter.

The " Laying on of Hands " in the New Testament signified that Christ is now no isolated and separate Individual, but Head of the Church—His Body—and that the Spirit in anointing upon the Head is for all the members in relatedness to Him and to one another; the Spirit being the power, the wisdom, the capacities, the qualifications, the energies, and the endowments for the Body's functioning as a heavenly Body. Hence, with the Laying on of Hands *at the beginning* the Spirit *demonstrated for all time* that Christ and His members are one for the accomplishment of eternal counsels. This is no ordinance, it is Christ corporately expressed.

It is in this way that all doctrine and practice must be seen. Not as things in themselves, but as features of the Living Person, and they

41

must be kept in that relationship.

Thirdly; and here we come to the principle which lies at the heart of all. Nothing that is in the New Testament can be taken and reconstructed into a system just because it is there. There is no system of doctrine and procedure which lies within that vast compass called "Christianity," however divergent or contradictory, however nominal or extreme, however fantastic or doubtful, but bases itself upon Scripture, and supports itself by the New Testament. It is no guarantee that there will be life because a framework, a body, has been put together and built up according to the exact technique of the New Testament. Many efforts have been made to reconstruct the "New Testament Church" in the belief that the nearer to the model the surer and fuller the Divine commitment. But it just doesn't work! The order of the New Covenant is just the reverse of the Old. Then God wrote upon tablets of stone and presented it as a tangible and objective completeness. In the New, the Spirit of God—*dwelling within*—writes upon the heart and mind. Then God appeared in unapproachable and unendurable glory so that men were devastated by His presence. Now "God . . . hath shined into our hearts to give the light of the knowledge of the glory of God in the face of Jesus Christ" (see II Cor. iii-iv-v).

The *face of Jesus Christ.*

The *glory of God* in the face of Jesus Christ.

The *knowledge* of the glory of God in the

face of Jesus Christ.

The *light* of the knowledge of the glory of God in the face of Jesus Christ.

In our hearts the light of the knowledge of the glory of God in the face of Jesus Christ.

Now, the crucial point is this. The principle of the New Covenant is a first-hand individual revelation of Christ as the knowledge of God in terms of glory in the heart of the believer. Every individual believer only comes into true Christianity by a revelation of Christ in his or her heart, so that the knowledge of Christ is all their own, and as real as when God commanded light to shine in darkness. But that is not all. That shining must be progressive. Christ is far too vast to be seen in more than minute degrees at any one time. The bulk of the New Testament is taken up with getting Christians to see what an immense realm it is into which they have come, and how they must go on; and that is the object of the letter under consideration.

Christianity can only be kept living and fresh and full of impact as Christians are living in an ever-growing apprehension of Christ as the Holy Spirit reveals Him in the heart.

This apprehension may only come as necessity is laid upon us by reason of suffering and trial. Capacity will increase by the stretching of suffering (see chapter xii, and read " child-training " for " chastening "). There is no succession in Christianity other than that of

the revelation of Christ to the heart by the
Holy Spirit. ·It is not a system to be perpetu-
ated, but a life to be possessed. The value of
the Scriptures is that they contain depths and
fulnesses which have never yet been fathomed;
and when we speak of " revelation " we do
not mean anything extra to them, but of that
which is in them, but only known by the inward " writing " and " shining " of the Holy
Spirit. The great peril into which Christendom has fallen is that of stultifying the
vastness of Christ by putting Him into a
framework of credal statements, each one of
which seeks to be the beginning and end of
the matter. Moreover, the Church and its
work have been reduced to a formula, and no
room is left for anything that goes beyond that
formula. It is just possible—and indeed it
has sometimes happened—that the Lord should
throw such a freshness and fulness of light
upon some Scriptural statement of truth as to
transform and revolutionise it and lead out
into an altogether new life and ministry; and
this without any contradiction of its essential
and true meaning. There is such a thing as
holding down the truth in tradition, as well as
holding down the truth in unrighteousness
(Rom. i. 18).

Let us try to summarise what we have said
and meant.

(1) It is doubtful whether a full and complete
system of doctrine and procedure can be
reconstructed from the New Testament,
so that on all matters we have a precise

answer to every question as to what should be done, and how it should be done at any given time. There certainly are basic and fundamental truths, but the Holy Spirit is still needed.

(2) It is, moreover, doubtful whether the Lord meant that there should be such a complete verbal framework; so that everything could be applied, repeated, and duplicated mechanically.

(3) The only living way to the realisation of the Divine thought and intention is by an apprehension of spiritual principles. When these principles are grasped, then the object, the means, and the methods of their expression are *livingly* appreciated.

For instance:—

(a) Sonship. When we recognise that sonship is a *full* Divine thought, and not just an initial one, as in birth, we shall then have the motive for " pressing on to full growth." It is a principle.

(b) Corporate union, life, and service. When we see the *corporate* principle as governing spiritual fulness, and that it is not possible for any unit of the Body of Christ to come to fulness apart from relatedness with other members, then we really have apprehended the true nature of the work, way, and end of God, and, amongst other things, we have the most powerful motive for fellowship.

(c) The Holy Spirit's revelation in terms of

life. " The law of the Spirit of life " is the principle of all that is of God. A thing can be in the Bible, and we can have read it a thousand times, but until the Holy Spirit makes it life to us it will be unfruitful. Hence, there is a place and need for an inward revelation of the Word of God, and this is the only true succession. Nothing can be preserved alive through generations save as every one entering its realm does so on the basis of such a personal, inward, living, and *growing* revelation of the truth, so that the *origin* and *beginning* is constantly repeated in experience.

These are principles. The Epistle to the Hebrews has been called the Book of the Open Heaven, and this is its meaning.

Chapter Five

"Them that have faith." "Now faith . . ."

YOU will have read many books and heard many addresses on the classic Hebrews Eleven: " The heroes of faith "; " The Roll-call of the Faithful "; and it is doubtful whether this chapter has ever been dealt with, in whole or in parts, without *examples* of and encouragement to faith being the point focused upon. And rightly so. But not often do we hear or read anything on it which makes the whole context of the letter the object. The chapter is usually taken in itself, with the first words of what follows often added.

What we desire to indicate here is that Chapter xi is really the Apostle's gathering up of his whole theme as he begins to round off his letter. He has presented Christ " crowned with glory and honour." God's Son in unique-ness of sonship; and then he has shown the Divine thought of securing and bringing to glory many sons, not sharing that uniqueness, but being made partakers of His incarnation and through " adoption," i.e., " child plac-ing." He has shown that everything of God in this dispensation is of a spiritual and heavenly nature, and not temporal and earthly. He has urged that spiritual fulness in Christ is the goal of the believer's calling, and that it is terribly possible to fail of it, with grievous consequences.

Now, as to all this, and its values for God's people, he shows, by triumphant examples, that faith is the link between calling and destiny, between Divine thought and its realisation.

The Supreme Feature of the Life of Faith

is that the people of God are tested by their position. There is no more testing position than that to which believers are called in this dispensation. God has not promised us anything on this earth in this dispensation which will be our vindication before men, the literal and material justification of our abandonment of all for Him. The nearer we get to the Divine thought the further away do we get from what can be " written up," pointed to, and advertised as the result of our work. Such things belong to the elementary stages of life, and God never prolongs them. His most abiding and solid work is underground where the sensation hunter cannot get at it, and where the publicity department will be hard put to it. If faith *is* really *faith,* and if the end times are to be more testing as to faith than any others (and the Scriptures say emphatically that it will be so) then there will be much less in the consummation of things to relieve faith by sight than at other times. But this principle holds good at all times *when God is after something more than the superficial.* The people mentioned in our chapter were all

48

tested by their position. This is most clearly seen in Abraham and in Israel with Moses. God was there and then acting on the line of material responses to faith, but they were severely tested by the position in which they were placed by God's act.

This is a spiritual age, and it is that fact which constitutes the test which *very few* Christians are prepared to accept. If anything becomes big, or if it can be made so: if names of world fame and titles of worldly import-ance sponsor it, or if they can be persuaded to do so: how much is made of it all! How very gratified is that flesh when things appear to be going well! Yes, yes, we are still so much of this earth, and we have failed to see how very small the biggest thing here is when seen from even ten thousand feet up, to say nothing of God's throne and His spiritual measure.

What our writer is really saying is that real measure is that of faith, because the realm into which we are now called is one in which there is nothing apart from faith. The first stage is now of faith, and so is every subsequent increase. The whole dispensation is an im-mense advance upward in Divine thought, and sets the background for something much more inward than ever before. In the previous dis-pensations everything was outward and tan-gible—sacrifices, altars, meeting places, priests, vestments, feasts, rewards, etc.; but in this age all these things are gathered into the all-inclu-sive " In Christ," and are essentially spiritual aspects of the One Heavenly Man; to be known, enjoyed, and comprehended only by faith. The long generations of sentient gratification in religious things were in the very blood of these Hebrews, and they craved for the seen, the felt, the heard, the physical and emotional system of the past. Thus, all that is said from the beginning of the epistle is carried up to the most spiritual of all attributes —faith, which worketh by love.

The encumbering weights impeding the running in the race of Chapter xii. i are the legal aspects of external Law. The " sin which doth so easily beset " is doubt or unbelief, ' unfaith '; for " whatsoever is not of faith is sin."

Thus sin, in this letter, is resolved into a matter, not of morals, but of how much we reverse the nature of the dispensation by putting temporal elements and ideas in the place of spiritual. It may never have occurred to many that ritual, vestments, and ecclesiastical regalia and forms may be sin in this respect, that they undermine, supplant, or weaken the truly spiritual, and, rather than help faith, only act as crutches which keep people from having " their senses (spiritual faculties) exercised " (Heb. v. 14).

This leads on in the unbroken sequence of thought to what is—in our unfortunate, mechanical divisions of chapters—in Chap. xii. Here the " fathers of our flesh," and the " Father of spirits " are compared. Child-training (" chastening ") unto " son receiving " (lit.

" placing as sons ") has to do with our spirits;
not firstly with our bodies, or our souls. The
spirit is the very new man himself with which
God is linked by new birth. All God's pater-
nal attentions are taken up with this " inner
man of the heart." Spirit cannot really be
fed with temporal things. The soul may be
greatly stimulated by blessings in the temporal
realm, but it is here that one of the most vital
and far-reaching distinctions is made by the
Word of God, and one most grievously overlooked by the vast majority of Christians;
and especially is it the point of default by the
majority of Christian leaders. It is thought
that if there is much soul stimulation along
the lines of emotion, feeling, and ' zeal ' or
enthusiasm : reason, argument, information to
the mind : and action, work, drive, volition :
this is essentially the mark of spiritual life.
In the New Testament it is the other way
round; there was a deep inward work of the
Holy Spirit in those days, before the effects—
the instruction or teaching, the zeal, and the
works. To put the cart before the horse in
this matter may be just Satan's great illusion
by which he brings about the most deadly reactions, so that the afterward is more hopeless
than before. It may be well at this point to
give a reminder that Satan's point of the conquest of man was man's soul—reason, argument: desire, feeling : volition, choice, action.
Through and by his soul man capitulated to
a course of unbelief, which severed his *spirit*
from fellowship with God. (God is spirit, not

soul. When God is referred to as having soul, it is only speaking after the manner of men, not actually the truth about God.) The undoing or destroying of the works of the devil in man and in a new race will be by rebirth of man's spirit in union with God by the Holy Spirit, and by that being " joined to the Lord, one spirit " to make for the full growth of a spiritual man (Heb. v. 14, vi. 1. R.V.) thus bringing the soul into captivity with its moods, variations, and its inherent weakness toward doubt. The " dominion " of chap. ii is now reserved unto *spiritual* people, and this is the heart of the whole letter to the Hebrews with its particular connection, as it is the heart of the whole New Testament in its manifold application.

The " placing as *sons*," which is the issue of " child-training " is spiritual " full-growth." Here is the link between chapters xi and xii. It was not only what those heroes of faith did through faith, but what they attained unto. There was a Divine " perfection " as the goal of fellowship with God. The word " perfect " (Gk. " complete ") is used eight times in this letter.

" To make the captain of their salvation perfect " (ii. 10).

" Having been made perfect, he became . . . the author of eternal salvation " (v. 9).

" The law made nothing perfect " (vii. 19), etc.,

and thus, having shown the object of God, and incidentally of this letter, the writer brings us to two consummate statements:

a. " Apart from us they should not be made perfect " (xi. 40).
b. " Ye are come . . . to the spirits of just men made perfect " (xii. 23).

We leave the second till later, only noting again where completeness lies.

So, with all their faith and its manifold and wonderful expression two things issued:

a. They "received not the promise," but " died (still) in faith." They awaited completion or completeness; the full fruit of their faith had yet to ripen and be gathered.
b. " The spirits of (these) just men made perfect." " Apart from us they should not be made perfect " (made complete). Note: This is not numerical completeness; that we were necessary to be added to them. That *might* be true, but it is not what is meant here. It is their own completeness.

Something then has happened between their dying and our time. Yes; their faith was, in its essence, prospective. It looked on. See statements as to this in the record of Chap. xi, etc. What did it look on to? Well, with greater or lesser clearness and definiteness it linked with the Christ, their Vindicator, their Redeemer, their Prince. This *link* of faith— not abstract faith, but its Divine Object— made it justifying faith; " it was accounted unto (them) for righteousness." Hence they are " just," or justified men, and their faith

53

carried them over centuries to the Justifier, to our day; and in the " perfect "—finished, full and final—work and speech of God in Christ (Heb. i. 2) they, with us who have faith, are made complete, and their spirits are in the rest of faith. This is all so much of a piece with the whole letter that we are considering, as will be seen.

So " Faith is the assurance (confidence, giving substance to) of things hoped for, a conviction of things not seen." Someone has translated it " the title deeds " of things hoped for. Then the inheritance is now—at length—in possession.

In our next chapter we shall have something more to say on this matter, drawing upon Chap. xi, as we move to the second part of Chap. xii.

Chapter Six

" SOME BETTER THING "

IN our last chapter we came to the matter
of " completeness " as the governing
object of the faith of all those mentioned in
Hebrews xi. " Apart from us they should not
be made perfect (complete)." Now we take
that up in relation to the clause which precedes
it. " God having provided (foreseen) some
better thing concerning us." We pointed out
that this being " made perfect " or complete
had to do with justification or righteousness
by faith. " All . . . . had witness borne to
them through their faith ", (" Abraham believed God, and it was reckoned unto him for
righteousness ", " Wherefore . . . it was reckoned unto him for righteousness "; Rom. iv.
3, 22, etc.) thus making them " just men "
(Heb. xii. 23) first potentially through faith,
and then actually when the object of faith,
the Christ, had come and made the work of
righteousness perfect. We now have to carry
that faith further as to its results.

In an earlier chapter we have dealt with
' sonship ' as the supreme Divine revelation,
brought out so much in this letter to the
Hebrews. We have to return to that for a
little while in our present connection. It is
tremendously impressive how much referred to

in Chapter xi directly relates to Christ in type and figure, and then how large a place sonship has there.

No one will dispute the typical factor of Abel, as to the virtue of the blood of Christ (xii. 24); of Isaac, as he that was raised from the dead; of Joseph, as he who was exalted to " the right hand of the Majesty on high " —three stages in the course of Christ. But sonship lies either patent or latent in so much. We shall not take this up in detail, but instances are clear in the case of Abraham and Isaac; of Jacob and Joseph; of the birth of Moses, etc. The point, however, is that sonship and spiritual fulness are the same thing, and that is what this letter is all about. Faith is shown to be the basis of spiritual completeness and therefore it leads to sonship.

To indicate something of the nature of this sonship we take one person out of Chapter xi —David. No doubt David's faith is there connected with " obtaining promises " (v. 33). See II Samuel vii. 11, 12; I Chron. xxii. 9, etc. These promises had to do with a son, one Divinely marked out from among many sons (I Chron. xxviii. 5). This son was going to be the fullest example in type of God's thoughts as to sonship that the Bible contains. But there was a point of transition in David's life. After many years of chastening—child-training—numerous and varied experiences of suffering and trial and proving the Lord's faithfulness, the point was reached where the one passion of his life came immediately into view. For this he had prayed, longed, and planned. For this he had been in quest, and it had so possessed him as to make him determine not to go up into his bed, nor give sleep to his eyes until his quest was successful. We might truly say that for David to live was that house for God. And now, at long last, he divulges to Nathan the prophet what was in his heart. Nathan, knowing that God was with David, gave him instant encouragement to do all that was in his heart, only to have to go back a little later at the Lord's command and withdraw that encouragement and tell David that he was not to be allowed to fulfil his desire nor carry out his life ambition *for the Lord*. What a blow! What a shattering disappointment! What an opportunity for being offended with the Lord! And what an occasion for faith to freeze, and for despair to overwhelm him! Not he, but his son, should build the house. If this whole matter had been a personal interest, if it had been for his own gratification, well might he have been embittered and spent his closing days in brooding over and nursing his disappointment. But no! He is too big a man for that. So long as the Lord gets the house it matters not who builds it, nor whether David is allowed to have any hand in it. Moreover, he will give his own treasure to help it forward. What a magnificent triumph over the smallness of man!

David Passes to Sonship

So David passes from the child-training

through faith's ultimate test into sonship; and no one, after all, ever thinks of David without that grand issue of his life—the Temple and its service; and no one ever thinks of Solomon without remembering that he was the son of David. And more, how often is Christ referred to as " son of David."

Thus we can see something of the nature of sonship; it is spiritual stature, measure, greatness. It is fulness born out of discipline. Carry this back into Hebrews xi and xii. Spiritual stature is determined very largely by disinterested devotion to the Lord's interests, by how little we come into the picture, and by how much we are ready to serve the Lord's ends without any gratification to ourselves, without having our hand in it. " By faith . . . David . . . obtained promises."

What we have said above forms a fitting setting for what we have as the application of the message as found in verses 1-3 of Chapter xii.

The Race, the Runners, the Witnesses, the Captain

Before we can proceed we must correct a possible doctrinal error. The Apostle truly employs a common spectacle as his illustration. The stadium, the course, the runners, the onlookers, and the captain. But he would not have us to think that he means that the " cloud of witnesses " are those " with Christ " who are all conscious of and interested in our lives here in this world. There is nothing in the Scriptures to support this idea, and we can only believe that it would *not* be " far better " if they knew all about our wavering faith and impersistent progress. Put yourself in their place! Rather would the Apostle have us think of them as having borne witness in their lives, and in some way linked with us in the way of faith, so that their ultimate interests and ours are one. But *conscious* observers of our course—No! They do say that, in all ages, not only in this age, faith has been the law and governing factor. Faith links all ages in one goal—fulness. Well then, this is a course to be run, and everything that makes for weakness in the running must be repudiated.

We have already pointed out that in the context of the whole letter the " weight " is the legal system. " They bind heavy burdens and grievous to be borne, and lay them on men's shoulders " (Matt. xxiii. 4). This refers to the endless definitions and interpretations of the Law made by the scribes or lawyers, which just keep men bound to burdens of legal impositions. No one can move freely in legalism, Jewish or Christian. The " sin which doth so easily beset " we have seen may represent the formalism which is lifeless, and to which religion is so persistently and easily susceptible.

But it may be of wider application. Weights may be anything which has the effect of bearing us down. Seeing that it is the *spirit* that is the object of fulness, the weight would be whatever hangs heavily upon our spirit. There are many things of spiritual anxiety and strain for which God has provided a remedy, and this letter refers to some of them. All-inclusively union with Christ is to find " rest unto your souls." " My burden is light." " There is . . . no condemnation to them that are in Christ Jesus. For the law of the Spirit of life in Christ Jesus made . . . free from the law of sin and of death." " We who have believed do enter into . . . rest." What burdens your spirit so that you cannot run? There is something somewhere in God's Word that will relieve you of that.

" The sin which doth so easily beset." I find that these last five words are what is required in English to express one Greek word. That word means " standing round about." Linked with the race course it may refer to people or things which are not really a part of the race, but just stand around and—because they are not in the business—get in the way of those who are. They are " sins " in the sense that they would weaken faith and slow down spiritual progress. What is there in our lives, having an influence upon our spiritual progress, which really does not belong to this business? We must each answer that question as to our own case. The Lord's word is " lay aside every weight " and thrust away the unrelated hindrances, like a runner brushing aside the obstructing people on or around the course. Do not be put off or put back. Faith is the test of all. What effect has this or that on faith?

That will decide what is to be done with it.

The Captain

When the Apostle bids his readers to look unto Jesus, the author and finisher of (our) faith, he really says more and other than our translations convey.

Firstly, it is " looking *beyond* or *onward* unto Jesus." In xi. 26 Moses is said to have looked ' beyond ' (same preposition) unto the recompense of reward.

Then it is " unto *Jesus*." This is the title of the incarnation and earthly life, and its use here indicates—as the next words show—that this faith course was taken up and completed in one Who was " in all points tempted like as we, sin apart." A Man in utter dependence upon God, never employing His deity for His own support, has compassed the whole course of faith triumphantly; and inasmuch as He did it by the same Eternal Spirit as is given to us—no more, no less—it shows that *it can be done*, and there is no *need* for failure.

" The author and perfecter of faith." There is no " our " in the original text. Literally it is " the foremost leader of faith." This word is the same as in ii. 10—" to make the foremost leader of their salvation perfect through sufferings." " Perfect through sufferings." Now we are back to our word " perfect " (= complete), and He Who has been made complete along the same way of faith as we are called to traverse is our " perfector, ' i.e., the One Who makes complete. In Him this faith way was initiated, and in Him it is completed.

Now then, the exhortation, so full of doctrine. If we look at the way, or the difficulties, or at ourselves, and become occupied with them, we shall not finish the course; and even if we do, it will be slow and jerky. The focal point of faith here is to link ourselves by it with the triumphant Lord, with His perfected work, and reckon His triumph ours. It is not abstract and merely psychological, but there is a definite Divine Object—a Living Person—Whose work the Holy Spirit is ready to make good in us. When the Apostle comes to his benediction in xiii. 20 he will use the phrase " Make *you* perfect (complete) in every good thing." We leave that for the moment, with but this remark—faith fastened upon Jesus and His embodiment of a perfect work is the basis upon which " the God of peace " makes *us* perfect.

Chapter Seven

The Approaching Great Shaking

AS the writer of this letter (to the "Hebrews") approaches its conclusion; after repeatedly giving great and terrible warnings as to the peril of failure to apprehend the full purpose and meaning of God in Christ, he gathers all up into a prophetic forecast which is itself the inclusive warning.

"*He hath promised, saying, Yet once more will I make to tremble not the earth only, but also the heaven. And this, Yet once more, signifieth the removing of those things that are shaken, as of things that have been made, that those things which are not shaken may remain*" (*xii.* 26-27).

It is necessary for us to be sure that this has still a future application, and was not fulfilled in the destruction of Jerusalem and the dispersion of the Jews which was imminent when the letter was written. Undoubtedly it had a partial fulfilment in that terrible event, but, as is so often the case in prophecy, was there not a double aspect, as there unquestionably was in two outstanding instances in the New Testament? One is the case of our Lord quoting Isaiah lxi at Nazareth, and stopping at "the year of the Lord's favour," not going on to "the day of vengeance of our God"

(Luke iv. 18-19). The other is the quotation from Joel on the Day of Pentecost (Acts ii. 16-21). This prophecy was obviously not wholly fulfilled on that occasion, but only partially so.

If we look at the passage in Haggai (ii. 6) quoted in Hebrews, we shall see ample reason for doubting its already fulfilment.

" Yet once, it is a little while, and I will shake the heavens, and the earth, and the sea, and the dry land; and I will shake all nations; and the precious things of all nations shall come; and I will fill this house with glory, saith the Lord of hosts. . . . The latter glory of this house shall be greater than the former."

Not one part of that prophecy has yet been fulfilled literally. If the apostle employed that prophecy in relation to the *destruction* of the Temple rather than to its filling with glory and peace, there remains much to be desired both as to Biblical usage, interpretation, and fulfilment. A spiritual interpretation of the Day of Pentecost would get nearer to the features—i.e., heaven and earth shaken : the sea and dry land (the multitudes of mankind): the nations; and the nations yielding treasures; the house filled with glory, etc. But even so we are left with the future aspect of the passage in Hebrews xii.

The sense of verse 28 is that we are in process of receiving a kingdom which cannot be shaken, but this corresponds to verse 5 of Chapter ii : —

*" Not unto angels did he subject the in-
habited earth to come, whereof we are
speaking."*

The whole of this paragraph should be
carried over to " the kingdom which cannot
be shaken " together with " partners of a
heavenly calling " (iii. 1). It will then be seen
that the " once more," lit. " only once," in its
universal sense must yet lie ahead, and doubtless in relation to the Lord's coming again.

The last verse of Chapter xii seems to clinch
this argument—" for our God is a consuming
fire," and surely it belongs to the events of
which Peter wrote : —

*" The day of the Lord . . . in the which
the heavens shall pass away with a great
noise, and the elements shall be dissolved
with fervent heat, and the earth and the
works that are therein shall be burned up.
Seeing that these things are thus all to be
dissolved . . ." (II Pet. iii.* 10).

Some of these phrases are very intelligible to
us, and we are quite sure that Peter knew
nothing about atomic bombs—" elements dissolved with fervent heat " ; but the Holy Spirit
did, and does ! (It is well to read the whole
of this chapter from Peter.) Peter's words in
his first letter (iv. 17) are also very relevant to
Hebrews xii. 26, where he says that

*" The time (is come) for judgment to
begin at the house of God."*

Having, then, as we think, good ground for
believing that the great shaking still lies ahead,
we are able to say something with regard to its

object, its need, and its call.

The Object of the Shaking

In the light of this entire letter, and, indeed, in the light of the entire New Testament revelation, the one Object by which everything is ultimately tested and judged is Christ, as being the constitution of everything in a spiritual way. God's one inclusive purpose is to have everything constituted according to Christ. This must be organic, the very nature and essence of Christ. It cannot be by imitation, duplication, or organisation. It can only be by conception, not observation. This kingdom " cometh not with observation." Therefore it must be spiritual. It must come from within by ' inbirth.' Thus, the measure of Christ as the spiritual life and nature of everything or anything working from within is the basis and standard of all Divine judgments. It will not be sound doctrine, extra truth, devoutness, zeal, many works, etc., but just Christ Himself, known, lived, and expressed, in the power and grace of the Eternal Spirit. In a word, it will be a matter of our true spiritual life as spiritual people in living and growing identification with Christ by the Holy Spirit. God has reduced His whole judgment to this. " He will judge the world by (or in) . . . Jesus Christ," and this is not just official, but spiritual—Christ is not only the Judge, but the standard of judgment. This is why the Book of the Revelation, which is a book of judgments, first of the Church, and then of the nations, begins with a full-length presentation of Christ the Living One. Then it shows that judgment is not so much as to *things*, more or less good or bad, but what is Christ or what is inimical to Him constitutionally.

The Need for the Shaking

We have been at pains in our earlier chapters to show that Christianity has become, very largely, another Judaism, an outward system and a historic tradition. But it has become more than this. In its principles, methods, and means, it has largely become conformed to this world or age. Were we wanting to deal with the negative or defective aspect of things, it would not be difficult to write whole chapters on the weaknesses of present-time organised Christianity; but we would rather use our time and space on the positive line. Let us, however, appeal to our brethren in responsibility to think again and seriously before the Lord as to the true nature and origin of much that goes to make up the means of propaganda and publicity of work for God. Let us take account of such things as the prominence given to human honours, glories, titles, reputations, distinctions. That men have gained these or been given them in various spheres of life—politics, philanthropy, industry, adventure, war, sport, entertainment, science, art, or education—may be quite all right in itself, but that these things should be so largely used as the ground of appeal may just imply that Christ is not sufficient as standing on His own merits,

E   67 but must be surrounded by these natural embellishments (?). Must Christ be recommended or His servants accepted because of some human association of the word " great " in some earthly connection?

Again, let us be very careful, for the same purpose, of the encroachment of the entertainment feature of sacred service. " Lovers of pleasure " is an end-time characteristic, and the age is running headlong thither. Is it necessary to go with the age in order to attract? Is the Gospel dependent upon this " make-up " for its effectiveness and appeal?

Once more: let us watch that we are not carried away by the illusion of bigness. Many a once powerful instrument of God—personal or collective—has lost its spiritual value and impact when it has become big or popular. There is a Satanic snare in bigness, and we may by this illusion lose our very faculty for seeing just where God is doing his deepest work, and how. Often, God's truest work is hidden. It is becoming difficult, if not impossible, for many servants of God to believe or understand that anything of real account can be done unless it is well known and in the public eye.

When David put the Ark upon a new cart and things went just so far and then came to an ignominious and tragic impasse, it was not due to a lack of sincerity, devotion, zeal, energy, or wholeheartedness, but because he had all unwittingly drawn up from his subconsciousness an idea and method which had originated with the Philistine diviners. Those diviners had once put the Ark upon a new cart to send it back into Israel. David had fled in an hour of weakness to dwell in the land of the Philistines, and had been infected with the methods and means of that world. When God made the breach upon Uzzah that he died before the Lord it would have been too hard and severe, in the light of the zeal for the Lord, if there had not been some extra factor. That factor was the hand of another spiritual system back of "this present evil world" of which the diviners were the representatives and servants, and whom God had already plagued and cursed. (Read the story in I Samuel v, vi, xxvii, II Sam. vi). There was no reason why Uzzah should be spared and the Philistines destroyed if the same factor obtained in both cases. No amount of zeal can save us in the end if the principles are false. But note how subtle it all was. There was not the remotest idea that things were basically wrong. The idea of bringing up the lArk (the Testimony) to its right and full place was right and according to God's mind. The earnestness and utterness left nothing to be desired. The motive and its passion were wholly commendable. But somewhere, somehow, Antichrist (in principle) was hidden in the constitution of things: the energy of the flesh, the soul-life actuated or taken charge of by that which was not the Spirit of God. If the soul, which is the natural side of man's being, is *predominant*, on any or all of its sides—intellectual, emotional, or volitional—then the door is wide open to deception; and deception, being what it is, does not mean that there is no zeal for God, but rather that it is zeal but not according to knowledge. It is only as the child of God lives in and is governed by the Holy Spirit through his renewed spirit—not *firstly* his soul—that he will be made aware of " the things that differ," even in his service for God. David eventually was shown what the Holy Spirit had indicated in the Scriptures as to God's principles of service, and he found by tragic experience that spiritual principles are more important than zeal and energy, although these latter were no less when the true basis was established. Satan is very subtle and will espouse our zeal for God if by so doing he can eventually bring shame and dishonour into God's testimony.

God sees through it, and would warn us of it. The trouble so largely is that, as in David's case, the drive and abandon associated with a great idea for God just ride rough-shod over quiet waiting upon God and enquiry of Him as to His mind concerning the means and methods to be employed. The point at which disaster will befall very much that is engaged in for God in all sincerity is that which leaves no time for quiet detachment, for unhurried waiting upon God. There may be prayer, but it is prayer with a drive of work behind it, instead of the other way round. The question is, Did you get that method, that means, that programme in the secret place with God, direct from Him? Have you put everything back until all heat and hurry have been subjected to the judgment of the Holy Spirit? Or are you just getting on with it because it is for the Lord?

Do you think that judgment is upon men and things as such? Was there not enough genuine devotion to the Lord in David, Uzzah, and all the others to prevail against that terrible breaking in of God? Would the Lord not be slow to anger if that were all? Oh, why then this severity of God? Why must judgment begin at the house of God? It cannot be because of a greater or lesser degree of Christian goodness or zeal. There must be something more in it than that! Yes, there is, and we have touched upon it. The " eyes of flame " (Rev. i. 14), " the consuming fire," have beheld an insinuation—in principle or element—of the great Evil One, who will deceive even to the point of simulating Christ or " an angel of light," in order that—sooner or later—the real Christ impact shall be neutralised.

This is all so relevant to our consideration in these chapters, and is undoubtedly behind the terrible nature of the warnings in this letter. We could never over-emphasise or exaggerate the terrible consequences to Christians and Christian work of failure to take sufficient account of the significance in verse 12 of Chapter iv linked with verse 9 (last part) of chapter xii.

But when all has been said both there and

here, *will* you stop, *can* you stop, to get a sure place in the Spirit, or are you so involved, committed, driven, that the " still small voice " of the Spirit has no chance of being heard ? It is in this whole realm of things that the great shaking will have its *first* effect. I was recently told in America on very good authority that fifty per cent. of the missionaries who go to the mission field never return there after their first furlough, they cannot stand up to it. If that proportion were only half the truth it would be a startling—though small— sample of what the great shaking will mean in the matter of discovering how much there really is of Christ back of all early enthusiasm and well-meaning intentions. Not less zeal, devotion, and energy, but more depth, spiritual measure, and Divine understanding lies behind the appeal of this letter—" Let us go on to full growth."

With that appeal we shall deal particularly in our next chapter.

Chapter Eight

The Reiterated Appeal

VERY early in this letter to the Hebrews the writer, having made a many-sided and very great comparison and contrast between the greatest persons and things of the old dispensation and Jesus the Son of God, launches an inclusive appeal and warning in superlative terms. " How shall we escape if we neglect so great salvation? " Throughout the letter he applies that in various connections, but he does so as always governed by that last clause

" So Great Salvation "

So that is what it is all about! Salvation. *Great* salvation. *So great* salvation ! As there cannot be two salvations, this one and some other, but this one is really what God intends by salvation, it is as well that we look again at what has been said in these pages as to the greatness of Christ, the greatness of our calling, the greatness of our intended destiny, and the greatness of our responsibility. One thing ought to emerge from this consideration, that is, that salvation is a much greater thing on the side of its *unto* than on the side of its *from*. That is, there is much more in God's purpose for man than to save him from sin, judgment, death, and hell. However great redemption is, it is only to get man back to the place where the original full intention of God can be proceeded with. It is a very costly ' fall ' that has happened to man, but his recovery has far more in it than the recovery itself. The Gospel of Salvation as it is usually preached is so largely occupied with man himself and the immediate advantages and benefits of being saved. To promise, and get him to, heaven is about the limit. The " so great salvation " has immense issues bound up with it and includes all the superlatives and " mysteries " of Paul's unparalleled unveilings of " the eternal purpose." Salvation's greatest aspect is what it is unto, however great may be what it is from. If more of this greatness had broken upon the preachers, and were the mighty motive of their preaching, as it was in Paul's case, and others, the impact upon men would need little of the upholstery mentioned in our last chapter.

It is in the light of this more positive aspect that our writer so repeatedly appeals, urges, and warns, and it is now our intention to close our meditations by surveying these calls quite briefly.

While the writer was too moved by his theme to stop for systematising his matter, it may help if we do something in that way. We can therefore, quite without straining, put these reiterations into three connections—A, B, and C.

It is assumed by this letter that those to whom it was written were believers in the Lord Jesus and that they had given themselves over to Him. They are called " holy brethren " (iii. 1) which implies consecration to Christ.

On this assumption the writer bases his appeals and warnings.

A. The Basis of Consecration

This basis is seen in the first series of appeals governed by the words " Let us."

i. (iv. 1) " *Let us fear.*"

If the consecration to the Lord is a genuine one upon an adequate apprehension of His superiority to all others, it will have in it this element of holy fear. The context shows that it is the great prospect which has come into view with Christ that creates such a fear lest it should be missed. Holy fear should always be a feature of a Christian's life; not fear of judgment; not dread of the Lord; but fear lest there might be a missing of *all* that is implicit in the call of grace. The presence of such an exhortation is itself enough to prove that just to have accepted Christ is not enough to guarantee the attainment (to use Paul's word) of all that which is included in our having been " apprehended by Christ Jesus."

ii. (iv. 11) " *Let us give diligence* "; literally " hasten."

This bears upon the time factor, especially the spiritual time factor. " So long as it is called To-day " or " To-day, if ye shall hear " is the ground of appeal here. The lack of urgency and diligence will have two effects. God's actual time opportunity—which is never shown to be other than now—may be missed; and, or, our capacity or ability to make good all that can be apprehended may slip past, and we be found like ships stranded on a mud bank.

iii (*iv*. 14) " *Let us hold fast* "; literally
" grasp."

It is so easy to lose grip and firmness of
hold, and become loose or slack. You have
made a confession; reaffirm, and do not let
its full meaning and value slip out of your
hand, or be taken from you. Close your hand
tightly upon it against all that would steal it
from you.

iv. (*iv*. 16). " *Let us . . . with boldness*."

False fear, timidity, uncertainty, or any
member of that large family of Doubt, will
keep us away if possible. The Throne of Grace
is there. The Blood has opened the way. The
High Priest in all sympathy holds out God's
hand to take yours. Why be hesitant, doubtful, wavering? Staying away means only to
be more and more involved in despondency
and Satan's accusations. Make the bold
plunge of faith in God's mercy and love; give
Him credit for meaning what He says, and
" draw near."

B. The Development of Consecration

i. (*vi*. 1). " *Let us go on . . .* "

The real value of this exhortation is found
in the implication of the Greek word used.
It is the same word as in Acts ii. 2 (" rush-
ing ") and II Peter i. 21 (" moved "). It
really means to be borne along by another.
This would indicate that God is moving on,
the Spirit of God is going forward. He is not
tarrying or delaying, but with great energy is
pursuing His goal. Let us fall in with Him.

Let us be caught in His goings. Let us yield to His energies. Let us not be left behind by the Lord . " Full-growth " is His goal; let us not remain infants or immature.

ii. (x. 22). " Let us draw nigh."

This is not the same as No. iv. above. That was a matter of adjustment of ourselves to being received. This is unto communion following the adjustment. In the one we need not, and must not, stand without, asking whether, peradventure, we dare approach. In the other, we should not come with reserves that will keep us from entering positively into the communion that is there for us.

iii. (x. 23). " Let us hold fast."

Again, this is not the same as No. iii. above. That was taking hold, taking a firm grip. This is maintaining our hold. It is a matter of tenacity as to " our hope," " that it waver not." This goes right to the root cause of this whole letter. It is a costly and difficult way. It is " outside the camp, bearing his reproach." We made a confession. Perhaps we weakened. Having tightened our grip, let us not weaken again, but be pertinacious.

iv. (x. 24). " Let us consider one another."

Rather " study " one another, with a view to

(a) Emulating the good in one another.

(b) Inciting one another to good ; to love and good works. In short, let us take account of one another with a view to positively helping one another toward the goal—not to noting one another's faults and defects and so retard-

77

ing their progress and our own.

C. The Characteristics of Consecration

Having made his appeal for renewed consecration, and having shown what consecration is, by the same phrase—" Let us "—the writer proceeds to a series of exhortations which indicate the kind of person a really consecrated person will be; what is necessary as characterising such an one.

i. (xii. 1). *" Let us lay aside."*

If we really mean business in relation to this " heavenly calling " (iii. 1) we must and shall look at everything from the standpoint of whether it is positive or negative as relating thereto. Does this thing help? If not it must go. For it to hinder, or retard, or make heavy going is its condemnation. The course must be as clear as we can make it, and anything or anyone not in the real business, but just obstructing or loitering, must be pushed aside. This will apply to ' the luggage of life '; it will apply to distractions and diversions; it will also apply to discouragements and disheartenments. There is no place for temperamentalism and moodiness in this race, and the easily-besetting sin of doubt and mistrust will bring the pilgrim quickly to the Slough of Despond.

ii. (xii. 1). *" Let us run."*

Not talk about consecration; not be interested in it; not be merely a member of the ' Consecration Committee '; not be an expert in the technique of athletics, knowing about running and runners, courses, rules, outfit, and prizes; but " Let us *run*," let us *do* it. How many know all the teaching and doctrine of consecration who are slow starters, or poor runners, always needing to be urged, encouraged, get refreshments, or have a rest! Let us get on with it, and " with patience." *Keep* on with it.

iii. (*xii.* 28). " *Let us have (or take) grace whereby we may serve . . . .*"

Here the Greek word for serve suggests that it is return for something received. Grace is a great blessing and benefit. The grace which has called us with *such* a " heavenly calling," into *such* a ' partnership ' (iii. 1) surely creates a responsibility born of indebtedness. Let us take this grace with grateful hearts and prove our sense of indebtedness by service.

iv. (*xiii.* 13). " *Let us go forth unto him without the camp.*"

In appreciation of the supreme greatness of Christ and of the grace bestowed upon us, let us show that we are not ashamed of Him, but rather are prepared to suffer with Him and share His reproach. If we are really consecrated to Christ we shall be glad to stand by Him while and where He and His fullest interests are excluded, even from the Christian-Judaistic system which is more for itself than for Him.

v. (*xiii.* 15). " *Let us offer up a sacrifice of praise continually.*"

This is the topstone, the crown, of consecration. Reproach and rejection, yes, and all else involved; but is He worth it? Will the end justify it? Sonship, dominion, partnership with Christ crowned with glory and honour, God's House for ever; these are the things held up to view in this letter. If we have really seen *Him*, and what partnership with Him means, so that we are abandoned to Him, we shall be in that priestly course of singers which —in David's constituting—never ceased. This letter is so largely on the line of the House and the Priesthood and the Sacrifice, so that it is not surprising that it should end on the " twenty four courses of the singers " by implication—a course for the whole circuit of the sun, day and night. " A sacrifice of praise continually," or " a sacrifice of perpetual praise."

Thus fourteen times in this letter the appeal is made against any and every failure to be always characterised by an active outreach after God's fullest thought for His people. The spirit of Caleb is so à propos to it all; he " wholly followed the Lord," and at an advanced age requested hill country and a mountain to prove that he was still of that mind, and that the Lord honours such with supplies of spiritual vitality. He had seen that God had made known what was His mind for His people and that was what mattered. He—Caleb—would not accept anything less. He would not talk about that being ' the ideal, but quite impracticable, ' or ' the state of things being what it is—in ruins—we must accept it, and make the best of a bad job. ' Any such talk would be to Caleb treachery or betrayal: disloyalty to the Lord : an admission that God had intended something, but it had proved unworkable and must be scrapped for something less. The mind of Caleb was *that;* the majority might take the other attitude, but until God gave another and modified revelation of His purpose, though he were the only one to " go on " he was going on. This attitude, spirit, and activity God fully honoured, and not only did Caleb inherit, but Judah came into their inheritance because of his faithfulness. And Judah stands for something in the Divine thought!

While " Hebrews " and " Ephesians " still remain a part of the Bible, that is what God means for His people, even if but a comparatively few " go on." It can only mean serious and grievous loss to take any other attitude. Hence with the repeated " Let us " the writer links a repeated warning note " Lest." The nine occurrences of this warning note are worth considering. They cover every form of possible cause of failure—from the lack of alertness necessary to grasp the mooring as the vessel is carried by the current either out to sea or on to the rocks, to a definite hardening of heart against the appeal " To-day, if ye shall hear his voice." This last is an appeal to Christians, not *here* to the unsaved as it is almost exclusively used by preachers.

All this, then, brings us back to our starting point—the implications of this letter—and should cause us to examine modern Christianity and our own position to see if it is a set system, a tradition, an inheritance; or whether it is really—and *now*—bringing to the Land and the goal, the fulness of Christ.

The
Stewardship
of the
Mystery
(Vol. 1)

Publisher's note:

The Stewardship of the Mystery (volume I)
originally published from
39 Honor Oak Road, London in 1940

The year of publication as given is from when, in the
author's bimonthly magazine *A Witness and a
Testimony,* a first notice of this book or booklet
appeared. Very many of the titles published had
already appeared earlier as articles or series in that
magazine.

Where a new title's date of publication is not known, +
signifies the year of the magazine article or series from
which, some unspecified time later, that new
publication was reproduced.

1998 Christian Books Publishing House / SeedSowers
P O Box 285
Sargent
GA 30275

Preface to Second Edition

This is a volume of messages given in Conference. They are retained in their spoken form. It is important that the reader should remember this, and the attitude should be rather that of one who is listening to, and watching, a speaker, than that of one who is taking account of literary style. It is marked Vol. I. The ground covered is comprehensive; no one subject being dealt with very fully. Volume II is being revised for reprinting. It deals more specifically with some of the matters mentioned in Vol. I.

The reprinting of these volumes (for some time out of print) is because of repeated requests for them.

The messages are in harmony with—if only a poor echo of—the heart-expression of the Apostle who provides the title—". . . whom we proclaim, admonishing every man, and teaching every man . . . that we may present every man perfect (complete, entire) in Christ; whereunto I labour . . ." (Col. i. 28-29). May this ministry be prospered unto that end.

T. A-S.

Forest Hill,
　London.
1964

Contents

CHAPTER I

The Purpose of the Ages

". . . No one knoweth the Son, save the Father . . ."—Matt. xi. 27.

". . . It was the good pleasure of God . . . to reveal his Son in me . . ."—Gal. i. 15-16.

". . . I count all things to be loss for the excellency of the knowledge of Christ Jesus my Lord . . ."—Phil. iii. 8.

". . . That I may know him . . ."—Phil. iii. 10.

"Having made known unto us the mystery of his will, according to his good pleasure which he purposed in him unto a dispensation of the fulness of the times, to sum up all things in Christ . . ." —Eph. i. 9-10.

That little clause in verse 10 is the word which will govern our meditation—ALL THINGS IN CHRIST.

These scriptures speak for themselves. As we listen to the inner voice of the Spirit in these fragments of the Divine Word, surely we shall begin to feel a sense of tremendous meaning, value and content. We should feel like people who have come to the doors of a new realm full of wonders— unknown, unexplored, unexploited.

The Necessity for Revelation

We are met at the very threshold of that realm with a statement which is calculated to check our steps for the moment, and if we approach with a sense of knowing or possessing anything already, with a sense of contentment, of personal satisfaction, or with any sense other than that of needing to know everything, then this word should bring us to a standstill at once: ". . . no one knoweth the Son, save the Father. . . ." Maybe we thought we knew something about the Lord Jesus, and that we had ability to know; that study, and listening, and various other forms of our own application and activity could bring us to a knowledge, but at the

—9—

outset we are told that ". . . no one knoweth the Son, save the Father. . . ." All that the Son is, is locked up with the Father, and He alone knows.

When, therefore, we have faced that fact, and have recognised its implications, we shall see that here is a land which is locked up into which we cannot enter, and for which we have no equipment. There is nothing in us of faculty to enter into the secrets of that realm of Christ. Then following the discovery of that somewhat startling fact of man's utter incapacity to know by nature, the next fact that confronts us is this: ". . . it was the good pleasure of God . . . to reveal his Son in me. . . ." While God has all that locked up in Himself, in His own possession, and He alone has the knowledge of the Son, it is in His heart, nevertheless, to give revelation. And, given the truth that we are so utterly dependent upon revelation from God, and that all human faculty and facility is ruled out in this respect, since such revelation can only be known by a Divine revealing after an inward kind, we are making it to be very evident that everything is of grace when we renounce all trust in works, when we turn away from self-sufficiency, self-reliance, from all confidence in the flesh, and any pride of advance and approach.

Read these two passages in the light of what Paul was when known as Saul of Tarsus, before the Lord met with him, and afterward as Paul the Apostle, and you will gain something more of their force. Saul of Tarsus would have called himself a master in Israel, one well learned in the Scriptures, with a certain strength of self-assurance, self-confidence, and self-sufficiency in his apprehension and knowledge of the oracles of God. Even such a one as he will have to come to the recognition that none of that is of avail in the realm of Christ; where he realises that he is utterly blind, utterly ignorant, utterly helpless, altogether ruled out, and needing the grace of God for the very first glimmer of light; to come down very low, and say: ". . . it was the good pleasure of God . . . to reveal his Son in me. . . ." That is grace.

That marked the beginning; and for this present meditation we are considering the unexplored fulness of what God has Himself placed within His Son, the Lord Jesus, actually and in purpose, as being the object of His grace toward us. His grace has led Him to seek to bring us by revelation into all that knowledge which He Himself possesses as His own secret knowledge of His fulness in His Son, the Lord Jesus. ALL THINGS IN CHRIST.

Paul's Revelation of Christ

It is never our desire to make comparisons between Apostles, and God forbid that we should ever set a lesser value upon any Apostle than that which the Lord has set upon him; yet I think that we are quite right in saying that, more than any other, Paul was, and is, the interpreter of Christ; and if we take Paul as our interpreter, as the one who leads us into the secrets of Christ in a fuller way, we mark how he himself embodies and represents that of which he speaks. It is the man himself, after all, and not just what he says which brings us to Christ in fuller and deeper meaning.

The thing that has been very much pressing upon my own heart in this connection is Paul's ever-growing conception of Christ. There is no doubt that Paul's conception of Christ was growing all the time, and by the time Paul reached the end of his earthly life, full, and rich, and deep as it had been, Paul's vision of Christ was such as to lead him to cry even at that point, ". . . that I may know him. . . ." Yes, at the beginning it had pleased God to reveal His Son in him, but at the end it was still as though he had known nothing of Christ. He had come to discover that his Christ was immeasurable beyond his thought and conception, and he was launched into eternity with a cry on his lips: ". . . that I may know him. . . ."

I believe (and not as a matter of sentiment) that will be our eternal bliss, the nature of our eternity, namely, discovering Christ. Paul as we have said, had a great knowledge of Christ. At best here we find ourselves shrivelling into insignificance every time we approach him. How many times have we read the letter to the Ephesians! I am not exaggerating when I say that if we have read it for years, read it scores, hundreds, or even thousands of times, every sentence can hold us afresh each time we come back to it. Paul knew what he was talking about. Paul's conception was a large one, but even so he is still saying at the end, ". . . that I may know him. . . ." I do not think we shall know Christ in fulness immediately we pass into His presence. I believe we are to go on—governed by this word, "the ages to come"—discovering, discovering, exploring Christ. That ever-growing conception of Christ was the thing which maintained Paul in life, and maintained Paul's ministry in life. There was never any stagnation with him. He never came to any point or place where there was the suggestion that now he knew. What he seems to say is this: I do not know anything yet, but I see dimly, yet truly, with the eye of the spirit, a Christ so great, so vast as to keep me reaching out, moving on. I press on; I leave the things which are behind; I count all things as refuse for the excellency of the knowledge of Christ Jesus, that I may know Him. In this growing conception of Christ, Paul moved a long way from the position of the Jewish teacher, or of the Jew himself at his best.

Paul began with the Jewish conception of the Messiah, whatever that was. It is quite impossible to say what the Jewish conception of Christ was. You have indications of what they expected the Messiah to be and to do, but there is nothing to indicate exactly what their conception of the Messiah was in fulness; it was undoubtedly a limited one. There is a great deal of uncertainty betrayed by the Jewish thought beyond a certain point about their long-looked-for Messiah. Their Messiah represented something earthly and something temporal; an earthly kingdom and a temporal power, with all the earthly and temporal advantages which would accrue to them as people on this earth from His kingdom, from His reign, from His appearing. That is where we begin in our consideration of Paul's conception of Christ. This Jewish conception, it is true, did not confine the thought of blessing to Israel alone, but allowed that Messiah's coming was, through the Jews, to issue in blessing to all nations; yet it was still earthly, temporal, limited to things here. If you read the Gospels, and especially Matthew's Gospel, you will see that the endeavour of these Gospels, so far as Jewish believers were concerned, was to show that Christ had done three things.

Firstly, how that He had corrected their ideas about the Messiah.

Secondly, how that He had fulfilled the highest hopes that could have been theirs concerning the Messiah.

Thirdly, how that He had far transcended anything that ever they had thought.

You must remember that these Gospels were never written merely to convince unbelievers. They were written also to believers, to help the faith of believers by interpretation. Matthew's Gospel, written as it was at a time of transition, was written in order to interpret and confirm faith in Christ by showing what Christ really was, what He really came for, and in that way to correct and adjust their conceptions of the Messiah. Their conceptions of Him were inadequate, distorted, limited, and sometimes wrong. These records were intended to put them right, to show that Christ had fulfilled the highest, and best, and truest Messianic hopes and expectations, and had infinitely transcended them all. You need Paul to interpret Matthew, and Mark, and Luke, and John; and he does it. He brings Christ into view as One in whom every hope is realised, every possibility achieved. Were they expecting an earthly kingdom, and deliverance and blessing in relation thereto? Christ had done something infinitely better than that. He had wrought for them a cosmic redemption; not a mere deliverance from the power of Rome or any other temporal power, but deliverance from the whole power of evil in the universe—"Who delivered us out of the power of darkness, and translated us into the kingdom of the Son of his love." Matthew had particularly stressed the fact of the kingdom, but the Jewish idea of the kingdom with which he was confronted was so limited, so earthly, so narrow. With a new emphasis Paul, by the Spirit, brings into view the nature and immensity of the kingdom of the Son of God's love.

Now we can see something of what deliverance from our enemies means. We shall not follow that through, but pass on with just that glimpse of it. Such an unveiling as this was a corrective. It revealed a fulfilment in a deeper sense than they had expected, but it was a transcendence of their fullest hope and expectation. Paul interpreted the Christ for them in His fuller meaning and value. He himself had begun on their level. Their conception of Christ had been his own. But after it pleased God to reveal His Son in him a continuous enlargement in Paul's knowledge of Christ began through an ever-growing unveiling of what He was.

Of course, as Saul of Tarsus, Paul never believed that Jesus of Nazareth was the Messiah. This takes us a step further back in his conception. He believed that Jesus was an imposter, and so he sought to blot out all that was associated with Him in the world.

Paul, then, had to learn at least two things. He had to learn that Jesus of Nazareth was the Messiah, but he also had to learn that Jesus of Nazareth far transcended all Jewish conceptions of the Messiah, all his own ideas, all his own expectations as bound up with the Messiah. He not only learned that He was the Messiah, but that as Messiah He was far, far greater and more wonderful than his fullest ideas and conceptions and expectations. Into that revelation he was brought by the grace of God.

The Progressiveness of Revelation as Illustrated in Paul

I do not think the point needs arguing, for it is hard to dispute that there are evidences of progress in Paul's understanding and knowledge of Christ, and it is clear that progress and expansion and development in his knowledge of Christ led to adjustment. Do not misunderstand. They did not lead to a repudiation of anything that Paul had stated, nor to a contradiction of any truth that had come through him, but they led to adjustment. As his knowledge of Christ grew and expanded Paul saw that he had to adjust himself to it.

This is a point at which many have stumbled, but it is a matter about which we should have no fear. There are so many people who are afraid of the idea that such a man as the Apostle Paul—or any man in the Bible who was Divinely inspired—so utterly under the power of the Holy Spirit should ever adjust himself according to new revelation. They seem to think that this necessarily means that the man changes in such a way as to leave his original position and more or less repudiate it. It does not mean anything of the kind.

Take an illustration. Paul's letters to the Thessalonians were his first letters. In those letters there is no doubt whatever that Paul expected the Lord to return in his lifetime. Mark his words: ". . . we that are alive, that are left unto the coming of the Lord. . . ." In his letter to the Philippians,

—14—

Paul has moved from that position, while in his letters to Timothy that expectation is no longer with him: ". . . I am already being offered, and the time of my departure is come. I have fought the good fight, I have finished the course. . . ." He had anticipated Nero's verdict. He knew now that it was not by way of the rapture that he himself was to go to glory. Are we to say that these two things contradict one another? Not at all! In going on with the Lord, Paul came into fuller revelation about the Lord's coming, and of his personal relationship thereto, but this did not set aside or change any fact of doctrine which had been expressed earlier in his letters to the Thessalonians. All that had been set forth there was fully inspired, given by the Holy Spirit, but it was still capable of development in the heart of the Apostle himself, and as he saw the fuller meaning of the things that had come to him earlier in his life, so he found that in practical matters he had to adjust himself. No fresh revelation, nor advance in understanding, ever placed him in the position of having to repudiate anything that had been given him by revelation in earlier days. It is a matter of recognising that these differences are not contradictions but the result of progressive, supplemental revelation, enlarging apprehension, clearer conception through going on with the Lord. Surely these are evidences that progress in Paul's understanding and knowledge led to adjustments.

The Eternal Purpose of God in His Son

Now the great effect of Paul's discovery concerning the Lord Jesus on the Damascus road was not only to reveal to him the fact of His Sonship (he undoubtedly discovered there that Jesus of Nazareth was the Son of God, as his words in Gal. i. 15-16 show), but to lift Christ right out of time and to place Him with the Father in the "before times eternal." That does not perhaps for the moment appear to be very striking, but it is a very big step toward what the Lord wants to say to us. Christ has been lifted out of time. The "time" Christ, that is, His coming into this world in time, becomes something like a parenthesis; it is not the main thing. It is the main thing if we look at the whole in the light of the fall and need for recovery, but not the main thing from the Divine standpoint originally. I want you to grasp this, because it is at this point that we come into that greatest of all revelations that have been given to us concerning the Lord Jesus. This effect of his experience on the Damascus road, this lifting of Christ right out of time and placing Him in eternity, came in Paul's conception to be related to eternal purpose, and in eternal *purpose* there was no fall and no redemption. That is, so to speak, a bend down in the line of God through the ages. God's line was to have gone straight without a bend, without a break, but when it came to a certain point, because of certain contingencies which were never in the *purpose*, that line had to go down, and then up and on again. The two ends of that line are on the same eternal level. You may, if you like, conceive of a bridge across that bend, and of Christ thus filling the bend, so that what was from eternity is not interrupted at all in Him; it goes on *in Him*. The coming to earth and all the work of the Cross is something other, the result of a necessity by reason of these contingencies; but in Christ from eternity to eternity the purpose is unbroken, uninterrupted, without a bend. There is no hiatus in Christ. This came to be related to purpose. That is a great word of Paul's: "According to the eternal purpose which he purposed in Christ Jesus our Lord . . ." (Eph. iii. 11); ". . . called according to his purpose" (Rom. viii. 28). These are eternal conceptions of Christ, and this purpose, and these Divine counsels were related to the universe, and to man in particular. Let us get across that bridge for a moment, leaving the other out; for I want you to notice the course that the letter to the Ephesians takes. The letter begins with eternity. It says much of things that were before the world was, and it comes back to that point. Just in between it speaks of redemption, and it never speaks of redemption until it has the past eternity in view. Redemption comes in to fill up that gap and then we go on to eternity again.

Now just leave the gap for a moment. Of course it concerns us tremendously and we shall have to come back to it, because everything is bound up with redemption so far as we are concerned in the eternal purpose; but leave it for a moment and turn your attention in this other direction. It is stated definitely and clearly that the whole plan of God without redemption was completed in those eternal counsels concerning His Son, Jesus Christ, and in that plan the ages were created: "... the fulness of the times ..." is the phrase used here in our translation.

I have heard such phrases in the New Testament as these interpreted as being the dispensations as we now know them in the Bible; the dispensation of Abraham, the dispensation of the Law, the dispensation of Grace. I wonder if that is right? Mark this expression: "... through whom also he made the ages" (Heb. i. 2; R.V.M.). Let us think again. Are we right in saying that applies to what we call the dispensations as they are shown to us in the Bible? Without being dogmatic about it, I have a question. Are we to say that in those eternal counsels of God, in relation to the eternal purpose of God concerning His Son, a dispensation of Law had a place, an age like the Old Testament age, those periods of time from Adam to Abraham, Abraham to Moses, Moses to David, David to the Messiah? Are those the ages referred to? Did God create those in relation to the eternal purpose? Remember all this creative work was in, and through, and unto His Son, according to *the eternal purpose.*

There are ages upon ages yet to come. There are marks through eternity which are not "time" marks in our sense of the word, but represent points of emergence and development, of progress, increase, enlargement. Had you and I been born on the Day of Pentecost, and were we then to have lived through until the return of the Lord (that is a dispensation according to this world's reckoning and order) we should never have discovered all the meaning of Christ. We should have discovered something and have reached a certain point in the knowledge of Christ, but we should then want another age under different conditions, to discover things which it would never be possible to discover under the conditions of this life; and when we had made good that next possibility, probably beyond that there would be new possibilities. There will be no stagnation in eternity—"... of the increase of his government ... there shall be no end ..." (Isa. ix. 7).

Now leave the sorry picture of this world's history from the fall to the restitution of all things aside, and you have the launching of ages in which all God's fulness in Christ could be revealed and apprehended progressively, on through successive ages, with changing and enlarging conditions, and

—17—

facilities, and abilities. That is the meaning of spiritual growth. Our own short Christian life here, if it is a right one, moving under the power of the Holy Spirit, is itself like a series of ages in brief. We start as children, and acquire what we can as children. Then we come to a point where we have increased capacity, where our spiritual senses are exercised. This again issues in a larger apprehension of Christ, and then a little later, as we have gone on, we still find these powers enlarging, under the Holy Spirit, and as the powers enlarge we realise there is more country to be occupied than ever we imagined. As children we thought we had it all! That is, of course, one of the signs of childhood and of youth. The saving thing in our old age is that we recognise there is a vast realm ahead of us to beckon us on and to stop us from settling down. That is eternal youth!

Thus, leaving the whole of this broken-down state in the creation, you can see the creating of ages in Christ, by Christ, through Christ, according to God's eternal purpose that all things should be summed up in Him; not just the "all things" of our little life, of our individual salvation, but the "all things" of a vast universe as a revelation of Christ, all being brought by revelation to the spiritual apprehension of man, and man being brought into it. What a Christ!

That is what Paul saw; and this may well be summed up in his own words: ". . . the excellency of the knowledge (that knowledge which excels) of Christ Jesus my Lord." It is Paul the aged saying, "that I may know Him." Christ is lifted right out of time, and time, so far as Christ was concerned, was only related to eternity by the necessity of redemption unto the eternal purpose.

We must break off here for the time being, but in so doing let me say this, that with his ever-growing conception of Christ, there was a corresponding enlargement in his conception of believers. Believers came to assume a tremendous significance. The saving of men from sin, death, and hell, and getting them to heaven, was as nothing compared with what Paul saw as to the significance of a believer now. All that which he has seen concerning Christ in His eternal purpose— eternal, universal, vast, infinite—now relates to believers: "Even as he chose us in him before the foundation of the world, that we should be . . . unto the praise of his glory" in the ages to come (Eph. i. 4, 12). Believers also are lifted out of time, and are given a significance altogether beyond anything here. We shall have to speak further of that.

There was a third thing. He was able rightly to apprise the range and place of redemption. Redemption could be seen in its full compass and as being something more than what is merely of time. It is called "eternal redemption." Redemption is something more than the saving of men and women from sin and their sinful state. It is getting behind everything to the ultimate ranges of this universe, and touching all its powers; linking up with the eternity past and the eternity yet to be, and embracing all the forces of this universe for man's redemption. Paul is able rightly to apprise the meaning, value, and range of redemption, and also to put it in its right place, and that is important.

Now these are big things. They all need to be broken up, and the Lord may enable us to do this, but if you cannot grasp what has been said you will be able to appreciate this, that Christ is infinitely bigger than you or I ever imagined. That is the thing that comes to us so forcibly through Paul. He started with a comparatively small Jewish Messiah; he ended with a Christ so far beyond all that ever he had yet seen or known, that his last cry is, ". . . that I may know him . . ." and that will take all eternity. What a Christ!

It is Christ who will lift us out, Christ who will set us free; but let me say this, that it will not be by His coming and putting His hands under us and lifting us out, but by being revealed in our hearts. How did Paul come out of his narrow Jewish conceptions about the Messiah? Simply by the revelation of Christ in him, and as that revelation grew his liberation increased. There were some things which he did not shake off for a long time. He clung to Jerusalem almost to the last. He still had a longing for his brethren after the flesh, and made further attempts for their deliverance on national grounds. But at last he saw the meaning of the heavenly Christ in such a way as to make it possible for him to write the letter to the Ephesians, and the letter to the Colossians, and then Judaism as such, Israel after the flesh, ceased to weigh with him. It was the revelation of Christ which was emancipating him, leading him out, freeing him all the time. In that way Christ is our Deliverer and

Emancipator. It is just the Lord Jesus that we need to know. Everything small will go as we see Him. Everything of earth and time will go as we see Him, and in the background of our lives there will be something adequate to keep us through difficult and hard times. We shall see the greatness of Christ and the corresponding greatness of our salvation "... according to his eternal purpose. . . ."

CHAPTER II

The Manifestation of the Glory of God

READING: Heb. i.

As the first thing in this meditation upon Christ, we have been occupied with the ever-growing conception of Him that marked the life of the Apostle Paul. We saw first how that Paul as a Jew had himself shared the very earthly and narrow conception of Messiah so common to his race, with all its thought of a temporal kingdom, privilege, and position, and how for him this conception came to be shattered by the revelation which he had of the Lord Jesus while journeying on the road to Damascus.

This crisis marked the beginning of an ever-growing knowledge of Christ. There Paul had learnt, not only that Jesus of Nazareth was Himself the long-expected Messiah, but that He was also the Son of God, who from before times eternal had been in the bosom of the Father. Christ was thenceforth to him no longer just a figure of time; and we marked how that by further revelation this fact came to be related to what Paul frequently calls purpose; the purpose of God, the Divine counsels—". . . who worketh all things after the counsel of His will. . . ." That is related to the "before times eternal," and in that purpose, in those Divine counsels from eternity, very many things are found to which Paul refers. We saw that these Divine counsels (this eternal purpose) concern the universe, and man in particular, and that both the universe and man are gathered up into His Son: "according to his good pleasure which he purposed in him unto a dispensation of the fulness of the times, to sum up all things in Christ, the things in the heavens, and the things upon the earth." That led us to consider a point which requires perhaps stating afresh, or at least a reiteration, to which therefore we now proceed.

These eternal counsels (this eternal purpose of God) represent the straight line of God through the ages, and as we are considering them have nothing to do with redemption. That is another line, an emergency line. We were saying that this fulness of the times, of the ages or seasons, represents God's eternal method of unfolding His fulness, and of bringing men into that fulness. They are stages of growth, of progress, of development concerning His Son, and, as we have said, all this was intended to be a straight line through the ages. These other ages of which we read, the ages of this world according to present conditions, are quite another line and introduce another expression of purpose. They were brought in, if we may put it figuratively or imaginatively, in this way: the Godhead in counsel laid the plan for all the future ages of the ages from eternity to eternity, and in that plan everything was clear and straightforward. There would be a progressive unveiling of God in the Son, and a progressive bringing of the universe into that fulness. But then God reached a point where He had to say, because of His foreknowledge (we speak imaginatively): But we know what will happen. We know that at a certain point the man whom We create will fail, will break down. That will mean a long period of disorder, disruption, chaos, and We must provide for that. There the whole plan of redemption was introduced, and the Lamb was slain from before the foundation of the world. That is another line of purpose. Thus the ages of this present world had to be introduced; the age before Law, from Adam after the fall to Moses, an age governed by certain things; then the age of Law up to Christ; then the age or the dispensation of the Church. These were not in the original plan. It is necessary to say that, because, were it otherwise, it would make God responsible for sin, and you might say: Well, if God had planned all that, the fall was bound to be; God had to bring about the fall! But that is not true. None of us would lay it to God's charge that He had planned the fall in order to make redemption necessary. That is another line of purpose, of planning according to the foreknowledge of God. The first line of purpose was not that, and, as we said, you start on a level and then reach a point where, because of failure and sin, there is a dip in the line, and in that dip, in that gap the whole story of redemption is seen. Christ bridges it and links up the first purpose, and its realisation, from eternity past to eternity to be. Coming in the likeness of sinful flesh, but without sin, the Redeemer stands in the gap and carries the purpose of the ages straight on in Himself. The present dispensations are, shall we say, subsidiary in their nature, and were brought in because of an emergency. God never intended it to be like that. Let us be quite clear on that point.

The fact which stands out clearly for us, and which is one of tremendous value, is that God intended that there should be ages, times, periods in which there should be increasing revelation, manifestation, and apprehension of Himself. Perhaps it sounds speculative, but let us ask: Now what would have happened if the fall had never taken place? If man had survived his testing in the garden and had not broken down, what would have happened? I believe man would have grown, grown, grown in his apprehension and knowledge of God, grown in his personal expression of God. God would have thus secured a progressive, ever-developing expression of Himself and, seeing that God is what He is, there would have been no limit to this; it could have gone on through successive ages, with movements in this universe into ever greater fulnesses of God.

We are not speaking of individual man but of collective man. That is what God intends, and that is what will be. Bridge the gap. Get right across the whole gap that has been filled by the redemptive programme, and take the matter up at the point where redemption is complete. Get back on to God's first level, triumphant over the enemy, and take things up there. What are you going to have? You are going to have a progressive, ever-growing expression of the fulness of God displayed in ages, in ever-widening circles of the revelation of God. It is not possible to comprehend the fulness of God. It will take eternity to express that.

All that fulness is in Christ; and our point at the moment is, how great is that fulness! What a Christ we have! It will take eternity to discover Christ. There is no small meaning about that statement. We recall the words of the Lord Jesus Himself: ". . . no one knoweth the Son, save the Father. . . ." That, of course, does not merely imply a question of identification, that no one knows who Christ is except the Father. It signifies what Christ stands for in the history of this universe, all that He is in His position in it. I believe it is unto an understanding of that that the Lord is calling us. The Lord wants us to come to a new understanding and apprehension of His Son, Jesus Christ, and that apprehension is our way out, our way up, our way to fulness. This, as we have said, came to be related to purpose, to Divine counsels concerning the universe, and man in particular.

The Personification of the Divine Thought in a Being

Its central meaning was in relation to a type of created being called man, and man is an expression of Divine thought, an image and likeness of something conceived in the mind of God. These are the eternal counsels issuing in eternal purpose, the counsel of His will. Now let us break that up.

God thought thoughts. You and I think thoughts, thoughts that correspond to our mental constitution, our nature, our make-up. One thinks after one manner because he is made that way, another after another manner because he is made that way. Our thoughts are the expression of our nature, our constitution, our disposition; in a word, our make-up. "For as he thinketh in his heart, so is he . . ." (Prov. xxii. 7). The thought is the man in essence. God thought thoughts. Those thoughts were God in essence. They were the projected mind of what God is like, what God thinks, what God is. Those thoughts were projected toward an object called man; that man should be an expression, a living personification of God's thoughts.

God desired desires. Now of man it is equally true that as a man desires in his heart so is he. We desire according to our inclinations, according to our preferences, according to what we feel to be best. Our desires express ourselves. God's desires are an expression of His own nature, His own being, His likeness. Those desires were centred in man, that man should be a living embodiment of God's heart, God's desire; desiring one desire with God, thinking one thought with God; one in mind, one in heart with God.

God willed a will. Our wills always betray us. What we will is the unveiling, the disclosing of what we are after, what we mean, what we intend. That is true of God. God willed a will, and that will was God, after the nature of God, the essence of God's nature, disposition, intention. That will of God was focused upon man, that man should embody the will of God and express it in personal living expression; living in the will of God, living by the will of God, his whole being gathered up in one inclusive and positive expression: Thy will, O God! There was to be a created being called "man" after that order, to be in that moral-spiritual sense the image of God, the likeness of God. This was not to share Deity, but to have the moral nature of God; the spiritual nature of God in mind, and heart, and will reproduced in man, expressed in a creation. That is where God's thought rested, and that is God's purpose. He would have it to be fruitful and multiply and replenish the earth; to grow and expand; morally and spiritually to reach out into all spiritual realms and fill the universe. Moral forces are forces which go far beyond the individual in which they rest or are centred.

The Lie and Its Outworking

Now you can see why Satan sought to capture man, and why he went about it in the manner that he did. It is as though he said: Set aside God's mind, God's will, God's desire! In other words, Accept mine instead! Now what have you? The expansion of that thing from a man to a universe! Those moral forces which are other than God intended are cosmic forces now. They have gone far beyond the individual, far beyond the family to a race, and out beyond a race to all the encircling realms of the cosmos. There is a will other than God's impregnating the very atmosphere. There are other desires, other feelings, other thoughts, all against God.

See, then, the awful alternative. See how far-reaching this matter is. Had man been true to God's expressed thoughts, His expressed desires, His expressed will; had man, in other words, been true to himself as out from the hand of God, which was to be true to God, this whole world, this whole cosmos to-day would be an expression of God's thought, desire, and will. What a world! What a universe! But what is it now? Such a thing as a thousand leagues of nations will never set it right. Man has let loose something in this universe by his treachery, his complicity with God's enemy, which must work itself out until this creation is an expression through and through of that which has revolted against God: and it will compass its own doom. What a difference! It is working out in that way. Try to arrest war. How futile! It is the working out of that thing: "only there is one that restraineth now, until he be taken out of the way." When that restraint is fully removed, you will see this whole creation as one leavened lump, seething with anarchy and self-destruction. God never intended that.

Do you see God's thought for man, God's intention, God's purpose? It was to express Himself through the universe. With this dispensation and creation just the opposite is expressing itself, and will do so until the end. This is not God's thought, God's desire, God's will; this is anarchy. It is against God, against His purpose, against His creation. Blessed be God, we are out of that creation, because we are in Christ, and Christ bridges the gap. He takes up the original intention. In Him you have God's thoughts, God's desires, God's will perfectly expressed, and we are in Him, a new creation in Christ Jesus. Now what is our business? To learn by the Holy Spirit to live after God's thoughts, according to God's desires, and in God's way. That lies ahead of us for our further consideration. It is only hinted at for the moment.

Conformity to Christ Essentially Moral and Spiritual

You see the result was intended to be a created corporate race as an expression of that which was, in essence, God. I do not mean Deity, I mean that which was intended in moral essence; the kind of thoughts God thinks, the kind of desires God desires, the kind of will God wills. God intended a created corporate race as an expression of Himself in that sense. You see it in Christ. You have the meaning of Christ when you see all that. This is what Christ means. This is the interpretation of Christ. How great a Christ!

Paul sees Him lifted altogether out of time, sees Him related to God's purpose; His express image, the effulgence, the very essence of God. Yes, His Deity included the moral essence of God. The expression of God in an Image morally constituted after God, that is Christ.

—26—

It is a great thing to see Christ, and then to see that we were chosen in Him to be like that, ". . . conformed to the image of His Son." The first representation of that thought, that mind, that heart, that will of God, was the Son; and the Son was *not created but begotten*. Man was created to be conformed to the image of the Son, but the Son was not created. He was the only begotten of the Father; unique, standing alone, inclusive, conclusive.

Those are not mere words. In the creation according to God there will be nothing but what is of Christ. It is important to realise that. That will govern a good deal that we may have yet to say. Thank God, you and I will not be as we are. It is not to be Christ *and* us; all is to be Christ. That is to say, Christ will be so corporately expressed that, the question of Deity apart, the moral and spiritual essence of Christ will utterly govern every other unit in the universe. It will be Christ in that sense; one great universal, collective, corporate Christ! Yes, there will be multitudes which no man can number, yet so conformed to the image of Christ that, looking at any one or all of these, spiritual conformity to Christ will be seen. We are not saying that Christ is to lose His individuality, to be absorbed in some inclusiveness where all His own personal distinctiveness ceases; we are saying that, when conformed to His image, we are to be as one great person, the Body of Christ perfected, a corporate and collective expression of what Christ is.

Paul refers to that when, with tremendous faith representing a tremendous victory and ascendancy, he said: ". . . we henceforth know no man after the flesh" (2 Cor. v. 15). It represents a victory of no mean order. In our dealings with the Lord's children, for instance, Paul means that, notwithstanding all that we may find of inconsistency and failure, because of what they are by nature, we are to focus all our attention upon Christ in them, and because they are Christ's, and He is in them, make His indwelling the ground of all our relations with them, keeping our eyes off the other altogether; we are to know them after Christ and not after the flesh. It will not be difficult in the ages to come, for then there will be nothing but what is of Christ in us. We shall see Christ in one another, we shall be fully conformed to His image. The Lord hasten that day!

What a Christ! See His position in God's purpose. See the universal, eternal Christ, embracing all, excluding all; excluding all that in character is unsuitable to God, and not out from Him, and including in Himself as the Son all that has become conformed to His image. Christ inclusive of creation, for all things were created for Him. They will be His, but as morally purged and made suitable to Him. That is why He refused them at the hands of the Devil. "All these things will I give thee, if thou wilt fall down and worship me" (Matt. iv. 9). He disdains the offer. Costly as the path would be—and He knew it—He would not be caught by that proposal. In effect He says: I will have them, but I will have them when all the trouble and the heart-break have gone. That is the effect of it; the whole creation included in Christ: but what a Christ!

One of the great governing factors and features of the new creation in Christ is deathless life. In the present creation at its best death reigns, decay reigns. Deathless life! There is no death at all in that new creation.

All the ages are included in Christ. Yes, there are ages yet to be—". . . that in the ages to come. . . ." Those ages are being included in Christ. That means that Christ will give them their character. They are to take their nature, their character from Christ, and inasmuch as they are ages, it means that progress, development, increase, expansiveness, extensiveness is all a matter of going on and enlarging unto Christ. The ages are made for Him, and the ages to come are for the showing forth in us of God in Christ. All the Divine fulness is in Christ. These are statements in the Word.

The Gift of Eternal Life

In the creation of man at the first one great factor was suspended. Perhaps it was the most important factor, and it was suspended pending man's probation and testing. What was it that so entirely depended upon how man issued from the probation and testing? It was eternity of life; life from the Divine standpoint; what God means by life. This was suspended pending the trial of man, and it introduces a further great factor of the Word of God—namely, the revelation of God. This represents the great governing question in history from Adam onward. The great governing question is this: In whom can that which is called eternal life dwell? We know that eternal life is not mere duration of being. It is a kind of life; it is God's life, Divine life, the life of the ages. In whom can that life dwell? That is the great governing question of history. The answer to the question is Christ: ". . . in *him* was life. . . ." He is the life. But then, we behold Him not only as personal, individual, separate, but corporate; the creation in Christ.

That concludes the first stage and begins the next. Up to that point everything, so far as this present time is concerned, is one great question. In this redemption period, brought in as a second line of Divine arrangement, the whole matter of our response to God's call, of our acceptance of Christ, and of union with Him is in the balance. One big question hangs over this dispensation: Who will respond? To many He has had to say, ". . . ye will not come unto me . . ." (John v. 40). The question is settled once the life is within; you have started at that point where Adam broke down, and have immediately been lifted out of the gap, out of the bend; you have been brought up there in Christ and have come right into the straight line of the eternal purpose which, in its realisation, will be a universe full of Christ: "Unto a dispensation of the fulness of the times, to sum up all things in Christ. . . ."

Are you asking what this is all about? If you are not yet clear it can be put into very few words. It is to bring the greatness of Christ into view, that is all. Now we need that there should happen to us, in the grace of God, what happened to this man who came into this ever growing, inexhaustible conception of Christ. We recall his own words: ". . . it was the good pleasure of God . . . to reveal his Son in me. . . ." You may have heard all this: it may have sounded more or less wonderful; you may know the truth, in an intellectual way; but there is all the difference between that and the way in which Paul knew it. Paul's way of knowing brings emancipation.

Have you ever seen a fly in a bottle? Round and round it goes, beating itself from side to side, rising, falling, until you really ache as you watch that fly. You saw it rise a little and your hopes rose with it, and then you saw it go down, trying to find a way out, beating itself to death. Then up, up, climbing and reaching the top, out and away! That is the difference.

You and I with all our head knowledge, our mental knowledge of a great spiritual realm, find it a hopeless thing if in reality we are living down in this creation. To-day it would be easy to despair, to drop down into things as they are. Look out into the world for prospects for the Church, prospects for the Gospel, prospects for the Lord. Look at the state of the Church itself. Bring the letter to the Ephesians down into this world! You will give it up and say: It is a wonderful conception, but impossible. Try to realise it down on this level and you beat yourself to despair. Note Paul as he looks out over the churches which he had seen brought into being and sees them breaking up, and the men for whom he had suffered turning against him. Paul would have despaired in his heart, had he been living down here. What were the prospects in such conditions? But he got up into the heavenlies in Christ Jesus and saw that this was a heavenly thing, an eternal thing. Read the Ephesian letter again and mark how it starts: "Blessed be the God and Father of our Lord Jesus Christ, who hath blessed us with every spiritual blessing in the heavenlies in Christ; even as he chose us in him before the foundation of the world, that we should be holy and without blemish before him in love: having foreordained us unto adoption as sons through Jesus Christ unto himself, according to the good pleasure of his will, to the praise of the glory of his grace, which he freely bestowed on us in the Beloved: in whom we have our redemption through his blood, the forgiveness of our trespasses, according to the riches of his grace . . ." (Eph. i. 3-7).

These are the words of a man with his life-work tumbling to pieces and all his old friends for whom he had sacrificed himself turning against him. What has he seen? The eternity, the universality of Christ, ALL THINGS IN CHRIST. Paul is not living in this world now, but living in Christ. It is the only way out. It is the way of life, the way of hope, the way of assurance in a day like this when things close down. Christ is the way out: ". . . in the heavenlies *in Christ* . . ."; ". . . chose us *in him* before the foundation of the world. . . ." Again we say: What a Christ!

Let us dwell much upon the Lord Jesus, for everything for us is in Him.

Chapter III

A Man After God's Heart

Reading: Ps. lxxxix. 19-20; Acts xiii. 22; Heb. i. 9; I Sam. xiii. 14.

The Bible abounds with men. It abounds with many other things, with doctrine, with principles; but more than anything else it abounds with men. That is God's method, His chosen method, His primary method of making Himself known. These men who were in relationship with God, with whom God was associated, bring distinctive features into view. Not in any one man is the whole man acceptable, every feature to be praised, but in every man there are one or more features that stand out and distinguish him from all others, and abide as the conspicuous features of that man's life. Those outstanding distinctive features represent God's thought, the features which God Himself has taken pains to develop, for which God laid His hand upon such men, that throughout history they should be the expression of certain particular traits.

Thus we speak of Abraham's faith, of Moses' meekness. Every man is representative of some feature wrought into him, developed in him, and when you think of the man the feature is always uppermost in your mind. Our attention is drawn, not to the man as a whole, but to that which marks him in particular. So by one apostle we are called to recollect the faith of Abraham, while another will bid us remember the patience of Job. These features are God's thoughts, and when all the features of all the men are gathered up and combined, they represent Christ. It is as though God had scattered one Man over the generations, and in a multitude of men under His hand had shown some aspect, some feature, some facet of that one Man, and that one Man is able to say, "Ye search the scriptures, because ye think that in them ye have eternal life; and these are they which bear witness of me . . ." (John v. 39). There is a Man spread over the

Bible, and all who have come under God's hand, have been apprehended for the purpose of showing something of His thought, which in its fulness is expressed in His Son, the Lord Jesus. Recognising that, we are better able to appreciate the words we have just read, which in the first instance related to David, but are clearly seen to reach beyond to a greater than David. Read again Ps. lxxxix and you cannot fail to see that two things merge into one another: "I have laid help upon one that is mighty; I have exalted one chosen out of the people." You have to look for a greater than David for the complete expression of that. In the words "I have laid help upon one that is mighty . . ." we have one of the great foundations of our redemption. A greater than David is here. David in those principal features of his life under God's hand was an expression of God's thought concerning Christ. You cannot say that of David's life as a whole. You cannot carry the statement, "I have found . . . a man after my heart . . ." through the whole of David's life, and say that when David was guilty of this and that particular thing which marred his life this was after God's heart. We have to see exactly what it was, in and about David, which made it possible for God to say that he was a man after His own heart. It was just that which indicated Christ, pointed to Christ. It is only that which is Christ which is after God's heart.

The Divine Purpose from Eternity

"The Lord hath sought him a man after his own heart . . ." (I Sam. xii. 14). Remembering our previous meditations, we shall find a large setting for a statement like that. It speaks of the creation of man, of the Lord seeking to have a man-race, a corporate man in whom His own thoughts and features are reproduced in a moral way. The Lord has ever sought Him that man. It was the seeking of such a man that led to the creation. It was the seeking of such a man that led to the Incarnation. It is that seeking of a man which has led to the Church, the "one new man." God is all the time in quest of a man to fill His universe; not one man as a unity, but a collective man gathered up into His Son. Paul speaks of this man as ". . . the church which is his body, the fulness of him. . . ." That is the fulness, the measure of the stature of a man in Christ. It is the Church which is there spoken of, not any one individual. God has ever been in quest of a man to fill His universe.

The Likeness Is Moral and Spiritual

God thinks thoughts, desires desires, and wills wills, and those thoughts, and desires, and wills are the very essence of His moral being, and when He has thus reproduced Himself in this sense, He has a being constituted according to His own moral nature; the man becomes an embodiment and personification of the very moral nature of God; not of the Deity of God, but the moral nature. You know what it is in life to say that anything or anyone is after your own heart. You mean they are just exactly what you think they are and what you want them to be for your own complete satisfaction. The man after God's heart is like that to Him.

Devoted to the Will of God

There is a third thing which defines that to some degree, which puts its finger upon the root of the matter. What is the man after God's heart? What is it that God has sought in man? The verse in Acts tells us: ". . . who shall do all my will" (Acts xiii. 22). If you look at the margin you will see that "will" is plural: ". . . all my wills"—everything that God desires, everything that God wills, the will of God in all its forms, in all its ways, in all its quests and objectives. The man who will do all His wills is the man after God's heart, whom God has sought. The words are spoken, in the first place, of David. There are several ways in which David as a man after God's heart is brought out into clear relief.

Firstly, David is set in striking contrast with Saul. When God had deposed and set aside Saul, He raised up David. Those two stand opposite to one another and can never occupy the throne together. If David is to come, then Saul must go. If Saul is there, David cannot come. That is seen very clearly in the history, but let us note that in this we are confronted with basic principles, not merely with what is historic and to do with persons of bygone days. Before God there are two moral states, two spiritual conditions, two hearts, and those two hearts can never be in the throne together, can never occupy the princely position at the same time. If one is to be prince, or in the place of ascendancy, of honour, of God's appointment, the other heart has to be completely put away. It is remarkable that even after David was anointed king there was a considerable lapse of time before he came to the throne, during which Saul continued to occupy that position. David had to keep back until that regime had run its course, until it was completely exhausted, finished, and then put aside.

It would be a long, though profitable study, to go over Saul's inner life as shown by his outward behaviour. Saul was governed by his own judgments in the things of God. That is one thing. When God commanded Saul to slay Amalek—man, woman, beast, and child; to destroy Amalek root and branch, it was a big test of Saul's faith in God's judgment, God's wisdom, God's knowing of what He was doing, God's honour. If God commands us to do something which on the face of it would seem to deny something in God's own nature of kindness, and goodness, and mercy, and we begin to allow our own judgment to take hold upon God's command and to give another complexion to the matter, to take obedience out of our hearts, we have set our judgment against God's command. In effect we have said: The Lord surely does not know what He is doing! Surely the Lord is not alive to the way His reputation will suffer if this is done, the way people will speak of His very morality! It is a dangerous thing to bring our own moral judgment to bear upon an implicit command of the Lord. Saul's responsibility was not to question why, but to obey. We recall Samuel's word to Saul: "Behold, to obey is better than sacrifice, and to hearken than the fat of rams" (I Sam. xv. 22). The man after God's heart does all His wills, and does not say: Lord, this will bring You into reproach! This will bring You into dishonour! This will raise serious difficulties for You! On the contrary, he replies at once: Lord, You have said this; I leave the responsibility for the consequences with You, and obey. The Lord Jesus always acted so. He was misunderstood for it, but He did it.

Saul was influenced in his conduct by his own feelings, his own likes and dislikes, and preferences. He blamed the people, it is true, but it was he himself who was at fault after all. It was his judgment working through his sentiments. In effect he said: It is a great pity to destroy that! Here is something that looks so good, that according to all standards of sound judgment is good, and the Lord says destroy! What a pity! Why not give it to God in sacrifice? Now we know that it is true of the natural man that there are these two aspects, a good side and a bad. Are we not, on our part, often found saying, in effect, Let us hand the good to God! We are quite prepared for the very sinful side to go, but let us give the good that is in us to the Lord. *All* our righteousnesses are in His sight as filthy rags. God's new creation is not a patchwork of the old; it is an entirely new thing, and the old has to go. Saul defaulted upon that very thing. He reasoned that the best should be given to God, when God had said, "Utterly destroy."

The man after God's own heart does not make blunders like that. His interrogation of himself is: What has the Lord said? No place is given to any other enquiry: What do I feel about it? How does it seem to me? He does not say: It is a great pity from my standpoint. No! The Lord has said it, and that is enough. God has sought Him a man who will do all His wills.

So we could pursue the contrast between Saul and David along many lines. We are led to one issue every time. It all points in one direction. Will this man surrender his own judgments, his own feelings, his own standards, his entire being to the will of God, or will he have reservations because of the way in which *he* views things and questions God?

An Utter Rejection of the Flesh

There is another way in which David stands out as the man after God's own heart, and it is this with which we are especially concerned, and with which we will conclude this meditation. It is that which is to be noted in the first public action of David in the valley of Elah. We refer, of course, to his contest with Goliath. This first public action of David was a representative and inclusive one, just as the conquest of Jericho was with Israel. Jericho, as we know, was representative and inclusive of the conquest of the whole land. There were seven nations to be deposed. They marched round Jericho seven times. Jericho, in spiritual and moral principle, was the embodiment of the whole land. God intended that what was true of Jericho should be true of every other conquest, that the basis should be one of sheer faith; victory through faith, possession through faith.

David's contest with Goliath was like that. It gathered up in a full way everything that David's life was to express. It was the comprehensive disclosure or unveiling of the heart of David. He was a man after God's own heart. God's ground of approval in His choice of men is shown to us in His words to Samuel with reference to another of Jesse's sons: "Look not on his countenance, or on the height of his stature . . . the Lord looketh on the heart" (I Sam. xvi. 7). In the case of David, the heart that God had seen is disclosed in the contest with Goliath, and it was that heart which made David the man after God's own heart all the rest of his life. What is Goliath? Who is he? He is a gigantic figure behind whom all the Philistines hide. He is a comprehensive one, an inclusive one; in effect, the whole Philistine force; for when they saw that their champion was dead they fled. The nation is bound up with, and represented by, the man. Typically what are the Philistines? They represent that which is very near to what is of God, always in close proximity, always seeking to impinge upon the things of God; to get a grip, to look into, to pry, to discover the secret things of God. You will recall their attitude toward the Ark when it came into their hands. They were ever seeking to pry into the secrets of God, but always in a natural way. They are called "uncircumcised." That is what David said about Goliath: "this uncircumcised Philistine." We know from Paul's interpretation that typically that means this uncrucified natural life, this natural life which is always seeking to get a grip on the things of God apart from the work of the Cross; which does not recognise the Cross; which sets the Cross aside, and thinks that it can proceed without the Cross into the things of God; which ignores the fact that there is no way into the things of the Spirit of God except through the Cross as an experienced thing, as a power breaking down the natural life and opening a way for the Spirit. There is no possibility whatever of our knowing the secrets of God except by the Holy Spirit, and the Holy Spirit "was not" (we use the word in the particular meaning of John vii. 39) until Calvary was accomplished. That must be personal in application, not merely historic. The uncircumcised Philistines simply speak of a natural life which comes alongside the things of God, and is always interfering with them, touching them, looking into them, wanting to get hold of them; a menace to that which is spiritual. Goliath embodies all that. All the Philistines are gathered up into him. David meets him, and the issue, in spiritual interpretation, is this, that David's heart is going to have nothing of that. He sets himself that all things shall be of God, and nothing of man. There shall be no place for nature here in the things of God, but this natural strength must be destroyed. The Philistines become David's lifelong enemies, and he theirs.

Do you see the man after God's heart? Who is he? What is he? He is a man who, though the odds against him be tremendous, sets himself with all his being against that which interferes with the things of God in an "uncircumcised" way. That which contradicts the Cross of the Lord Jesus, that which seeks to force its way into the realm of God other than by the gate-way of the Cross is represented by the Philistine. Who is this uncircumcised Philistine? David's heart was roused with a mighty indignation against all that was represented by this man.

That constitutes a very big issue indeed. It has not merely to do with a sinful world. There is that in the world which is opposed to God, positively set against God, a sinful state that is recognised and acknowledged by most people. That is all against God, but that is not what we have here. This is something else that is to be found even amongst the Lord's people, and which regards nothing as too sacred to be exploited. It will get into an assembly of saints in Corinth and call for a tremendous letter of the Apostle about natural wisdom, the wisdom of this world expressing itself as the mentality even of believers, and thus making the Gospel of none effect. This spirit that is not subject to the Cross creeps in and associates itself with the things of God, and takes a purchase upon them. It is not so much that which is blatantly, obviously, and conspicuously sinful, as the natural life which is accounted so fine according to human standards. The Lord's people have always had to meet that in one form or another. Ezra had to meet it. Men came and proffered their help to build the House of God: and how the Church has succumbed to that sort of thing! If anybody offers their help for the work of the Lord, the attitude at once taken is: Oh, well, it is help, which is what we want; let us have all the help we can get! There is no discrimination. Nehemiah had to meet it. There is some help that we are better without. The Church is far better without Philistine association. That is the sort of thing that has assailed the Church all the way through. John, the last surviving Apostle, in his old age writes: ". . . but Diotrephes, who loveth to have the pre-eminence . . . receiveth us not . . ." (3 John 9). You see the significance of that. John was the man of the testimony of Jesus: "I John, . . . was in the Isle that is called Patmos, for the Word of God and the testimony of Jesus." The great word of John's writings is "life": "In him is life . . ." (John i. 4); ". . . this life is in his Son" (I John v. 11). Diotrephes could not bear with that. If Christ is coming in, Diotrephes, who loveth to have the pre-eminence, must go out; if he that loveth to have the pre-eminence is coming in, then Christ is kept out.

The man after God's own heart is the man who will have no compromise with the natural mind; not only with what is called sin in its more positive forms, but all that natural life which tries to get hold of the work of God and the interests of God, to handle and to govern them. This has been the thing that has crippled and paralysed the Church through the centuries; men insinuating themselves into the place of God in His Church.

You see what David stands for. He will take the head off that giant. There has to be no compromise with this thing; it must go down in the name of the Lord.

The Price of Loyalty

Now notice this, that for his devotion David had to suffer. This man, who alone saw the significance of that with which he had to do, this man who alone had the thoughts of God in his heart, the conceptions of God, the feelings of God, the insight of God; this man who alone amongst all the people of Israel in that dark day of spiritual weakness and declension was on the side of God, seeing things in a true way, has to suffer for it. As he came upon the scene, and, with his perception and insight into what was at stake

—38—

betraying itself in his indignation, his wrath, his zeal for the Lord, began to challenge this thing, his own brethren turned upon him. How? In the cruellest way for any such man, the way most calculated to take the heart out of any true servant of God. They imputed wrong motives. They said in effect: You are trying to make a way for yourself; trying to get recognition for yourself; trying to be conspicuous! You are prompted only by personal interests, personal ambitions! That is a cruel blow. Every man who has come out against that which has usurped God's place in any way, and stood alone for God against the forces that prevail, has come under that lash. To Nehemiah it was said: You are trying to make a name for yourself, to get prophets to set you on high and proclaim through the country that there is a great man called Nehemiah in Jerusalem! Similar things were said to Paul. Misrepresentation is a part of the price. David's heart was as free from any such thing as any heart could be. He was set upon the Lord, the Lord's glory, the Lord's satisfaction, but even so, men will say: It is all for himself, his own name, his own reputation, his own position. That is more calculated to take the heart out of man than a good deal of open opposition. If only they would come out and fight fairly and squarely in the open! But David did not succumb; the giant did! May the Lord give us a heart like David's, for that is a heart like His own.

We see in David a reflection of the Lord Jesus, who was eaten up by zeal for the Lord's House, who paid the price for His zeal, and who was, in a sense above all others, the Man after God's own heart.

CHAPTER IV

Putting on the New Man

READING: Rom. v. 12, 15-19; Eph. iv. 13, 20-24; Col. iii. 9-11.

Here the Word says we have put off the old man, or more literally, that we have laid down or laid aside the old man. The same word is found in Heb. xii. 1—"therefore . . . lay aside every weight, and the sin which doth so easily beset us. . . ." We have laid down, or put off, the old man. So often those words are used by us in a merely personal connection. We speak of "our old man"; by which we mean this sinful nature of ours which rises up under provocation. That aspect, of course, is included in the initial act of faith's repudiation, but that is not all that is meant by the statements before us. It is included; but what we have here is something very much more.

The Significance of the Term "Old Man"

Rom. v. explains what is meant. The old man is a racial order, represented by its racial head, Adam. It is an order. That corporate, collective Adam, as apart from God, having departed from God, is a kind of order which can no longer be accepted by God, which has passed out of God's thought and God's acceptance, and stands contrary to His mind. That is the order into which we are born, and to which all that we are by nature belongs, and it is spoken of as a corporate, collective entity. It is important to remember that, not only is the Body of Christ one, but the Body of Adam is one; that is, that all in Adam are also a corporate being. It is a man, a kind of man, a type of man expressed world-wide; and we are said to have put off that man, the old man; we have laid him aside, laid him down. We have laid him in the grave in the same way that we lay a corpse there. The body of one who has departed this life is laid aside. It is no longer the place in which he dwells. He has laid aside that body, and we follow up and likewise lay it aside. Now as believers we have put off, have laid aside the Adam type, the Adam order, the Adam system, this one great collective man of a certain kind, of a certain order.

The New Man

Then it is further said that in Christ we have put on the new man. That also is often thought to be a merely personal affair, an individual matter. That is to say, the new man in our conception is a kind of new personal life and nature. That is true, but it is far more than that. In the letter to the Ephesians, the Apostle is speaking of the new man which is the Church, "the Christ" as it is literally expressed in I Cor. xii. 12. Christ is one with all His members, as the Head joined to the body, all the members making one body, one new man. It is a collective, corporate man, a man of a new order which is not Adam, but Christ: "where . . . Christ is all, and in all" (Col. iii. 11). Before it was Adam who was all, and in all, but now in this new creation it is Christ who is seen to be all, and in all. The Apostle well expresses what is meant when he writes: "But ye did not so learn Christ; if so be that ye heard him, and were taught in him, *even as truth is in Jesus*" (Eph. iv. 20, 21). It is a great embodiment of Divine truth in a Person, and we are represented as having divested ourselves of the one body, of old Adam, and as having invested ourselves with this body of Christ, with the new man.

(a) The Primary Feature

That includes a good many things. If you look at the context of this passage you will observe some of them. It includes the nature of Christ. That is why, after mention has been made of putting on the new man, the Apostle proceeds almost immediately with words like these, "Be ye therefore imitators of God, as beloved children; and walk in love, even as Christ . . ." (Eph. v. 1, 2). The new corporate man is the embodiment of the love of Christ. That is the first thing. This love must have an individual expression, for what is said to be true of the whole body is only so in the degree in which it is found to be true of the individual member. Let us recognise that, when we speak of the Church, or the Body of Christ, or make use of this alternative title, the "new man," we are speaking of that which is the embodiment of Christ's love; and when we say we are putting on, or have put on, the new man, we mean that we have put on the love of Christ.

To walk in love, then, is one thing that is involved. The Body is built up in love; the Body is constituted by love; the Body is the means of expression of Christ's love. If you take the figure and follow it, you will see how impossible it is to escape the fact. Were you to find a body without a head, it might be said that you had found a body; but it would be a very mutilated body! It really could not in the full sense be called a body. The Lord Jesus has not such a Body. For a full expression of the meaning of "body" must have head and members all together, properly adjusted and related. Now Christ cannot be said to be love as the Head, and His members be viewed apart from Him. The Body is one; Christ in expression is inclusive of His members, and that involves a nature. That nature is love: therefore ". . . as beloved children . . . walk in love, even as Christ also loved you. . . ."

Love is not the only feature in this new nature. We use it simply by way of indicating that this nature does imply a new Body-disposition. You and I need to be more before the Lord for a Body-disposition. The disposition of this new man is the disposition of love. Let us ask the Lord for the increase of this disposition in the Body of Christ. All that is other than that is still the old man, and he has to be put off. When anything that is not of the love of Christ springs up amongst us as the Lord's people, in any form whatever—and there are many forms of thoughts, and feelings, and words; words of criticism, words of judgment—love has to put it off. If you and I are found with such a thing as a spirit of criticism one toward another, that is of the old man, the old Adam, and he has to be put away. We have to recognise that the Lord has put old Adam in the grave. Then we have to follow up and say: To the grave you go; you belong there! The new man, then, speaks of a new nature, and of a new disposition. We all need more of this "new man" disposition, that we may walk in love.

(b) A Corporate Consciousness

Then this new man, being corporate and collective, being related and inter-related in this way, represents a life of fellowship. It demands a corporate consciousness which is one of the most important things. In the Lord's purpose everything depends upon this corporate life. The Lord Himself can never reach His end by individuals, and you and I can never reach that ultimate end as individuals. While it is true that Adam, the old man, is a corporate unity, the consciousness of the old man is not a corporate consciousness; it is an independent consciousness, a divisive consciousness. We must have a corporate consciousness in order to reach God's end. There are quite a number of the Lord's own dear children who remain far too long in a state of spiritual immaturity. They never grow much beyond childhood spiritually. You may know such for years, and find them to be just the same simple children to-day as when you first knew them. Now, it will be said: It is very right and proper to be a simple child of the Lord! Well, let us always have a childlike spirit, let us always seek to be of a pure, simple spirit before the Lord, but let us remember that there is a difference between childlikeness and childhood. There is all the difference between keeping that simplicity, purity, openness, teachableness of the child, and a delayed understanding, an overdue ability to grasp spiritual things and to assimilate food for those more advanced in years. The trouble with so many people, or the cause of their own delayed maturity, is that they are merely going their own sweet way; that is, they are butterflies, simply flitting from one thing to another with no corporate life, no related life. A butterfly is quite a pretty thing as it flits about, but there is all the difference between a butterfly and a bee. A bee too may go from one thing to another, but it does so to very good purpose. The bee's life is a corporate life, the butterfly's is not a corporate life; it is an individual life.

Delayed maturity, stunted spiritual growth, is very often due to this lack of a corporate sense of life which is bound up with the life of the Lord's people in a definite and positive way. That is the way of enlargement. That is the law of the new man. We arrest our spiritual growth when we set aside the necessity for a life that is linked with the people of God in quite a definite way. That is a background in Ephesians. The whole of the fourth chapter is devoted to this vital matter. The new man is there set forth as the church, the Body of Christ, and this new man is to grow unto the measure of the stature of the fulness of Christ. It is the corporate man that grows to that stature; individuals cannot do so. Only in relatedness do we move into the fulnesses of Christ.

Beware, then, of missing that very important law of spiritual enlargement. This is what is meant by putting on the new man. We are right, then, in asking the question, Have we really put on the new man? Have we really put on a Body-consciousness, a related-consciousness, a fellowship-consciousness that belongs to the new man? It may not always be possible for us to enjoy the immediate, local, geographical fellowship of a large company of the Lord's people, but that is not the point; we are talking about a consciousness.

(c) A Disposition

Again, it is a disposition. It is the setting aside of everything individual, personal, separate, as such, and putting on that consciousness of relationship in which everything is for the Body, and in the Body, and by the Body. It is by this fellowship of spirit that the Lord gains His end and we come to the Lord's end.

It is very sad to see the results of failure to recognise that. There are some, of whose devotion to the Lord we have no question, but the thing that pains us is that they have not grown one fraction of an inch since we first knew them years ago. At least, there is no sign of larger capacity. They are just exactly the same as they were. Such as these are never to be found making a supreme effort for a relatedness of a definite kind with the Lord's people. They flit about from one thing to another, and they say: I am not going to settle down in any one particular fellowship of the Lord's people! I am going to keep free! I am going to move about and keep in touch with everything that there is! That may be very good from one point of view; and you must not misunderstand and suppose it to be said that we are not to be in sympathetic touch with all that is of the Lord. But there is something else which is necessary to building up, and that is a concrete relationship with the people of God. It is necessary to the Lord for fuller revelation. What do we not owe in the matter of revelation to this very thing! For revelation the Lord must have the Body spiritually expressed. It is tremendously important to know that. It is there that the Lord's ministry functions. Eph. iv is a great ministry chapter. You lose all isolation and departmentalism in ministry when you have the Body in realised expression, when everyone is found occupying some place of spiritual value in the work of the Lord; not according to the technical terms that man is wont to use with reference to such work, but where everyone represents something of spiritual value, where everyone is a minister before the Lord in some way. Whether you recognise it or not, it is a fact, and unfortunately a great deal of loss is suffered because it is not realised how greatly obedience on the part of every one of us affects the issue.

I will tell you how to test it. Is there going to be something personal for the Lord by a corporate means, say a conference? I venture to say that there are not many people who are spiritually associated with that who do not know some aspect of the Devil's rage and pressure in connection with it. You do not have to provoke the Devil in any way. It is one conflict and not only are the more evidently responsible individuals in ministry affected, but the conflict reaches to those whom we do not connect with ministry in that specific sense. In our thought we so often limit the ministry to this one expression of it. Those who have ordinary home and domestic duties may haply think of them as something quite other, and not as part of the ministry, but the conflict finds its way in there. It gets into your personal consciousness, into your business, apart from your being in any more immediate way involved in what is going on. It is because you are spiritually related to a testimony, because you have come in a spiritual way into the Body of Christ, recognising what the Body of Christ is. Whether you have understood the truth or not in any large measure, you have put on the new man and you are suffering as a part of one man.

Now that is not only a fact which perhaps we recognise in a painful way, but it is a privilege. Paul said, "I . . . fill up on my part that which is lacking of the afflictions of Christ in my flesh for his body's sake, which is the church" (Col. i. 24). There in your homes, in your business, in what you would call the back places, you meet with the conflict. It is for the Body's sake. Out there, far away from others, you are meeting the impact. That is the proof that every part of this Body is a partaker in this ministry. The whole is being served by every part in a spiritual way putting on the new man.

While it involves us in the cost, in the suffering, it equally means that we come into the good and the value; for no few members can come into blessing without all who are in spiritual relationship receiving benefit. If one member suffers, all the members suffer; if one member rejoices, all the members in some way rejoice, in some way come into the good of it.

God's Quest Is a Man

You will see that this is very closely related to what the Lord is seeking to bring to us in these days. We are still speaking of it in very general terms, but the presentation of the Lord's mind ought to be very clear to us. It is a man that God is after. That man is represented by His Son, and the Church is His expression as His Body. This new man is the universal manifestation of what Christ is—one Lord, one Life, one Love. It is important, lest you should make a mistake in interpretation, to recognise that there is a difference between the word used in Ephesians and that in Colossians. In Ephesians we read of putting on the new man, in Colossians we read of having put on the new man. In Ephesians the word *kainos* means something that never was before, something altogether new. This Church never was before; this corporate man according to Christ never existed before, it is something new. In Colossians another word is used which simply means "fresh," not necessarily altogether new. You will see the significance of the different word if you look at the context. There is a freshness of mind, a freshness of spirit that is to be a mark of those who are in Christ. But our word at this time has to do with the former word, which is *kainos*, the new man, the man that never was before. There is an old man who was before, and he has to go. Here is another man that never was before, and he has to be put on.

This new man is after God. That takes us back to our previous meditation, God thinking His thoughts, desiring His desires, and willing His wills, all of which express His own nature, and all of which are focused upon a created being called "man": ". . . which after God hath been created . . ." (Eph. iv. 24). That is a marvellous expression. You know how we speak of certain works of men, and use that word. We say, After Landseer! We mean that it is a reproduction of Landseer. Now here is a new man which after God is created in righteousness. The Lord teach us the meaning more clearly of so learning Christ.

CHAPTER V

His Excellent Greatness

READING: I Kings iv. 1, 7, 20-34, x. 1-9; Matt. xii. 42.

Some of the passages which have provided the background for our meditations have referred very definitely and precisely to the excellence and exceeding greatness of the Lord Jesus. One basic passage of tremendous implication is that which came from His own lips: ". . . no one knoweth the Son, save the Father. . . ." That is a declaration, in other words, that only the Father knows the Son, knows who the Son is and what the Son is; only the Father knows all that the Son means. Along with that we have the profound statement of the Apostle Paul: ". . . it was the good pleasure of God . . . to reveal his Son in me. . . ." That relates to the beginning of his life in Christ Jesus, and it was a revelation which was destined to become so full that after all his years of learning, after all his discovery of Christ, at the end he is still to be found crying from his heart, ". . . I count all things to be loss for the excellency of the knowledge of Christ Jesus my Lord: for whom I suffered the loss of all things, and do count them but refuse, that I may gain Christ . . ." (Phil. iii. 8). It indicates clearly that even at the end the Apostle recognised that there was a knowledge of Christ still available to him which was beyond anything that had yet come to him, and such knowledge was more precious and more important than all other things. We often sing in one of our hymns, "Tell of His excellent greatness"—"Behold, a greater than Solomon is here."

Our difficulty always will be to comprehend, to grasp, to bring that excellent greatness, that transcendent fulness within the compass of practical everyday life and experience. Yet it is necessary that this should be, and our approach to that fulness must be of such a kind as to render it of immediate value to us; for all that vast range of power and fulness, although so far beyond our comprehension, is yet for our present good and advantage. There are some features in this account of Solomon's greatness which foreshadow this greatness of the Lord Jesus, a greatness which, as we have said, is for our present benefit.

(1) Supreme Dominion

We mark that it is said of Solomon that he was king over all Israel and that he had dominion over all the region beyond the river; and a greater than Solomon is here. The first feature, then, is this of his supreme dominion, his excelling lordship, kingship, sovereignty. That is of tremendous practical value. It operated, as we see, in two realms; he was king over all Israel, and he had dominion over all the region *beyond* the river.

Those statements suggest that the Lord Jesus is not only King within the compass of those who acknowledge Him as Lord, His own saved ones, but that, in spite of what may seem, He is King in a far wider sense. We are moving much in the realm of Ephesians in our consideration, and in Ephesians it is the universal sovereignty of the Lord Jesus that is brought before us, not only His relation to the Church. He is Head over the Church which is His Body, He is Lord there, but He is, in addition, far above all rule and authority, principality and power. He is *now* universal Lord. It does not appear like it; everything would seem to contradict the fact; but we need to be given sight to see that the kingship, the lordship, the universal dominion of the Lord Jesus at this present time does not necessarily mean that all are enjoying that lordship, nor that for all within the universe is it a beneficent reign. But even if that be the case, it does not alter the fact. There are other things which also point to the fact in a very positive way.

Of course, our trouble is that we take such short views. We are children of a span of time, and that span of time is of such great importance with us that our view of things is so narrow. If we could but take the long view, and see things from God's standpoint, how different would be the result in our own hearts. In saying that, we have in mind the widespread denial of the kingship, the lordship, the sovereignty of the Lord Jesus Christ. This period of the world's history is called the day of His rejection and there is a verse of a hymn that commences thus:

Our Lord is now rejected,
And by the world disowned.

But it is not so easy a matter to put the Lord Jesus aside.
Men may reject, nations may reject, may seek to put Him
out, deny Him a place, repudiate His rights, refuse to
acknowledge His claims and His lordship, but that does not
get rid of Him. God has set His king upon His throne. Of
the Son He has said, "Thy throne, O God, is for ever and
ever . . ." (Heb. i. 8). Nothing can upset that. The attitude
of men, the attitude of the world, cannot interfere with that,
cannot depose the Lord Jesus. It may be said: That is a statement, but how will you prove it? Well, there are evidences.
We have evidence that He is Lord, that He is holding things
in His own sovereign hand, that *nothing can take His place.*

The Witness of History

Look at history and see what has tried to take the place
of the Lord Jesus in sovereignty; tried to do what only the
Lord Jesus could do; tried to bring about a state of things,
to accomplish which is put into the power of the Son alone,
and see how far those efforts have succeeded. Anything
which seeks to bring about a state of things which the Lord
Jesus alone can establish is doomed. You can see it repeated
through history again and again. World dominion has been
sought by one and another. Things which were ideals, magnificent conceptions for the world, have been attempted, and
they have all failed, all broken down. Kingdoms and empires,
despots, dictators, monarchs, have risen to a tremendous
height, some of them having great sway, but the empire has
broken and passed, the reign has broken down. So you have
these things coming and going all the way through history;
and, mark you, the whole matter is related to the Lord Jesus.

Read the Book of Daniel again, and you will perceive the
realm in which we are moving. There you have the prophetic
unveiling of world empires; Babylonia, the empire of the
Medes and Persians, then that of the Greeks, and on to the
great Roman Empire; they all pass in review, and pass away.
The lesson of the Book of Daniel is this, that there is but *One*
whom God has appointed to be universal Lord, and that no
one else can hold that place. Others may go a long way, but

they can never gain that place, and so they must pass. We may yet see great powers coming into being, vast ranges of territory under one sway, but all this will pass. The matter is held in the hands of the Lord Jesus. All this endeavour is doomed from its birth to go so far, and then pass out. The Lord Jesus alone can have world dominion. He alone can bring universal peace. He alone can bring prosperity to all nations. That is held in reserve for Him and His reign. Till then there will be fluctuations and variations in world fortunes, but it will all pass.

This passing, this breakdown, this confusion, this deadlock is all because the course of things is in His hands, and He is holding it all unto Himself. He is King! He is Lord! It is a tremendous thing to recognise that the very course of the nations, the very history of this world, is held in the hands of the Lord Jesus unto His own destined end. God has for ever set His Son as the only one to be full, complete, and final Lord of His universe, King of kings and Lord of lords, with a beneficent sway and reign over all the earth. Peace and prosperity is locked up with the Lord Jesus, and He holds the destiny of nations unto that. Men may attempt it of themselves, and they may go a long way to usurp His place, but the end is foreseen, foreshown. He must come whose right it is, and *of His kingdom there shall be no end.* It has commenced in heaven; it is already vested in Him and held in His hands. That is how we must read history. That is how we must read our daily papers. That is how we shall be saved from the evil depression and despair that would creep into our hearts as we mark the state of things in this world. All is being held by Him to a certain end. The meaning is that *nothing* can take the place of the Lord Jesus.

You can apply that in various ways, and in different directions. It explains the history of the so-called church, the history of Christendom. Why is it that what professes to be of Christ, but in reality is not, breaks down, continually breaks down all the way through history? Simply because it is something assuming the place of Christ, which is not of Christ. Failure is written upon it from the beginning. Everything that is not of Christ is going to break down; and it does break down. Though a thing may begin with Christ and evidence a measure of Christ, immediately it moves beyond the range of Christ and becomes of man, its end is in view.

That is the explanation of things which God has raised up in relation to His Son, things which were pure and true, but of which, because of the blessing resting upon them, men have taken hold. Whenever this has been done the end of these things has come into view, that is, as a spiritual force. Why is this? It has gone beyond Christ, it has gone outside of Christ, and nothing can take the place of Christ. Oh, how necessary it is to abide wholly in Christ, to be wholly of Christ, according to Christ, governed by the Holy Spirit. He operates His sovereignty against the success, the prosperity, the final triumph of anything and everything that is not of Himself, and if we want the sovereignty of the Lord Jesus on our side, then we have to be utterly on the side of the Lord Jesus; otherwise that sovereignty works against us. The world confusion, and the world trouble, and the world despair, is all a mighty evidence that Jesus is Lord, because it is a world that is trying to get on without Him, but cannot do so. No! He says it cannot be done. He says: I am essential! I am indispensable! If you would have it otherwise, then you must learn that without Me it cannot be done.

We could spend all our time considering Solomon's dominion and kingship. He was king over Israel, and had dominion over all the land beyond the river. But we must pass on to consider another feature in which Solomon foreshadows the excellency of the Lord Jesus.

(2) The Bounty of Solomon's Table

"And Solomon's provision for one day was thirty measures of fine flour, and three score measures of meal; ten fat oxen, and twenty oxen out of the pastures, and an hundred sheep, beside harts, and gazelles, and roebucks, and fatted fowl." That is a great day's feast for Solomon! What does this speak of, if not of the bountifulness of Solomon. This is no mean fare, no starvation diet! "A greater than Solomon is here."

When by the Holy Spirit we really come into the knowledge of the Lord Jesus, there is no need to starve spiritually. Oh, the tragedy of starving believers, with such a King! The tragedy, the unspeakable grief of children of the Lord spiritually starving! The fact is there is a fulness for His people which far excels that of Solomon.

Read the Gospel by John again with this one thought in mind, and you will see how the truth receives confirmation from the earthly life of the Lord Jesus. Take Chapter VI, with its great incident of the feeding of the multitude, all leading up to the spiritual interpretation: "I am the bread. . . ." His disciples broke down in faith at one point, and He was amazed: "Do ye not yet perceive, neither remember the five loaves of the five thousand, and how many baskets ye took up? Neither the seven loaves of the four thousand, and how many baskets ye took up?" (Matt. xvi. 9-10). He was amazed at their failure to understand that in Him was not only enough, but abundance. There is something wrong with us if we have not discovered it to be so. The fulness of Christ is for our spiritual satisfaction. There is abundance of food.

Again, consider not only the pathetic tragedy, but the wicked tragedy of starvation. What is it that is keeping the Lord's people out of fulness? Very largely it is prejudice, the Devil's trick of putting up the barrier of prejudice between the need and the supply. Oh, the wickedness of the Devil in coming in by these works of blinding to starve the Lord's people. There is bread in Christ. He is an inexhaustible fulness for the spiritual life. We know that we shall come to the same position as Paul, when he cried, ". . . that I may know him. . . ."—that is, to a consciousness of there being a knowledge beyond anything that we have yet attained unto, and where everything is counted as nothing compared with that. This is not mere words, it is true. There is bread in the Lord Jesus; there is bread in His house. This is where He is superior to Solomon. There is bread for a mighty host, a company capable of doing greater justice to His fare than ever Solomon's household could do. If they had sat down to his bounty, they could have gone so far and no farther, but our appetite will go on. We have a spiritual capacity which is growing, and growing all the time, unto the fulness of Christ. Solomon's bounty, then, is another feature by which He foreshadows the excellent greatness of the Lord Jesus. We touch but briefly on a third.

(3) The Glory of Solomon

The glory of Solomon is proverbial. Even the Lord Jesus spoke of it as being so: "Consider the lilies of the field, how they grow; they toil not, neither do they spin: yet I say unto you, that even Solomon in all his glory (and they knew what his glory was) was not arrayed like one of these" (Matt. vi. 28, 29). But what was Solomon in his glory compared with the Lord Jesus? What is the glory of the Lord Jesus? Inclusively it is the revelation of the fulness of God, the glory of God in the face of Jesus Christ.

That may not sound very practical, but let us mark that this glory of Solomon was closely associated with his wisdom; his wisdom indicated the nature of his glory. There was something beyond the glory. This glory was not mere tinsel, or mere show, but was the fruit of a great wisdom that God had given him. It was the wisdom of Solomon that issued in his glory and his fame. What may be said of his wisdom? He spoke three thousand proverbs, he wrote many songs; he spoke of trees, and of beasts, and of birds, of creeping things, and of fishes. They are all very practical things. How did he speak of them? He invested everything in the creation with a meaning. If he speaks of trees, he will give you a secret, give a meaning to the trees, from the cedar in Lebanon (trees in the Word of God all have a significance) to the hyssop that springeth out of the wall. We know of what hyssop speaks as we first meet with it away back in Exodus and Leviticus. We know what the cedars of Lebanon stand for, and all the trees in between the two equally bear a meaning. Solomon gave the secret significance, the Divine meaning. Then he spoke of beasts, and we know that the Bible speaks of many beasts, and they all have a significance. He spoke of fowls also, and of creeping things, and of fishes. He unfolded the secrets of the creation, and invested everything in the creation with a deeper meaning. To be able to do that is proof of no mean wisdom.

Wherein is the Lord Jesus superior? Well, after all, Solomon's was only poetic wisdom in those realms. The Lord Jesus has practical wisdom; in this sense, that everything is laid hold of by Him in relation to His purpose, and made to serve that purpose. Oh that we could see and believe that at all times in our experience! So many things come into our lives. What a diversity! What a range! How mysterious some things seem to be! How strange it is that the Lord's own people have so many more experiences, both in number and variety, than anyone else. It seems that almost anything that can happen to a person, happens to a believer. You wonder sometimes, if anything else is possible. Have we not exhausted the whole store of possible experiences? That is how we question. There is not one thing in the life of a child of God but what is controlled and governed by a deeper meaning in relation to His purpose. We recall Paul's statement: "And we know that to them that love God all things work together for good, even to them that are called according to his purpose" (Rom. viii. 28). The more accurate translation is, God worketh in all things good. God invests everything with a meaning, for those who love Him, and are the called according to His purpose. The wisdom of God lays hold of everything and gives to it a value. It may be that only eternity will reveal to us the value of some things, but we must believe that, inasmuch as our lives are wholly under His government, there is nothing without a meaning, nothing without a value. His wisdom is governing everything.

It is when we come to realise that, to accept and believe it, that we find rest in our hearts, and find ourselves on the way to gain rather than loss. When we revolt against these things, then we are in the way to rob ourselves of something. But when we come into line with the Lord in these things we find, firstly, rest in our hearts, and then the discipline produces something of value. It is gain, not loss; it is good, not evil. This is wisdom. That is better than having so many poems; it is practical. A greater than Solomon is here! That is the glory of the Lord Jesus. How does His wisdom work out to His glory? You and I go through a painful experience, a mysterious experience; we can see no good in it; we can only see harm in it. We are led to look to the Lord, to believe that although we cannot see, cannot understand, He knows; and we trust Him. We come through the trial, and our eyes are enlightened about the purpose of it, and we worship. Oh, we never saw that such a thing as that could produce this! We never, never imagined that this value could result from it. The thing which seemed to be for our undoing is the thing that has brought us into a greater fulness of the Lord. That is His glory.

Remember that His wisdom is governed by His love. That is a great point with Solomon. It was the heart of Solomon which was behind his wisdom. It was a wise and understanding heart (not brain). Now look at Solomon. Two women bring a babe to him. Solomon is watching. For what is he watching? For something that he knows out of his own experience. Read the story of Solomon's birth. Read that little clause about his mother's special love for him. Solomon was the darling of his mother's heart, and Solomon knew what mother love was. He knew what the love of a mother for her babe was, and he watches those two women. He has the keen eye of a mother or her child upon those two women, and he says to one at his side: Take this sword and divide the child in two. That does not sound very much like a mother heart; but he is watching. Then he sees the mother heart leap, and hears her cry: No! I had rather that the other woman had the child than that you should hurt it! And Solomon knew who was the mother of that child. That is the wisdom of Solomon which is actuated by his love.

Supremely does this characterise the Lord Jesus. Oh, it seems at times that the way He goes to work is hard, but it is actuated by His love. It may be strange and mysterious, but love is in it; there is a great heart behind it all.

When at the direction of Solomon the Ark was brought into the sanctuary, and set there in its appointed place, speaking of the Lord coming into His rest and satisfaction, we are told that this symbolic realisation of the Lord's end in rest was attested from heaven, and that Solomon turned his face to the people and blessed them. God has come into His rest in His Son, into full satisfaction, and then the Son, in whose face is the glory of God, turns to us in blessing: ". . . the glory of God in the face of Jesus Christ" (2 Cor. iv. 6). A greater than Solomon is here.

The Lord give us a new apprehension of His Son.

CHAPTER VI

The Heavenly Man—The Inclusiveness and Exclusiveness of Jesus Christ

We have under consideration a phrase from the letter to the Ephesians, "ALL THINGS IN CHRIST": ". . . unto a dispensation of the fulness of the times, to sum up all things in Christ . . ." (Eph. i. 10). That is the great general vision that is occupying us, and we will now begin to break it up into its parts.

To begin with, it is supremely important that we should recognise that there is one basic and all-governing factor with God, which is a supreme matter for our knowledge, and that is the inclusiveness and exclusiveness of His Son, Jesus Christ.

Everything intended and required for the realisation of Divine purpose and intention is in, and with, Christ, not only as a deposit, but all *is* Christ. That is the inclusiveness of Christ.

Then, on the other hand, nothing but what is of Christ is accepted or permitted by God in the final issue. That is the exclusiveness of Christ. However God may seem in His patience and long-suffering, in His race and mercy, to be bearing with much, even in us His people, which is not of Christ; however, much He seems for the time being to allow, it is of supreme importance that we settle it once for all that God is not really allowing it. He may extend to us His forbearance, His long-suffering, but He is not in any way accepting what is not of Christ. He has initially said that it is dead to Him, and He is progressively working death in that realm. So that in the final issue, not one fragment anywhere that is not of Christ will be allowed. Christ excludes everything that is not of Himself. That is God's ruling of the matter.

The Church to be what Christ Was and Is as the Heavenly Man

In view of what we have just said, it is of the utmost importance for real effectiveness that we should realise that the Church is intended to be what Christ was, and is, as the Heavenly Man. Only that which is of Christ, the Heavenly Man, is eternally effective. Therefore, the more there is of Christ, the more effectiveness there is from God's standpoint. That means that what was, and what is, true of Him as the Heavenly Man, as to His being, as to the laws of His life, as to His ministry and His mission, is to be true of the Church. (When we speak of the Church, of course, we speak of all the members as forming the Church.)

Do you notice that we are speaking of Christ as the Heavenly Man, and not of His co-equality with the Father in Deity? We are not saying that the Church is to be, in the same sense as Christ, God incarnate, occupying the place of Deity; we are speaking of the Heavenly Man. Christ was, and is, a *Heavenly* Man. The Church in Him is also a heavenly man, one "new man." It is not to be thought of as Jew and Greek, circumcision and uncircumcision, bond and free, a combination of earthly elements, of various aspects of human life as here on this earth. These and all other earthly distinctions are lost sight of and set aside, and one "new man" is brought in, where "Christ is all, and in all" (Col. iii. 11).

Christ has never been, in His essential nature, of the earth. He had a relationship to Israel, a relationship to man here; He has a judicial relationship to this earth, but in His essential nature He never has been earthly. He is the Lord from heaven. He takes pains to stress the fact, and to keep it clearly in view: ". . . I am from above . . ." (John viii. 23).

Now as Christ in His essential nature never was of the earth, neither is the Church. The Church has never been an earthly thing in God's thought. That is where the gap is bridged. Paul takes you right back, and shows you that the Church is in the heavenlies before ever the fall took place. In Christ we are made to bridge the gap created by the fallen ages. Before the world was, Christ existed with the Father, literally and personally. The Church existed in the fore-knowledge of God before the world was, though not literally in the same way that Christ did; that is, this is not a rein-carnation, but, in the foreknowledge of God, the Church was as actual before time as it is now, or ever will be. Whenever Paul speaks of the Church, he always speaks of it as though it were complete. He never speaks of a completing of it. Much has to be done to add the members, to bring it to its numerical completeness, and its spiritual and moral completeness and perfection, but while Paul has much to say about spiritual growth and increase, he yet speaks of the Church as though it were already completed. He is viewing it from the heavenly, eternal, Divine standpoint, from the standpoint of the foreknowledge of God. There in that foreknowledge of God, and that foreordaining according to foreknowledge, the Church existed as a complete whole with the Father and the Son before times eternal. Then came the break, the gap, the dip down; but in Christ it is bridged, and the Church is seen as a continuous thing in the heavenlies, above it all.

The Church is seen as being literally formed in this dispensation, but it is as immediately translated to heaven. Immediately we come into Christ, we are seated in the heavenlies in Christ: "God . . . when we were dead through our trespasses, quickened us together with Christ . . . and raised us up with him, and made us to sit with him in the heavenlies . . ." (Eph. ii. 6). It does not say that we are to be placed there at some future date. Before ever we believed, we became a heavenly people from God's standpoint. We were cut clear of this world, translated out of this kingdom of darkness into the kingdom of the Son of His love, and ceased to be earthly, immediately we came into Christ. We are lifted right back on to the level of the original purpose, and linked up with the first thought of God in Christ. We become the corporate heavenly man, even as He is the Heavenly Man in person.

We are called upon to recognise our link with the eternal and the heavenly, and to take things up from there. There would not be that terribly anomaly of "worldly Christians," if only this were apprehended. Look at all that has to be dealt with because of failure to keep the testimony pure for the Lord's people. Worldly Christians! What a contradiction to the Divine thought! How impossible it is to accept anything like that! Let us repeat, we are called upon to recognise our link with the eternal and heavenly, and to take things up from there. It is not the case that we are struggling, working, striving to be a heavenly people; now aiming at such a state, and hoping that at some time it will be realised, but we are a heavenly people, and we must take things up from that standpoint.

The convert, the young child of God, must remember that by his union with Christ he becomes entirely a heavenly part of Christ from the first, linked with everything heavenly and eternal. Everything here is to be as out from another realm. That should be kept in view. We should have a very different kind of believer if that were always kept to the fore. That is God's standpoint, God's mind.

This, then, brings us to the point at which that eternal and heavenly relationship is resumed. It is not the commencement but the resumption in Christ of something that was broken off, interrupted, and which ought never to have suffered such an interruption.

Nothing But What Is of Christ Allowed by God in the Ultimate Issue

Before we deal with the point of resumption, we will spend a few moments in looking yet further at the implication of what has been emphasised already. Nothing but what is of Christ is allowed by God in the ultimate issue. Now, because that is true, all the activities of God in discipline are introduced and pursued. All the discipline which comes by failure, for example, is followed out. Failure is in the way of God's thought now, a necessity as it were. Lives reach a point, and then are unable to get beyond that point; there is a going on so far in a measure of blessing, and then the state of things changes, the kind of blessing that has been is withheld, and a state of things ensues which has but one issue, that of an absolute necessity for a new position in the Lord. It is not that the Lord blesses what is not of Christ in such a period, but in His grace and mercy He blesses us, in order to lead us on in Christ: then, when we have come to a place where we have a certain knowledge of the Lord, the Lord suspends that outward blessing, and we pass into a time of trial, of conscious failure, defeat, arrest, helplessness, and we are found before long in that realm saying: My need is of a new place with the Lord, a new experience of the Lord, a new knowledge of the Lord. All that has been, has been very wonderful, but it is as nothing now, and the need now is of a new place with the Lord.

That will go on to the end. The experience is not relative to the early stages alone, but continues throughout the course. How many of us have cried, Lord, we need a new position! What is this? It is the outworking of this law, that with God nothing but what is of Christ is allowed. Only that which is of Christ can be effective, and our experience means that more of the mixture has to go, and Christ has to take its place. Failure leads to that.

The same thing applies with regard to work, to great movements. The history of a movement is like that of the individual. Even that which has been blessed of God comes to the place where, as a movement, as a collective instrumentality, it knows that the old days have passed, and for that which now obtains, and that which is before, a new position is necessary. Unfortunately so many try to live upon the past, try to go on upon a reputation, a history, and will not confess to the fact that things have changed and that God requires something more. If only they would face up to that, how much more glorious in its effectiveness would be the future, than ever the past has been. But there you have the interpretation of the experience. However it is apprehended by those concerned, the fact remains that God applies this law, that in the end, when everything has been said and done, and when all these present ages have run their course, in God's ages of the ages there will be nothing but what is of Christ. He is seeking to bring the Church to that goal, to be the fulness of Him that filleth all in all. It cannot be the fulness of Christ while anything else is there.

How manifold is the application of this truth! How many a detail it touches, and how ashamed it should make us! If we really do see it, if it really strikes our hearts, we shall be greatly humbled. Inwardly we shall feel thoroughly disgusted with ourselves as in the light of this we think of *our* assertiveness, of *our* strength, of *our* activity in the things of God, of all that has been of ourselves in this realm. The putting forth of strength is only effective in the proportion in which it represents a measure of Christ. We puny folk on this earth stand up and think we are of some account! What insignificant people we are if viewed from the heavenlies! The Lord looks down upon us and sees us trying to make names for ourselves in His things; dominating other lives; manipulating, putting our hands upon them. It is all pride, all conceit, all self in some form. The aspects of it are countless.

The Lord looks at it and says, No, it is not of Christ; therefore, in the final issue it has to go! That is why He breaks us, and empties us, and brings us down to the place where we cry from a deep, heart-broken consciousness: Lord, unless Thou doest it, it is impossible! Unless Thou dost speak the word, my words are useless! That is why He works in that way. The Lord in His sovereignty sees to it that we meet with plenty of things to keep us humble.

The Lord keeps us humble through the difficult people He sets around us, and whom He does not take away however much we cry to Him to do so, even though in themselves they are all wrong and an apparent menace to the Lord's interests. They serve to keep us humble and dependent. The Lord does that sort of thing, all in keeping with this law, that everything in us must be of Christ. Christ fills the universe for God. If He sees anything but what is of Christ, it cannot have a place. Only His Son can fill all things, excluding everything else. Oh, how humbly we need to seek of the Lord that there shall be nothing about us that, as of ourselves, presses itself upon others—our manner, our mannerisms, our presence, our conduct, our spirit, even our voice. The Spirit would oft-times check us and cause us to walk softly. None of us has attained to very high levels in this matter, and we are all having to acknowledge failure. The Spirit is dealing with us in that way. If even in our dress, or in any other thing, *we* come into view as the Lord's children, the Holy Spirit would seek to bring us to a place of sensitiveness, where He can say: That is bringing yourself into view! That is out from you! Now, get covered, get hidden! That thing excludes Christ!

God has determined from all eternity that this universe shall be filled with Christ, the Heavenly Man, through that corporate heavenly man joined to Him as its Head. He is getting rid of the Jew in us, of the Greek in us, and constituting us according to Christ, conforming us to the image of His Son. Blessed be God! the moment we come to the place where the last remnants and relics of what is not of Christ fall from us, then He will be displayed in us; He shall come to be glorified in the saints. It is Christ who is to be glorified, not ourselves; yet so close is the relationship that He is to be glorified in us. The Lord hasten the day!

CHAPTER VII

The Heavenly Man as the Instrument of the General Purpose

The Heavenly Man personally is presented to us by the Apostle John in a fuller way than by any other of the New Testament writers. Paul advances to the corporate Heavenly Man. That does not mean that Paul does not present the personal Heavenly Man, for he undoubtedly does, particularly in his letter to the Colossians; but he advances from the personal Heavenly Man to the corporate Heavenly Man, which is the Church, His Body.

May we repeat one thing. Christ, actually and literally, was with the Father before times eternal, and the Church, not actually and literally, but in foreknowledge and fore-ordination, was also with the Father and the Son before times eternal. The fullest unveiling of the Church, which comes to us through the Apostle Paul, reveals it as already complete, but we know it to be a fact that it was in no sense completed when Paul wrote. It was not finished numerically and it was anything but finished spiritually and morally, yet he speaks of it as though it were the most complete, the most perfect thing in the universe. He is standing, as it were, at God's side, and God views the Church from the eternal standpoint, that is, as outside of time.

The Restoration of Heavenly Relationship

Recognising, then, that Christ and the Church are revealed as being with the Father from all eternity, we next see that by reason of that which has taken place in the fall, and which was anticipated in the redemptive line of purpose, Christ comes into time, and is born in time in relation to redemption, and that redemption is said to be from "this present evil age." The Authorised Version renders it "world," but the change is important. It is not from a place that we are redeemed, but from an age, and it is perfectly clear what that age is. It embraces all the intermediary sections or dispensations. The present evil age runs from Adam to the new heavens and the new earth. There is a coming glorious age. To be redeemed out of this present evil age, means that the Church, which belongs to eternity and not to this age, is to be redeemed out of it. It shows how Christ, by redemption, brings back into the straight line of what is eternal and outside of time, into the eternal counsels and purposes of God concerning His Son. By the redemption that is in Christ Jesus, which is a redemption from this evil age, the Church is redeemed unto that other age, that eternal age. So the birth of Christ is related to the redemption of the purchased possession, the redemption of the Church.

Coming to John, firstly with regard to Christ's entry into time, we find that John has three things to say about Christ.

(i) John sets Christ in eternity.

"In the beginning was the Word, and the Word was with God, and the Word was God" (John i. 1). That is Christ outside of time.

(ii) He shows Christ's coming into time.

"And the Word became flesh and tabernacled among us . . ." (John i. 14).

(iii) Christ is revealed as being also in heaven while here.

This third thing which is stated in John's Gospel is declared by the Lord Himself, and combines both of the other two things. The Son, who is here in the flesh, is at the same time in heaven. There is the uniting of the two spheres. While He is here, He is still in heaven; while He is in time, He is still in eternity. "No man hath ascended into heaven, but he that descended out of heaven, even the Son of man, which is in heaven" (John iii. 13). That is the Heavenly Man as presented to us by John; Christ on earth, and at the same time still in heaven.

Now, in Christ, that becomes true of the Church, and is true of every member of the Church. In Christ we are here, and at the same time in heaven. We are in time, but we are also in eternity. The question arises, how can this be? It is a statement which needs explaining.

This brings us to the point where eternal and heavenly relationship is resumed. That relationship was broken off, interrupted. In Christ, as representative Man, it is resumed, taken up again. With Him it has never been interrupted. The interruption had to do with man, but through union with Christ that relationship—howbeit in a fuller way—is resumed, or restored to man. What is the point at which this resumption takes place? It is what is known amongst us as being born anew, or from above. Its law and its main spring is eternal life.

Israel and the Promises

Two things were evidently related in the Jewish mind. These were (i) The kingdom of heaven, and (ii) Eternal life. Nicodemus asked what he must do to enter the kingdom of heaven. Another ruler, probably of the same school as Nicodemus, and perhaps of the same rank, asked this question: "Master, what shall I do to inherit eternal life?" (Luke x. 25). These things were evidently accepted by the Jews as a promise. The Lord Jesus recognised and referred to that expectation when He said, "Ye search the scriptures, because ye think that in them ye have eternal life . . ." (John v. 39). There was a quest for eternal life, an expectation, a hope of eternal life, a persuasion that eternal life was a promise to be realised. These two things were linked together in their mind. Christ associates this hope with Himself and says concerning the testimony of the Scriptures, ". . . these are they which bear witness of *me*." To such as can receive it, He indicates that He Himself is the way or ladder into heaven, the necessary means of getting there. We are, of course, referring to John i. 51. Now read verse 47:

> "Jesus saw Nathanael coming to him, and saith of him, Behold, an Israelite indeed, in whom is no guile!"

Here is a pure Israelite. What can you say to a pure Israelite who is looking for the kingdom of heaven and eternal life, a man who is true, a man who is honest? The Lord has seen him under the fig tree, really pouring himself out in quest of the kingdom of heaven and eternal life, if what the Lord Jesus said to him is a clue to what was going on in his heart. He was of those who looked for the blessings of Israel.

Let us pause for a moment, and insert Ps. cxxxiii here in brackets. "Behold, how good and how pleasant it is for

—64—

brethren to dwell together in unity! . . . for there the Lord commanded the blessing, even life for evermore." How does the blessing come? Whence is this hope, this expectation of the blessing? Our question takes us back to the promise made to Abraham: ". . . in thee shall all the families of the earth be blessed" (Gen. xii. 3). These Israelites were looking for the blessing of Abraham. But note what is further said: ". . . in Isaac shall thy seed be called" (Gen. xxi. 12). What does Isaac represent? Life from the dead, Divine life. The blessing of Abraham is life. Now note the words of the psalm: ". . . for there the Lord commanded the blessing, even life for evermore." So you see that what they were in quest of was the blessing which had these two aspects, the kingdom of heaven, and eternal life.

In Nathanael we see an Israelite indeed in whom there is no guile, a pure man in a right quest. The Lord says to a man like that, "Ye shall see the heaven opened, and the angels of God ascending and descending upon the Son of man." Are you in quest of the kingdom of heaven? "Ye shall see the heaven opened. . . ." Are you wanting to get through? You will need a ladder, a way, a means, a vehicle: "Ye shall see . . . the angels of God ascending and descending upon the Son of man."

Nathanael knew exactly to what the Lord was referring. An Israelite indeed, in whom there was no guile, was Nathanael! Let us recall the incident to which the Lord referred. "And Jacob . . . lighted upon a certain place . . . and he took one of the stones of the place, and put it under his head, and lay down in that place to sleep. And he dreamed, and behold, a ladder set up on the earth, and the top of it reached to heaven; and behold the angels of God ascending and descending on it. And, behold, the Lord stood above it, and said . . . I am with thee, and will keep thee whithersoever thou goest. . . . And Jacob awaked out of his sleep, and he said . . . How dreadful is this place! this is none other but the house of God, and this is the gate of heaven" (Gen. xxviii. 10-17)—Bethel, the House of God: the House of God, the gate of heaven. The Lord Jesus appropriates that and says, in effect: "I am the House of God, I am the gate of heaven. Thou shalt see heaven open through Me.' Do you want to know how to reach heaven? Two things have to be considered; one is the fact of union with Christ, the other is that which is bound up with union with Christ—namely, eternal life.

Man by Nature an Outlaw

Let us stay with that for a moment. "Ye shall see the heaven opened. . . ." Such a statement implies that the heavens have been closed. That, again, carries with it the fact that for man eternal life has also been put behind a closed heaven. Even for Nathanael, even for Nicodemus, even for a pure-hearted Israelite that is true by nature. Their longing is for an opened heaven. They are stretched out for the kingdom of heaven, but it is closed.

We know quite well that to everyone by nature, heaven is a closed realm. But a closed heaven is not God's thought for us. We belong to heaven. Christ belongs to heaven. The Church belongs to heaven. Yet the very place to which we belong is closed to us. The place with which we are related in the eternal counsels and purpose of God is closed to us by nature. That has its most terrible manifestation in those moments of the Cross, when the Lord Jesus, standing in the place of man in his sinful state, cried, "My God, my God, why hast thou forsaken me?" Heaven is closed to Me; the place to which I belong, My heaven, My home, is closed to Me! I am an outcast from heaven!

Such is the state of man by nature, shut out from heaven, the place for which he was made, the place which belongs to him in the purpose of God. The Lord says to Nathanael, "Ye shall see the heaven opened." There is far more meaning in the phrase we so often use, "an open heaven," than we have recognised. What is it to enjoy an open heaven? It is to be at home in fellowship with the Lord; it is to have a heavenly life; it is to have all the heavenly resources at our disposal; all that heaven means is open to us, and we have come into that for which God brought us into being, which he intended to be ours from all eternity; that is an opened heaven. "Ye shall see the heaven opened. . . ." Then the quest of the heart is satisfied, the promise realised. The principle of the opened heaven, or of the heavenly life, is what is called eternal life in Christ. Christ is the Heavenly Man, coming into time.

Christ and the Church

We have said once or twice that the Church is to be what the Heavenly Man was, and is, as to His being, as to the laws of His life, as to His ministry. Everything that is true about Him as the Heavenly Man has to become true of the Church. Thus, seen as the Lord Jesus, as the Heavenly Man, was born here in time, so also is the Church, the corporate Heavenly Man, to have a birth here in time, and on the same principle as Christ was born.

How was Christ born? You will realise that we are leaving the question of Deity on one side. We are not touching that side at all. In the sense in which Christ was God incarnate, Immanuel, God with us, God manifest in the flesh, that is not true of us as members of the Church. That is understood. We are talking about the Heavenly Man, not of the Divine Son, not of Godhead. So that what is true of Him as the Heavenly Man as to His birth, has to be true of the whole Church in every part. Let us look at the birth of the Lord Jesus and mark how it is characterised by three things.

(i) The Word Presented

We go back to Luke, for Luke enlarges upon what John says. John compasses it all in one statement: "And the Word became flesh, and tabernacled among us. . . ." It is Luke who gives us the fullest description of the Word being made flesh, the birth of Christ. We will not read the whole story, but we mark first of all how that the angel went to Mary, and began to present Mary with a statement. He made his statement to her, and then waited. In her perplexity she asked a question. He answered her question, and again waited. Then came the response: "Behold, the handmaid of the Lord; be it unto me according to thy word" (Luke i. 38). First of all the word offered: that is the first step in His birth, the word presented, the statement made. Then the angel waited. What are you going to do with it? How are you going to react to it? The word presents a challenge, always a costly challenge. That word is going to lead outside of the world, and is to bring the liberty of the world. Mary weighs the cost while the angel waits. The battle is fought, the storm for a moment rages, and then it is over, and in calm deliberateness, she responds, ". . . be it unto me according to *thy word.*"

Do you see what it means to be begotten of the word of God? The first step in this new birth, the first step into this heavenly life, is our attitude toward the presented word of God, and that will be found to govern every step in the heavenly life. Such is the nature of the first step, and it is equally that of every subsequent step. All the way through the Lord will be presenting us with His word, and with it a challenge, a cost, a price to be paid, and there will be conflict over it: Are we prepared to go that way? Are we prepared to accept that word? Are we prepared for what that word means, for what it involves? On the response to what is presented depends our knowledge of the heavenly life. From beginning to end it is like that.

That is why the Lord never first explains everything to unsaved people. Doctrine followed for believers but was never given for unbelievers. Clear, concise statements were made to unbelievers. To them there was a presenting of facts, boldly and deliberately. "This is God's will. This is God's word. This you must do. Explanation will come later. Now, heaven is going to remain closed, or is going to be opened; the question of your entry into a heavenly life hangs in the balance as you decide what is to be your response to God's word. You will be born of that word, if you respond to it, begotten by the word of truth." So the first thing is the word offered, and then, after some difficulty and conflict, accepted, received, surrendered to: ". . . be it unto me according to thy word."

(ii) The Word Germinating

What is the next step? The Spirit makes the word to germinate within. The Spirit generates within by means of the word. That is the second thing to be noted in the case of Mary, the Spirit generating, or implanting. Not until the word has found a response can that word become a living thing within. That is why an unsaved person can never know the meaning of the Word of God. The meaning of any word of God demands the inward work of the Holy Spirit to make it live, to make it germinate, and response to it opens the way for the Spirit.

(iii) The Word (Christ) Formed Within Initially and Progressively

That is the third step. It is very simple when presented like that, but this is the way into heaven, into eternal life. Mark you, this is something other than of Mary, her race, and her nature. By the Holy Spirit there was a complete coming in between all that Mary was by nature and that Holy Thing. It is a very important matter, moreover, for us to recognise that in exactly the same way are we born anew. When Christ was born of Mary, or when Christ was (may we use the word?) generated in Mary, there took place in Mary something that was altogether above nature. Mary had a long natural lineage, and in that lineage there were all sorts of people, including several harlots. But when the Holy Spirit came in and formed Christ in her, He set all that aside and cut it off. That blood did not come into Christ. Remember that! He did not inherit aught of that, whatever it was, whether high or low, good or bad. The Holy Spirit cut it off, and Christ was something other than that, distinct: ". . . that holy thing. . . ." You can never say that of anything that is inherited of the blood of Rahab, or of Ruth the Moabitess. It is something other.

Christ in us is something other than ourselves. That is what makes us heavenly. Flesh and blood cannot inherit the kingdom of heaven. That is our natural stream, our natural history, the whole course of our Adamic relationship, which cannot inherit the kingdom of heaven. It is only what is of Christ that will inherit the kingdom of heaven. It is Christ in us who is to us the hope of glory, and the only hope of glory. This is something other than of Mary, and her race and nature, something other than of ourselves. This which is begotten of God is of the Holy Ghost. You and I ever need to discriminate between what is of Christ in us and what is of ourselves, and not to get these things mixed. Nothing that is not of Christ is going to find acceptance. Everything has to measure up to Christ, to pass through the sieve of Christ, and the sieve is a very fine one; for everything has to go through the test of death, and death is a tremendous test. Is there anything that death can lay hold of? If there is, it will lay hold of it. All that is subject to death will succumb to death, and this old creation is nothing else but that. Christ is not subject to death; He cannot be holden of it, for there is nothing in Him upon which death can fasten. That is our hope of glory, Christ in us. This Holy Ghost dividing between Mary and Christ, between ourselves and Christ, this fundamental division made by the Holy Ghost, must be kept constantly in mind, for only as we do that can God reach His end. Mark you, God can reach His end far more rapidly where that discrimination is maintained, than He can where it is overlooked. That is the importance of believers being instructed of the Lord concerning that which is essential unto His purpose.

Christ was other than the rest of men in that respect. Even from childhood He had another consciousness, as we have occasion to note when He is at the age of twelve. Not finding Him in their company, His earthly parents sought Him, and found Him in the temple, and claimed Him as son: "Son, why hast thou thus dealt with us? behold, thy father and I sought thee sorrowing." To this He replied, ". . . wist ye not that I must be in my Father's house?" (Luke ii. 48-9). It is a reproof, but at the same time a disclosure of another consciousness. "Thy father and I . . ."—". . . my Father's house. . . ." That is not Joseph's house. Here is the setting of one Father over against the other, and of the one above the other. It is a heavenly consciousness, an eternal consciousness, a mark that He is "other," as begotten of the Holy Ghost.

When, begotten of the Holy Ghost, we come at once back into our eternal relationship with God in the Son, a new consciousness springs up within us, a consciousness that was not there before. This "new man" which has been put on, has a new consciousness as to heavenly relationships.

All that is embraced in the words "eternal life." We know that eternal life does not merely imply the fact of duration; it means a kind of life. That eternal life, that life from above, that Divine life in Christ, carries with it all that relates to the Heavenly Man.

Consider the Heavenly Man personally again. "In him was life . . ."; "For as the Father hath life in himself, even so gave he to the Son also to have life in himself . . ." (John v. 26). In the Gospel of John, the Lord Jesus says much about Himself as the Heavenly Man, possessing heavenly life, and that heavenly life was the seat of the heavenly nature and the heavenly consciousness; it was through that heavenly life that He conducted Himself as He did. He was alive unto God by that life which He possessed, and this is seen in His being able to know God, to know the movements of God, the directions of God, the gestures of God, the restraints of God. It was all gathered up in that life. That is the principle of His life as of His birth. It is the principle of our birth, and alike the principle of our life as the corporate Heavenly Man.

The Gift of the Holy Spirit

That life is by the Holy Spirit. It is always related to a Person; it is not an abstract, a mere element. It is inseparable from the Person, which Person is the Holy Spirit; and the Holy Spirit is the Spirit of Jesus. When you come to the book of the Acts, you have a great deal disclosed about the gift of the Holy Spirit. If you look at it closely you will see that the coming of the Holy Spirit was invariably related to spiritual union with Christ. Pentecost marked the end of a physical relationship with the Lord Jesus as in the flesh, the end of that extraordinary period of His post-resurrection appearances. It is the beginning of an inward, spiritual relationship with Christ. We may mark the same feature at Caesarea; they believed, and the Holy Spirit was given. At Samaria, again, hands were laid upon those who had believed, and the Holy Spirit was given. And one of the most interesting things in the book of the Acts is that incident at Ephesus. When Paul came to Ephesus, he found certain disciples, and discerned something unusual in their condition, or was it something lacking? To them he says, "Did ye receive the Holy Ghost when ye believed?" (Acts xix. 2, R.V.). That is the correct translation, not "since ye believed" as in the Authorised Version. That in itself assumes that believing implies the receiving of the Spirit. The two things go together. Paul could not quite understand this situation. It was something abnormal. Here were those who professed to believe in Christ, and who in a way had believed in Christ, but that which should go alongside of true faith was not there. Paul found himself confronted by a condition he had never met with before, and on his putting them to the question, "Did ye receive the Holy Ghost when ye believed?" they made answer, "Nay, we did not so much as hear whether the Holy Ghost was. . . ." So Paul further enquires, "Into what then were ye baptised?" to which they replied, "Into John's baptism." Ah! now we have the clue. "John baptised with the baptism of repentance, saying unto the people, that they should believe on him which should come after him, that is, on Jesus." So they had been baptised into John's baptism, unto an objective, future Christ; not baptised into Christ, but baptised toward Christ. Those are two different baptisms altogether. Paul commanded them to be baptised into the Name of the Lord Jesus, laid his hands upon them, and the Holy Ghost was given. Those two things go together. Union with Christ is shown to involve the receiving of the Spirit. That is not intended by the Lord to be something later on in the spiritual life; it should mark the commencement.

If in the book of the Acts there are particular elements which throw up the whole matter into such clear relief, such as accompanying signs, those signs were only the Lord's way of emphasising for all the dispensation what it means, that union with Christ involves the receiving of the Holy Spirit. How do you know? Well, He has shown it to this dispensation by bringing it out into clear relief in that way. He has laid it down so that no one can fail to see it. If you become occupied with the signs (tongues, etc.), but miss their signification, you will fail to see that those outward marks, those demonstrations, were only allowed as accompaniments, in order to emphasise the basic truth, namely, that union with Christ was now established. The gift of the Holy Spirit was the seal and proof of this. On what ground? By believing in Christ, by being baptised into Christ, eternal life is received in the Holy Spirit. And that life has heavenly capacities, within it are the powers of the age to come; and when in the ages to come its powers are fully released, we shall be endued with powers which far transcend our present powers. The age to come has been foreshadowed in tokens at the beginning. It may be that from time to time those powers are made manifest in the healing of the sick even now, but let us not fasten upon those tokens and make a doctrine of tokens and signs, begin to gather them up and systematise them, and make them the object of our quest. Let us remember that they are the tokens of something else, and you can have the "something else" apart from the tokens. When in truth you are baptised into Christ, you receive the Spirit of life in Christ, and in that life you are at once brought back into your heavenly relationship with the Heavenly Man; you become part of the corporate Heavenly Man.

It is what Christ is in us by His Spirit that determines everything. It determines all the values, settles for ever the question of effectiveness, answers all the questions and problems. I wish we had had this understanding, this knowledge sooner. If only we could have this as the foundation of our life from the beginning, what a lot we should be saved from.

Ministry is the expression of life, and not the taking on of a uniform and a title. Once I thought that to be in the ministry was to go into a certain kind of work, to come out of business, and, well, be a minister! So one got into the thing. Many, many are labouring and toiling in it, breaking their hearts, afraid to leave that order of things, lest they should be violating what they conceived to be a Divine call. Many others cannot get out of it because it is a means of livelihood, and they too are breaking their hearts. It is all false. Ministry is not a system like that. Ministry is the expression of life, and that is but saying in other words that it is the outworking of the indwelling of Christ. Disaster lies before the man or woman who ministers on any other ground than that. When the Lord gets a chance in us, and we really will trust Him on that ground, take our position there, He will show us that there is ministry enough for us; we shall not have to go round looking for it. The real labour so often is to get us down to that ground, the delivering of us from this present evil age even in its conception of the ministry, unto the heavenly ministry.

The Lord Jesus is our pattern. You see the spontaneous ministry, the restful ministry of that Heavenly Man. I covet that! It does not mean that we shall become careless, but it does deliver us from so much unnecessary strain. That is how it should be. May the Lord bring us to it; the Heavenly Man with the heavenly life as the full heavenly resource.

CHAPTER VIII

The Heavenly Man as the Source and Sphere of Corporate Unity

READING: Eph. iv. 1-16, 30-32; Ps. cxxxiii.

Here we have a Psalm which, on the one hand, presents an imperfect or partial entering into the spirit of the blessing of which it speaks, and, on the other hand, a prophecy; a type and prophecy of the full blessing to come, and a present but imperfect enjoyment of the meaning of the blessing. As a type and prophecy of the full blessing to come, it indicates the basis of the blessing, and the wonderful beneficent elements of the blessing. Read the Psalm backward and you will at once see what the basis is: "... there the Lord commanded the blessing, even life for evermore." Where was the blessing given? "Behold, how good and how pleasant it is for brethren to dwell together in unity!"—"... there the Lord commanded the blessing, even life for evermore." Between the first and the last verses the beneficent influence and effect of the blessing is seen, which blessing is based upon two things. One of these is brought to our notice in the preceding Psalm. You will recognise that these are "Psalms of Ascents." That, again, speaks of the partial enjoyment of the meaning of the blessing. The people are going up to Zion; they are in caravan, in procession, coming up from the distant parts with their eyes and their hearts all toward Zion in expectation, in hope; Zion the city of their solemnities; Zion the joy of all the earth; Zion the unifying centre of all their life; Zion in the ways of which they were but which was also in their hearts as a way—"... in whose heart are the high ways to Zion" (Ps. lxxxiv. 5).

The Unifying Centre

Now you see Zion is there as a great unifying factor. People from all directions are coming in procession. Some have joined the caravan at various places as it has moved on from

—74—

its most distant point, and they find that although they may never have met before on earth; although they may only just have come into touch with one another for the first time in their lives; although their paths may lie far apart in ordinary life, their sphere of life and service be divided and separate, Zion makes them a unity. Immediately the thoughts of Zion are in their hearts, immediately they think of Zion and move toward Zion, all scatteredness, separateness, divisiveness passes out, and they are as one man. Zion has unified them.

Now let us mark what is brought before us in Ps. cxxxii:

> "Surely I will not come into the tabernacle of *my* house, nor go up into *my* bed; I will not give sleep to *mine* eyes, or slumber to *mine* eyelids; until I find out a place for the Lord, a tabernacle for the Mighty One of Jacob. . . . Arise, O Lord, into thy resting place; thou, and the ark of thy strength. . . . This is my resting place for ever: here will I dwell; for I have desired it. I will abundantly bless her provision: I will satisfy her poor with bread" (Ps. cxxxii. 3-8, 14-15).

The first factor in the basis of the blessing is God's satisfaction, God finding His satisfaction: "Arise, O Lord, into thy resting place. . . ." Here we have the Lord coming to rest in His House. This is not to be interpreted mentally in a literal way. It is a case of the Lord having a ground of perfect satisfaction, the Lord having things according to His own mind, His own heart, the Lord just finding what He has been seeking all the time: "This is my resting place for ever. . . ." The Lord has been provided with that which answers to His own heart's desire, and it is therefore possible to say to Him, "Arise, O Lord, into thy resting place. . . ."

David's concern was that the Lord should be satisfied first of all. You will notice from the passage we have quoted that he sets aside all that is his own. With David, the Lord takes first place.

Christ—God's All and Ours

Let us carry that over to the New Testament for interpretation, for it is there that we shall find the spiritual meaning. We are meditating upon "ALL THINGS IN CHRIST," and

—75—

amongst these things, and by no means least, is God's satisfaction, God's coming to rest in His Tabernacle. That is what was in point when the Spirit, descending in the form of a dove, lighted upon the Lord Jesus. The dove returning to her rest in the Ark typified the Spirit coming to rest in Christ, the satisfaction of God: "This is my beloved Son in whom I am well pleased" (Matt. iii. 17). I find My rest, I am perfectly satisfied, here I have all My desire. So the Spirit as a dove, the symbol of peace and rest, lighted upon Him. The Lord Jesus answers to all the desire of God's heart, and in Him God enters into His rest.

When you and I set aside all our interests, and focus and concentrate all our concern upon the Lord Jesus, so that He has first place, has all, we have provided God with His rest in our lives, thus paving the way for the blessing. "There the Lord commanded the blessing. . . ." Where? Firstly, where He found His rest, His satisfaction, His joy. The Lord does not bless you and me as our natural selves. The Lord will not bless my flesh, nor your flesh. The blessing of the Lord comes to rest upon His Son as within us: ". . . the anointing which ye received of him abideth in you . . ." (I John ii. 27). Remember that the blessing of the Lord, the anointing, the precious ointment, is upon the Head. It comes down to us only as from the Head, by way of the Head, and it is when Christ by His Spirit has come to rest in us that the blessing rests there. The blessing rests upon Him in us, and that is why it abides. Thank God, it abides. This, if we do but recognise it, is one of the chief blessings of our life in union with the Lord. We in ourselves do not abide for five minutes! We can be as changeable as the weather. In the morning we may be one man, and in the afternoon another, and in the evening quite another. We may be as many different people in the course of the week as there are days. At one time we feel splendid spiritually and think we shall never, never be down again, but it is not long before we are right down. We vary like that; we become familiar with every movement that this human life is capable of knowing. If we live in that soul-life of constantly changing moods, oh, what a distressing life it is. But the anointing which you have received abideth. Why is this? Because it abides upon Him, not upon us, and He is "the same, yesterday, and to-day, and for ever." There is no changing on the part of the Lord Jesus in us. With Him, there is no variableness, neither shadow cast by turning. Oh, the changes that sweep over our lives because of the change-ableness of this human life; but there He is in us ever the same. We may have a thousand moods in as many hours, but He never changes, He is always the same. The anointing abides upon Him in us. Oh, that we should live in Christ, live in the anointing, live in that unvarying fact of God in Christ, unchangeable. He does not love us in the morning and turn against us in the afternoon. However we may feel it to be so, such is not the case. "I have loved thee with an everlasting love." Our moods would lead us to conclude that to-day the Lord loves us, and to-morrow that He is against us; to-day that the Lord is with us, to-morrow that He has departed from us. That is our infirmity. That is of ourselves and not of the Lord. The Lord is not us, in that way. The Lord is not our moods, our feelings, our sensations, or our lack of sensations. The Lord is the same always, the same faithful, unchangeable God, and the anointing abideth. It does not come and go. It does not rise and fall. It is not in and out, up and down, one day this and the next day that; it abides.

The enjoyment of that is only possible when Christ is the focal point of our lives. God comes to rest in His Son, and finds His satisfaction there. You must come there in order to find God's rest, and then the blessing is there. The Lord commands the blessing in the place where He has His rest, that is, in the Lord Jesus. But then Christ is in you: ". . . thou, and the ark of thy strength." That is Christ in you, the hope of glory.

Christ as God's Rest in the Heart

So then, the first aspect of the basis of the blessing is that of our knowing God's rest in His Son, Jesus Christ, in our own lives. He Himself put it in language which had to be more or less symbolic, or parabolic. "Take my yoke upon you, and learn of me; for I am meek and lowly in heart; and ye shall find rest unto your souls" (Matt. xi. 29). "Come unto me, all ye that labour and are heavy laden, and I will give you rest" (verse 28). We know what that means in the spirit. When we were children we may have thought it to be a word for labouring men in life's labours and toil, but we have come to know that this labouring and being heavy laden has mainly to do with these changeable moods of ours. We are labouring against the current, the tide, the stress of our own instability, our own uncertainty, our own oft-doubting and questioning, our feelings: and it is a labour when you live in that realm! The Lord Jesus says, ". . . I will give you rest." How will He do this? Well, He will come into you, take up His abode in you as the seat and centre of the deepest satisfaction, and you need have no more question. Are you straining and struggling over the question of whether the Lord is satisfied with you? You had better cease from it, because He never will be. If you are looking and longing for that day when the Lord is going to be perfectly satisfied with you, you are looking for a very distant day. If you are hoping that some day the Lord will be very pleased with you, and then you will be very happy, that day is not coming this side of glory. What we have to realise—and it is a truth so often repeated, and yet not grasped enough by our hearts—is that the Lord is never going to be satisfied with us as in ourselves, but He is already perfectly satisfied with His Son whom He has given to dwell in our hearts as the seat of His satisfaction, and we are accepted in the Beloved. Then the blessing comes. We see how the blessing works out.

Dwelling Together in Unity

Now we come to the second aspect of the basis of the blessing.

"Behold how good and how pleasant it is for brethren to dwell together in unity!" (Ps. cxxxiii. 1).

We have seen it in the illustration, the foreshadowing, namely, of Zion uniting all hearts, making all one, drawing away from everything personal, everything sectional. Now when the heart is centred upon the Lord Jesus, we have the greatest power and dynamic against division, against separateness, against everything that keeps us apart, and when the Lord Jesus is our central, supreme object, and it is toward Him that our hearts go out, then we come into a unity. You cannot have personal interests and at the same time care for the interests of the Lord. David makes that perfectly clear.

"The tabernacle of *my* house," that is one thing; and if I consider that, then I shall not be set upon a house for the Lord; if I am set upon that, then I shall not find a place for the Lord's rest. If I am seeking to satisfy *my* desire, giving sleep to *my* eyes, and slumber to *my* eyelids, then the Lord's interests will take a second place. But when I set myself aside, with all that is personal, and I am centred upon the Lord, and when all the others do that too, we shall find our perfect uniting centre in Christ. That is what it is to dwell in unity.

Now Eph. iv is the great New Testament exposition of Ps. cxxxii: "*There is* one body. . . ." Read the passage without the italicised words: ". . . Giving diligence to keep the unity of the Spirit in the bond of peace . . . one body, and one Spirit . . . one Lord, one faith, one baptism, one God and Father of all, who is over all, and through all, and in all" (verses 3-6). Oneness in Christ as a body fitly framed together is what is portrayed. How is this perfect unity reached? By all that is individual and personal being left, by the Lord being the focal centre, and by our giving diligence to maintain the unity in that way; keeping all personal things out, and keeping Christ and His interests always in view: ". . . till we all attain unto the unity of the faith, and of the knowledge of the Son of God, unto a full-grown man . . ." (verse 13). Dwelling together in unity in that way, is the result of His being the sole and central object of all our concerns. This is not visionary, imaginative, merely idealistic, it is very practical. You and I will discover that there are working elements of divisiveness, things creeping in amongst us to set us apart. The enemy is always seeking to do that, and the things that rise up to get in between the Lord's people and put up a barrier are countless; a sense of strain and of distance, for example, of discord and of unrelatedness. Sometimes they are more of an abstract character; that is, you can never lay your hand upon them and explain them, and say what they are; it is just a sense of something. Sometimes it is more positive, a distinct and definite misunderstanding, a misinterpretation of something said or done, something laid hold of; and of course, it is always exaggerated by the enemy.

How is that kind of thing to be dealt with in order to keep the unity of the Spirit? Rightly, adequately on this basis alone, by our saying, "This is not to the Lord's interests; this can never be of value to the Lord; this can never be to His glory and satisfaction; this can only mean injury to the Lord." What I may feel in the matter is not the vital consideration. I may even be the wronged party, but am I going to feel wronged and hurt? Am I going to stand on my dignity? Am I going to shut myself up and go away, because I have been wronged? That is how nature would have it, but I must take this attitude: "The Lord stands to lose, the Lord's Name stands to suffer, the Lord's interests are involved in this; I must get on top of this; I must get the better of this; I must shake this thing off and not allow it to affect my attitude, my conduct, my feelings towards this brother or sister!' There must be the putting aside of that which *we* feel, and even of our rights for the Lord's sake, and a getting on top of this enemy effort to injure the Lord's testimony. That is giving diligence to keep the unity. That is the power of a victory over divisiveness, and is the victory for unity, and *there* the Lord commands the blessing. That is the way of eternal life. The other way is manifestly the way of death, and that is what the enemy is after. Until that difference is cleared up, all is death, all is withered and blighted. Life is by unity, and unity can only adequately be found in Christ being in His place as the One for whom we let go everything that is personal. We might not do it for the sake of anyone else. We might never do it for the sake of the person in view. We do it for His sake, and the enemy is defeated. There the Lord commands the blessing.

Such, then, is the twofold aspect of the basis of the blessing. Firstly, God's ground of satisfaction and rest must be equally our own, namely, His Son; and, secondly, we must dwell together therein.

Take the great illustration in the second chapter of the book of the Acts. Here is the greatest exhibition of the working of this truth that the world has ever seen. "But Peter, standing up *with* the eleven. . . ." There are brethren together in unity! The Lord also has entered into His rest. By the Cross the Father has found His satisfaction in the Son; the Lord has entered into His heavenly Tabernacle. All is rest now in heaven: God is satisfied, the reconciling work has been done in the Blood of the Cross, peace has been made, and

God has entered into His rest in the perfect work of redemption. Now the eyes of all the apostles are on the Lord Jesus, and as they stand up He is in full view. Peter has left all those personal things behind. They have all left the personal things now, and their whole object is Christ. Standing up now, their testimony is all to Christ, and they are one, united in Him; and there the Lord commanded the blessing, even life for evermore, such blessing as was like the precious ointment coming down from the head to the skirts of the garment.

The figure is perfect, as a figure. There is the Head, the Lord Jesus, and the Father has commanded the blessing in the pouring of the eternal Spirit upon the Head. Now as all these members are ranged under the Head, centred in the Head, held together in the Head, the blessing comes down to the skirts of His garment, and it is ". . . like the dew of Hermon that cometh down upon the mountains of Zion. . . ." That is the effect of the blessing, that is the effect of life for evermore. What is the dew of Hermon? If you had lived in that country, you would know the value of the dew of Hermon. It is a parched and shrivelled land, with everything dry and becoming barren, and then the dew of Hermon comes down and everything revives, everything is refreshed, everything lifts up its head and lives again. It is the beneficent result of the blessing; life, freshness, hope, reviving, fruitfulness. There the Lord commanded the blessing.

Do you see the way of life, the way of fruitfulness, of reviving, of refreshing, the way of blessing? Two things are basic. These are our coming to the place of God's rest in His Son, and our letting go of everything that is of ourselves in the interests of His Son, and finding our all in Him. Thus are we drawn together by our mutual love for the Lord. Oh that we had more of the expression of this. I think that is why the Lord is bringing the matter before us; not for the message to be merely as a blessed prospect, a word that has a happy ring about it and that gives us a certain amount of uplift while it is being spoken, but for it to be a strong call from the Lord. Do we want the blessing? Do we want life for evermore, life more abundant? Do we want refreshing, and fruitfulness, and reviving, and uplift? Do we want that others also should get the blessing through us? Look at Pentecost. Pentecost is the outworking of Ps. cxxxiii; for there brethren were dwelling together in unity, centred upon the Lord, and in the Lord, and the Lord commanded the blessing.

There is nothing very profound in this, but it is of no less importance on that account. It is yet another way of bringing the Lord Jesus into view, of showing Him as the centre, as supreme. But, oh, it is a call from the Lord, a serious and solemn call from the Lord to our hearts. The way of fruitfulness, the way of blessing, the way of freshness, the way of joy is to be in this way that is under the blessing of the Lord, because we have found our rest where He has found His, in the Lord Jesus; because the object of our hearts, for which we have set aside all lesser objects, all personal interests, is the object of His own, even His Son, our Lord Jesus Christ. There the Lord commands the blessing, even life for evermore.

May He be able to do that with us. Oh, that it might be said in days to come as never hitherto: "... *there* the Lord commanded the blessing, even life for evermore," because of these two great governing realities, both of which are centred in the Lord Jesus.

CHAPTER IX

The Heavenly Man and Eternal Life

It is Christ as the Heavenly Man that is our consideration at this time, and we have been seeing that the main spring of the being of the Heavenly Man is eternal life. "In him was life . . ." (John i. 4); ". . . as the Father hath life in himself, even so gave he to the Son also to have life in himself . . ." (John v. 26). It is eternal life, Divine life, life from God, a special kind of life; not merely extensiveness of life, but a nature of life. The main spring of his being as the Heavenly Man is eternal life. The Lord Jesus, as the Son of God, was ever appointed to be the Life-giver. From eternity that life was in Him for creation.

Eternal Life in View from Eternity

The words in the Gospel of John, used by the Lord Jesus, that it was given to Him of the Father both to have life in Himself, and to give that life unto whomsoever He willed, carry us back again into the "before times eternal." Here they relate to redemption, but that is not where the matter of life-giving, of God's intention with regard to life begins. We are shown in a figurative way that right at the beginning, before there was any fall, and therefore before there was any practical necessity for redemption, God's thought was eternal life, and when from fallen man He shut off the tree of life, He is seen to do so on this ground: ". . . lest he put forth his hand, and take also of the tree of life, and eat, and live for ever . . ." (Gen. iii. 22). Now God had made that provision. Eternal life was there in the thought and intention of God, but this eternal life was for a certain kind of man, and the Adam that came to be, as separated from God, ceased to stand in God's view as the being in whom eternal life could reside, and so that was reserved. It was maintained in the Son; for the tree surely is but a figure of Christ. When we get to the end of the Scripture the tree is seen again. Christ is the "tree of life." Christ is the repository of that life, and here He comes forth in man-form as the last Adam as the kind of man in whom that life can be.

Through union with Him now by redemption, that life that is in Him is deposited in the believer himself; not as apart from Christ, but in Christ in the believer. It never departs from Christ. The Apostle states that this life *is* in His Son, and was given to us. We have eternal life, and this life is in His Son. It is Christ resident within in the person of His Spirit in whom the life is, and it is never possessed apart from Him.

We have been saying that the Lord Jesus, as the Son of God, was ever the appointed Life-giver. Of course, He can only so be known as Redeemer. He could have been known as the Life-giver apart from redemption, but now on account of man's condition through the fall, He can only be known as the Life-giver according as He is known as Redeemer. So that what we have to do with now, here in time, is redemption and life, redemption unto life.

Redemption Related to the Eternal Purpose

Here we want again to speak for a few moments of that main line of eternal purpose which the Lord is seeking to bring us to, and to bring to us. Because it is so great, and lifts us so much out of that with which we are more entirely occupied in time, that is, our salvation, our redemption, and all that is associated with it; because it takes us out of that and puts us into so much larger a realm, it is quite natural that we should have difficulties and not be able to grasp it immediately. That is how we are finding it, and that is what is making necessary a return to this main emphasis.

Look again intently at the word redemption. The word itself carries an implication. Redemption implies a bringing back. The question immediately presents itself: Brought back to what? And to what place? There is something that, for the time being, has been lost. It has ceased to remain in its original relationship, in its original position. It has to be brought back, reclaimed, restored, redeemed. Then there must have been a place and a position, and that is our main point.

We are seeking to say at this time, that before ever there was a fall, and even before this creation was, there was a counsel of God issuing in a purpose, and the straight line of that purpose through the ages was intended to work out progressively to a universal display of God in man, through His Son. So, through the Son, He created all things. Everything that was created in heaven and in earth, and in the universe came, through the Son, to be "Son-wise" itself, God expressed and manifested in terms of "Son." In relation to that, we were ". . . foreordained . . . unto adoption as sons . . ." (Eph. i. 5).

If you read the Word carefully you will descry Adam in the condition of a child, rather than of a son; a child under probation, under test; and because he failed under the test, he never came to the maturity of a son. Some of us are familiar with the New Testament teaching on the difference between a child of God and a son. Adam is in the infancy of God's thought, God's intention. He has to grow, to develop, to expand, to mature, to come to full stature; and we are not saying that the one test was the only one, the final test unto his maturity, but it was the first one. The whole plan of growth, of progressive development unto a full-grown, corporate man, does not necessarily rest upon redemption. It rests upon the eternal purpose, the eternal counsels. The straight line of things would have gone right on apart from any redemptive plan at all, and would have been realised. If Adam had not fallen, the eternal purpose would still have been realised, because it is all eternally vested in the Son. Now inasmuch as man is included, Adam was included. Adam failed and, with him, the race. Then a redemptive plan must come in; just as complete a plan in the counsels of God, but one developed or projected because of something that went wrong. We cannot say the fall was right, but it occasioned a plan, a perfect plan, a wonderful plan, and when God made the plan, when in His eternal counsels He was projecting this whole scheme of creation and intention and purpose, then the attitude, as we read back into those counsels, was undoubtedly this: "We know, because We cannot help knowing, being what We are, all-knowing, how things will go. We know that Our first thought will not be immediately realised, that there will be this bend down, this break. We therefore project this further plan of redemption by which We come down into that bend and bring things right up again on to Our level. We fill it up; but in so doing We will not lose, We will gain. This work of the adversary, all this tragedy, this suffering shall not take from Our original plan and thought, shall not diminish it one whit, neither shall it just mean that in the end We come back to Our level; We will come back with added glories, and these will be the glories of grace." God always reacts to the work of the Devil in that way; to get more than He had before, through suffering. Suffering is not God's will any more than sin is God's will, but in the sufferings of His own people He always secures something more than was there before. It is not only that He keeps even with the Devil, God is always "more than conqueror." That means that He obtains added glories as the result of the interference of His enemy, whatever may be said of that. This is so in the details of the individual experience, but in its fulness, in its whole movement, that interference occasioned the whole redemptive system and plan.

We recognise that, but that is not at the moment the thing with which we are dealing. Were it so, we should be speaking on the glories of redemption. But the Lord has laid this burden of His eternal thought for man upon our hearts at this time, and we do not believe that for one moment we are taking away from the glories of redemption, or putting redemption into a place of less value than it should have. If it seems to you that we are brushing that aside, or putting it into a secondary place, it is not that we are seeing less value in it than there is. God forbid! How are we to know God at all apart from it? At the same time, what we have in view is God's Son. It is not redemption, but the Son of God, this Heavenly Man, as representing God's full thought for man, and for the universe, with which we are dealing. The Son of God as Redeemer is but one expression of the Son, and one which, while so full of glory, and ever to be the theme of the redeemed through the ages of the ages, has become painfully necessary here in time. It speaks of tragedy. It speaks of Divine heart-break, of God suffering. This, however, as we have said, is not our main consideration at the present time, but in these meditations we are occupied with Christ as the Heavenly Man.

The Lost Treasure

We have said that we can only know Him as the Life-giver now in terms of redemption, as the Redeemer: ". . . the Son of man came to seek and to save that which was lost" (Luke xix. 10). What do we understand by that Scripture? Of course, in Gospel terms we have painted pictures of lost sheep, and we have thought of the individuals who are out and away from the Lord, as that which is lost. Well, that is quite true, but you have to be far more comprehensive than that in interpreting the scripture. God has lost something, and the Son of Man has come to recover that which God has lost. What is it that God has lost? Listen again: "The kingdom of heaven is like unto a treasure hidden in the field; which a man found, and hid; and in his joy he goeth and selleth all that he hath, and buyeth that field" (Matt. xiii. 44). What is the treasure? What is the field? The field is the world, the treasure is the Church. That treasure is hid, and the Lord Jesus paid the price for the crown rights of the whole creation in order to have the Church which was in it. Christ acquired by redemption, by paying the price, universal rights in order to secure that treasure, the Church. This it was that was lost. What is the Church? The Church is the one new man, the fulness of the measure of the stature of a man in Christ. It is the corporate heavenly man, the expression of Himself in corporate form, His inheritance in the saints. That is a very precious treasure.

The Church is not the only thing, but it is the central thing. The Lord Jesus has acquired the rights of the universe, and there will be other things in addition to the Church. There will be the nations walking in the light thereof. There will be a redemption that goes far beyond the Church, but the Church is the central thing. He has found that, and it was this lost treasure that dictated His course, and governed Him in paying the price. That is a tremendous thought. The Church is so precious to Him as to make Him willing to pay the price for the whole universe, in order to have it. That is the focal point. The Church is the key to redemption. It is that which is coming to the perfect image of Christ. All else will be secondary. There will be a reflection of Christ through the Church; His light will fall upon all else; what

He is will come to rest upon all else; all else will take its character from what He is in the Church, but the Church will be at the centre: ". . . the nations shall walk amidst the light thereof . . ." (Rev. xxi. 24). It is a tremendous thing to live in this dispensation when the Lord, though having acquired the rights of the universe, of the whole creation, by His Cross, is specifically concentrated upon the treasure now, to get it out of the creation.

"The kingdom of heaven [it should be in the plural, the kingdom of the heavens] is like unto a treasure hidden in the field; which a man found, and hid. . . ." The Lord is doing a secret work in relation to the Church. It is always a dangerous thing to bring what we conceive to be the Church out into a conspicuous place, and make a public thing of it. The real Church is a secret, hidden company, and a hidden and secret work is going on in it. That is its safety. When you and I launch out into great public movements, displaying and advertising, we expose the work of God, and open it to infinite perils. Our safety is in keeping where God has put us, in the hidden, secret place with Himself. That by the way.

"The kingdom of heaven (the heavens) is like unto. . . ." What is the significance of that phrase? It means that the whole heavenly system is focused upon the Church. It is the centre of the heavenly system. All that "the heavens" means, in this spiritual sense, is interested in the Church, is concerned with the Church, the treasure in the field. Why is this? Because, again, the Church is the *heavenly* man in Christ.

Take the Lord Jesus in person, as the Heavenly Man. The whole universe is interested in Him. At His birth heaven is active; the hosts of heavenly beings break through in relation to Him. Hell also is active and, through Herod, seeks to destroy this birth and all its meaning. You find that right on through His earthly life all the universe is centring its attention upon Him, and is related to Him, so that in His death the sun hides its face, the earth quakes, and there is darkness over the face of it. The whole universe is bound up with this One.

Thus the kingdom of the heavens, all the heavenly system, is concerned with this treasure in the field, because of its eternal significance, relationship, purpose. That is an immense thing. Now, of course, you are able to appraise more perfectly the value and meaning of redemption. To see the background of things is not to take away from redemption, it is to add marvellously to it. It is to give to redemption a meaning far removed from that of just being saved as a unit here and getting to heaven. That is a big thing, of course, that saving of the individual. But when we see the redemption that is in Christ Jesus in the light of God's eternal background, how immense a thing it is! If you want really to appreciate, and rightly appraise redemption, you have to set it where Paul set it, and see that it is cosmic. The coming into redemption on the part of every single individual is a coming into something immense, a far bigger thing than the redemption of the individual himself. All the powers and intelligences of the universe are bound up with, and interested in, this redemption. We believe that in order rightly to appreciate and enjoy the things of God, it is necessary to get their universal and eternal background, and not take them as something in themselves. That is how Paul saw redemption.

Eternal Life the Vital Principle of Redemption

The vital principle in redemption has to be implanted. Redemption is not something objective, something that is done for us. It is that, but it is not just that. It is not merely a system carried through, but redemption embraces a vital principle which has to become implanted in the believer, and the vital principle in redemption is eternal life, the life of the ages. So that redemption, bringing with it its vital principle, at once swings us back into relation with Christ before times eternal as the appointed Life-giver, and then we are carried right through with deathless life. Redemption itself, by itself, that principle of eternal life, expresses itself in the bringing back to the place where God can do what He found it impossible to do with the first Adam, to the place where He can give eternal life. When we come into redemption, all the ages of this world are wiped out as a matter of time, and we find ourselves at once made eternal beings, linked back there with the timeless God. The vital principle of redemption is eternal life to be implanted in the redeemed.

The next thing, working out from that, is that this vital principle of redemption makes the perfect redemption which is in Christ Jesus progressive in us. In Christ our redemption is perfect. We have a full redemption in Christ. His being in glory betokens that redemption is complete, full and final. But when the vital principle of redemption, that is, eternal life, is introduced into us through faith, this, which is perfect in Christ as redemption, takes up a progressive course in us as that principle of life. Redemption becomes progressive in us by life. That life is a progressive thing. We only come to the understanding and the enjoyment of the full redemption as the life increases in us. It is the work of redemption life in us which is going to bring us to the fulness of redemption. That is going to be proved true in spirit, mind, and body. We are going to enter into the fulness of redemption that is in Christ's present heavenly, physical body. His body, His present heavenly physical body, is a representation, a standard of the redemption of our complete humanity. We are going to be made like unto His glorious body. By what principle is this to be accomplished? By the working of that redemption life in us progressively.

The Twofold Law of the Life

Now, how does that redemption life in us operate? It operates in two ways. On the one hand, it operates to cut us off from our own natural life as the basis of our relationship with God. That is a big thing, and a big work, and a very deep work. So many in spiritual infancy and immaturity are making their own natural life, energies, resources, enthusiasms, and all such things, the basis of their relationship with the Lord both in life and service. It is a mark of immaturity. We know quite well that the young believer is always full of tremendous enthusiasm, and thinks it to be the real strength of his union with God, and that it really does represent something in relation to God. When presently the March winds begin to blow, and the blossom is carried away, such as these think the Winter has come instead of the Summer. They think they have lost everything. They ask, What has happened to me? The words of the hymn are perhaps heard upon their lips:

"Where is the blessedness I knew
When first I saw the Lord?"

But you do not get the fruit until the blossom has gone. It is the Summer, not the Winter, that follows the blowing away of the blossom. Of course, we all like to see the blossom in its time, but we should have some strange feelings if we saw the blossom there all through the Summer. We should say: "There is something wrong here, it is time that blossom went." We look closer, and we see something in its place, full of promise, and of much more value. This early blossom may be a sign of life, but it is not the life itself. A sign of early life belongs to the early Spring, showing that the Winter is past and resurrection is at work. It is a sign but it is not the thing itself, and it passes with spiritual infancy. These early enthusiasms are not the real basis of our union with God, but are signs of something that has happened in us. They are of ourselves, they are not of God. He is something other than that. He is not going to blow away. The life is working and will show itself in stronger and deeper forms.

All the way through this life we have to learn the change from what is, after all, ourselves in relation to God, to what is God Himself in us. There is a great deal that is of ourselves in relation to God, and I expect there will be in some measure right to the end. There is still something of our minds at work on God's things. We may be thinking that they are God's thoughts, God's mentality, but there is still much that is of our human mind, the mental make-up of ourselves in relation to the things of God, and we shall always find that God's mind is other than that, and we have to give place to new conceptions of the Lord. In will and in heart it is just the same.

We have been speaking of the body. This law of life works to the removing of our natural basis in relation to the Lord, so that even in our physical being we come on to the Lord in relation to His things, and the Lord becomes even our bodily life in relation to heavenly things. That is a fact. Therein is the testimony, that we are brought progressively, on the one hand, to the place where, in the Lord's things, we have no life in ourselves, where even physically we are faced with impossibility. It always has been so from God's standpoint, but we have been thinking that we were doing quite a lot because we had not been brought to the point where the consciousness of natural inability was allowed to overtake us. Now we have come to the place where, in greater or lesser degree, we realise that in the things of God we "cannot," even physically.

But if, on the one hand, eternal life operates to cut us off from our natural life as the basis of our relationship with God, on the other hand, it is perfectly wonderful what is done. It is "the Lord's doing, and it is marvellous in our eyes." The Lord even comes in as our physical life to the doing of more than would have been possible to us at our best, and certainly far beyond the present possibility, because He has made us known that as men we are nothing, even at our best. Life does that. Life forces off one system and brings on another, making room for it as it goes.

That, I believe is what the Lord meant when He said, "I am come that they might have life, and that they might have it *more abundantly*" (John x. 10). We have thought that just to mean that we are to have abundance of exuberance. We are always asking for life more abundant that we might feel wonderfully elated and overflowing and energetic. The Lord is pre-eminently practical, and more abundant life means that, having life, you will find the need of more to lead you a little further, and you will need it abundantly as you go on, because that life alone can bring you into the fulness. And it is His will that there should be the full provision of life unto the full end, because the purpose is such an abundant purpose. The life is commensurate with the purpose.

All that and much more is bound up with this basic statement that the active principle of redemption is eternal life, and that while that redemption is perfect in Christ it is progressive in us by the principle of life, and that to come into the fulness of redemption for spirit, mind and body there has to be a constant increase of redemption life. This life is redeeming us all the time. It is redeeming us from this present evil age, from all that came in with Adam. Full redemption will be displayed when Christ appears, and we with Him, when seeing Him we shall be like Him. It will simply be the manifestation of that life which is His eternal life in us. Oh, the possibilities of that life to transfigure! As we look at the

Lord Jesus on the Mount of Transfiguration we see the full display of the life which the Father gave to dwell in us. It blazes forth in its fulness there, and shows you what kind of a man that man is in whom Divine life is fully triumphant. He is a man full of glory, full of perfection; and when we see Him we shall be like Him.

The word for us as we close is this, that He has called us unto eternal life. We must lay hold on eternal life daily for spirit, and mind, and body.

CHAPTER X

The Heavenly Man and the Word of God

READING: Matt. iv. 4; John vi. 63, 68, viii. 47, xiv. 10; I Pet. i. 23, 25; Heb. iv. 12-13; I John iv. 17.

You will notice that what is said in the first four of these passages arises out of the fact that the Lord Jesus was the Heavenly Man. In the temptation in the wilderness, as recorded in the passage in Matthew, we see that it was following the opening of the heavens and the attestation from the Father, "This is my beloved Son . . ." that the enemy made his challenge to all that this designation of Christ as the Heavenly Man implied. "If thou art the Son. . . ." The temptations had their foundation in the fact of the heavenliness of the Lord Jesus. In the passages in John's Gospel the same feature is seen. As we have already noted, John keeps in view the heavenliness of the Lord Jesus all the way through, from the first words of his Gospel to the end. The challenge of the Lord Jesus carries that same meaning: "Believest thou not that I am in the Father. . . ." The Heavenly Man is brought before us at this point in relation to the Word of God.

We closed our previous meditation by dealing with the vital principle of redemption, and we were saying that that principle, which is eternal life, makes the redemption that is perfect in Christ, progressive in us. Redemption is introduced into us with the receiving of eternal life, and as the life operates, works, and increases, we come increasingly into the good of redemption. The real values of redemption become ours in experience by the operation of the life of the Redeemer in us, the Redeemer operating in us by His own life.

Christ the Beginning of the Creation of God

In John xx. 22 we have an incident recorded which has given rise to a certain measure of perplexity: ". . . he breathed on them, and saith unto them, Receive ye the Holy

Ghost. . . ." We perhaps want an explanation of that act, and of those words, and I think the explanation is that what He did and said was in pattern, and not immediately in actuality; that is, it was a representative act on the part of the last Adam. John xx sees us on resurrection ground with the Lord Jesus. We remember that it is written, "The first man Adam became a living soul. The last Adam became a life-giving spirit" (I Cor. xv. 45). That must, in spiritual reality, relate to His resurrection. Not in the full sense was He a life-giving spirit before the Cross, neither was He the last Adam before the Cross. All that was represented by, and summed up, in Him, but in the sense of generation, this only begins on resurrection ground. There in the fullest sense He becomes the last Adam, a life-giving spirit. So on resurrection ground He performs this representative or pattern act, and utters these representative words as the last Adam, fulfilling in the spiritual sense the words of Rev. iii. 14, ". . . the beginning of the creation of God." In the literal sense He was that at the beginning of this world. He was the beginning of the creation of God. That does not mean that He was the first one created by God; it means that He began the creation of God literally then, as to this world.

In the new creation He is taking that place in the spiritual sense: ". . . the beginning of the creation of God." In the beginning of the literal creation there was a breathing into man of the breath of lives. Now, as the last Adam, as a life-giving spirit, He breathes upon them. It is a typical act. It is the last Adam acting in a pattern-way in relation to the first members of the new creation, the beginning of the creation of God. He is typically infusing eternal life into the new creation. It is only a typical act, because the Spirit was not yet given. The full expression of it came later at Pentecost.

The Heavenly Man in Relation to the Word of God

Here is life in relation to the Heavenly Man in the full sense. We now come to bring all this life principle in the Heavenly Man into relation to the Word of God. The Word of God is very closely related to this life, and this life is very closely related to the Word of God, both of them as in the Heavenly Man, the life and the Word. So much is this so that they are not things in Him, but He is them. He is the Word, and He is the life; the life and the Word are in Him as His very being. Yet the Word is utterance as well as person. If you have taken the trouble to study the technique of the point that is raised in the use of the words "Logos" and "rema," you know how difficult it is always to differentiate between the two. You know how they run into one another, and how very often they meet and are one. So it is that the person has the word and the word is the word of the person. There is a difference, and yet they are both bound up with the person. We shall see as we go on what it means.

(a) Begotten by the Word

In the first place, as we have been saying, the Lord Jesus as the Heavenly Man was begotten through the Word. The angel visited Mary and presented her with the Word of God, and waited for her to respond to it before there was any living result, and when, after consideration and fighting her battle through the problem and the difficulty, and the cost of it, she responded, "Behold, the handmaid of the Lord; be it unto me according to thy word," then the living Christ was implanted.

(b) Tested by the Word

In the temptation in the wilderness, it is clearly indicated to us that, in the background of things, it was the Word of God that was governing the Lord. Every temptation was met with the Word of God: "It is written. . . ." Life was contingent upon the Word of God: "Man shall not live by bread alone, but by every word that proceedeth out of the mouth of God" (Matt. iv. 4). In the Heavenly Man the life question is bound up with the Word of God. If you take the opposite of that, you know that the earthly man dies because he refuses the Word of God; his life depends upon the Word of God and his attitude toward it. Here the last Adam is taken up on the same basis, and inasmuch as He met the three temptations with the Word of God, it is perfectly clear that His life was bound up with the Word of God. It was the Word of God that was governing this whole experience, and its issue. The Heavenly Man was being assailed with a view to tearing Him out of His heavenly life, as it were, by getting

Him in some way to refuse, or violate, or ignore the Word of God. He maintained His position as the Heavenly Man in life on the ground of the Word of God.

(c) Governed by the Word

Not only was He begotten through the Word, and tested by the Word, but in the third place, Christ was governed throughout the whole of His life by the Word of God. All the Law and the Prophets apply to Him. Said He to Jewish leaders, "Ye search the scriptures, because ye think that in them ye have eternal life; and these are they which bear witness of me" (John v. 39). The suggestion there does not immediately affect our consideration, but is worth noting. In effect He was saying: In your searching of the Scriptures for eternal life, it is the Person in the Scriptures that you need to know; it is in Him in whom the Scriptures are gathered up that eternal life is found. That is the force of the statement: ". . . these are they which bear witness of me." Again, when with the two on the way to Emmaus after His resurrection, it is said of Him that "beginning from Moses and from all the prophets, he interpreted to them in all the scriptures the things concerning himself."

We mark the fact, then, that all the Scriptures applied to Him. He embodied and fulfilled all the Scriptures. How often will He say, while here on the earth, concerning a certain movement, a certain act, a certain experience, a certain statement, ". . . that the scriptures might be fulfilled. . . ." If you have never taken out every instance in which that occurs, you should do so. It is worth gathering up.

The Relation of the Holy Spirit to the Word of God and the Heavenly Man

Now I want you to note this. The Lord Jesus, in the whole of His life, was being governed by the Word of God. How necessary it was, then, for Him to walk in the Spirit, so that the Word of God should be fulfilled. Now what does that mean? Take, for example, the Old Testament. Do you suppose for one moment that every statement in the Old Testament was always present in the mental consciousness of the Lord Jesus, and that when He went to do something He referred to His manual, and said: "Now shall I do this, or shall I do that? What does the Scripture say I ought to do?" Yet every part of the Scripture was controlling His life, and there was a sense in which He was responsible for everything there. It all applied to Him. But He was not carrying all the Scriptures in His head, nor even in a book, and referring to His memory or His manual for His conduct, His utterances, His acts, His experiences, for what He allowed and what He did not allow, for what He did and what He did not. Although the Word of God was with Him richly, although He would have had a great knowledge of the Scriptures—and that becomes perfectly clear as we read His utterances—that is not the way in which the Word of God governed Him; as though He had to call Scriptures to remembrance on every occasion and to act accordingly. He was moving in the Spirit of life, and as He did so He moved according to the Word of God. When necessary the Spirit of life brought the Word of God to His remembrance, and He was able to use it. How He did use it! But apart from any quoting of Scripture, and apart from any present memory of the particular passage which governed any given incident, the Spirit was moving with life, in relation to the Word of God. He was governed by the Word of God, so that even when, as Man, He was helpless upon the Cross, unable to do anything, it says of those very conditions, ". . . that the scripture might be fulfilled. . . ." Again, it is recorded that when He was dead on the Cross, and they came to break the legs of those crucified, finding Him already dead, they break not His legs, ". . . that the scripture might be fulfilled, A bone of him shall not be broken" (John xix. 36). That Man is under the government of the Word of God in everything because of the Spirit possessing, because of the Spirit directing, and the Spirit taking responsibility.

I can see a danger there, and am going to safeguard what we are saying, but let us first of all stress this law. If we are walking in the Spirit, and are moving according to the life of the Heavenly Man, our lives will be ordered according to the Word of God. Sometimes we shall not know the scripture that applies to a given moment, but we shall know of something happening; we shall know that at that point we were checked; it was as though within us something said: That is not right, you will have to correct that statement;

there is a flaw in that, and you will have to make that good. How often we have known that. Afterwards we have discovered where we were mistaken. The Spirit of life does not let anything that is contrary to the Word of God pass, if we are walking in the Spirit. Surely that should be a great comfort to us, and a great help.

The Word of God Never to Be Set Aside

But there is a danger of which we need to beware. What we have said does not mean that we can take up a course of trying to walk in the Spirit, and neglect the Word of God. We cannot say: Well, to walk in the Spirit is all we need and we shall be according to the Word of God; we need not bother about that. There are a lot of people who live in what they call their "spirit." They "get it from the Lord." They get something, and act upon it, and afterwards it is discovered that it is a direct violation of the Word of God. How often we have met that. People get things "from the Lord," and do something which they think they got from the Lord, and it is as clear as possible that the Word of God is positively against what they have done.

Thus the matter needs safeguarding. "Let the word of Christ dwell in you richly in all wisdom . . ." (Col. iii. 16) as a basis for the Holy Spirit. If, however, you are doing that you will not always have the exact passage to hand to govern the thing of the moment, but the Holy Spirit will be making good in you what He knows to be the Word of God, and holding you up. How true that is. Some of us have found that our natural memories have in great measure broken down. Very often a misquotation of Scripture does not touch doctrine at all, but the point is this, that there is a governing Intelligence which makes us know the Word of God, though we may not be able for the moment to give a particular passage in its exact phrasing or call it to mind. We are governed by it if we belong to the Heavenly Man. "As he is, so are we in this world" (I John iv. 17). Here is the Heavenly Man governed by the Word of God, inasmuch as there was life in Him.

What is true of the Head, is to be true of the members. If we are to be joined to the Heavenly Man, we become parts of that corporate Heavenly Man, and that same life is in us, and we shall walk by the Word. We shall be governed by the Word through the Spirit of life that is in the Word, and that Spirit of life is all-knowing, all-intelligent. I wish that all the Lord's people lived on that basis. It would save us from all that deadly heresy-hunting kind of thing, from always being suspicious, little, doctrinal watch-dogs, keeping a look-out for anything that is erroneous, and producing a blight of death over everything. If we were but living in the Spirit, we should know in our hearts whether a thing were right or not, without projecting our analytical minds into things; the Spirit would bear witness in our hearts. That would be life and salvation. The other is a miserable existence for everybody.

Now you see the Heavenly Man, eternal life, and the Word governing throughout. What a difference there is between being governed by the letter and being governed by the Spirit. We may have the book; may possess all the letter; and may be constantly exclaiming, "To the law and to the testimony!" We may thus become very legal, checking up on the letter all the time. The Lord Jesus did not thus act, nor did the Apostle Paul. Zealous as they were for the Scriptures, for the Word of God, utterly governed by the Word of God, the thing which mattered with them was the living Word. Said our Lord Jesus: ". . . the words that I have spoken unto you are spirit, and are life"; ". . . the flesh profiteth nothing" (John vi. 63). We can kill with the letter. We can kill with the Word, as the Word. Surely we want to be delivered from dealing with the Scriptures as words, as letters, and to be brought into the place where it is the Spirit in the Word giving life. What a difference there is between those two realms. One leads to nothing but death, paralysis, to the chilling and blighting of everything; the other leads to a positive condemnation, to judgment which is necessary to slay the thing that is evil. It does not leave things in that blighted state without any meaning, which is all too often the case when it is merely a thing of the letter.

So you get the twofold aspect of the Word unto growth in Christ. Firstly, the Word is a Spirit-breathed utterance. That is what the Word of God must be, and not just something that has been written. Secondly, the Spirit of life associated with the Word. This raises a very big question, a question that perhaps it is almost dangerous to open in public in these days, and to answer which maybe would require a good deal of explanation. The question is this: How far is the written Word, as it stands, the Word of God? This Book can be taken hold of and the same fragment used in fifty different ways at the same time. The same passage of Scripture can be the basis of a dozen different things, all of which are mutually exclusive and contradictory. Which of these dozen or fifty is the Word of God? You can take Scripture as the letter like that, out from this Book, and you can say: This is the Word of God! How are you going to prove it? All these different people take the Word of God, and get a different meaning with a different result, act in a different way, and justify a different course, and the same Word has brought about terrific conflict and opposition between different sections of people. How far is it the Word of God as it stands? My point is this, that I believe that something extra is necessary to make that the Word of God in truth, in fulness, and that is the Spirit of life in it. That Spirit of life (we are thinking of the Holy Spirit now, not an unintelligent abstraction) must Himself use, and apply, that Word, to make it the Word of God. I do not believe that you can get any Divine result by simply quoting scripture as scripture. The Holy Spirit has to come into that Word, express Himself as in it, and make it live before you get the Divine result, because of the object in view. A living Heavenly Man is not made by mere words, even though they be words of Scripture. That is what people have tried to do. They have tried to make the Church by words of Scripture, constitute the Church by what is here as written, and so you have half a dozen different kinds of Churches, all standing on what they call the Word of God, and the thing does not live. It is a living, Heavenly Man that God has in view, and to produce that, the Spirit must operate through the Word. "The words that I have spoken unto you are spirit, and are life," said the Lord to His disciples. "Lord, to whom shall we go? Thou hast the words of eternal life." On the part of Peter, the spokesman of these latter words, this was a word of discrimination. The Scribes and Pharisees had the Scriptures. They claimed that everything they had and held was in the Word of God. Ah yes, but they knew them not as the words of eternal life.

There is a difference. This life is in His Son. It has to be in a living relationship to the Lord Jesus that the Scriptures are made effective.

The Sovereignty of God in the Creative Word

That works, in the first place, sovereignly in the direction of the unsaved. You may take the Word of God as it is written and preach it, but you have to leave the whole matter to the sovereignty of the Spirit. Preach it to a crowd of fifty, a hundred, a thousand, and to nine hundred and ninety-nine of the thousand the thing is as dead as anything can be. They see nothing, they feel nothing, but one in the thousand is sovereignly touched. That word is something more than an utterance, than letters, that word is spirit and life. That is no accident, no chance, but a sovereign act. The Spirit of God has come into the Word in relation to that one. That is the foolishness of preaching, in a sense, that you have to preach, and have no guarantee that the many will be touched by the Word of God. You have to commit yourself to the waters, and believe that God will somewhere come into the Word and touch some life, though the majority should be left untouched. That is the extra element, the Spirit of life in the Word of God, sovereignly acting in relation to the unsaved.

That, of course, is the creative Word, and brings us to see that in the Heavenly Man the Word of God is God's act, and not just God's statement. In the Heavenly Man the Word of God is never a statement alone, it is an act. We say many things, and then we look round for the result, with the thought in our minds, "What is the value of all this?" You have never, never to look for the result of God's Word in the Heavenly Man; it is there. You may not see it, but it is there. The Word in relation to the Spirit of life in Christ is an act; something is done; and when that Word has come by the Spirit of life, those to whom it has been directed by the intelligent Spirit can never again be the same, though they may seem to go on in the old way: ". . . the word that I spake, the same shall judge him in the last day" (John xii. 48). Something has been said; the Word has come, and the thing is done, never to be undone. Sooner or later those concerned are going to come right up against that, and it is all going to be dated back to the hour when the Spirit gave expression to the Word. That is a tremendous fact. That is the value of giving the Word in the Spirit, because it is an act. It is creative. It is something done, not something said. Oh, to recognise that the Word in the Holy Ghost is something done, not merely something said. God's Word is always God's act: ". . . the worlds have been framed by the word of God . . ." (Heb. xi. 3). The Word of the Lord *is* a blessing. It is not just saying, The Lord bless you. It is a blessing in itself; it brings the blessing. It is an act.

The Life Principle Established in the Case of the Saved

In the saved there is another side. The first side is creative, sovereign. Now in the case of the saved, where those concerned are the Lord's people, the operation of the Spirit in relation to the Word of God is no longer purely sovereign. In the case of believers the Word is not given with a view to bringing about creation, for that is done. We stand because of the Word of the Lord spoken sovereignly by the Spirit into our hearts, having thus been made His children, begotten by the Word of God. That is a sovereign act, but from that time onward, that which is sovereign ceases and growth is by the Spirit of life in the Word; but upon a basis that there is life in us to correspond to the life in the Word. The life in the one, or in the company, concerned is the basis of growth according to the Word of the Lord, which has life in itself. Take a simple illustration from our use of natural food. No matter how you may feed a corpse, you will get no development, no kind of growth. It is of no use feeding a dead man. There must be some life in a man that corresponds to the life in the food, takes hold of it, works with it, co-operates with it, before there can be growth. That is what we mean by the activity which bears the mark of sovereignty in the main ceasing. The sovereign act is something apart from ourselves; it is the grace of God to sinners who can give nothing back. Now that the life is in us our growth is on the basis of the life within us co-operating with the life in His Word. You can preach to people who have not much light, and preach in the Holy Ghost, and may not get very much result because of the limited measure of life that is in them. But you get tremendous response to a living word when people are all alive unto the Lord, when there is life in them. Growth comes that way, the life in us corresponding to the life in the Word, forming the Heavenly Man.

The Spirit-accompanied Word imparts life, quickens into life where there is a dead state, and does it sovereignly; but the Spirit-accompanied Word requires a response in the spirit in the case of those who have already been sovereignly brought into relation to Christ through the Word. The same life in the Word governs our lives as governed our new birth. The Lord Jesus was begotten truly of the Holy Ghost, the Spirit of life, but by the Word, or through the Word. Now, for the governing of His life, the same life through the Word operated as in the birth; that is, the same life that brought into being must be in the Word which governs the life, to bring that being to full growth. It is the life principle which is so important. It is this newness, this freshness that is of such account—if you like, this originality. Do not misunderstand; we are not using that word in the natural sense. We mean that in the birth by the Spirit of life there is something that never was before; it is original, new. We are a new creation in Christ Jesus. We call it the "new birth." It is not just something fresh, recent, but something that was not before.

In relation to the Word it has to be like that. The Word must come with all the force of something that never was before. There has to be a sense of Divine originality and freshness about it that is bringing to wonder, amazement. Again, you can test that. When the Word is in the hands of the Holy Spirit, though you may have read a passage a thousand times, and have had something from that word, you can come back to it again and say: Well, I never saw that before! Why, this is alive with meaning and value beyond anything before! There is all the difference between that, and the stale stuff that we put into books as the result of our Bible study. The Lord would have His ministers in the realm where their handling of the Word of God is in life. It is the Heavenly Man being governed by the heavenly life in the Word, so that everything is constantly new, constantly fresh, constantly original.

How true that is to experience. There have been times when we thought we knew all about a certain thing in the Bible; we have talked about it tremendously, and it has been ɔur theme for a long time. Then a period of time has elapsed when we have left it, and the Spirit of the Lord has led us to that again, and it is as though we have never seen that truth before. We find that we can come back to the old themes, as they are called, with such a newness. Other people may not realise what is going on in us. They may hear what amounts to the old things again, but they say: "There is such a new meaning, a new grip, that it is quite clear the Holy Spirit has not finished with that matter, and has more to say to us about it." We have to be careful how we react mentally to things like that. We are so often tempted to take this attitude: Oh, well, I have spoken of that so often that people must be tired of it! The Holy Spirit is saying: You say it again; do not take any notice of what they think; if they have heard it a thousand times, you say it! And when you do so, there is something done which, with all the earlier utterances of the same thing, has never been done before. Be careful of pigeon-holing anything in the Word of God, and saying that we have exhausted that. If you are dealing with the themes of the Bible, as such, you may as well pigeon-hole the whole thing right away. If you are moving in the Spirit with the Word of God, there will never be a time when any part of the Word of God becomes obsolete. It is the same new life that never was before, which came into us to constitute us a part of the Heavenly Man, which is so governed by the Word all the way along, unto constant increase, constant growth.

Remember, then, that it is a matter of life. Remember that doctrine comes out of life, and not life out of doctrine. The Church comes out of life, and not life out of the Church. It is not attachment to doctrine, nor attachment to the Church, but attachment to the Heavenly Man in a living way that is the vital necessity; and then you will get the doctrine and the Church. In the Word as we have it, the doctrine came after the life. The Church existed before the doctrine of the Church was given. Attachment to the Heavenly Man produced the doctrine of the Church. The Church came about by a living relationship, not by taking up a revelation of what the Church was, and seeking to put it into operation. Life comes first of all, and where life is found the rest will follow. It is of no use trying to impose the doctrine of the Church, or any other doctrine, upon people, if they are not alive unto the Lord. The Lord knows what He is doing. You cannot go about the world anywhere, not even amongst Christian people, with your full doctrine, your full revelation, and have the assurance that, as you give it out, they are going to leap to it. You have to go where the Spirit leads you, for the Spirit knows exactly where there is a sufficiency of life to have prepared the ground, and what can respond to that which you have to give. How we would like to go out into the world and talk to all the Lord's people of what He has shown us, and give them the revelation of the Body of Christ! We should go and organise great gatherings and get people together, only to find that they look at us blankly and exclaim: This is strange doctrine! You cannot do it like that. Increase has to be on a basis of life; because doctrine does not come first, but life. You cannot get the Church by trying to get it! There has to be life, and life by its working forms the Church, becomes the realisation of the Church. The reversal of that order only leads to Babylon.

What is Babylon? Babylon represents the loss of the authority of the Word of God as a living thing. It was in the reign of Jehoiakim, the king who took his penknife and cut up the Word of God, that Judah began to be carried away into Babylon. When he repudiated the living authority of the Word of God, all the vessels of gold and silver were carried off to Babylon. It is a parable. It means that the Lord's people come into bondage, into captivity, into death, are out of the place of the Lord's appointment, and the Lord's ministry is not going on in life, because the vessels have departed, have all been taken away. Right up to that time they were going on with their sacrifices, going on with their Levitical order. But that is not the point. You can have the form of things, the system, and yet go to Babylon. It is the Word of the Lord as a spiritual and living thing, which keeps you free, clear, strong, out of Babylon.

CHAPTER XI

The Heavenly Man and the Word of God

(contd.)

READING: John i. 14, xiv. 10; Col. iii. 16-17; Rev. xix. 13.

In the course of our previous meditation, we noted the relationship of the Holy Spirit to the Word of God and the Heavenly Man, and before we pass on to further considerations it may be well to sum up that relationship under three or four specific heads.

The Holy Spirit Related to the Word of God and the Heavenly Man

(a) In Birth. We observe, then, that the Holy Spirit is related to the Word of God in the birth of the Heavenly Man. The Word was presented to Mary, and it created for her a problem. In the human realm there was perplexity as to how the realisation of this thing could be; how she should attain unto that; how this wonderful presentation and unveiling of possibility and meaning, purpose and intent, and Divine thought could ever become a realised thing. That was her problem. The angel answered her enquiry and cleared her perplexity with one statement: "... the Holy Ghost shall come upon thee ..." (Luke i. 35). So we see that, related to the Word of God, there was the Spirit, in this birth.

The Holy Ghost did not take up the Word to make it a realised thing in Mary until she had committed herself to the Word. That is always a law. But when she committed herself deliberately to the Word, then the Holy Ghost took up the realisation of the meaning, the implication, the content, the purpose of that Word.

(b) In Conflict. In the same way the Holy Spirit was associated with the Word of God in the conflict. When the Spirit had come upon the Lord Jesus, as the Heavenly Man, at Jordan, He was led of the Spirit into the wilderness, to be tempted of the Devil. Being led of the Spirit, governed

by the Spirit, actuated by, and moving in, the Spirit, the Word of God was, by the Spirit, the instrument for the overthrow of the enemy, and for the ultimate advance rather than the arrest of the Heavenly Man. You notice that there is the mark of enlargement, because when the Devil left Him, it says, ". . . Jesus returned in the power of the Spirit . . ." (Luke iv. 14). There is the mark of enlargement, the sign of increase through this that has happened. The Spirit was associated with the Word in the conflict, unto victory, and unto enlargement.

(c) In Ministry. The same was true in the ministry of the Lord Jesus: ". . . the words that I speak unto you I speak not from myself; but the Father abiding in me doeth his works" (John xiv. 10). The words are the issue of an indwelling activity of the Father, by the Spirit.

We are speaking solely of Christ as the Heavenly Man now, not of Christ in His Deity and Godhead, as the Son of God in the highest sense. In His ministry, by the anointing, by the indwelling Spirit of the Father, there are activities going on in Him which result in words coming from Him. But they are not from Him apart from the Father, they are not from Him out of relationship with the Spirit, they are coming from the inward activities and energies of the Spirit of the Father. The Spirit is producing the words by His operations in the life. That is why they are always practical words, that is, words of practical effect. We will come back to that presently.

(d) In the Life. What was true in His spoken ministry, and in these other ways, was also true in His life. His life was a continuous and spontaneous fulfiling of the Scriptures, not by continuous reference to them, but through the indwelling of the Spirit, who had the Scriptures in possession, having Himself given them, and inspired them. They are eternal, and the Spirit in Him was moving in such a way that the Scriptures were being fulfilled all the time. On many occasions the statement is made to indicate that fact: ". . . that the scriptures might be fulfilled. . . ." So He was energised and actuated in His life, and in all its incidents, by the Spirit in relation to the Word. The Heavenly Man is governed by the Word of God through the Eternal Spirit. That is true of Him personally.

Now that is true also of Him corporately. The corporate Heavenly Man is the result of the same process. The Church, His Body, in its every part, is brought into being by the Word, firstly presented, and then contemplated, considered, responded to, and the Holy Ghost taking it up and making it a living thing. The result is the Church, the Body of Christ, the corporate Heavenly Man.

That is how the Church comes into being, and to contemplate any kind of thing called the Church, which does not come in by the operation of the Holy Spirit through the Word of God, is to contemplate something that does not exist in the thought of God. Set the Word of God aside and you will have no Church. What you will have is something that is utterly false. Set the Holy Ghost, in relation to the Word of God, aside, and you destroy what you are trying to build up.

That is viewing it in a very general way, but for us it becomes an immediate matter that our very being, as a part of Christ, issues from exactly the same principle as operated in His incarnation, the Word and the Spirit co-operating.

A Reiteration of the Divine Purpose—The Principle of Incarnation

Let us break this up, going back a little in thought. God requires a Man for the expression of His thoughts. To put that in another way, God has never meant just to utter words, statements; to make Himself known and give expression to Himself by verbal utterances. There is a great deal more hanging upon that than appears for the moment, but that is the simple fact, that God has never intended to make Himself known by statements, by words, by verbal utterances. That is why it is infinitely perilous to be occupied with teaching as teaching, and to take up teaching as teaching, to take up things said, and think that because we have the thing said to us we have the thing itself. We never have! Many people have all the things that have been said, but they have not the thing itself. There is such a position to come to as that of learning, and never coming to a knowledge of the truth. That is a position of great peril. Yes, for twenty, thirty, forty, fifty years we may have heard all that there is, and know it all, and yet never have come to a knowledge of the truth. It sounds like a contradiction, but it is possible, or the Word of God would not say so. What is the trouble? Where is the flaw? That is what we are trying to see now.

Now, as we have said, God never intended to try to make Himself known, to give expression to Himself, by words, by statements, by mere utterances, that is, by things said. For the expression of His thoughts God requires a Man. The Word, therefore, becomes flesh; for the man God desires must be the product of His Word in an inward way; that is, life must be related to truth, and truth must be related to life.

Again, there is the terrible danger of speaking apart from the Word of God having been inwrought. There is a fascination about the great truths, and connected with this there is a danger, especially if you happen to be in what is called "ministry." The danger is that of getting hold of truths, of doctrines, of themes, of subjects, of things in the Word of God, and all the time talking about them. You go and hear something fresh, and it is a new idea, and so off you go to give it out. In reality you are collecting material for your ministry in that way, and there is a terrible danger in so doing. It is going to put you and your hearers into a false position. As we have already said, it will make things top-heavy. You are building teaching upon something that is not life, that is not growth. It is simply a case of putting teaching on to people, and presently the whole thing will topple over, down will come your edifice, and you will wonder what is the matter. It is only life that counts. You have to lay a foundation, but there must be an excavating, an upheaving, a breaking up, an inworking, before you can add teaching. That is why doctrine followed the working of grace in the heart, in the New Testament. The word of grace was begun, and then the Lord explained by the doctrine what He had been doing. It is often thus with ourselves. The Lord takes us through something which we cannot understand, and which to us, while we are passing through it, is a deep, dark, terrible experience, but afterward He explains it to us in His Word, and we are brought into a full interpretation of what we have gone through. It is far better to have it so.

The receiving of the Word of God by the Old Testament prophets is described by the Hebrew verb *hayah*, which means "happened." Thus the literal rendering of the Hebrew is, The word of the Lord *happened* unto so and so. In our translation this is expressed by the word "came": The word of the Lord *came* to so and so. It is an event, not just a verbal utterance. That is how it has to be through us to others. That is why the Lord said, ". . . the words that I have spoken unto you are spirit, and are life . . ." (John vi. 63). There is an event with His words, not always in the immediate consciousness of those spoken to, but, as we have already pointed out, something is done, and it will come to light one day. Upon that everything in destiny hangs. God speaks, and something is effected one way or the other. Thus the Word of God is not merely a saying, a speech, it is an event.

The full value is given to the Word of God when it is incorporated in a body. That is, of course, patent in the case of the Lord Jesus Himself. The full value of the Scriptures was reached when they were incorporated in Him personally, when it could be said, "And the Word became flesh, and tabernacled among us . . . full of grace and truth" (John i. 14).

The Word of God and a Living Assembly

On the corporate side there is something to be recognised which perhaps may occasion difficulty for the moment, but which is nevertheless true, and something that must be taken into account, and be remembered, that the Word of the Lord in a living assembly has special value and power. If you have not seen that mentally, and recognised that as a truth, possibly you have known it as an experience, as a fact. In a living assembly of the Lord's people, with the Word of the Lord in the midst, what power that Word has, and what value. But how unprofitable it is to try to preach the Word in the midst of an assembly that is not living, but dead and dry. It may be the Word of the Lord, and, so far as the preacher is concerned, it may be in the power of the Holy Ghost, but of how little profit it is. When you get an assembly really alive unto the Lord, a body throbbing with life, what value, what power, what fruit there is in the Word. It was true in the case of the Lord Jesus. There you have a living One, with the Word of God in Him, and you see how, so far as He was concerned, the Word was spirit and life. The Word had special value in Him, because in Him was life.

—111—

That is a true principle in relation to the Heavenly Man, as corporately set forth. You have there a living body, with the Lord's life and the Lord's Word in the midst, running, having free course, and being glorified. On the outer fringe of that company there may be the unsaved, and others who are not alive to the Spirit, but the fact that the Lord has a nucleus of living ones in the midst gives to the Word something of value, which makes it far more powerful, far more effective, than where this is not the case. This is a thing that those who minister in the Spirit know all about in experience. If the Word is ministered in a fairly large company, not very far advanced, and not having learned the language of the Spirit, and anything is said very much beyond early simplicities, they look at you almost open-mouthed, and think you are talking a strange language. But when the Word has been released and there have been two or three who are alive to the Word, it has taken on power, and these people, although not perhaps understanding the terminology, have become alive to something. Some of you when preaching may have looked round the congregation to find one co-operating spirit, and the Word has found release. If there is a nucleus in the midst of a realm of death, or comparative death, the Word of God has a special value by reason of a Holy-Spirit-actuated unit. It is there that we have to see the importance of being alive unto the Lord for the ministry.

We have been dealing with the fourth chapter of Ephesians, where we read of the Heavenly Man giving gifts; apostles, prophets, evangelists, pastors and teachers, for the perfecting of the saints unto the work of the ministry. The saints are to minister. Now here is a way in which the saints minister. All the saints do not come up on to the platform and give the message, but they marvellously minister when they co-operate with the ministry, and really the ministry of the apostle or prophet, evangelist, pastor or teacher, is fulfilled by the living company. It is a poor look-out for the one who is ministering, if there is not a company to fulfil the ministry like that, by spiritual co-operation. In that way the Lord gets through with a revelation of Himself. How much more can the Lord reveal Himself when He has a living company.

The Lord seemed severely limited when He was here, so that He could never say all He wanted to say: "I have yet many things to say unto you, but ye cannot bear them now" (John xvi. 12). Nor, again, could He do what He wanted to do: "And he did not many mighty works there because of their unbelief" (Matt. xiii. 58). But, given a living company, there is no end to the possibilities. The Lord can reveal and express Himself there. The Lord needs a Man, a heavenly Man for His self-revelation, the expression of His thoughts, and the full value is only given to the Word when it is incorporated in a body.

Christ and the Word of God Are One

Now we come much closer. The thing that must be said at once is, that by the Holy Spirit the Word is Christ. It is not a statement of things, it is the expression of a Person. What we mean to say is, that we have to take the same attitude toward the Word, that we take toward Christ. We have to face the Word of the Lord in the same way that we face the Lord Himself. It is not something of the Lord presented to us in words, but it is the Lord Himself coming to us. We cannot reject any part of His Word and keep Him. We cannot divide between the Lord and His Word. People seem to think that they can take some of the things the Lord has said and leave others. The Word is one. The Word is the Lord. To refuse the Word in any part, is to refuse the Lord, is to limit the Lord, is to say, in effect: Lord, I do not want You! Lord, I will not have You! It is not that we will not have the Word, but that we will not have the Lord Himself, for the two are one: "His name is called The Word of God." "The Word became flesh. . . ." You cannot get in between, the two are one. He is the Word of God. God does not come to us in statements, He comes to us in Person, and the challenge is to take an attitude, not towards the things said, but towards the Lord Himself.

The Necessity for Heart Exercise

The question that arises in most of our hearts when we have been hearing a great deal is, How is that to become our life? How is that to become a part of us? How are we to become the living expression of that? That is the question which should arise, at any rate. Let us remind ourselves, and those for whom we have responsibility in ministry, that it is possible to be ever learning, and never coming to a knowledge of the truth. We can attend conferences, go right through every meeting, and mentally take in all that is said, and go away with it in our minds, or have it in our note-books, and then have to come back to another conference to get more, and then to another, and still another. We look back over the years of conferences and begin to take stock, and we ask ourselves the question: What is the result of all this? I remember that on such and such an occasion, such and such a thing was spoken about, and on another occasion something else; these have been the things which have been the subject of the various conferences; and now, what does it represent? That is a very solemn question. Is it that we know these things; that is, if they were repeated, should we take the attitude: Well, we have heard that before; we know that! That is what we mean by ever learning, ever learning, without maybe ever coming to the knowledge of the truth, in the sense in which that word "knowledge" is used. What are we going to do? How is all this to be translated into something more than words, more than thoughts, more than ideas, more than truths as truths, more than teaching, so that it really does become incorporated, expressed in a Man? It can be, and it must be. Exactly the same principle must operate as when Christ was born of Mary. It means that the Word presented has to lead us to exercise of heart. That is what happened with Mary. She immediately entered into an exercise of heart about it. You know what measure of exercise has resulted from your hearing of the Word. Consider it thus: What does that mean? What does that involve? What cost will that entail? What is that going to lead to? Is that the will of God for me? The need is of a present, direct, and deliberate taking up of the Word, and facing it, contemplating it, entering into exercise of heart about it. That is the first step towards incarnation of the Word.

Having looked at it, having been exercised by it, we must take a deliberate step in relation to it in faith. That is necessary. You will never get anywhere unless you do. When, having faced that Word, weighed it, looked at it in the light of God's will for you, and having come to a position you take a deliberate attitude, if it is to be towards the Lord, the attitude must be: "Behold, the handmaid of the Lord (behold, the servant of the Lord); be it unto me according to thy word." "I do not know how it can be; it seems an impossible thing, too high for me, but be it unto me." That is faith. Mary did not stand back and say: Well, it is a wonderful revelation, far too great for me; I do not believe it can ever be, I cannot really accept it! Wonderful as it was, and impossible as it was on any other ground but God, with the sheer impossibility of its ever being on any natural ground, she said: Nevertheless, be it! That is faith. It is not according to what I think is possible, what I feel to be possible, what seems to me to be possible, but "according to thy word." It is according to the Word, and that Word is not an impossible thing! If You have spoken, You do not speak impossibilities, You do not challenge me with impossibilities! "... be it unto me according to thy word." It is a committal of faith, a deliberate act of faith in relation to the Word, that is required.

How many of us have so acted over things which we have heard? How many of us have got away and, in exercise of heart, said: "Lord, that is a tremendous thing, and for me in a natural way it is quite impossible; but it is Your Word, therefore, be it unto me. I stand on it, and I stand for it, You make it good. I can do no more than say, Yes, and I believe God." There is a great deal in a transaction like that. Without that we do not grow. Without that we are ever learning and never coming to a knowledge of the truth. Without that so much of the truth becomes merely mental in its apprehension, and is not living, is not effective.

However much we have failed in the past, there is something to be done in this matter. When the Lord has been speaking to us, we should make it our first business to get apart with Him. You would not believe the heart-break it is, to one who has been pouring out that Word, to find that almost before he has finished his message, and the gathering is closed, people are talking on all the trivialities of their domestic and business affairs, on things that can quite well wait. It is not as though there were any serious or critical situation to be enquired into, but mere talk ensues along the lines of ordinary, every-day things. Our point is that there has to be a deliberate transaction with the Lord, if that Word is to become an expression of God in a life; and God can never be satisfied with anything else. God can never be satisfied with mere statements, but only with the man as a living expression of His words.

The Relation of the Word to the Cross

That is why the Word is always related to the Cross. The Apostle Paul uses this phrase: "For the word of the cross is . . . the power of God" (I Cor. i. 18). It is the power of God. It is the wisdom of God. We know that the word used is the "Logos" of the Cross. The Logos is the combination of a thought and expression in a personal way. It is the Word in a Person, related to the Cross. That is why it is put in this way by the same Holy Spirit of knowledge and understanding, in the book of the Revelation: "And he is arrayed in a garment dipped in blood: and his name is called The Word of God" (Rev. xix. 13). You see the two things, the garment sprinkled with blood, and His name "The Word of God." Then you look into the letter to the Hebrews, and you will remember that in chapter ix. 19, you have these words: ". . . he took the blood of the calves and the goats, with water and scarlet wool and hyssop, and sprinkled both the book itself, and all the people. . . ." There is the Word and the Blood. It is the Cross that gives the working power to the Word.

The Cross of the Lord Jesus is a tremendously effective thing. The Cross of the Lord Jesus, in its spiritual value, will break down everything that stands in God's way. It will clear the ground of the old creation. It will destroy the power of the enemy and his works. The Cross is a tremendous thing for breaking down, destroying, overthrowing. The Cross, on its resurrection side, knows no bounds to power: ". . . the exceeding greatness of his power to us-ward who believe, according to that working of the strength of his might which he wrought in Christ, when he raised him from the dead . . ." (Eph. i. 19-20). The Cross has these two sides, the breaking down side and the raising up side, and it is in the power of the Cross of the Lord Jesus that the Word of God finds its effectiveness. He becomes the Word of the Cross, and the garment sprinkled with blood is the garment of Him who

—116—

is "The Word of God," and as "The Word of God" He gets His power by way of the Cross. Christ crucified is the power of God. When the Cross has its place in our lives, the Word of God is tremendously potent. An uncrucified preacher is an ineffective and unfruitful preacher. Ministry in the Word of God from any but a crucified minister or vessel is impotent, fruitless, barren. Find the crucified man giving the Word of God, and you know it will be effective, fruitful, powerful.

Take Jeremiah as a great Old Testament illustration. If ever there was a crucified man in spirit, it was Jeremiah. He bears the marks of a crucified man right from the beginning. If you want to know what a crucified man is, read the first chapter of Jeremiah's prophecy, and you will see him indicated at once. Read right through Jeremiah, and you will see a life-size portrait of a crucified man. Turn to chapter i. 4-6:

> "Now the word of the Lord came unto me, saying, Before I formed thee in the belly I knew thee, and before thou camest forth out of the womb I sanctified thee; I have appointed thee a prophet unto the nations."

Any natural, uncrucified man would leap at that, and say: My! I am somebody! What power is entrusted to me! What a life-work I have!

> "Then said I, Ah, Lord God! behold, I cannot speak: for I am a child."

Such is the reaction of a crucified man to a great prospect set before him by the Lord. See what a crucified man can be when the Lord has him in His hands—verses 9-10:

> ". . . I have put my words in thy mouth: see, I have this day set thee over the nations and over the kingdoms, to pluck up and to break down, and to destroy and to overthrow; to build, and to plant."

There is the Cross in the word of the crucified man: ". . . my words in thy mouth . . ." destroying, overthrowing, plucking up, casting down. That is the power of the Cross. The Lord does that with regard to ourselves. The Cross works havoc in our flesh. It brings us to an end. But there is another side of the Cross, and that is to build, and to plant. That is the working of the Cross in resurrection. Thus we have the Word in the mouth of a crucified man. It is the Word of the Cross in effect. It is Christ crucified, the power of His Cross bringing into view a heavenly Man, through the embodiment of the Word of God. The Cross gets rid of that other man who looms so large, and who is to be summed up in Antichrist, the super-man, who will sit in the very temple of God giving out that he is God; some great one of this old and cursed creation, so lifted up in pride that he assumes the very place of God. The Cross casts him out, and brings God's man into view, greater than he. Over against Antichrist is Christ, and there is no comparison. The Cross brings in that Man by putting out the other. All that is in us of that other man the Cross brings to nought, and thus makes room for the revelation of the Heavenly Man, both personally and corporately, and gives to us a ministry which is the result of the work of His Word within. It is a ministry which is a work, not a ministry of statements. That is why we have stressed the words in John xiv—". . . *the words* that I say unto you I speak not from myself: but the Father abiding in me doeth *his works*." The Father dwelling in Him was doing His works. The words that He speaks, He is not speaking from Himself, they are coming out of the Father's works. Thus, it is not a case of truth, teaching, words, ideas; it is a ministry (evidenced, maybe, by words, but by "words, which the Holy Ghost teacheth") resultant from inward works, the works of the Spirit within. The Lord lead us more into that.

Chapter XII

Taking the Ground of the Heavenly Man

Reading: Col. ii. 16-23; iii. 1-11. Eph. iv. 13-15.

There is one particular application of this whole vast, comprehensive truth which we feel we should stress at this time. It has to do with our taking the ground of the Heavenly Man. Whether you consider Him personally or corporately in the Word, you will see that the one thing which is being pointed out as absolutely necessary, is that the ground of the Heavenly Man shall be taken; that is, that man shall come on to the ground of the Heavenly Man. God has nothing to say to men, nothing to do with them, on any other ground than that of the Heavenly Man. His attitude is that, if you want Him to speak to you, to have anything to do with you, you must come on to His ground, which is that of the Heavenly Man. You have to leave your own ground of nature, whatever be your thought of it, and you have to come on to His ground. You must leave the ground of the earthly man, the fallen Adam, leave natural ground, and come on to the ground of the last Adam, on to heavenly ground, which is spiritual ground.

If you were to take that thought, and begin to read again the Gospel by John, and then go on into the Epistles, especially those of Paul, although it is not confined to them, you would see that this is the one thing all the way through, and it would give you a wonderful opening up of the Word.

Christ the Sole Ground of God's Dealings with Man

We begin, then, by seeing that the Father has set forth the Son as His ground of dealing with men, and He will deal with no man on any other ground: ". . . him the Father, even God, hath sealed" (John vi. 27). Jesus of Nazareth was anointed by God. Now that is God's ground: "This is my beloved Son, in whom I am well pleased" (Matt. iii. 17); "This is my beloved Son . . . hear ye him" (Matt. xvii. 5). He has set forth the Son, and if you want to have anything to do with God at all, if you want Him to have anything at all to do with you, you have to come on to the ground of the Son, the ground of the Heavenly Man. God meets us in Him. God takes up His work with us there on that ground. God carries on His work with us on that ground alone. For all God's interest and activity with us, Christ is the first and the last. He is set forth, sealed, anointed, and there only shall we find an opened heaven.

Referring again to Jacob and his dream, we read: "And he lighted upon a certain place, and tarried there all night. . . . And he dreamed, and behold a ladder set up on the earth, and the top of it reached to heaven; and behold the angels of God ascending and descending on it. And, behold, the Lord stood above it, and said . . ." (Gen. xxviii. 11-13). The Lord took that up, as you remember, with Nathanael, and said: ". . . ye shall see the heaven opened, and the angels of God ascending and descending upon the Son of man" (John i. 51). The Lord communes with man by way of that ladder, which is the Son of Man, and by way of His Son alone; He speaks to us at the end of these times "in His Son, whom He appointed heir of all things." I think it hardly needs stressing that this is where we begin, and this is what the Father has done. He has made the Heavenly Man, His Son, the sole ground upon which to meet man.

The Meaning of the Divine Appointment of the Son

In using the term "Heavenly Man," we are doing something more than just referring to a Divine Person, the Son of God. We are implying a great order of Man, a kind of Man, constituted by all heavenly features, resources, faculties. Everything about this Man is heavenly, and of practical value. Nothing in Him is without meaning, without value. It is something of an applied kind; that is, everything that is in Christ is of use, of heavenly use for us, of heavenly value, of practical meaning. That is why we speak of Him as the Heavenly Man, the kind God has in view. God can only deal with that kind, and that is why we have to leave our own ground and get on to Christ's ground, because God can only deal with that kind. That is what is meant by the so familiar phrase, "Believe on the Lord Jesus Christ . . ." (literally, believe on to the Lord Jesus Christ). This is not the mere taking of an attitude toward Him and saying: Of course I believe Him, I believe He is a perfectly trustworthy one. No! It is the committing of oneself, a stepping on to His ground, taking the ground of the Heavenly Man. Until that is done there is no hope at all. In order to do that, we have to leave our own ground, and that is not so simple as it sounds. It is a life-long education. There may be one act in the beginning, where in that first initial sense we believe on to the Lord Jesus Christ; where we step over on to Him in faith and commit ourselves to Him and trust Him, but for the rest of our lives we shall be learning what it is to leave our own ground and take His. As we do that we come to His fulness, the fulness of the stature of Christ. It is as we learn to leave our own ground and take the ground of the Heavenly Man that this can be. We have plenty of opportunities every day we live in which to do that. It is a life-long course, though there is that initial act in the beginning of which we have spoken.

The Truth Illustrated in the Case of (a) Nicodemus

Take some examples. Nicodemus presents himself to the Lord Jesus as interested in Divine things, interested in what he calls the kingdom of God. He feels that Jesus can tell him something, and give him some information. "Rabbi, we know that thou art a teacher come from God . . ." (John iii. 2). Well, You can tell us something! The Lord does not begin to give him information. He does not begin to satisfy his inquiries, and to open up to him Divine secrets. He makes no response to that inquiry, but He says, in effect: Nicodemus, ruler of the Jews as you are, you have to leave that ground and to come on to another ground altogether; you must be born anew.

As you follow out the meaning of that conversation, and of what the Lord said, you see perfectly clearly that He is only saying in other words, You have to come on to My ground. You must be where I am, before you can know what I know. You want to know what I know. Well, I cannot tell you, but you will know it if you are born again; you will have My heavenly knowledge when you occupy My heavenly ground. You can only occupy My heavenly ground by being born from above as I have been. It is a heavenly man's ground for a heavenly man's knowledge. You must leave your own ground. What, leave my ground? What is wrong with my ground? I am a good, upright Israelite, a faithful teacher of the Law! Yes, but you have to leave that ground, the Lord Jesus would say; I am not now dealing with a man and his standing with the Law, I am dealing with you, Nicodemus, a ruler in Israel; you have to leave your ground and come on to Mine.

That is what is clearly to be inferred from John iii and the same principle can be followed throughout the Gospel. That is the law which is being applied all the way through.

(b) The Inquiring Greeks

You come to chapter xii and you read: "Now there were certain Greeks among those that went up to worship at the feast: these therefore came to Philip . . . and asked him, saying, Sir, we would see Jesus" (John xii. 21). Then the disciples came and told the Lord Jesus that there were certain Greeks wanting to see Him. What did the Lord Jesus reply? Did He say: Very well, I will come and show them Myself! No! "Jesus answereth them, saying, The hour is come, that the Son of man should be glorified. Verily, verily, I say unto you, Except a grain of wheat fall into the earth and die, it abideth by itself alone; but if it die, it beareth much fruit" (verses 23-24). Did they want to see Him? They must come on to His ground. What is that ground? Heavenly ground, resurrection ground. It is not the ground of this creation, but you must needs die to get on to this ground. It is not the ground of this earthly life, but you must die to that. Those Greeks could never "see" Him if their thought of Him were as of someone of interest here on this earth; if they had come to see someone of whom they had heard wonderful things, and were looking for a wonderful man who has been performing miracles; if He were as one of the sights of Jerusalem for which they had come to the feast, one of the people to get into touch with. They must leave that ground altogether, and leave it through death (we will come back to that again presently); then they shall see Him by corporate relationship: ". . . if it die, it beareth much fruit." One corn of wheat turned into an ear—and a harvest. That is how the Lord Jesus can

be known, by our becoming a part of the corporate Heavenly
Man, through death and resurrection. You have to leave the
natural ground if you want to see Him. It is not by the contemplation of Him as a historical figure that you see Him;
you only see Him by resurrection-union with Him, on the
ground of the Heavenly Man.

How true that was with the disciples themselves. He was
with them by the space of three and a half years, and yet
they really did not know Him, and did not "see" Him; but
after He had gone from them, they saw Him and knew Him.
The knowledge was something far transcending that of the
days of His flesh.

(c) Peter and the Gentiles

Come further, over into the early chapters of the book
of the Acts, and you come to that paragraph in the history
of first things in the Church, where Peter has been fasting
and praying. He falls into a trance and sees the heaven
opened and a sheet let down from heaven. In it are all manner of four-footed beasts and creeping things; and a voice
says to him, "Rise, Peter; kill and eat" (Acts x. 13). To this
Peter replied, "Not so, Lord; for I have never eaten anything
that is common and unclean" (verse 14). We know what it
is related to. Away up country there is a devout man with
very little light, reaching out with all his heart to know the
Lord more perfectly, to go on with God; hungry for the Lord,
but not knowing the way. In his reaching out for the Lord,
he is visited by an angel, and told that if he sends to a certain place, at such and such an address, there is a man there
named Peter, who, if he but calls for him to come, will tell
him what he needs to know. Meanwhile in connection with
that man, who is not a Jew, who is not of Israel, and who
is outside the covenant, the Lord is having these dealings
with Peter. Now, to Peter, that man would be as one of those
reptiles, those creeping things, as unclean meat, because he
was outside Israel. Peter says, "Not so, Lord. . . ." Now Peter
must leave that ground. That is his old Jewish ground, and
he must leave it and come on to the ground of the Heavenly
Man. What is the ground of the Heavenly Man? It is that
where there is neither Jew nor Greek, where these distinctions are not to be made. You are not to make these distinc-

tions, Peter! You are not to stand off like this, saying, I am a Jew and he is not a Jew; we have no relationship! Fellowship is the mark of the Heavenly Man, and there these distinctions are lost sight of. You must come off your earthly, historic, traditional ground, Peter, on to the ground of the Heavenly Man.

The Lord made it perfectly clear that Peter had to do it, and that the issues were very serious and critical if he did not. Peter had the grace of obedience to leave his own ground, and he went up to Caesarea and met with one of the greatest surprises of his life in that he found that the Lord was there! He had to report to the other Jewish apostles that, though he had gone with all fear and misgiving, he found the Lord there. Yes, the Lord was on the ground that He Himself had provided, the ground of the Heavenly Man. We shall always meet the Lord on that ground. Leave your own ground, and come on to My ground, and I will meet you there and show you something which will surprise you. So it was in this case: "Who was I, that I could withstand God?" The Lord had given them the Spirit, and I had to get off my ground, and get on to the Lord's ground, the ground of the Heavenly Man.

(d) Paul and Israel

What was true of Peter had to be true of Paul. I think Paul was a long time in getting thoroughly off his own ground. He clung to Israel as long as he could. Other things there were that had quickly become clear, and his going out to the Gentiles had very largely moved him away even from this ground, but he was still clinging to it in measure. That vow, and that going up to Jerusalem which led him into such trouble, was all the fruit of his clinging to Israel, esteeming his brethren after the flesh above others. He did not easily let go. But when at length Paul let go of that ground, then he was able to write the letter to the Ephesians. The letter to the Ephesians is the glorious expression of heavenly ground having been reached in fulness. Is it not that? Ephesians deals with being in the heavenlies in Christ. It speaks of the stature of the fulness of Christ. The full-grown man is the Heavenly Man. At long last he has finally quitted his own ground, that of tradition, nature, birth, natural hope, and now, being on the ground of the Heavenly Man, he has such a fulness to pass on. He says—and it invests these words with such richness when you see what they represent of the position to which he himself has come—"And put on the new man, which after God hath been created in righteousness and holiness of truth" (Eph. iv. 24). On this heavenly ground, there can be neither Jew nor Greek. You must leave the ground of the Jew, leave the ground of the Greek. On this ground there can be neither circumcision nor uncircumcision. You have to leave both those grounds. On this ground there can be neither barbarian nor Scythian, neither bondman nor freeman, but Christ is all, and in all. That is the ground of the Heavenly Man.

All Natural Ground Must Be Forsaken

In this dispensation God is not meeting Jews as Jews, and Gentiles as Gentiles, and a great many are making the mistake of thinking that He is. His Word to the Jew is: You must leave your Jewish ground, and stand before God, not as a Jew, but as a man, and until you take that ground God has nothing to say to you; you will not have any light whilst you persist in coming before God on your own ground. The same has to be said to everyone else. We have to leave our own ground in every way.

As that applies in these directions nationally, it applies in every other thing. Are you going to answer the Lord back: But I am this or that, or something else; or, But I am not this or that. It is not what you are, but what the Son is, that is of account. Come on to His ground. The Lord will not meet you on the ground of what you are, whether it be good or bad; He will meet you on the ground of the Heavenly Man. Do you answer back, I am so weak! The Lord is not going to meet you on that ground; He will meet you on the ground of His Son. That is what the Holy Spirit means by such words as He speaks through Paul: ". . . be strengthened in the grace that is in Christ Jesus" (2 Tim. ii. 1). God hears us exclaim, But I am so weak, Lord! but He does not pay any heed to what we mean to indicate by that confession, which is: Come down on to the ground of my weakness and pick me up! He says, You forsake that ground, and come on to the ground of My Son, and you will find strength there. I am so foolish,

Lord! The Lord says: You will remain foolish until you get on to the ground of My Son, who is made unto you wisdom.

That applies all the way along. We take our own ground before the Lord and are surprised that the Lord does not lift us right out of our own ground and put us into a better position, but He never does. We shall stay there for ever, if that is our attitude. The Lord's word to us is: Forsake your own ground and come on to My ground. I have provided a Heavenly Man who is full of all that you need; now come on to that ground. It does not matter what you are, or what you are not. There everything is adjusted and made good.

The Witness of the Testimonies to the Truth: (a) Baptism

This is the meaning of the testimonies of baptism and the laying on of hands, as mentioned in Hebrews vi. Those testimonies go together. Baptism is, on the one hand, leaving your own ground of nature, dying to your own ground and being buried. So far as your own natural ground is concerned, that is finished with: "Ye died...." You have parted from your own ground of nature. In your baptism, on the other hand, you were raised together with Christ, and you have come on to the ground of Christ, the Heavenly Man. "Having been buried with him in baptism, wherein ye were also raised with him through faith in the working of God, who raised him from the dead." It is thus that the truth of which we have been speaking is set forth in Colossians. And the Apostle goes on to urge the recognition of it. "If ye died with Christ from the rudiments of the world, why, as though living in the world, do ye subject yourselves to ordinances?..." Ye died! Ye died! You are now on other ground, the ground of the Heavenly Man. In resurrection you were raised together with Christ; seek, therefore, those things which are above.

May we just say here, lest some fall into a peril which we recognise in making such a statement, that amongst the things mentioned it says that you died to being under bondage to the Sabbath. That is quite true as a legal thing, as a part of a legal system imposed upon you; you have died to that, and you are no longer in bondage to that. But, mark you, we do not believe that a risen man, a spiritual man, will violate the principle of the Sabbath. We do not believe that a really spiritual man will do that. There is that portion of our time which is the Lord's portion, that which must be set aside for the Lord apart from all other things in the matter of time, that which must give the Lord His place and give a clear space for the Lord's things in our week. It is a settled law of a spiritual character that lies behind the ordinance of the Sabbath. I cannot believe for a moment that a man who is under the government of the Holy Spirit will treat every day alike, and turn the Sabbath day into a day of personal pleasure and gain. The Holy Spirit would check a spiritual man on such a matter, at the same time keeping him free from the legal Sabbath, so that he holds it unto God and not as a part of a legal religious system.

Now we say that in parenthesis to safeguard what has just been expressed against an unwarranted conclusion. Oh, well, I can do as I like because I am not under the Law, someone will say. Oh no ! Not at all! We can have the Holy Ghost now in resurrection, and on the ground of the Heavenly Man we shall be kept right by the Lord in these matters.

You see that baptism sets forth, on the one hand. our having forsaken our own ground of nature, through death, and, on the other hand, our having come on to the ground of the Heavenly Man in resurrection.

(b) The Laying on of Hands

But then we come to the laying on of hands. That immediately follows baptism in the scripture of Heb. vi. What is the significance of the laying on of hands? It witnesses to our coming on to the ground of the corporate Heavenly Man, the one Body, so that in the laying on of hands there is the testimony borne between two or three, or more, by an act of identification, that we are not isolated units, but that we are a collective or corporate body, the corporate Heavenly Man. The ground of the Lord Himself was that of the one Body, that of the corporate Heavenly Man. There is no doubt that it is in that life of oneness in the Spirit, as the life of the Heavenly Man, that we find the greater fulnesses of Christ. There is always something more in two than in one. There is always something more of the Lord in relatedness than in isolation. The Lord indicates this very clearly when by the writer to the Hebrews He says: "Not forsaking the assembling of ourselves together, as the custom of some is, but exhorting one another; and so much the more, as ye see the day drawing nigh" (Heb. x. 25). Why should it be said "as ye see the day drawing nigh"? Because it is the day of the fulness, the day of the consummation. Our coming together "so much the more" in view of that day makes possible the Lord's giving so much the more unto that final fulness. We need it so much the more as we get near the end, and near the beginning of "the day." The ground of the Heavenly Man, personal and corporate, is the ground that we have quite definitely to take.

In Christ, the Heavenly Man, everything lives. The ruling principle of the Heavenly Man is eternal life. Everything lives in Him. We have been saying that in Him the Word of God lives. On the ground of the Heavenly Man, the Word becomes alive. Get on to that ground and you will prove that things are really alive. Forsake your own ground and take His, and you will find life. Put it to the test if you like. If you keep your ground you will die, or you will remain in death. You say: But Lord, I am so weak! Well, stay on that ground and see whether you do not die. Lord, I am so foolish! Well, stay there, and see how much life you enjoy. The realm of "what I am" is the realm of death. And even though it be the other kind of "I" that thinks itself to be something, that is, a certain self-satisfaction, self-fulness, it is death. The ground of "what I am," whatever it may be, is the ground of death. It is not the ground of the Heavenly Man. Get on to the ground of the Heavenly Man and you find life. Forsake your own ground and take His, and it will be life.

If you get upset, offended, and go off and sulk, and nurse your grievance, you will die. Are you expecting the Lord to come out to you there and intreat you: Oh, do not be so upset, do not make so much of it! The Lord will do nothing of the kind. He does not follow us out like that. He says to us: You will have to forsake that ground and come back to My ground! You will die out there! And you know it is not until you get over your huff and come back on to the Lord's ground that you begin to live again. Heavenly things are practical, not mythical. On any other ground than the Lord's ground there is death. If we separate ourselves, forsake that fellowship, that association which is our spiritual relationship in the will of God, we shall begin to lose, and become like Thomas. We are outside, losing ground, and our lives will become small, shrivelled, miserable. The Lord will not go out after a Thomas. The Lord never followed Thomas out. When the other disciples came together and Thomas was not with them, because he was offended, the Lord did not seek him out and say, Come along, Thomas! The Lord met them when they were together, and it was not until Thomas came in where they were that he met the Lord, and came into life, and came to see how silly he had been. Then Thomas fell down and said, "My Lord and my God." That is his confession to having been a fool.

If we separate ourselves and go off for any cause whatever, we shall die. The Lord will not come out to us in life. He will be saying to us all the time: You must forsake that ground and come back again to where I can meet you, to where your life is. That is the ground of the corporate Heavenly Man. The Lord teach us the meaning of that.

CHAPTER XIII

The Corporate Expression of the Heavenly Man

READING: Eph. iii. 17-21, iv. 1-10.

The fact that the Lord Jesus is the Heavenly Man is touched upon at various points in this reading. Here in chapter iv we have the statement that "He ... ascended far above all the heavens ..." while all that follows in the chapter is related to the present expression of the Heavenly Man as here in the world.

We have already noted this feature in John's Gospel; for we have there seen the Heavenly Man in person as both present here in the world and at the same time in heaven. We now meet with it again in Ephesians, but this time in a wider sense; for here we have to do with the corporate expression of the same Heavenly Man in His Body, the Church.

These two are one, not merely by their relatedness, but by their very life; one in their resources, one in their mind, one in their consciousness, one in their nature, one in the laws of their life, one in their purpose, one in their method, one in their times. There is nothing which relates to them as the Heavenly Man in which they are not one. It is not just the oneness that springs from an understanding or an agreement, but that which is the result of being one in substance, one in essence.

Again, we are speaking of Christ as the Heavenly Man, and not of Him as God. In this corporate expression it is not a case of the Body acting for the Head, of the Church acting for the Lord. There is no independence nor separate responsibility. It is the Lord Himself continuing His own life and work in and through His Body; the whole is one Man. Not that the Lord has given up a personal identity and ceased to be a separate person, but as out from His very heavenly manhood He has given His own substance, His own constituents, His own life, to constitute a Body which is so one with Him, in this utter way, as to be part of Himself. That is the

Body of Christ as set forth here. That is the Heavenly Man corporately expressed.

The Body, the Church, was never meant to be something in itself, but from eternity was always intended to be "the fulness of him that filleth all in all." Therefore it has no existence apart from Him, nor has it existence apart from God's purpose in Him. These facts, simple as they are in statement, are very profound, and very searching in their meaning. They govern and determine what the Church is. Nothing which bears the name "Church" (in the New Testament acceptation of that term) and is not the continuation of His Son in this universe, exists in the thought of God.

Now this involves several things, and these are presented in the chapter we have before us.

One Life in Christ

Firstly, this involves the one life that by the Holy Spirit is in all the members of Christ. "There is . . . one Spirit"; "Giving diligence to keep the unity of the Spirit. . . ." There is the one life by the Holy Spirit. Only thus does Christ come to His fulness in His Body, does the Church fulfil the Divine thought for its existence, come to the Divine end.

We have already sought to see how the Heavenly Man in person was in every detail governed by the Spirit, inasmuch as upon such a government depended the fulfilment of the whole revelation of God concerning Him. All the Scriptures which had gone before pointed to Him, and waited for their fulfilment in Him, and He was to be the fulfilment of all those Scriptures to a detail. It would have been an impossible, overwhelming, crushing responsibility to have taken that on mentally, to have felt a consciousness every instant of His life that He was responsible for everything that was written in the Scriptures. To have had that on His mind would have been an intolerable burden impossible of bearing. He would have been the most introspective person that had ever lived. Every moment He would have been asking: Am I doing the right thing? Am I doing it in the right way? Am I doing what I ought to be doing according to that Book, that standard? But His life, being governed by the anointing, being under the control of the Spirit, meant that He spontaneously, and by the inward consciousness that was

His through the Holy Spirit as to what was, and what was not, the mind of God, did fulfil the whole revelation.

Now what was true of Him personally has to be true of Him in the corporate sense. Here is a revelation concerning Jesus Christ which has come out of the eternal counsels of God, a revelation of vast meaning, a destiny, a great spiritual, heavenly system summed up in Him, and which is to be expressed, to be wrought out, to be realised in Him corporately as in Him personally. But how is it possible for us to fulfil it, to realise it, to attain unto it; for it to have its fulfilment and its expression in us? Only on the basis of the one life by Holy Spirit in all. That is what gives force to the exhortation in this very letter to ". . . be filled with the Spirit." That gives the real meaning and value to the whole teaching concerning the Holy Spirit—the receiving of the Spirit, walking in the Spirit, being led by the Spirit—because only so can that which has been produced by the mind of God, concerning His Son, and which is to have its full realisation in the Body of Christ, be reached. How necessary, then, for us all to live in the Spirit. It is not enough that some of us should live in the Spirit; it is important that all should do so, and that none should walk after the flesh.

An Inter-related and Inter-dependent Life

The second thing, which is really a part of the same truths, but with perhaps a rather closer application of it, is the need for a recognition of, and diligence to keep, an inter-related and inter-dependent life. It is something to be recognised first of all, to be taken account of, and then something we are to be diligent to maintain. That is to say, all the members of Christ are related; there is an inter-relationship. We are not so many separate parts, fragments, individuals, we are all related; and not only so, but we are all dependent on one another. For God's end, for God's purpose, we cannot do without one another. On any level other than that we might be able to do without one another. If we were living on any natural level, we could perhaps say of some people, that we could do without them, but when we come into the light of God's purpose, then we are governed by an inter-dependence. We find that we need one another, that we are dependent upon one another, in respect of God's fulness. Of this fact we have a clear indication in the words "strong to apprehend *with all the saints.*" We cannot apprehend apart from the rest. No one of us will ever be able to apprehend the whole. We need the strength of all saints to apprehend with all saints.

This is not only a statement of fact, but a truth by which we are immediately put to the test. Do we say: Well, we have seen the Body of Christ, we have seen the Church! As to whether we have seen that aright, will be proved by whether we realise our inter-dependence. If any one of us should ever take the attitude that we can dispense with another member of Christ, or be of that spirit, such a one has not truly seen the Body of Christ. Maybe there has been a seeing of something, but not the Body of Christ; it has not been seen that this Body is to be the fulness of Christ. For that fulness all saints are needed. The Lord Jesus in His own way, His own parabolic way, was putting His finger upon principles and laws all the time—"See that ye despise not one of these little ones . . ." (Matt. xviii. 10); "Inasmuch as ye did it not unto one of these least . . ." (Matt. xxv. 45). This is not just a community kind of thing, a fraternity; we are face to face with a law, when it is said that it will take all saints to come to, and to express, His fulness. If we have seen the Body of Christ we must have seen the inter-relatedness and the inter-dependence of all members, and must be living on the basis that the Body is one.

The Apostle exhorts to diligence in relation to that. We must recognise that the Body is one, and then give diligence to keep the unity of the Spirit. I expect the Apostle, by the time he wrote his letter, well knew how much diligence that required. He was beginning to see how easy it was for Christians to dispense with one another, to take the attitude that they could do without one another, or without certain ones at any rate; how easy it was for them to fall apart, to take a careless attitude, to be anything but diligent in keeping the unity.

This maintaining of the unity is a positive thing. It represents a being on full stretch for something. It is not just a case of our desiring it, wanting it, of our considering it to be the best thing and even necessary, but of our applying it. It takes application to give diligence to keep the unity of the Spirit.

This is what is meant by being "renewed in the spirit of your mind," which, again, is unto the putting on of the "new man," the corporate Heavenly Man. Thus in the passage before us, the practical exhortation immediately follows: "Wherefore, putting away falsehood, speak ye truth each one with his neighbour: for we are members one of another." The renewing of the spirit of the mind works out in each one speaking truth with his neighbour, in the putting away of all falsehood. Why tell yourself a lie? We would not do that deliberately. What would be the point in my telling myself something that is not true? What would be the sense of my left hand doing my right hand an injury, seeing that ultimately both must suffer? Similarly "we are members one of another." In the other mind, the mind of the old man, which is mentioned here, there is a lack of this sense of corporate life, this inter-dependence, this inter-relationship, where it is recognised that everyone is necessary, indispensable. You can put people off in that realm; you can get rid of them, can gain your end, gain an advantage by just suspending the truth. But here we are dealing with one entity, and that entity must not be conflicting, must not be different things but one thing. We must be renewed in the spirit of our mind by putting on this new corporate Heavenly Man.

These verses are worth our noting again in the light of what we are saying:

"... If so be that ye heard him, and were taught in him, even as truth is in Jesus: that ye put away, as concerning your former manner of life, the old man, which waxeth corrupt after the lusts of deceit; and that ye be renewed in the spirit of your mind, and put on the new man, which after God hath been created in righteousness and holiness of truth. Wherefore, putting away falsehood, speak ye truth each one with his neighbour: for we are members one of another" (Eph. iv. 21-5).

That is the new mind of the "new man," which is renewed in the spirit on the principle, the law, the reality of inter-relatedness and inter-dependence.

I need you; you are indispensable to me. I can never realise my destiny, the purpose of my being, apart from you. What, then, is the point in my telling you lies? If there is someone without whom our destiny, the purpose of our being, our whole objective is impossible, is lost, and, in the face of such a fact, a deceptive, lying relationship, what a contradiction! That is the force of the words here. "We are members one of another," therefore we must have a one mind; and speaking truth one with another is a mark of the "new man," the Heavenly Man who has only one mind. Lies all speak of contrary minds.

Gifts in Christ

The third thing that this implies is that for the progressive realisation and expression of this Heavenly Man in time and in eternity, the heavenly Head has given gifts.

"When he ascended on high, he led captivity captive, and gave gifts unto men. (. . . He that descended is the same also that ascended far above all the heavens, that he might fill all things.)" Eph. iv. 8-10.

There is the Heavenly Man in person as the heavenly Head, giving gifts among men for the progressive realisation and expression of Himself as the corporate Heavenly Man.

Now we must break that up and look at this parenthesis in verses 9 and 10. It carries with it this fact that He descended before He ascended. He did not have His beginnings here. Of course we know that, but this is the argument of the Apostle; His origin was not here. By His ascending it is to be understood that He first descended. There is the Heavenly Man coming down and being here among men, the Heavenly Man in incarnation; He came down out of heaven. Having descended, He ascended, that He might fill all things. The whole universe is to be filled with the Heavenly Man.

Now you have to get that background before you can understand and appreciate what follows about these gifts. In relation to that filling of all things by the Heavenly Man, there is to be the increase of the Body. This chapter is all of a piece. Christ is not here as separated from His Body. Here the Heavenly Man in person and the corporate Heavenly Man are brought together as one in purpose. Earlier in the letter the Apostle has shown how before times eternal, in the thought of God, this Heavenly Man has come out of heaven to be found here, but whilst here, is still in heaven.

Now He personally is to be the universal fulness, and that fulness is to be by the Church: ". . . glory in the church and in Christ Jesus unto all generations, unto the ages of the ages." In relation to that universal filling there is to be this increase of the Body: ". . . in whom each several building, fitly framed together, *groweth* into a holy temple in the Lord. . . ." In the letter to the Colossians there is a very similar word:

> ". . . And not holding fast the Head, from whom all the body, being supplied and knit together through the joints and bands, increaseth with the increase of God" (Col. ii. 19).

He is to fill all things by His Body, which is His fulness. Then the Body must grow, the Body must make increase, the Body must add to its stature, until it comes to the full measure of Christ. Now with a view to this increase, the heavenly gifts are given by the Heavenly Man to this heavenly Body.

Then I want you to notice another thing. These gifts are themselves a measure of Christ: "But unto each one of us was the grace given according to the measure of the gift of Christ" (Eph. iv. 7). The gifts are a measure of Christ, and therefore they are all intended to produce the fulness of Christ, to lead to that fulness. In their own way they represent a fulness of Christ ministered in the Body. They are to make up the full measure.

Having seen that, we are able to look at the gifts mentioned.

Authority in Christ

"And he gave some apostles . . ." (it does not say "to be" apostles). Then we need to know what the apostle represents as a measure of Christ. What is his value in bringing the fulness of Christ by way of the Body, the Church, the corporate Heavenly Man? It is impressive to recognise that the apostle stands first on account of the value associated with the apostle. What are apostles? There is one word which expresses the meaning of apostles, and that word is "authority." Authority comes first.

We know that grammatically speaking the word means "one sent." But look again to see its signification in the Word of God. Take the word wherever you find it and see what is in it. Look, for example, at the parable of the house-holder who planted a vineyard. He sent unto them his servants to receive of the fruit. They came with his authority, and the wicked husbandmen, in slaying the servants, wholly repudiated the master's authority. You see, the application to Israel there is so piercing. The point of the parable is that they were refusing to acknowledge the authority of God in Christ. When the owner of the vineyard comes himself to deal with the situation he will miserably destroy the husbandmen. On what ground will he do this? Because he did not get his own personal gratification in the fruits? No! Because they had refused to recognise his authority in his son—". . . he sent unto them his son. . . ." Wherever you find the "sent" of the Lord, you find the authority of the Lord. That is an apostle.

As you carefully consider the matter of apostleship, you will see that everything that constituted an apostle represented what made for authority. An apostle was a specially constituted servant of the Lord. There was a very rigid Law governing apostleship (so far as the Twelve were concerned), that an apostle must have seen the Lord in resurrection. He could not be an apostle if the Lord had not appeared unto him, for he had not had first-hand knowledge of the risen Lord. That first-hand knowledge of the risen Lord invested him with an authority. It was a matter of the Lord having Himself appeared unto him.

If you turn to the letter to the Hebrews you will find that the Lord Jesus is spoken of as God's Apostle and High Priest. The very phrase at once carries us back in thought to the writings of Moses, and we mark how it combines what God has set forth in Moses and Aaron respectively. Moses as the apostle, and Aaron as the high priest, represent two aspects of the Lord Jesus. Moses represents authority. From the beginning of God's using of Moses, right to the end, Moses represented the authority of God. The rod which was Moses' rod, became the rod of God, and by that rod the authority of God was displayed. The authority of God was so much vested in him that God was able to say to him, regarding Aaron, ". . . thou shalt be to him as God" (Exod. iv. 16).

We see later how that worked out. When there were those who tried to displace Moses, or tried to take an equal place with him, see how the authority found expression. Moses never had to fight for his position. When the dispute arose touching his position, being the meekest of men, he just said to the Lord, in effect: Lord, am I here by Your authority, or am I not? Have I grasped this position? Have I sought authority, or have You put me here with it? I count on You to let it be known whether my position is of my own taking, or whether of Your appointing. The Lord called the people to the door of the tabernacle and took up the case of Moses, and you know what happened. It was because of what he represented as an apostle.

"All authority hath been given unto me in heaven and on earth. Go ye therefore . . ." (Matt. xxviii. 18). Thus an apostle is one who stands in Divine authority for the setting up, and the carrying on, of the Divine testimony. You can see that in Moses. The Lord appeared unto Moses and spake with him face to face. No one else came into that realm. Even though they came up into the Mount, they did not come into exactly the same place as Moses. It was with Moses that the Lord communed and spake as a man speaks to his friend, face to face. Then for ever after, the one thing that governs Israel is this: ". . . as the Lord spake unto Moses. . . ." At the end of the constituting of the tabernacle, there is a whole chapter in which some seven or eight times this one phrase occurs: ". . . as the Lord commanded Moses." It speaks of authoritative government by what had come in through Moses, God's apostle. Well, in that authority he set up the testimony, and maintained it; the authority was his to that end.

Or, again, take the Apostle Paul, who perhaps above all others stands out as an apostle, and you see that his commission and his authority was, first of all, for the setting up of the testimony everywhere, and then for the maintaining of the testimony. He says to the Corinthians that, if he comes to them in the authority that he has received, it will go ill with some of them, because he is invested with this authority to maintain the testimony in purity.

Now what does this say to us? It is the Lord! This is the factor of Christ's heavenly authority in the corporate

Heavenly Man. That may be administered through individuals. The point is that it is a feature of the Heavenly Man, and is active in the Church. We are face to face with the fact that Christ in His heavenly authority is in the Church for the setting up of His testimony, and the maintaining of it. Where the Lord's testimony is by the Holy Ghost, there the authority of the Lord is, and people have to reckon with that.

Of course, while we have to take these things to heart in our own personal lives, we are saying them as to those who have to instruct others. As the Lord's servants, you cannot have too clear a recognition of how definite is this operation of the authority of Christ in His Body. None can anywhere come into relationship with that corporate expression of Christ, which is constituted by the Holy Ghost, without becoming responsible for the Lord's testimony which is there, and if you violate it you suffer. You cannot just attach yourself, and escape the implications. If you make a breach of the testimony, of the oneness of the Body of Christ, when you have been brought into real touch with it, and do not put that right, you will die. You may die physically. You may have a tragic end. You will undoubtedly go through sufferings and chastening; because you have not become a member of a movement, something merely of man; you have come into the place where the custodianship of eternal purpose is invested in the Holy Ghost working in the spirit of apostleship, and the authority of Christ is there. This is the precise meaning of those searching words in the first letter to the Corinthians: "For this cause many among you are weak and sickly, and not a few sleep." "Not discerning the Lord's body" (I Cor. xi. 30). You have come into a realm where things are not to be taken as mere doctrine, as an organisation, as something of man with which you can do as you like; you have to come to the place where the authority of Christ is an operating reality. It is a terrible thing to get into the House of God if you are not of a mind to become suitably conformed.

That is one side, and a terrible side. But there is another side that makes for heart rest and assurance for those who carry extra responsibility in the house of God, where it is possible to say: "Well, we have not to bear the full responsibility that properly is in the hands of the Holy Ghost, in the authority of Christ, to meet that which is contrary to the truth, and to the law of the house of God." We need not be anxious, in that sense, because it is our responsibility. The heavenly Lord has put a functioning of His authority in the Church. There may be a disputing of that authority in the vessel. Hell may dispute, as at Philippi, or at Ephesus, or many another place, and may show its hand in vehement antagonism and resistance. But what is the issue? Every time the authority of Christ triumphs.

The establishment of the testimony throughout the Roman Empire through the Apostle Paul, is a marvellous manifestation of the supreme Lordship of Jesus Christ over all powers. It is not just a case of getting the better of man's mentality, of overcoming prejudice and difficulties amongst men; it is the conquest of the evil forces of hell. Cosmic forces are beaten and broken when the testimony is established through an apostle. It is the fact of Christ's heavenly authority in the Body, by the Spirit. Christ truly expressed in the assembly really cannot be set aside without suffering.

The Mind of God in Christ

Now what are the prophets in the assembly? In a word, the prophet is the instrument for the expression of the mind of the Lord, and this is usually set over against the expression of the mind of man. Of very great moment is the injunction we have noted already, ". . . be renewed in the spirit of your mind. . . ." Because, in the corporate Heavenly Man, the Body, the mind of the Lord is to predominate, to operate, to be supreme. The Lord's mind is the only mind in this "new man," this Heavenly Man. You must be renewed in the spirit of your mind, if you are to come to the Lord's mind. The Lord's mind comes through an instrument called a prophet. He is the interpreter of the mind of the Lord. He brings into the Body the knowledge of the mind of the Lord. That, as we have said, involves the setting aside of the mind of man.

We are thinking, of course, of how the Old Testament prophets are a source of confirmation of what we have just said; for if you examine the point, you will find that they come before the people in relation to the rights of God in His House. Those rights were being set aside by His people. The mind of man was taking the place of the mind of God, and that worked out usually to very great evil, so that before long the very rights of God were denied Him in His own House, amongst His own people.

Take Elijah as an example. Elijah stands out pre-eminently amongst the prophets in relation to the rights of God, and Carmel is the great crisis as to Baal's rights and God's rights in Israel. Elijah is the instrument for establishing the rights of God in an utter way, unto the complete destruction of that other mind, represented in the prophets of Baal. Those rights are expressed in terms of God's mind for His people, and so all the prophets bring in the mind of God, interpret it, keep the mind of God before God's people, and do battle in relation to it, that God shall have His place, have things according to His mind.

This, again, is a functioning of the Heavenly Man in His Body, to keep things according to the mind of God. We are not thinking, at the moment, particularly of people whom we may think to call prophets amongst us. We are not thinking of office, but of function. Vital functioning is what is before us, and anyone who is anointed and endowed by the Holy Spirit to keep God's thoughts clear in the midst of His people, to make His people know the mind of God, so that God gets His place and His rights, and all other minds are set aside, is fulfilling the ministry of a prophet. We are so apt to start at the other end, with the technical line of things, that of appointing prophets. Let us look at the function, not the man, and let us see that it is Christ who is the Prophet, and that in this character He ministers through some whom He gives for the expression of the Divine mind as in Himself. It is quite possible to combine these functions in one individual.

The Heart of God in Christ

Now what are the evangelists? In a word, the evangelist is the one to make God known through the Gospel, to disclose the heart of God in grace, and the function of the evangelist is to secure material for the expression of the Heavenly Man corporately. Thus we begin with authority in Christ, Christ in the place of supreme authority far above all heavens. Then we have the mind of God in Christ. Here we have the heart of God in Christ. The Gospel of grace is to secure increase by gathering material for the corporate Heavenly Man.

Resources of God in Christ

We now come to the pastors and teachers. These two are brought together. The material is being gathered, the corporate Heavenly Man is being progressively brought into being and coming to His eternal completeness. Now while the material is being gathered, and the corporate Heavenly Man is being progressively brought together, the next need is for pastors and teachers, and the function here is that of the adjustment and fitting of that Heavenly Man. Adjustment is brought about by teaching, by instruction. The purpose of the instruction is to adjust us, to bring us into our place, into our right relationship, to bring us into an understanding of Christ, of our relationship to Him, and of our relationship to one another in Him. The instruction has to do with such matters as the believer's resources in Christ, and all that is signified by the Heavenly Man. This is the work of the teacher. The pastor is one whose function is to fit, to shepherd, to nurture. Building up by right adjustment to revealed truth is what we have here.

But all does not end there. The apostle, the prophet, the evangelist, the pastor and teacher, are given in order that the corporate Heavenly Man, deriving the values of these functions, shall itself minister to its mutual building up; for the making complete of the saints unto the work of the ministry, unto the building up of the Body of Christ. Mutual building up, mutual ministry, is to result from these gifts. Because we are receiving the benefits of this ministration in Christ to us, we have to make those benefits a mutual ministration, so that the Body builds itself up, increases with the increase of God, each separate part in due measure making increase.

If this sounds like technique to you, may we urge you to get away from teaching, and anything like a system of truth, and get the Lord in view. Keep the Lord Himself in view, and see that the one thing which governs all is Christ's coming into ever greater fulness of life and expression in this universe by means of the Church which is His Body.

CHAPTER XIV

I. Judas—The Indwelling of Satan in Its Outworking
II. The Heavenly Man—The Indwelling of God

READING: John xiii. 21-33; Eph. iii. 17-19; Col. i. 25-27.

We are to view the Lord Jesus in relation to the first Adam, and all that came in through that which happened with the first Adam in his fall, not only as this has reference to man and his condition, but to all that which Adam's act of disobedience let into this universe, and into this world. That act of disobedience opened the door at which the forces of evil were standing, waiting for access. Adam was that door. They could never have got in but for Adam, but he opened the door by his disobedience, and the forces of evil rushed into God's creation, and took up a position of great strength, to bring about in it a state of things contrary to God, and that in the most powerful and terrible way. To all of that, to the powers themselves, and the state brought about through their being let in, and all the consequences thereof, the Lord Jesus was, and is, God's answer. But there was a secret about Him, a secret which spiritual intelligences alone could really discern, and this was that God was in Him. He was a Man, but He was far more than that; He was God. In these meditations our concern has been with what the Lord Jesus is as Son of Man, God's Man, the Heavenly Man, in whom God was, and is. That secret, that mystery hidden from the ages, hidden from men, is the greatest factor to be reckoned with.

So far as the enemy was concerned, his main objective with the Lord Jesus was to seek to get in between Him and that Divine relationship; to drive a wedge in and in some way to get Him to move on a ground apart from that inner, deepest reality of the Father. The meaning of the temptations in the wilderness is that they were an attempt to drive that wedge in between, to get Him to act apart from the Father, to move on His own human ground. The enemy knew quite well that, if only he could succeed in getting Him to do that, he would accomplish with the last Adam what he had accomplished with the first, and would have re-established his dominion and again gained the mastery. The secret of Christ's victory was that He was so one with the Father, that in everything He was governed by the Father within, dwelling in Him. The life of the Heavenly Man, the Son of Man, again and again bids us heed the question that once came from His own lips: "Believest thou not that I am in the Father, and the Father in me?" (John xiv. 10, 11). It was on that basis that He lived His life and met the enemy, and because He remained on that basis the enemy was incapable of destroying Him.

Many times attempts were made by the Devil to destroy Him, both directly and through men, but it was impossible while He remained on that basis, and this He did right to the end, and triumphed because of that inward relationship, that upon which He was living deliberately, consciously, persistently: the Father was in Him, and He and the Father were one; He dwelt in the Father, and the Father dwelt in Him.

But—and this is one of the main points that we want the Lord to show us at this time—that was the great secret, the wonderful secret which men could not read; for He Himself said, ". . . no one knoweth who the Son is, save the Father . . ." (Luke x. 22). John, writing his epistle long years after, said, ". . . the world knoweth us not, because it knew him not" (I John iii. 1). The world knew Him not. In His own prayer recorded by John, we have these words: "O righteous Father, the world knew thee not, but I knew thee . . ." (John xvii. 25). It was on the basis of the secret relationship that there was to be a glorifying of Him. The glorifying of the Lord Jesus was bound up with that secret.

Now we want to know what the glorifying of the Son is, the glorifying of the Heavenly Man. We will again first take up the question in relation to the Heavenly Man in person, and then see how the same thing applies to the corporate Heavenly Man.

"When therefore he was gone out, Jesus saith, Now is the Son of man glorified, and God is glorified in him; and God shall glorify him in himself, and straightway shall he glorify him" (John xiii. 31-32).

We need not be concerned for the moment with the form of the statement. It sounds a little involved and difficult, but let us take the central comprehensive statement: "Now is the Son of man glorified, and God is glorified in him. ..." It is upon the word "now" that everything hangs, and the Lord Jesus put into that little word a tremendous meaning. To what does that word relate? "When therefore he (Judas) was gone out, Jesus saith, *Now* is the Son of Man glorified."

The Rejected Natural Man

I confess that Judas was a problem to me for many years, but I think I am getting near the truth about him, and this passage seems to give us the clue. The problem, of course, has its occasion in the statement of the Lord Jesus that He knew whom He had chosen: "Did not I choose you the twelve, and one of you is a devil?" (John vi. 70). He chose Judas and brought him into association with Himself, in such a way that he had all the advantages of the others and all the facilities that were theirs; all the benefits of the others were open to him. There is no trace of partiality. He has placed Judas apparently upon exactly the same footing, excluding him from nothing which was open to the rest, all deliberately, consciously, knowing what He was doing, and knowing all the time what Judas was. Then all finally heads up to this statement, "Now is the Son of man glorified. ..."

I do not know how best to put it, and wish I had language and wisdom to express this, that would capture your hearts as it has captured mine; for I am inwardly glorying in what is brought to us here. To begin with, this represents the full development of man under the kindness of God: ". . . for he maketh his sun to rise on the evil and the good, and sendeth rain on the just and the unjust" (Matt. v. 45). God has shown no partiality amongst men. He has made it possible for all men to enjoy His benefits. He has shown unbelieving, Godless, rebellious men great kindness. He has not discriminated. All men may know His kindness and His goodness. Man is thus represented in Judas, who in this figurative way is here set in relation to the Lord, so that what is available to those who are really the Lord's is available to him; He can come into it, it is open to him. The Lord has not shown any partiality. Yet man, living under the beneficent, merciful and gracious will, purpose, thought, and desire of God, can develop to this.

Let us seek to explain that. Man has been tried under every condition from the beginning. First of all he was tried under innocence. How did he behave? He failed. Then in his fallen state he was tried again, without law. How did he get on? He failed again. Then he was tried under law, but failed as before. Man has failed under every condition. He has been tried by God in every state and appointment, and has utterly failed. The end has always been a tragedy. No matter what attitude God takes toward man, in himself he is a failure and will work out to the most dreadful tragedy.

Look at Israel. What is the attitude of the Lord toward Israel? How marvellous is the way the Lord dealt with Israel. Look at the patience of God with Israel, the kindness of God with Israel, the ground upon which Israel was set before Him. In effect, God said: You have only to show something of faithfulness to Me and you will immediately receive blessing. Some of us have wished we could get blessing as instantly as Israel did when they were true to the Lord. They were subjects of such special care, but they failed. Their condition and treatment is figuratively set forth in the unprofitable fig-tree, that bore no fruit in spite of years of care. Justice demanded that it be cut down without delay, but still further opportunity is given: "Let us dig about it and dung it this year also." Let us show kindness for another year! But it is just as big a failure. So man, tried under every condition, brought into touch with the beneficent will of God, is yet a failure.

Judas gathers up man, man to whom is open all that God has, man who is brought into touch with all the good and perfect will of God, and yet in himself the most awful failure; for this man, when he comes to his fulness, will betray his Lord, he is so hopeless. Man in himself, even though the mercies of God may go out to him, will arrive at this. This is a fearful end. "Yea, mine own familiar friend . . . which did eat of my bread," says the Psalmist, "hath lifted up his heel against me" (Ps. xli. 9). Thus will this man do amidst the very wealth of the grace of God.

Here is Judas representing one who has been brought into touch with the Lord, and to whom all the blessings are open that are open to the rest of the Lord's own, and this is how he turns out. It is a picture of man in himself. Is it not true? The full development of old Adam, of the first Adam, in whom God does not dwell, is here shown to us. Just at the point where this man is surrounded with all the advantages, all the facilities, all the blessings, all the opportunity, all that could have been his, just at that point he goes out to betray his Lord: ". . . and it was night" (John xiii. 30). There is a world of meaning in that.

The Heavenly Man of God's Election

Instantly that man has gone out the Lord Jesus says, "Now is the Son of man glorified. . . ." What does this mean? This is God's answer to all that. God has another Man, whose path is to be wholly different from that tragedy, that dark calamity, a Son of Man who can be glorified. God has prepared His own Man to take the place of this other man, as soon as he has reached his end: and what an evil end it is! Do you see what is signified in the end of Judas? When he goes out God brings in His Man who can be glorified.

Do you see why the Lord Jesus chose Judas? Do you see why it is that when he was gone out Jesus said, "Now is the Son of man glorified"? There is the one who represents the Adam man and what he comes to in spite of all God's grace and mercy which is at his command. Until there is something in him other than himself, that is what he comes to. And just when that nature, that man, that race is seen in its full awfulness, its full outworking, lifting its heel in treachery against the God of all grace; just when that man reaching fulness goes out into the dark, the eternal night, God begins His new day by bringing in His new Man to take his place.

What is the secret? What kind of man will be glorified? We have seen the man who cannot be glorified, who goes out into the darkness. What kind of man is he who can be glorified? What is the principle and secret of His glorifying? It is that God is in him. What is the glorifying of the Lord Jesus? It is the breaking forth and manifesting of the Father in Him, of that secret which makes Him other than the type represented by Judas. The hope of glory in His case, the certainty of glory, was the Father dwelling in Him. "Now is the Son of man glorified, and God is glorified in him. . . ." That is a full-orbed statement about the glorifying of the Son of Man. It is remarkable that this statement should be found in the Gospel by John, in which the Lord Jesus is pre-eminently set forth as the Son of God.

The Glorifying of the Corporate Heavenly Man

Now, of course, we come to feel the benefit and the power of this, when it is transferred from the personal Heavenly Man to the corporate Heavenly Man. So the Apostle says: "That Christ may dwell in your hearts through faith . . ." (Eph. iii. 17); ". . . Christ in you, the hope of glory . . ." (Col. i. 27). We read at the beginning of the letter to the Ephesians that we are ". . . a habitation of God in the Spirit" (ii. 22). What does this mean in its value and out-working? This Body, so created and living upon that fact, is as indestructible as Christ Himself, is as certain of victory as was Christ. On the principle that Christ dwells in the heart by faith, this Body can enter into wrestling with principalities and powers, world rulers of this darkness, spiritual hosts of wickedness in the heavenlies, and come out victor on the field.

What is the secret of the glorifying of the Church, His Body, the corporate Man, and what is the nature of the glorifying? It is the same thing. It is the manifestation of the secret, the coming out from secrecy into open display of that which is true, of Christ within. During the course of this dispensation, the secret is in the Church, in the members of Christ, but ". . . the world knoweth us not, because it knew him not" (I John iii. 1). Looked at from the outside we are very little different from any other people in the world. Yet the secret is there, and this secret means that if you touch that one, or that church, you touch God. "Saul, Saul, why persecutest thou me?" said the Lord, when Saul was touching His members. He is in His members. You have to reckon with Him. They are indestructible, they cannot be destroyed.

We are not talking about the destroying of the body. The true Church is an indestructible entity. When Satan has done his worst, that Church will still stand triumphant, and will abide for ever, when he and all his shall have been banished from the universe.

At the end of this dispensation which has held this hidden secret, there will be an unveiling of the Christ in His Church, when it appears with Him in glory, and it will be glorified on the same principle as that on which He was glorified.

The Essential Basis of the Believer's Everyday Life

Now, there is something that we have to take to our own hearts out of these inclusive factors. We have to live all the time on this basis that we have set forth, and as we do so the enemy's power is absolutely rendered nil. Our trouble is that we do not live upon this basis. We live so much upon ourselves. We live upon our own feelings, our own conditions, our own state, anything and everything that is ourselves, and because we do that we are simply played with by the Devil. When we get into our own mood, what a mess he makes of us. When we get into our own feelings, or our own thoughts what havoc there is. Anything that is ourselves, if we get into that, and live on that, will give the enemy an opportunity to do as he likes. Whenever believers get down into themselves, on to the ground of what they are, if it is only for a moment, they begin to lose their balance, their poise, their rest, their peace, their joy, and they are tossed about of the Devil at his will. They may come to the place where they even wonder whether they are saved. Let us remember that the part of us which still belongs to the fallen creation, and will not survive, is the playground of the enemy, and it is of no use our trying to make it survive.

We have, for instance, a physical life. Within the compass of this natural, physical life as a part of the old creation, anything is possible. Mental darkness is possible. The upsetting of our nervous system can be of such a kind as to make us feel that hell rages in our very being. Anything is possible of moods, and feelings, and sensations, or of utter deadness and numbness, and if we live in that realm the Devil plays havoc. He encamps upon such things at once, if we take our natural condition as the criterion. There is no hope of glory in that natural realm.

How is the enemy to be defeated, to be nullified, to be robbed of his power? On the same principle as in the life of the Lord Jesus, by our living on the Father. We must live on the indwelling Christ. Our attitude will have to be continually toward the Lord: Lord, in me Thou art other than I am; Thou art not what I am; Thou art other than this mood, than this feeling, than this absence of feeling; Thou art other than all these thoughts, other than I am! I am dead, so far as my feelings are concerned, but Thou art other than that, Thou art living! I am feeling dark, Thou art the light, and Thou art in me! This is me, this is not the Lord! If only you and I will learn steadily (it will take time, it will be progressive) to live on in Christ, on what He is, on the fact that He is other than we are—not upon our experience of this, but the naked fact that He is within us—if we will steadily learn to live on that basis, by that great Divine reality, then the enemy has nothing in us. The Lord Jesus was able to say, ". . . the prince of the world cometh; and he hath nothing in me . . ." (John xiv. 30). What was the adversary looking for? He was looking for the Lord Jesus to be living somewhere in Himself, consulting His own feelings, leaning to His own understanding, following His own judgments, His own will. If we could have caught Him there, he would have had something in Him and disturbed the balance of His life. The Lord Jesus was able to say, ". . . I live because of the Father . . ." (John vi. 57); I live by the Father, not on what I am. He could say that as a perfect, sinless being, living none the less in dependence upon the Father all the time. Of this we have His own testimony: "The Son can do nothing of himself . . ." (John v. 19); ". . . the words that I say unto you I speak not from myself: but the Father abiding in me doeth his works" (John xiv. 10). He lived all the time on the basis of the Father dwelling within, and because of that the enemy had no ground whatever.

This is the lesson of life for us. For any glory within now, or for any hope of glory in the great day of the manifestation, the sole ground of expectation must be Christ in us; because the glory is simply the manifestation of the Father within.

The Church, a Mystery of a Divine Indwelling

Now concerning the corporate expression of this Heavenly Man, in the letter to the Ephesians the Apostle tells us that something is going on in the unseen, the purpose of which is stated thus: ". . . that now unto the principalities and the powers in the heavenly places might be made known through the Church the manifold wisdom of God. . . ." I wonder what that means? I do not know altogether, but I think I can see something of what it means. I believe the unseen intelligences are watching to see how they can get an advantage. They are watching with all their cunning, their diabolical wit and wisdom and ingenuity, with all their superhuman intelligence, to see how they can get an advantage, how they can make a stroke, if by any means they can get the upper hand of this baffling creation, the Church. Unto the principalities and powers the manifold wisdom of God is being made known by the church. How is this being accomplished? A clause from a verse in the first letter to Timothy will, I think, help us towards the answer. "And without controversy great is the mystery of godliness; He who was manifested in the flesh, justified in the spirit, seen of angels, preached among the nations, believed on in the world, received up in glory." A part of the mystery here spoken of is this somewhat obscure statement that He was "seen of angels." I cannot be satisfied with the thought that this just means that the heavenly angels saw Him, either when He was in the flesh, or after His resurrection. This seems to say to my heart (of course I cannot prove it, but I am comparing scripture with scripture, and taking into account that it is the Holy Spirit who has disclosed this fact and brought it to our knowledge) that these other angels, these spiritual intelligences who had watched for a chance against His life, seeking an advantage, using their cunning, saw now who He was, saw the full meaning of His being, and why they had never succeeded in compassing their design, but had been compelled to learn their impotence regarding Him. They know now, because the secret is out. This Man is other than the first Adam; He is different from the first Adam! They got their chance with the first Adam and they took it, and into that race they brought the diabolical wisdom of which the Apostle says, "This wisdom is . . . devilish [demoniacal]" (Jas. iii. 15).

These intelligences had been waiting for an opportunity to bring in their wisdom in this other Adam, this last Adam, and they could not get it. They were beaten and defeated at every point, and now the secret is out, and they see One over whom they could gain no advantage. Why was this? Because of the Father dwelling in Him. It is to this same truth that Paul refers when He says that Christ crucified, so far from being the wisdom of this world, is the wisdom of God. His wisdom far transcends the wisdom of this world, which in its nature is demoniacal. God is still further displaying His manifold wisdom to principalities and powers through the Church, the Body of Christ, the corporate Heavenly Man. How is this being accomplished? By the mystery of Christ within, defeating their every plan, their every scheme, by the great reality of the indwelling Lord whose wisdom is so much greater than theirs.

Oh that we could live upon the great reality, the great essential, the great secret of the very being of the Church according to God's mind, that basic secret of Christ within; not upon what we are at any time, but what Christ is. If you take that position you will be in a position of wisdom that outwits all the cunning of the Devil, and outmatches all his power.

Put it to the test; for it is open to practical proof at any time. If when you are next feeling desperately bad and hopeless and full of evil in yourself, as though all that you had believed in no longer held water and everything had gone to pieces, and all the sensations are upon you that it is possible for one to have, till you could well believe that you are lost; if, when this is so, you will take the position that it is all to do with your poor, broken down creation, and that Christ in you is other than that, and by faith stand on Him, the Devil's power is destroyed, his wisdom is outwitted, and there is glory. That is the lesson we have to learn. Christ in you, and in the Church as the habitation of God through the Spirit, is the symbol of glory, of victory, of power and wisdom. Blessed be God, there are seasons when this reaches out to our feelings and we enjoy the realisation that the Lord is in us, but it is not always so. An attack of indigestion can

—152—

have the strangest effect upon our spiritual life, so far as our consciousness is concerned. The slightest little thing can come along and change the whole situation if we allow ourselves to go out into *things*. What things the enemy puts up, to draw us out into them! He is busy setting traps everywhere, contriving situations all round us, always ready with something to upset us. How cleverly arranged it is, just at the time when we are least wanting to be upset. Go home from a time with the Lord amongst His people, feeling gloriously uplifted, and probably when you get across the doorstep there is something waiting for you!

How are you going to outwit the Devil, outmanoeuvre him, defeat him? By not going out into things. It is not easy; but not to go out into things, not to be drawn into the realm of the old creation so as to become involved in it, but to stand upon the ground that the adversary has to meet the perfection of Christ, is the sure way of his defeat, though we may have to bear with the difficult situation, and endure the pain and pang of it for quite a considerable time. But our position is that Christ is more than that, Christ in us is stronger than that, and falling back upon faith within, reaching out to Christ within as equal to this situation, we must repudiate it. David comes to our rescue so much in this realm. You will remember that on one occasion he was saying all sorts of depressing, hopeless things because the situation looked so utterly impossible; and then he recollected himself and said, "This is my infirmity; but I will remember the years of the right hand of the Most High" (Ps. lxxvii. 10). To-day I have blue spectacles on! This is my way of viewing things! This is how things affect me! This is me, it is not the Lord! Let us attribute things to their right quarter, and give to Caesar the things that are Caesar's, and to God the things that are God's.

I am certain that here is the key to everything; the key to everything is Christ in you, Christ in me, Christ in His Body, and that to be lived upon by faith. It is the key to the superior wisdom, to outwit and outmatch the enemy. He will be defeated if we live on Christ and refuse to live on our own ground. The Lord make it clear to us.

CHAPTER XV

The Man Whom He Hath Ordained

READING: Rom. viii. 29; Gal. iv. 19; Eph. ii. 15-16; I Cor. i. 24-30; xii. 13; Gal. iii. 27-28; Acts xvii. 31.

"Inasmuch as he hath appointed a day, in the which he will judge the world in righteousness by the man whom he hath ordained; whereof he hath given assurance unto all men, in that he hath raised him from the dead" (Acts xvii. 31).

The words "the man whom he hath ordained" take us back to the point where we commenced our contemplation of things, into the counsels of God before times eternal. It was then that the Man was ordained. The history of this world, then, is to be gathered up, to be summed up in that Man; its destiny is to be determined in Him.

Let us make a few comprehensive, and yet quite concrete statements in relation to this fact.

Firstly, *God's explanation of the universe is a Man.* If we want to know the meaning of the universe, we must look at a Man: and if we look at that Man whom He hath ordained, and see Him with the eyes of our hearts enlightened, through a spirit of wisdom and revelation in the knowledge of Him, we shall see Him as God's explanation of the universe.

Secondly, *God's answer to everything that has resulted from Adam's fall is a Man.* That is comprehensive. It is quite beyond our working out; but it does not matter at what point you touch the outcome of Adam's fall, or what phase of the result you touch, you will find that God answers in a Man, in this Man. You may take any one of the issues of the Fall as you see them expressed at different points, representing a state full of difficulty, full of complexity, full of tragedy apparently, and ask, How is this to be dealt with, to be remedied? God's answer is a Man, and this Man whom He hath ordained.

I do not want to launch out upon a course of illustration, but I will give you one example of what I mean by this. Take Babel. Now Babel is a problem: the scattering of the people, the confounding of the language, and all the result of Babel in nations and diversities of tongues, with all the weakness that issues from that—a determined and intended weakness—is a problem of considerable magnitude. It was a sovereign act of God, against a certain kind of strength which would take charge of the world apart from God. But Babel itself represents a very big problem, and a complex state of things, as being in itself something which God never intended. It is the outworking of the Fall, and the expression of a curse. It has to be dealt with. The whole thing has to be cleared up. It can never abide if God is to have things as He intended. What is the answer to Babel? It is a Man. It is this Man. All that situation, that confusion, that tragedy, that evil, will be eventually cleared up in a Man. There will be in that Man a unity of all that is divided and scattered. There will be in that Man a coming to one understanding. We have the earnest of all this now in Christ. There is such a thing as spiritual misunderstanding, and it does not matter whether we can understand one another in our human language or not, we can all understand by the Holy Spirit the same thing, and speak an inward language. There is a oneness of understanding, and the full assurance of understanding in Christ. I merely instance it and do not stay to work it out.

Thirdly, *God's proclamation to men, in respect of their salvation, their satisfaction, their fulness, is a Man.* We will break that up in a minute or two.

Fourthly, *God's object, in all His dealings with His own, is a Man.* The object of all the Lord's strange and mysterious dealings, and of all His painful dealings with His own, is a Man, and He is entirely governed by His view of that Man in all He does with us. Nothing in all His dealings is something in itself, but it is all related. He has His eye all the time upon a Man, and He acts in relation to us with that Man in view.

No experience of ours, under the hand of God, is an incident by itself. It does not come into our lives because of this, or that, or something else as apart. If we go wrong, God does not chastise us for this or that as a thing in itself. God's chastisements are not incidental, are not detached, are not apart, but in relation to an object, the object in His eye, a Man.

God's dealings, not only with His own, but with the world, which are different kinds of dealings, are in relation to that Man. If we were able to recognise what that means, and apply it, bring it into the realm of applied truth, it would considerably help us in our everyday life.

Now in those statements we have comprehensively set forth God's object, the great governing reality. Everything is explained by a Man, and in a Man, and that Man interprets the history and the destiny of the universe. It could be put in other ways, and a great deal more from the Word of God could be cited to show how this is so, but we have to go on to break it up further.

God Has Not Evolved or Produced a Religion

God has not evolved or produced a religion, that is, a system of religious teaching and practice. That is where so many have gone astray, and, as a consequence, you get the clever and scholarly works on the religion of the Semites, and all that sort of thing. To these are added works on comparative religions, with Judaism and Christianity included. The whole matter is reduced to comparative values in the religions of the world, as to which is the best, and if it can be proved, as many have tried to show, that Judaism was better than all the ancient religions, and Christianity better than both ancient and modern religions, then it is to be concluded that Christianity is the religion for the world. This is a missing of the point. It is not a thing that we are likely to be caught in, but we have to recognise this truth for ourselves, and see where men have gone astray. God has not evolved or produced a religion: God has presented a Man.

God Has Not Presented a Set of Themes

God has not presented us (in the first instance) with a set of truths, themes, subjects, although the Bible may be full of these. He has not presented us with them, but with a Man. We are never called upon to preach salvation to anybody: we are called upon to preach Christ, and the salvation that is in Christ Jesus: ". . . it was the good pleasure of God . . . to reveal his Son in me, that I might preach *him* among the Gentiles . . ." (Gal. i. 15, 16). Any truth, any doctrine, any theme, any subject which is not a revelation of Christ, and a ministration of Him, and which does not bring into Christ and make Christ Himself greater and fuller in the life, has missed its intention, has been divorced and separated from the purpose of God, and does not stand with God at all. God has not presented us, in the first instance, with a set of truths, themes, subjects, though there be found great themes in the Word of God, such as atonement, redemption, and the many others; He has presented us with a Man. Everything with God from eternity to eternity is inseparably bound up with a Man.

Perhaps you are wondering what is the practical value of saying such things. The practical value is this, that you never come into the meaning and value of the things, even should you deal with them all your life long, if they are taken as things in themselves. The only dynamic in any truth is the living Christ. Sanctification is Christ, even as justification is Christ. These are not things to be taken and stated, laid hold of and appropriated as things in themselves: *Christ* is made unto us sanctification and redemption.

Now one or two qualifying statements need to be made alongside of that. While it is true that God has not presented us, in the first instance, with truths, and so on, but with a Man; while it is true that God has not evolved religion, but presented a Man; while we are called to preach, not salvation, but the Saviour, we must remember that, even that, it is not with a Man officially that we have to do, but with what He is personally. By officially, we mean it is not the office that He occupies as Redeemer, Saviour, Mediator, or any other of the designations which may be given Him, representing His official work, with which we have to be concerned. That is not the first thing, but the Man Himself. We are not saved by coming to Him in His official capacity as Saviour, we are saved by vital union with Him as a person.

It is not by our objective vision of the Man that we receive all God's meaning. There is great meaning and great value in Christ, viewed objectively; that is, as having summed up in Himself all that we need, and our holding fast by the fact of the completeness of everything in Christ. There is a real value for the heart in that, but it is not in having to do with the Man objectively alone, but subjectively, that we come into the Divine intention. The full hope of Christ is not Christ in salvation, but Christ in you. There are the values associated with Christ in salvation, but such a conception may be no more than of the official values of Christ as placed out there. The practical values of Christ are only known subjectively; they are what He is in Himself, and not what He is in office. You will see what we mean as we go on. It is very important for those of us who have responsibility in the things of God to recognise these differences.

Vital Union with Christ the Basis of God's Success

The point is this, that the basis of God's success is vital union with Christ, what we sometimes speak of as identification with Christ. God depends for His success entirely upon Christ within, and therefore, as we have said before, the one thing that God is after, and the one thing that the Devil is against, and will counter by every means of substitution, imitation, counterfeit, and so on, is getting Christ within men. Oh, how far things can go, and yet fall short of that! This is where the importance comes of recognising the difference between doctrine—even the doctrine of salvation—and the Man, the Person. We can preach the doctrine to men and get an assent, the consent of the mind to the doctrine, so that we have our catechumens, our classes for instructing converts in the doctrine; and when they have come to the place where they say, Now I understand the doctrine, it is all clear to me now! we think they are ready to be brought into the Church. The matter is much simpler than that; and it must be more than that. You cannot educate anybody into the kingdom of God, not even with Christian doctrine. No one ever passes into the kingdom of God by understanding Christian doctrine intellectually. You may have all that, and yet have a serious breakdown before long. You may have an awful condition amongst your so-called converts in the face of all that. It may be found in the long run that they were never really saved, though they were baptised on the grounds that they understood all that you could say to them about Christian doctrine. Thus, on the one hand, perfectly honest people may make a grave mistake, and, on the other hand, the Devil is out to give a tremendous amount of what comes just short of new birth. He will readily allow things to go so far, provided they do not go that far. But once that thing is really done, you have the basis for everything. You have the basis for the doctrine in a living way, the basis of complete assurance, the basis for everything, once Christ is within. God's objective is reached with regard to the starting point, and everything is possible. That is what I mean by the difference between doctrine and the Person, between the official and the personal. The basis of God's success is Christ in you, union with Christ, identification with Christ in an inward way. This is laid down in the Word of God as the principle upon which God works in this dispensation from first to last.

The Perfection of the Divine Provision Seen in Relation to (a) The Problem of Human Life

Let us take some of the passages to which we have referred at the commencement of our meditation, and see how they are but a following out of this very principle laid down as the basis upon which God works through this dispensation. Turn to Gal. iii. 28:

> "There can be neither Jew nor Greek, there can
> be neither bond nor free, there can be no male and
> female: for ye all are one man in Christ Jesus."

This is the way in which God solves the problem of human life. As we find human life on this earth to-day, it really is a problem. It is up against that problem that all those well-intentioned people who have round-table conferences of an International character always come. You call your round-table conference, and you have your representatives of the different nations of the earth, East and West, North and South; you have your different representatives of the social realm, your working man, as he is called, and your aristocrat, your capitalist, the employer and the employee; and in order to get different points of view, you will have your male and your female. You laboriously work: a proposition is made, but someone from the other end of the earth cannot accept that; it is not suitable to their realm of life, to what obtains

—159—

in their nation. Then, of course, the employee cannot bring himself to see the point of view of the employer, neither the employer the point of view of the employee; and there is not a little difficulty in a man seeing a woman's point of view. How many round tables have been held, and how many of them have been successful? The amazing thing is how men go on with their conferences! As long as we have been living, men have been having conferences, and what is the upshot? Every one gets just so far, and then there is deadlock. But they will have another one, and they will go on to the end trying to solve the problem of human life on that level of discussion, of conference.

Now God is perfectly aware of the whole situation. He is far more aware of the difficulties and the problems than anyone else. From His standpoint there are a great many more factors and features in the whole situation than have ever been manifested to men. But He has a solution, an infallible solution, and one which has fully proved itself wherever received. What is God's solution to the problem of human life? It is a Man.

(b) The Problem of Race

Here we have it: ". . . neither Jew nor Greek. . . ." That is the national problem. If you are familiar with the background of Galatians, you know that it was a national problem that gave rise to that letter. Jewish believers were assuming a status above other believers. They were saying, Well, we are the Jews, and they are the Greeks; we stand in one realm and they in another! We, as the Jews, have certain privileges and advantages, which they have not: we stand in a more favoured position than they do; we are altogether superior! Greeks or Gentiles are spoken of by Jews as "the dogs," the outsiders. How are you going to deal with the national problem? You will never finally solve that problem by a round-table conference. It is that problem which is so pressing in the world to-day, between the superior and the inferior races, between those who have the advantage and those who have not the advantage.

God's solution to the problem is a Man. In Christ there can be neither Jew nor Greek. Has not the Man solved the problem? You and I who come on to the ground of the Heavenly Man, who forsake the earthly ground, forsake the national ground, and come on to the ground of Christ, find blessed fellowship. Oh, what perfect fellowship! What profitable fellowship! What prospects loom up in view; how fruitful it all is! So far from being a way of a loss, it is blessedly full of value. What a tragedy that even so many of the Lord's own people have not forsaken national ground. What prejudices and implied limitations there are through pride. How they limit, how they blight, how they keep out the fulness of Christ, and make God's intention impossible. Get off that ground on to the ground of God's Heavenly Man, where there can be neither Jew nor Greek, and the national problem, as a part of the human problem, is solved.

(c) The Social Problem

Then further it is said, ". . . there can be neither bond nor free. . . . " The social problem is dealt with, the problem of the master and the slave. How are you going to solve the problem of the employer and the employee? You will only solve it in the Man, but in Him you will solve it in truth. Then, if the Jew thinks that nationally he has an advantage over the Greek, and if the master thinks he has an advantage over the servant, and, as is often the case, particularly in the East, the man thinks he has the advantage over the woman, how are you to get over these problems? God's salvation is a Man. You do not, of course, get rid of the facts; the distinctions are not abolished here on the earth—and God forbid that we should attempt such a thing—but on the ground of the "new man" we are made as one. There we meet on a different ground altogether. *In Christ* there can be neither Jew nor Greek, neither male nor female, neither bond nor free, neither superior nor inferior: advantages and disadvantages disappear.

(d) The Religious Problem

The Apostle refers again to both the national and social problems, as you notice, in Colossians iii. 11, but he also expands a little: "Where there cannot be Greek and Jew, circumcision and uncircumcision. . . ." Here he is perhaps putting his finger a little more firmly upon the Jew and the Greek problem. He is now stressing, not only the national, but the religious problem. How acute that was. In Christ there is no religious advantage over others; no one is in a position of less advantage on religious grounds than others. Then he speaks of barbarian and Scythian. This is a further reference to the racial question. These represent different levels of civilisation and cultivation, and the Apostle is clearing up the problem by saying that in Christ such distinctions have no place.

(e) The Problem of Human Destiny

Then another aspect of this is brought before us in the passage in I Cor. i. 24, 30:

> "But unto them that are called, both Jews and Greeks, Christ the power of God, and the wisdom of God. . . . But of him are ye in Christ Jesus, who was made unto us wisdom from God, and righteousness and sanctification, and redemption. . . ."

Here is another problem, that of human destiny, and this is gathered up into two words, and words that are frequently repeated, wisdom and power, power and wisdom. The question here at Corinth is a reflex of Greek philosophy, which had crept in with its subtle and pernicious suggestions. The question is that of reaching the super-man status. That is the question of philosophy—the highest wisdom and the greatest power. Wisdom and power are the two constituents of the super-man. Philosophy has always had in view the thought of man reaching his destiny, the idea that man has a great destiny. Man has indeed a meaning, a great meaning; there is bound up with man a great idea. With many of the Pagans, the idea was that of the deification of humanity, of man slowly evolving until he becomes deified. So that the great man is to be worshipped. Their heroes were worshipped as approximating to their ideal, and this was all a movement toward the ultimate deification of humanity, and the characteristics of this supreme super-man, as thus conceived of, were wisdom and power. They were always stretching out for a superior wisdom to bring them into a place of superior power, and thus to realise the great destiny of man. The problem of human destiny was dealt with in the light of wisdom and power.

—162—

That lies behind the world to-day. Is it not this that we are meeting with now in dictators, in men who would dominate the world? It is a case of wisdom and power reaching such an attitude of human status that everything is brought under the dictator's dominion. He is regarded as the embodiment of the world's highest wisdom and greatest power. That is man. Such will be the Devil's man on the human level.

The question of human destiny is quite a living one for us. It is just as real and important and right a question for believers as it is for the world. It is not the world which is really in line with the destiny of man. There is no getting away from the fact that man has a marvellous destiny. God created man with an object far greater than anything the princes of this world have ever conceived, and so the question of human destiny is a right and a proper one, and perhaps one of the greatest. But the question which goes with it is, How is the end to be reached? Wisdom is quite right. This "one new man" is to display the manifold wisdom of God unto all supernatural intelligences, to be the embodiment of Divine wisdom on all its sides. Power is quite right. There is no doubt at all that this one "new man" is to be the instrument of the exercise of the infinite power of God, to be a display of God's mighty power. These things are a right consideration for us: they present a legitimate question, the problem of how to reach the super-man status. That was the question with the Greeks all the time. The answer of God through His Word is a Man whom He hath ordained. The answer is Christ within, the power and the wisdom. Christ within, in the power of death and resurrection, solves the problem of human destiny.

This world has tried to solve this problem by numerous systems of philosophy. If you sit down to investigate any one of them, you will find it is an attempt to solve the problem of human destiny, the meaning of man, and the meaning of the universe, and how man and the universe are to reach their predestined end. The world is full of systems of philosophy which are seeking to answer this question. The Lord answers it in a simple and direct way, and says that the solution to the problem is a Man, and that Man, in the power of death and resurrection, dwelling within. How are you and I to realise God's predestined purpose? This is the answer: ". . . Christ in you, the hope of glory" (Col. i. 27). But this is Christ within as the wisdom and power of God. This wisdom is so simple. What does Christ within mean in relation to that great ultimate purpose of God? It is the earnest of that to which the Apostle by the Spirit elsewhere gives expression: ". . . foreordained to be conformed to the image of his Son . . ." (Rom. viii. 29); and again: ". . . until Christ be formed in you . . ." (Gal. iv. 19). When that is done the world will be occupied by a great corporate Man of God's own kind, and the end will be reached. That Man is Christ, in His fulness—His Body.

How then are you going to solve these problems? Well, Plato will tell you all about it in his Republic! Oh, the laws and the regulations! Oh, the observances! See all that you have to take account of, to do, and not do, to institute, and carry out. It is all a tremendous system to bring man up to standard. The Lord's answer is a very much simpler one than that. Let Christ but dwell within, and He will work to bring you up to His own level. Give Him a chance within, and you will be conformed to His image; Christ will be fully formed in you. And when that is true of the whole Body, you have the one new, universal Man. Is that not wisdom? Oh, the poor philosophers! How they have exhausted their brains, and many of them have gone mad in the attempt to solve the problem of human destiny. The Lord's wisdom is so simple. Christ in you is the wisdom of God. That is how the whole problem is met. You have not to think everything out, plan it all, work to a colossal system of rules and regulations and observances; you have simply to let the Lord within have His way, and the end is sure. The problem of the universe is solved without any mental exhaustion. It is a matter of life. The foolishness of God is wiser than men, and the wisdom of God so simple. Men are spending the centuries wearing themselves out, and what is the result? Look at it to-day. What a sad picture of the upward progress of humanity! But God is effecting His purpose, and in the unseen there is a Man growing that is to fill the universe. God's way is so simple and so effective. If you want to solve the question of wisdom and power, this is it. Wisdom is the question of "how." Then it becomes a question of ability when you know how. Christ within is both the "how," and the "ability."

All this, and much more (the Word is full of it and we shall never exhaust it all) comes back to the one thing: ALL THINGS IN CHRIST. God's answer to everything, God's explanation of everything, God's means of realising everything is a Man, "the man Christ Jesus." When this world has run its evil course, this inhabited earth will be judged *in* a Man. Men will be judged by what their inward relationship is to that Man. The question at the judgment will never be of how much good or bad, right or wrong, more or less, is in a man; it will turn upon this one point, Are you in Christ? If not, more or less makes no difference. God's intention, God's proclamation is that all things are in His Son. Are you in Him? Why not? The basis of judgment is very simple. It is all gathered up in a Man, and what is in that Man of God for us. That is the basis of judgment. It all comes back to the very simple, and yet comprehensive and blessed truth, that it is what Christ is that satisfies God, reaches God's end, and meets all our need. It is all summed up in a Man, "the man Christ Jesus."

The Lord continue to open our eyes to see His glorious and Heavenly Man, who is also the Divine Servant.

The Stewardship of the Mystery
(Vol. 2)

Publisher's note:

The Stewardship of the Mystery (volume II)
originally published from
39 Honor Oak Road, London in 1964

The year of publication as given is from when, in the
author's bimonthly magazine *A Witness and a
Testimony*, a first notice of this book or booklet
appeared. Very many of the titles published had
already appeared earlier as articles or series in that
magazine.

Where a new title's date of publication is not known, +
signifies the year of the magazine article or series from
which, some unspecified time later, that new
publication was reproduced.

1998 Christian Books Publishing House / SeedSowers
P O Box 285
Sargent
GA 30275

Foreword

In the year 1939 we published two volumes on *The Stewardship of the Mystery*. Volume I, the larger of the two, covered wider ground under the title *All Things in Christ*. This latter was reprinted and republished and is still available. Volume II was more specific in relation to Paul's ministry and the Church. This second volume has been out of print for some time, and although we have had so many requests for it, there has been a strange restraint from reprinting it in its original form. But there has been a growing burden to put into writing the *essence* of that particular ministry of "The Mystery" and, under this pressure which we believe to be of God, we have written this volume which, although changed in various respects from the former Vol. II, is a concentration of that "Revelation" to the Apostle. In the overwhelming presence of so great an unveiling it would be an impossible thing to give an adequate presentation and, although so burdened and urged, the end finds us with a deep sense of failure. We can do no more than "cast this bread upon the waters" and trust that it may reach some prepared hearts as a message from God in a timely way. It is not an *exposition* that is needed, but a *revolution* similar to that which took place in the Apostle when "it pleased God to reveal His Son in him." May the prayer in Eph. i. 17-21 be answered in the case of many readers.

T. Austin-Sparks

Forest Hill, London
1966

Contents

CHAPTER ONE

Introductory

Near the Journey's End

The last phase of his pilgrimage has arrived. The end of the journey is in sight. The course has been well-nigh run; and what a course it has been! The faithful servant, the war-scarred warrior, the greatest of Christ's missionaries, church builders, and stewards of the heavenly riches, will soon receive "the crown of life" laid up for him. His "journeys oft" are soon to give place to "the rest that remaineth." His "labouring more abundantly" is practically over. He gives expression to a hope that he may yet visit some of his most beloved converts (Phil. ii. 24). (Some believe that this hope was realised, and that, for a short period of release, he travelled still further afield. But we have no definite record of this in the New Testament.) He is now in imprisonment in Rome, and Luke concludes his record with the period there "in his own hired house." This man, who saw the sovereignty of God in every vicissitude of his life, did not fail to do so in this arrival in Rome and sojourn there, so different from what he had hoped for and expected (Rom. i. 15).

Disappointment and God's Appointment

Taking stock of his situation, he was not long in arriving at the conclusion that, in that Divine sovereignty, this would make possible the realisation of another strong desire that had been in his heart, but which could not be fulfilled while on his many travels. Letters, longer or shorter, he had written, each of which had been written in relation to some particular need and situation. Not one of them went—other than by a passing reference—outside of that special demand. During his long journeys, when plying his trade to support himself and make it impossible for critics to rightly say that he lived on his converts; and by special and extraordinary experiences, such as being "caught up into the third heaven

—7—

(in a vision or dream) and hearing unspeakable things" (2 Cor. xii. 1-4); not omitting that two years in the Arabian Desert; several years alone in Tarsus soon after his conversion; and a long imprisonment in Caesarea; all this gave him much time for meditation and for the Lord to speak to him. In this way an immense accumulation of spiritual knowledge became stored up in his heart. Being so sure, as he often said, that this "revelation" was a "stewardship" for "the Body of Christ," he would doubtless be hoping for a time when he would have leisure and detachment enough to unburden his spirit in writing. We now know that such a time and opportunity just *had* to come, for the fruit of that has been an unspeakable blessing to the Church during these many centuries.

Well, as we have said, strange as the Providence may have seemed when first he looked round his apartment, and, not least, his Roman guard and chain, he soon realised that this could be the great opportunity for which he had been waiting. It would very strongly appear that as this realisation came to him, and perhaps in the long nights when visitors had gone, he became almost overwhelmed by the uprush of that store of revelation. We so conclude from the way and manner, as well as the substance of what he then committed to writing. He had those churches in Asia immediately in mind (though the Lord had much greater intentions) and what he wrote was intended to be circulated among them; probably a blank space being left for filling in with the particular name, such as: "to the saints which are at . . ." (the name "Ephesus" does not occur in earliest manuscripts). There is little doubt, however, that this overflow of heart had a special direction for that so great and spiritually influential church at Ephesus. This may be of secondary importance in view of the so-much-greater Divine intention by this inspiration.

The Overflowing Heart

It is his manner that means so much as a first impression. Our sub-title is an example of that manner. The Letter (to the Ephesians, so-called) is written in terms of the superlative. Look at some of these superlatives: "The exceeding greatness of his power" (i. 19); "the fulness of him that filleth all in all" (i. 23); "the exceeding riches of his grace" (ii. 7); "the unsearchable riches of Christ" (iii. 8); "the breadth and length and height and depth," "the knowledge-surpassing love of Christ," "all the fulness of God" (iii. 18, 19); "exceeding abundantly above all that we ask or think" (iii. 20); "far above all the heavens, that he might fill all things" (iv. 10); "the fulness of Christ" (iv. 13); "a glorious church, not having spot or wrinkle or any such thing" (v. 27).

Are we not right in saying that the man was just unable to contain his fulness? Then, not only his phrases, but his grammatical form. He will start on a course, and then, when an extra thought comes into his mind, he will diverge and go off at a tangent, not picking up the earlier thread again until some way after. The longest sentence, without a "period" or full stop, in the New Testament occurs in this Letter. He is too full and too eager to stop for literary technicalities. The flood-gates are open, and, like a torrent, he is pouring out this fulness so long pent up. When we come to consider the nature of his revelation we shall understand better why he was so expressive in superlatives. At the moment we are just registering the force of his anxiety to get it out at last.

To dwell a little longer on this Letter.

Some may not agree with us, and some may think that we are exaggerating when we say that this Letter is

The Greatest Document ever Penned

We shall have to substantiate that opinion, but we shall not have altogether failed when we have finished.

When we say "greatest," of course we do not mean in length, but in intrinsic value and content.

This is the crown and consummate essence of Paul's ministry. It is the climax of his mission.

Here are a few comments of outstanding Christian scholars:

For one such it is "the consummate and most comprehensive statement which even the New Testament contains of the meaning of the Christian religion, blending as nowhere else its evangelical, spiritual, moral and universal elements."

Or from another:

"The sublimest communication ever made to men was made from a Roman prison by one who in his own esteem was 'the very least of all the saints.' "

"This Epistle is one of the noblest in the New Testament."

"A divine Epistle glowing with the flame of Christian love, and the splendour of holy light, and flowing with fountains of living water."

"The most heavenly work of one whose very imagination is peopled with things in the heavens."

"In this, the divinest composition of man, is every doctrine of Christianity; first, those doctrines peculiar to Christianity; etc."

"It is emphatically the Epistle of the Ascension. We rise in it, as on wings of inspiration, to the divinest heights. Word after word—and thought after thought—now 'the heavenlies,' now 'spiritual,' now 'riches,' now 'glory,' now 'mystery,' now 'plenitude,' now 'light,' now 'love,' seem, as it were, to leave behind them 'a luminous trail' in this deep and shining sky."

"It is the most advanced, the most sublime, the most profound, the most final utterance of Paul's Gospel."

Let us hasten to say that our own appraisal is not the result of reading such estimates as the above, for these are of much later discovery. We have reached our own conclusion after many years of reading and meditating in this Letter, and Paul's ministry in general. But we are so glad to have our judgment confirmed or checked by men of so much greater knowledge than our own.

Thus far we have only introduced the Letter. Its content, teaching and message will occupy the main space, while still remaining so vastly beyond our comprehension. Before we take our plunge into those deeps, and never get much further than the surface, we shall have of necessity to give some attention to the man himself, and to how the man and his ministry are one thing. Before so proceeding, let us remind our readers of one or two obvious, but impressive facts.

When the Apostle Paul set himself to write this Letter, he had no idea that he was writing Holy Scripture—the Bible (in part). His sole thought and desire was to confirm and supplement that "whole counsel of God" which he "had not shunned" to declare to—and through—Ephesus and Asia Minor during the two years that he was there (Acts xix). It was a *Letter* that—in his own mind—he was writing, and that to a location and a need. It could never have occurred to him that what he was writing would be read by an ever-growing number of people through nearly twenty centuries; that it would go into a world the size of which he knew nothing; that people of every race under heaven would have it translated into their own language or dialect; that it would divide Christendom world-wide into the largest opposing schools of theology and interpretation; that people of God in every time and realm would feed eagerly upon it; that bookstores in every country would have their shelves growingly bulged with "Expositions," "Commentaries," "Sermons," etc., on this "Letter"; and that, finally, such appraisals as we have given above would be attached to that piece of personal correspondence! He would not only never have imagined this as possible, but would have had a shock of astonishment if he *could* have foreseen it. What a vindication of his testimony! What a justification of his sufferings! What an unveiling of God's sovereignty and grace! What an inspiration and strength this should be to any who may be suffering in fellowship with Christ, and what a proof of the truth of his own words: "Your labours are not in vain in the Lord"!

CHAPTER TWO

The Man in the Message

This is not intended to be a "Life of the Apostle Paul," but has rather to do with the particular *significance* of this servant of Jesus Christ. While there are those vital and essential factors in his case which must be true of every servant of Christ, and which are basic to every fruitful ministry (as we shall later mention), everything about Paul indicates that he was indeed "a chosen (elect) vessel," foreknown, foreordained and selected. This was true particularly in the nature of the ministry for which he was "apprehended." The same nature of ministry may—in measure—be the "calling" of others, but it was pioneered in Paul. All the Apostles stood on common ground where the fundamentals of the faith were concerned: the Person of Christ; the work of Christ; redemption; justification; sanctification; the world commission to preach salvation in Christ to all the world; the coming again of the Saviour, etc. They had the same foundation. Each one may have had "grace according to the measure of the gift of Christ"; that is, according to their personal gift, whether Apostle, Prophet, Evangelist, Pastor or Teacher, each had "grace"—anointing, enablement—corresponding to the responsibility, but on "fundamentals," i.e. foundation matters, they were agreed and one. Whatever we may say in distinguishing Paul, we would not for a moment take one small fragment from the great ministry of John, or Peter, or James, or others. Never could our New Testament suffer the loss of those ministries, and elsewhere we have gloried in them. When all has been said as to their value—and it would be an immense "all"—we still have to affirm that there was, and is, that which is unique and particular in what came through Paul. Let us hasten to say a very significant and helpful thing before we proceed.

It would never have been possible for Paul to understand his pre-conversion life until he came under the hand of Jesus Christ. That vocation with which he was called when Jesus became his Lord throws so much illumination upon the sovereignty of God in his past history. This is a principle which will help so many people and servants of God, and it shows how immensely important it is that Jesus shall be—not only Saviour—but Lord. We shall see this more fully later. Paul's Jewish birth, upbringing, training, education and deep embeddedness in something from which he would be extricated by the power of God, and something which was going to be shown no longer to be what God needed, is in itself of tremendous educative value. Why God, in His foreknowledge, should put a man deeply into something which does not ultimately represent His mind contains a point to be noted. Many there are who argue that, because they have ample reason to know that God put them into a certain way, work, form, association, there they are to abide for ever, willy nilly. Paul's history says No to that argument. God's ways in his case came to show that He may do a thing like that, and all His sovereignty may truly be in it, but only for a purpose, and a temporary purpose; namely, to give a deep and thorough first-hand knowledge of that which is really at best a limitation upon the full purpose of God. It is necessary for an effective servant of God to have personal knowledge of that from which people are to be delivered. Abraham must know Chaldea; Moses must know Egypt; David must know the falsehood of Saul's reign. So Paul must know the proscribed Judaism, so that he can speak with *authority*, the authority of personal experience. Were we the Psalmist, we should put "Selah" there. "Think of that!"

But we must underline two aspects of this principle. We are referring to what was definitely within the Divine "working of all things after the counsel of His own will," and "according to his purpose." Paul was not changing his God at conversion, Jehovah was his God for ever. The change was in the *method* of God. It was still God working. We say this because no one can say that, because they were born and brought up in this or that, therefore "Providence" (meaning God) intended that to be their way for always. We *must* be as we are and where we are by the sovereignty of God, and we *must* know that any major change is equally definitely of God, and the only alternative to making it is clear disobedience to the presented will of God. It has to be a *must*, or a missing of the way. It certainly will make

—13—

demands upon faith's walk with God, because the element of *apparent* contradiction may be present. We do not know what mental and soul battles Paul had. It is not recorded that in facing the immense revolution he reasoned with the Lord—"Well, Lord, by Your own sovereignty I was born a Jew, and that with more than general terms: 'of the stock of Israel, of the tribe of Benjamin, a Hebrew of the Hebrews ... a Pharisee.' And now, Lord, You are requiring me to take a course which repudiates all that and contradicts it. It is not like You, Lord, to contradict Yourself; it seems so inconsistent. It is not as though I have not been God-fearing and have been without faith in You." The change *was* so revolutionary as to seem to be two contrary ways in the same God. Here was a very big occasion to "trust in the Lord with all thine heart, and *lean not upon thine own understanding.*" We could cite the cases of many servants of God who have been brought to such a crisis between reason and faith when God was demanding a decision which *seemed* to contradict all His former leading. Some of these have come to be very greatly vindicated by obedience. Some have lived to be examples of having missed the way, or God's best.

All this has had to do with God's sovereign preparation and equipment of a servant so that that servant should truly know by deep experience what he is talking about and what the differences are. This then, in brief, as to his Jewish relationship.

But this man was elected and destined to be God's special messenger to the *nations,* not just to *a* nation. The nations were mainly under Roman government and Greek culture and language. Through his father Paul inherited Roman citizenship and Freemanship, and by his birth and upbringing in Tarsus he had both the Greek language and a first-class familiarity with Greek life and culture. These three things—Jewry, Roman citizenship and Greek language —took him with facility and ease into practically the whole world. But, added to all this natural qualification was that without which Paul would never have been the real factor that history testifies to; he was anointed with the Holy Spirit. Sometimes the anointing has made up for much natural deficiency in education and birth, and men have made spiritual history who would never have been recognised on merely natural grounds. The Lord took very real care that Paul could never make his natural advantages the ground of his *true* success. This was implied or indicated in the first recorded words of the Lord about him (to Ananias) after his conversion: "I will show him how many things he must suffer for my name's sake" (Acts ix. 16).

The sovereignty of God is many-sided and has many ways. It is only when the full story is told that a true explanation is seen. At the beginning and in the course there can be room for many a "why?" A Moses and a Jeremiah may start off with what they are convinced is a definite handicap and contradiction, but history justifies God and in the end His wisdom is vindicated. When God says "He is a chosen vessel," He knows all about the clay of which the vessel is made. As we go on, the two implicit things just referred to will become increasingly apparent. One, that the messenger and his message are one thing; the message is in the man's constitution and very history under the hand of God. And two, the man is not just recognised for his natural qualifications alone, but pre-eminently because God has anointed him for his position and work. No man can be in any but a completely false position who speaks without what he says being born out of real experience. Only, for instance, may a man speak of brokenness if he himself has been broken. Paul's ministry throughout came from a continuous history with God in deep and usually painful experiences of conflict. It was "the spoil of battle." It is absolutely imperative that it should be obvious and manifest that any position, function and ministry on the part of anyone in relation to Christ should be by anointing, and that the impression made and the conclusion drawn by others is that "that man is clearly anointed for that job!" Anointing simply means that God is most evidently with the person concerned in what they are doing and in the position that they hold. To be out of position is to be out of anointing in that particular. We cannot select, choose, decide our place and function. That is an organic thing, and just as it is awkward for a leg to try to do the work of an arm in the human body, so there will always be something wrong when we assume a work or position for which the sovereignty of the Spirit has not chosen us. With all the adversities and oppositions, it is the most helpful thing to know that we are where we are by Divine appointment and not by our own will. It is a good thing when we know what *our* function is, and what it is not, and act accordingly! There are sufficient functions in the body corporate for every member to have a quite definite one under the one anointing, and the function will as naturally express itself as an eye sees, an ear hears, a hand grips, and so on, *if* the head (the Head) is in full and right control. Paul, then, has much to teach us on this matter, first by his life and then by his writings. At this point we are brought back to where we diverged from the message to the man, and we must now consider that differentiation of function for which Paul was particularly chosen and apprehended.

Paul's Distinctive Vocation

That there was a difference and peculiar importance in Paul's ministry has a number of strong evidences and attestations. He knew it himself and often referred to it, both as to its substance and the way in which he received it. This is expressed in such words as these:

"the stewardship (R.V. margin) *of that grace of God which was given me to you-ward";*
"how that by revelation was made known unto me the mystery . . . whereby . . . ye can perceive my understanding in the mystery of Christ"; "Unto me . . . was this grace given . . . to make all men see (bring to light—R.V. margin) what is the stewardship of the mystery" (Eph. iii. 2-4, 8, 9).

While Paul does not say that he alone had had the "mystery" made known to him, he does claim that, as a stewardship, a ministry, it was revealed to him in a distinctly personal and direct-from-heaven manner. He claimed that he was divinely apprehended for this particular ministry. What that revelation was has to spread itself over all that we shall yet write. At the moment we are concerned with the *fact* of Paul's specific vocation.

Not least among the evidences of this was the fury, invective, hatred, malice and murderous cruelty of the devil and his forces focused upon this man, relentlessly. It was sheerly because of what was coming through him and not just because of his personality. It began and broke loose on the same issue before Paul was the apprehended vessel of it. To see and understand this we have to go back to the one man who had previously seen what Paul was shown. We refer to Stephen as the first Christian martyr and we are deeply moved when we read the account of his death. But how little Stephen has been understood, and how blind we have been to the real meaning of his death—his destruction by Satan-controlled men.

Stephen—the Precursor of Paul

A thoughtful consideration of Stephen's discourse before the Jewish Sanhedrin will show that Stephen was like a "preface," an introduction, to Paul's ministry. If Stephen had lived, there is little doubt that he and Paul would have been in a mighty partnership in the Stewardship of the Mystery. This, of course, supposes that the Lord did not foresee that Stephen *would* die, and that, in that foreknowledge, He did not mark down Paul for the alone steward of this ministry in its fulness. The Divine sovereignty has rarely been evidenced more than in Saul's presence with Stephen at the time of the latter's death, although an accomplice in it. As we move with Stephen through that long discourse, following his mind from Abraham through Isaac, Jacob, the Patriarchs, Joseph, Israel, Moses, Egypt, the Exodus, Sinai, the Tabernacle, the Wilderness, Joshua, David, Solomon, the Temple, the Prophets, up to Christ, the "Righteous One," there is one thing that is in Stephen's mind throughout, and that one thing is the key to everything and that which— more than anything else—explains, defines and characterizes Paul and his ministry. That one thing is that God is ever, from eternity to eternity, pressing on to an all-comprehending goal. Through human failure, human and Satanic obstruction and attempted frustration; by a variety and multitude of ways, means, and persons, in all generations and ages, God is ever going on. His desired and selected instruments may become a hindrance rather than a help. Nations, empires and systems may oppose and obstruct; circumstances may seem to limit Him, but—given time—He is found not to have given up, but still to be going on. He has set Himself a purpose and a goal, and that goal will be reached. Let Jewry "always resist the Holy Ghost" as Stephen says; so much the worse for Jewry. That is the tremendous upshot of Stephen's discourse. Within that inclusiveness there are other features. God's purpose is a heavenly one, a vast one, a spiritual one, an eternal one. Neither the Tabernacle, with all its inner beauty and symbolic embodiment of Divine thoughts; nor the Temple of Solomon with all its magnificence and glory; nor Solomon himself with his stunning wisdom and overwhelming wealth—says Stephen—can remotely approximate to that toward which God is moving in relation to His Son. That is not "made with hands." That is not of the earth. That is not God's House (Acts vii. 48, 49). The Holy Ghost—says Stephen, in effect—is moving on, ever on to this so-much-greater in every way. Stephen, in one glorious hour met the devastating force of that with which Paul contended all his life, namely the incorrigible disposition of *God's people* to bring what is essentially heavenly down to earth and fix it there; to crystallize spiritual things into man-made systems; to lay hands upon what is of God and make it something of man, something exclusive and legal under man's control. Stephen's stand for, and testimony to, this "Heavenly Vision" (*that* became Paul's phrase) brought him into the most violent and vicious hatred of vested religious interests, so far as systems were concerned, and Satan's fiercest jealousy behind all. Touch religious traditions and established orders and you will find the same thing that Stephen met, a jealousy which issues from blindness to the vastly greater purpose of God. In *some way* you will be stoned! by ostracism, exclusion, closed doors, suspicion and misrepresentation, all of which are traceable in the case of Paul.

Have we said enough about Stephen to justify and establish our statement that he was—so to speak—Paul in advance? Stephen himself is an example of God going on in spite of hell and men, as Paul *was* the going on of God in fulness when men put Stephen away. We look back to our beginning statement that a major evidence of the particular ministry for which Paul was chosen is the vehemence of Satanic antagonism.

All that we have said, and much more, will, of course, come out in our consideration of the ministry of Paul himself, but I am sure that we are beginning to see something of his significance.

Still ahead of our contemplation of the crowning and consummate ministry of Paul the Apostle, there are several matters of considerable value which may make a brief chapter of helpfulness by themselves.

CHAPTER THREE

Spying Out the Land

On two occasions, when Israel was contemplating entering the Land of the Covenant and Promise, spies were sent over beforehand. The first was disastrous because it was the decision of the people governed by self-interest, and although Moses complied and the Lord acquiesced, the secret motive was eventually betrayed. After long and deep discipline the principle of "the delight of the Lord" was present and faith triumphed. The spies can go with approval and blessing when the motive is that of the Lord's glory, not man's. We would believe that the move from First Corinthians chapter x to Ephesians, Philippians, Colossians, corresponds to that change from the first to the second spying out of the Land. May ours answer to the second as we contemplate the glorious Land!

Of the preliminary considerations these are some:

(1) Paul himself was—when writing—aware that what he had been shown by the Lord was beyond his power of utterance. The very phrase "unsearchable riches" implies this. It could be correctly translated "untraceable," or "unexplorable." Beyond tracing, beyond exploring, beyond searching out. Paul knew himself to be attempting an impossible task. He requested these believers in Asia to pray for them "that utterance may be given unto me in opening my mouth, to make known . . . the mystery . . ." (Eph. vi. 19). He was labouring to speak the unspeakable, to fathom the unfathomable, to comprehend the incomprehensible. The paradox of preaching the unpreachable characterizes these final Letters. If that was true of *that* man, what can *we* do more than behold at a distance!

(2) What Paul *did* and did *not* set himself to do. Paul—in these final writings—did *not* set himself to write a treatise on this or that theme, subject, or doctrine. There is all the difference *in this respect* between "Ephesians" and "Galatians" or "Romans." No particular threat to the faith

—19—

led him—as in those Letters—to write this the greatest of all, although that may have been partly true of "Colossians." In "Ephesians" Paul is not "reasoning," arguing, debating. He is not setting down his "Philosophy of Christianity." He had a wide and rich knowledge of the philosophies and religious ideas of the world in which he had moved. But he is not minded to deal with these or to compare the other religions with Christianity. What Paul *did do* in this Letter to Asia and, through Asia, to all whom Asia touched (and unconsciously to us) was to make a mighty proclamation. Here we have a man making a proclamation. He is just giving out, with a heart too full for articulation, an "utterance." It is like an imperative broadcast for which the microphone is too small and inadequate. This is not something that he had thought out and was the product of his great brain. He attributed it to a "revelation" given him by the initiative of God. This that he is penning is a vital and, in a sense, a consummate presentation of the long process of God's self-disclosure, and it embodies God's full and final revelation of His eternal purpose. It is because it is of this nature that Paul falls on his knees and prays a special prayer for his readers (i. 15-17). It is because of a fixed and unalterable law and principle which he has enunciated so clearly and emphatically elsewhere (I Cor. ii. 14-16) that spiritual things, things of the Spirit, can only be understood by spiritual people, people of the Spirit. We have to come on this later, but all that is before us in this Letter will be little or not more than written mysteries if we do not pray this same prayer on this same necessity before we go any further.

(3) The last Letters, being so inclusive in substance, naturally gather up in allusion, if not in restatement, many of the matters touched on incidentally in former Letters. So, in allusion, we have vital points in Romans, Corinthians, Galatians, etc. It would require much time and space to trace and tabulate the instances. Some great words will be indicative, such as "Redemption," "Spiritual," "Sons," "Grace," "Adoption," "Fore-ordained," etc.

(4) Our method will be different from that usually employed in studying these (and other) Letters. In order that Bible students may obtain a quick, easy and simple grasp of the books, the Letters are usually reduced by Bible

teachers to outlines according to the content and subjects mainly mentioned. This is a very valuable and helpful method. So we have such helpful outlines and analyses (of Ephesians) as Dr. Campbell Morgan's *The Church—I. The Heavenly Calling. II. The Earthly Conduct,* each of these two sections being divided into three more. Or we have Miss Ruth Paxon's *The Wealth, Walk and Warfare of the Christian*; or that little book by Watchman Nee, *Sit, Walk, Stand.* We have not an idea that we can at all improve on such, but that is not the method which we are employing, and we hasten to say so. From the following you will not be given a "bird's eye view," as we usually describe a general look at things; unless it is an eagle's eye which sees vast ranges from great altitudes. In this sense "Ephesians" does take up the eagle aspect of the Cherubim—mystery and heavenliness. Our method will be—as it were—to hover over some of the eminences rising from this landscape, or, to keep to our title, to stand and gaze with wonder at some of "the unsearchable riches of Christ" which are presented in these final writings, especially in "Ephesians."

This, then, is what we meant by "Spying out the Land." At most we can but glimpse the greatnesses which are embodied in this Letter. But if we could see them, free from all prejudice, bias and natural influences, we should return with the same wonder and assurance as did the spies of the second investigation.

CHAPTER FOUR

The Unsearchable Riches

We shall not get very far into the practical meaning and import of this great unveiling until we have the key in our hand. Once we have that key everything will be explained as to its purpose and value. Strangely enough, that key is in the form of a small prefix which—unfortunately—does not appear in our translations. It occurs twice in "Ephesians" (in major connections); four times in "Colossians"; once in "Philippians"; in both letters to Timothy; and in "Hebrews" (whether Paul actually wrote "Hebrews" is not discussed, but we have no hesitation in saying that his influence and conception are definitely in it). In our translation we have the word *knowledge* in Eph. i. 17 and iv. 13; in Col. i. 6, 9, 10; iii. 10; and in Phil. i. 9. But in these and the other letters mentioned the word (in the Greek) has the little prefix *epi*. *Epi* means "full," and while "to know" occurs alone in many places in the New Testament, it means—usually—the beginning of knowledge, such as "This is life eternal, that they should know thee the only true God, and him whom thou didst send, Jesus Christ" (John xvii. 3). But when we have moved on from the beginning and are come to the more mature state as in Paul's later Letters, that which is set before us is "Full Knowledge" *(Epi-gnosis)*. What Paul prays for therefore in Ephesians i. 17 is that believers who have already advanced in knowledge may still come to *full* knowledge. That is the word of maturity. This then is the key to all that is presented here, and what is presented is that which constitutes full knowledge. All that we will add until later is that this knowledge, or full knowledge, is not mental, intellectual, academic, obtained by reading, study, hearing (although it *might* come *through* such), but, as Paul emphasizes, it is by revelation of the Holy Spirit. For us now, since the Scriptures were completed, revelation is not something *extra to* the Scriptures, but revelation or illumination as to what is *in* the Scriptures; and that is inexhaustible. Back to that later.

Let us note some of the

Major Features of the Ultimate Discourse

As to how the Apostle came by the full knowledge which he had, we can only say two things which are made known. One was the more general, "a spirit of wisdom and revelation in the full-knowledge of him, the eyes of your heart being enlightened..." etc. That is the birthright of every believer, but it belongs to obedience to all truth or light already given. It is what John refers to: "the anointing which ye received ... teacheth you concerning all things" (1 John ii. 27). But, in Paul's case, because of his special "stewardship" he was given special revelations, as when he was caught up (in vision, dream or trance) into the third heaven and heard unspeakable things (2 Cor. xii). If we follow this illumined and inspired mind of the Apostle, we shall be led into and through "ages" from eternity past to eternity yet to be. We shall be given a glimpse of what took place in each of these eras, and what the characteristic of each was, is, and will be.

There are four of these eras referred to:

i. "Before times eternal";

ii. from creation to Christ—the Old Testament era;

iii. from the Incarnation to the consummation of the age;

iv. "the ages of the ages."

Between i and ii there is an event which has affected the whole course and character of things from i to iii, as we shall see.

Before Times Eternal

It is to be noted that the Apostle had barely begun this Letter (to the "Ephesians") and opened the flood-gate of this pent-up revelation, than he carried his readers away back past all time and landed them in what he called "before the foundation of the world." It is language which he used more than once: "before times eternal" (2 Tim. i. 9; Titus i. 2). Having taken that long flight back over centuries and millennia, he intimated what in that dateless past took place. Two things are indicated and stated. In the counsels of the Godhead, the Son of God was designated and appointed the eternal Sphere of all that would be of God. "In Him" is the definition (Eph. i. 4). Two hundred times the Apostle uses that term in varying forms in his writings. The writer of the Letter to the Hebrews states the same thing in precise words: "whom he appointed heir of all things" (Heb. i. 2). This is not knowledge exclusively Paul's. Both John and Peter speak of the same thing as to the eternal position of the Son of God. But Paul unfolds so much more of that designation. There, then, first in the "before times eternal," the Son of God— now given the name which became His so long after, "Our Lord Jesus Christ" (Eph. i. 3)—was determined the inclusive realm of all that which would belong to God. As a race would be "in Adam" (1 Cor. xv. 22); as a nation would be in the single seed of Abraham (Rom. iv. 13, etc.); and as the harvest is in the single grain of wheat, so the Son of God would be the content of all that which would eventually be of God. So the Apostle links with the Person the persons: "He chose *us* in him." This was in the Divine deliberations. We are not unfamiliar with this concept. Jesus Himself made reference to it: "for the elect's sake. . . ," ". . . so as to lead astray, if possible, even the elect" (Matt. xxiv. 22, 24). "Shall not God avenge his elect. . . ?" (Luke xviii. 7), etc. Peter also uses the term (1 Pet. i. 1). In those eternal counsels there was determined and secured a "people," a "body," a "nation," which just had to be to justify the appointment of the Son. No, we are not going to launch into a discussion of "predestination" or "foreordination." All that we will say just at this point is that two things govern this matter of the Divine election. One is that it is corporate; it is a "Body" and, just as a physical body was prepared for God's Son in incarnation—"a body didst thou prepare for me" (Heb. x. 5)—so a corporate "Body" was prepared for Him. It was as essential as it is for a spirit to have a body for all practical purposes. (More on this later.) The other governing thing is that this election is not to salvation, willy nilly, but to *purpose*. This is fundamental to this whole Letter to the "Ephesians." See how large and powerful a place the "eternal purpose" has in Paul's mind and writings. It is that "purpose" that determines so much in God's ways! The exhortations, the admonitions, the encouragements, the warnings, the entreaties, are all related to "His purpose" *in salvation.* How vastly much there is bound up with that drawing aside of the veil upon those eternal counsels! Out of them come the deliberations and activities of God: "who worketh all things after the counsel of his will," "according to the good pleasure of his will" (Eph. i. 11, 5, etc.). See also Romans viii. 28-30.

We must, however, remember that there is one absolutely pre-eminent and predominant matter which determines everything and from which and to which *all things* are related. This is the one thing which explains everything which is in this Letter and all Scripture. It is the place of God's Son. That indeed does explain the Calling, the Conduct and the Conflict. This, then, in and from eternity past, stands over all time and eternity to be; affecting, determining, governing "all things." To substantiate this it is only necessary to pass an eye through this Letter and to note how often the Lord Jesus is actually mentioned. His personal name is mentioned some forty-four times, in addition to which note the many pronouns—"He," "Him," "His" and "Whom."

It has often been said that the criterion by which truth or error in any system of religious teaching is determined is the place that it gives to the Son of God, Jesus Christ. That is a very sound criterion.

CHAPTER FIVE

The Tragic Interlude

We have mentioned that between the "before times eternal" and the first era of time there took place something which has affected in a tragic way the whole course of events. The Bible has much to say in relation to that, but Paul in his final three Letters (excluding those to Timothy, Titus and Philemon) gives a very strong place and meaning to that event. We refer to the invasion into the universe of

The Great Schism

As to the particular Letter with which we are occupied, there are three allusions to this cosmic disruption.

The first, and this is a supreme factor in the significance of Christ, is in a very brief phrase. The fuller context is this (chapter i. 9, 10): *"having made known unto us the mystery of his will, according to his good pleasure which he purposed in him* (Christ) *unto a dispensation of the fulness of the times, to sum up all things in Christ, the things in the heavens, and the things upon the earth; in him, I say. . . ."* The clause we want is "to sum up all things in Christ."

The word (one long Greek compound) "to sum up" means "to bring back and to gather around the main point," that is, "in Christ." It is to re-gather the "all things." In the companion letter, Colossians, Paul says: "For in him were all things created, in the heavens and upon the earth" (i. 16). This means that originally all things were in God's Son. That it should be necessary to say that in the fulness of the times all things would be *re*-gathered or brought back into Him clearly means that something happened to take things out of Him, or away from Him. Oh, what a lot there is that points to that! Jesus said He came "to seek and to save that which was *lost.*" He gave a parable of wicked husbandmen who slew the heir in order to appropriate the inheritance. He said that "All that came before me are thieves and robbers" (John x. 8). It is an aspect of truth which has an immense amount of teaching in the Scriptures. Something was done to rob God's Son of His place and rights in the eternal purposing of God, making it necessary to re-gather, re-cover, re-unite. Back to that later.

The second thing pointing to that great event and breaking in of disruption is the *state,* the condition against which the purpose revealed in this Letter stands. It is a horrible picture.

"Dead through your trespasses and sins," "Ye walked according to . . . the prince of the power of the air, of the spirit that now worketh in the sons of disobedience . . . in the lusts of our flesh . . . by nature children of wrath" (Eph. ii. 1-3). "At that time separate from Christ *(note that)* . . . having no hope and without God in the world" (ii. 12). ". . . as the Gentiles also walk, in the vanity of their mind, being darkened in their understanding, alienated from the life of God . . . being past feeling . . . lasciviousness . . . uncleanness . . ." (iv. 17, 19). How did all this come about when all things were in God's Son originally? All this is outside of, and apart from, Christ! Surely we can say of this: "An enemy hath done this."

Very well: let us pass to the third thing in this Letter indicative of the great schism. How well known the words are, but how little known their vast, sinister context. "Our wrestling is not against flesh and blood, but against the principalities, against the powers, against the world-rulers of this darkness, against the spiritual hosts of wickedness in the heavenly places." "Stand . . . withstand . . . having done all, stand'" (Eph. vi. 12-14).

Relations between the Son of God and some evil Power and his hosts have been so ruptured and disrupted that there can be no appeasement, no compromise, no fellowship, until that evil system has been destroyed beyond remedy. That great schism began somewhere outside of this earth; it then invaded the earth, and it has been the source and cause of all the schisms and disruptions in history. The Bible labels that responsible one Satan, the Devil.

For some time rationalism, liberal theology, psychology and certain philosophers ridiculed the existence of a personal Devil, and what the Bible attributes to him was explained as just neuroses and complexes; that is, evil is not anything to do with evil spirits or a "Satan," it is nervous disorder, or at most good in the making. Demonology is only a form of mythology. So, Satan played a master trick by persuading men to believe that he does not exist. But the world has had some shocks in recent history and there has been a positively terrible unmasking of the most awful malignity in this world and in human behaviour. Not only in those realms which are called "savage," "uncivilized," and "backward," but for sheer devilry, wickedness and calculated cruelty, nothing has ever been worse than that among what have been thought to be "cultured" and "advanced" peoples. Their very scientific "advancement" (?) has been employed for the most unspeakable horrors. We could write many pages on this line, but we refrain. The Bible is terribly vindicated as the course of this world proceeds, and not least in its unveiling of an evil personal power which is ill-disposed towards mankind and particularly to those who have allied themselves with God's Son. The battle for unity is a painful and heart-rending conflict. The disruption of nations proceeds apace, and among God's people there is nothing too sacred to escape this cosmic determination to disrupt the smallest approximation to Divine fellowship. Of course, there are many "societies" and "fraternities" which are left alone, but it is no compliment if Satan is not disturbed. Let us make no mistake about this matter. The Bible leaves us in no doubt that, at the end of the age, every element in the universe will assume unmistakable features of intensification. This, of course, is only logical if the end is fulness in every connection. Whatever your interpretation of Rev. xii may be, we have to note that Satan's shortening tenure of power is marked by his coming down to the earth with great wrath (Rev. xii. 12).

But to return to "Ephesians," the great summary of spiritual history. We most note particularly that the Apostle brings out in full and definite statement that the Church—the Body of Christ—is involved in this war of the ages and all that he has written he heads up in this. It is as though he would say: "All that I have been saying regarding the eternal counsels of God; the place and purpose of the Elect—the Body of Christ; the redemption of that Body and its uniting with its Head; its life, character, walk, and work in this dispensation; and the great goal and established purpose of

God to ultimately reunite all things in Christ is *the* object and occasion of an immense, untiring, and ever-intensifying cosmic conflict, in which unseen and countless evil forces are bitterly antagonising the purpose and all related thereto." Paul says that it is because of the ministry committed to him to make all this known that he is in bonds and imprisonment. He shows that this antagonism of spiritual intelligences will be levelled at all that relates to that stewardship, and implies that if ministries are not just "departments" or aspects of Christianity, but all of a *corporate whole,* solidly bent upon a single object (Eph. iv. 13), this *corporate* character will constitute the most serious menace to that evil kingdom as to draw out its venomous and every-sided effort to break it up and neutralise it. The Apostle defines this opposition as "wiles of the devil." He then sets over against each other the armour of God and the wiles of the devil. It is God's provision for meeting Satanic "wiles." By symbolic means he shows the nature of the "wiles." On the positive, Divine side the points of attack are shown to be "Truth," "Righteousness," "Peace," "Faith," "Salvation," "The Word of God." Against every form of subtle lying God provides the girding of the Spirit of TRUTH. He provides "The RIGHTEOUSNESS of God which is through faith in Jesus Christ." Against fear which makes the going, the feet, unsteady and unsure He provides "The PEACE of God, which passeth all understanding." Against the suggestions, ideas, thoughts, imaginations and reasonings which assail the mind—the head, He provides SALVATION by Grace. Against the attacks upon the trustworthiness of the promises of God He supplies the Holy Spirit to answer back and retaliate with the sure WORD. "Over all," and related to all, He says "in all your taking, take the big shield of FAITH." But *note,* God does not put all this provision on His people; He provides it and then says to them, "Take unto you." There *must* be an act on their part, for the element of passivity is not consistent with such warfare. Would to God that, when these fiery darts began to fly, we instinctively reached for the appropriate weapon of defence! Perhaps we ought *consciously* to have them always on.

As we have said that in his last Letters Paul gave a strong place to this conflict of the ages, we cannot close this chapter without a reference to "Philippians." In "Colossians" it is obvious (see i. 13, 20; ii. 15), but in "Philippians" it is more by inference and allusion. We believe that when Paul, writing of the self-emptying of the Son of God, said that "although he was equal with God, he thought it not something to be grasped (held on to) to be equal with God, but emptied himself" (ii. 6), the Apostle was alluding to the ambitious pride of "Lucifer" to be like the Most High (Isa. xiv. 14; Luke x. 18). If this is a right interpretation (cf. 2 Pet. ii. 4 and Jude 6), then the scene in Phil. ii, in keeping with so much other teaching in the New Testament, is that of the Son of God becoming the Son of Man, taking man-form to fight out this battle with the usurper.

> "A final Adam to the fight
> And to the rescue came."

And Paul, a "good soldier of Jesus Christ," in the same letter (Phil. iii) goes on to show that the way of victory is the way of "counting all things as loss."

Let us sum up.

"Before the foundation of the world" Divine counsels took place which are called "The good pleasure of his will," "The mystery of his will," "The purpose of him who worketh all things after the counsel of his will," "The eternal purpose" (Eph. i. 4, 5, 9, 11; iii. 11). In those deliberations certain very definite decisions were made. These decisions were two-fold.

1. The Son of God was "appointed heir of all things." The sphere and realm of all things (Heb. i. 2; Eph. i. 10, 11).

2. An Elect people was "chosen" in the Son to be the complement of Him; to be the corporate vessel of His expression and administration, termed His Body, His Bride, His Church, etc.; vocation being the idea of that election and predestination (Eph. i. 4, 23; v. 25-32; iv. 1).

3. Subsequent to that two-fold appointment and election, a revolt took place among heavenly beings in great number, led by one in very high position, probably very near the top. Pride and jealousy over the Son's appointment were the causes of this revolt, the place of "equality with God" being aspired to by that high one. The one, and the hosts in complicity with him, were cast out of heaven and "kept not their first estate" (Jude 6, A.V.). The schism, rupture, and divi-

sion in heaven with the wrath of God upon them inspired an eternal and deathless enmity in that leader against God's Son, and mankind as the intended and potential vessel of His glory. So mankind was struck at early after creation, and the special enmity was focused upon the line of those who maintained faith in God and bore any characteristic features of God's Son. As primarily, so through all the ages, the one object and activity of that evil adversary has been to disrupt, divide, disintegrate humanity, and most particularly the "elect," the people of God. By such an object the purpose is to neutralise God's purpose and its appointed and chosen vessel. In this intensifying battle the true Church is shown to be deeply involved. God has made a full provision for the Church to meet and stand against that great enemy. That is a general summary of the actual teaching and implications of one aspect of this "Letter to the Ephesians."

CHAPTER SIX

The Era of the Hidden Secret

"In other generations was not made known unto the sons of man."

"From all ages hath been hid in God" (Eph. iii. 5, 9).

"Which hath been hid from all ages and generations" (Col. i. 26).

It will be noticed that we have chosen the alternative word to the one in the relevant Scriptures, that is, "Secret" instead of "Mystery." Our reason for so doing is to avoid the necessity of spending a lot of time in explaining that Paul was not thinking in terms of the pagan mystery religions and making Christianity another such, with differences. Neither was he thinking of something mysterious. We have heard people speak of "mystical Christianity" and of "the mystical Body of Christ." Such terms, we feel, are dangerous, because they open the mental door to mysticism which is false spirituality. Mysticism leads multitudes of people into a wholly false and deceived position as regards Christianity. We want to say here with great emphasis that, contrary to many false definitions of the Letter to the Ephesians, that Letter is in another world altogether from mysticism! It is intensely real and practical, and there are no illusions about it. To use the word "Secret" is to be easily understood, whereas "mystery" *suggests* to the ordinary mind something remote from comprehension. By "Secret" the simple meaning is that something was not made known, but hidden, or kept in reserve. This will be more fully defined as we go on. In this chapter we are mainly concerned with *the fact* of the secret, not with the nature of it, which will be *the* subject of the chapter to follow. As to the fact, by that we mean that it did definitely exist and was ever and in all things *the* great *reality* in the mind of God. Indeed, it was implicit, if not explicit, in all the ways and means of God. It was no myth, but a positive reality. It was the hidden *meaning* of God's ways, and of the means that He employed. We, to whom the "secret" or "mystery" has now been disclosed, find it very difficult indeed to use the Old Testament without giving that meaning. But to the people of that dispensation, with a few exceptions of partial enlightenment, only the events, the instruments, and the objects were known. They did things and employed things because they were commanded to do so. Their entire system—given by God—was objective, outward. Even where and when there was sincerity, devoutness, reverence, and zeal, it was to an outward form and with outward means. The heart could be in it, and there could be strong conviction that it was right, and yet, withal, true spiritual understanding was absent. That lack of spiritual understanding could—and often did—mean *mis*understanding, and that misunderstanding led to hard and even cruel behaviour.

This fact comes out in a glaring way in the days when God's Son was here in the flesh. It would almost seem that the Spirit of Truth had—among other things—the deliberate intention in inspiring the Gospels to expose this terrible fact that men could be fiercely and utterly committed to the outward and objective things of tradition, ritual, dogmas, etc., and at the same time be utterly remote from their spiritual meaning and value. The Apostle of whom we are speaking just now was formerly one of these people. He said that he "verily thought that he *ought* to do many things contrary to Christ," and he did vehemently what he believed his understanding of his Bible demanded. It is just at this point that the Apostle focused his revelation as to the change in the Divine economy from one era to another. This is the significance of his words regarding the mystery being hidden from ages and generations. He knew, and no one knew better than he, the nature and features of that Old Testament economy. It was an economy of externals: ritual, vestments, liturgies, formalities, particular places, e.g. buildings and localities; men dressed differently from other men; names and titles, religious classes, and the thousand-and-one other things which went to make up the religious system; orders, adornments and procedure. It was the system of the visible, tangible, temporal, and palpable. Very wonderful, elaborate, attractive, impressive; the processions of high priests, priests and attendants, with robes, mitres and censers, etc.

It was so familiar to Paul in his former life, and it was just *the* things, beside which there was nothing comparable.

Now, something had happened which made it all a system of shadows without the substance: it had—for him—receded from reality, and it belonged to a past and disposed of childhood. Yes, so he described it in his Letter to the Galatians. For him, any carry-over of that kind of thing was failure in apprehension of God's mind; failure in "growing up"; failure in spiritual understanding; a clinging to childish things: in a word, contradiction to the very meaning of Christ and the advent of the Holy Spirit. With Paul the revolution was radical and, while he loved the people in that proscribed system, he felt keenly the falsehood of their position. It will be in our next chapter that we shall seek to show what it really was that was hidden from the people of that era and from those who carried the features of that era beyond God's appointed time into a new and completely different era, even to our own time.

We are at present dealing only with the inclusive *fact* of the hiddenness. There are one or two matters to which we must refer in particular. One has to do with what was *not* hidden in that era. This is necessary in order to arrive at the essential "Secret."

The coming and expectation of the "Messiah," the "Christ" (the same word in different languages) was certainly no mystery. That "Seed" had been foretold immediately sin entered (Genesis iii. 15) and Moses had prophesied the rising of the Prophet (Deut. xviii. 15). References to the Coming One are many: His birth, His life, His anointing, His sufferings and His glory.

Then there was no secret as to salvation being preached to the Gentiles. That is not an exclusively New Testament truth, nor a part of the Mystery now revealed. The same is true as to the Kingdom of God. That is not made known as a fact for the first time in the New Testament. There are other things also in the New Testament which are *quite apparent* in the Old.

One other thing needs to be emphasised as not changing with the two eras. It is the basic law of all that relates to God. Some confusion has come into the minds of many in relation to the change from law to grace. When everything has been rightly said as to our being no longer under the Law, but now under grace, the idea has slipped in that the fundamental principle has changed with the dispensations. This is not so. The principle, or law, which is the same in every era is faith. Faith was no less *the* governing law in the Old Testament than it is in the New; and no more in the New than in the Old. In that age it was not the works by themselves that justified. Neither in Abel, Enoch, Noah, Abraham, nor any other of the army mentioned in Hebrews xi was it what they did that found the way through to God (although there was a significance in what they actually did), it was faith in God that was virtuous. Works without faith are as ineffective as faith without works. There is no conflict between Paul and James. They are only the two sides to one thing. (Perhaps James *was* more of a legalist than Paul.) The key to every approval in the Old Testament is "He believed God." It is so very clear that God placed this law beneath and behind everything. Very big changes exist in the two dispensations, it is true. In the old, God blessed in temporal and material ways. Obey God; be faithful to God's commands, and blessing will be upon "thy basket and thy store"; your family and your field. Prosperity will be on your labours and there will be facilitation of your success. But underneath all that there was the law of faith. It is unchanging with times and economies. Paul has not been shown a new principle. This has nothing to do with his "revelation" in particular. The "secret" lies beyond that, although his doctrine of justification was admittedly revolutionary and upsetting. He really only made faith in the finished work of Jesus Christ dominant and thereby its closure of an old order of things. Of course, much time and space is required to elucidate Paul's doctrine of justification, but that he has done for us. We are saying that "the mystery" as revealed to Paul particularly is not a new idea as to the law of faith, although the basis of faith may be literally changed from men's works to Christ's finished work. Works themselves do not justify, but the justified man works the works of faith.

It is important and helpful to know that, in the old era, God was not working with a different *mind* from that which belongs to this present era. His mind is unchanging in its nature and purpose. If His method and means change, his thoughts and object remain the same from eternity to eternity. Because in one era He hides these essential concepts, it does not mean that they are not implicitly in all that He chooses and uses. What comes to light in the subsequent dispensation is not new in the sense of never having been before in the goings of God. It is only what God has been consistently working toward all along. So, when the secret is out, we are able to see it in the ways of God with persons and people and things from the beginning. There are no afterthoughts with God.

"The sovereign rule of heaven is like

A TREASURE which A MAN found in a field, and HID it, and in his joy he sold everything that he had, and BOUGHT that field" (Matt. xiii. 44—Free translation).

CHAPTER SEVEN

The Secret Revealed

". . . it hath now been revealed unto his holy apostles and prophets in the Spirit";
"According to the purpose of the ages (R.V. margin) *which he purposed in Christ Jesus our Lord"* (Eph. iii. 5, 11).

As we now arrive at the very heart of the whole matter, it is necessary to repeat, firstly, that the Apostle Paul does not claim exclusiveness in the revelation of the long hidden mystery. While he certainly and positively does claim that it was revealed to him in a specific and particular way, and that his revelation constituted him a particular "steward," and that he was chosen and dealt with by the Lord in a way which especially related to this purpose, yet he includes "his holy apostles and prophets" in the knowledge of the long-hidden, but now unveiled, secret. It *is* evident that Paul did have a fuller "understanding" and perhaps a unique apprehension of it, but it is not difficult to find at least partial traces of this knowledge in Peter and John, as it was also true in Stephen.

We must also emphasize that Paul's was not a *different* Gospel from that preached by the others, and certainly Paul did not have two Gospels, one concerning "Salvation" and the other concerning "The Mystery." How often have we heard Christians say that they are only interested in "the simple Gospel," "the Gospel of salvation," and that they are *not* interested in "deeper teaching or truth." Paul would have been both surprised and grieved to hear such language, for his "Gospel" was one, and he would say that the fullest and deepest revelation is the Gospel. There can only be tragic and grievous loss and weakness resulting from failure to see that "the whole counsel of God" is the Gospel. The position so much to be deplored in great numbers of Christians is so largely due to fallacy: the fallacy that it is unwise, if not futile, to give the greatness and immensity of God's revelation in

Christ to either the unsaved or to young Christians. Let them be made aware of the vastness of that to which they are called! A little Christ and a little Christianity will produce little Christians! Some of the best and strongest Christians that we have known came to the Lord in gatherings where the greatness of Christ was being unfolded to *Christians*, and Christians in responsibility. "Back to the simple Gospel" can be a snare and a sop to those who do not really mean business with God!

At the time of writing this we are in the midst of having work done on our present home. Hammers and drills are making such a noise as to almost deafen. The workmen are explaining, "This house *is* well built. The bricks are not just put together with ordinary sand cement, but with concrete, and it is very hard work to make a hole." God's building is like that, whereas men build—not for eternity—but for the present. But, mark you, it is not just deep *teaching* that we advocate, but Holy Spirit unveiling of Christ.

That brings us to *the* message and substance of this letter in particular. Standing before it we find ourselves facing some of the greatest questions and problems with which men have been, and still are, wrestling in the realm of Christianity. This letter answers them, but how few there are who see the answer, and fewer still who—if they glimpse it—are prepared to follow it. In a time of well-nigh worldwide war there have been those countries which have taken no share in the conflict and have missed the honours because "they were not free to participate." Internal complications, divisions, and commitments bound their hands and made them neutrals. Fear, self-interest, and failure to recognise the great moral interests kept them as "isolationists." Let us at once affirm that "The Letter to the Ephesians" represents the greatest religious crisis in the history of the world. It tells us that, out from the past eternity has come the revelation of a secret which God had kept hidden from all previous ages. The revelation has introduced and inaugurated a dispensation of greater importance and significance than any age before it. It tells us that for the ministering of this revelation God chose, prepared and appointed an instrument of a particular kind; one formed by God in a particular way. This instrument—Paul—was never ordained or appointed to this work by men, although he was recognised and "sent forth" by the Church. He was never taught or prepared for his work by man. He received everything direct and at first hand from Heaven. He was dealt with by the Lord in a way that wholly corresponded with the purpose for which he was chosen. The Letter which is before us goes to the heart of a matter which has been growingly occupying the most serious consideration of all Christendom and is the matter which is perhaps more to the fore today than any other. It is the matter of very real consequence to all Christians but, unfortunately, it has been lifted above the ordinary person by a highbrow term which is so widely employed. The word or term which has been so much used since about the year 1900 is "Ecumenical," a word from another language. Of course, something impressive is lost if its simple meaning is employed, which is "worldwide"; and its present instrument is what is known as "The World Council." This "Council" is laboriously applying itself to discover a solution to the chaos and complications of divisions in Christendom. For centuries the various sections—called "Denominations" or "Churches"—of Christendom have tenaciously held to the position that they were each originated and justified on a basis of Scriptural authority. Every division has made that claim, and finds its strength in that conviction. Now the slogan of the "World Council," or Ecumenical Movement, is "these man-made divisions" which must be got rid of. For one of its great convocations the subject chosen was "The Order of God and the Disorder of Man.' This was subsequently changed to "Man's Disorder and God's Design." But every attempt to resolve this problem, whether it be in general or even among evangelicals, meets with unsolvable difficulties, and the only recourse is to tolerate or compromise on matters of serious account. So a *number* of compromises have to be introduced into the programme for unity. The great problem of divisions in Christianity is as hopeless of solving *by human recourses* as are the many inter-racial problems.

This, then, is the tremendous situation which this Letter deals with and answers. We have already seen that this great spirit of schism had its beginning far back at some dateless point in Heaven, dividing angelic hosts into two irreconcilable camps; later it involved the earth and has had a long, long history, gaining momentum in ever multiplying and intensifying wars. Then it invaded Christianity and the entail is grievous indeed. So, it is no small thing that this Letter deals with and to which it gives the answer.

We have also seen that the heart of this whole matter is reached and touched by one phrase which sums up the purpose of God at the end. That phrase is: *"Unto a dispensation of the fulness of the times, to sum up* (reunite) *all things in Christ, the things in the heavens, and the things upon the earth; in him, I say . . ."* (Eph. i. 10). But, while we may embrace that as the end, beyond this age, our concern is for *this* age. Is there no way or hope for at least an approximation to that now? The Letter would surely leave us in our dilemma if it only pointed to a future age and had no answer to the present tragedy. But it has the answer. This answer is given by several means and ways. Perhaps the simplest, most direct, and most helpful way will be to let Paul himself be the answer. Seeing that the Apostle makes such strong and categorical claims as to his own personal revelation, it will be best to examine that revelation, and what it did in this man's life. We noted at the end of chapter four that the personal name of Jesus Christ is mentioned some forty times in this short letter, plus all the pronouns "He," "Him," "His," "Whom." This, in itself, is the strong clue. In his Letter to the Galatians Paul made the statement in these words:

"An apostle (not from men, neither through man, but through Jesus Christ, and God the Father . . .)";

"Neither did I receive it from man . . . but through revelation of Jesus Christ";

"It was the good pleasure of God . . . to reveal his Son in me" (Gal. i. 1, 12, 15, 16).

In the Letter to the Ephesians which is our present consideration the Apostle makes much of revelation; indeed, he bases all the "full knowledge" upon a "spirit of wisdom and revelation." Very well, then; the answer to this great question which is before us and which is the occasion of all this feverish discussion and deliberation in Christendom is found in the *revelation* and apprehension of God's Son. It is wholly a question as to whether or not God's Son has been really seen by an operation of the Holy Spirit.

The kind of seeing to which we refer is an epoch, an encounter, a revelation, a crisis. There is no power on this earth which could have changed that rabid, fanatical, bigoted Saul of Tarsus, a "Pharisee of the Pharisees," into "the apostle of the Gentiles" (Rom. xi. 13, A.V.); the fierce and intolerant persecutor and destroyer of everything and everybody related to Jesus of Nazareth into His greatest friend, advocate and devotee! Argument would not have done it. Neither persuasion nor persecution nor martyrdom would have effected it. But it was done! That "conversion" stood the test of all the persecutions, sufferings, and adversities possible to man for the rest of his life. Moreover, it provided the substance of the greatest of all apostolic ministries; so intrinsic as to have extended and exhausted all efforts, through many centuries, to fathom, explain and comprehend. What did it? Paul would answer, "It pleased God ... to reveal his Son in me"; or, in other words, "I have seen Jesus Christ."

Right at the foundation and root of this man's life was a "seeing" which split his life in two and emancipated him from the tightly bound fetters of a mighty tradition. He said, "The God of the great creative fiat who said Let light be, and there was light, shined into my heart, and in that act and light I saw the glory of God in the face of Jesus Christ" (2 Cor. iv. 6). In that face Paul saw God's eternal purpose as to man. He saw God's method of realising His purpose. He saw the vast *significance* of God's Son in creation and in the universe: and he saw—in that One—the Church as His Body.

We cannot make too much of this matter of revelation, illumination, seeing. It is basic in salvation (Acts xxvi. 18). It is essential to effective ministry (2 Cor. iv. 6) and it is indispensable to full knowledge and full growth (Eph. i. 17). Jesus made a tremendous amount of spiritual seeing, as a reading of John's Gospel will show. "Eyes" were—in His teaching—a criterion of life or death. Indeed, a fundamental and preeminent work of the Holy Spirit has to do with spiritual enlightenment and that supremely as to the significance of God's Son, Jesus Christ. It is all in the Scriptures, but still

—41—

our eyes may be holden. Let us be quite categorical in stating that we can never see the Church until we have seen the Son of God, and we cannot *truly* see the Son of God without seeing the Church. This is *the* point in the incident at Caesarea Philippi (Matthew xvi. 16-18). Leave all your debate of whether Peter is the Rock on which the Church is built and light on the real key to what Jesus said: "Flesh and blood hath not revealed it unto thee, but my Father which is in heaven." "My Father in heaven *revealed* it"; revealed what? "Thou art the Christ, the Son of the living God." What then? "Upon *this* rock I will build my church; and the gates of Hades shall not prevail against it." Can anything built upon Peter, even converted Peter, withstand the power of hell or death? It is who Jesus Christ is, revealed from heaven, that is foundational to the Church, and "other foundation can no man lay" (1 Cor. iii. 11).

"Ephesians" is tremendously contemporary, that is, up-to-date. In our time it is customary, practically instinctively, for Christians meeting for the first time to ask, or be asked, "What denomination, or mission, or society do you belong to?" Some such question is almost inevitable. The "Church" (?) is designated by a national, a doctrinal, a colour, a "State," a "Free," a personal name (e.g. Wesley, Luther, Calvin, Mennonite, etc., etc.) title. If the Apostle Paul were to step into Christendom today and be asked such a question as to "association," membership, he would open his eyes wide and look with pained astonishment and say, "Oh, brother, I have seen Jesus, the Son of God, and in seeing Him I have seen the Church, and in that only true Church there is not this mix-up of nationalities, colours, names, social or cultural differences and distinctions." "In Christ Jesus . . . there can be *neither* Greek nor Jew, there can be *neither* bond nor free, there can be no male and female; for ye are all one man in Christ Jesus" (Gal. iii. 28). ". . . where there *cannot* be Greek and Jew, circumcision and uncircumcision, barbarian, Scythian, bondman, freeman: but Christ is all and in all" (Col. iii. 11). He would add, "there cannot be Paul, Apollos, Cephas, or any other name." The very least that such a seeing of Christ would do would be to revolutionise our phraseology, our manner of speaking.

A little incident might be to the point here. The writer heard it told by a well-known servant of God. In one of the Southern States of America the street cars are divided for "Coloured" and "White" travellers, and the rule of separation is strict. A car was about to start from the stopping-point and the "coloured" section was quite full. The "white" also was full, but for one place. That place was next to a well-dressed and apparently well-to-do lady. An old, feeble and very poor coloured man hobbled to the car and begged the conductor to let him on because his son was seriously ill and he must get to him quickly. The conductor pushed the old man away, saying there was no room. The old man begged again to be allowed on, and was hardly treated by the conductor. The lady turned to the conductor and said, "Let him come and have this seat by me." The conductor objected, saying that it was against the law. But the lady insisted and enforced her wish. When the old man got off, another woman said indignantly to the lady, "Why did you allow that— nigger to come into our section?" The lady answered, "I am a servant of Jesus Christ, and my Master is colour-blind." A simple and touching story, but a profound exposition of the New Testament doctrine of The Body of Christ.

Paul's revelation of Christ is "there cannot be. . . ." Not, "all these are in the Body as what they are on this earth." Given that all are truly born again and "baptized in one Spirit into one body," there is the foundation for gathering *above* the very real problems of the natural. Of course, there really is no other true Church. We remind you again of the *very* great place that Christ holds in Paul's very being and in his Letters, and, of course, this will determine everything.

How many things to which we give such importance would lose that importance and just recede from a first, or even secondary, place if truly we saw the Lord! What change in manner of speech and conduct would just happen without effort if we truly saw Him *in the Spirit*! Costly, yes costly. All true light costs. So the man in John ix found, but ask him whether he would exchange his new sight for the old acceptance. Read again Paul's evaluation of his revelation of Christ in Philippians iii.

But let us insist and stress very strongly that, although Christ in all His fulness has been revealed and presented in the New Testament, that same New Testament makes it very clear that, *through the Word* and by the Holy Spirit, that objective presentation has to have a subjective counterpart in the heart—the spirit—of the believer. It will tell us that it was for this purpose that the Holy Spirit came; for this very purpose we have the indwelling Spirit. Paul earnestly prayed for already well-taught believers that they might be given a Spirit of revelation in the full knowledge of Christ. This open-heaven endowment and given spiritual faculty is meant for all believers. But remember, the demand is for an absolutely pure and honest spirit and a preparedness to accept and go through with all that is involved. Here, the Cross, that is, Christ crucified, in its deepest application to self-interest in every form is the rock of Offence, or the Chief Corner Stone; stumbling and falling or building and rising. Any pride, prejudice, or reserve will find us out sooner or later in that we shall have been side-tracked from the fullest intention of God in calling us. It will be a tragedy, if, in the end, we are found to be in a "back-water," a *cul-de-sac*; perhaps snug and free from all the stresses of the battle, but—from heaven's standpoint—*out!* Such a possibility was an ever-present dread of Paul. "Lest, having heralded others, I myself should be rejected"; and there is much more like that. "If by any means. . . ," he says.

We must return to the great matter of the "Mystery," for there are things related thereto in our Letter which need clarifying. In all his Letters Paul uses this word some twenty times.

1. The mystery (secret) of the blindness which has happened to Israel. Rom. xi. 25.
2. The mystery of the wisdom of God. 1 Cor. ii. 7.
3. The mysteries of God. 1 Cor. iv. 1.
4. The mysteries of speaking in tongues. 1 Cor. xiv. 2.
5. The mystery of the Rapture and change of body. 1 Cor. xv. 51.
6. "The mystery of his will." Eph. i. 9.
7. The mystery made known to Paul. Eph. iii. 3, 4.
8. The fellowship of the mystery. Eph. iii. 9.
9. The mystery of the union between Christ and the Church. Eph. v. 32.

10. The mystery of the Gospel. Eph. vi. 19.
11. The mystery which hath been hid. Col. i. 26.
12. The mystery of Christ within or in the midst. Col. i. 27.
13. The mystery of God—Christ. Col. ii. 2; iv. 3.
14. The mystery of iniquity. 2 Thess. ii. 7.
15. The mystery of the faith. 1 Tim. iii. 9.
16. The mystery of Godliness. 1 Tim. iii. 16.
(Some of the above are duplicated.)

It looks as though there are many mysteries, but if we look again we shall find that, at least in the majority of cases, the mystery relates—*in some way*—to Christ and the Church. There are *very* few exceptions to this, and when it comes to Paul's particular conception it is not in the plural, but "*The* mystery," and invariably it is connected with Christ personal and Christ corporate.

The next thing that we must take account of in this connection is Paul's particular viewpoint. It is from above. Five times in this Letter to the Ephesians he uses the phrase "in the heavenlies" (i. 3, 20; ii. 6; iii. 10; vi. 12) and in that form it is found nowhere else. This is one of the most difficult of Paul's phrases for any of us to understand. We are not altogether helped by other phrases referring to heaven, such as "every knee should bow, of things in heaven . . ." (Phil. ii. 10). The translation "in the heavenly places" is not too fortunate. But let us look at the various references.

1. The present realm and nature of the believer's blessings in the heavenlies. i. 3.
2. Christ is now seated in the heavenlies "above all rule, and authority, and power, and dominion, and every name . . ." i. 20, 21.
3. The position of Christ is said to be that also of the Church. ii. 6.
4. There are principalities and powers in the heavenlies which are having made known unto them, through the Church, the manifold wisdom of God. iii. 10.
5. The warfare of the Church is not now in the realm of flesh and blood, but in the heavenlies with principalities and powers, etc. vi. 12.

Very well then, what have we? Just this: there is a realm or sphere above and around the material, the sense and tangible realm, where spiritual interests are supreme, where rival spiritual activities go on. Great forces are at work in that realm, and they have a constitution, system or organisation suitable to this purpose. It is a divided realm between celestial and demonic principalities. On the one side there is both interest in and co-operation with Christ's interests in the Church. On the other side there is not only bitter and relentless hostility to those interests, but an impact upon this world, "this darkness," which is intended to destroy both the people and the earth as the inheritance of God's Son. We know that natural elements above the earth have a powerful influence upon the *physical* life here. In the same way there are spiritual intelligences and forces which exert a tremendous influence upon the moral and spiritual life in this world. It is in this realm that Paul sees several things belonging to "the Mystery." One, that, amidst the strife, confusion and all that seems to the contrary, God is working out a "Purpose" which, because He is absolute Lord, will not just have to contend with adverse forces, but will both show His superiority and make the adverse forces serve the furtherance of that Purpose. This is the long view and the above view of the heavenlies.

Then, because Christ risen and exalted is "seated at God's right hand," He is in that position representatively and inclusively of the Church. The Church, therefore, is "seated together with Him in the heavenlies"; that is, in the present and ultimate good of His sovereignty.

Further, the blessings of believers are now, not as under the old economy, temporal, material, sentient, but "spiritual." "The riches of his grace"; "the riches of his inheritance"; "the riches of his glory"; "the unsearchable riches of Christ," etc.—these are all phrases in "Ephesians." These blessings are for a Church and its members who have—through union with Christ in His death and resurrection—been spiritually delivered and emancipated from "this present evil world" as the sphere of their natural life, ambition and resource, and whose hearts are "set on things above" (Col. iii. 1-3). If you have really come into the good of such "riches," then you have proportionately come into the heavenlies. While we are

—46—

right in mentally conceiving of "the heavenlies" as being a realm, we must not confine the idea to geography. Like "the Kingdom of Heaven," it is a sphere or realm in which spiritual factors, principles or laws and conditions obtain and take pre-eminence. That is why we used the word "proportionately." Geographically we are, or we are not, in a realm, a country; but spiritually we can be more or less in the *nature, character* and good of that realm. It is not a matter of definition of terms, but of spiritual accord, harmony, adjustment, agreement. In a time of great blessing we can just say, "It was as though we were in heaven." It is a spiritual position in oneness with spiritual realities. While it *seems* so difficult to explain, it is really only the fact and development of that which every *truly born-again* believer knows without explanation; namely, that something has happened by that new birth which has changed their consciousness of belonging and gravitation, so that a break has taken place *in them* with one realm and what belongs to it, and a union has come about with an entirely new realm and its content. They sense that they belong somewhere else and that there is a spirit in them which gravitates there and to those things. The New Testament has all the language and words for this, but it is the inward awareness that is the ground of learning the *meaning*. The development of that "law of the Spirit of life in Christ Jesus" (Rom. viii. 2) by discipline—maybe trial and error—or triumph, is the way of the "transforming by the renewing (making anew) of the mind" (Rom. xii. 2). It is the Church's and the believer's normal course.

But we have not yet brought the present aspect of Paul's revelation into sufficiently clear relief. So as not to overload this chapter we will divide it, and continue in a separate one.

CHAPTER EIGHT

The "Mystery" Revealed *(Continued)*

In the wonder and amazement of this unveiling we must be clear as to its *exact* nature and meaning. To do this we must put our finger upon key phrases which precisely embody and define it. We have found the statement which gives the ultimate and consummate issue: it is in Eph. i. 10. Can we find in that same Letter a phrase which brings that end into history, that is, the operation leading to that end? I think that we can. It is a fragment in the section marked as verses 13 to 22 of chapter ii: "one new man." That whole section is an enlargement of that fragment and it should be carefully read as such. There have been hints of this in other Letters of Paul, but here he gathers all together, and not only so but—as we should expect if his mind was ranging the "ages" and the secret hidden in them—the whole Bible is comprehended.

As to other hints, we have such classic and impressive instances as Rom. v. 12-19. Here the two generic and racial heads are set over against one another—the "one man" Adam, and the "one man" Christ; and the context shows the significance of each. Another tremendous instance is set in that chapter of amazing enlightenment, 1 Cor. xv. It is at verse 45: "The first man Adam became a living soul. The last Adam became a life-giving spirit" (see the immediate context). In "Ephesians" the Apostle first refers to the personal Christ, and then proceeds to the corporate "one new man." In an earlier passage both of these aspects have been mentioned: 1 Cor. xii. In verse 3 "Jesus" and "Jesus is Lord" is personally mentioned; in verse 12 the phrase "so also is the Christ" (the article is in the original) makes the member and the Head identical *for the practical purpose of expression* (context): "Now ye are the body of Christ" (verse 27). The uniting is by the "One Spirit" on Head and members.

It is in "Ephesians" that this "One new man" is revealed fully. If this is "the mystery hid from ages and generations," although existent all the time, we can now see, in the light of "the making known," how this has been the governing concept all through the Bible, that is, Manhood according to Christ.

At the beginning God said, "Let us make man"—MAN. The Psalmist cried, "What is man?"—MAN? In the Incarnation Christ's favourite designation of Himself was "Son of Man." In redemption there is "one mediator also between God and men, himself man" (1 Tim. ii. 5). In reconstitution there is the Pattern "Second man" (1 Cor. xv. 47). In exaltation and glory the Psalmist's question is answered in Jesus: "What is man?" (Psalm viii. 4; Heb. ii. 6). In consummation there is "One new man"—Man. There are foreshadowings in the Old Testament. Adam was "a figure of him that was to come" (Rom. v. 14). "The *man* Moses" (Num. xii. 3). David was "a *man* after God's heart" (Acts xiii. 22). These are only instances taken from many, and their character or function bears respectively features of Christ.

So, over all the Bible history, there is the shadow of a Man, both individually and corporately. The Divine concept of MAN governs all God's ways: in creation, Incarnation, mediation; in the Cross as setting aside one type of man to make way for another; in the resurrection as the New Man—the "firstborn from the dead"—accredited; in the exaltation of Jesus as the New Man instated; in the coming again of "The Son of Man" to remove the remnants of Christ-rejecting humanity and establishing the new order; in the Church in terms of corporate manhood, the vessel and vehicle of Christ's completeness and manifestation. All this is what Paul saw in "the face of Jesus."

The Church itself is not the "Mystery" revealed to Paul, but the Church as the Body of Christ—The One New Man—in which all distinctions other than Christ are non-existent; this was the revelation. It *had* to be a revelation from heaven for such a rabid, committed, fanatical Jew, with all his ancestry , descent, "birth," tradition, training and "blood" to come genuinely to the place where he could say with conviction "where there is *neither* Greek nor Jew, etc.; where all walls of partition are broken down; where there is neither circumcision nor uncircumcision; where there are no 'children' and 'dogs,' but 'all are one in Christ Jesus'" (Greek: "One *person* in Christ Jesus"—the gender is masculine).

How very much of the New Testament is illuminated in the light of this "New Man" concept! Indeed, it covers all of the meaning of true Christianity. It gives the real meaning to the new birth (John iii). It explains the Person and character and work of Christ. It is what the Apostle meant when he said "If any man is in Christ, there is a new creation" (2 Cor. v. 17, R.V. margin). And it explains those consummate words in Rom. viii. 29: ". . . foreordained to be conformed to the image of his Son"; and Eph. i. 5: ". . . foreordained unto adoption as sons through Jesus Christ." All this and much more indicates what is the specific purpose, work and nature of this present dispensation. The work in the "groaning creation" is with a view to "the manifestation of the sons of God" (Rom. viii. 19-23).

Comprehensively, the Spirit of God who "brooded upon the face of the waters" (Gen. i. 2) is now at work upon a "new creation in Christ." But with a profound and significant difference. In the old creation everything began and proceeded from the outside toward the centre—Man. In the new creation everything begins and proceeds from the inside, and the "outer man," the body, is the *final* phase of redemption and new creation: "The redemption of our body" (Rom. viii. 23; 1 Cor. xv., etc.).

The work of the Spirit of God has four aspects in this dispensation.

1. The securing of the new man. This is the evangelizing and apprehending of the individuals. In evangelism the ultimate purpose should ever be kept in mind, otherwise there will be weakness in the "converts" due to an inadequate motive.

2. Through the securing, the rebuilding of the new man. In the old creation God built up the man—"formed out of the dust of the earth." ("The first . . . is of the earth, earthy"—1 Cor. xv. 47.) In the new creation God begins with the spirit of man, proceeds to the soul and completes with the body. Everything in the new creation is basically and essentially spiritual. See 1 Cor. ii. The "inward man" is the renewed—born anew—spirit of man, to be "renewed day by day." Here enters all the teaching on the Holy Spirit and the believer's

life in the Spirit, as having been "born of the Spirit," and "is spirit" (John iii. 6).

3. Then follows all the discipline, training and growth of the new man. The Spirit of God works to a Pattern—"the image of his Son"; "until Christ be (fully) formed in you" (Gal. iv. 19); "God dealeth with you as with sons" (Heb. xii. 7). It is a long and hard transition from the "old man" to the "new," but the end governs all God's dealings and ways with His own, namely the "image" or "likeness" which was the primal concept in man's creation. "Let us make man in our image, after our likeness" (Gen. i. 26); "I shall be satisfied, when I awake, with thy likeness" (Ps. xvii. 15).

4. Then, finally and fully, the Spirit of God is working to constitute the "one new man," Christ corporately expressed; "the body of Christ," "the fulness (complement) of him"; "the measure of the stature of Christ," "the full-grown man."

All this comes out at last in full and clear revelation in that Letter of finality, "Ephesians." It is the Man concept from eternity to eternity, and that concept has, like a shadow, been over all God's history with man and man's history with God. Hidden from their eyes in all the strange, inexplicable and mysterious ways of God in individual men of faith and a peculiar people and nation, it has now been revealed to the sons of men, in Christ, that

"God having foreseen some better thing concerning us . . . apart from us they should not be made perfect (complete)" (Heb. xi. 40).

CHAPTER NINE

The Church Local

It is of considerable importance to note that, although the "Letter to the Ephesians" is a majestic presentation of the Church in its entirety, ranging every dimension of the eternities and realms and ages and setting forth the profound councils of God, the Letter was sent to local churches. This fact has some very challenging and searching implications. We must remind our readers that there is such a thing as a positive and definite revelation of what the Church is and therefore of the basis of its unity. It may be something to take note of that there is such a worldwide concern for and activity in relation to the unity of Christians, and such concern should find us in full heart sympathy with it. The big difference is between a massive effort on the one hand to solve the problem from the outside by trying to stick all the broken pieces together and in some way make them fit, and on the other hand a concern to recover the spiritual power which will make for a spontaneous coming and fitting together. The one is the organised, composite collection and assemblage, as of a machine; the other is the organic, spontaneous relationship of a corporate life. The former will come unstuck repeatedly. The latter will eventually emerge "a glorious church, not having spot or wrinkle or any such thing."

But what about the Church as locally represented? We must remember that when Paul wrote this Letter and sent it to the churches in localities, he was very well aware of the trends, or even the actual movements toward "departure" and breakdown in the churches. He had foretold it as to Ephesus when he left the elders of that church near the ship on his way to Jerusalem: "I know that after my departing grievous wolves shall enter in among you . . . and from among your own selves shall men arise . . . to draw away . . . after them" (Acts xx. 29, 30). That was incipient division. But here from his prison in Rome he will write, "all that are in Asia (in *Asia*) turned away from me."

Two Letters will soon be written to Timothy (who was probably in Ephesus) which will deal with the beginnings of the change from primal Christianity to all that it has become now. They were intended to warn against the ecclesiasticism, clericalism, ritualism, sacramentalism, etc., which have invaded the Church and changed its primitive character. No, Paul's head was not in the clouds and his feet off the earth when he deliberately wrote this Letter as to what the Church is. No doubt his reference to the spiritual warfare was because he knew so well that the battle was on in particular relationship with this very matter, showing of how great a consequence it is to the Satanic forces. It is impressive how any stand for a true expression of the Body of Christ is fraught with more conflict than anything else. If it is a congregation, that is, a number of individual Christians resorting to a given place for "Public Worship," without any corporate Church life and order; or if it is a Mission Hall mainly for preaching the Gospel to the unsaved; or, again, if it is a preaching centre where people go to hear a well-known preacher—all these will go on in the quiet way with little opposition from within or without. But, let there be a movement in the direction of a real corporate expression of a Holy Spirit constituted testimony to Christ corporate, then the battle is on and nothing will be untried to break *that* up, discredit it, or in some way nullify *that* testimony.

The Book of Nehemiah is a very good illustration of this many-sided hostility. Again we point to "Ephesians" as relating vicious spiritual antagonism to the essential purpose of the Letter. In this first particular, the universal is transferred to the local, and the local takes character from the universal. A true representation of the elect Body of Christ is a standing menace and ominous sign to the Satanic Kingdom because it is the Church which—at last—is going to dispossess and supplant the "world-rulers of this darkness" and govern with Christ. Would to God that God's people would view all their divisions and internal troubles in this light, instead of always attributing them to "second causes"! This is the first implication in Paul's passing to local churches the *whole* immense revelation of "The Mystery." There are several other features and factors in this Letter which carry such tremendous significances. There is that factor which the Apostle mentions with one of his superlatives. "The exceeding greatness of his power to usward who believe, according to that working of the strength of his might which he wrought in Christ, when he raised him from the dead . . ." (i. 19). "And you did he quicken, when ye were dead" (ii. 1). The church locally represented should be and should embody the testimony to "the power of his resurrection." It should, *in its history and constant experience*—as more than doctrine—declare that Christ is risen.

The impression primarily given should be one of livingness. The testimony should be that, although you may be jaded, weary, too tired even to make the journey; disheartened and despondent; physically, mentally and spiritually drained—you come away renewed, refreshed, reinvigorated and lifted up. The activity of Divine life has just resulted in a spiritual uplift. Note the way in which that has been said: "the activity of Divine life." We have *not* said: "the life of human activity." There is an illusion or delusion in much Christianity and in many "churches" that activity is essentially spiritual life. Hence, stunts, programmes, attractions, "special efforts," and an endless circle of "specials." All this is too often with a view to giving the impression of life, or even creating or stimulating "life." It may be the life of works, and not the works of life. Life will work, but works are not always life. That was the indictment of the church at Ephesus: "I know thy works . . . but . . ." (Rev. ii. 2). Divine life is spontaneous and not forced. The dead (spiritually) *are* raised, and not by artificial means. The Lord of the Church is the risen Lord, and His attestation is resurrection life. So "the power of his resurrection" should be the hallmark of a truly New Testament church. So often we quote our Lord's own words, almost as a formula: "Where two or three are gathered together in my name, there am I." At the same time the atmosphere may be heavy, uninspiring and devoid of a ministration of Divine life. Is this really consistent with the presence of the risen Lord?

We proceed with the implications of this Letter. If the church local is a true microcosm of the Church universal, then this Letter will show us that in the local representation there should—and can—be abundance of wholesome and upbuilding food. Our Letter has fed and stimulated believers through many centuries, and still the food-values are unexhausted.

The ministry in a true local expression of the Body of Christ should be an anointed ministry, and because it is such, no hungry soul should ever go away unfed. Not just studied and "got up" addresses or discourses, but a message from heaven making it possible for people to say, "We have been truly fed today." This means that the Lord's people, being nourished, are growing in *spiritual* stature, capacity, and responsibility. Not just increasing in mental knowledge or doctrine, but really knowing the Lord. The criterion of a church's value is the measure of Christ Himself in His members. This is not mere idealism, it is the normal state of a truly Holy Spirit constituted church in any place. Paul's use of the word "riches" in this Letter indicates how spiritually wealthy any company of the Lord's people should be.

We have earlier shown that the man behind the Letter is, in his spiritual history, identical with his message. We shall now seek to show that, in several respects, the history of the Church, universal and local, should follow that spiritual history of the Apostle.

1. The church in any locality should be born out of heaven. It is the aggregate or corporate fellowship of born-from-above believers. What, then is to be true of every individual believer must be true of the corporate company. That goes right to the very root of the Church conception, and it will be as well if we settle it here and now that, in the Scriptures, no other such thing is known or recognised as having a right to that name—Christian Church. That will sift our consideration down from an immense amount that takes the name but is not *the* true thing. Christendom or Christianity has become a colossus of a thing which is the home of every kind of bird in creation. To try to make a unity of such is a trick of him whose "fowls of the air" they are; *naturally*, some better, some worse, but far from all born again or from above (John iii. 5-13). This just means that every local company of believers, right at its beginning as such, should be something done by the sovereign Holy Spirit. Inasmuch as the Church takes it character from its "Head," its "First-born," its "Chief Cornerstone," the "Foundation," it must in every representation have its origin in heaven and embody the life of heaven. That means that formation by man's action is ruled out. It is not an "institution," it springs out of life.

It should be possible to say of any local church—or the Church in any locality—"That was an act of God." Mark you, we are seeking to get right to the root of this matter of what the Church is, and what it is not. The former is our real concern. Study what—in the Gospels—Jesus said about Himself and about men, and you have the key to what the church really is.

2. That leads to the next thing as to the "local church." If the Church was *born* of the Holy Spirit, it was born out of the travail of God's Son; then the law of travail must lie right at the origin of any true representation of both. In the New Testament the Church universal and the churches local came out of real travail. The travail, agony, and pain of Christ gave birth to the Church at Pentecost. Those who were its nucleus were baptized into His passion. They suffered the breaking of their souls when Jesus died. Hence their ecstatic joy when He rose again. John xvi. 21-22 was literally fulfilled in their case. That needs no enlarging upon. But what of the churches? Can we put our finger upon a New Testament church which was not born out of and into suffering? Immediately such a church was in view the battle for its very life, its very existence, began. Stonings, imprisonments, lashes, chasings, intrigues, slanders, persecutions of every kind lay at the emergence of every such potential representation of Christ corporately. Someone had to pay a price and the churches were the price of blood and tears. *When power is lost, perhaps through neglect, foolishness, strife, division, formalism, or the loss of the sense of the value of the truth, or for any other reason, the only way of recovery will be that of a fresh baptism into sorrow, remorse, tears and travail.* This is surely the right interpretation of the Second Letter to the Corinthians after the First. This also surely is the key to the situation in most of the churches in Revelation ii-iii. It is definitely implied in the case of Laodicea. A church which does not suffer for its life is, by all the laws of nature and grace, a weak and ineffective church.

3. Still pursuing the line of Paul's history and the Church, we have to say that a local expression of the Church—and all its members—must be the result of an encounter with God in Christ. Any corporate or personal ministry which is to be as fruitful as was Paul's, even in a more limited degree, must

have such an encounter at its beginning. The Cross and the Resurrection of Christ were such for the nucleus, the representative company. The Cross was devastating and desolating to all the self-sufficiency, self-assurance, self-confidence, pride, ambition, and presumption of man. The Resurrection was the invasion and taking over of the life of *Another*. This is so clearly seen in the case of the man who, more than any other, represented that nucleus, namely Simon Peter. He was a man broken and shattered by the Cross, but reconstituted on another basis by the Resurrection. As to the great unveiling of the "Mystery" of Christ and His Body—the Church— Paul's devastation and very survival was by this encounter on the road to Damascus. Such an encounter, sooner or later, personal and collective, must lie at the foundation of a true corporate life. It may be at the beginning or it may be later. It may be a recovery necessary after failure. Many a church, and many a servant of God, has had history cut in two by such an encounter. Before it, an ordinary, limited and comparatively powerless ministry. After it, a release and enlargement, with much spiritual fruitfulness. A little book published by the Moody Press, Chicago, called *Crises Experiences in the Lives of Noted Christians* is an example of this in a number of instances.

4. *If the Church universal is above all earthly differences, then the local church ought to be super-national, super-denominational, super-interdenominational, in spirit, fellowship, and outreach.* We have often said that Christ *cannot* be confined or fitted exclusively to any category that is of this world. His temperament overlaps all the categories. His nationality, time, teaching and person suit and meet the need of all, but He cannot be the sole property of any. We have seen works of man's artistic imagination purporting to depict the great scene in Revelation v: "And the number of them was ten thousand times ten thousand, and thousands of thousands." In the artist's portrayal, with all the good meaning in the world, the artist painted in people of every nation, colour, physique, dress, complexion, age and stature. Well, as we have said, the motive and intention was good, but who can describe resurrection bodies? "Fashioned like unto his glorious body" (Phil. iii. 21 A.V.); "It is raised a spiritual body" (1 Cor. xv. 44). We can be quite sure that everything

—57—

that has come in as the result of man's failure, causing estrangement and what is "foreign," will be gone for ever.

The point is that if Christ and what is of Him by the Holy Spirit is the constitution of the Church, then our meeting, our fellowship, our communion *must* be on the ground of that which is of Christ in all believers. We are referring to the basic life of all true Christians. When it comes to the work of the Lord, there may be *things* which we *cannot* accept, while we still hold to the ground of one life. This is surely the meaning of the Lord's Table. In "Ephesians" Paul sees only one Church, while he knows all about the many churches. There may be a million loaves and cups and tables in true evangelical Christianity in every nation under heaven. But the Lord only sees one loaf and one cup. Even when the local loaf is broken and "divided among yourselves," the Lord still only sees one loaf. Christ can be shared but not divided; He remains one Christ in "ten thousand times ten thousand" believers who share His life. When the Lord does something in us and thereby changes our mind about former acceptances, the temptation and battle can so easily be to become separate *in spirit* from those who—as yet—have not been so changed, and then the almost incorrigible inclination sets in to make a "sect" of that particular complexion or experience. While there may be real values and *vital* values in God's dealings with us which we strongly desire all others to know and experience, we must never make our experience a wall between us and all true children of God. The only way of hope and prospect is to shut our eyes to much that may offend our spiritual sensibilities (providing it is not sinfulness in the life) and to get on with the positive course of as much fellowship in Christ as is possible by the grace of God, always avoiding like the plague any attitude or talk which can be justifiably interpreted as spiritual superiority. Misunderstandings because of ignorance, prejudice or insufficient investigation are inevitable, but even such must not be allowed to close our hearts and turn us in on ourselves. While the wall of the New Jerusalem *does* mean a definite limit to and demarcation of what is "within" and what is "without" *as to Christ,* we must remember that it is "twelve thousand furlongs" in every direction, which symbolism is intended to signify how great Christ is and, therefore, how great His Church is.

When Paul set himself to write the First Letter to the Corinthians, he knew that he was going to deal with the partisan and sectarian spirit. He therefore opened the Letter with the true ground and range of Christian fellowship: "Sanctified in Christ Jesus, called saints, with all that call upon the name of our Lord Jesus Christ in every place, their Lord and ours." In this same dimension he closed the Letter to the "Ephesians": "Grace be with all them that love our Lord Jesus Christ in uncorruptness."

5. If it is true, as we have been trying to show, that Paul's history embodied the principles of the revelation that became his "Stewardship," one further feature of that history must be noted and taken up in the church local. That is, an overmastering apprehension of Christ. "I was apprehended by Christ Jesus" (Phil. iii. 12). The word "apprehended" is a strong word. It means to be arrested, overpowered, appropriated and brought under control. It is the word used in John i. 5 regarding light and darkness: "And the darkness overcame (apprehended) it (the light) not." It is also used in relation to the power of demons in possession. As the outcome of this apprehending, Paul always spoke of himself as "the prisoner of Jesus Christ" and "the bond-slave of Jesus Christ" and as "bearing branded in his body the marks of Jesus." This experience, born of an event, meant for Paul the loss of all independence, self-direction, self-government, and the rule of the world. It meant the absolute Lordship of Christ. Here was a man who had one overmastering concern for Jesus Christ. Not for a this or a that, but for a Person. His first ejaculation on the encounter was "Who art thou, *Lord*?", and in capitulation he followed up with "What shall I do, *Lord*?" That Lordship was no mere doctrine to him, it was a complete mastery. Very personal; for of the many double calls in encounter with God, such as "Abraham, Abraham!", "Jacob, Jacob!", "Moses, Moses!", "Samuel, Samuel!", "Martha, Martha!", "Simon, Simon!", the last was by no means least: "Saul, Saul!" Such a real sense of being called with a purpose *must* be a constituent of and in any true local church. To lose the sense of vital vocation, purpose and destiny is to lose dynamic and to become an existence rather than an impact.

CHAPTER TEN

The All-Inclusive Goal

"Till we all attain unto . . . the measure of the stature of the fulness of Christ" (Eph. iv. 13).

Everything before this and after it in this Letter has its focus upon this clause. Do you ask, "What is this whole Letter about?" The answer is in four words: "The Fulness of Christ." The two usages of this word "Fulness" by the Apostle in this Letter not only sum up the whole Letter, but present the most wonderful and remarkable thing in this wonderful document and, indeed, the most wonderful thing in the Bible. In chapter i, verse 23, the astounding statement is that the Church, which is the Body of Christ, is "the fulness of him that filleth all in all." That seems clearly to mean that Christ can no more be full as Head without His body to make Him complete: that He needs and depends upon His body for His self-realisation and self-expression. Closer still: He "filleth all in all" and yet requires His body in order to fulfill His filling. The body *is* the fulness, the completing of Him. In iv. 13 the finality of that truth is pushed along a line to a future climax. *"Till* we all attain" is linked with a vari-sided provision of functions. We are informed that, on His return to heaven—"When he ascended on high"—the Lord Jesus forthwith "gave gifts unto men." These were *personal* gifts, or gifts as persons, and they were men taken captive by Him. But these men were the expression of various functions: "Apostles, Prophets, Evangelists, Pastors and Teachers"—different functions, each one given "grace according to the measure of their gift," but *all together* bound and energized by *one* object. The Apostle—inclusive; the other three (Pastors and Teachers being one function) making up one interrelated and interdependent ministry. These are *not* different "Schools" or categories working apart, but only different aspects or functions of one body. There has to be mutual recognition, mutual evaluation and mutual co-operation. The separating of these functions can only result in an unbalanced condition, and lack of balance always results in weakness and loss. To give an unbalanced emphasis to evangelism is only to have immature Christians. To give out-of-proportion weight to teaching may result in the introversion which is divorced from objective concern for men's salvation.

In a *local* assembly, constituted by the Holy Spirit, for its full-growth, all of these *functions* should be present. Those who minister should know what their particular gift, grace and anointing is; and the assembly also ought to know it. Things are thrown into confusion when there is a trying to be and do what the anointing is not meant for. What pathetic, and even tragic, situations come about when men try to be that for which they are not anointed! A leader must be *obviously* anointed for that function, and the anointing must be accepted and acknowledged. The same must be true of all other parts of the one ministry. But each personal gift *must*—and this is absolutely imperative—*must* keep the one inclusive goal in view, and definitely contribute to it—"The fulness of Christ," because it is a "measure of the gift of Christ." The question may arise as to knowing what our particular function is. The answer in general will, of course, be that as we seek to be a responsible member of the body, in the local church, we find that the Holy Spirit "burdens" us and exercises us in a particular way. Note: this is not official. That is, it is not by our being appointed by men, or by our assumption, but by our spontaneous and voluntary exercise in concern for Christ's interests in His body. The Lord save His body, and its ministering members, from the pathetic scene of ministries which are not the definite projecting of *"He gave . . ."*; *He* gave; not man chose, appointed, or "opened the platform" to *anyone* who would take it. The "giving" of the ascended Lord is selective, specific and deliberate.

We must here indicate something very precious and helpful in this connection in New Testament procedure. It is indicated in 1 Tim. iv. 14 and implicit in various other instances. "Neglect not the gift that is in thee, which was given thee by prophecy, with the laying on of the hands of the presbytery." The "Presbytery" here does not necessarily mean special Apostles, but surely 1 Tim. v. 17—"Let the elders that rule well." True, Paul did speak of "the gift of God, which is in thee through the laying on of my hands" (2 Tim. i. 16). It would seem clear that, at some time, there was a praying over the members of Christ's body, and in the praying the Holy Spirit constrained to ask for some particular qualification by which the persons concerned would make a specific contribution to the ministry in the body. Elsewhere Paul exhorted Timothy to "do the work of an evangelist, make full proof of thy ministry" (2 Tim. iv. 5, A.V.), and to Archippus he sent a specific message that he should "take heed to the ministry which thou hast received in the Lord, that thou fulfil it" (Col. iv. 17). It might be a very good thing if *all* ministries were the result of such specific action in prayer! There would be a much greater "attaining unto the fulness of Christ," and much less of the ineffective and unprofitable "wisdom (or otherwise) of men."

Our passage in Eph. iv. 13 indicates that the body, whether universal or locally represented should, by the ministries, be making progress toward the ultimate fulness. The words are "the building up of the body of Christ." "Edifying" in the Authorised Version is misleading because it conveys the idea of "Headifying." While it is corporate growth, it, of course, must be true of each member. While Paul mixes his metaphors, at one time speaking of a Temple and the next of the body, he eventually comes down fully on the body as "the full-grown man," and what he means by building up is seen in iv. 14: "no longer children." It is the transition from childhood in which the persons concerned are always having to be nursed and, like children, draw attention all the time to themselves, to becoming such as can take spiritual responsibility and care for others, with the outward-looking concern for the other members of the body. It is a matter of coming into an increasing measure of Christ.

"Till . . ." represents process and progress; "we all attain" is the corporate object; "the fulness of Christ"—the goal reached.

From chapter iv, verses 10 to 15, we are thrown backward to the election, the calling, and vocation, to the relevant conduct and walk, and onward to the conflict and the demand for "standing." Everything relates to and focuses upon "Attaining unto the fulness of Christ."

CHAPTER ELEVEN

Conclusion

THE BASIS OF ALL

Having pointed to the inclusive goal, we cannot close without a further special emphasis upon the inclusive basis. The question that will be in most minds is, How shall all this be made good in the Church, the churches and the individual? There *is* an answer, but it will challenge us to the depth and at every point in our lives. Much—perhaps everything—will depend upon how seriously we are concerned for God's purpose, and therefore how ready we are to put aside all prejudice, superficiality, scepticism, familiarity and perhaps our traditions. It is the universal resort of the Apostles. Were things other than they should be in their days? Was there a condition in the church in Rome that *demanded* such a tremendous corrective as that great Letter to them? Was there a state of things in Corinth—divisions, carnalities, disorders, rivalries, dissensions, and worse, calling for such a corrective as the First Letter to the church there? Was there an incipient movement of reprobation from grace to legalism with all the entail of loss of glory in Galatia? Was there a "fly in the beautiful ointment" at Philippi? Was there a threatening of a false spirituality in the form of mysticism at Colossae? Yes, all this and other things, threatening the testimony of the churches and their influence in the world. The Apostles did not excuse, condone or accept it. Their whole attitude was "These things ought not to be." How did they approach these situations? Had they one common basis and means of approach and remedy? Yes, they had! In every case it was the same.

To Rome it was: Rom. vi. 3-10; xii. 1, 2.
To Galatia: Gal. ii. 20; v. 24; vi. 14.
To Philippi: Phil. ii. 5-8.
To Colossae: Col. ii. 11, 12; iii. 3.

Well, there it is, plain, clear and positive: the Cross of Jesus Christ brought by the Holy Spirit right to the root and foundation of the life of every believer. A foundational crisis and thereafter an inworking and an outworking. "We," "Ye," "I"—all the pronouns of direct application. Christians believe in the Holy Spirit. Very many desire to know the Holy Spirit as a reality and power in their lives. But it should really be understood and recognised that the Holy Spirit is committed and wedded to the Cross. His coming awaited the work of the Cross. Only after the symbolic representation of the Cross in death, burial and resurrection with Christ in baptism—*so understood*—did the Holy Spirit take His place in power in the lives of the first believers. Because the taproot of everything that the Cross was meant to deal with is the self-life, the self-principle, the New Testament word for which is "the flesh," the Holy Spirit leads those under His government into the experiences which are calculated to expose and bring to the Cross the self-life of the child of God. It is a primary and inseparable part of the Holy Spirit's business to make good and real the meaning of the Cross.

This is not popular to the flesh, but it is the gateway to spiritual fulness, and the deeper the Cross, the greater the measure of resurrection life, power and light. This touches the whole realm and range of Satan's authority. Power over him is inseparable from the Cross. Therefore he will do everything possible to undercut, set aside, belittle and discredit the Cross. The Person of Christ and the Cross of Christ have been the ground of the most bitter controversy in the history of Christianity. Of course, they are really one thing. It is the Person who gives the Cross its real meaning and value, and it is the Cross that vindicates the Person; provided that by the Cross is meant the death, burial *and* resurrection to glory. The Scriptures cited earlier and many others make it quite clear that the Cross of Christ is something more than an historic event of long ago. It is something that has to become very real in the *experience*, and not only in the doctrine, of the Christian. But who could survive the Cross in what it meant in the case of Jesus Christ? It rent, devastated and desolated Him, soul and body, heart and mind. For Him it was a going out into outer darkness and forsakenness. All the eternal agony was concentrated into a few hours and a last terrible moment. There is no other creature in God's universe who could go through that and survive. Thank God, no other creature is ever required to go all that way: He went it for us. And yet there is an aspect of that which concerns our being "united with him by the likeness of his death" (Rom. vi. 5) and "always bearing about in the body the putting to death of Jesus" (2 Cor. iv. 10 Margin) and a "fellowship of his sufferings"; a drinking at the cup which He drained. This working of His death in the Church and in the believer will be progressive. The law of nature, which is only another way of speaking of the law of God, is more life, more fruit, more growth, by recurrent Winter and Spring, alternating experiences of death and life, every cycle unto increase. This is the law of the Cross (John xii. 24). God is not a God who believes in theories; He is immensely practical.

One of the greatest enemies to fulness is superficiality. This is an age of "quick returns," easy gains, least trouble, everything with as little effort, trouble and cost as possible. Depth is a lost dimension. Stamina is a minus quality. That is why God allows wars and nature's upheavals and difficulties. Heaven is only going to be entered through tribulation is the principle of the Cross which God is sustaining before men's eyes. It will be those who share *His* travail who will share His reign.

 SeedSowers

THE WORKS OF T. AUSTIN-SPARKS
The Centrality of Jesus Christ... 19.95
The House of God... 29.95
Ministry... 29.95
Service.. 19.95

COMFORT AND HEALING
A Tale of Three Kings *(Edwards)*..................................... 8.95
The Prisoner in the Third Cell *(Edwards)*........................ 7.95
Letters to a Devastated Christian *(Edwards)*................... 5.95
Healing for those who have been Crucified by Christians *(Edwards)*........ 8.95
Dear Lillian *(Edwards)*... 5.95

OTHER BOOKS ON CHURCH LIFE
Climb the Highest Mountain *(Edwards)*........................... 9.95
The Torch of the Testimony *(Kennedy)*.......................... 14.95
The Passing of the Torch *(Chen)*.................................... 9.95
Going to Church in the First Century *(Banks)*................. 5.95
When the Church was Young *(Loosley)*.......................... 14.95
Church Unity *(Litzman, Nee, Edwards)*.......................... 14.95
Let's Return to Christian Unity *(Kurosaki)*.................... 14.95

CHRISTIAN LIVING
Final Steps in Christian Maturity *(Guyon)*...................... 12.95
The Key to Triumphant Living *(Taylor)*.......................... 9.95
Turkeys and Eagles *(Lord)*... 8.95
Beholding and Becoming *(Coulter)*................................. 8.95
Life's Ultimate Privilege *(Fromke)*................................. 7.00
Unto Full Stature *(Fromke)*.. 7.00
All and Only *(Kilpatrick)*.. 7.95
Adoration *(Kilpatrick)* 8.95
Release of the Spirit *(Nee)* 5.00
Bone of His Bone *(Huegel)* 8.95
Christ as All in All *(Haller)* 9.95

Please write or call for our current catalog:

SeedSowers
P.O. Box 285
Sargent, GA 30275

800-228-2665
www.seedsowers.com